PLASTIC CANVAS
FOR ALL SEASONS ™

Edited by Lisa M. Fosnaugh

the Needlecraft Shop

Plastic Canvas for All Seasons™

EDITOR	Lisa M. Fosnaugh
ART DIRECTOR	Brad Snow
PUBLISHING SERVICES DIRECTOR	Brenda Gallmeyer
ASSISTANT EDITOR	Sue Reeves
ASSISTANT ART DIRECTOR	Nick Pierce
COPY SUPERVISOR	Michelle Beck
COPY EDITORS	Nicki Lehman
	Mary O'Donnell
	Judy Weatherford
TECHNICAL EDITOR	June Sprunger
GRAPHIC PRODUCTION SUPERVISOR	Ronda Bechinski
GRAPHIC ARTISTS	Debby Keel
	Edith Teegarden
PRODUCTION ASSISTANTS	Marj Morgan
	Judy Neuenschwander
PHOTOGRAPHY	Tammy Christian
	Don Clark
	Matthew Owen
PHOTO STYLISTS	Tammy M. Smith
	Tammy Steiner
PUBLISHING DIRECTOR	David McKee
MARKETING DIRECTOR	Dan Fink

Printed in China
First Printing: 2007
Library of Congress Control Number: 2007921365
Hardcover ISBN: 978-1-57367-264-1
Softcover ISBN: 978-1-57367-265-8

Every effort has been made to ensure the accuracy and completeness of the instructions in this book. However, we cannot be responsible for human error or for the results when using materials other than those specified in the instructions, or for variations in individual work.

DRGbooks.com

1 2 3 4 5 6 7 8 9

WELCOME!

As the seasons change from warm summer days to chilly winter nights, you'll love stitching these darling plastic canvas designs.

Celebrating all that's to love about each season, this book features designs from brightly colored coaster sets to adorable tissue toppers. Also included are wall art, ornaments and sit-arounds.

Welcome spring with delicate florals and darling bunnies for Easter. Feel the summer heat with a touch of patriotism and the brilliant color of the tropics. Delight in the crisp autumn air with harvest pumpkins and colorful leaves. Warm up for winter with cozy Santa designs and sparkling snowflakes.

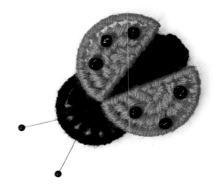

You'll want to stitch each and every design to add a little cheer to your home throughout the seasons! These projects are also fabulous to stitch for a friend or loved one as a cherished gift.

I know you'll love stitching these cheerful designs for the seasons! Happy Stitching!

SPRING SPLENDOR

8 Egg Basket Coasters

11 Cute as a Bug Fridgie

12 An Irish Blessing

14 Lil' Birdie Mini Easter Basket

19 Darling Baby Album Cover

20 Wallflowers

23 Baby Chick Favor

24 Simply Spring

26 Dancing Ladybugs

SUMMER SENSATIONS

32 Touch of the Tropics

35 Under the Sea Tissue Topper

36 Mischievious Monkey Coasters

38 Pretty Parrot

41 Summer Gift Bag

42 Farm Friend Towel Hanger

44 Liberty Angel

47 Dragonfly Box

50 Lighthouse Seascape Calendar

54 Pinwheel Roses

56 Sunflower Blackboard

AUTUMN ACCENTS

62 Autumn Angel

66 Autumn Glow Votive Candle Screen

68 Harvest Friends Candleholder

73 Autumn Leaves

76 Scarecrow Gift Bag

78 Log Cabin Coaster Set

80 Seasonal Welcome Sign

87 Batty Mobile

88 Boo Table Runner

92 Tiny Treat Bags

95 Pumpkin Basket Party Favor

97 Trick-or-Treat Wall Hanging

99 Jack-o'-Lantern Tissue Topper

102 Faith & Phillip

WINTER WONDERS

116 Santa Card Box

122 Santa Door Hanger

129 Rudolph Tissue Topper

132 Holiday Frame & Ornament Set

135 Christmas Tree Doorstop

138 Joyful Coaster & Gift Bag

140 O Christmas Tree

142 Musical Christmas Stocking

144 Charming Chalets

146 Variations on a Theme

148 Celebrate Winter Tissue Topper

150 Country Snowman Welcome

154 Sensational Snowman

159 Wild & Wacky Lights

160 Glistening Snowflakes

163 Heart & Bear Frame Set

166 Heart Coasters

168 Swinging Along in Love

170 Heart Air Freshener

173 Special Thanks   **174** Stitch Guide   **176** Buyer's Guide

SPRING SPLENDOR

EGG BASKET COASTERS

The delicate cutout designs on the front of this basket show off the brightly colored eggs within.

DESIGNS BY JANELLE GIESE

Skill Level
Advanced

Size
Egg Coasters: 3³⁄₈ inches W x 4³⁄₈ inches H (8.6cm x 11.1cm)
Basket: 6 inches W x 5¾ inches H x 1⅝ inches D (15.2cm x 14.6cm x 4.1cm)

Materials
- 1 sheet clear 7-count canvas
- 1 sheet almond 7-count plastic canvas
- Uniek Needloft plastic canvas yarn as listed in color key
- Kreinik Heavy (#32) Braid as listed in color key
- DMC #3 pearl cotton as listed in color key
- DMC #5 pearl cotton as listed in color key
- #16 tapestry needle
- Hot-glue gun

Project Note
The diamond and triangle symbols represent Continental Stitches.

Instructions
1. Cut four coaster front pieces, basket back, basket sides and basket handle from clear plastic canvas according to graphs (pages 9 and 10). Cut one 24-hole x 10-hole piece from clear for basket base.

2. Cut four coaster back pieces and basket front from almond plastic canvas according to graphs (pages 9 and 10), carefully cutting away blue lines on basket front.

3. Stitch one coaster front as graphed working uncoded area with pink Continental Stitches. Work star pink Straight Stitches over lavender and pink yarn Continental Stitches where indicated.

4. Stitch one coaster front replacing pink with baby blue, lavender with sail blue and star pink with star blue. Stitch one replacing pink with baby yellow, lavender with yellow and star pink with star yellow. Stitch one replacing pink with moss, lavender with fern and star pink with star green.

5. Whipstitch coaster fronts to unstitched coaster backs, using

the darker color of yarn on each egg.

6. Continental Stitch basket base with camel. Stitch remaining basket pieces with yarn following graphs.

7. When background stitching is completed, using medium beige gray #3 pearl cotton, Overcast or wrap edges and bars of egg indicated on basket front, then work lines of Backstitches across bands.

8. Using heavy (#32) braid, work embroidery on front. Work remaining embroidery on basket pieces with ultra dark beaver gray #5 pearl cotton.

Assembly
1. Using camel, Whipstitch basket sides to ends of basket handle, then Whipstitch assembled sides and handle to basket front and back, making sure to match placement points (red dots).

2. Using fern, Whipstitch front, back and sides to basket base.

3. Overcast top edge of back, remaining top edges of front and remaining edges of handle with camel.

4. Place one egg behind cutout work of front. Lean remaining eggs to sides of basket for background color. ●

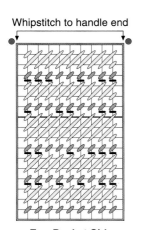

Whipstitch to handle end

Egg Basket Side
10 holes x 17 holes
Cut 2 from clear

Egg Basket Front
38 holes x 30 holes
Cut 1 from almond,
cutting away blue lines

COLOR KEY

Yards	Plastic Canvas Yarn
4 (3.7m)	Lavender #05
6 (5.5m)	Baby yellow #21
7 (6.5m)	Fern #23
7 (6.5m)	Moss #25
4 (3.7m)	Sail blue #35
6 (5.5m)	Baby blue #36
3 (2.8m)	Eggshell #39
13 (11.9m)	Beige #40
14 (12.9m)	Camel #43
4 (3.7m)	Yellow #57
6 (5.5m)	Uncoded area on egg is pink #07 Continental Stitches

Heavy (#32) Braid

2 (1.9m)	Star yellow #091 Straight Stitch
2 (1.9m)	Star pink #092 Straight Stitch
1 (1m)	Star mauve #093 Straight Stitch
2 (1.9m)	Star blue #094 Straight Stitch
2 (1.9m)	Star green #9194 Backstitch and Straight Stitch
	Star pink #092 Lazy Daisy Stitch
	Star mauve #093 Lazy Daisy Stitch
	Star yellow #091 French Knot

#3 Pearl Cotton

3 (2.8m)	Medium beige gray #644 Backstitch

#5 Pearl Cotton

4 (3.7m)	Ultra dark beaver gray #844 Backstitch

Color numbers given are for Uniek Needloft plastic canvas yarn, Kreinik Heavy (#32) Braid and DMC #3 and #5 pearl cotton.

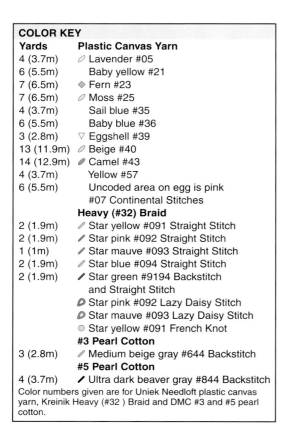

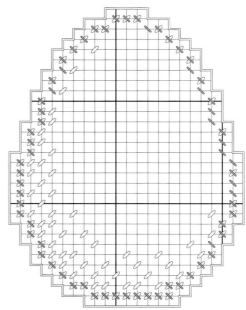

Egg Basket Coaster
22 holes x 29 holes
Cut 4 from almond for backs
Do not stitch
Cut 4 from clear for fronts
Stitch 1 as graphed
Stitch 1 replacing lavender with
sail blue, pink with baby blue
and star pink with star blue
Stitch 1 replacing lavender with
yellow, pink with baby yellow
and star pink with star yellow
Stitch 1 replacing lavender with
fern, pink with moss
and star pink with star green

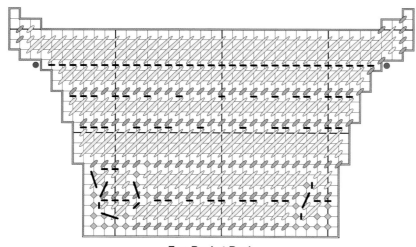

Egg Basket Back
38 holes x 22 holes
Cut 1 from clear

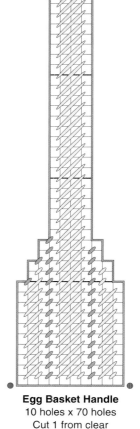

Egg Basket Handle
10 holes x 70 holes
Cut 1 from clear

CUTE AS A BUG FRIDGIE

Decorate your fridge or other magnetic surface with this tiny magnet. You can also use the motif as a package add-on.

DESIGN BY GINA WOODS

Skill Level
Beginner

Size
1¾ inches W x 2¼ inches H (4.4cm x 5.7cm), including antennae

Materials
- 1 (5-inch) Uniek QuickShape plastic canvas heart
- 2 (4-inch) Uniek QuickShape plastic canvas radial circles
- Worsted weight yarn as listed in color key
- #16 tapestry needle
- 6 (4mm) black beads
- 2 small black ball-head straight pins
- Hand-sewing needle
- Black sewing thread
- Small piece of magnetic strip
- Hot-glue gun

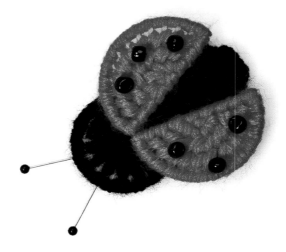

Instructions
1. Cut ladybug body from plastic canvas heart shape and ladybug wings from 4-inch plastic canvas radial circles according to graphs (page 28), cutting away gray areas.

2. Stitch and Overcast pieces following graphs.

3. Using hand-sewing needle and black thread, attach beads to wings where indicated.

4. Using photo as a guide, glue wings to body. Push pins into back of stitches at top of head. Place beads of glue on back of pins to secure.

5. Glue magnetic strip to back of assembled ladybug. ●

GRAPHS ON PAGE 28

AN IRISH BLESSING

Add warmth and cheer to your decor with a gorgeous Irish-themed sign complete with a loving blessing.

DESIGN BY ANGIE ARICKX

Skill Level
Beginner

Size
13½ inches W x 9⅞ inches H (34.3cm x 25.1cm)

Materials
- 1 sheet 7-count plastic canvas
- Uniek Needloft plastic canvas yarn as listed in color key
- #16 tapestry needle

Instructions

1. Cut plastic canvas according to graph.

2. Stitch and Overcast piece following graph, working uncoded area in center with eggshell Continental Stitches.

3. Hang as desired. ●

COLOR KEY		
Yards	**Plastic Canvas Yarn**	
16 (14.7m)	☐	Holly #27
10 (9.2m)	■	Forest #29
59 (54m)	☐	Eggshell #39
9 (8.3m)	☐	Lilac #45
11 (10.1m)	■	Purple #46
	Uncoded area is eggshell #39 Continental Stitches	
	✎	Holly #27 Straight Stitch
Color numbers given are for Uniek Needloft plastic canvas yarn.		

An Irish Blessing
89 holes x 65 holes
Cut 1

LIL' BIRDIE MINI EASTER BASKET

Cute and cuddly, this delightful little basket is sized just right to hold mini Easter treats.

DESIGN BY DEBRA ARCH

Skill Level
Intermediate

Size
8½ inches W x 6⅝ inches H x 3⅜ inches D (21.6cm x 16.8cm x 8.6cm)

Materials
- 1 sheet 7-count plastic canvas
- 1 (4-inch) Uniek QuickShape plastic canvas radial circle
- 1 (6-inch) Uniek QuickShape plastic canvas hexagon
- 1 (6-inch) Uniek QuickShape plastic canvas heart
- Red Heart Kiss bulky weight yarn Art. E727 as listed in color key
- Uniek Needloft plastic canvas yarn as listed in color key
- #16 tapestry needle
- 2 (⅜-inch/10mm) round black shank buttons
- Button shank remover
- Clean soft toothbrush
- Hot-glue gun

Instructions

1. Cut front, back, tail and basket side from 7-count plastic canvas according to graphs (pages 15, 16 and 17), cutting out slit in back where indicated.

2. Cut feet from plastic canvas hexagon; cut wings and beak from plastic canvas heart (page 17), cutting away gray areas.

For basket base, cut the three outermost rows of holes from 4-inch plastic canvas radial circle. Basket base will remain unstitched.

3. Following graphs and using 2 strands ice blue yarn through step 4, stitch and Overcast wings. Stitch and Overcast top part of tail as indicated, leaving bottom section unstitched. Stitch body pieces and basket side.

4. Whipstitch body front and back together around side and top edges; Overcast bottom edges. Do not Overcast slit on back.

5. Whipstitch side edges of basket together, then Whipstitch bottom edge to unstitched base; Overcast top edge.

6. Slide tip of needle between stitches to loosen and free up loose fibers of ice blue yarn. Use toothbrush to carefully brush up nap.

7. Using lemon yarn, stitch and Overcast beak; Backstitch and Overcast feet.

8. Use shank remover to cut shanks from buttons. Using photo as guide throughout, glue buttons to head for eyes where indicated on graph. Glue wings, beak and feet to body.

9. Apply a thin line of glue to back side of tail along bottom edge of stitching, then insert tail into slit on body back. ●

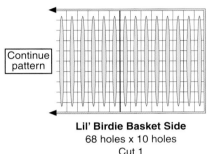

Lil' Birdie Basket Side
68 holes x 10 holes
Cut 1

Continue pattern

COLOR KEY

Yards	Bulky Weight Yarn
83 (75.9m)	☐ Ice blue #3865 (2 strands)
	Plastic Canvas Yarn
5 (4.6m)	☐ Lemon #20
	⁄ Lemon #20 Backstitch
	● Attach button eye

Color numbers given are for Red Heart Kiss bulky weight yarn Art. E727 and Uniek Needloft plastic canvas yarn.

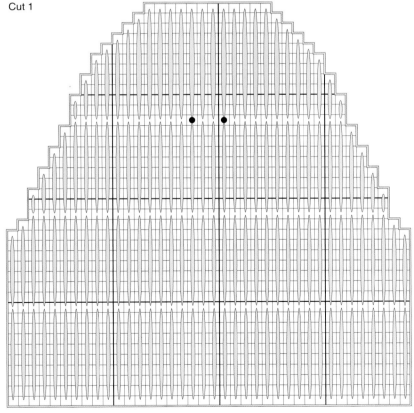

Lil' Birdie Body Front
38 holes x 39 holes
Cut 1

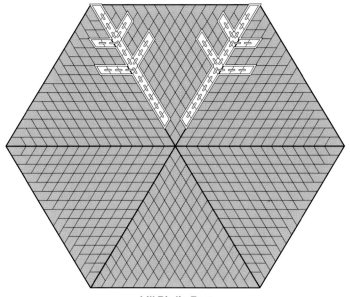

Lil' Birdie Feet
Cut 1 each from plastic canvas hexagon,
cutting away gray area

Lil' Birdie Body Back
38 holes x 39 holes
Cut 1

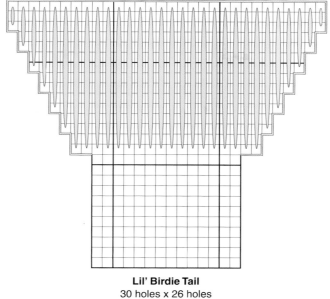

Lil' Birdie Tail
30 holes x 26 holes
Cut 1

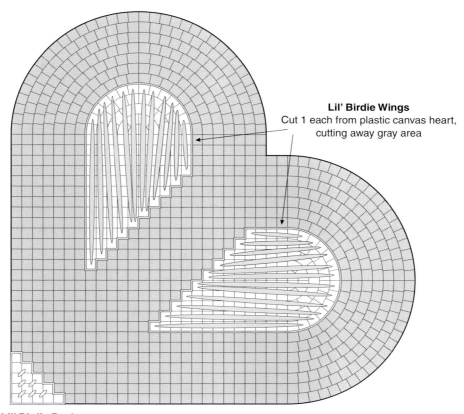

Lil' Birdie Wings
Cut 1 each from plastic canvas heart,
cutting away gray area

Lil' Birdie Beak
Cut 1 from plastic canvas heart,
cutting away gray area

DARLING BABY ALBUM COVER

Keep your treasured baby photos safe and sound with a stitched album cover.

DESIGN BY CYNTHIA ROBERTS

Skill Level
Beginner

Size
7¼ inches W x 5½ inches H x 2⅝ inches D (18.4cm x 14cm x 6.7cm)

Materials
- 1 sheet 7-count plastic canvas
- Worsted weight yarn as listed in color key
- #16 tapestry needle
- Photo album for 4 x 6-inch (10.2 x 15.2cm) photos

Instructions

1. Cut plastic canvas according to graphs (this page and page 29). Cut two 47-hole x 21-hole pieces for album sleeves.

2. Stitch front following graph, working uncoded areas on white background with white Continental Stitches and uncoded areas on green background with light green Continental Stitches. Stitch back and spine with light green Slanted Gobelin Stitches following graphs.

3. Whipstitch spine to top edges of front and back. Whipstitch sleeves to front and back around side and bottom edges from dot to dot: Overcast remaining edges of album. Do not Overcast remaining sleeve edges.

4. Slide cover of purchased photo album in sleeves of stitched photo album cover. ●

GRAPHS CONTINUED ON PAGE 29

COLOR KEY	
Yards	**Worsted Weight Yarn**
38 (34.8m)	☐ Light green
7 (6.5m)	■ Dark green
3 (2.8m)	▨ Pink
2 (1.9m)	■ Blue
2 (1.9m)	▨ Lavender
1 (1m)	▨ Yellow
19 (17.4m)	Uncoded areas on white background are white Continental Stitches Uncoded areas on green background are light green Continental Stitches

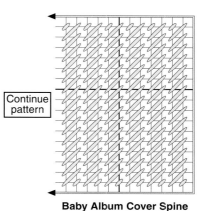

Baby Album Cover Spine
47 holes x 17 holes
Cut 1

Continue pattern

WALLFLOWERS

Bring the beauty of flowers to life when you add this framed masterpiece to any room of your home.

DESIGN BY ALIDA MACOR

Skill Level
Beginner

Size
Fits 10 x 13-inch (25.4cm x 33cm) frame

Materials
- 1 sheet 7-count plastic canvas
- Uniek Needloft plastic canvas yarn as listed in color key
- DMC #3 pearl cotton as listed in color key
- #16 tapestry needle
- 7 (4mm) yellow beads
- 7 (1–1¾-inch/2.5–4.4cm) artificial flowers in coordinating colors
- Hand-sewing needle
- Yellow sewing thread or embroidery floss
- 10 x 13-inch (25.4 x 33cm) piece white cardboard
- 10 x 13-inch (25.4 x 33cm) picture frame

Project Note
Always begin and end pearl cotton under yarn stitches. Use a small starting knot where needed.

Instructions
1. Cut plastic canvas according to graph (page 22).

2. Stitch piece following graph, filling in around flowers, leaves and vase with white Slanted Gobelin Stitch pattern. Do not Overcast edges.

3. When background stitching is completed, work fern and forest green Backstitches and Straight Stitches for flower stems.

4. Remove center of each artificial flower, then place one bead in center of each flower and attach where indicated, using hand-sewing needle and yellow thread or floss.

5. Place white cardboard behind stitched piece in frame. ●

COLOR KEY	
Yards	**Plastic Canvas Yarn**
15 (13.8m)	▦ Lavender #05
7 (6.5m)	▦ Fern #23
24 (22m)	☐ Orchid #44
1 (1m)	▦ Lilac #45
9 (8.3m)	■ Mermaid #53
4 (3.7m)	☐ Pale peach #56
	⁄ Fern #23 Backstitch and Straight Stitch
	#3 Pearl Cotton
30 (27.5m)	☐ White
1 (1m)	⁄ Forest green #989 Backstitch and Straight Stitch
	◉ Attach artificial flower

Color numbers given are for Uniek Needloft plastic canvas yarn and DMC #3 pearl cotton.

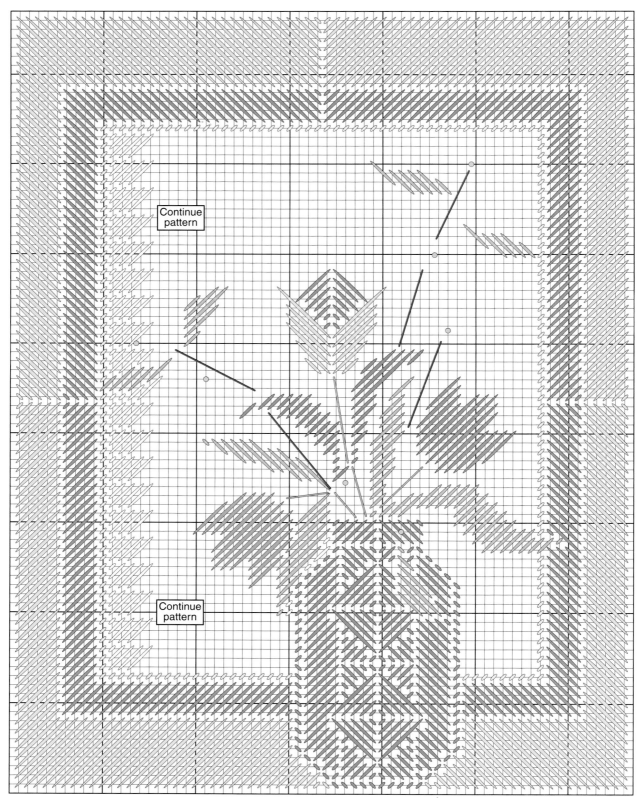

Continue
pattern

Continue
pattern

Wallflowers
67 holes x 87 holes
Cut 1

BABY CHICK FAVOR

Stitch up several of these tiny chicks to give to guests at your next Easter gathering. Fill them with candy for an extra-special treat.

DESIGN BY MARY T. COSGROVE

Skill Level
Beginner

Size
2 inches W x 2⅞ inches H x 3⅜ inches D (5.1cm x 7.3cm x 8.6cm)

Materials
- ½ sheet 7-count plastic canvas
- Uniek Needloft plastic canvas yarn as listed in color key
- #16 tapestry needle

Instructions

1. Cut plastic canvas according to graphs.

2. Stitch pieces following graphs, overlapping four holes of side as indicated before stitching; work uncoded area on chick with yellow Continental Stitches.

3. Overcast top edges of side, including egg and chick. Work bright blue Backstitches when Overcasting is completed.

4. With wrong sides facing, Whipstitch side to base. ●

COLOR KEY

Yards	Plastic Canvas Yarn
1 (1m)	■ Black #00
5 (4.6m)	□ White #41
1 (1m)	▨ Bright orange #58
2 (1.9m)	▨ Bright blue #60
4 (3.7m)	▨ Bright purple #64
1 (1m)	Uncoded areas are yellow #57 Continental Stitches
	⁄ Yellow #57 Overcast
	⁄ Bright blue #60 Backstitch

Color numbers given are for Uniek Needloft plastic canvas yarn.

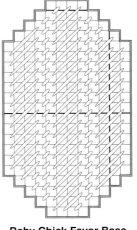

Baby Chick Favor Base
12 holes x 21 holes
Cut 1

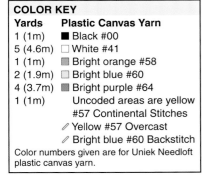

Overlap

Overlap

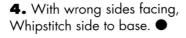
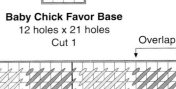

Baby Chick Favor Side
60 holes x 18 holes
Cut 1

SIMPLY SPRING

Cute daisy embellishments add charm to this matching floral cell-phone case and key-chain motif.

DESIGNS BY LEE LINDEMAN

Skill Level
Beginner

Size
Cell-Phone Case: 2³⁄₈ inches W x 4⁵⁄₈ inches H x 1 inch D (6cm x 11.7cm x 2.5cm), excluding ribbon

Key-Chain Motif: 2½ inches W x 2¾ inches H (6.4cm x 7cm), excluding ribbon

Materials
- ²⁄₃ sheet 7-count plastic canvas
- Uniek Needloft plastic canvas yarn as listed in color key
- #16 tapestry needle
- Daisy buttons:
  2 (1-inch/2.5cm)
  2 (¾-inch/1.9cm)
- 27 inches (61cm) ¼-inch/7mm-wide red satin ribbon
- Button shank remover
- Hot-glue gun

Instructions

1. Cut plastic canvas according to graphs.

2. Stitch pieces following graphs, working uncoded areas on case front and back, and on key-chain motif with holly Continental Stitches.

3. Using holly throughout, Overcast inside and outside edges of key-chain motif. Whipstitch side edges of case gusset to side and bottom edges of case front and back from arrow to arrow, easing as necessary to fit. Overcast all remaining edges.

4. If buttons have shanks, cut off shanks with shank remover. Glue buttons to pieces where indicated on graphs.

5. Cut one 12-inch (30.5cm) length red satin ribbon. Thread through hole on key chain motif, then tie in a knot next to plastic canvas. Use ribbon to attach keys.

6. Thread remaining length of ribbon from inside to outside on back piece where indicated on graph. Tie ribbon around belt or purse straps. ●

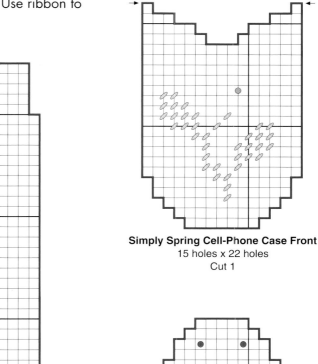

Simply Spring Cell-Phone Case Front
15 holes x 22 holes
Cut 1

Simply Spring Key-Chain Motif
16 holes x 18 holes
Cut 1

COLOR KEY

Yards	Plastic Canvas Yarn
4 (3.7m)	☐ Fern #23
25 (22.9m)	■ Holly #27
	Uncoded areas are holly #27 Continental Stitches
	⦿ Attach large daisy button
	⦿ Attach small daisy button
	● Attach red satin ribbon

Color numbers given are for Uniek Needloft plastic canvas yarn.

Simply Spring Cell-Phone Case Gusset
6 holes x 55 holes
Cut 1

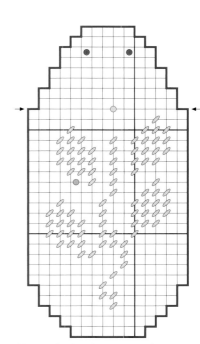

Simply Spring Cell-Phone Case Back
15 holes x 30 holes
Cut 1

DANCING LADYBUGS

Tiny ladybugs look fabulous on this mini tissue holder that's sized for your purse or car console.

DESIGN BY TERRY RICIOLI

Skill Level
Beginner

Size
Fits pocket-size tissue package

Materials
- ½ sheet 7-count plastic canvas
- Uniek Needloft plastic canvas yarn as listed in color key
- 6-strand embroidery floss as listed in color key
- #16 tapestry needle
- 8 (5mm) movable eyes
- Self-adhesive hook-and-loop fastener
- Hand-sewing needle and white sewing thread (optional)
- Hot-glue gun

Instructions

1. Cut one top, one bottom and two ends from plastic canvas according to graphs, cutting out hole on top only, leaving bottom intact.

2. Cut two 32-hole x 7-hole pieces for sides and one 4-hole x 6-hole piece for tab.

3. Stitch top as graphed, working uncoded areas with fern Continental Stitches. Stitch bottom entirely with fern Continental Stitches.

4. When background stitching on top is completed, work black floss Straight Stitches on ladybugs.

5. Continental Stitch remaining pieces with fern.

6. Using fern through step 7, Overcast inside edges of top. Whipstitch top and bottom to sides and one end.

7. Whipstitch second end to top only. Overcast remaining edges of this end, Whipstitching tab in place where indicated while Overcasting. Overcast all remaining edges of holder, including tab.

8. Attach hook-and-loop fastener to tab and to back. If desired, use hand-sewing needle and thread to tack fastener firmly in place.

9. Glue movable eyes to ladybug heads where indicated on graph. ●

TOUCH OF THE TROPICS

Serve up cold drinks in style with these brightly colored coasters that are reminiscent of a tropical resort.

DESIGN BY MARY T. COSGROVE

Skill Level
Beginner

Size
Coasters: 4⅝ inches square (11.7cm)
Holder: 5 inches W x 6¼ inches H x 1½ inches D (12.7cm x 15.9cm x 3.8cm)

Materials
- 1½ sheets 7-count plastic canvas
- Uniek Needloft plastic canvas yarn as listed in color key
- #16 tapestry needle
- 9 x 12-inch sheet CPE Inc. white #0650 Stiffened Eazy Felt
- Fabric glue

Instructions

1. Cut plastic canvas according to graphs (pages 33 and 34). Cut felt slightly smaller than coasters.

2. Stitch pieces following graphs, working uncoded areas on white background with bright pink Continental Stitches, uncoded areas on peach background with bright orange Continental Stitches and uncoded areas on blue background with bright blue Continental Stitches.

3. When background stitching is completed, work Straight Stitches and Running Stitches where indicated.

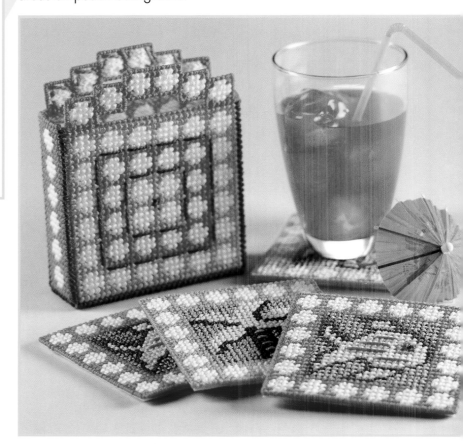

4. Overcast coasters. Whipstitch holder front and back to sides, then Whipstitch front, back and sides to base. Overcast remaining edges.

5. Using fabric glue, attach felt to backs of coaster. Allow to dry. ●

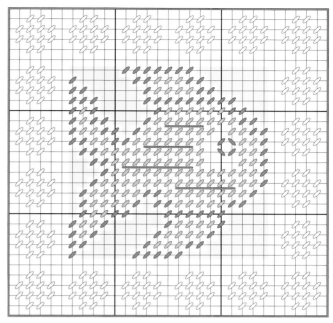

Touch of the Tropics Fish Coaster
30 holes x 30 holes
Cut 2

COLOR KEY

Yards	Plastic Canvas Yarn
4 (3.7m)	■ Holly #27
41 (37.5m)	□ White #41
9 (8.3m)	■ Bright green #61
9 (8.3m)	■ Bright purple #64
24 (22m)	Uncoded areas with peach background are bright orange #58 Continental Stitches
10 (9.2m)	Uncoded areas with blue background are bright blue #60 Continental Stitches
31 (28.4m)	Uncoded areas with white background are bright pink #62 Continental Stitches
	╱ Bright orange #58 Straight Stitch and Overcast
	╱ Bright pink #62 Straight Stitch and Overcast
	╱ Bright purple #64 Running Stitch

Color numbers given are for Uniek Needloft plastic canvas yarn.

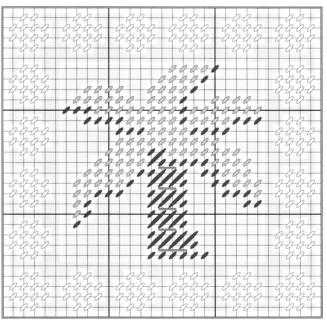

Touch of the Tropics Tree Coaster
30 holes x 30 holes
Cut 2

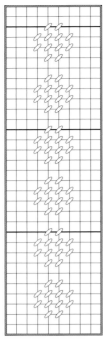

**Touch of the Tropics
Coaster Holder Side & Base**
9 holes x 32 holes
Cut 3

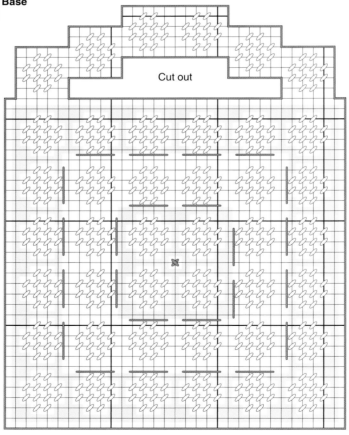

Cut out

**Touch of the Tropics
Coaster Holder Front & Back**
32 holes x 41 holes
Cut 2

UNDER THE SEA TISSUE TOPPER

Fun and fanciful fish swim amongst the shells and seaweed on this bold tissue topper.

DESIGN BY PATRICIA KLESH

Skill Level
Beginner

Size
Fits boutique-style tissue box

Materials
- 1½ sheets 7-count plastic canvas
- Worsted weight yarn as listed in color key
- 6-strand embroidery floss as listed in color key
- #16 tapestry needle

Project Note
Depending on size of boutique-style tissue box, this topper may be a very tight fit.

Instructions
1. Cut plastic canvas according to graphs (page 58).

2. Stitch pieces following graphs, working uncoded areas on sides with light blue Continental Stitches.

3. When background stitching is completed, use full strands (4 plies) yarn to Straight Stitch fish tail and fins and to work French Knot eyes.

4. Use 2 plies yarn to work Backstitches and Straight Stitches on seashells. Work medium yellow floss Straight Stitches on seaweed.

5. Overcast inside edges on top with light blue and bottom edges of sides with black. Using black, Whipstitch sides together, then Whipstitch sides to top. ●

GRAPHS ON PAGE 58

MISCHIEVOUS MONKEY COASTERS

Bring the zoo to your home with this quick-to-create monkey coaster set.

DESIGN BY CHERYL GOODSELL

Skill Level
Beginner

Size
Monkey Coasters: 4⁷⁄₁₆ inches W x 3⁷⁄₈ inches H (11.3cm x 9.8cm)
Cage Holder: 5 inches W x 4¼ inches H x 1¾ inches D (12.7cm x 10.8cm x 4.4cm)

Materials
- 1½ sheets clear 7-count plastic canvas
- 1 sheet black 7-count plastic canvas
- Worsted weight yarn as listed in color key
- #16 tapestry needle

Instructions

1. Cut eight coasters from clear plastic canvas according to graph. Four will remain unstitched and be used for backing.

2. Cut cage holder front, back and sides from block plastic canvas according to graphs, cutting out areas indicated on front and back. Cut one 31-hole x 10-hole piece for cage holder base from black plastic canvas. Base will remain unstitched.

3. Stitch four coasters and cage front, back and sides following graphs.

4. When background stitching is completed, use block to Backstitch mouths and white to Straight Stitch eye highlights.

5. Using dark brown, Whipstitch one unstitched backing to each stitched monkey.

6. Using light brown, Whipstitch cage front and back to cage sides, then Whipstitch front, back and sides to unstitched base. Overcast top edges.

7. Store monkey coasters in cage holder. ●

COLOR KEY	
Yards	**Worsted Weight Yarn**
15 (13.8m)	▨ Dark brown
6 (5.5m)	☐ Medium brown
3 (2.8m)	■ Black
20 (18.3m)	Uncoded areas are light brown Continental Stitches
	⁄ Light brown Overcast and Whipstitch
	╱ Black Backstitch
1 (1m)	⁄ White Straight Stitch

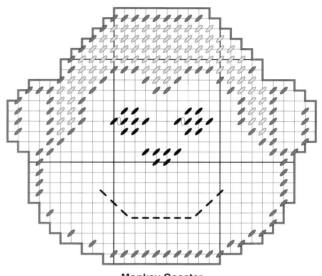

Monkey Coaster
29 holes x 25 holes
Cut 8, stitch 4, from clear

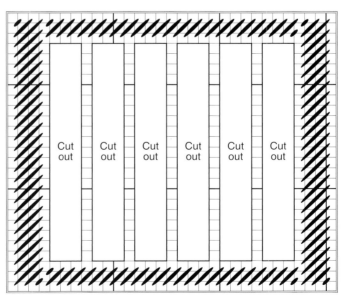

Cage Holder Side
10 holes x 27 holes
Cut 2 from black

Cage Holder Front & Back
31 holes x 27 holes
Cut 2 from black

PRETTY PARROT

Multicolored yarn adds dimension and interest to this tropical-themed design. You don't need to worry about complicated yarn changes.

DESIGN BY MARY T. COSGROVE

Skill Level
Intermediate

Size
6³⁄₈ inches W x 11¹⁄₈ inches H, including hanger (16.2cm x 28.3cm)

Materials
- 1½ sheets 7-count plastic canvas
- Red Heart Classic worsted weight yarn Art. E267 as listed in color key
- Red Heart Kids worsted weight yarn Art. E711 as listed in color key
- #16 tapestry needle
- 1 yard (1m) plus 6 inches (15.2cm) 24-gauge icy lemonade #84510 Fun Wire from Toner Plastics Inc.
- 35 (8mm) round pink faceted beads
- 133 purple metallic E beads
- 2 black E beads
- Wire cutters
- Craft glue

Instructions
1. Cut plastic canvas according to graph (page 40), cutting out center area, forming parrot.

2. Stitch one piece as graphed. When background stitching is completed, use cherry red to work Backstitches on beak and Straight Stitches on tail.

3. Reverse remaining piece, then work stitches in reverse, adding cherry red embroidery when background stitching is completed.

4. Whipstitch wrong sides together along inside and out0side edges.

Beading
Notes: *Use a 1-yard (1m) length icy lemonade wire to thread on beads inside frame. Note that some bending of wire is needed in order to add amount of beads required.*

Begin and end each length by threading wire through holes indicated. Wrap end of wire around wire just below or above edge. At bottom of each length, cut wire and proceed to next length.

1. Begin at top left hole indicated. Thread on one pink bead, then four purple beads. Continue pattern eight more times. Add one pink and three purple beads, then thread wire through hole on tail and add another purple bead, one pink, four purple and one more pink bead before ending.

2. At next point at top, thread on one pink bead and four purple beads.

3. At next point at top, add one pink and one purple bead, ending at center of head. Proceed to bottom of parrot and add four purple and one pink bead. Repeat pattern one more time.

4. At next point, thread one pink bead, then four purple beads, ending at front of head. Begin next length at bottom of red part on breast and thread on four purple beads and one pink. Continue pattern four more times.

5. At final point at top, thread on one pink bead then four purple beads. Continue pattern 10 more times, then end with pink bead.

6. For hanger, attach 6-inch (15.2cm) length of wire at one point indicated at top. Thread on four purple, one pink and four purple beads. Attach end of wire at remaining point indicated.

7. Glue black beads to head for eyes where indicated on graph. ●

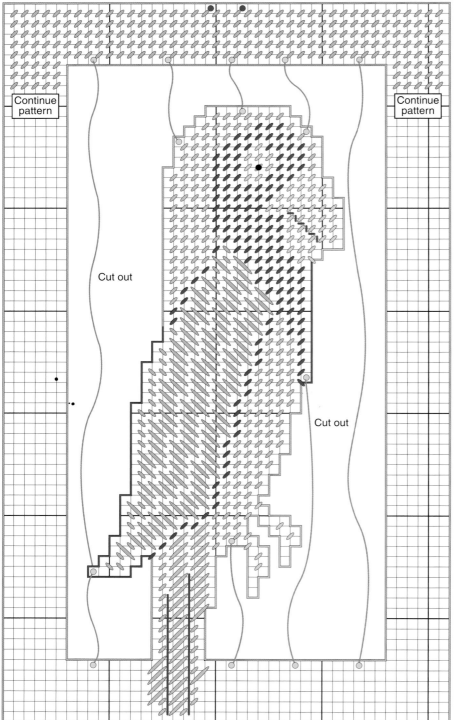

COLOR KEY

Yards	Worsted Weight Yarn
9 (8.3m)	Parakeet #513
6 (5.5m)	Cherry red #912
4 (3.7m)	Yellow #2230
39 (35.7m)	Bikini multi #2945
╱	Cherry red #912 Backstitch and Straight Stitch
●	Attach black bead
○	Attach wire for beading
●	Attach wire for hanger

Color numbers given are for Red Heart Classic worsted weight yarn Art. E267 and Kids worsted weight yarn Art. E711.

Continue pattern

Continue pattern

Cut out

Cut out

Pretty Parrot
42 holes x 70 holes
Cut 2
Stitch 1 as graphed
Reverse 1 and work
stitches in reverse

SUMMER GIFT BAG

Give a cherished friend a gift with an extra bonus—
a plastic canvas motif. The detachable motif is the perfect size
for use as a summertime coaster.

DESIGN BY CYNTHIA ROBERTS

Skill Level
Beginner

Size
Motif: 4⅛ inches square
(10.5cm)

Materials
- ⅓ sheet 7-count plastic canvas
- Worsted weight yarn as listed in color key
- #16 tapestry needle
- 1 yard black 6-strand embroidery floss
- Gift bag larger than motif
- Repositionable adhesive

Instructions
1. Cut plastic canvas according to graph (page 59).

2. Stitch piece following graph, working uncoded areas with off-white Continental Stitches. Overcast with off-white.

3. When background stitching and Overcasting are completed, use a full strand yarn to work black Running Stitches between motifs and light green Straight Stitches at bottom of birdhouse motif.

CONTINUED ON PAGE 59

FARM FRIEND TOWEL HANGER

Add some down home on the farm fun to your kitchen by decorating with this cheeky chicken.

DESIGN BY DARLENE NEUBAUER

Skill Level
Beginner

Size
10½ inches W x 11⅜ inches H (26.7cm x 28.9cm), excluding metal ring

Materials
- 2 sheets 7-count plastic canvas
- Worsted weight yarn as listed in color key
- Sport weight yarn as listed in color key
- #16 tapestry needle
- 7-inch gold metal ring
- 1-inch white bone ring

Instructions

1. Cut plastic canvas according to graph. Back will remain unstitched.

2. Stitch front with worsted weight yarn following graph, working uncoded areas with Continental Stitches as follows: white background with white and yellow background with yellow.

3. When background stitching is completed, work medium pink and black sport weight yarn embroidery.

4. Sew white bone ring to back piece near top edge of scarf area.

5. Place front over back, matching edges; Whipstitch together, placing gold metal ring between pieces where indicated at arrows and Whipstitching around ring. ●

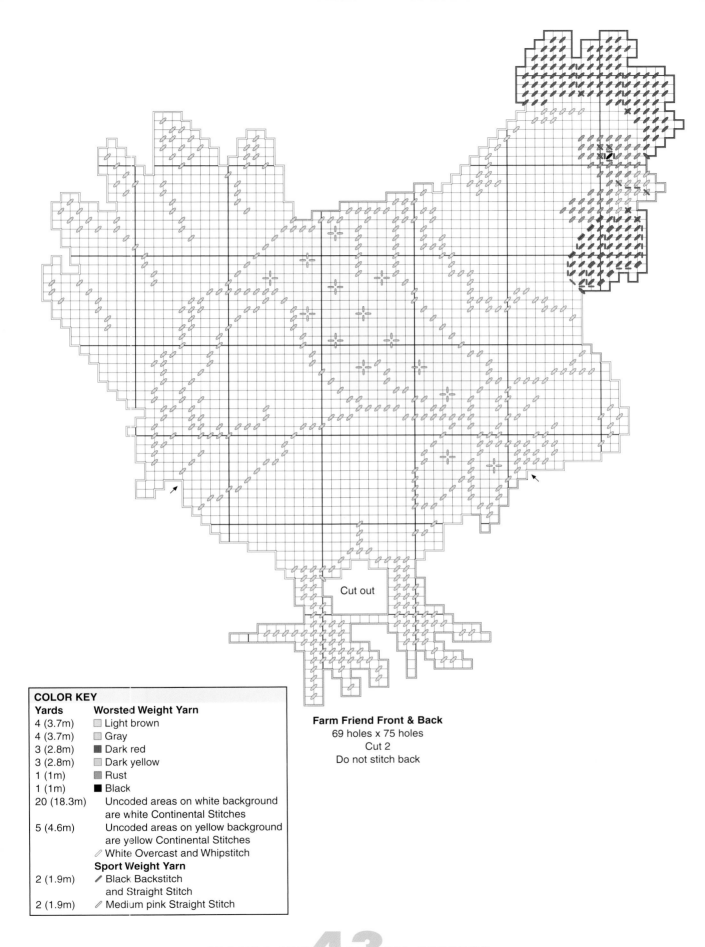

COLOR KEY

Yards	Worsted Weight Yarn
4 (3.7m)	☐ Light brown
4 (3.7m)	☐ Gray
3 (2.8m)	■ Dark red
3 (2.8m)	☐ Dark yellow
1 (1m)	■ Rust
1 (1m)	■ Black
20 (18.3m)	Uncoded areas on white background are white Continental Stitches
5 (4.6m)	Uncoded areas on yellow background are yellow Continental Stitches
	⟋ White Overcast and Whipstitch
	Sport Weight Yarn
2 (1.9m)	⟋ Black Backstitch and Straight Stitch
2 (1.9m)	⟋ Medium pink Straight Stitch

Farm Friend Front & Back
69 holes x 75 holes
Cut 2
Do not stitch back

Cut out

LIBERTY ANGEL

Your patriotic pride will shine bright when you create this loving little angel.

DESIGN BY KATHY WIRTH

Skill Level
Beginner

Size
8⅝ inches W x 11⅞ inches H (21.9cm x 30.2cm)

Materials
- 1 sheet 7-count stiff plastic canvas
- Red Heart Classic worsted weight yarn Art. E267 as listed in color key
- 4mm Rainbow Gallery Plastic Canvas 7 Metallic Needlepoint Yarn as listed in color key
- #16 tapestry needle
- 2½-inch (6.4cm) wooden star
- 13 inches (33cm) 20-gauge white cloth-covered wire
- Gold spray paint
- Hot-glue gun

Instructions

1. Cut plastic canvas according to graphs (page 46), cutting out holes in letters B and R.

2. Spray wooden star with gold paint. Allow to dry.

3. Overcast letters with red metallic needlepoint yarn.

4. Stitch and Overcast angel and wings following graphs, working uncoded area across arms with soft navy Continental Stitches. Do not Overcast edges at center of wings and head edges at Lark's Head Knots.

5. When background stitching is completed, work French Knot eyes with 2 plies black yarn. Use 4 plies black yarn to work Lark's Head Knots around head edges where indicated, leaving ½-inch tails. Use needle to divide yarn strands to "frizz" hair. Trim as needed.

6. Use photo as a guide through step 7. For hanger, insert wire ends behind stitches in hands where indicated with arrows. Bend back small amount of wire on each end to secure to hands. Glue to fix firmly in place.

7. Position wings behind angel, then glue in center and behind hands. Glue star behind head. Glue letters to front of hanger, spelling the word "LIBERTY." ●

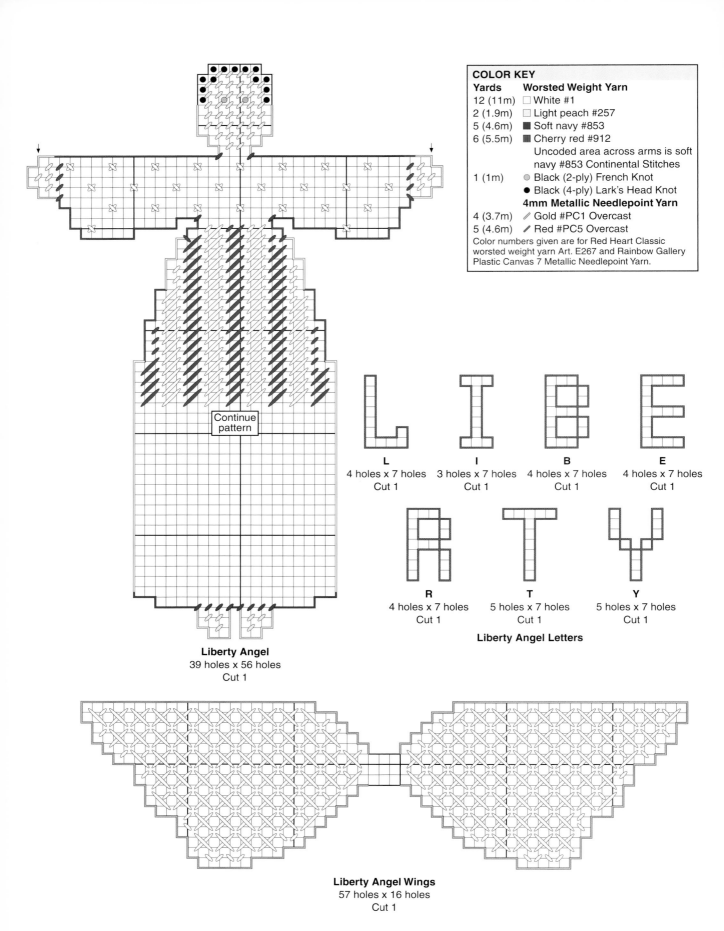

COLOR KEY

Yards	Worsted Weight Yarn
12 (11m)	☐ White #1
2 (1.9m)	☐ Light peach #257
5 (4.6m)	■ Soft navy #853
6 (5.5m)	■ Cherry red #912
	Uncoded area across arms is soft navy #853 Continental Stitches
1 (1m)	● Black (2-ply) French Knot
	● Black (4-ply) Lark's Head Knot

4mm Metallic Needlepoint Yarn

4 (3.7m)	✦ Gold #PC1 Overcast
5 (4.6m)	✦ Red #PC5 Overcast

Color numbers given are for Red Heart Classic worsted weight yarn Art. E267 and Rainbow Gallery Plastic Canvas 7 Metallic Needlepoint Yarn.

Continue pattern

Liberty Angel
39 holes x 56 holes
Cut 1

L
4 holes x 7 holes
Cut 1

I
3 holes x 7 holes
Cut 1

B
4 holes x 7 holes
Cut 1

E
4 holes x 7 holes
Cut 1

R
4 holes x 7 holes
Cut 1

T
5 holes x 7 holes
Cut 1

Y
5 holes x 7 holes
Cut 1

Liberty Angel Letters

Liberty Angel Wings
57 holes x 16 holes
Cut 1

DRAGONFLY BOX

Add natural beauty to any setting with this lovely, linen-look box.

DESIGN BY ADELE MOGAVERO

Skill Level
Beginner

Size
5 inches square x 5½ inches H (12.7cm x 14cm)

Materials
- 2 sheets 7-count plastic canvas
- Uniek Needloft plastic canvas yarn as listed in color key
- Kreinik ⅛-inch Ribbon as listed in color key
- #16 tapestry needle

Instructions

1. Cut plastic canvas according to graphs (pages 48 and 49). Cut one 33-hole x 33-hole piece for base. Base will remain unstitched.

2. Stitch lid top and sides following graphs, working uncoded areas with beige Continental Stitches.

3. For sides, use lilac to work base of dragonfly bodies first following body base stitching graph (page 49). Complete body by working lilac stitches in opposite direction following box side graph, covering body base stitches and watching carefully in which holes the stitches begin and end.

4. Stitch remaining areas on sides, working uncoded areas with beige Continental Stitches.

5. When background stitching is completed, embroider flowers on lid top, lid sides and box sides with purple and mermaid yarn; Straight Stitch antennae with amethyst ribbon.

6. Using beige throughout, Whipstitch box sides together, then Whipstitch sides to base. Overcast top edges.

7. Using moss throughout, Whipstitch lid sides together, then Whipstitch lid sides to lid top. Overcast bottom edges. ●

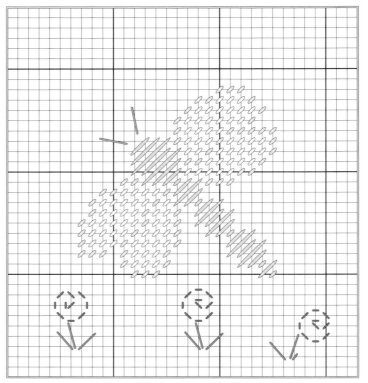

Dragonfly Box Side
33 holes x 36 holes
Cut 4

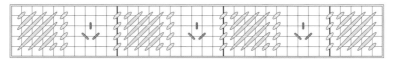

Dragonfly Box Lid Side
35 holes x 5 holes
Cut 4

COLOR KEY	
Yards	**Plastic Canvas Yarn**
20 (18.3m)	☐ Baby yellow #21
30 (27.5m)	☐ Moss #25
30 (27.5m)	☐ Lilac #45
130 (118.9m)	Uncoded areas are beige #40 Continental Stitches
	⁄ Beige #40 Overcast and Whipstitch
10 (9.2m)	⁄ Purple #46 Backstitch and Straight Stitch
10 (9.2m)	⁄ Mermaid #53 Backstitch
	¹⁄₈-Inch Ribbon
2 (1.9m)	⁄ Amethyst #026 Straight Stitch

Color numbers given are for Uniek Needloft plastic canvas yarn and Kreinik ¹⁄₈-inch Ribbon.

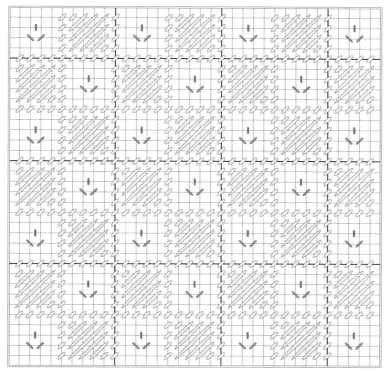

Dragonfly Box Lid Top
35 holes x 35 holes
Cut 1

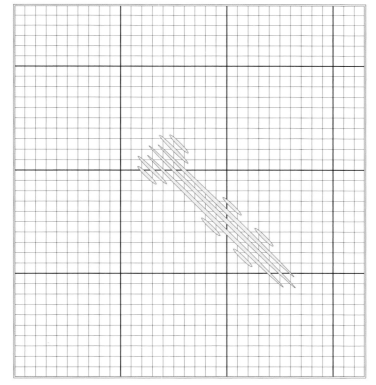

Dragonfly Body Base Stitching

LIGHTHOUSE SEASCAPE CALENDAR

Make every day a breezy one at the beach when you count down the days with this nautical calendar.

DESIGN BY CAROLE RODGERS

Skill Level

Beginner

Size

10½ inches W x 13½ inches H (26.7cm x 34.3cm)

Materials

- 3 sheets 7-count plastic canvas
- Uniek Needloft plastic canvas yarn as listed in color key
- #16 tapestry needle
- 36 inches (91.2cm) white hook-and-loop strip
- Hot-glue gun

Instructions

1. Cut ledge front, month and number pieces, and seascape front and back from plastic canvas according to graphs (pages 52 and 53). Cut one 42-hole x 2-hole piece for ledge back. Seascape back will remain unstitched.

2. Stitch seascape front following graph, working uncoded areas with Continental Stitches as follows: green background with fern, yellow background with silver, white background with white and blue background with bright blue. Leave area at center bottom unstitched as indicated.

3. When background stitching is completed, work black Backstitches for birds' wings and at lighthouse side, burgundy and red Backstitches on windows and white Straight Stitches for fence rails.

4. Place two ledge front pieces together, then place ledge back behind front pieces, aligning bottom and side edges. Continental Stitch pieces with fern, working through all three layers. Overcast around side and top edges of ledge front from blue dot to blue dot.

5. Stitch calendar numbers following graphs, working uncoded areas with fern Continental Stitches.

6. For months, stitch one for May as graphed working uncoded areas with fern Continental Stitches. For each remaining month, center and stitch the three-letter abbreviation for month first using letters given (page 53), then fill in with fern Continental Stitches.

Assembly

1. Place front seascape over back seascape, matching edges. Whipstitch together following graph, attaching bottom edges of ledge pieces where indicated with brackets at center bottom while stitching. Whipstitch side edges of ledge pieces to front and back where indicated at fern lines.

2. Cut hook-and-loop tape in 12 (2-inch/6.4cm) lengths for months and 12 (1-inch/2.5cm) lengths for numbers. Center and glue soft side of tape in place to back side months and numbers.

3. Display months and numbers on ledge as in photo.

4. Hang seascape as desired. ●

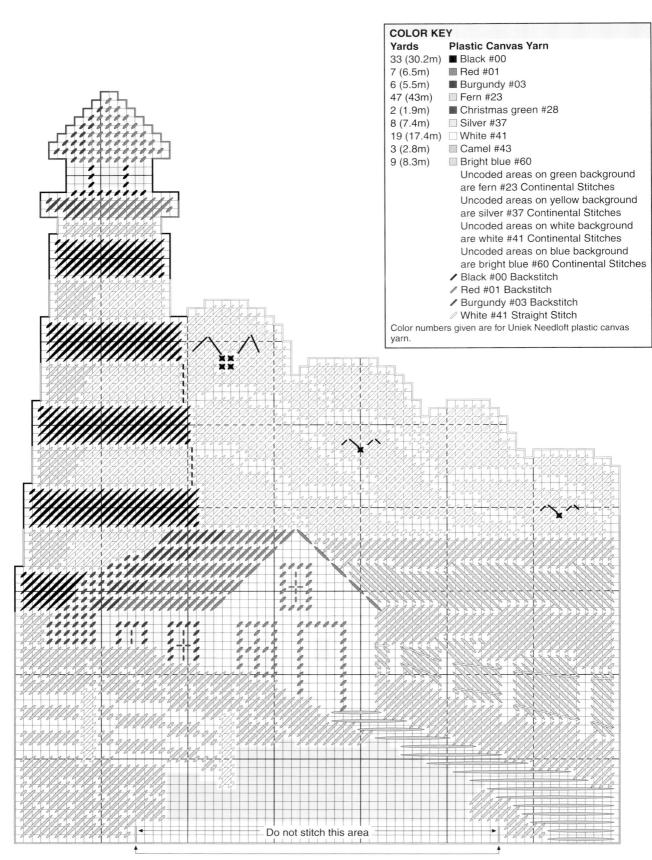

COLOR KEY

Yards		Plastic Canvas Yarn
33 (30.2m)	■	Black #00
7 (6.5m)	■	Red #01
6 (5.5m)	■	Burgundy #03
47 (43m)	■	Fern #23
2 (1.9m)	■	Christmas green #28
8 (7.4m)	■	Silver #37
19 (17.4m)	□	White #41
3 (2.8m)	■	Camel #43
9 (8.3m)	■	Bright blue #60

Uncoded areas on green background
are fern #23 Continental Stitches
Uncoded areas on yellow background
are silver #37 Continental Stitches
Uncoded areas on white background
are white #41 Continental Stitches
Uncoded areas on blue background
are bright blue #60 Continental Stitches

✦ Black #00 Backstitch
✦ Red #01 Backstitch
✦ Burgundy #03 Backstitch
✦ White #41 Straight Stitch

Color numbers given are for Uniek Needloft plastic canvas
yarn.

Do not stitch this area

Lighthouse Seascape Front & Back
70 holes x 90 holes
Cut 2
Stitch front only

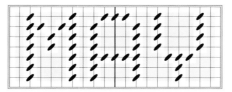

Lighthouse Seascape Month
20 holes x 8 holes
Cut 12
Stitch 1 as graphed
Stitch 1 for each remaining month

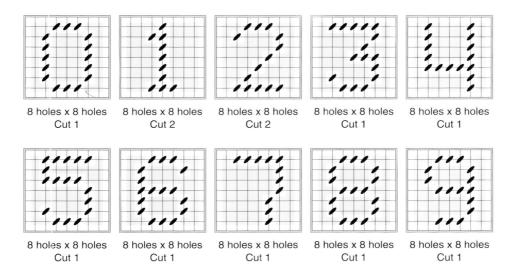

| 8 holes x 8 holes | 8 holes x 8 holes | 8 holes x 8 holes | 8 holes x 8 holes | 8 holes x 8 holes |
| Cut 1 | Cut 2 | Cut 2 | Cut 1 | Cut 1 |

| 8 holes x 8 holes | 8 holes x 8 holes | 8 holes x 8 holes | 8 holes x 8 holes | 8 holes x 8 holes |
| Cut 1 | Cut 1 | Cut 1 | Cut 1 | Cut 1 |

Lighthouse Seascape Calendar Numbers

Lighthouse Seascape Ledge Front
42 holes x 3 holes
Cut 2

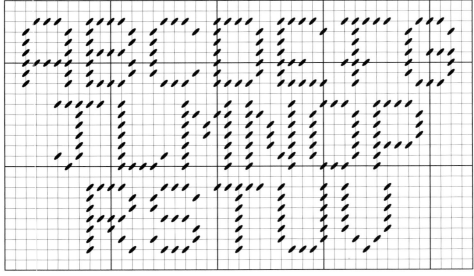

Lighthouse Seascape Months Letters

PINWHEEL ROSES

Both a pinwheel and a pretty rose, the motif on this topper will surely be a conversation piece.

DESIGN BY KATHY WIRTH

Skill Level

Intermediate

Size

Fits boutique-style tissue box

Materials

- 1½ sheets 7-count plastic canvas
- Red Heart Classic worsted weight yarn Art. E267 as listed in color key
- 4mm Rainbow Gallery Plastic Canvas 7 Metallic Needlepoint Yarn as listed in color key
- #16 tapestry needle

Instructions

1. Cut plastic canvas according to graphs.

2. Stitch pieces following graphs, working uncoded areas with white Continental Stitches.

3. Overcast inside edges of top with purple metallic needlepoint yarn. Using light lavender throughout, Overcast bottom edges of sides; Whipstitch sides together, then Whipstitch sides to top. ●

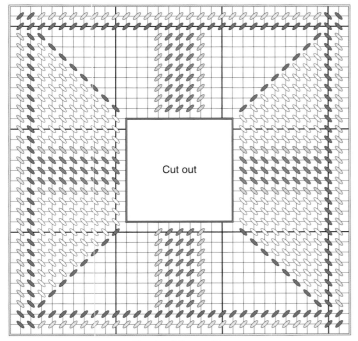

Pinwheel Roses Top
32 holes x 32 holes
Cut 1

Pinwheel Roses Side
32 holes x 37 holes
Cut 4

SUNFLOWER BLACKBOARD

Hang this gorgeous chalkboard in your entryway or kitchen to leave important notes for your family.

DESIGN BY CYNTHIA ROBERTS

Skill Level
Beginner

Size
9 inches W x 10⅛ inches H
(22.9cm x 25.7cm)

Materials
- 1 sheet 7-count plastic canvas
- Worsted weight yarn as listed in color key
- #16 tapestry needle
- Small amount of raffia
- 4 (⅝-inch/1.6cm) butterfly buttons
- Button shank remover
- 6 x 8-inch (15.2 x 20.3cm) blackboard
- Chalk
- Hot-glue gun

Instructions
1. Cut plastic canvas according to graph.

2. Stitch and Overcast frame following graph, working uncoded areas with beige Continental Stitches.

3. When background stitching is completed, work Running Stitches just inside checkered border with 2 plies black. Work Backstitches

around each sunflower with 1 ply copper.

4. Using photo as a guide through step 5, center and glue stitched frame to blackboard. Tie raffia in a bow and glue to upper left corner of beige and sunflower border. Tie one streamer around chalk. Trim ends of raffia as desired.

5. Remove shanks from butterfly buttons. Glue one butterfly in center of raffia bow, then glue one butterfly in each corner of beige and sunflower border.

6. Hang as desired. ●

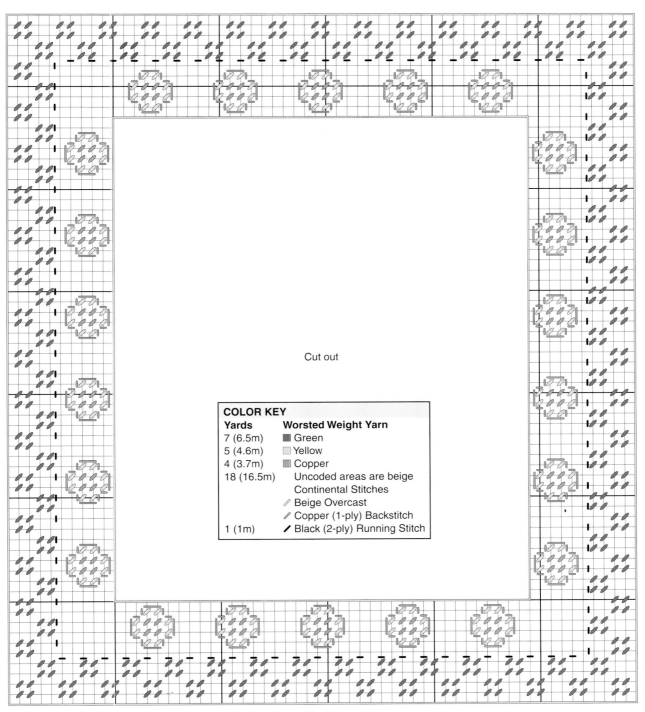

Cut out

COLOR KEY

Yards	Worsted Weight Yarn
7 (6.5m)	■ Green
5 (4.6m)	□ Yellow
4 (3.7m)	▨ Copper
18 (16.5m)	Uncoded areas are beige Continental Stitches
	⁄ Beige Overcast
	⁄ Copper (1-ply) Backstitch
1 (1m)	✦ Black (2-ply) Running Stitch

Sunflower Blackboard Frame
59 holes x 67 holes
Cut 1

UNDER THE SEA TISSUE TOPPER

CONTINUED FROM PAGE 35

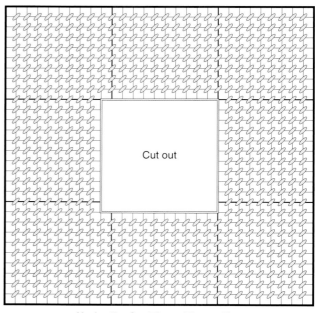

Under the Sea Tissue Topper Top
29 holes x 29 holes
Cut 1

Cut out

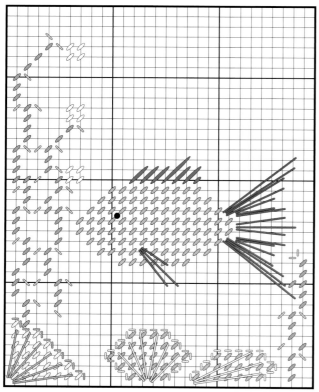

Under the Sea Tissue Topper Side
29 holes x 37 holes
Cut 4

COLOR KEY	
Yards	**Worsted Weight Yarn**
65 (59.5m)	☐ Light blue
8 (7.4m)	▨ Orange
6 (5.5m)	▨ Olive green
3 (2.8m)	☐ Peach
2 (1.9m)	■ Yellow-gold
2 (1.9m)	▨ Light tan
2 (1.9m)	▨ Rose
1 (1m)	☐ White
	Uncoded areas on sides are light blue Continental Stitches
7 (6.5m)	✎ Black Overcast and Whipstitch
3 (2.8m)	✎ Bright orange (4-ply) Straight Stitch
	✎ Yellow gold (4-ply) Straight Stitch
	✎ Peach (2-ply) Backstitch and Straight Stitch
	✎ Light tan (2-ply) Backstitch and Straight Stitch
	✎ White (2-ply) Backstitch Straight Stitch
	● Black French Knot
	6-Strand Embroidery Floss
4 (3.7m)	✎ Medium yellow Straight Stitch

SUMMER GIFT BAG

CONTINUED FROM PAGE 41

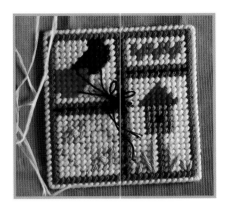

4. Use 2 plies yarn to work yellow French Knots on flowers and light green Backstitches on flower and bird motifs.

5. Cut black floss in four equal lengths. For balloon tails, thread needle with one length; knot end. Bring needle from back to front where indicated at blue balloon, pulling length through to knot. Repeat for yellow and red balloons, using two more lengths.

6. To tie balloon tails together, bring ends of remaining length from back to front through holes indicated with red dots. Tie in a bow around balloon tails. Trim ends as desired.

7. Apply repositionable adhesive to back of stitched motif, then adhere to gift bag as desired. ●

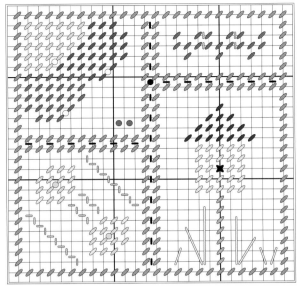

Summer Gift Bag Motif
27 holes x 27 holes
Cut 1

COLOR KEY	
Yards	**Worsted Weight Yarn**
5 (4.6m)	▨ Medium green
2 (1.9m)	☐ Light green
1 (1m)	☐ Yellow
1 (1m)	■ Red
1 (1m)	■ Royal blue
1 (1m)	■ Dark red
1 (1m)	☐ Pink
1 (1m)	▨ Rust
1 (1m)	▨ Medium blue
1 (1m)	■ Black
7 (6.5m)	Uncoded areas are off-white Continental Stitches
	⁄ Off-white Overcast
	⁄ Light green (4-ply) Straight Stitch
	⁄ Light green (2-ply) Backstitch
	✄ Black (4-ply) Running Stitch
	○ Yellow (2-ply) French Knot
	● Black (4-ply) French Knot
	○ Attach balloon tail
	● Attach bow

AUTUMN ACCENTS

AUTUMN ANGEL

Sweet as can be, this precious angel will add seasonal cheer to your home.

DESIGN BY LAURA VICTORY

Skill Level

Intermediate

Size

14⅞ inches W x 20½ inches H x 1¼ inches D (37.8cm x 52.1cm x 3.2cm), excluding flowers

Materials

- 3 sheets 7-count plastic canvas
- Uniek Needloft plastic canvas yarn as listed in color key
- 6-strand embroidery floss as listed in color key
- #16 tapestry needle
- 2 (8mm) black beads
- 1-inch/2.5cm-wide cream lace:
    14-inch (35.6cm) length
    9-inch (22.9cm) length
- 4 (1¾-inch/4.4cm) sunflowers with leaves
- Excelsior
- 2 (½-inch/1.3cm) orange buttons
- 11⅞ x ¹⁵⁄₁₆-inch (30.2 x 2.4cm) plastic foam disk
- Craft knife
- Curly doll hair in desired color
- Straw doll hat
- Powdered blush
- Hand-sewing needle
- Black, pumpkin and cream sewing thread
- Hot-glue gun

Instructions

1. Cut plastic canvas according to graphs (pages 64 and 65). Cut two 7-hole x 28-hole pieces for sides and one 33-hole x 7-hole piece for base. Body back will remain unstitched.

2. Stitch sides and base with bittersweet Continental Stitches. Stitch remaining pieces following graphs, leaving bottom portion of wings unstitched as indicated.

3. When background stitching is completed, work bittersweet Backstitches for mouth and pumpkin Backstitches for shoe straps. Use 2 plies very dark brown floss to outline squares on front with Backstitches.

4. Overcast head around side and top edges from dot to dot. Overcast legs around side and bottom edges from dot to dot. Overcast heart portion of wings, leaving bottom edges of wings unstitched as indicated on graph.

5. Using hand-sewing needle throughout, attach beads to head for eyes with black thread. Attach buttons to shoes with pumpkin thread, placing one button where indicated for leg on right and remaining button on other side of shoe for leg on left (see photo).

Assembly

1. Using eggshell throughout, Whipstitch bottom edge of head to top edge of body front. Place base along bottom edge of front, then Whipstitch legs to base and front where indicated.

2. Using bittersweet through step 3, Whipstitch remaining edges of base and body front together. Whipstitch sides to front along straight side edges. Overcast remaining edges of body front.

3. Whipstitch back to sides and base. Overcast remaining edges of base and sides. Remaining edges of back will remain unworked.

4. Glue unstitched portion of wings to back side of body front where indicated.

5. Using hand-sewing needle and cream thread, run a gathering stitch across top edge of 14-inch (35.6cm) length of lace. Gather to fit across bottom edge of body above legs and sew in place. Repeat with 9-inch (22.9cm) length, sewing to neckline.

6. Cut plastic foam to fit body shape, then insert in body.

Finishing

1. Using photo as a guide through step 3, apply blush to cheeks.

2. Evenly space and glue three sunflowers down front of body. Glue curly doll hair around side and top edges of head. Glue or sew sunflower to straw hat, then glue or sew straw hat to head.

3. Glue excelsior over plastic foam behind wings, completely covering foam.

4. Hang as desired. ●

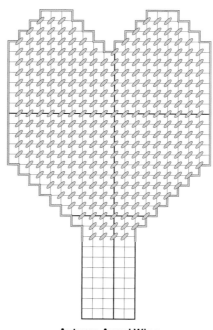

Autumn Angel Wing
19 holes x 30 holes
Cut 2

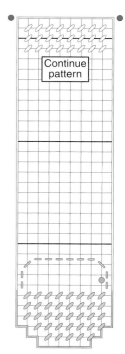

Continue pattern

Autumn Angel Leg
9 holes x 32 holes
Cut 2

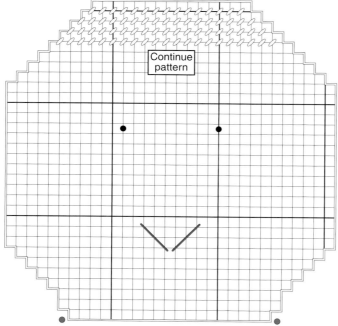

Continue pattern

Autumn Angel Head
31 holes x 31 holes
Cut 1

COLOR KEY

Yards	Plastic Canvas Yarn
20 (18.3m)	▨ Rust #09
20 (18.3m)	▨ Tangerine #11
40 (36.6m)	▨ Pumpkin #12
29 (26.6m)	▢ Eggshell #39
43 (39.4m)	▨ Bittersweet #52
	⟋ Pumpkin #12 Backstitch
	⟋ Bittersweet #52 Backstitch
6-Strand Embroidery Floss	
16 (14.7m)	⟋ Very dark brown (2-ply) Backstitch
	● Attach bead
	● Attach button

Color numbers given are for Uniek Needloft plastic canvas yarn.

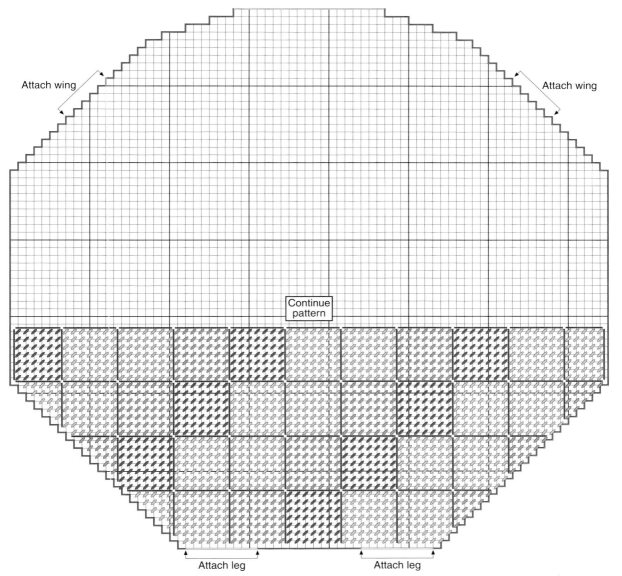

Attach wing

Attach wing

Continue pattern

Attach leg

Attach leg

Autumn Angel Body Front & Back
75 holes x 70 holes
Cut 2
Stitch front only

AUTUMN GLOW VOTIVE CANDLE SCREEN

Light up the night with a votive enclosed by this brilliant autumn leaves candleholder.

DESIGN BY TERRY RICIOLI

Skill Level
Beginner

Size
5 inches square

Materials
- 1 sheet 7-count plastic canvas
- Uniek Needloft plastic canvas yarn as listed in color key
- #16 tapestry needle

Project Note
Please use caution. Plastic canvas and plastic canvas yarn will melt and burn if they get too hot or come in contact with a flame. Never leave a lighted candle unattended. Recommended for decorative purposes only.

Instructions

1. Cut plastic canvas according to graphs.

2. Stitch corners following graph. Stitch side 1 as graphed, Overcasting inside edges with red.

3. Stitch side 2, replacing yellow with red and red with pumpkin; side 3, replacing yellow with pumpkin and red with bittersweet; and side 4, replacing yellow with bittersweet and red with yellow.

4. Using maple throughout, Whipstitch sides to corners, placing sides in numerical order. Overcast top and bottom edges. ●

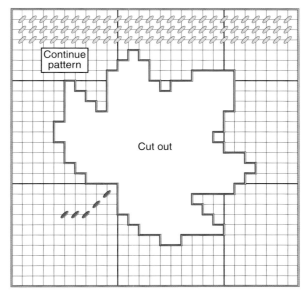

Autumn Glow Votive Candle Screen Side
27 holes x 27 holes
Cut 4
Stitch side 1 as graphed
Stitch side 2 replacing yellow with
red and red with pumpkin
Stitch side 3 replacing yellow with
pumpkin and red with bittersweet
Stitch side 4 replacing yellow with
bittersweet and red with yellow

Continue
pattern

Cut out

COLOR KEY

Yards	Plastic Canvas Yarn
7 (6.5m)	■ Red #01
7 (6.5m)	Pumpkin #12
12 (11m)	▨ Maple #13
7 (6.5m)	Bittersweet #52
7 (6.5m)	☐ Yellow #57

Color numbers given are for Uniek
Needloft plastic canvas yarn.

**Autumn Glow Votive
Candle Screen Corner**
3 holes x 27 holes
Cut 4

HARVEST FRIENDS CANDLEHOLDER

Light up your home with this charming candleholder that uses a battery-powered tea-light candle. No fuss, no muss!

DESIGN BY JANELLE GIESE

Skill Level
Beginner

Size
6¼ inches W x 8¼ inches H x 3¼ inches D (15.9cm x 21cm x 8.3cm)

Materials
- 1 sheet clear stiff 7-count plastic canvas
- 1 sheet brown 7-count plastic canvas
- ¼ sheet orange 7-count plastic canvas
- Uniek Needloft plastic canvas yarn as listed in color key
- Kreinik ⅛-inch Ribbon as listed in color key
- #5 pearl cotton as listed in color key
- #16 tapestry needle
- Battery-operated tea-light candle
- 1⅛ inches high x 1⅞ inches in diameter (2.9cm x 4.8cm) glass tea-light candleholder
- 6 x 3¼-inch (15.2 x 8.3cm) piece felt in coordinating color
- Aquarium gravel
- Powdered blush
- Cotton swab
- Thick white glue

Project Note
The diamond, heart, star, triangle and inverted triangle symbols designate Continental Stitches.

Instructions
1. Cut one each of motif front, base top support and base bottom support from clear stiff plastic canvas according to graphs (pages 70 and 72). Support pieces will remain unstitched.

2. Cut one each of motif back, leaf ring, base top, base bottom and base side from brown plastic canvas according to graphs (pages 70 and 72). Base bottom will remain unstitched.

3. Cut one leaf ring liner from orange plastic canvas according to graph (page 72). Liner will remain unstitched.

4. Cut felt slightly smaller than base bottom. Set aside.

Motif Front
1. Stitch motif front following graph, working Continental Stitches in uncoded areas as follows: tangerine on peach background, cinnamon on white background, forest on green background, royal on blue background, beige on yellow background. Do not stitch Whipstitch line or below line at this time.

2. Use a full strand (2 plies) yarn to work embroidery through step 3 as follows: black at cat's nose; red for hat brim; rust for scarecrow's buttons, eggshell for crow's eyes; camel for cornstalks.

3. For corn tassels, work only the first three Lark's Head Knots on the left over intersections indicated. Trim tails to ½ inch (1.3cm). Remaining three Lark's Head Knots will be stitched later.

4. Use 1 ply yarn to work embroidery through step 6, working yellow Straight Stitches for crow's bottom beak and eggshell Straight Stitches at crow's wing and top knot.

5. Work eggshell Pin Stitches for highlights on cat's eyes. Bring yarn up in hole indicated above stitch, go down through black yarn, splitting stitch, and back through same hole in which stitch originated.

6. Combine 1 ply each of cinnamon and beige to Straight Stitch straw accents at head, collar, hands and feet.

7. Work remaining embroidery with gold ribbon and black pearl cotton following graphs, wrapping French Knots on crow's eyes two times.

Base & Leaf Ring

1. Place base top support under base top, then stitch as one following graph, working uncoded areas outside blue Whipstitch line with cinnamon Continental Stitches. Do not stitch blue Whipstitch line or area inside blue line.

2. Stitch side following graph.

3. Stitch leaf ring, overlapping two holes on sides before stitching and working Continental Stitches in uncoded areas as follows: tangerine on peach background, cinnamon on white background.

4. Work black pearl cotton embroidery when background stitching is completed.

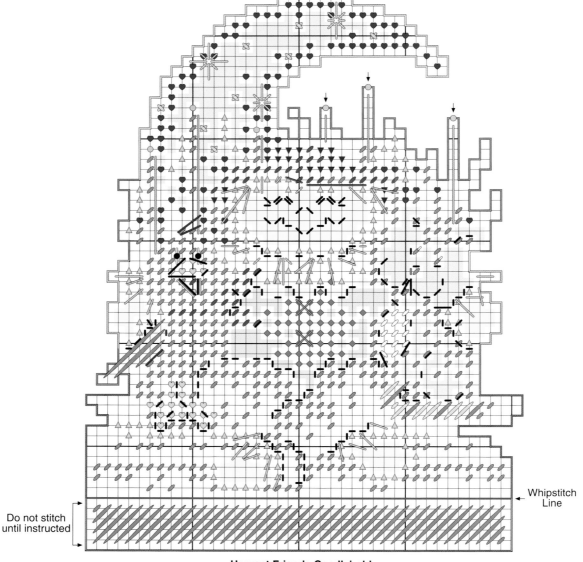

Whipstitch Line

Do not stitch until instructed

Harvest Friends Candleholder
Motif Front & Back
41 holes x 54 holes
Cut 1 from clear stiff
Stitch as graphed
Cut 1 from brown
Do not stitch until instructed

5. Place leaf ring liner inside leaf ring, aligning top edges and placing side edges together at seam of leaf ring. ***Note:*** *Some peaks on ring will be adjacent to valleys on liner and therefore will not match. Bottom edge of liner will be above bottom edge of ring.*

6. Whipstitch top edges of ring and ring liner together, Overcasting top edges of ring adjacent to valleys on liner. These valleys will remain unstitched.

Assembly

1. Placing ring seam at back and using cinnamon, Whipstitch bottom edge of leaf ring to blue Whipstitch line on base top.

2. Using cinnamon, Whipstitch back edge of assembled base top to Whipstitch line on motif front. Reverse motif back and work Continental Stitches along Whipstitch line.

3. Place motif pieces together, matching edges. Whipstitch together above Whipstitch line with colors indicated on graph. Work Lark's Head Knots along edges at arrows. Apply a dab of glue inside each knot to secure, then trim tails to ½ inch (1.3cm).

4. Turn motif over to back side and work rust Slanted Gobelin stitches below Whipstitch line, working through both layers.

5. Whipstitch base side to motif below Whipstitch line with rust; Whipstitch to base top with cinnamon, easing as necessary to fit curved edges of base top.

6. Place base bottom and base bottom support pieces together. With brown canvas at the bottom, Whipstitch curved edge of base bottom to side with cinnamon, working through all three layers and easing as necessary to fit.

7. Fill base with aquarium gravel, then Whipstitch back edge of base bottom to bottom edge of motif with cinnamon, working through all four layers.

Finishing

1. Glue felt to bottom of base.

2. Use cotton swab to apply small amount of blush to scarecrow's cheeks.

3. Place tea-light candleholder and tea light candle in leaf ring. ●

COLOR KEY	
Yards	**Plastic Canvas Yarn**
7 (6.5m)	⬭ Black #00
2 (1.9m)	⬭ Red #01
4 (3.7m)	▼ Burgundy #03
13 (11.9m)	⬭ Rust #09
3 (2.8m)	⬭ Tangerine #11
1 (1m)	◆ Christmas green #28
1 (1m)	◯ Eggshell #39
7 (6.5m)	△ Camel #43
2 (1.9m)	♥ Dark royal #48
2 (1.9m)	♡ Yellow #57
	Uncoded areas on peach background are tangerine #11 Continental Stitches
18 (16.5m)	Uncoded areas on white background are cinnamon #14 Continental Stitches
1 (1m)	Uncoded areas on green background are forest #29 Continental Stitches
2 (1.9m)	Uncoded areas on blue background are royal #32 Continental Stitches
4 (3.7m)	Uncoded areas on yellow background are beige #40 Continental Stitches
	╱ Cinnamon #14 Overcast and Whipstitch
	╱ Black #00 (2-ply) Straight Stitch
	╱ Red #01 (2-ply) Backstitch
	╱ Rust #09 (2-ply) Straight Stitch
	╱ Eggshell #39 (2-ply) Straight Stitch
	╱ Eggshell #39 (1-ply) Straight Stitch and Pin Stitch
	╱ Camel #43 (2-ply) Straight Stitch
	╱ Yellow #57 (1-ply) Straight Stitch
	╱ Cinnamon #14 (1-ply) and beige #40 (1-ply) combined Straight Stitch
	◯ Camel #43 (2-ply) Lark's Head Knot
	⅛-Inch Ribbon
6 (5.5m)	⬜ Gold #002
	╱ Gold #002 Straight Stitch
	#5 Pearl Cotton
6 (5.5m)	╱ Black Backstitch and Straight Stitch
	● Black (2-wrap) French Knot
Color numbers given are for Uniek Needloft plastic canvas yarn and Kreinik ⅛-inch Ribbon.	

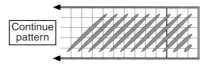

**Harvest Friends
Candleholder Side**
63 holes x 5 holes
Cut 1 from brown

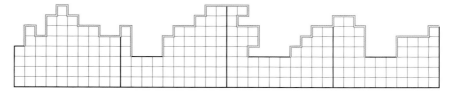

**Harvest Friends Candleholder
Leaf Ring Liner**
40 holes x 8 holes
Cut 1 from orange
Do not stitch

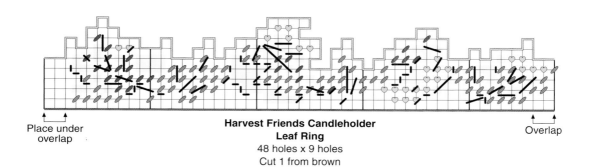

Place under
overlap

**Harvest Friends Candleholder
Leaf Ring**
48 holes x 9 holes
Cut 1 from brown

Overlap

Back Edge

Do not stitch
area inside
blue line

Harvest Friends Candleholder Base
40 holes x 20 holes
Cut 1 from brown for base top
Cut 1 from clear stiff for base top support
Stitch as 1
Cut 1 from brown for base bottom
Cut 1 from clear stiff for base bottom support
Do not stitch

AUTUMN LEAVES

Autumn leaves have never been so pretty. You'll love decorating your home with this delightful topper.

DESIGN BY ANGIE ARICKX

Skill Level
Beginner

Size
Fits family-size tissue box

Materials
- 1½ sheets 7-count plastic canvas
- Red Heart Classic worsted weight yarn Art. E267 as listed in color key
- Red Heart Super Saver worsted weight yarn Art. E300 as listed in color key
- #16 tapestry needle

Instructions

1. Cut and stitch plastic canvas according to graphs (pages 74 and 75).

2. Using medium thyme, Overcast inside edges on top, and bottom edges of sides and ends. Whipstitch sides to ends, then Whipstitch sides and ends to top. ●

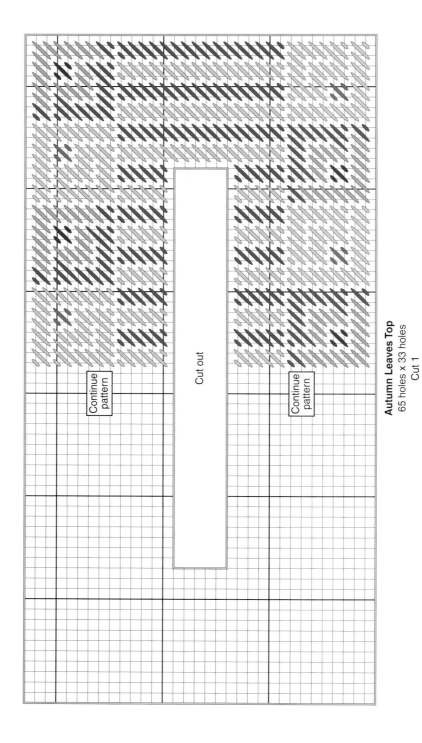

Autumn Leaves Top
65 holes x 33 holes
Cut 1

Cut out

Continue pattern

Continue pattern

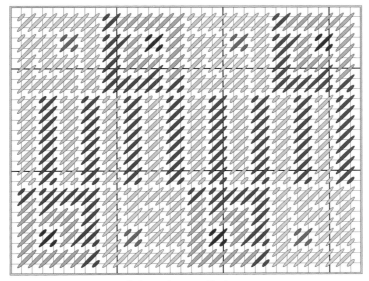

Autumn Leaves End
33 holes x 26 holes
Cut 2

COLOR KEY

Yards		Worsted Weight Yarn
3 (2.8m)	■	Bronze #286
16 (14.7m)	▨	Copper #289
16 (14.7m)	□	Gold #321
3 (2.8m)	■	Mid brown #339
39 (35.7m)	▨	Medium thyme #406
32 (29.3m)	■	Dark sage #633

Color numbers given are for Red Heart Classic worsted weight yarn Art. E267 and Super Saver worsted weight yarn Art. E300.

Continue pattern

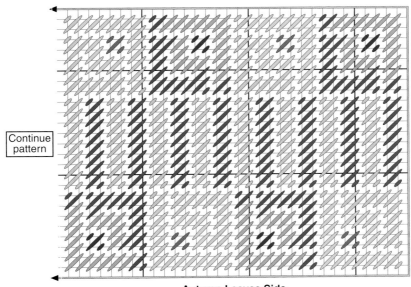

Autumn Leaves Side
65 holes x 26 holes
Cut 2

SCARECROW GIFT BAG

Delight a favorite friend or loved one with a seasonal gift presented in a decorated gift bag.

DESIGN BY MARY T. COSGROVE

Skill Level
Beginner

Size
6 inches W x 5¼ inches H (15.2cm x 13.3cm), excluding hair and bows

Materials
- ⅓ sheet 7-count plastic canvas
- Uniek Needloft plastic canvas yarn as listed in color key
- #16 tapestry needle
- 8 x 10½-inch (20.3 x 26.7cm) bittersweet gift bag
- 4 (1¼ x 9½-inch/3.175 x 24.1cm) strips striped or patterned scrapbook paper to coordinate with gift bag
- 2 (1-inch/2.5cm) strips adhesive-backed hook-and-loop tape
- Paper glue

Instructions
1. Cut scarecrow head from plastic canvas according to graph.

2. Stitch and Overcast head following graphs, working uncoded areas with holly Continental Stitches.

3. When background stitching is completed, work bittersweet Backstitches and Straight Stitches where indicated.

4. For straw hair, work five 1-inch (2.5cm) gold Turkey Loop Stitches on each side of hat where indicated and three 1-inch (2.5cm) loops at top of hat where indicated. Cut loops.

5. Cut ½ yard (0.5m) length each of moss and holly yarn. Form each length in four 1½-inch/3.8cm-loop bows. Using gold yarn, securely tack center of bows to bottom of head with three stitches where indicated.

6. Center scrapbook paper strips evenly spaced on bag front; glue in place. Allow to dry.

7. Adhere hook-and-loop tape to back of head and to center front of bag, then attach head to bag front. ●

COLOR KEY		
Yards	**Plastic Canvas Yarn**	
4 (3.7m)	☐ Baby yellow #21	
2 (1.9m)	☐ Moss #25	
4 (3.7m)	■ Bittersweet #52	
6 (5.5m)	Uncoded areas are holly #27 Continental Stitches	
	╱ Holly #27 Overcast	
	╱ Bittersweet #52 Backstitch and Straight Stitch	
2 (1.9m)	╱ Gold #17 Turkey Loop Stitch	
	╱ Attach bows	
Color numbers given are for Uniek Needloft plastic canvas yarn.		

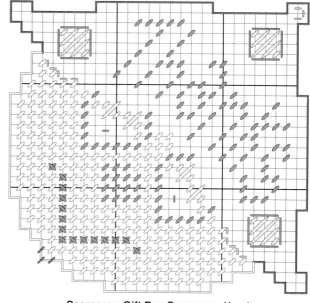

Scarecrow Gift Bag Scarecrow Head
28 holes x 28 holes
Cut 1

LOG CABIN COASTER SET

Stitch this handsome coaster set for Dad to enjoy during quiet evenings in the den.

DESIGN BY LAURA SCOTT

Skill Level
Beginner

Size
Coasters: 3⅞ inches square (9.8cm)
Coaster Box: 4¼ inches square x 1¾ inches H (10.8cm x 4.4cm)

Materials
- 1 sheet 7-count plastic canvas
- Uniek Needloft plastic canvas yarn as listed in color key
- #16 tapestry needle
- 9 x 12-inch sheet brown self-adhesive felt

Instructions

1. Cut plastic canvas according to graphs. Cut one 27-hole x 27-hole piece for coaster box base. Base will remain unstitched.

2. Cut one piece of felt to fit each coaster, bottom of base and top of base inside box. Set aside.

3. Stitch pieces following graphs. Alternating maple and brown yarn, Overcast coasters and top edges of box sides. Using maple, Whipstitch box sides together, then Whipstitch sides to unstitched base.

4. Adhere felt to wrong sides of coasters, to bottom of base and to base inside box. ●

COLOR KEY		
Yards		**Plastic Canvas Yarn**
7 (6.5m)	■	Burgundy #03
24 (22m)	▨	Maple #13
15 (13.8m)	■	Brown #15
2 (1.9m)	▨	Gold #17
6 (5.5m)	■	Forest #29
2 (1.9m)	□	Camel #43

Color numbers given are for Uniek Needloft plastic canvas yarn.

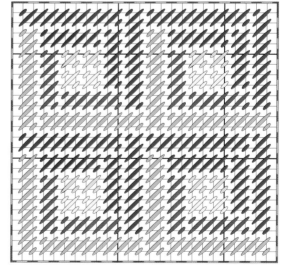

Log Cabin Coaster
25 holes x 25 holes
Cut 4

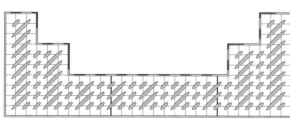

Log Cabin Coaster Box Side
27 holes x 10 holes
Cut 4

SEASONAL WELCOME SIGN

Celebrate the changing seasons with this welcome sign, featuring interchangeable add-ons.

DESIGNS BY TERRY RICIOLI

Skill Level
Beginner

Size
Welcome Sign: 9¼ inches W x 4 inches H (23.5cm x 10.2cm), excluding seasonal motifs

Seasonal Sign: 8⅜ inches W x 3½ inches H (21.3cm x 8.9cm), excluding seasonal motifs

Hanging: 9¼ inches W x 11¾ inches H (23.5cm x 29.8cm), excluding seasonal motifs

Materials
- 2 sheets clear 7-count plastic canvas
- 2 sheets coordinating light colored 7-count plastic canvas
- Uniek Needloft plastic canvas yarn as listed in color key
- #16 tapestry needle
- 8 inches (20.3cm) gold or silver chain
- 12 (10mm) jump rings to match chain
- 2 S-hooks or S-clasps to match chain (approximately 15 x 25mm)
- 4 (⅝-inch/1.6cm) hook-and-loop circles
- Needle-nose pliers
- Hot-glue gun

Instructions

1. Cut one each of all sign fronts, and all seasonal motifs from clear plastic canvas according to graphs (pages 82–86).

2. Cut one each of all five sign backs from light colored plastic canvas.

3. Stitch sign fronts following graphs, working uncoded backgrounds with Continental Stitches as follows: welcome and fall with eggshell, spring with orchid, summer with pale peach, winter with white.

4. Whipstitch sign fronts and backs together following graphs.

5. Stitch and Overcast motifs for each season following graphs, reversing tangerine and watermelon colors on two summer butterflies. Stitch one fall leaf as graphed; stitch remaining leaves, replacing red with pumpkin and burgundy with maple.

6. Using photo as a guide, glue two motifs to corresponding season's sign. Glue one loop circle from hook-and-loop circles to back of each remaining motif. Glue one hook circle to welcome sign where indicated on graph.

7. Using needle-nose pliers, open jump rings and attach to signs where indicated on graphs.

Note: Welcome sign has four jump rings. Each seasonal sign has two jump rings.

8. Attach chain to jump rings at top of welcome sign. Close all jump rings.

9. To hang signs, slip S-hooks or S-clasps through jump rings at bottom of welcome sign and at top of each season's sign. Attach corresponding motif for each season to welcome sign. ●

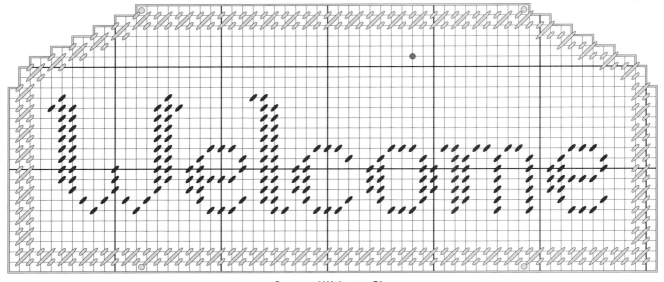

Seasonal Welcome Sign
61 holes x 26 holes
Cut 1 from clear for front
Stitch as graphed
Cut 1 from coordinating
light color for backing
Do not stitch

COLOR KEY	
Yards	**Plastic Canvas Yarn**
8 (7.4m)	■ Red #01
2 (1.9m)	■ Burgundy #03
5 (4.6m)	□ Lavender #05
2 (1.9m)	□ Tangerine #11
4 (3.7m)	Pumpkin #12
6 (5.5m)	■ Maple #13
10 (9.2m)	■ Holly #27
4 (3.7m)	■ Forest #29
8 (7.4m)	■ Royal #32
7 (6.5m)	□ Camel #43
8 (7.4m)	□ Mermaid #53
2 (1.9m)	■ Watermelon #55
24 (22m)	Uncoded areas on welcome and fall signs are eggshell #39 Continental Stitches
12 (11m)	Uncoded area on winter sign is white #41 Continental Stitches
12 (11m)	Uncoded areas on spring sign and flowers are orchid #44 Continental Stitches
12 (11m)	Uncoded area on summer sign is pale peach #56 Continental Stitches
○	Attach jump ring
●	Attach hook circle

Color numbers given are for Uniek Needloft plastic canvas yarn.

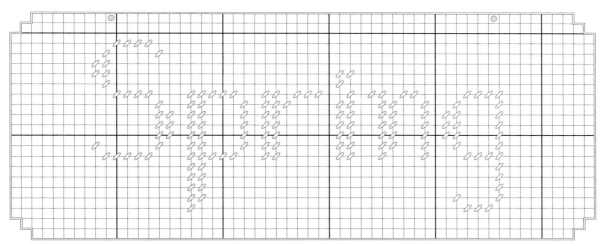

Seasonal Welcome Spring Sign
55 holes x 22 holes
Cut 1 from clear for front
Stitch as graphed
Cut 1 from coordinating
light color for backing
Do not stitch

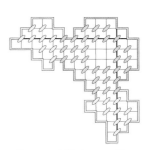

**Seasonal Welcome Sign
Spring Flower**
12 holes x 12 holes
Cut 3 from clear

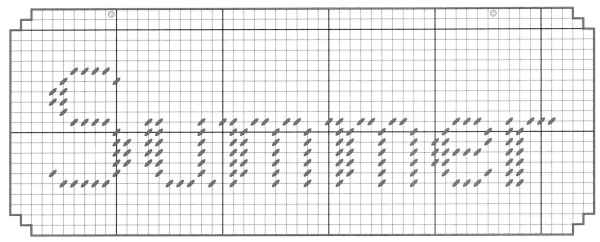

Seasonal Welcome Summer Sign
55 holes x 22 holes
Cut 1 from clear for front
Stitch as graphed
Cut 1 from coordinating
light color for backing
Do not stitch

**Seasonal Welcome Sign
Summer Butterfly**
12 holes x 12 holes
Cut 3 from clear
Stitch 1 as graphed
Stitch 2 reversing tangerine
and watermelon colors

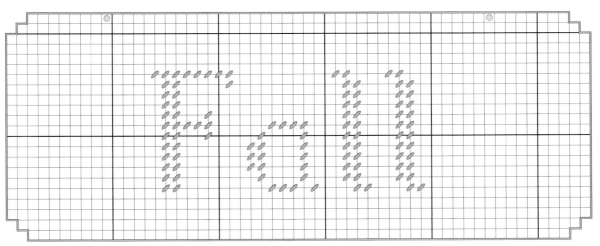

Seasonal Welcome Fall Sign
55 holes x 22 holes
Cut 1 from clear for front
Stitch as graphed
Cut 1 from coordinating
light color for backing
Do not stitch

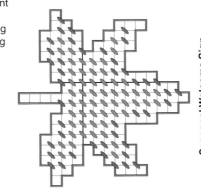

**Seasonal Welcome Sign
Fall Leaf**
17 holes x 16 holes
Cut 3 from clear
Stitch 1 as graphed
Stitch 2 replacing
red with pumpkin and
burgundy with maple

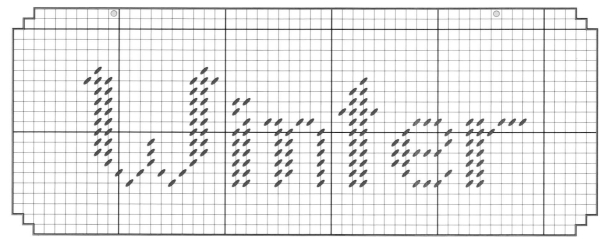

Seasonal Welcome Winter Sign
55 holes x 22 holes
Cut 1 from clear for front
Stitch as graphed
Cut 1 from coordinating
light color for backing
Do not stitch

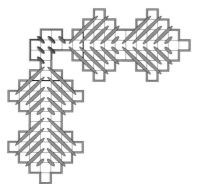

Seasonal Welcome Sign
Winter Holly
17 holes x 17 holes
Cut 3 from clear

BATTY MOBILE

Cute and not scary, this positively batty mobile will swing and spin in the autumn breeze.

DESIGN BY GINA WOODS

Skill Level
Beginner

Size
4¼ inches in diameter (10.8cm), excluding hanger

Materials
• 1 Uniek QuickShape 5-inch plastic canvas star
• 1 Uniek QuickShape 4-inch plastic canvas radial circle
• Worsted weight yarn as listed in color key
• #16 tapestry needle
• Small amount black felt
• 2 (8mm) movable eyes
• Hand-sewing needle
• Black sewing thread
• Hot-glue gun

Instructions
1. Cut frame from radial circle, and bat body and wings from plastic canvas star according to graphs (page 113), cutting away yellow areas.

2. Using pattern given, cut two bat ears from black felt.

3. Stitch and Overcast pieces following graphs.

4. Using photo as a guide, glue wings and ears to back of body and eyes to body front.

5. Using hand-sewing needle and black sewing thread, attach bat to frame where indicated on graphs.

6. For hanger, cut desired length of dark plum yarn. Thread ends through stitching on back of mobile where indicated with arrow. Either knot ends or glue to secure. ●

GRAPHS ON PAGE 113

BOO TABLE RUNNER

Add some ghostly fun to your Halloween get-together when you stitch this spooky, yet cute table runner.

DESIGN BY KAREN MCDANEL

Skill Level
Beginner

Size
40½ inches L x 10½ inches W (102.9cm x 26.7cm)

Materials
- 3 sheets 7-count plastic canvas
- Worsted weight yarn as listed in color key
- #16 tapestry needle

Instructions

1. Stitch pieces following graphs (pages 90 and 91), working un-coded areas on blue background with white Continental Stitches and continuing orange stitch pattern through center of pieces, adjusting as needed to fit around ghosts and black lettering.

2. When background stitching is completed, work black Backstitches for mouths and French Knots for eyes on ghosts.

3. Using black throughout, Whipstitch end pieces to center piece. Overcast all remaining edges. ●

Whipstitch this edge to center piece

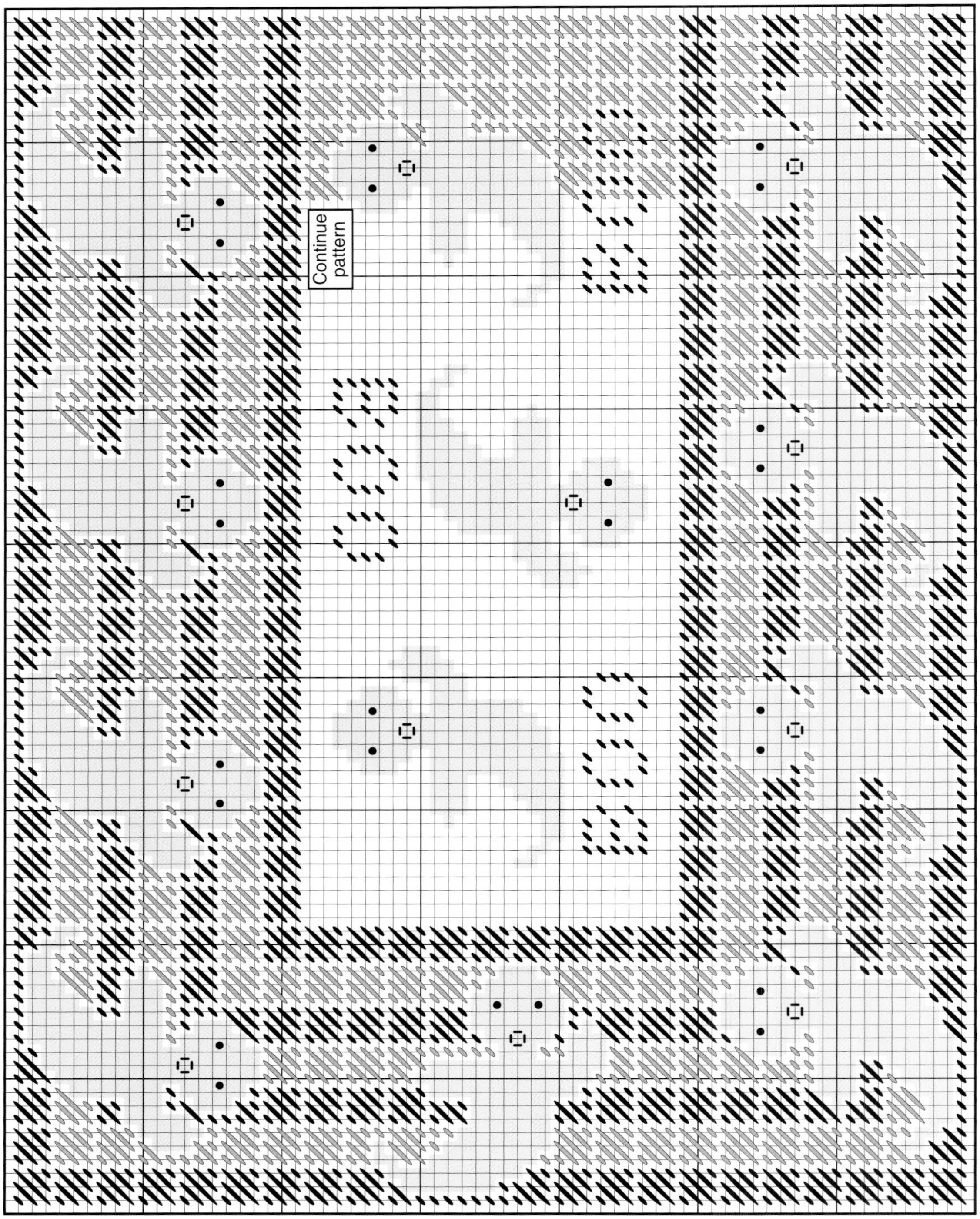

Continue pattern

Boo Table Runner End
90 holes x 70 holes
Stitch 2

COLOR KEY

Yards	Worsted Weight Yarn
115 (105.2m)	▨ Orange
90 (82.3m)	■ Black
80 (73.2m)	Uncoded areas on blue background are white Continental Stitches
	╱ Black Backstitch
	● Black French Knot

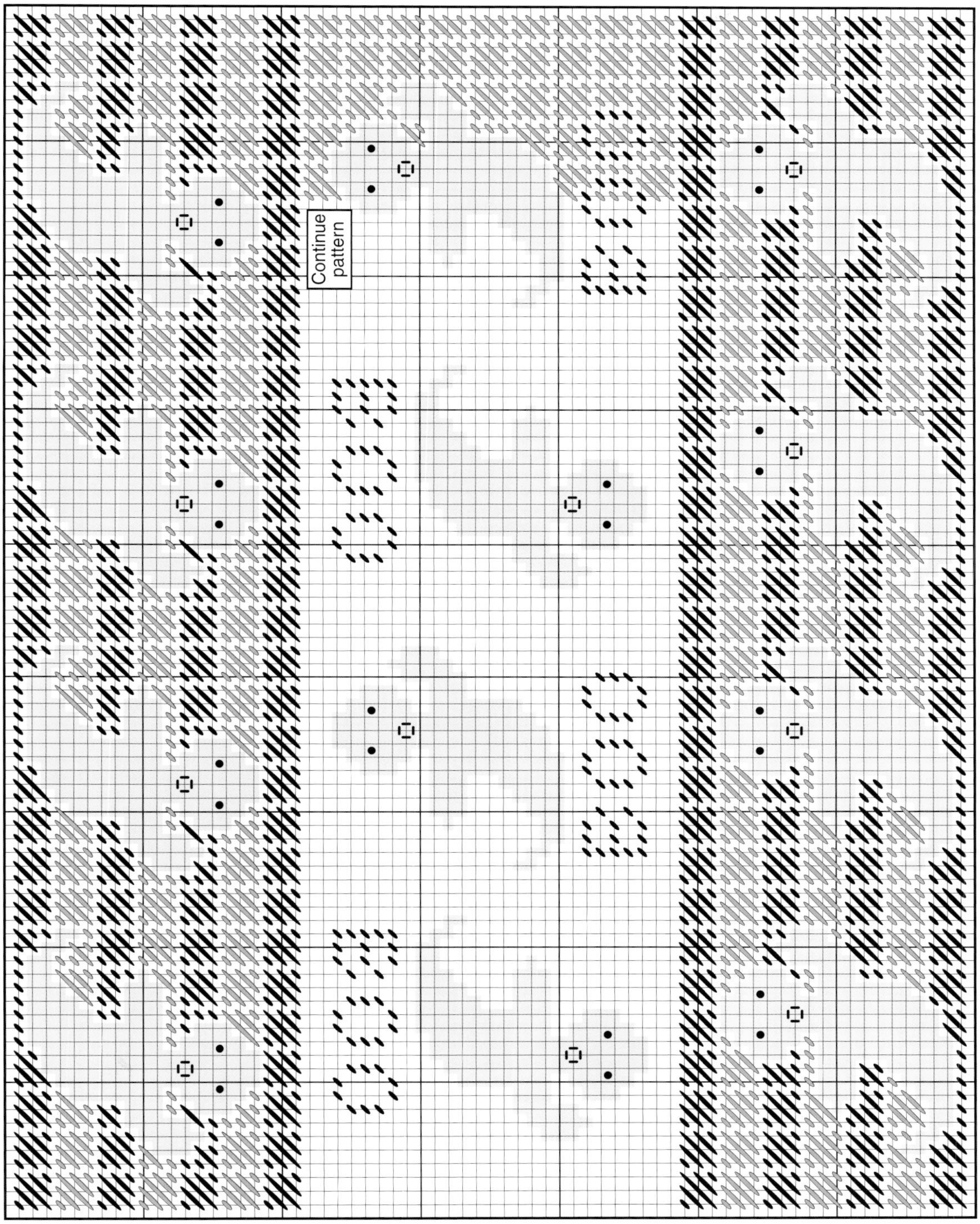

Continue pattern

Boo Table Runner Center
90 holes x 70 holes
Stitch 1

TINY TREAT BAGS

This tiny trio is sized just right to fill with miniature candy bars or wrapped candies.

DESIGNS BY KAREN MCDANEL

Skill Level
Beginner

Size
3⅜ inches W x 4⅛ inches H x 2⅜ inches D (8.6cm x 10.5cm x 6cm), excluding handles

Materials
Each Bag
- ⅔ sheet 7-count plastic canvas
- Worsted weight yarn as listed in color key
- #16 tapestry needle
- 24 inches (61cm) ¼-inch (0.6cm) white cord
- Transparent tape

Instructions

1. Cut plastic canvas according to graphs (pages 93 and 94), cutting out openings for handles on fronts, backs and supports.

2. Align support pieces behind openings on each front and back, then stitch pieces following graphs, working through both layers at top and working Continental Stitches in uncoded areas as follows: ghost and jack-o'-lantern fronts and backs with orange, and witch's face with light green.

3. Overcast openings and top edges of fronts, backs and sides. Whipstitch fronts and backs to corresponding sides, then Whipstitch fronts, backs and sides to corresponding bases.

4. For each bag, cut cord in half. Place transparent tape around ends, then thread ends from right side to wrong side through openings on front and back. Tie each end in a knot on wrong side. ●

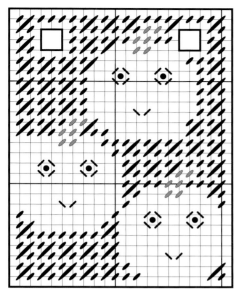

Tiny Treat Jack-o'-Lantern Bag
Front & Back
21 holes x 27 holes
Cut 2

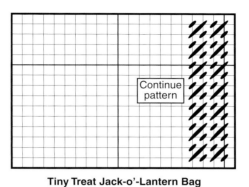

Tiny Treat Jack-o'-Lantern Bag
Base
21 holes x 15 holes
Cut 1

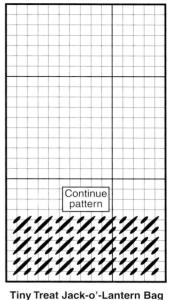

Tiny Treat Jack-o'-Lantern Bag
Side
15 holes x 27 holes
Cut 2

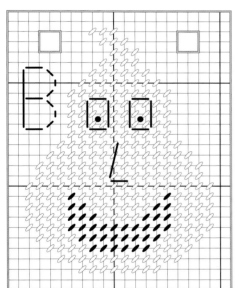

Tiny Treat Ghost Bag
Front & Back
21 holes x 27 holes
Cut 2

COLOR KEY

Yards	Worsted Weight Yarn
64 (58.5m)	Orange
40 (36.6m)	Black
9 (8.3m)	White
2 (1.9m)	Emerald green
	Uncoded areas on ghost and jack-o'-lantern fronts and backs are orange Continental Stitches
3 (2.8m)	Uncoded area on witch's face is light green Continental Stitches
	✁ Black Backstitch
3 (2.8m)	✁ Medium gray Straight Stitch
	● Black French Knot

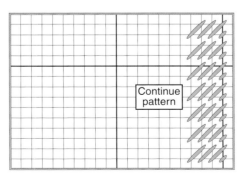

Tiny Treat Ghost Bag
Base
21 holes x 15 holes
Cut 1

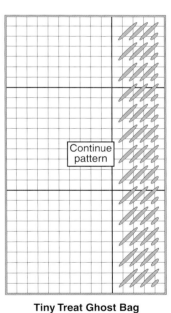

Tiny Treat Ghost Bag
Side
15 holes x 27 holes
Cut 2

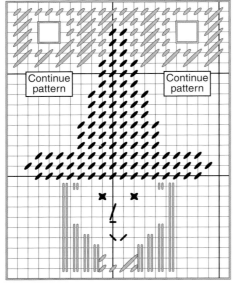

Tiny Treat Witch Bag
Front & Back
21 holes x 27 holes
Cut 2

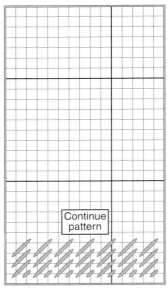

Tiny Treat Witch Bag
Side
15 holes x 27 holes
Cut 2

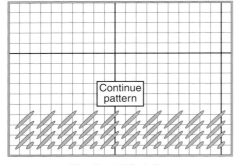

Tiny Treat Witch Bag
Base
21 holes x 15 holes
Cut 1

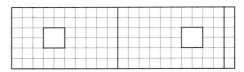

Tiny Treat Bag Support
21 holes x 6 holes
Cut 2 for each bag

COLOR KEY	
Yards	**Worsted Weight Yarn**
64 (58.5m)	▨ Orange
40 (36.6m)	■ Black
9 (8.3m)	□ White
2 (1.9m)	■ Emerald green
	Uncoded areas on ghost and jack-o'-lantern fronts and backs are orange Continental Stitches
3 (2.8m)	Uncoded area on witch's face is light green Continental Stitches
	╱ Black Backstitch
3 (2.8m)	╱ Medium gray Straight Stitch
	● Black French Knot

PUMPKIN BASKET PARTY FAVOR

This is one pretty pumpkin! Decorated with eyelashes and a coy smile, this favor basket will be a favorite.

DESIGN BY PATRICIA KLESH

Skill Level
Beginner

Size
3⅛ inches W x 3¾ inches H x 1⅝ inches D (8cm x 9.5cm x 4.1cm), excluding eyelashes

Materials
- ½ sheet 7-count plastic canvas
- Worsted weight yarn as listed in color key
- #16 tapestry needle
- Black doll eyelashes
- Hot-glue gun

Instructions
1. Cut plastic canvas according to graphs (page 113). Cut one 14-hole x 10-hole piece for base.

2. Stitch base with orange Continental Stitches. Stitch and Overcast handle. Stitch front, back and sides following graphs, working uncoded areas on front with orange Continental Stitches and working back entirely with orange Continental Stitches.

3. Whipstitch sides to front and back from dot to dot, then

Whipstitch front, back and sides to base. Overcast top edges.

4. Using photo as a guide throughout, center and glue han-

dle to sides of basket on inside. Trim eyelashes to about ¾ inches (1.9cm) wide. Center and glue above eyes. ●

GRAPHS ON PAGE 113

TRICK-OR-TREAT WALL HANGING

Enjoy the Halloween season with a wall hanging featuring an old-time favorite.

DESIGN BY PATRICIA KLESH

Skill Level
Beginner

Size
7⅛ inches W x 20½ inches H (18.1cm x 52.1cm)

Materials
- 1 sheet 7-count plastic canvas
- Worsted weight yarn as listed in color key
- #16 tapestry needle
- 18 inches (45.7cm) ¼-inch/7mm-wide black satin ribbon
- 9 inches (22.9cm) ¼-inch/7mm-wide orange satin ribbon
- Hot-glue gun

Instructions

1. Cut plastic canvas according to graphs (this page and page 98).

2. Stitch and Overcast pieces following graphs.

3. Using photo as a guide through step 6, center and glue bottom 4¼ inches (10.8cm) of ribbon band to back of trick-or-treat bag.

4. Glue candy corn to ribbon band above bag.

5. Cut black ribbon in half. Thread one length through top center hole of ribbon band. Tie ends together in a knot to form a loop for hanging.

6. Place orange ribbon and remaining length black ribbon together. Tie in a bow and glue to ribbon band top below hanger. ●

COLOR KEY		
Yards	**Worsted Weight Yarn**	
39 (35.7m)	☐	Light tan
25 (22.9m)	■	Black
12 (11m)	▨	Orange
6 (5.5m)	☐	Yellow
1 (1m)	☐	White
	●	Attach ribbon hanger

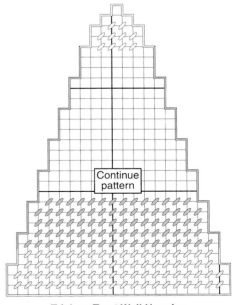

Trick-or-Treat Wall Hanging
Candy Corn
21 holes x 28 holes
Cut 3

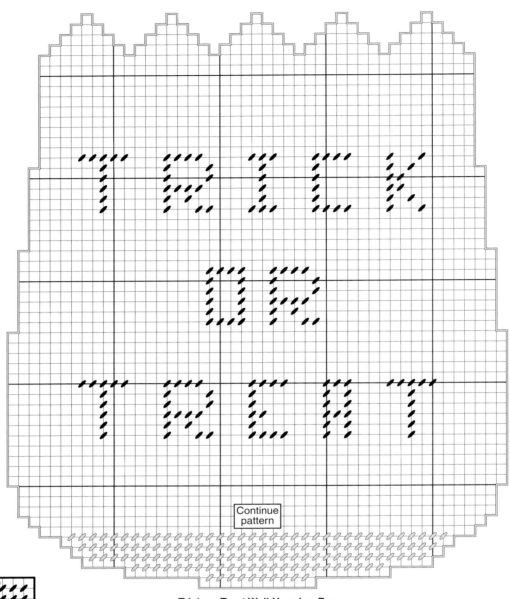

Trick-or-Treat Wall Hanging Bag
47 holes x 56 holes
Cut 1

Continue pattern

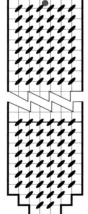

**Trick-or-Treat Wall Hanging
Ribbon Band**
7 holes x 90 holes
Cut 1

COLOR KEY

Yards	Worsted Weight Yarn
39 (35.7m)	☐ Light tan
25 (22.9m)	■ Black
12 (11m)	▨ Orange
6 (5.5m)	☐ Yellow
1 (1m)	☐ White
	● Attach ribbon hanger

JACK-O'-LANTERN TISSUE TOPPER

Add some spookiness to your decor with this frighteningly fun pumpkin tissue topper.

DESIGN BY ANGIE ARICKX

Skill Level
Intermediate

Size
9¼ inches W x 7⅜ inches H x 5 inches D (23.5cm x 18.7cm x 12.7cm); for boutique-style tissue box

Materials
- 1 artist-size sheet 7-count plastic canvas
- Uniek Needloft plastic canvas yarn as listed in color key
- #16 tapestry needle
- Hot-glue gun

Instructions
1. Cut plastic canvas according to graphs (pages 100 and 101), carefully cutting out eight holes in spiderweb. Cut two 9-hole x 9-holes pieces for stem front and back and two 8-hole x 9-hole pieces for stem sides.

2. Continental Stitch stem pieces with Christmas green.

3. Following graphs throughout, stitch and Overcast spiders and webs. Stitch remaining pieces, working uncoded areas with bright orange Continental Stitches.

4. Using Christmas green throughout, Whipstitch stem front and back to stem sides, then Whipstitch bottom edges to corresponding edges of panel opening. Overcast top edges.

5. Using Christmas red throughout, Whipstitch long edges of panel to front and back around side and top edges from blue dot to blue dot. Overcast bottom edges.

6. Using photo as a guide, glue spiderwebs and spiders in place. ●

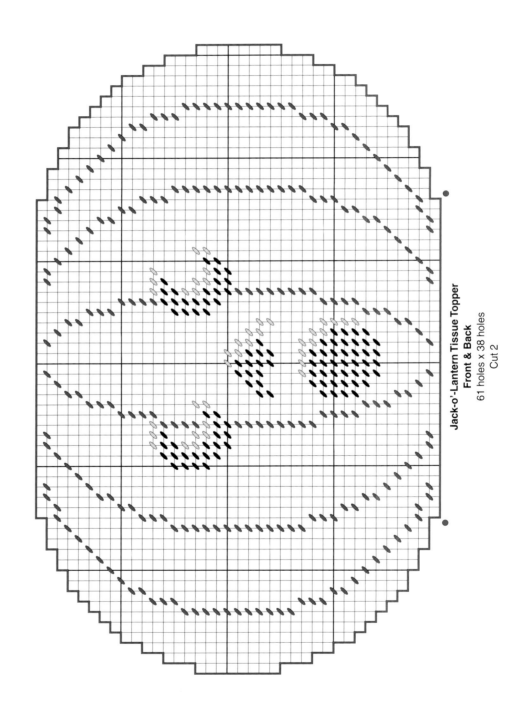

Jack-o'-Lantern Tissue Topper
Front & Back
61 holes x 38 holes
Cut 2

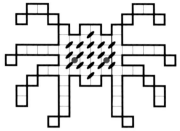

Jack-o'-Lantern Tissue Topper Spider
16 holes x 12 holes
Cut 2

COLOR KEY

Yards	Plastic Canvas Yarn
10 (9.2m)	■ Black #00
21 (19.3m)	■ Christmas red #02
6 (5.5m)	■ Christmas green #28
10 (9.2m)	□ Silver #37
2 (1.9m)	▨ Yellow #57
120 (110m)	Uncoded areas are bright orange #58 Continental Stitches
	● Christmas red #02 French Knot

Color numbers given are for Uniek Needloft plastic canvas yarn.

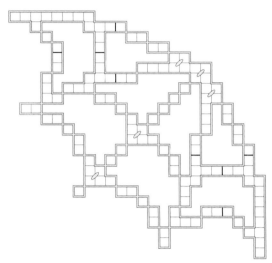

Jack-o'-Lantern Tissue Topper Spiderweb
24 holes x 24 holes
Cut 2

Center

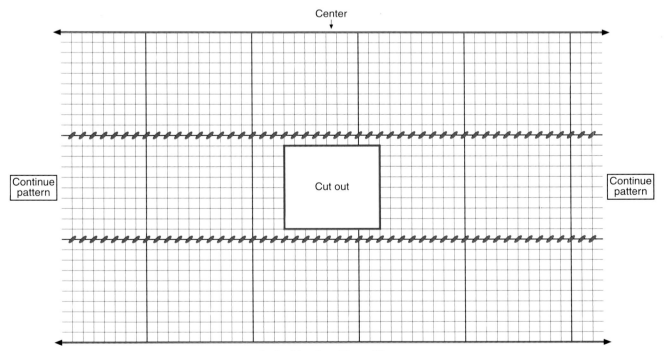

Continue pattern

Cut out

Continue pattern

Jack-o'-Lantern Tissue Topper Top & Side Panel
135 holes x 30 holes
Cut 1

FAITH & PHILLIP

These darling Pilgrim friends will be the perfect centerpiece for your Thanksgiving feast.

DESIGN BY DEBRA ARCH

Faith

Skill Level
Intermediate

Size
5 inches W x 10¾ inches H x 5½ inches D (12.7cm x 27.3cm x 14cm)

Materials
- 2 sheets 7-count plastic canvas
- 2 (4-inch) Uniek QuickShape plastic canvas radial circles
- 6-inch Uniek QuickShape plastic canvas radial circle
- Red Heart Classic worsted weight yarn Art. E267 as listed in color key
- Red Heart Super Saver worsted weight yarn Art. E300 as listed in color key
- #16 tapestry needle
- 9 inches (22.9cm) ¼-inch/7mm-wide black satin ribbon
- 2 (8mm) black cabochons
- 9⅛-inch/23.2cm-tall potato chip canister with lid (optional)
- 2 cups sand (optional)
- Rose blush
- Cotton swab
- Hot-glue gun

Instructions

1. Cut plastic canvas according to graphs (pages 105–108), cutting away blue areas on 6-inch and 4-inch radial circles. Base will remain unstitched.

2. Following graphs throughout, stitch and Overcast collar. Stitch remaining pieces, using two strands mid brown to Straight Stitch hair.

Assembly

1. Whipstitch side edges of body pieces together forming back seam. Whipstitch unstitched base to body with gray heather. Fill potato chip canister with sand if desired. Glue on canister lid. Insert canister in body. Whipstitch top in place with mid brown.

2. Use photo as a guide throughout assembly. Glue center front of collar under face. Bring collar sides to back so inside corners meet at back seam, approximately 2¼ inches (5.7cm) from bottom edge. Glue collar in place, leaving inside corners free.

3. Thread ends of a length of white yarn from back to front through holes indicated on collar and tie in a bow; trim ends.

4. Overcast arms and hands, folding hands where indicated and Whipstitching hands together from blue dot to blue dot.

5. For each sleeve cuff, Overcast both straight side edges. Fold cuffs over wrists and Whipstitch angled bottom edges together. Glue shoulders of arms in place under collar, centering hands in front.

6. For hat, Whipstitch edges A together, forming back seam. Whipstitch edges B to edge C. Overcast remaining edges. Glue hat to top of head.

7. For top tuft (bangs), loosely wrap a strand of mid brown around three fingers five times. Remove from fingers and tie in center. Repeat this procedure for remaining tufts, wrapping seven times for side tufts and 15 times for back tuft. Glue all in place.

8. Tie black satin ribbon in a bow and glue to collar where indicated on graph. Glue cabochons to face for eyes where indicated.

9. Using cotton swab, apply blush to cheeks.

Phillip

Skill Level
Intermediate

Size
5½ inches W x 11¾ inches H x 6¼ inches D (14cm x 29.8cm x 15.9cm)

Materials
- 1½ sheets 7-count plastic canvas
- 4-inch Uniek QuickShape plastic canvas radial circle
- 2 (6-inch) Uniek QuickShape plastic canvas radial circles
- 9-inch Uniek QuickShape plastic canvas radial circle
- Red Heart Classic worsted weight yarn Art. E267 as listed in color key
- Red Heart Super Saver worsted weight yarn Art. E300 as listed in color key
- Kreinik ⅛-inch metallic ribbon as listed in color key
- #16 tapestry needle
- 9 inches (22.9cm) ¼-inch/7mm-wide black satin ribbon
- 2 (8mm) black cabochons
- 9⅛-inch/23.2cm-tall potato chip canister with lid (optional)
- 2 cups sand (optional)
- Rose blush
- Cotton swab
- Hot-glue gun

Project Note
Use two strands when stitching with mid brown and black metallic ribbon.

Instructions
1. Cut plastic canvas according to graphs (pages 109–112), cutting away blue areas on 4-inch, 6-inch and 9-inch radial circles. Base will remain unstitched.

2. Following graphs throughout, stitch and Overcast jacket bottom, collar, hatband and hatband buckle. Stitch remaining pieces.

Assembly
1. Whipstitch side edges of body pieces together forming back seam. Whipstitch unstitched base to body with black yarn. Fill potato chip canister with sand if desired. Glue on canister lid. Insert canister in body. Whipstitch top in place with mid brown.

2. Use photo as a guide throughout assembly. Wrap jacket bottom around body at top of black yarn trousers so that side edges meet in center front; glue in place. *Note: There will be a gap in front where edges meet.*

3. Overcast arms and hands, folding hands where indicated and Whipstitching hands together from blue dot to blue dot.

4. For each sleeve cuff, Overcast both straight side edges. Fold cuffs over wrists and Whipstitch angled bottom edges together. Glue shoulders of arms in place at top of gray heather jacket on body, centering hands in front.

5. Wrap collar around body over shoulders at top of jacket so that top of angled edges meet at center front; glue in place. *Note: There will be a small space in front where edges meet.*

6. Whipstitch side edges of hat crown together, forming back seam. Whipstitch hat top to top edge of hat crown. Whipstitch bottom edge of hat crown to inside edge of hat brim. Overcast outer edge of hat brim. Glue hat to top of head.

7. Whipstitch side edges of hatband together, forming back seam. Slide hatband down over crown of hat, aligning back seams; glue in place. Glue buckle to center front of hatband.

8. Tie black satin ribbon in a bow and glue to center front of collar where top edges meet. Glue cabochons to face for eyes where indicated.

9. Using cotton swab, apply blush to cheeks. ●

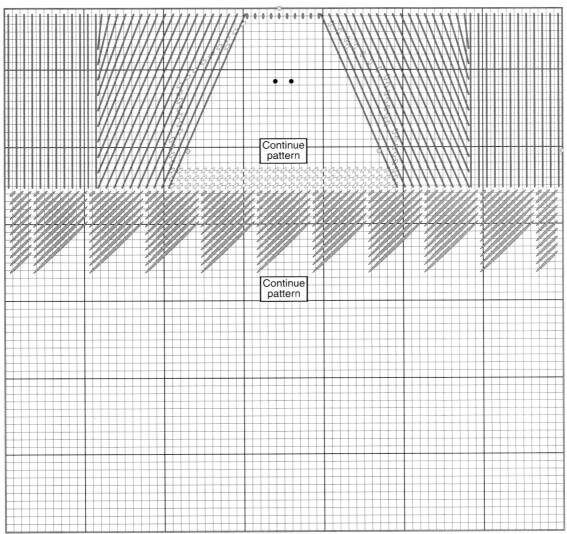

Faith Body
70 holes x 68 holes
Cut 1

COLOR KEY	
FAITH	
Yards	**Worsted Weight Yarn**
60 (54.9m)	☐ White #311
44 (40.3m)	▦ Mid brown #339
50 (45.7m)	▦ Gray heather #400
15 (13.8m)	☐ Baby pink #724
	✎ Mid brown #339 (double-strand) Straight Stitch
	○ Attach hair tuft
	● Attach white yarn tie
	● Attach cabochon
	● Attach satin ribbon bow

Color numbers given are for Red Heart Classic worsted weight yarn Art. E267 and Super Saver worsted weight yarn Art. E300.

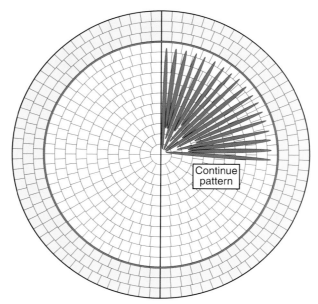

Continue
pattern

Faith Top & Base
Cut 2 from 4-inch radial circle,
cutting away blue area
Stitch top only

Faith Sleeve Cuffs
4 holes x 21 holes
Cut 1 each

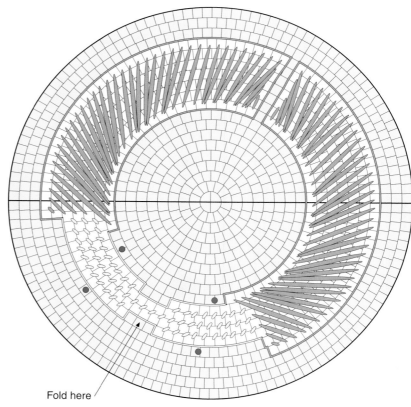

Fold here

Faith Arms & Hands
Cut 1 from 6-inch radial circle,
cutting away blue areas

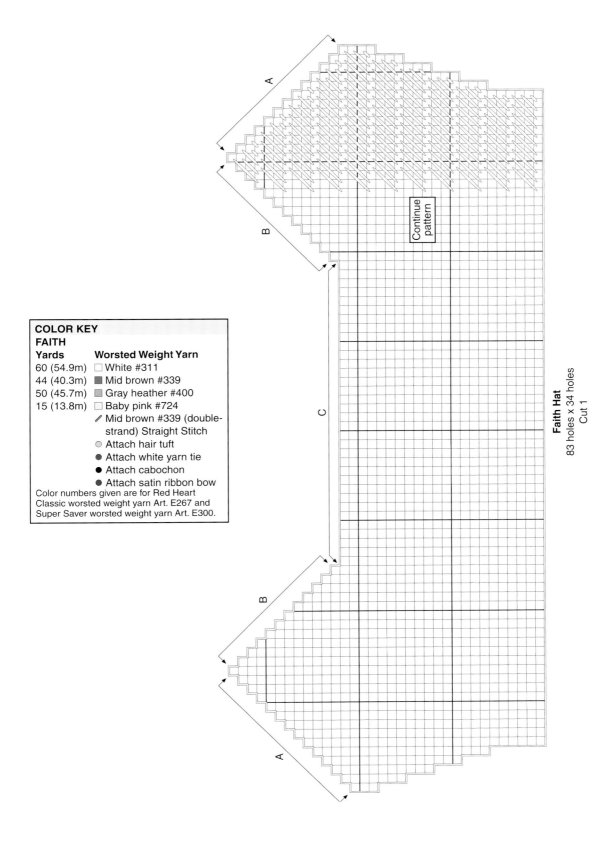

COLOR KEY
FAITH

Yards	Worsted Weight Yarn
60 (54.9m)	☐ White #311
44 (40.3m)	■ Mid brown #339
50 (45.7m)	▨ Gray heather #400
15 (13.8m)	☐ Baby pink #724
	✎ Mid brown #339 (double-strand) Straight Stitch
	◯ Attach hair tuft
	● Attach white yarn tie
	● Attach cabochon
	● Attach satin ribbon bow

Color numbers given are for Red Heart Classic worsted weight yarn Art. E267 and Super Saver worsted weight yarn Art. E300.

Continue pattern

Faith Hat
83 holes x 34 holes
Cut 1

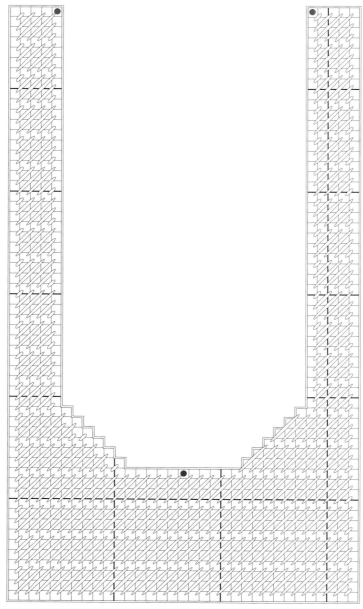

Faith Collar
33 holes x 58 holes
Cut 1

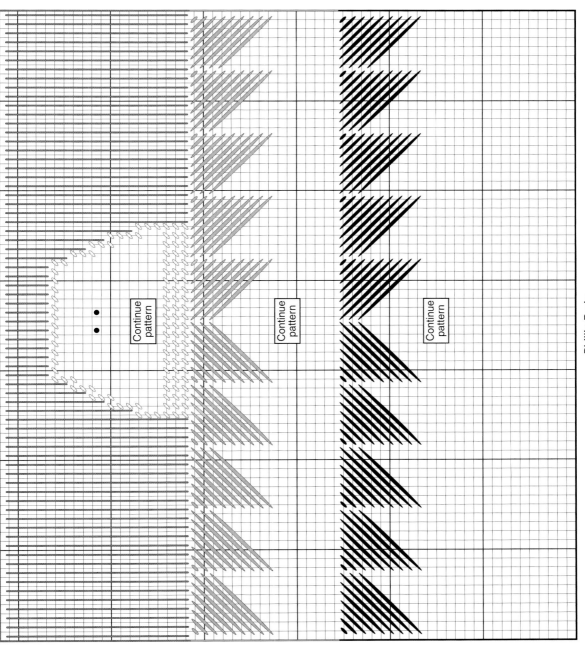

Phillip Body
70 holes x 62 holes
Cut 1

Continue pattern

Continue pattern

Continue pattern

COLOR KEY
PHILLIP

Yards	Worsted Weight Yarn
40 (36.6m)	■ Black #12
17 (15.6m)	☐ White #311
80 (73.2m)	▨ Gray heather #400
15 (13.8m)	☐ Baby pink #724
27 (24.7m)	╱ Mid brown #339 (double-strand) Straight Stitch and Whipstitch

¹/₈-Inch Metallic Ribbon

	▨ Black hi lustre #005HL (double strand)
27 (24.7m)	● Attach cabochon

Color numbers given are for Red Heart Classic worsted weight yarn Art. E267 and Super Saver worsted weight yarn Art. E300, and Kreinik ¹/₈-inch metallic ribbon.

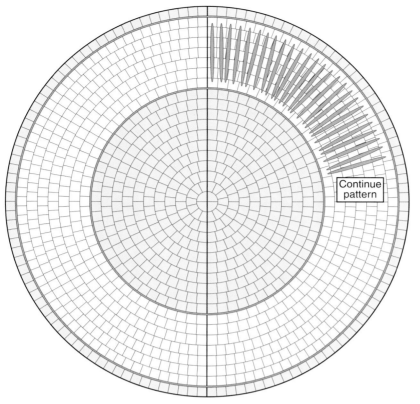

Phillip Hat Brim
Cut 1 from 6-inch radial circle,
cutting away blue areas

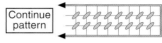

Phillip Hatband
70 holes x 3 holes
Cut 1

Phillip Hatband Buckle
4 holes x 4 holes
Cut 1

Phillip Hat Top
Cut 1 from 6-inch radial circle,
cutting away blue areas

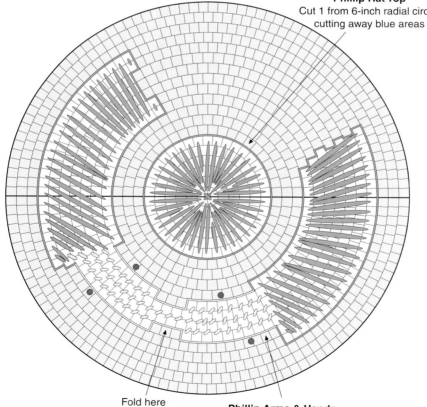

Fold here

Phillip Arms & Hands
Cut 1 from 6-inch radial circle,
cutting away blue areas

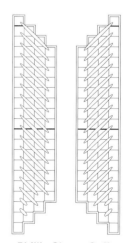

Phillip Sleeve Cuffs
4 holes x 21 holes
Cut 1 each

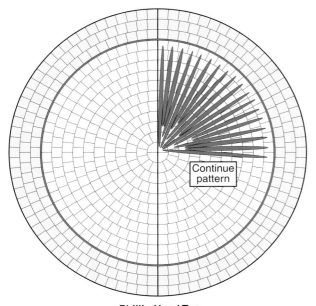

Phillip Head Top
Cut 1 from 4-inch radial circle,
cutting away blue area

Continue
pattern

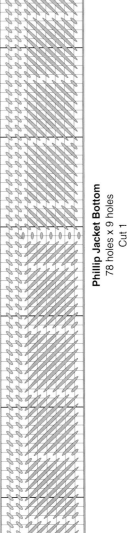

Center Back →

Phillip Collar
79 holes x 9 holes
Cut 1

Center Back →

Phillip Jacket Bottom
78 holes x 9 holes
Cut 1

COLOR KEY
PHILLIP

Yards		Worsted Weight Yarn
40 (36.6m)	■	Black #12
17 (15.6m)	□	White #311
80 (73.2m)	▨	Gray heather #400
15 (13.8m)	□	Baby pink #724
27 (24.7m)	⁄	Mid brown #339 (double-strand)
		Straight Stitch and Whipstitch

¹/₈-Inch Metallic Ribbon

	▨	Black hi lustre #005HL (double strand)
27 (24.7m)	●	Attach cabochon

Color numbers given are for Red Heart Classic worsted weight yarn Art. E267 and Super Saver worsted weight yarn Art. E300, and Kreinik ¹/₈-inch metallic ribbon.

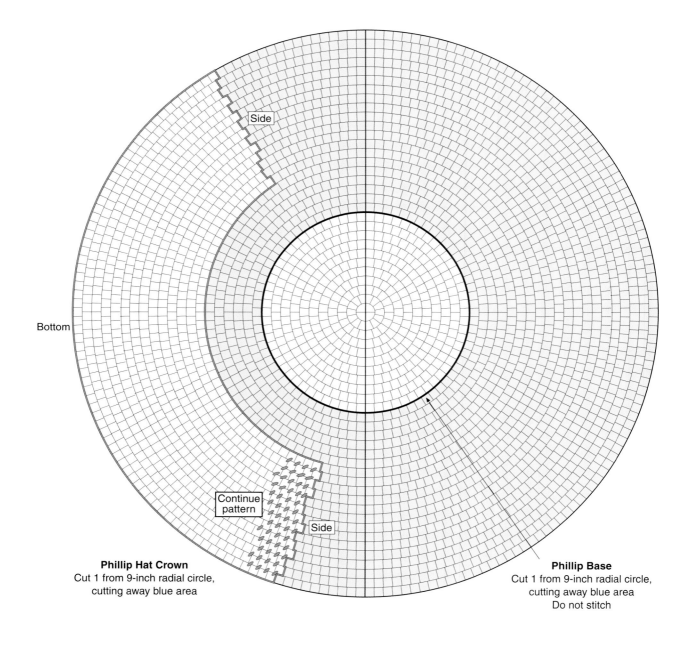

COLOR KEY
PHILLIP

Yards	Worsted Weight Yarn
40 (36.6m)	■ Black #12
17 (15.6m)	□ White #311
80 (73.2m)	▒ Gray heather #400
15 (13.8m)	□ Baby pink #724
27 (24.7m)	⁄ Mid brown #339 (double-strand) Straight Stitch and Whipstitch
	¹⁄₈-Inch Metallic Ribbon
	▒ Black hi lustre #005HL (double strand)
27 (24.7m)	● Attach cabochon

Color numbers given are for Red Heart Classic worsted weight yarn Art. E267 and Super Saver worsted weight yarn Art. E300, and Kreinik ¹⁄₈-inch metallic ribbon.

Side

Bottom

Continue pattern

Side

Phillip Hat Crown
Cut 1 from 9-inch radial circle,
cutting away blue area

Phillip Base
Cut 1 from 9-inch radial circle,
cutting away blue area
Do not stitch

PUMPKIN BASKET PARTY FAVOR

CONTINUED FROM PAGE 95

COLOR KEY

Yards	Worsted Weight Yarn
13 (11.9m)	Orange
3 (2.8m)	Green
1 (1m)	Black
1 (1m)	Dark red
1 (1m)	Pink
	Uncoded areas on front are orange Continental Stitches

**Pumpkin Basket Party Favor
Front & Back**
20 holes x 17 holes
Cut 2
Stitch front as graphed
Stitch back entirely with
orange Continental Stitches

**Pumpkin Basket
Party Favor Side**
10 holes x 15 holes
Cut 2

Continue pattern

**Pumpkin Basket
Party Favor Handle**
34 holes x 4 holes
Cut 1

BATTY MOBILE

CONTINUED FROM PAGE 87

Bat Body
Cut 1 from plastic canvas star,
cutting away yellow areas

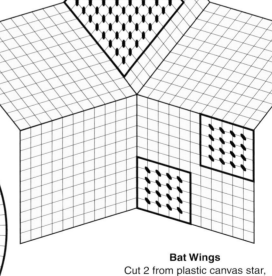

Bat Wings
Cut 2 from plastic canvas star,
cutting away yellow areas

Continue pattern

Bat Mobile Frame
Cut 1 from 4-inch radial circle,
cutting away yellow area

COLOR KEY

Yards	Worsted Weight Yarn
6 (5.5m)	Black
3 (2.8m)	Dark plum
2 (1.9m)	Medium purple
	Attach bat to frame

Bat Ear
Cut 2 from
black felt

WINTER WONDERS

SANTA CARD BOX

Keep your holiday cards close at hand by storing them in this decorative Santa box.

DESIGN BY DEBRA ARCH

Skill Level
Intermediate

Size
9¼ inches W x 13¾ inches H x 4 inches D (23.5cm x 34.9cm x 10.2cm)

Materials
- 2 sheets stiff clear 7-count plastic canvas
- 1½ sheets black 7-count plastic canvas
- Red Heart Classic medium weight yarn Art. E267 as listed in color key
- Red Heart Super Saver medium weight yarn Art. E300 as listed in color key
- Red Heart Plush medium weight yarn Art. E719 as listed in color key
- Moda Dea Dream medium weight nylon fur yarn Art. R113 as listed in color key
- Moda Dea Cheerio medium weight chenille yarn Art. R112 as listed in color key
- Kreinik ⅛-inch Ribbon as listed in color key
- #16 tapestry needle
- 2 (8mm) black cabochons
- 6 (¾-inch/1.9cm) silver stars
- Rose blush
- Cotton swab
- Hot-glue gun

Project Note
Use 2 strands when stitching with snow or winter white.

Instructions
1. Cut one each of front, back, base, mustache, hat and hat brim and two each of arms and mittens from clear stiff plastic canvas according to graphs (pages 118–121).

2. Cut one each of back, base and front from black plastic canvas for lining according to graphs. Lining pieces will remain unstitched.

3. Stitch one arm and one mitten for right side of box following graphs. Reverse remaining arm and mitten for left side and work stitches in reverse.

4. Stitch remaining clear stiff pieces following graphs, working uncoded areas on white background with linen Continental Stitches and uncoded areas on yellow background with light peach Continental Stitches. Straight Stitch beard and mustache with winter white.

5. When background stitching is completed, Straight Stitch nose with light peach. Work letters and Running Stitch border on front with black ribbon.

6. Overcast mustache. Overcast top edges of arms from dot to dot. Overcast curved edge of mittens from dot to dot.

7. For hair, wrap 1 strand winter white yarn around three fingers 10 times. Remove from fingers and tie in center with a short piece of yarn. Cut through loops on one end. Glue looped end above face on back piece where indicated on graph.

Assembly
1. Place front lining behind box front and base lining under box base, then Whipstitch front pieces to base pieces with linen. ***Note: Stitched base piece should be facing up.***

2. Following graphs, Whipstitch bottom edges of arms to base pieces. Place straight edge of one mitten along corresponding side edge of front (see photo). Using black, Whipstitch front pieces, arm and mitten together through all four layers. Whipstitch remaining arm and mitten to opposite side.

3. Place back lining behind box back, then Whipstitch bottom edges to back edges of base pieces, working through all four layers.

4. Whipstitch arms to back pieces. Whipstitch remaining edges of box back and back lining pieces together around side and top edges.

5. Overcast hat and hat brim edges around bottom side and top edges between dots. Place hat behind hat brim, then Whipstitch hat and brim together with snow along bottom edges between dots.

6. Place hat on back where indicated on graph with green lines. Glue center top portion of hat in place, then glue sides of brim flush with sides of back where indicated at brackets. ***Note:*** *Bottom edge of brim will be raised slightly over Santa.*

7. Glue cabochons to face for eyes where indicated. Glue one

star to front and remaining stars to hat brim where indicated.

8. Using cotton swab, lightly apply blush to cheeks on both sides of nose. Glue mustache in place. ●

Back Edge

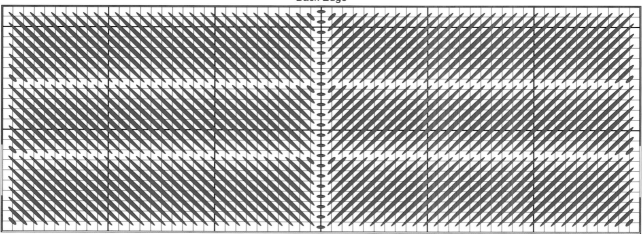

Santa Card Box Base
60 holes x 22 holes
Cut 1 from clear stiff
Stitch as graphed
Cut 1 from black for lining
Do not stitch

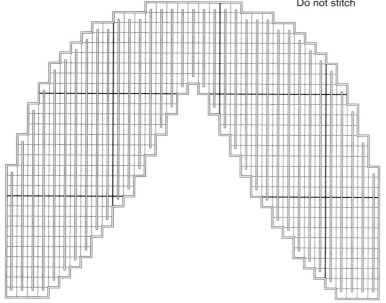

Santa Card Box Mustache
35 holes x 29 holes
Cut 1 from clear stiff

COLOR KEY

Yards	Medium Weight Yarn
20 (18.3m)	□ Snow #8010 (2 strands)
15 (13.8m)	■ Black #9002
65 (59.5m)	■ Red #9907
15 (13.8m)	Uncoded areas on yellow background are light peach #257 Continental Stitches
55 (50.3m)	Uncoded areas on white background are linen #330 Continental Stitches
	╱ Linen #330 Whipstitch
	╱ Light peach #257 Straight Stitch
45 (41.2m)	╱ Winter white #3101 (2-strand) Straight Stitch

⅛-inch Ribbon

6 (5.5m)	╱ Black #005 Backstitch, Straight Stitch and Running Stitch
	● Attach hair
	● Attach cabochon
	★ Attach star

Color numbers given are for Red Heart Classic medium weight yarn Art. E267, Super Saver medium weight yarn Art. E300 and Plush medium weight yarn Art. E719; Moda Dea Dream medium weight yarn Art. R113 and Cheerio medium weight yarn Art. 112; and Kreinik ⅛-inch Ribbon.

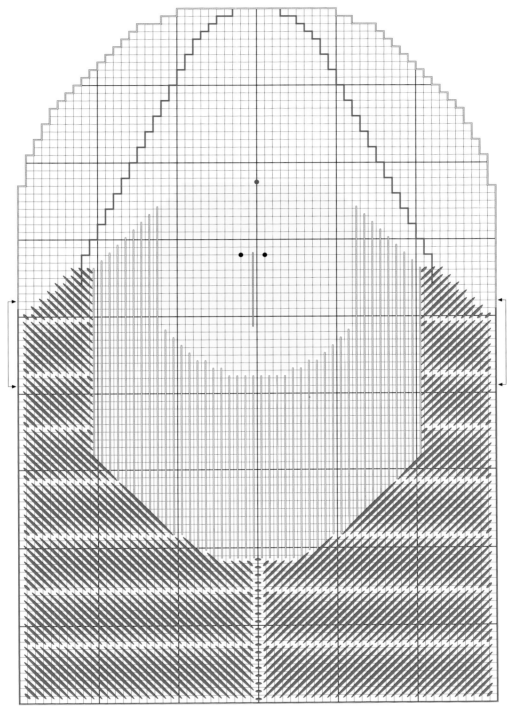

Santa Card Box Back
60 holes x 90 holes
Cut 1 from clear stiff
Stitch as graphed
Cut 1 from black
Do not stitch

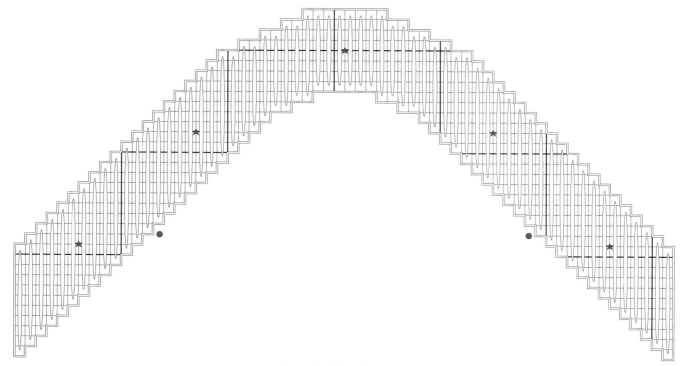

Santa Card Box Hat Brim
62 holes x 34 holes
Cut 1 from clear stiff

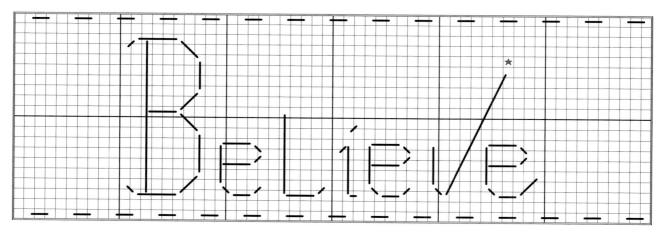

Santa Card Box Front
60 holes x 20 holes
Cut 1 from clear stiff
Stitch as graphed
Cut 1 from black for lining
Do not stitch

COLOR KEY

Yards	Medium Weight Yarn
20 (18.3m)	☐ Snow #8010 (2 strands)
15 (13.8m)	◼ Black #9002
65 (59.5m)	◼ Red #9907
15 (13.8m)	Uncoded areas on yellow background are light peach #257 Continental Stitches
55 (50.3m)	Uncoded areas on white background are linen #330 Continental Stitches
	⟋ Linen #330 Whipstitch
	⟋ Light peach #257 Straight Stitch
45 (41.2m)	⟋ Winter white #3101 (2-strand) Straight Stitch
	¹/₈-inch Ribbon
6 (5.5m)	⟋ Black #005 Backstitch, Straight Stitch and Running Stitch
	● Attach hair
	● Attach cabochon
	★ Attach star

Color numbers given are for Red Heart Classic medium weight yarn Art. E267, Super Saver medium weight yarn Art. E300 and Plush medium weight yarn Art. E719; Moda Dea Dream medium weight yarn Art. R113 and Cheerio medium weight yarn Art. 112; and Kreinik ¹/₈-inch Ribbon.

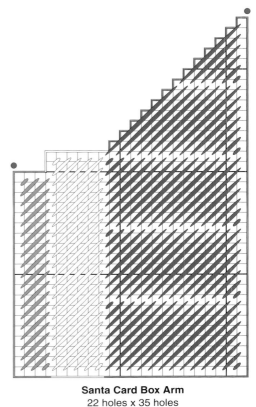

Santa Card Box Arm
22 holes x 35 holes
Cut 2 from clear stiff
Stitch 1 as graphed for right side
Reverse 1 for left side and
work stitches in reverse

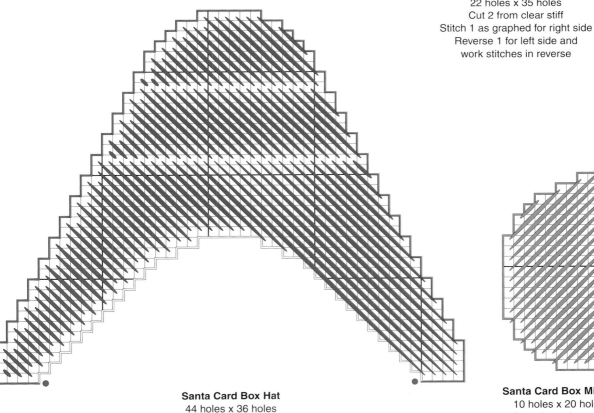

Santa Card Box Hat
44 holes x 36 holes
Cut 1 from clear stiff

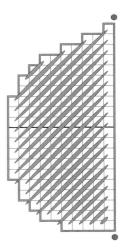

Santa Card Box Mitten
10 holes x 20 holes
Cut 2 from clear stiff
Stitch 1 as graphed for right side
Reverse 1 for left side and
work stitches in reverse

SANTA DOOR HANGER

Dress up your door with jolly old St. Nick, complete with his bag of toys!

DESIGN BY KATHLEEN HURLEY

Skill Level

Intermediate

Size

13½ inches W x 30 inches H (34.3cm x 76.2cm), excluding bird and holly sprig

Materials

- 4 sheets 7-count plastic canvas
- Uniek Needloft plastic canvas yarn as listed in color key
- Chenille yarn as listed in color key
- Uniek Needloft metallic craft cord as listed in color key
- #3 pearl cotton as listed in color key
- #16 tapestry needle
- 1-inch (2.5mm) white pompom
- 3 (³⁄₈-inch/9mm) red jingle bells
- 5mm black cabochon
- 12 inches (30.5cm) ⁷⁄₈-inch/ 23mm-wide green polka dot grosgrain ribbon
- 12 inches (30.5cm) ¼-inch/7mm-wide white satin ribbon
- 9 inches (22.9cm) ³⁄₈-inch/ 9mm-wide red plaid ribbon
- Hot-glue gun

Instructions

1. Cut plastic canvas according to graphs (pages 124–127), cutting out area by shoulders and hat pompom on top section.

2. Stitch and Overcast Santa pieces following graphs, overlapping top and bottom sections with middle section where indicated on graphs. Work uncoded areas with Continental Stitches as follows: pink background with burgundy, green background with forest, peach background with pale peach and yellow background with ivory.

3. Work two Straight Stitches per hole where indicated for Santa's cheeks, eyebrows, mustache and nose, and for candy cane, ball, teddy bear's hat and doll's shoes.

4. Work embroidery at eyes, mouths and patch.

5. Stitch and Overcast cardinal and holly sprig, working two stitches per hole where indicated. Work one holly Straight Stitch down center of leaves on holly sprig when background stitching and Overcasting are completed.

6. Use photo as a guide through step 8. Tie green grosgrain ribbon in a bow, trimming ends as desired. Center and glue to neck of teddy bear. Tie white satin ribbon in a bow, center and glue to neck of doll. Glue white ribbon tails to doll.

7. For pony reins, thread plaid ribbon from front to back where indicated on graph; tie ends in a knot. If desired, glue ribbon to door hanger to secure.

8. Glue cabochon to cardinal for eye, then glue bells in a cluster to red area of holly sprig. Glue cardinal and holly sprig to door hanger. ●

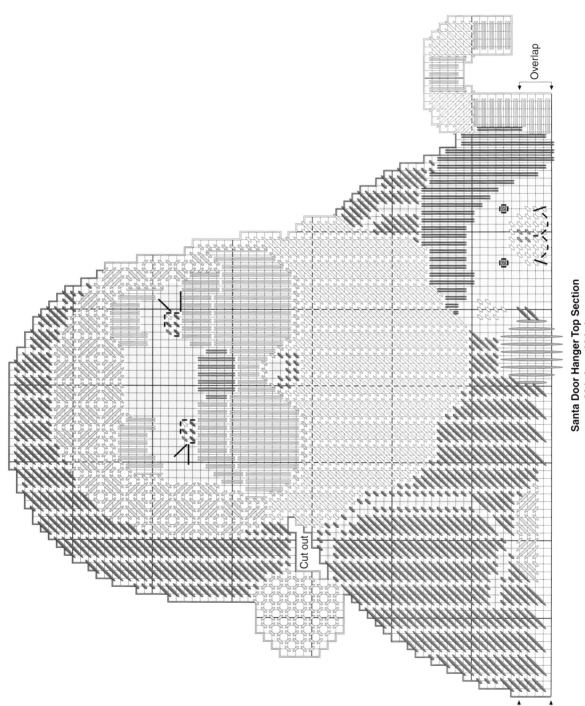

Santa Door Hanger Top Section
88 holes x 68 holes
Cut 1

Overlap

Cut out

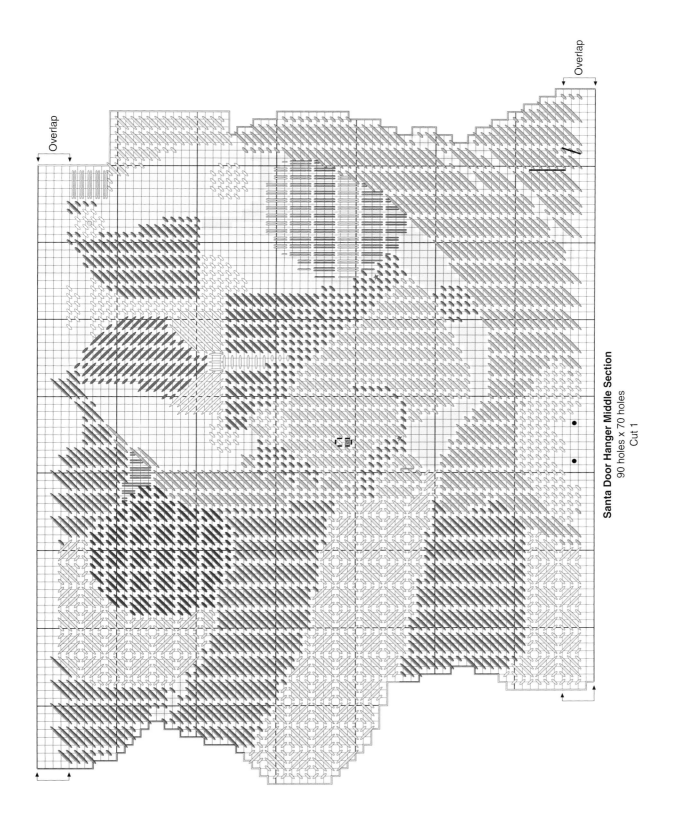

Overlap

Overlap

Santa Door Hanger Middle Section
90 holes x 70 holes
Cut 1

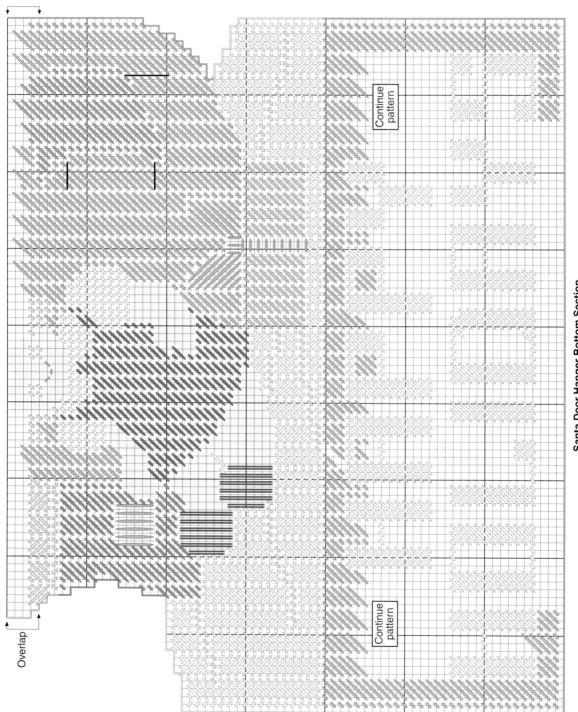

Santa Door Hanger Bottom Section
90 holes x 70 holes
Cut 1

Continue pattern

Continue pattern

Overlap

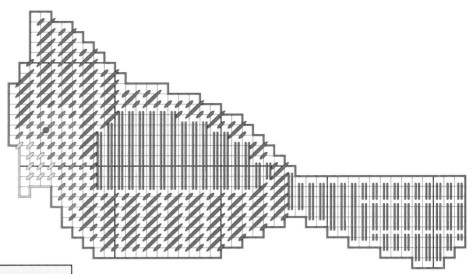

Santa Door Hanger Cardinal
43 holes x 25 holes
Cut 1

COLOR KEY

Yards	Plastic Canvas Yarn
5 (4.6m)	■ Black #00
49 (44.8m)	■ Red #01
6 (5.5m)	□ Christmas red #02
6 (5.5m)	□ Pink #07
7 (6.5m)	□ Maple #13
3 (2.8m)	■ Cinnamon #14
63 (57.7m)	■ Holly #27
6 (6.5m)	■ Forest #29
12 (11m)	■ Royal #32
3 (2.8m)	□ Silver #37
44 (40.3m)	□ White #41
6 (5.5m)	■ Purple #46
6 (5.5m)	■ Bittersweet #52
6 (5.5m)	□ Yellow #57
2 (1.9m)	Uncoded areas with pink background are burgundy #03 Continental Stitches
	Uncoded areas with green background are forest #29 Continental Stitches
8 (7.4m)	Uncoded areas with peach background are pale peach #56 Continental Stitches
	╱ Black #00 Straight Stitch
	╱ Red #01 Straight Stitch
	╱ Pink #07 Straight Stitch
	╱ Holly #27 Straight Stitch
	╱ Royal #32 Straight Stitch
	╱ White #41 Straight Stitch
	╱ Purple #46 Straight Stitch
	╱ Bittersweet #52 Straight Stitch
	╱ Yellow #57 Straight Stitch

Chenille Yarn

Yards	
48 (43.9m)	□ White
5 (4.6m)	□ Ivory
24 (22m)	Uncoded areas with yellow background are camel Continental Stitches

Metallic Craft Cord

Yards	
2 (1.9m)	■ Gold #55001
1 (1m)	□ Green #55004

#3 Pearl Cotton

Yards	
2 (1.9m)	╱ Black Backstitch and Straight Stitch
1 (1m)	╱ Red Backstitch
	● Black French Knot
	★ Attach plaid ribbon
	● Attach cabochon
	○ Attach pompom

Color numbers given are for Uniek Needloft plastic canvas yarn and metallic craft cord.

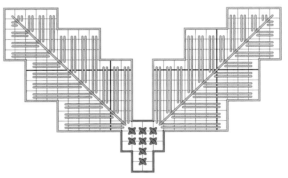

Santa Door Hanger Holly Sprig
26 holes x 16 holes
Cut 1

RUDOLPH TISSUE TOPPER

Sweet as can be, this tissue topper features everyone's favorite reindeer.

DESIGN BY CHRISTINA LAWS

Skill Level
Beginner

Size
Fits boutique-style tissue topper

Materials
- 2 sheets 7-count plastic canvas
- Worsted weight yarn as listed in color key
- #16 tapestry needle
- Hot-glue gun

Instructions

1. Cut plastic canvas according to graphs (this page and pages 130 and 131).

2. Stitch and Overcast head and muzzle following graphs, working uncoded areas with medium brown Continental Stitches.

3. When background stitching is completed, work black Backstitches for mouth and white Straight Stitches on eyes.

4. Stitch tail pieces following graph, working tail back as graphed. Stitch tail front entirely with medium brown Continental Stitches. Whipstitch wrong sides of front and back together.

5. Stitch front, back, sides and top following graphs. Overcast inside edges of top, and bottom edges of front, back and sides. Whipstitch front and back to sides. Whipstitch front and back to top from blue dot to blue dot; Whipstitch sides to top.

6. Using photo as a guide, center and glue muzzle to head, then center and glue head to front. Center and glue tail at top edge of back. ●

Rudolph Tissue Topper Side
33 holes x 39 holes
Cut 2

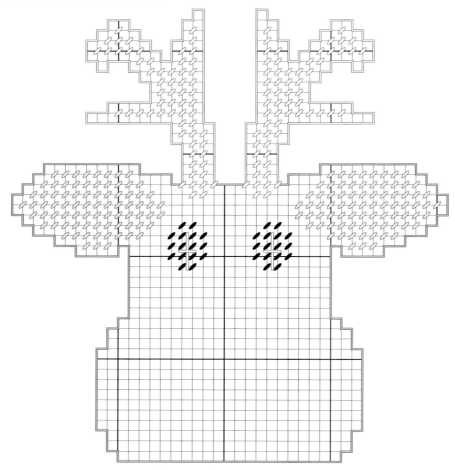

Rudolph Tissue Topper Head
41 holes x 44 holes
Cut 1

Whipstitch to back

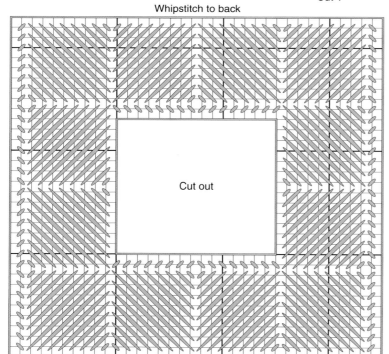

Cut out

Whipstitch to front

Rudolph Tissue Topper Top
35 holes x 33 holes
Cut 1

COLOR KEY

Yards	Worsted Weight Yarn
70 (64m)	Medium brown
15 (13.8m)	Black
4 (3.7m)	Cream
2 (1.9m)	Tan
2 (1.9m)	White
1 (1m)	Red

Uncoded areas on head and muzzle are medium brown Continental Stitches
✏ Black Backstitch
✏ White Straight Stitch

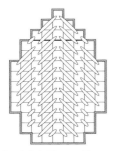

**Rudolph Tissue Topper
Tail Front & Back**
9 holes x 13 holes
Cut 2
Stitch 1 as graphed
for back
Stitch 1 entirely with
medium brown Continental
Stitches for front

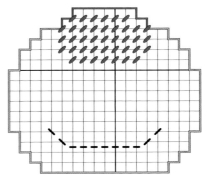

Rudolph Tissue Topper Muzzle
18 holes x 16 holes
Cut 1

Rudolph Tissue Topper Front & Back
33 holes x 43 holes
Cut 2

HOLIDAY FRAME & ORNAMENT SET

Display your favorite photo and your holiday spirit with this coordinating frame and ornament set.

DESIGNS BY SANDRA MILLER MAXFIELD

Skill Level
Beginner

Size
Frame: 11½ inches W x 9¾ inches H (29.2cm x 24.8cm)
Ornaments: 3½ inches W x 5½ inches H (3.5cm x 14cm)

Materials
- 1 sheet 7-count plastic canvas
- Worsted weight yarn as listed in color key
- Metallic craft cord as listed in color key
- #16 tapestry needle

Instructions

1. Cut plastic canvas according to graphs (this page and page 134), cutting away blue lines on ornament hangers.

2. Stitch and Overcast frame following graph, working uncoded areas with red Continental Stitches.

3. Center and attach photo behind opening as desired. Hang as desired.

4. Bend hangers so ends overlap blue shaded areas on caps of ornaments, then stitch and Overcast as graphed, working through both layers on cap. Do not stitch bent portion of hangers. ●

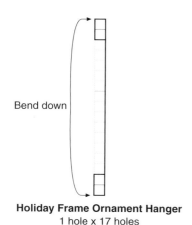

Bend down

Holiday Frame Ornament Hanger
1 hole x 17 holes
Cut 2,
cutting away blue lines

COLOR KEY	
Yards	**Worsted Weight Yarn**
23 (21.1m)	■ Red
24 (22m)	■ Green
21 (19.3m)	□ Light green
3 (2.8m)	■ Dark red
	Uncoded areas are red Continental Stitches
	✏ Red Backstitch
	Metallic Craft Cord
4 (3.7m)	▨ Solid gold

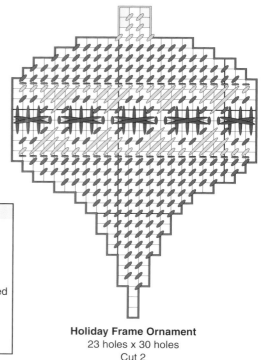

Holiday Frame Ornament
23 holes x 30 holes
Cut 2

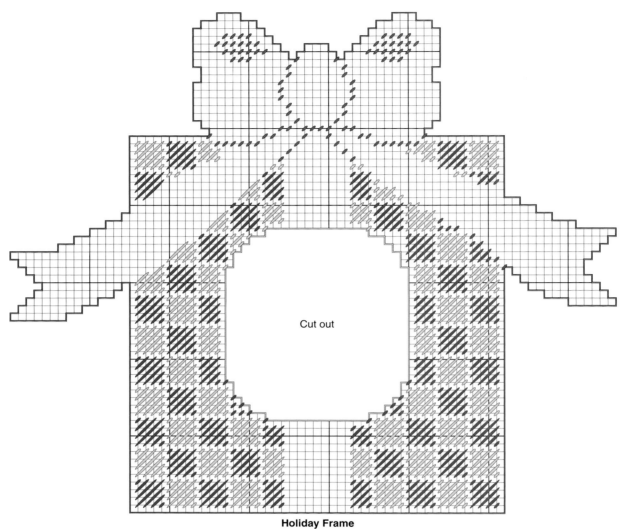

Cut out

Holiday Frame
76 holes x 65 holes
Cut 1

COLOR KEY

Yards	Worsted Weight Yarn
23 (21.1m)	■ Red
24 (22m)	■ Green
21 (19.3m)	▨ Light green
3 (2.8m)	■ Dark red
	Uncoded areas are red
	Continental Stitches
	╱ Red Backstitch
	Metallic Craft Cord
4 (3.7m)	▨ Solid gold

CHRISTMAS TREE DOORSTOP

Keep your door open for holiday guests with this cheerful doorstop.

DESIGN BY JOYCE MESSENGER

Skill Level
Intermediate

Size
Approximately 5⅝ inches W x 8½ inches H x 5¼ inches D (14.3cm x 21.6cm x 13.3cm), including tree, swag and banner

Materials
- 2 sheets 7-count plastic canvas
- Worsted weight yarn as listed in color key
- Metallic craft cord as listed in color key
- #16 tapestry needle
- 29 (5mm) faceted beads in assorted colors
- Brick or zip-close bag filled with sand, gravel or other weighted material
- Hot-glue gun

Project Note
If metallic cord has a white core, the core may be removed for easier stitching. Use tweezers or fingertips and pull; core slips out easily.

Instructions
1. Cut plastic canvas according to graphs (pages 136 and 137). Base will remain unstitched.

2. Stitch and Overcast banner, star and swag, working uncoded background on banner with white Continental Stitches.

3. Stitch tree branches following graph, reversing two before stitching. For center branch, Whipstitch wrong sides of two branches together along all edges except edges within brackets. Overcast remaining two branches along all edges except edges within brackets.

4. Stitch doorstop front, back, sides and top following graphs, working uncoded areas with pewter Continental Stitches.

5. Work red and pewter embroidery on banner. When working gold metallic cord stitches for tree garland, work stitches over edges and seams, then allow longer stitches to drape as shown on graph.

6. Using pewter throughout, Whipstitch front and back to sides, then Whipstitch front, back and sides to top and base, inserting brick or weighted material before closing.

7. Using Christmas green and with right sides facing, Whipstitch center and side tree branches together along edges inside brackets.

8. Use photo as a guide through step 9. Open branches and glue wrong sides of side branches to doorstop front, making sure bottom edges of tree and doorstop are even. Glue beads to branches as desired.

9. Glue star to front at top of tree. Glue swag and banner to top front. ●

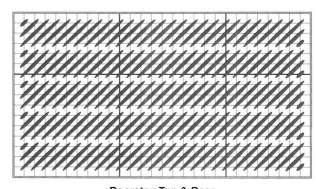

Doorstop Top & Base
28 holes x 16 holes
Cut 2
Stitch top only

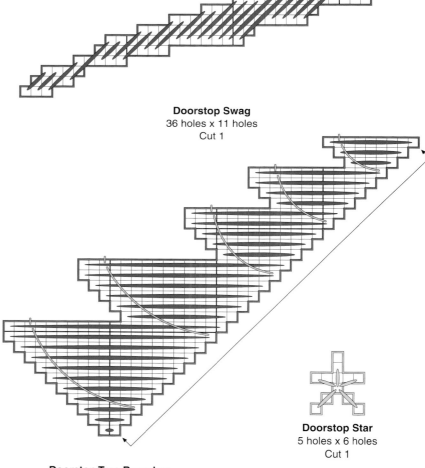

Doorstop Swag
36 holes x 11 holes
Cut 1

Doorstop Star
5 holes x 6 holes
Cut 1

Doorstop Tree Branches
39 holes x 29 holes
Cut 4, reverse 2

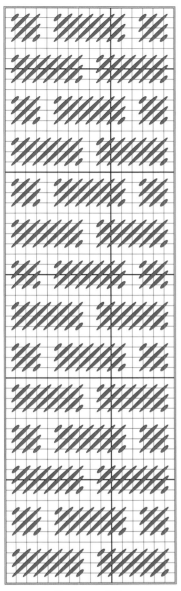

Doorstop Side
16 holes x 56 holes
Cut 2

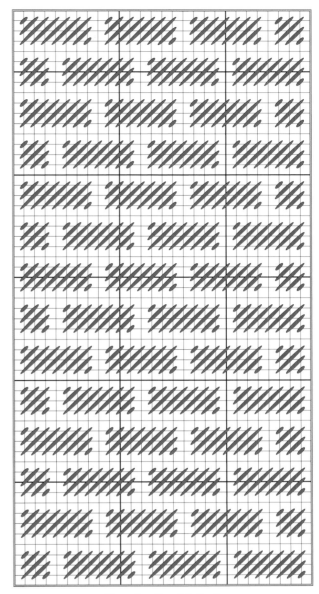

Doorstop Front & Back
28 holes x 56 holes
Cut 2

COLOR KEY

Yards	Worsted Weight Yarn
52 (47.6m)	■ Red
40 (36.6m)	☐ Pewter
22 (20.2m)	■ Christmas green
4 (3.7m)	Uncoded background on banner is is white Continental Stitches
	Uncoded areas on doorstop pieces are pewter Continental Stitches
	⁄ White Overcast
	⁄ Red Backstitch
	⁄ Pewter Backstitch
	Metallic Craft Cord
3 (2.8m)	☐ Gold

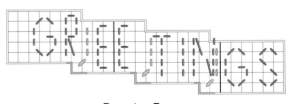

Doorstop Banner
26 holes x 8 holes
Cut 1

JOYFUL COASTER & GIFT BAG

Give an extra gift to loved ones when you present them with a coaster-embellished gift bag. You can stitch up extra motifs for a whole set.

DESIGN BY CYNTHIA ROBERTS

Skill Level
Beginner

Size
Coaster: 4⅛ inches (10.5cm) square

Materials
- ½ sheet 7-count plastic canvas
- Worsted weight yarn as listed in color key
- Metallic craft cord as listed in color key
- DMC 6-strand metallic embroidery floss as listed in color key
- #16 tapestry needle
- Brown paper gift bag
- Small amount red raffia
- Hot-glue gun

Instructions

1. Cut plastic canvas according to graph.

2. Stitch and Overcast coaster and gift bag motif following graph, working uncoded areas with off-white Continental Stitches.

3. When background stitching is completed, work black and light green yarn and gold metallic floss embroidery.

4. Center and glue motif to center front of gift bag. Tie a small bunch of raffia in a bow around bag handle. ●

COLOR KEY

Yards	Worsted Weight Yarn
6 (5.5m)	☐ Gold
2 (1.9m)	■ Dark red
1 (1m)	■ Forest green
1 (1m)	■ Christmas green
1 (1m)	■ Red
1 (1m)	☐ Light green
1 (1m)	■ Brown
6 (5.5m)	Uncoded areas are off-white Continental Stitches
	╱ Off-white Overcast
1 (1m)	╱ Black Running Stitch
	╱ Light green Backstitch and Running Stitch
	● Black French Knot

Metallic Craft Cord

| 1 (1m) | ☐ Gold |

6-Strand Metallic Embroidery Floss

| 2 (1.9m) | ╱ Gold #5282 Backstitch and Straight Stitch |

Color number given is for DMC 6-strand metallic embroidery floss.

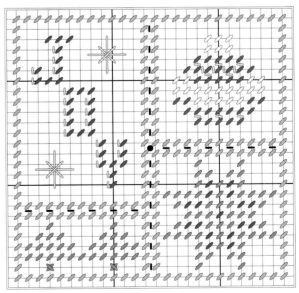

Joyful Coaster & Gift Bag Motif
27 holes x 27 holes
Cut 2

O CHRISTMAS TREE

The classic beauty of a decorated Christmas tree is wonderful when added to a quick-to-create tissue topper.

DESIGN BY ALIDA MACOR

Skill Level
Beginner

Size
Fits boutique-style tissue box

Materials
- 2 sheets 7-count plastic canvas
- Worsted weight yarn as listed in color key
- Uniek Needloft plastic canvas yarn as listed in color key
- #16 tapestry needle
- 56 (5mm) round metallic gold beads
- Hand-sewing needle
- Green sewing thread or floss to match green yarn
- Hot-glue gun

Instructions

1. Cut plastic canvas according to graphs.

2. Stitch pieces following graphs. Overcast inside edges of top and bottom edges of sides. Overcast side edges of top between dots. Overcast top tree edges on sides between arrows.

3. Using hand-sewing needle and green thread or floss, attach beads to trees on sides where indicated on graph.

4. Whipstitch sides together, then Whipstitch top to sides along unstitched edges. ●

O Christmas Tree Side
31 holes x 42 holes
Cut 4

COLOR KEY

Yards	Worsted Weight Yarn
56 (51.3m)	☐ White
6 (5.5m)	■ Red
1 (1m)	▨ Light brown
	Plastic Canvas Yarn
32 (29.3m)	■ Christmas green #28
	● Attach bead

Color number given is for Uniek Needloft plastic canvas yarn.

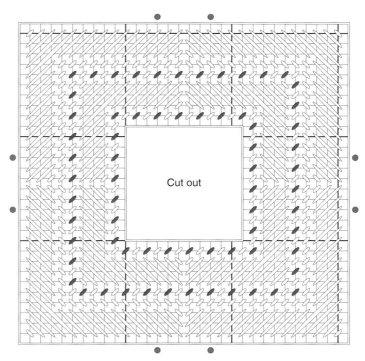

O Christmas Tree Top
31 holes x 31 holes
Cut 1

MUSICAL CHRISTMAS STOCKING

Featuring a pretty angel, this tiny stocking includes a small music button for a little extra cheer

DESIGN BY ALIDA MACOR

Skill Level
Beginner

Size
3 inches W x 4 inches H x ¾ inches D (7.6cm x 10.2cm x 1.9cm)

Materials
- ½ sheet 7-count plastic canvas
- Worsted weight yarn as listed in color key
- Darice metallic cord as listed in color key
- 6-strand embroidery floss as listed in color key
- #16 tapestry needle
- ¼ yard (0.2m) thin gold cord
- 15/16-inch (3.3cm) music button

Instructions

1. Cut plastic canvas according to graphs.

2. Stitch pieces following graphs, working brown floss French Knots for eyes when background stitching is completed.

3. Using pale pink yarn and with wrong sides facing, Whipstitch front and back to gusset around side and bottom edges, easing as necessary to fit. ***Note:*** *Holes marked with a green dot on stocking graphs are to be Whipstitched to two holes of gusset. Overcast top edges.*

4. For hanger, attach thin gold cord with a Lark's Head Knot through hole indicated on gusset. Tie ends together in a knot to form a loop for hanging.

5. Slip music button in toe of stocking. ●

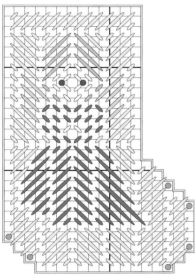

Musical Christmas Stocking Front
18 holes x 26 holes
Cut 1

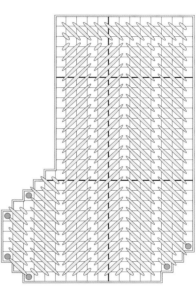

Musical Christmas Stocking Back
18 holes x 26 holes
Cut 1

COLOR KEY	
Yards	**Worsted Weight Yarn**
12 (11m)	☐ Pale pink
1 (1m)	☐ Peach
1 (1m)	▨ Light brown
	Metallic Cord
5 (4.6m)	▨ Blue/silver #3412-06
1 (1m)	☐ Gold/white #3412-11
	6-Strand Embroidery Floss
1 (1m)	● Brown French Knot
	● Attach hanger
Color numbers given are for Darice Metallic Cord.	

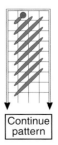

Continue pattern

Musical Christmas Stocking Gusset
4 holes x 69 holes
Cut 1

CHARMING CHALETS

Escape on a winter wonderland vacation when you stitch these tiny snow-covered chalets.

DESIGNS BY ANGIE ARICKX

Skill Level
Beginner

Size
Chalet A: 3½ inches W x 3¼ inches H x 2⅜ inches D (8.9cm x 8.3cm x 6cm)
Chalet B: 2⅞ inches W x 3⅛ inches H x 2⅛ inches D (7.3cm x 8cm x 5.4cm)

Materials
- ½ sheet 7-count plastic canvas
- Red Heart Classic worsted weight yarn Art. E267 as listed in color key
- #16 tapestry needle
- Hot-glue gun

Instructions

1. Cut plastic canvas according to graphs, cutting four chimney sides for each chalet.

2. Stitch pieces following graphs, working uncoded areas on chalet B pieces with mid brown Continental Stitches.

3. When background stitching is completed, work coffee Backstitches on chalet front, back and side pieces.

4. For chalet A, Whipstitch front and back to sides. Overcast top and bottom edges.

5. Overcast around side and bottom edges of roof pieces from blue dot to blue dot; Overcast chimney openings from arrow to arrow. Whipstitch top edges of roof pieces together.

6. Whipstitch chimney sides together. Overcast top and bottom edges.

7. Using photo as a guide, glue chimney in opening on roof, then center and glue roof on chalet.

8. Repeat steps 4–7 for chalet B. ●

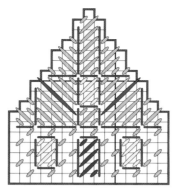

Chalet B Front & Back
15 holes x 17 holes
Cut 2

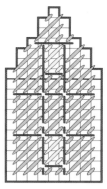

Chalet A Side
9 holes x 17 holes
Cut 2

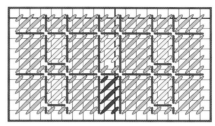

Chalet A Front & Back
19 holes x 11 holes
Cut 2

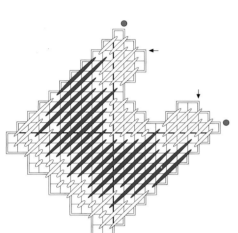

Chalet B Roof
20 holes x 20 holes
Cut 2

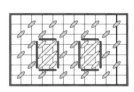

Chalet B Side
11 holes x 7 holes
Cut 2

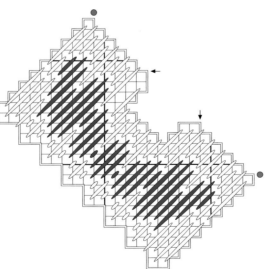

Chalet A Roof
24 holes x 24 holes
Cut 2

Chalet Chimney Side
3 holes x 6 holes
Cut 4 for each chalet

COLOR KEY

Yards	Worsted Weight Yarn
9 (8.3m)	☐ White #1
4 (3.7m)	☐ Maize #261
11 (10.1m)	▨ Warm brown #336
9 (8.3m)	■ Coffee #365
6 (5.5m)	■ Paddy green #686
4 (3.7m)	■ Country red #914
2 (1.9m)	Uncoded areas on chalet B pieces are mid brown #339 Continental Stitches
╱	Coffee #365 Backstitch

Color numbers given are for Red Heart Classic worsted weight yarn Art. E267.

VARIATIONS ON A THEME

Combine the crispness of white with the antique aura of ivory, and stitch a set of each of these doilies for truly versatile decorating!

DESIGN BY ALIDA MACOR

Skill Level
Intermediate

Size
9½ inches W x 9½ inches H
(24.1cm x 24.1cm)

Materials
• 1 sheet almond 7-count plastic canvas
• 1 sheet white 7-count plastic canvas
• Uniek Needloft plastic canvas yarn as listed in color key
• Worsted weight yarn as listed in color key
• #16 tapestry needle

Instructions

1. Cut plastic canvas according to graph.

2. Following graph, stitch and Overcast almond plastic canvas with eggshell; stitch and Overcast white plastic canvas with white. As much as is possible, avoid carrying yarn under unstitched areas. ●

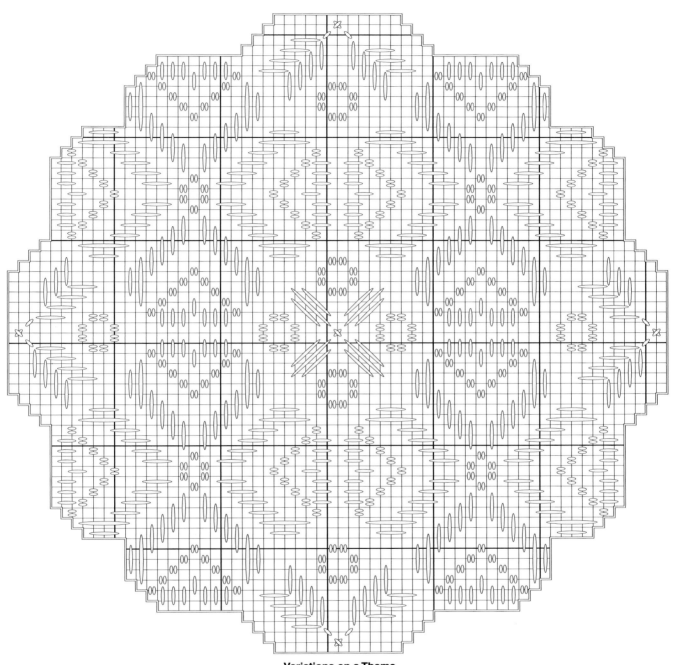

Variations on a Theme
62 holes x 62 holes
Cut 1 from almond, stitch as graphed
Cut 1 from white, stitch with white

COLOR KEY

Yards	Plastic Canvas Yarn
27 (24.7m)	☐ Eggshell #39
	Worsted Weight Yarn
27 (24.7m)	White

Color number given is for Uniek
Needloft plastic canvas yarn.

CELEBRATE WINTER TISSUE TOPPER

Chase away those winter blahs with a bright and colorful tissue topper that celebrates the beauty of winter.

DESIGN BY TERRY RICIOLI

Skill Level
Beginner

Size
Fits boutique-style tissue box

Materials
- 1½ sheets 7-count plastic canvas
- Uniek Needloft plastic canvas yarn as listed in color key
- #16 tapestry needle

Instructions

1. Cut plastic canvas according to graphs.

2. Stitch pieces following graphs, working Continental Stitches in uncoded areas as follows: pink background with red, green background with holly, white background with white.

3. When background stitching is completed, work black Straight Stitches for eyes on snowmen and white Backstitches and Straight Stitch for letters and snowflakes.

4. Using holly throughout, Overcast inside edges on top and bottom edges of sides. Whipstitch sides together, then Whipstitch sides to top. ●

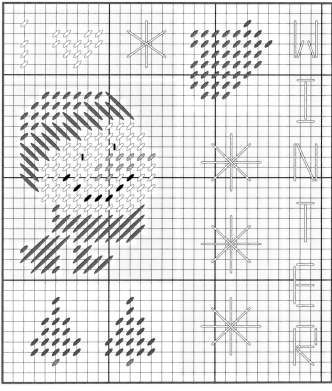

Celebrate Winter Tissue Topper Side
31 holes x 37 holes
Cut 4

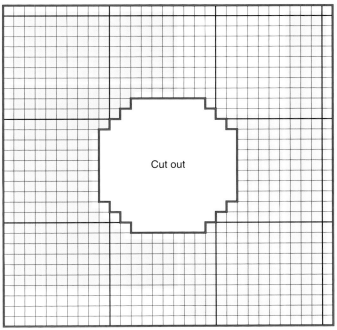

Celebrate Winter Tissue Topper Top
31 holes x 31 holes
Cut 1

COLOR KEY

Yards	Plastic Canvas Yarn
3 (2.8m)	■ Black #00
32 (29.3m)	■ Red #01
2 (1.9m)	▨ Pumpkin #12
1 (1m)	▨ Cinnamon #14
27 (24.7m)	■ Holly #27
25 (22.9m)	□ White #41

Uncoded areas with pink
background are red #01
Continental Stitches
Uncoded areas with green
background are holly #27
Continental Stitches
Uncoded areas with white
background are white #41
Continental Stitches

✐ Black #00 Straight Stitch
⟋ White #41 Backstitch
and Straight Stitch

Color numbers given are for Uniek Needloft
plastic canvas yarn.

COUNTRY SNOWMAN WELCOME

Welcome friends from far and wide when you adorn your door with this charming snow buddy!

DESIGN BY ROBIN PETRINA

Skill Level
Beginner

Size
12 inches W x 15¼ inches H (30.5cm x 38.7cm)

Materials
- 1 sheet 7-count plastic canvas
- Red Heart Classic worsted weight yarn Art. E267 as listed in color key
- Red Heart Super Saver worsted weight yarn Art. E300 as listed in color key
- #16 tapestry needle
- Hot-glue gun

Instructions

1. Cut plastic canvas according to graphs (pages 152 and 153).

2. Following graphs throughout all stitching, stitch and Overcast buttons, working two as graphed for body buttons. Stitch and Overcast remaining button for hat, switching light blue and country blue.

3. Stitch and Overcast remaining pieces, reversing one arm before stitching.

4. When background stitching is completed, use 4 plies black to work mouth and "holes" in buttons. Using 2 plies throughout, Straight Stitch white highlights on eyes; work gold French Knot for bird's beak and black French Knots for bird's eyes.

5. Cut four 2-inch (5.1cm) lengths of white yarn. Thread yarn from front to back through holes indicated at top of body bottom graph; knot ends on back side. Thread other ends from front to back through holes indicated at bottom of body center graph. Knot on back side, making sure lengths are even.

6. Repeat to attach head to body center with remaining two lengths of white yarn.

7. Using photo as a guide, center and glue one body button each to body center and bottom. Center and glue hat button to hat. Glue hat brim and nose to head.

8. Glue arms to back of body center. Glue bird to top right side of one arm, then glue bird tail to back side of arm just behind bird.

9. Hang as desired. ●

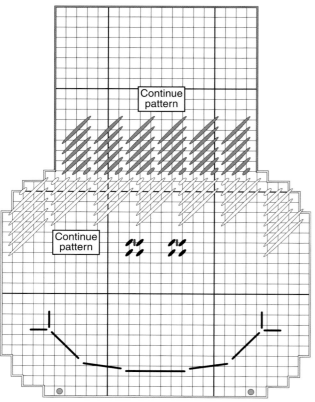

COLOR KEY

Yards	Worsted Weight Yarn
1 (1m)	■ Copper #289
27 (24.7m)	□ White #311
1 (1m)	■ Black #312
3 (2.8m)	■ Cafe #360
5 (4.6m)	□ Light blue #381
9 (8.3m)	■ Country blue #382
1 (1m)	■ Cherry red #912
	╱ White #311 (2-ply) Straight Stitch
	╱ Black #312 (4-ply) Backstitch
	● Black #312 (2-ply) French Knot
1 (1m)	○ Gold #321 (2-ply) French Knot
	● Connect parts with white yarn

Color numbers given are for Red Heart Classic worsted weight yarn Art. E267 and Super Saver worsted weight yarn Art. E300.

Country Snowman Head
29 holes x 38 holes
Cut 1

Country Snowman Button
7 holes x 7 holes
Cut 3
Stitch and Overcast 2
as graphed for body buttons
Stitch and Overcast 1 for hat button,
switching light blue and country blue

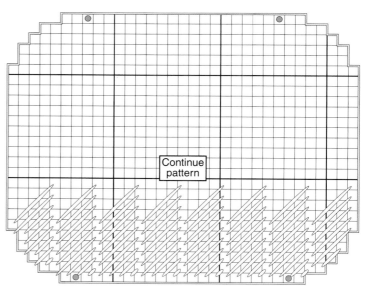

Country Snowman Body Center
33 holes x 26 holes
Cut 1

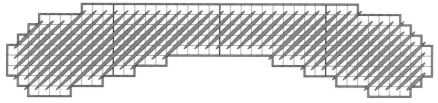

Country Snowman Hat Brim
40 holes x 9 holes
Cut 1

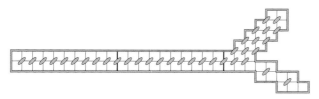

Country Snowman Arm
28 holes x 8 holes
Cut 2, reverse 1

Country Snowman Nose
5 holes x 5 holes
Cut 1

Country Snowman Bird
5 holes x 5 holes
Cut 1

Country Snowman Bird Tail
4 holes x 4 holes
Cut 1

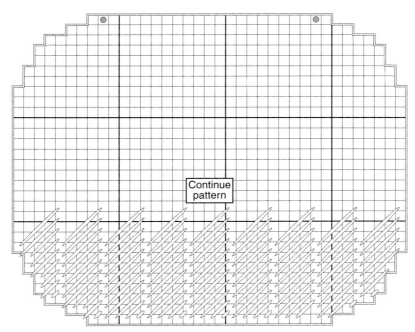

Continue pattern

Country Snowman Body Bottom
37 holes x 30 holes
Cut 1

SENSATIONAL SNOWMAN

Grab a coaster from this decorative snowman wall hanging. The "snowballs" are actually removable coasters!

DESIGN BY JANELLE GIESE

Skill Level
Advanced

Size
Snowman: 8³⁄₈ inches W x 20³⁄₄ inches H (21.3cm x 52.7cm)
Coaster: 3³⁄₄ inches W x 3³⁄₄ inches H (9.5cm x 9.5cm)

Materials
- 2 artist-size sheets clear stiff 7-count plastic canvas
- ²⁄₃ sheet white 7-count plastic canvas
- Uniek Needloft plastic canvas yarn as listed in color key
- DMC #3 pearl cotton as listed in color key
- #5 pearl cotton as listed in color key
- #16 tapestry needle
- 4 (³⁄₄-inch/1.9cm) white hook-and-loop circles
- 8 inches (20.3cm) 18-gauge steel wire
- White acrylic paint
- Paintbrush
- Spray sealer
- Hand-sewing needle
- White sewing thread or carpet thread
- Sawtooth hanger
- Thick white glue

Project Note
The diamond, heart, square, triangle and inverted triangle symbols designate Continental Stitches.

Preparation
1. Cut four coaster bases and two snowman pieces from clear stiff plastic canvas according to graphs (pages 156–158), joining top and bottom sections of snowman graphs before cutting each snowman as one 55-hole x 138-hole piece.

2. Cut four coaster tops from white plastic canvas following graph (page 158), cutting away blue areas. Coaster tops will remain unstitched.

3. Cut 22 (4-inch/10.2cm) lengths eggshell yarn for scarf fringe. Set aside.

4. Using photo as a guide, bend and curl wire as desired for headband on earmuffs, leaving ½ inch (1.3cm) on each end. Paint wire with white acrylic paint. Allow to dry. Seal with spray sealer. Allow to dry.

Instructions
1. Stitch coaster bases following graph. Using hand-sewing needle and white thread, center and sew one soft side of hook-and-loop circles to wrong side of each coaster base.

2. Place one coaster top on top of each coaster base and Whipstitch together along outside edges with white.

3. Place snowman pieces together and stitch as one following graphs, working uncoded areas on white background with white Continental Stitches. Do not stitch uncoded areas shaded with green.

4. Overcast snowman leaving scarf edges with Lark's Head Knots unworked.

5. Backstitch beak on bird with beige yarn. Using black pearl cotton, work embroidery where indicated, wrapping French Knot eyes on bird two times. Work light old gold pearl cotton French Knots for bird seed, wrapping needle two times.

6. For scarf fringe, attach 4-inch (10.2cm) lengths eggshell yarn, cut in step 3 of preparation, with Lark's Head Knots where indicated. Place a dab of glue behind each knot to secure. Trim fringe to ¾ inch (1.9cm).

7. Use hand-sewing needle and white thread through step 8. Sew hook side of hook-and-loop circles to shaded green areas on snowman.

8. Center and sew sawtooth hanger to top back of snowman. Sew ends of wire headband to back of earmuffs.

9. Attach coasters to snowman matching hook-and-loop circles. ●

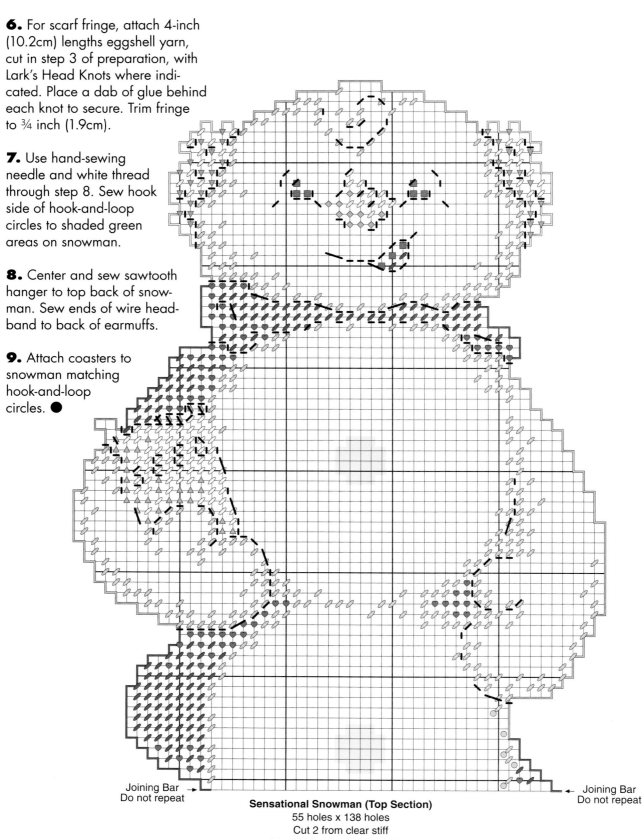

Joining Bar
Do not repeat

Joining Bar
Do not repeat

Sensational Snowman (Top Section)
55 holes x 138 holes
Cut 2 from clear stiff
Join with bottom section before
cutting each snowman as 1 piece

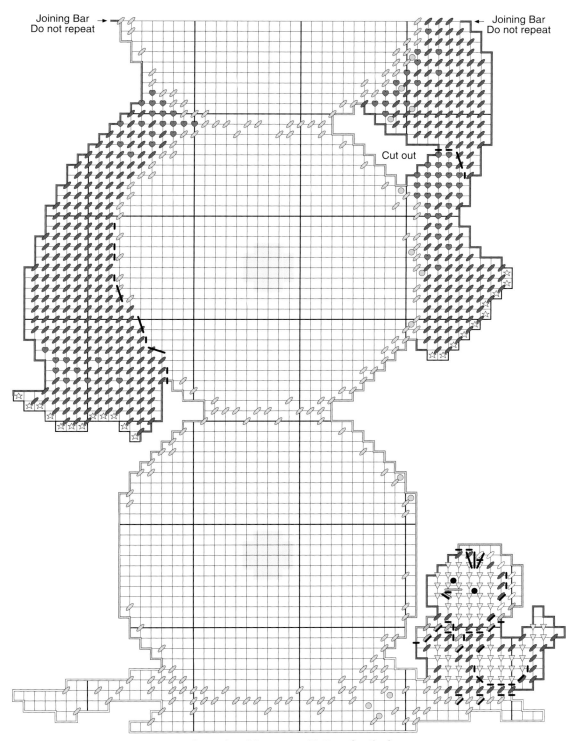

Cut out

Sensational Snowman (Bottom Section)
55 holes x 138 holes
Cut 2 from clear stiff
Join with top section before
cutting each snowman as 1 piece

**Sensational Snowman
Coaster Top**
24 holes x 24 holes
Cut 4 from white,
cutting away blue areas

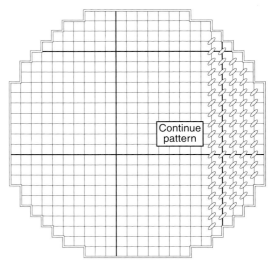

Continue
pattern

**Sensational Snowman
Coaster Base**
24 holes x 24 holes
Cut 4 from clear stiff

COLOR KEY

Yards	Plastic Canvas Yarn
1 (1m)	■ Black #00
17 (15.6m)	◢ Red #01
1 (1m)	▽ Christmas red #02
4 (3.7m)	♥ Burgundy #03
1 (1m)	⬮ Tangerine #11
1 (1m)	◆ Pumpkin #12
1 (1m)	▽ Sail blue #35
28 (25.7m)	⬮ Baby blue #36
18 (16.5m)	⬮ Silver #37
5 (4.6m)	⬮ Eggshell #39
2 (1.9m)	▲ Beige #40
75 (68.6m)	Uncoded areas with white background on snowman are white #41 Continental Stitches
	⬮ White #41 Overcast
	◢ Beige #41 Backstitch
	☆ Eggshell #39 Lark's Head Knot

#3 Pearl Cotton

1 (1m)	○ Light old gold #676 (2-wrap) French Knot

#5 Pearl Cotton

8 (7.4m)	◢ Black Backstitch and Straight Stitch
	● Black (2-wrap) French Knot

Color numbers given are for Uniek Needloft plastic canvas yarn and DMC #3 pearl cotton.

WILD & WACKY LIGHTS

Fun and funky, these brightly colored lights will bring a smile to your face.

DESIGN BY MARY T. COSGROVE

Skill Level
Beginner

Size
One light: 2⅛ inches W x 2¾ inches H (5.4cm x 7cm)
String of lights: 45 inches W x 3 inches H (114.3cm x 7.6cm)

Materials
• 1¼ sheets 7-count plastic canvas

• Uniek Needloft plastic canvas yarn as listed in color key
• Uniek Needloft metallic craft cord as listed in color key
• Kreinik Medium (#16) Braid as listed in color key
• #16 tapestry needle
• 3 yards (2.7m) 22-gauge icy kiwi #84741 Fun Wire by Toner Plastics Inc.
• ⅛-inch (0.3cm) dowel

Project Notes
Instructions and amounts given are for sample project. Sample has 18 lights.
Amounts needed for one light are as follows: 18 inches (45.7cm) black yarn, 3 yards (2.8m) yarn for main color of light, 18 inches (45.7cm) gold metallic craft cord, 12 inches (30.5cm) topaz medium (#16) braid. Project requires about 1 yard (0.9m) of wire for every six lights.

CONTINUED ON PAGE 171

GLISTENING SNOWFLAKES

Sparkle and shine your way through the winter months with this eye-catching centerpiece, featuring pretty snowflakes.

DESIGN BY LEE LINDEMAN

Skill Level
Intermediate

Size
5¾ inches W x 11¼ inches H (14.6cm x 28.6cm)

Materials
- 2 sheets 7-count plastic canvas
- Plastic canvas yarn as listed in color key
- #16 tapestry needle
- 7 (7mm) round crystal rhinestones
- 35 inches (88.8cm) ⅛-inch (0.3cm) wooden dowel
- 4 x 4-inch (10.2 x 10.2cm) wooden plaque
- Hand drill with ⅛-inch (0.3cm) bit
- White acrylic paint
- Small paintbrush
- Hot-glue gun

Instructions

1. Cut plastic canvas according to graphs (page 162), cutting away gray areas on snowflakes A, B and D.

2. Stitch and Overcast pieces following graphs, using full strand white for stitching on snowflakes C and E and 1 ply white for Overcasting on all snowflakes.

3. Cut dowel in seven pieces as follows: one 10¾ inches (27.3cm) long, one 7 inches (17.8cm), one 6½ inches (16.5cm), two 3¾ inches (9.5cm), one 2¼ inches (5.7cm) and one 1 inch (2.5cm).

4. Randomly drill seven holes ¼ inch deep in top of plaque.

5. Paint plaque and dowel lengths with white paint. Allow to dry.

6. Glue dowels in drilled holes, placing longest length in center and shorter lengths on outside.

7. With right sides facing up, glue snowflake A pieces together, placing spokes of top snowflake between spokes of bottom snowflake. Glue one rhinestone to center of assembled snowflake. Glue snowflake to center dowel.

8. Repeat step 7 with remaining snowflakes, gluing smaller snowflakes on shortest dowels and remaining snowflakes on mid-sized dowels. ●

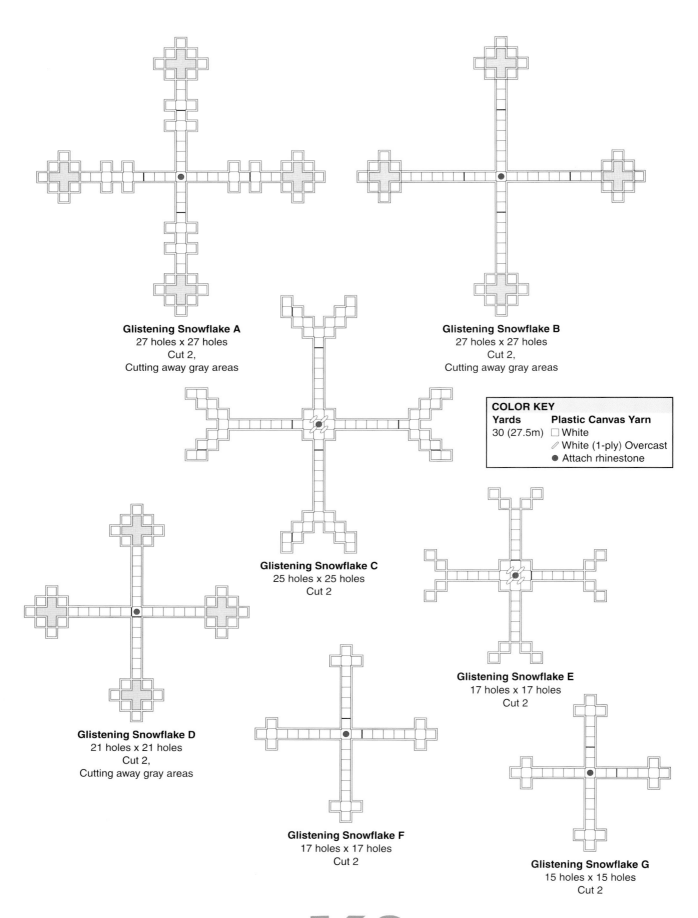

Glistening Snowflake A
27 holes x 27 holes
Cut 2,
Cutting away gray areas

Glistening Snowflake B
27 holes x 27 holes
Cut 2,
Cutting away gray areas

COLOR KEY

Yards	Plastic Canvas Yarn
30 (27.5m)	☐ White
	⁄ White (1-ply) Overcast
	● Attach rhinestone

Glistening Snowflake C
25 holes x 25 holes
Cut 2

Glistening Snowflake D
21 holes x 21 holes
Cut 2,
Cutting away gray areas

Glistening Snowflake E
17 holes x 17 holes
Cut 2

Glistening Snowflake F
17 holes x 17 holes
Cut 2

Glistening Snowflake G
15 holes x 15 holes
Cut 2

HEART & BEAR FRAME SET

Show someone how much you care by stitching this darling frame set as a Valentine's Day gift.

DESIGNS BY ANGIE ARICKX

Skill Level
Beginner

Size
Double Frame: 9¾ inches W x 7⅛ inches H x 2⅝ inches D (24.8cm x 18.1cm x 6.7cm)
Single Frame: 3⅞ inches W x 5⅛ inches H x 2¼ inches D (9.8cm x 13cm x 5.7cm)

Materials
- 1 sheet 7-count plastic canvas
- ¼ sheet 10-count plastic canvas
- Uniek Needloft plastic canvas yarn as listed in color key
- DMC #3 pearl cotton as listed in color key
- #16 tapestry needle
- #18 tapestry needle
- Double 5 x 7-inch (12.7 x 17.8cm) vertical acrylic photo frame
- 3½ x 5-inch (8.9 x 12.7cm) vertical acrylic single photo frame
- 5-inch (12.7cm) plush beige bear with movable joints
- 1½-inch (3.8cm) flocked beige bear ornament with movable joints
- Double-sided adhesive sheet
- Hot-glue gun

Instructions

1. Cut one single and two double frames from 7-count plastic canvas; cut hearts, flowers and leaves from 10-count plastic canvas according to graphs (pages 164 and 165).

2. Using #16 tapestry needle and plastic canvas yarn, stitch frames following graphs, working uncoded background on single frame with burgundy Continental Stitches.

3. Overcast inside edges with eggshell. Overcast outside edges with alternating colors of burgundy and eggshell.

4. Using #18 tapestry needle and pearl cotton, stitch and Overcast hearts, flowers and leaves, working uncoded background on large heart with medium coral Continental Stitches.

5. Making sure bottom edges are even, attach stitched double frames to front of double acrylic photo frame using ½-inch-wide strips of double-sided adhesive at top, bottom and along outer sides; use 2-inch-wide strip at center, attaching inner sides of both frames to the same strip.

6. Keeping bottom edges even, attach stitched single frame to front of single acrylic photo frame with ¼-inch-wide strips of adhesive along all edges.

7. Using photo as a guide through step 8, hot-glue large flowers and leaves to bottom outside corners of double frame. Glue large heart to 5-inch bear, then glue bear to center of frame.

8. Glue small flower and leaves to a bottom corner of single frame. Glue small heart to front of 1½-inch bear, then glue bear to remaining bottom corner. ●

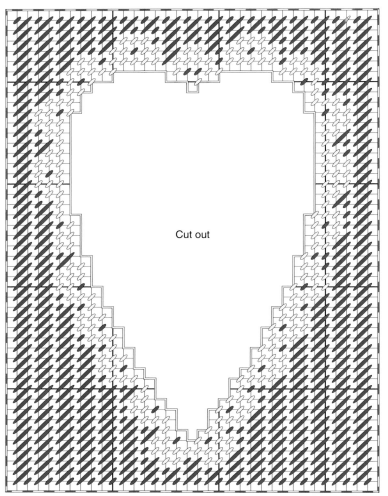

Double Heart Frame
35 holes x 47 holes
Cut 2 from 7-count
Stitch with yarn

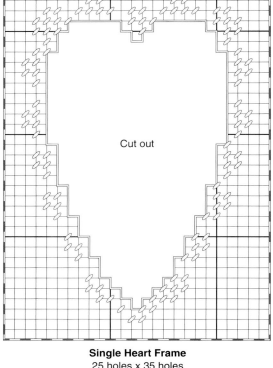

Single Heart Frame
25 holes x 35 holes
Cut 1 from 7-count
Stitch with yarn

Small Leaf
5 holes x 3 holes
Cut 2 from 10-count
Stitch with pearl cotton

Large Leaf
8 holes x 5 holes
Cut 4 from 10-count
Stitch with pearl cotton

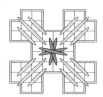

Large Flower
8 holes x 8 holes
Cut 2 from 10-count
Stitch with pearl cotton

Small Flower
5 holes x 5 holes
Cut 1 from 10-count
Stitch with pearl cotton

COLOR KEY	
Yards	**Plastic Canvas Yarn**
30 (27.5m)	■ Burgundy #03
20 (18.3m)	☐ Eggshell #39
	Uncoded background on single frame is burgundy #03 Continental Stitches
	#3 Pearl Cotton
7 (6.5m)	■ Medium coral #347
3 (2.8m)	☐ Coral #351
3 (2.8m)	■ Very dark olive green #730
2 (1.9m)	☐ Off-white
	Uncoded background on large heart is medium coral #347 Continental Stitches

Color numbers given are for Uniek Needloft plastic canvas yarn and DMC #3 pearl cotton.

Small Heart
7 holes x 6 holes
Cut 1 from 10-count
Stitch with pearl cotton

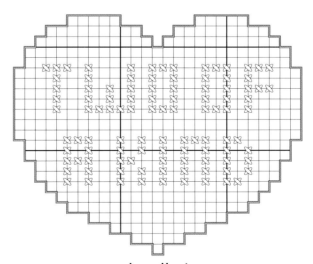

Large Heart
27 holes x 23 holes
Cut 1 from 10-count
Stitch with pearl cotton

HEART COASTERS

Bright metallic yarn and pretty shades of red and pink combine for a gorgeous coaster set you'll fall in love with!

DESIGN BY KATHY WIRTH

Skill Level
Beginner

Size
Coaster: 4⅞ inches W x 4⅞ inches H (12.4cm x 12.4cm)
Coaster Holder: 5¼ inches W x 5¼ inches H x 2⅝ inches D (13.3cm x 13.3cm x 6.7cm)

Materials
- 12 (6-inch) Uniek QuickShape plastic canvas hearts
- ¼ sheet stiff 7-count plastic canvas
- Red Heart Classic worsted weight yarn Art. E267 as listed in color key
- Red Heart Super Saver worsted weight yarn Art. E300 as listed in color key
- 4mm Rainbow Gallery Plastic Canvas 7 Metallic Needlepoint Yarn as listed in color key
- #16 tapestry needle
- 3 sheets white adhesive-backed felt

Project Note
When working with metallic needlepoint yarn, keep stitches flat and untwisted.

Instructions
1. Cut plastic canvas according to graphs (this page and page 172), cutting away yellow areas on coasters and coaster holder front and back. Four coasters and one each of holder front and back will remain unstitched and will be used as liners.

2. Cut four pieces felt slightly smaller than coasters and two pieces felt slightly smaller than holder front and back.

3. Stitch four coasters, two holder sides and one each of holder front and back following graphs.

4. Whipstitch one liner to back of each coaster with silver yarn. Apply felt to liner on each coaster.

5. Place one liner behind front; Whipstitch together with burgundy around rounded edges from blue dot to blue dot. Repeat with holder back. Apply felt to liners, keeping unstitched edges free for Whipstitching.

6. Using burgundy throughout, Whipstitch sides together along one short edge. Whipstitch sides to front and back along unstitched straight edges. Overcast remaining edges of sides. ●

CONTINUED ON PAGE 172

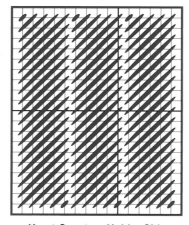

Heart Coasters Holder Side
16 holes x 20 holes
Cut 2 from stiff

COLOR KEY

Yards	Worsted Weight Yarn
66 (50.3m)	■ Burgundy #376
18 (16.5m)	□ Grenadine #730
	4mm Metallic Needlepoint Yarn
39 (35.7m)	□ Silver #PC2

Color numbers given are for Red Heart Classic worsted weight yarn Art. E267 and Super Saver worsted weight yarn Art. E300, and Rainbow Gallery Plastic Canvas 7 Metallic Needlepoint Yarn.

SWINGING ALONG IN LOVE

Have some whimsical fun on Valentine's Day with this darling ornament.

DESIGN BY PATRICIA KLESH

Skill Level
Beginner

Size
8 inches W x 11¾ inches H
(20.3cm x 29.8cm)

Materials
- ½ sheet 7-count plastic canvas
- Worsted weight yarn: 4½ yards (4.2m) pink and as listed in color key
- 6-strand embroidery floss as listed in color key
- #16 tapestry needle
- 12 inches (30.5cm) ¼-inch/7mm-wide white satin ribbon
- White chenille stem
- 2 (12mm) foil-backed red faceted rhinestone hearts
- Hot-glue gun

Instructions
1. Cut plastic canvas according to graphs.

2. Stitch and Overcast pieces following graphs, working un-coded background on heart with red Continental Stitches and un-coded areas on arrow with white Continental Stitches.

3. When background stitching is completed, work black floss embroidery on heart for eyes and mouth.

Finishing
1. Cut pink yarn in three 1½-yard (1.4m) lengths, then braid into one long length for rope. Thread one end of rope from back to front through hole indicated on right side of arrow; glue end to back side.

2. Thread other end from top to bottom through opening on right side of swing seat, then from bottom to top on left side of seat. Thread from front to back through hole indicated on left side of arrow. Adjust rope to desired length, making sure seat is level. Cut excess rope and glue to back of arrow.

3. Cut chenille stem in two 2-inch (5.1cm) lengths for arms and two 2½-inch (6.4cm) lengths for legs.

4. Thread about ⅜-inch (1cm) of arms from front to back through holes indicated on sides of heart; bend to back side.

5. Thread about ⅜-inch (1cm) of legs from front to back through holes indicated at bottom of heart; bend to back side. Bend at knees about ¾ inch (1.9cm) from heart. Glue heart rhinestones to bottom of legs for shoes.

6. Glue bottom edge of heart to swing seat. Bend "hands" on arms around rope.

7. For hanger, glue ends of white ribbon behind arrow where indicated with arrows. ●

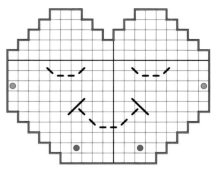

Swinging Along in Love
Heart
19 holes x 15 holes
Cut 1

COLOR KEY

Yards	Worsted Weight Yarn
11 (10.1m)	■ Red
3 (2.8m)	□ White
	Uncoded background on heart is red Continental Stitches
	Uncoded areas on arrow are white Continental Stitches
	6-Strand Embroidery Floss
1 (1m)	✦ Black Backstitch
	○ Attach rope
	◉ Attach arm
	● Attach leg

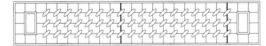

Swinging Along in Love
Swing Seat
23 holes x 4 holes
Cut 1

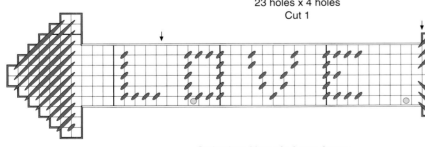

Swinging Along in Love Arrow
54 holes x 12 holes
Cut 1

HEART AIR FRESHENER

Add a fragrant touch to your home or vehicle with this tiny air freshener that also will show your love.

DESIGN BY DEBRA ARCH

Skill Level
Beginner

Size
3 inches W x 3¾ inches H (7.6cm x 9.5cm), including beaded hanger

Materials
- Small amount clear stiff 7-count plastic canvas
- Small amount bright pink 7-count plastic canvas
- Uniek Needloft plastic canvas yarn as listed in color key
- #16 tapestry needle
- 50 pearl glass E beads
- 15 inches (38.1cm) 26-gauge wire
- Cotton ball or 1¼-inch square white felt
- Hand-sewing needle
- White sewing thread
- Essential oil

Instructions
1. Cut one heart from clear stiff plastic canvas for front and one from bright pink for back according to graph. Back will remain unstitched.

2. Stitch front following graph. Overcast top edge of front between dots.

3. Using hand-sewing needle and white thread, attach beads to front where indicated.

4. For hanger, thread one bead on wire to midpoint. Fold wire in half with bead at center, then thread both ends of wire through remaining beads.

5. Thread wire ends through tapestry needle, then weave wire through stitches on wrong side, pulling taut until beads meet at center top edge of heart (see photo). Take a few more weaving stitches to secure. Trim excess wire. Bend beaded wire into a hook shape for hanging.

6. Whipstitch front and back together around side and bottom edges from dot to dot.

7. Put a few drops of essential oil on felt or cotton ball and insert in air freshener. ●

Air Freshener Heart
Front & Back
19 holes x 17 holes
Cut 1 from clear stiff for front
Stitch as graphed
Cut 1 from bright pink for back
Do not stitch

WILD & WACKY LIGHTS

CONTINUED FROM PAGE 159

Instructions

1. Cut plastic canvas according to graph. Cut wire in three 1-yard (0.9m) lengths.

2. Stitch and Overcast nine lights as graphed. Stitch three each of remaining lights, replacing Christmas red with Christmas green, royal and bright purple.

3. When background stitching is completed, work topaz braid Straight Stitches around eyes.

4. Twist one end of one length wire around dowel. Thread other end from back to front through first hole indicated at top of a Christmas red light to coiled end.

5. Thread wire from front to back through second hole indicated, leaving about 1 inch (2.5cm) of wire. Twist wire above top edge a few times to form a small loop for hanging.

6. Wrap wire around dowel 8–9 times, then add a royal light, following instructions for Christmas red light in steps 4 and 5. Continue wrapping wire around dowel and adding lights in following order: Christmas red, bright purple, Christmas red, Christmas green.

7. Wrap one end of second length of wire around twisted part of loop on Christmas green light. Wrap wire around dowel and add lights following steps 4–6.

8. Repeat for third length of wire, wrapping any remaining wire at final end around dowel.

9. Hang string of lights from loops on lights. ●

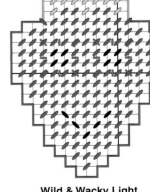

Wild & Wacky Light
14 holes x 18 holes
Cut 18
Stitch 9 as graphed
Stitch 3 each replacing
Christmas red with Christmas
green, royal and bright purple

HEART COASTERS

CONTINUED FROM PAGE 166

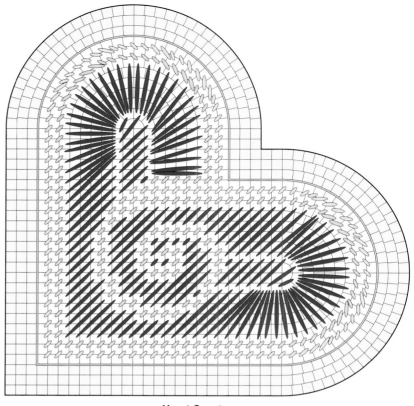

Heart Coaster
Cut 8 from plastic canvas hearts,
cutting away yellow area
Stitch 4

COLOR KEY

Yards	Worsted Weight Yarn
66 (50.3m)	■ Burgundy #376
18 (16.5m)	□ Grenadine #730
	4mm Metallic Needlepoint Yarn
39 (35.7m)	□ Silver #PC2

Color numbers given are for Red Heart Classic worsted weight yarn Art. E267 and Super Saver worsted weight yarn Art. E300, and Rainbow Gallery Plastic Canvas 7 Metallic Needlepoint Yarn.

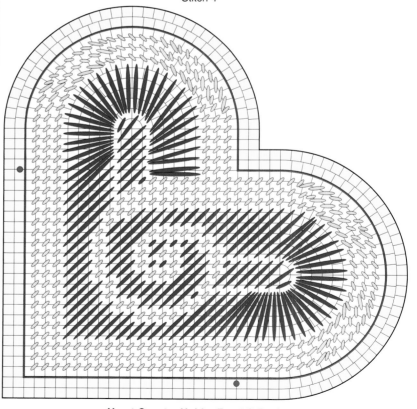

Heart Coaster Holder Front & Back
Cut 4 from plastic canvas hearts,
cutting away yellow area
Stitch 2

SPECIAL THANKS

We would like to acknowledge and thank the following designers whose original work has been published in this collection. We appreciate and value their creativity and dedication to designing quality plastic canvas projects!

DEBRA ARCH
Faith & Phillip, Heart Air Freshener, Lil' Birdie Mini Easter Basket, Santa Card Box

ANGIE ARICKX
An Irish Blessing, Autumn Leaves, Charming Chalets, Heart & Bear Frame Set, Jack-o'-Lantern Tissue Topper

MARY T. COSGROVE
Baby Chick Favor, Pretty Parrot, Scarecrow Gift Bag, Touch of the Tropics, Wild & Wacky Lights

JANELLE GIESE
Egg Basket Coasters, Harvest Friends Candleholder, Sensational Snowman

KATHLEEN HURLEY
Santa Door Hanger

CHERYL GOODSELL
Mischievous Monkey Coasters

PATRICIA KLESH
Pumpkin Basket Party Favor, Swinging Along in Love, Trick-or-Treat Wall Hanging, Under the Sea Tissue Topper

CHRISTINA LAWS
Rudolph Tissue Topper

LEE LINDEMAN
Glistening Snowflakes, Simply Spring

ALIDA MACOR
O Christmas Tree, Musical Christmas Stocking, Variations on a Theme, Wallflowers

KAREN McDANEL
Boo Table Runner, Tiny Treat Bags

JOYCE MESSENGER
Christmas Tree Doorstop

SANDRA MILLER MAXFIELD
Holiday Frame & Ornament Set

ADELE MOGAVERO
Dragonfly Box

DARLENE NEUBAUER
Farm Friend Towel Hanger

ROBIN PETRINA
Country Snowman Welcome

TERRY RICIOLI
Autumn Glow Votive Candle Screen, Celebrate Winter Tissue Topper, Dancing Ladybugs, Seasonal Welcome Sign

CYNTHIA ROBERTS
Darling Baby Album Cover, Joyful Coaster & Gift Bag, Summer Gift Bag, Sunflower Blackboard

CAROLE RODGERS
Lighthouse Seascape Calendar

LAURA SCOTT
Log Cabin Coaster Set

LAURA VICTORY
Autumn Angel

KATHY WIRTH
Heart Coasters, Liberty Angel, Pinwheel Roses

GINA WOODS
Batty Mobile, Cute as a Bug Fridgie

STITCH GUIDE

Use the following diagrams to expand your plastic canvas stitching skills. For each diagram, bring needle up through canvas at the red number one and go back down through the canvas at the red number two. The second stitch is numbered in green. Always bring needle up through the canvas at odd numbers and take it back down through the canvas at the even numbers.

Background Stitches

The following stitches are used for filling in large areas of canvas. The Continental Stitch is the most commonly used stitch. Other stitches, such as the Condensed Mosaic and Scotch Stitch, fill in large areas of canvas more quickly than the Continental Stitch because their stitches cover a larger area of canvas.

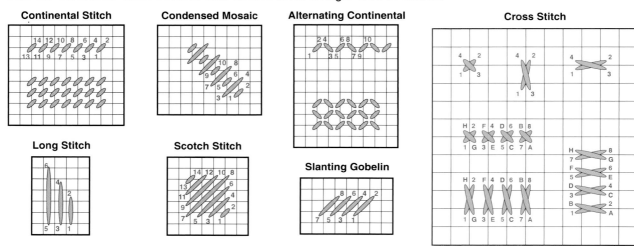

Continental Stitch

Condensed Mosaic

Alternating Continental

Cross Stitch

Long Stitch

Scotch Stitch

Slanting Gobelin

Embroidery Stitches

These stitches are worked on top of a stitched area to add detail to the project. Embroidery stitches are usually worked with one strand of yarn, several strands of pearl cotton or several strands of embroidery floss.

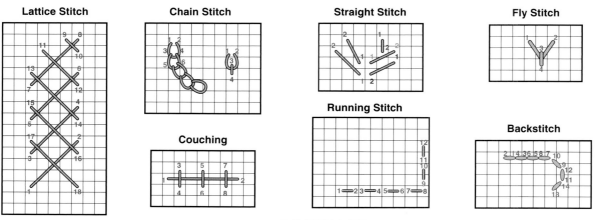

Lattice Stitch

Chain Stitch

Straight Stitch

Fly Stitch

Couching

Running Stitch

Backstitch

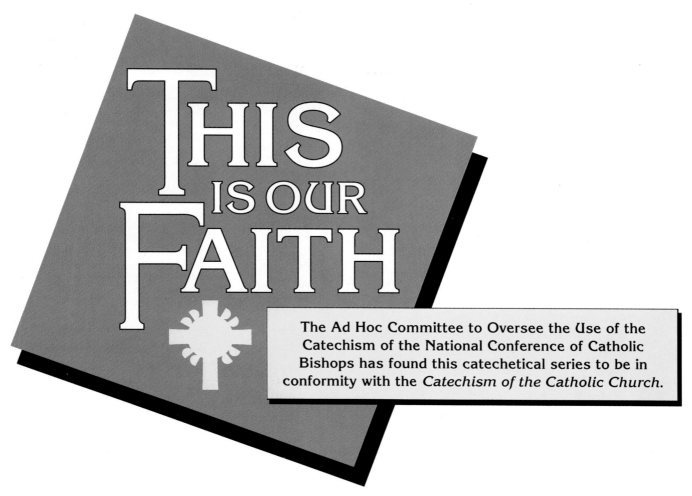

THIS IS OUR FAITH

The Ad Hoc Committee to Oversee the Use of the Catechism of the National Conference of Catholic Bishops has found this catechetical series to be in conformity with the *Catechism of the Catholic Church.*

Series Authors: Janaan Manternach
Carl J. Pfeifer

Teacher Edition Authors: Mary Beth Jambor
Kate Sweeney Ristow
Sister Carolyn Puccio, C.S.J.

Contributing Authors: Susan G. Keys
Maureen Shaughnessy, S.C.
Paula Lenz

Barbara Carol Vasiloff
Mary Mescher

Student Edition Authors: Jacqueline Jambor
Joan R. DeMerchant
Maureen Gallagher

Consulting Editor: Jean Marie Weber

SILVER BURDETT GINN
PARSIPPANY, NJ

Contents . . . .

Program Overview   T3

LET US PRAY   1

Beginning the Journey: Introductory Lesson   6a
Parent Preview Magazine   9

Reproduced pupil edition pages with complete lesson
plans and chapter organizers:

UNIT 1 Choosing Between Good and Evil   11
    Chapters 1–4
    Unit Organizer, Unit Review, Day to Day:
      Skills for Christian Living, *Opening*
    Doors: A Take-Home Magazine

UNIT 2 Following the Way of Love   61
    Chapters 5–8
    Unit Organizer, Unit Review, Day to Day:
      Skills for Christian Living, *Opening*
    Doors: A Take-Home Magazine

UNIT 3 Respecting God and People   111
    Chapters 9–12
    Unit Organizer, Unit Review, Day to Day:
      Skills for Christian Living, *Opening*
    Doors: A Take-Home Magazine

UNIT 4 Respecting Truth and Property   161
    Chapters 13–16
    Unit Organizer, Unit Review, Day to Day:
      Skills for Christian Living, *Opening*
    Doors: A Take-Home Magazine

UNIT 5 Celebrating and Serving   211
    Chapters 17–20
    Unit Organizer, Unit Review, Day to Day:
      Skills for Christian Living, *Opening*
    Doors: A Take-Home Magazine

Celebrating the Journey: Prayer Service   261

AMEN Section   262
    Chapters for celebrating feasts, seasons and people of faith

OUR CATHOLIC HERITAGE   327
    • What Catholics Believe   • How Catholics Live
    • How Catholics Worship   • How Catholics Pray

THE RESOURCEFUL TEACHER   365
    • Helps for the Teacher   • Resource Guide
    • Teacher's Reflections   • Publishers and Media Companies

Consultants
Linda Blanchette, Anita Bridge, Fred Brown, Rod Brownfield, Sister Mary Michael Burns, S.C., Patricia Burns, Bernadine Carroll, Mary Ellen Cocks, Sister Peggy Conlon, R.S.M., Mary Ann Crowley, Pamela Danni, Sister Jamesetta DeFelice, O.S.U., Sister Mary Elizabeth Duke, S.N.D., Mary M. Gibbons, Yolanda Gremillion, Sister Angela Hallahan, C.H.F., Alice T. Heard, Sister Michele O'Connoll, P.B.V.M., Sister Angela O'Mahoney, P.B.V.M., Sister Ruthann O'Mara, S.S.J., Sandra Okulicz-Hulme, Judy Papandria, Rachel Pasano, Sallie Ann Phelan, Sister Geraldine M. Rogers, S.S.J., Mary Lou Schlosser, Patricia Ann Sibilia, Margaret E. Skelly, Lisa Ann Sorlie, Sister Victorine Stoltz, O.S.B., Sister Nancy Jean Turner, S.H.C.J., Christine Ward, Judith Reidel Weber, Kay White, Elizabeth M. Williams, Catherine R. Wolf, Florence Bambrick Yarney, Kathryn K. Zapcic

Advisory Board
Rev. Louis J. Cameli, Philip J. Cunningham, Sister Clare E. Fitzgerald, William J. Freburger, Greer G. Gordon, Sister Veronica R. Grover, S.H.C.J., Rev. Thomas Guarino, Rev. Robert E. Harahan, Rev. Eugene LaVerdieré, S.S.S., Rev. Frank J. McNulty, Rev. Msgr. John J. Strynkowski

National Catechetical Advisor
Kathleen Hendricks

Nihil Obstat
Kathleen Flanagan, S.C., Ph.D., Censor Librorum
Ellen Joyce, S.C., Ph.D., Censor Librorum

Imprimatur
✠ Most Reverend Frank J. Rodimer, Ph.D.,
    Bishop of Paterson
    November 22, 1996

The *nihil obstat* and *imprimatur* are official declarations that a book or pamphlet is free of doctrinal and moral error. No implication is contained therein that those who have granted the *nihil obstat* and *imprimatur* agree with the contents, opinions, or statements expressed.

1 2 3 4 5 6 7 8 9 10 -W - 05 04 03 02 01 00 99 98 97

Dear Catholic School Teacher,

The teaching of religion is an important responsibility for all Catholic School teachers. We commend you for assuming this responsibility and are proud to be your partner in sharing the Catholic faith with children.

We are especially pleased to announce that the National Conference of Catholic Bishops' Ad Hoc Committee to Oversee the Use of the Catechism has found this new edition of *This Is Our Faith* to be in conformity with the *Catechism of the Catholic Church*. This means that *This Is Our Faith* has a breadth and depth of content wherein the presentation of Catholic doctrine is authentic and therefore suitable for catechetical instruction.

This sharing of faith includes many dimensions: the instruction in doctrine, Scripture, and morality; the experience of prayer and liturgy; the building of a value system; the ability to relate teaching to life; the knowledge of the rich heritage we share in time, place, and people; and the profound respect for and love of the Catholic Church. *This Is Our Faith* addresses each of these dimensions.

We take our responsibility to Catholic education seriously and once again we have consulted you, the classroom teacher, at every step along the way of the development of this revision. The next few pages will give you an overview of the new *This Is Our Faith*. We know that you will find in this program everything that a publisher can provide to support you in your important work.

Your commitment to Catholic education and to the children whom you teach is one that we share. This program has been created to be the best for you and for your class. It is to you that we dedicate this edition of *This Is Our Faith*.

Sincerely,

Raymond T. Latour
Vice President & Director
Religion Division

Content is important to Catholic Identity.

What content is included?

THIS IS OUR FAITH is a developmental program, based on Scripture and rooted in the teachings of the *Catechism of the Catholic Church*. While the content for each year centers on one particular theme, strands on Church, Sacraments, Trinity, and Morality are interwoven throughout the program. The presentation of doctrine has been increased in each chapter of this new edition.

Plus—chapter reviews and **expanded unit reviews** help you to evaluate student progress as you teach!!

The chart to the right outlines the doctrinal content of Grade 4.

TRINITY — THREE PERSONS ONE GOD

CREATOR/FATHER
God is merciful and forgiving.

God always forgives us when we are sorry.

God loves us even when we sin.

God is always with us.

God gives us grace, the gift of his presence and life.

Goodness and love come from God and are manifest in creation.

God calls us to love and respect ourselves and others.

The first three commandments teach us to place God first in our lives.

JESUS
Jesus came to bring God's forgiveness to everyone.

Jesus teaches about and explains God's laws.

Jesus was tempted as we are, but overcame temptation.

Jesus teaches us how to live according to the Beatitudes and the Commandments.

Jesus is the example of Christian life and love.

MORALITY
We sin when we choose to do wrong and turn away from God. We are called to choose between good and evil with the help of the Holy Spirit.

We show our love for God when we help those in need.

The Ten Commandments, the Great Commandment, and the Beatitudes are our guides for living the way of Jesus—a life of love and respect for God, truth, people, and property.

Evil spreads through the selfish acts of people.

We must love God above all things and love our neighbor as ourselves.

We will be happy if we live the Beatitudes.

THE BIBLE
The Bible teaches us about God's goodness in us and around us.

The Bible teaches us about choices and how to live good lives.

There is a total of seventy-three books in the Bible.

The books provide us with stories, poetry, prayers, and histories of people and events.

Our Church Celebrates Advent ... 264
Our Church Celebrates Christmas ... 272
Our Church Celebrates Lent ... 280
Our Church Celebrates Holy Week ... 290
Our Church Celebrates Easter ... 294
Our Church Honors Saints ... 302
Our Church Honors Mary ... 310
Our Church Celebrates Holy Days ... 316
In the Spirit of Jesus

Our Amen Section of Saints, Feasts and Seasons is still conveniently located in the back of the student book and has been expanded just as you requested. Every year your students will have the opportunity to celebrate the holy seasons of Advent, Lent, Christmas, and Easter in addition to other special feasts.

THE HOLY SPIRIT

The Holy Spirit helps us and guides us in times of temptation.

The Holy Spirit guides us to choose good rather than evil.

The Holy Spirit helps us live as Jesus did.

The Holy Spirit gives us special gifts of love, joy, peace, patience, kindness, unselfishness, faithfulness, gentleness, and self-control.

Jesus gives us the Holy Spirit as he gave the Holy Spirit to his disciples on Pentecost.

We celebrate this gift in the sacraments.

SACRAMENTS

We receive God's grace and the strength of the Holy Spirit in the sacraments.

In both individual and communal celebrations of Reconciliation, we show sorrow for our sins and receive God's mercy and forgiveness.

In addition to loving and sharing, the sacrament of Matrimony is a commitment to faithfulness.

In the sacrament of Reconciliation, or Penance, the Church celebrates our sorrow for sin and God's forgiveness.

In the Eucharist, the Church celebrates its unity in Jesus Christ.

The Eucharist helps us become the Body of Christ, the Church.

About the Mass

About Reconciliation

A complete chapter reviewing the basics of these sacraments.

CHURCH

The Catholic Church is the Christian community which celebrates the seven sacraments and recognizes the pope and bishops as its leaders.

The Church continues Christ's presence on earth.

The Church celebrates its unity in the Eucharist.

The Church cares for those in need and works to build a better world.

The Church community is the light of Christ and servant to the world.

All members of the Church are members of the Body of Christ.

PRAYERS AND PRECEPTS

Sign of the Cross
The Lord's Prayer
Hail Mary
Glory Be to the Father
Grace Before Meals
Grace After Meals
Morning Prayer
Evening Prayer
Act of Contrition
Prayer to the Holy Spirit
The Apostles' Creed

Prayers and precepts of the Church are used in lessons throughout the texts. Selected traditional prayers also appear in the front of the text in a section called Let Us Pray. Precepts also appear in a special end-of-text section designed to encourage their memorization.

RELIGIOUS VOCABULARY

Absolution
Bear False Witness
Beatitudes
Cheat
Conscience
Consequences
Corinthians
Covet
Disciples
Examination of Conscience
Faithful
Galilean
Grace
Greed
Heaven
High Priest
Honor

In Vain
Judas
Justice
Light of the World
Neighbor
Original Sin
Peacemakers
Reconciliation
Reign of God
Samaritan
Service
Temptation
Violence

Our Catholic Heritage, a special doctrinal section organized according to the four pillars of the *Catechism of the Catholic Church,* is included in each grade-level student book to provide you with the opportunity and resources necessary to teach and review basic Catholic teachings every year.

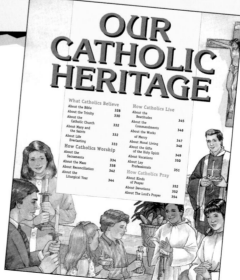

OUR CATHOLIC HERITAGE

What Catholics Believe
About the Bible
About the Trinity 328
About the 330
Catholic Church
About Mary and 332
the Saints
About Life 332
Everlasting 333

How Catholics Worship
About the
Sacraments
About the Mass 334
About Reconciliation 338
About the 342
Liturgical Year 344

How Catholics Live
About the
Beatitudes 345
About the
Commandments 346
About the Works
of Mercy 347
About Moral Living 348
About the Gifts
of the Holy Spirit 349
About Vocations 350
About Lay
Professionals 351

How Catholics Pray
About Kinds
of Prayer
About Devotions 352
About The Lord's Prayer 352
.... 354

What about prayer?

THIS IS OUR FAITH emphasizes prayer in all forms from traditional to spontaneous, from music to meditation, from the spoken word and formal liturgical prayer to the psalms and prayers of the heart. Children learn not only prayers, but how to pray alone, in a small group, within the classroom or school or in the church assembly. **Among other resources within THIS IS OUR FAITH, you will find the following:**

Praying with Gestures

Throughout the history of the Church, people have used a variety of gestures in their prayer. It has always been important to Catholics to pray with their bodies as well as with words. Bowing and genuflecting, kneeling and standing, making the sign of the cross and folding our hands have long been prayerful gestures used by Catholics.

Pray the following prayer with your class, using the prayer gestures your teacher suggests.

Leader: We begin our prayer in the name of the Father, and of the Son, and of the Holy Spirit.

All: Amen.

Leader: Loving God, you are Creator of all. We offer you the work of our hands, for we are your servants.

All: We are your servants.

Leader: Generous God, you give us all that we need. Let us help others obtain all that they need. We offer you the work of our hands, for we are your servants.

All: We are your servants.

Leader: God of all people, we are your servant Church. Help us to work toward making the world a better place, for we are your servants.

All: We are your servants. We will build a better world. And we will do it in the name of the Father, and of the Son, and of the Holy Spirit. Amen.

250   Prayer

▲ **Prayer pages** in each chapter of the student book provide instruction on and an experience of prayer each week.

INTERMEDIATE 3-6

PRAYERS FOR EVERY DAY

SILVER BURDETT GINN

▲
Prayers for Every Day is a wonderful resource for you. In it you will find prayers for every day of the year, as well as additional prayers to be said during special times and seasons.

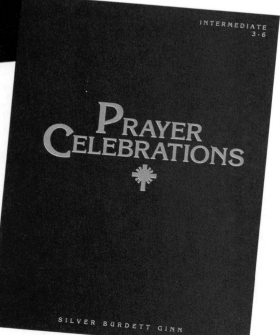

INTERMEDIATE 3-6

PRAYER CELEBRATIONS

SILVER BURDETT GINN

◄
Prayer Celebrations are resource books full of complete grade-level-specific prayer services ready to use with your class. Everything is done for you. All you need to do is read the special preparation page, duplicate the master sheet, and begin the celebration!

What about Sunday?

This brand-new supplemental program helps prepare children to better understand the Sunday readings. It provides ways to help children participate more fully in the Sunday liturgy—a need expressed by many teachers. Here's how to do it!

Each week, perhaps on Friday, distribute the student leaflets for Sunday. Then together, listen to the Word of God and follow the specific activities that will help the Word take on real meaning for children. They will be ready to listen and pray on Sunday!

This is indeed a true liturgical-year program! Each leaflet is brand-new and developed for each liturgical cycle!

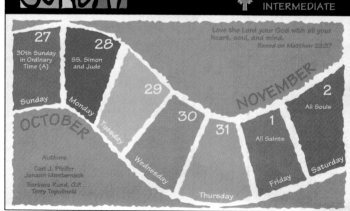

Background for the Teacher and a session outline are clearly and simply presented on each teacher folder—which also provides a handy storage unit for the student leaflets.

THIS IS OUR FAITH has always provided the best in Teacher Editions.

What's new in this one?

Chapter Organizers keep you on target and make planning quick and easy.

All content is correlated with the *Catechism of the Catholic Church*

Correlation to the **Catechism of the Catholic Church**
Paragraphs 356, 2258–2330, 2262, 2302, 2303, 2304, 2305, 2306, 2319, 2669

11 Respecting Life

Objectives

To help the students
- Understand the fifth commandment.
- Understand that Jesus taught against violence through both actions and words.
- Recognize violence in our world and ways to cope with it.
- Consider ways of living out the fifth commandment.
- Pray the Way of the Cross and review the chapter.

Chapter Outline

	Step 1 Learning About Our Lives	**Step 2** Learning About Our Faith	**Step 3** Learning How to Live Our Faith
Day 1	■ Review the commandments. ■ Study a cartoon. ■ Decide what to do. ■ Write answers to questions. *ABOUT 15 MINUTES*	■ Read about the fifth commandment. ■ Understand the vocabulary. ■ Review the doctrine. *ABOUT 10 MINUTES*	■ Draw a picture. ■ Review the lesson. *ABOUT 5 MINUTES*
Day 2	■ Listen to and discuss a story. *ABOUT 5 MINUTES*	■ Read a Scripture story. ■ Complete an activity. ■ Learn that Jesus is a model of nonviolence. *ABOUT 15 MINUTES*	■ Participate in a discussion. *ABOUT 10 MINUTES*
Day 3	■ Read and discuss a story. ■ Write a story ending. *ABOUT 15 MINUTES*	■ Read about the fifth commandment. *ABOUT 5 MINUTES*	■ Write about coping with violence. ■ Make a continuum from disrespect to violence. *ABOUT 10 MINUTES*
Day 4	■ Complete an activity. *ABOUT 5 MINUTES*	■ Read a Scripture story. ■ Study how violence happens. ■ Review the vocabulary. *ABOUT 15 MINUTES*	■ Consider how to work for nonviolence. ■ Review the fifth commandment. ■ Complete an activity. *ABOUT 10 MINUTES*
Day 5	**Prayer** Recall the Way of the Cross; read about praying the Way of the Cross; pray the Way of the Cross; invoke God's help; and sing together. **Review** Review the fifth commandment; review the chapter; and read the Scripture verse.		

Plan Ahead

	Preparing Your Class	**Materials Needed**
Day 1	Read through the lesson plan.	■ pencils or pens
Day 2	Read the lesson plan.	■ pencils or pens ■ news magazines ■ Bibles, one per student
Day 3	Read the lesson plan.	■ pencils or pens
Day 4	Read the lesson plan. If making the curriculum connection, review the song "World Peace Prayer" in THIS IS OUR FAITH *Hymnal.*	■ pencils or pens ■ writing paper
Day 5	Read the lesson plan. If you plan to hold the prayer service at the church, make all the necessary arrangements.	■ pencils or pens ■ Bible, cross ■ candle ■ copies of THIS IS OUR FAITH *Hymnal*

Additional Resources

As you plan this chapter, consider using the following materials from The Resourceful Teacher Package.
- *Classroom Activity Sheets* 11 and 11a
- *Family Activity Sheets* 11 and 11a
- *Chapter 11 Test*
- *Prayers for Every Day*
- *Projects: Grade 4*

You may also wish to refer to the following Big Book.
- *We Celebrate God's Word,* pages 12, 18

In preparing the students for the Sunday readings, you may wish to use Silver Burdett Ginn's *Getting Ready for Sunday* student and teacher materials.

Chapter Organizer 131b

131a **Chapter Organizer**

Also in each chapter you will find special feature boxes, giving you additional tips where you need them.

Focus On
provides background information for you on specific topics.

Curriculum Connection
helps you tie in what is being taught in Religion with other content areas.

Enriching the Lesson
includes extras—additional ideas to expand and enrich the lesson.

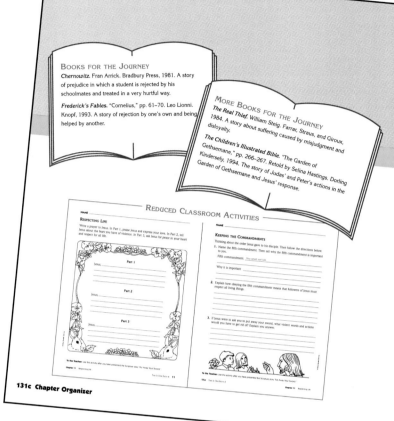

BOOKS FOR THE JOURNEY
Chernowitz. Fran Arrick. Bradbury Press, 1981. A story of prejudice in which a student is rejected by his schoolmates and treated in a very hurtful way.

Frederick's Fables. "Cornelius," pp. 61–70. Leo Lionni. Knopf, 1993. A story of rejection by one's own and being helped by another.

MORE BOOKS FOR THE JOURNEY
The Real Thief. William Steig. Farrar, Straus, and Giroux, 1984. A story about suffering caused by misjudgment and disloyalty.

The Children's Illustrated Bible. "The Garden of Gethsemane," pp. 266–267. Retold by Selina Hastings. Dorling Kindersely, 1994. The story of Judas' and Peter's actions in the Garden of Gethsemane and Jesus' response.

Background for the Teacher

YOU SHALL NOT KILL

Children are full of zest for living. They are curious about living things; animals and insects fascinate them. They feel a kinship with their pets. They prefer companionship to being alone. Children, however, like all humans, can at times exhibit a lack of compassion, even cruelty, toward others. It is from this context of mixed experiences that the students will approach the fifth commandment.

Whenever human life is hurt or destroyed, or the quality of life is so diminished that human rights are denied, the fifth commandment is violated. By this commandment we are called to revere, care for, and protect life as a sacred gift from the Creator. Sin against the fifth commandment, therefore, has been defined as a denial of human rights and a refusal to see life as a gift from God.

Originally, the fifth commandment was a prohibition against murder. For the people of Israel, capital punishment was justified, but the taking of innocent life was not acceptable. The taking of a life was seen as denying God's gift of life, and Yahweh's dominion over all life. Today, we realize that the fifth commandment reaches beyond murder into all the areas of respect for life.

Current teaching of respect for life has its roots in the Church's teachings regarding life: as persons created by God, we are all made in the image and likeness of God.

Therefore, there is an intrinsic dignity to the human person. Any action or attitude which diminishes the dignity of the human person is wrong.

THE PEACE OF JESUS

Jesus loved and respected all life. He sought out those whose lives were fractured and those who were viewed as castaways. In a society embroiled in violence, Jesus asserted the rights of all in a peaceful manner. Faced with a violent attack on himself, he refused to take up the sword and condemned the use of violence. The gospel accounts of the agonized Jesus in the garden, followed by his arrest, reveal him as strengthened by prayer. He greeted his enemies in full control of the situation. He was protective of the Apostles and allowed himself to be taken captive.

TODAY'S PROBLEMS

Jesus' example and teaching are of particular relevance in today's world. Civil wars rage in different parts of the world. People continue to suffer from prejudice and discrimination. The crime of abortion stands in direct opposition to the fifth commandment. Environmental issues facing all of us today are also the concerns of the fifth commandment.

Chapter Organizer 131d

Background for teachers provides excellent information for you on what is to be taught as well as insights into how to teach it.

Cultural Awareness
gives you needed information to aid students in their appreciation of other cultures.

Teaching Tips
provides just what you need—an extra idea, project, or help - just when you need it.

These new features plus our new size and easier to use format, along with our proven method of teaching—our three-step lesson plan—and a complete lesson every day makes this the best teacher edition ever!

You've always had great additional teacher resources.

What's new in this edition?

We've already told you about the *new* **Prayer Celebrations Book,** the *new* **Prayers for Every Day,** and the *new* **Getting Ready for Sunday** program.

Here's more!

▶ **Project Books**
One per grade give ideas and opportunities to enhance and expand learning.

▲ **Saints and Other Holy People**
provide excellent role models
for students.

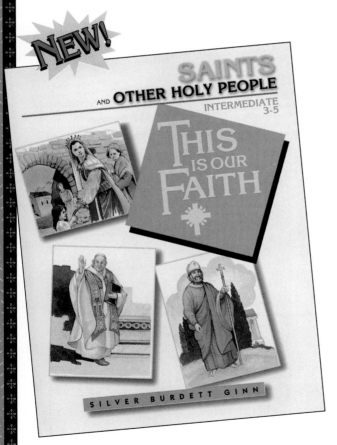

▶ **Saints Cards**
(32 of 6 Saints for each year)
Take-home cards for
each child to treasure.

Mother Katharine Drexel

Saint Frances Cabrini

Pope John XXIII

Saints Cyril and Method...

T10

VIDEO LIBRARY 1
THIS IS OUR FAITH

VIDEO LIBRARY 2
THIS IS OUR FAITH

VIDEO LIBRARY 3
THIS IS OUR FAITH

VIDEO LIBRARY 4
THIS IS OUR FAITH

VIDEO LIBRARY 5
THIS IS OUR FAITH

VIDEO LIBRARY 6
THIS IS OUR FAITH

VIDEO LIBRARY 7
THIS IS OUR FAITH

VIDEO LIBRARY 8
THIS IS OUR FAITH
SILVER BURDETT GINN

NEW!

◀ **Videos**
One per grade,
correlated to each unit!
(Ready in 1998)

▲ **Teacher Resource Package**
Includes Project Booklet,
Classroom Activities, Family
Activities and Letters in English
and Spanish, and Tests as well as
a handy tote to keep all your
resources together.

Familiar Resources Designed Especially for the 1998 Edition!

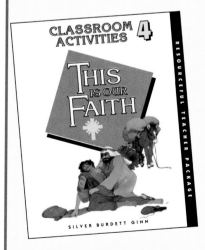
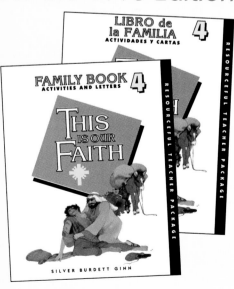
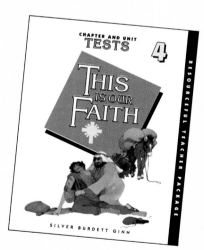

CLASSROOM ACTIVITIES 4
THIS IS OUR FAITH
SILVER BURDETT GINN
RESOURCEFUL TEACHER PACKAGE

LIBRO de la FAMILIA 4
ACTIVIDADES Y CARTAS
RESOURCEFUL TEACHER PACKAGE

FAMILY BOOK 4
ACTIVITIES AND LETTERS
THIS IS OUR FAITH
SILVER BURDETT GINN
RESOURCEFUL TEACHER PACKAGE

CHAPTER AND UNIT TESTS 4
THIS IS OUR FAITH
SILVER BURDETT GINN
RESOURCEFUL TEACHER PACKAGE

▲
Classroom Activities
two sheets for every chapter!

▲ **Family Activities and Letters**
(in English and in Spanish)
Ready to duplicate and send home!

▲
Tests
Both Chapter and Unit

And, as your students would say,

"What does THIS IS OUR FAITH have to do with real life?"

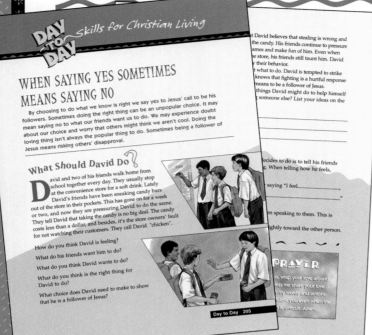

Living our faith goes well beyond the classroom experience into the everyday challenges and opportunities faced by each of our children every day. Each class begins with a life experience and ends with an integration of what has been learned into the child's life.

◀ **Day to Day: Skills for Christian Living**

At the end of each unit, two pages focus on the development of personal and moral skills in a sensitive and constructive way consistent with our Gospel values and Christian life. This is an infinitely practical feature that will help the faith and life to emerge as one.

◀ For each grade-level the gatefold invites students to journey together as a school community through faith and life!

THIS IS OUR FAITH provides a complete and comprehensive coverage of Doctrine, Scripture, Morality, Prayer and Review, all taught in age-appropriate and proven ways.

Including all of the resources you've used and loved—and many new ones that you've wanted.

Written with you in mind and backed by the very best service in publishing for Catholic schools.

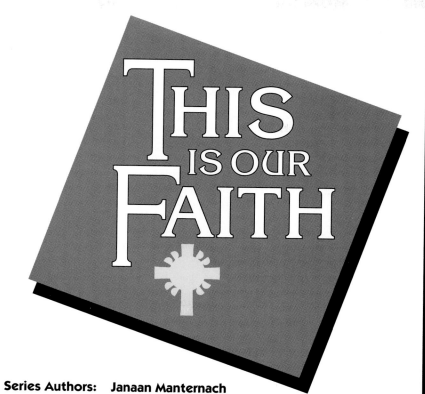

THIS IS OUR FAITH

Series Authors: Janaan Manternach
Carl J. Pfeifer

Authors: Jacqueline Jambor
Joan R. DeMerchant
Maureen Gallagher

Consulting
Editor: Jean Marie Weber

Contributing Authors: Kate Sweeney Ristow
Sister Carolyn Puccio, C.S.J.

SILVER BURDETT GINN
PARSIPPANY, NJ

THIS IS OUR FAITH
SCHOOL PROGRAM

Contributing Authors: James Bitney, Robert Hamma, Paula A. Lenz, Judene Leon, Yvette Nelson, Sister Carolyn Puccio, C. S. J., Anna Ready, Kate Sweeney Ristow, Barbara Carol Vasiloff, Sister Maureen Shaughnessy, S.C., Sister Cecilia Maureen Cromwell, I.H.M., Patricia Frevert, Mary Lou Ihrig, Sister Arlene Pomije, C.S.J., Sister Mary Agnes Ryan, I.H.M., Brother Michael Sheerin, F.M.S.

Opening Doors: *A Take-Home Magazine:* Peter H.M. Demkovitz, Janie Gustafson, Margaret Savitskas

Day to Day: *Skills for Christian Living:* Susan G. Keys

Advisory Board:
Rev. Louis Camelli
Philip J. Cunningham
Sister Clare E. Fitzgerald
William J. Freburger
Greer J. Gordon
Sister Veronica R. Grover, S.H. C. J.
Rev. Thomas Guarino
Rev. Robert E. Harahan
Kathleen Hendricks
Rev. Eugene LaVerdierre, S.S.S.
Rev. Frank J. McNulty
Rev. Msgr. John J. Strynkowski

Consultants: Linda Blanchette, Anita Bridge, Fred Brown, Rod Brownfield, Sister Mary Michael Burns, S.C., Pat Burns, Bernadine Carroll, Mary Ellen Cocks, Sister Peggy Conlon, R.S.M., Mary Ann Crowley, Pamela Danni, Sister Jamesetta DeFelice, O.S.U., Sister Mary Elizabeth Duke, S.N.D., Mary M. Gibbons, Yolanda Gremillion, Sister Angela Hallahan, C.H.F., Alice T. Heard, Sister Michelle O'Connor, P.B.V.M., Sister Angela O'Mahoney, P.B.V.M., Sister Ruthann O'Mara, S.S.J., Sandra Okulicz-Hulme, Judy Papandria, Rachel Pasano, Sallie Ann Phelan, Sister Geraldine M. Rogers, S.S.J., Mary Lou Schlosser, Patricia Ann Sibilia, Margaret E. Skelley, Lisa Ann Sorlie, Sister Victorine Stoltz, O.S.B., Sister Nancy Jean Turner, S.H. C. J., Christine Ward, Judith Reidel Weber, Kay White, Elizabeth M. Williams, Catherine R. Wolf, Florence Bambrick Yarney, Kathryn K. Zapcic

Nihil Obstat
Kathleen Flanagan, S.C., Ph.D.
Censor Librorum
Ellen Joyce, S.C.
Censor Librorum

Imprimatur
✠ Most Reverend Frank J. Rodimer
Bishop of Paterson
November 22, 1996

The *nihil obstat* and *imprimatur* are official declarations that a book or pamphlet is free of doctrinal and moral error. No implication is declared therein that those who have granted the *nihil obstat* and *imprimatur* agree with the contents, opinions, or statements expressed.

Acknowledgments

Excerpts from the "Dogmatic Constitution on the Church (Lumen Gentium)" reprinted from *The Documents of Vatican II* by Walter M. Abbott, S.J. Copyright © 1966 by permission of New Century Publishers, Inc., Piscataway, New Jersey.

Scriptural text used in this work are taken from the *New American Bible with Revised New Testament* Copyright © 1970, 1986 by the Confraternity of Christian Doctrine, Washington, D.C. and are used by permission of copyright owner. All rights reserved.

All adaptations of Scripture are based on the *New American Bible with revised New Testament.*

Excerpts from the English translation of *Rite of Marriage* © 1969, International Committee on English in the Liturgy, Inc. (ICEL); excerpts from the English translation of *Rite of Baptism for Children* © 1969, ICEL; excerpts from the English translation of *The Roman Missal* ©1973, ICEL; excerpts from the English translation of *Rite of Penance* © 1974, ICEL; excerpts from the English translation of *Eucharistic Prayers for Masses with Children* © 1975, ICEL; excerpts from the English translation of *Rite for Confirmation,* Second Edition © 1975, ICEL; excerpts from *Pastoral Care of the Sick: Rites of Anointing and Viaticum* © 1982, ICEL; excerpts from the English translation of *Book of Blessings* © 1988, ICEL. All rights reserved.

Contents ~~~~~~~~~~~~~~~

Let Us Pray   1

Beginning the Journey   7
A Preview of Grade 4: A Take-Home Magazine
following page 8

Unit 1 **Unit 1 Choosing Between Good and Evil**   11
1 Goodness from God   12
2 Evil in the World   22
3 Choices to Make   32
4 Choosing What Is Good   42
       Unit Organizer, Unit Review,
       Day to Day: Skills for Christian Living,
       Opening Doors: A Take-Home Magazine   52

Unit 2 **Unit 2 Following the Way of Love**   61
5 The Great Commandment   62
6 Happy Are Those...   72
7 The Reign of God Is Theirs   82
8 God's Commandments   92
       Unit Organizer, Unit Review,
       Day to Day: Skills for Christian Living,
       Opening Doors: A Take-Home Magazine   102

Unit 3 **Unit 3 Respecting God and People**   111
9 Worshiping God   112
10 Honoring Our Parents   122
11 Respecting Life   132
12 Being Faithful in Marriage   142
       Unit Organizer, Unit Review,
       Day to Day: Skills for Christian Living,
       Opening Doors: A Take-Home Magazine   152

Catechism of the Catholic Church

Since its publication in June 1994, the English translation of the *Catechism of the Catholic Church* has enjoyed a wide readership among Catholics throughout the United States. Parents and teachers will want to know how the chapter themes in THIS IS OUR FAITH relate to the content of the *Catechism*.

As a service, we have included a Catechism Reference Box at the beginning of each chapter in the Teacher Edition. We suggest that in preparing to teach the chapter, teachers first read the section "Background for the Teacher." For additional enrichment, you may wish to refer to the paragraphs in the *Catechism* that are indicated in the Reference Box.

Although the *Catechism of the Catholic Church* is not the only source of enrichment regarding doctrine, it can be most helpful in broadening our understanding of faith. We are encouraged to use it as a reference in our ongoing study of our Catholic tradition.

Unit 4 **Unit 4 Respecting Truth and Property**   **161**
  13 Respecting What Belongs to Others   **162**
  14 Respecting the Truth   **172**
  15 Our Merciful God   **182**
  16 Bringing God's Forgiveness   **192**
    Unit Organizer, Unit Review,
    Day to Day: Skills for Christian Living,
    Opening Doors: A Take-Home Magazine   **202**

Unit 5 **Unit 5 Celebrating and Serving**   **211**
  17 The Sacrament of Reconciliation   **212**
  18 Unity Through the Eucharist   **222**
  19 A Light to the World   **232**
  20 A Servant to the World   **242**
    Unit Organizer, Unit Review,
    Day to Day: Skills for Christian Living,
    Opening Doors: A Take-Home Magazine   **252**

Amen   **262**
  Our Church Celebrates Advent   **264**
  Our Church Celebrates Christmas   **272**
  Our Church Celebrates Lent   **280**
  Our Church Celebrates Holy Week   **290**
  Our Church Celebrates Easter   **294**
  Our Church Honors Saints   **302**
  Our Church Honors Mary   **310**
  Our Church Celebrates Holy Days   **316**
  In the Spirit of Jesus   **322**

Our Catholic Heritage   **327**
  What Catholics Believe   **328**
  How Catholics Worship   **334**
  How Catholics Live   **345**
  How Catholics Pray   **352**
  Glossary   **355**
  Index   **361**

Sign of the Cross	2	Morning Prayer	4
The Lord's Prayer	2	Evening Prayer	4
Hail Mary	3	Act of Contrition	5
Glory Be to the Father	3	Prayer to the Holy Spirit	5
Grace Before and After Meals	4	The Apostles' Creed	6

Learning Prayers

The students at this age probably have learned most of the prayers on this page. You may want to review these prayers by discussing the meaning of each line of every prayer and the meaning of each prayer in our daily lives.

Introducing the Prayers

Ask the students to look at the prayers on page 1. They are placed here as an easy-to-find reference for the students. You might use one of more of these prayers to open and close each class session.

Challenge the students to commit these prayers to memory and to pray them often. Suggest that they pray one or more of these prayers each night before falling asleep. Ask the students to suggest other times when they might say the prayers on this page.

Let Us Pray

The Lord's Prayer

Our Father, who art in heaven,
hallowed be thy name;
thy kingdom come;
thy will be done on earth
as it is in heaven.
Give us this day our daily bread;
and forgive us our trespasses
as we forgive those
who trespass against us;
and lead us not into temptation,
but deliver us from evil.
Amen.

Sign of the Cross

In the name of the Father,
and of the Son,
and of the Holy Spirit.
Amen.

Padre Nuestro

Padre nuestro, que estás en el cielo,
santificado sea tu nombre;
venga a nosotros tu reino;
hágase tu voluntad en la tierra
como en el cielo.
Danos hoy nuestro pan de cada día;
perdona nuestras ofensas,
como también nosotros
perdonamos
a los que nos ofenden;
no nos dejes caer en la tentación,
y líbranos del mal.
Amén.

Señal de la Cruz

En el nombre del Padre,
y del Hijo,
y del Espíritu Santo.
Amén.

2

Hail Mary

Hail Mary, full of grace,
  the Lord is with you.
Blessed are you among women,
  and blessed is the fruit
  of your womb, Jesus.
Holy Mary, Mother of God,
  pray for us sinners, now,
  and at the hour of our death.
Amen.

Ave María

Dios te salve, María, llena eres de
  gracia,
  el Señor es contigo.
Bendita tú eres entre todas las
  mujeres,
  y bendito es el fruto
  de tu vientre, Jesús.
Santa María, Madre de Dios,
  ruega por nosotros, pecadores,
  ahora
  y en la hora de nuestra muerte.
Amén.

Glory Be to the Father

Glory be to the Father,
  and to the Son,
  and to the Holy Spirit.
As it was in the beginning,
  is now, and ever shall be,
  world without end.
Amen.

Gloria al Padre

Gloria al Padre,
  y al Hijo,
  y al Espíritu Santo.
Como era en el principio,
  ahora y siempre,
  por los siglos de los siglos.
Amén.

3

Let Us Pray

Grace Before Meals

Bless us, O Lord,
and these your gifts,
which we are about to receive
from your goodness,
through Christ our Lord.
Amen.

Grace After Meals

We give you thanks
for all your gifts,
almighty God,
living and reigning
now and forever.
Amen.

A Morning Prayer

My God, I offer you today
all I think and do and say,
uniting it with what was
done on earth,
by Jesus Christ, your Son.
Amen.

Evening Prayer

Dear God, before I sleep
I want to thank you for this
day
so full of your kindness
and your joy.
I close my eyes to rest safe
in your loving care.
Amen.

Act of Contrition

My God,
I am sorry for my sins with all my heart.
In choosing to do wrong
and failing to do good,
I have sinned against you
whom I should love above all things.
I firmly intend, with your help,
to do penance,
and sin no more,
and to avoid whatever leads me to sin.
Our Savior Jesus Christ
suffered and died for us.
In his name, my God, have mercy.

(Revised Rite of Penance)

Prayer to the Holy Spirit

Come, Holy Spirit, fill the hearts of your
    faithful
and kindle in them the fire of your love.
Send forth your Spirit, and they shall be
    created;
and you will renew the face of the earth.
Amen.

Let us pray

Lord, by the light of the Holy Spirit
you have taught the hearts of your faithful.
In the same Spirit help us to relish what is
    right and always rejoice in your
    consolation. We ask this through Christ
    our Lord.
Amen.

Let Us Pray

The Apostles' Creed

I believe in God, the Father almighty,
    creator of heaven and earth;
I believe in Jesus Christ, his only Son,
    our Lord.
He was conceived by the power of the
    Holy Spirit and born of the Virgin Mary.
He suffered under Pontius Pilate, was
    crucified, died, and was buried.
He descended to the dead.
On the third day he rose again.
He ascended into heaven,
    and is seated at the right hand
    of the Father.
He will come again to judge the living
    and the dead.
I believe in the Holy Spirit,
    the holy catholic Church,
    the communion of saints,
    the forgiveness of sins,
    the resurrection of the body
    and life everlasting.
Amen.

Beginning the Journey

Introductory Lesson

Objectives

To help the students
- Get acquainted with one another.
- Desire to learn more about God's ways of love.
- Dedicate themselves to the journey of faith.

Lesson Outline

- Welcome the students.
- Complete a get-acquainted activity.
- Introduce the student text.
- Sign one another's books.
- Pray together.
- Conclude the session.

Plan Ahead

Prepare a special area in your room for prayer. Cover a table or desk with a cloth and place a candle on it. Have on hand a picture of Jesus and a Bible to use during the prayer service.

If possible, purchase a small cross pin for each student. Distribute these at the prayer service.

Materials Needed

- white construction paper
- pens or pencils
- a Bible
- a Bible stand
- a candle and matches
- a picture of Jesus
- a small cross pin for each student (optional)
- *Parent Preview Magazine*

Background for the Teacher

Becoming a Community

An ancient Chinese proverb tells us that "a journey of a thousand miles must begin with a single step." You and your fourth graders are about to begin an exciting journey together. The introductory session provides you, the teacher, with the opportunity to greet the students and to help them begin to know one another. Your goals for the year should be not only to teach the students to understand and appreciate the Church's rich tradition of moral example and teachings, but also to help them become a community of faith. Helping the students to get acquainted, to learn one another's names, and to feel comfortable with each other and their surroundings will help to ensure that your group is on the way to becoming a community.

During this session, invite the students to participate in the journey of faith. As Catholic Christians, we are like pilgrims on a long journey. Our ultimate destination, of course, is everlasting life and eternal happiness with God and with all those who have tried to love God in this life. While this concept is beyond the understanding of nine- and ten-year-old children, you can help them appreciate that they are called to grow closer to God and Jesus while they are learning more about the beliefs and traditions of our faith.

Following Jesus' Ways of Love

The journey theme is meant to help focus the attention of the young people and to illustrate in a memorable way this fact: The loving Jesus they meet in their studies is with them in all their life experiences. The world they find so interesting, so demanding, and sometimes so thrilling is *God's* world, made a new creation through Jesus and the Spirit.

The session concludes with a prayer experience in which the students will dedicate themselves to the challenging faith journey. They are invited to sign their names on the commitment page located on the inside front cover panel of the student text. They will also hear encouraging words from Scripture. These promises will assure the students that Jesus' presence and care will continue as they journey through life.

Starting the Year Right

Having a successful year begins long before the students arrive for the first session. To help you succeed, The Resourceful Teacher section of this book, beginning on page 365, includes

- notes on catechesis, faith, the role of the teacher, the *National Catechetical Directory,* and the *Catechism of the Catholic Church*
- a profile of the fourth-grade child
- tips on creating a healthy classroom environment
- suggestions for classroom management
- tips on good planning strategies
- ideas on using learning activities
- suggestions for assessing learning
- ideas for using prayer within the session
- tips on involving the community

Refer to The Resourceful Teacher section before planning your first session and whenever you need help throughout the year.

Beginning the Journey

We are on our way to learn more about God, about ourselves, and about life. As we begin our journey this year, name some things you would like to know about your world, about yourself, and about God. Then list them on the lines below.

Things I would like to learn about my world.

1. _____
   _____

2. _____
   _____

Things I would like to learn about myself.

1. _____
   _____

2. _____
   _____

Things I would like to learn about God.

1. _____
   _____

2. _____
   _____

7

Welcoming the Students

Greet the students warmly as they arrive. Introduce yourself and show them where they will be sitting. Ask the students to make name place cards, using white construction paper and crayons or felt-tip markers. Instruct them to fold the paper in half and write their names boldly in large letters below the fold.

Completing a Getting-acquainted Activity

Direct the students to write two "I am" statements about themselves on the place cards. Suggest the following examples: "I am the oldest child in my family"; "I am a soccer player"; "I am a good friend."

Encourage the students to introduce themselves and to share their "I am" statements. Then ask them to stand their place cards on their desks so that the names can be seen.

Introducing the Student Text

Distribute the texts. Give the students the opportunity to look through the books and to comment on them. Call attention to the introductory lesson on page 7. Ask a volunteer to read aloud the opening paragraph. Instruct the students to complete the activity. As they work, move about the room speaking individually with them about their responses. Afterward, invite them to share their responses with the class.

Signing One Another's Books

Tell the class that you are on a special journey together. Ask them to identify the purpose of your journey. Help the students to appreciate that the Christian life is like a journey in which we find our way to happiness with God and others. Ask a student to read aloud the paragraph at the bottom of the page. Encourage the students to sign one another's books. Be sure to participate in this activity with the class.

Praying Together

Ask the students to bring their books and pencils to the prayer area. Direct them to form a circle around the table.

Make the sign of the cross. Read from the text and hold the Bible up. Reverence the Bible by kissing it or bowing your head. Invite the students to reverence the Bible as you did. Enthrone the Bible and light the candle. Together, read the response from the texts.

Read the Scripture passage and have the class respond. Give one of the students a picture of Jesus to place on the table. After the next prayer and response, present each student with a cross pin (optional). Suggest that they wear the pin to show that they are followers of Jesus.

Read the final blessing, while you make the sign of the cross. Invite the students to respond by saying "Amen."

Direct the students to the gatefold. Read aloud the text at the top of the page. Ask the students to read silently the commitment. Explain that the commitment is a promise to learn more about God's ways of love. Invite them to sign their names in the text. Allow them to read aloud the commitment, adding their names.

You may also wish to invite the students to make paper footprints as a reminder of their commitment. Ask them to trace an outline of one of their feet onto construction paper. Encourage them to write "I want to learn to follow God's ways" on their paper footprints and cut them out.

Concluding the Session

Tell the group how happy you are that they have begun this year's journey with you. Remind them of their promises to learn more about God's ways of love. Send the students home with the *Parent Preview Magazine* from the student text. Collect the name place cards for the next session.

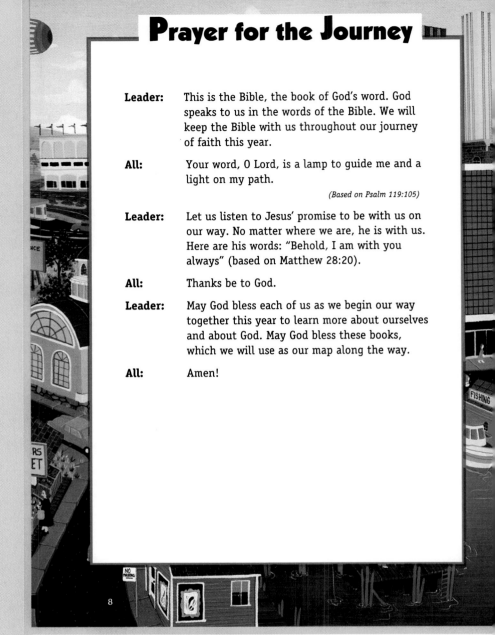

Prayer for the Journey

Leader: This is the Bible, the book of God's word. God speaks to us in the words of the Bible. We will keep the Bible with us throughout our journey of faith this year.

All: Your word, O Lord, is a lamp to guide me and a light on my path.

(Based on Psalm 119:105)

Leader: Let us listen to Jesus' promise to be with us on our way. No matter where we are, he is with us. Here are his words: "Behold, I am with you always" (based on Matthew 28:20).

All: Thanks be to God.

Leader: May God bless each of us as we begin our way together this year to learn more about ourselves and about God. May God bless these books, which we will use as our map along the way.

All: Amen!

8

THIS IS OUR FAITH

A Preview of Grade 4

SILVER BURDETT GINN • SCHOOL PROGRAM

OPENING DOORS
A Take-Home Magazine

THIS IS OUR FAITH

You are cordially invited...

Profile of the Fourth-Grade Child

No one knows your child better than you! It may be helpful and interesting to you as a parent or guardian, however, to explore some of the characteristics of the fourth grader.

Fourth graders

- enjoy reading.
- learn readily from their observations.
- need parents' and other adults' warmth and support.
- need sets of guidelines and rules to follow.
- need to belong to a group, particularly an understanding family group.
- act more independently than when they were younger.
- place great emphasis on friendships with people of the same sex.
- like being and doing things with friends.
- have a general willingness to share with each other more than they did when they were younger.

THIS IS OUR FAITH Grade 4 Program has been designed to reflect the doctrine presented in the **Catechism of the Catholic Church** at a level that is appropriate for the fourth-grade child.

4

© Silver Burdett Ginn Inc.

A Preview of Grade 4

The purpose of the *Parent Preview Magazine* is to introduce the parents of your students to THIS IS OUR FAITH, Grade 4. This preview invites the family to join their child on this year's journey of faith, while providing a brief summary of the material taught in Grade 4. Special emphasis is given to describing *Opening Doors: A Take-Home Magazine,* as well as to profiling the fourth-grade child.

Sending the Magazine Home

At the end of the first session, help the students carefully remove the preview magazine from their books. Explain to the students that this preview magazine will introduce their families to THIS IS OUR FAITH, Grade 4. Demonstrate how to fold the page, forming a four-page booklet. Encourage the students to bring the preview magazine home and to share it with their families.

to continue on the journey of faith you began on the day you presented your child for Baptism. As your fourth grader commits to this year's faith journey, you are invited as the primary educator in faith to journey along with your child, in whatever way is most comfortable for you. *This Is Our Faith* is privileged to assist you in this important task.

This Year in Grade 4

This year your fourth grader will learn about the Church's rich tradition of moral example and teaching. This tradition will provide motivation and direction for your child's moral growth. We begin the year with a look at Christian morality.

In Unit 1, your child will learn that God makes all things good. Your child will also learn that at times we are strongly tempted by evil. Sometimes we sin. However, Jesus gives us the Holy Spirit to help us choose good over evil.

As your child completes each unit of *This Is Our Faith*, you will receive *Opening Doors: A Take-Home Magazine*. Each magazine will include the following features to help you and your family share your faith.

A Closer Look

includes thought discussion starters, points for reflection, and an article relating the unit theme to a particular aspect of the Mass.

Being Catholic

explains a particular aspect of our Catholic heritage.

Growing Closer

suggests activities to help you and your family integrate your faith into everyday life.

And also . . .

Looking Ahead

A preview of the next unit of *This Is Our Faith*

UNIT 1

Choosing Between Good and Evil

What are some of the good things and bad things about our world?

Introducing the UNIT

Make two lists on the chalk-board titled *Good Things* and *Bad Things.* List the students' responses to the unit-focus question on page 11. Explain that in Unit 1 they will learn where good-ness comes from and how evil entered our world.

Vocabulary

grace
consequences
original sin
temptation
sin
conscience

Unit Aim

To help the students understand that the universe God creates is good but that evil enters into it through human selfishness.

Doctrinal Summaries

CHAPTER 1
All that God makes is good and shows his goodness, love, and presence with us. God is present here with us in our world. We call God's loving presence *grace*.

CHAPTER 2
The goodness of the world is spoiled by sin. Sin is part of each one of us. It has been part of the world since God's first people began to act selfishly. This first selfish act is called *original sin*.

CHAPTER 3
We are all tempted. Jesus was tempted, just as we are. Temptation is not a sin. We sin only when we choose to give in to temptation and turn away from God. With Christ's help we can overcome temptation.

CHAPTER 4
Jesus sends us the Holy Spirit to be our helper and our guide in our fight against temptation. The Holy Spirit helps us to know what is good for us. The Holy Spirit guides us to choose good rather than evil.

Note:
As you prepare this unit, you may wish to refer to the reference section, *Our Catholic Heritage,* beginning on page 327.

Additional resources for Unit 1 include: a Unit Test and a Family Letter as well as a video and selections from THIS IS OUR FAITH Music Program. You might also find it helpful to preview *Saints and Other Holy People* and *Prayer Celebrations* for possibilities to enhance the unit.

11

Goodness from God

Objectives

To help the students

■ Identify the good people and things in their lives.

■ Appreciate that creation reflects God's goodness.

■ Understand that since they are created in God's image, they are good.

■ Determine ways to be caretakers of God's creation.

■ Praise God for the wonder of creation and review the chapter.

Chapter Outline

	Step 1 Learning About Our Lives	**Step 2** Learning About Our Faith	**Step 3** Learning How to Live Our Faith
Day 1	■ Introduce the chapter. ■ Complete an activity. *ABOUT 12 MINUTES*	■ Read about God's gift of goodness. *ABOUT 8 MINUTES*	■ Complete an activity. *ABOUT 10 MINUTES*
Day 2	■ Discuss the beauty of the world. ■ Talk about the beginning of the world. *ABOUT 8 MINUTES*	■ Read and discuss a Scripture story. ■ Name ways to care for the world. *ABOUT 14 MINUTES*	■ Write about God's gifts. ■ Review the lesson. ■ Pray together. *ABOUT 8 MINUTES*
Day 3	■ Think about good people. *ABOUT 5 MINUTES*	■ Read about God's grace. ■ Learn the vocabulary. ■ Learn the doctrine. *ABOUT 15 MINUTES*	■ Complete an activity. ■ Write a wordgram. ■ Pray to God the Creator. *ABOUT 10 MINUTES*
Day 4	■ Identify signs of God's love. *ABOUT 7 MINUTES*	■ Read and discuss a biography. ■ Learn to follow Francis' example. *ABOUT 14 MINUTES*	■ Complete an activity. ■ Review previous lessons. *ABOUT 9 MINUTES*
Day 5	**Prayer** Present prayers of praise; understand "Canticle of the Sun"; and give thanks for God's goodness.		
	Review Identify true or false statements; complete the chapter review; and reflect on the Scripture verse.		

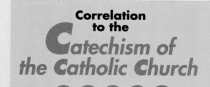

Plan Ahead

	Preparing Your Class	**Materials Needed**
Day 1	Read through the entire lesson plan.	■ pencils or pens
Day 2	Read the lesson plan. Decide if you want to make a class mural and make all the necessary preparations.	■ pencils or pens ■ butcher paper for murals ■ colored chalk
Day 3	Read through the entire lesson plan. If you plan to use "Amazing Grace," have copies of the THIS IS OUR FAITH *Hymnal* and recording available.	■ pencils or pens ■ lined paper
Day 4	Read through the lesson plan. If you choose to share the song "All Good Gifts," begin locating the recording right away. Gather posterboard and stickers if enriching the lesson.	■ pencils or pens
Day 5	Read through the entire lesson plan. Decide how you will utilize the "Canticle of the Sun" and make all the necessary preparations.	■ pencils or pens ■ prayer cloth ■ candle ■ Bible

Additional Resources

As you plan this chapter, consider using the following materials from The Resourceful Teacher Package.

■ *Classroom Activity Sheets 1* and *1a*

■ *Family Activity Sheets 1* and *1a*

■ *Chapter 1 Test*

■ *Prayers for Every Day*

■ *Projects: Grade 4*

You may also wish to refer to the following Big Book.

■ *We Celebrate God's Word,* page 2

In preparing the students for the Sunday readings, you may wish to use Silver Burdett Ginn's *Getting Ready for Sunday* student and teacher materials.

BOOKS FOR THE JOURNEY

Adam's Story. Louise Ulmer. Concordia, 1985. Poetic version of the Creation story.

The Random House Book of Poetry. "Nature Is," p. 21; "All Things Bright and Beautiful," by Cecil Francis Alexander, p. 22; "The Universe," by Mary Britton Miller. Selected by Jack Prelutsky. Random House, 1983. A compilation of poems for children.

MORE BOOKS FOR THE JOURNEY

The Dreamer. Cynthia Rylant. Blue Sky Press, 1993. A wonderful story of God's creation.

Francis, the Poor Man of Assisi. Tomie dePaola. Holiday House, 1982. A careful retelling of Francis of Assisi's story.

REDUCED CLASSROOM ACTIVITIES

NAME _____

GOODNESS FROM GOD

You and your detective partner are looking for an important message hidden in the grid below. The following letters are dead-end clues.

B   C   F   J   K   N   P   Q   U   V   W   X   Y   Z

By coloring all the boxes that contain those letters, you will solve the case.

C	F	Q	F	W	B	C	X	Z	Y
P	N	V	Z	C	Y	B	A	L	L
Q	W	T	H	A	T	J	N	Q	P
Z	B	Y	Q	X	F	W	J	V	K
N	U	P	Z	C	Z	Y	Q	W	F
G	O	D	F	J	N	Y	V	N	X
P	U	Y	X	J	Z	H	A	S	F
B	Y	M	A	D	E	Q	W	Z	V
Z	X	C	J	F	W	X	Y	I	S
C	F	Y	J	G	O	O	D	W	B

Write the message here.

All that God has made is good.

To the Teacher: This activity follows the Scripture story "The Story of Creation."

Chapter 1   Goodness from God   THIS IS OUR FAITH 4   **1**

NAME _____

QUESTION THE ANSWERS

To score points for this game, write the question for each answer given in the box. Score 500 points for each correct question you write.

1. What is grace?

   God's loving presence in our lives

2. Who is Saint Francis of Assisi?

   A good Christian who saw the goodness of God in the people and things around him

3. What is the sun?

   God set this in the sky to give light by day.

4. Who are human beings?

   They were made in God's image and likeness.

5. What is earth?

   What God called the dry land

6. What are the waters?

   God gathered this below the sky into seas and oceans.

7. Who are poor people?

   To be more like Jesus, Francis shared his money with these people of God.

8. What is October 4?

   On this day, we celebrate the life and example of Saint Francis.

Perfect score: 4,000   My score: _____

To the Teacher: This page reviews the content of the chapter and requires critical thinking.

1a   THIS IS OUR FAITH 4   **Chapter 1**   Goodness from God

Background for the Teacher

CHRISTIAN MORALITY

The theme for this grade is the Christian moral life. Christian morality is essentially a response to God's initiative, enabled by the activity of the Holy Spirit. So we begin with the visible evidence of God's initiative, namely ourselves and the world around us.

The students look at the good they know in themselves, in others, and in the world about them. This consideration of the treasures in their lives is important in their developing relationship with God. It allows the teacher to build a connection between the goodness of people in our lives and the goodness of God. Our response to God's goodness often begins with thanksgiving for the gifts that fill our lives. "Let them praise the name of the Lord, for he commanded and they were created" (Psalm 148:5).

GRACE

Creation reflects God's presence. The stories of Creation from Scripture are poetic explanations that help us see truth about God. They are not meant to be scientific reports. They underscore the supreme goodness of God. "For from the greatness and the beauty of created things their original author . . . is seen" (Wisdom 13:5).

The Genesis accounts show that God gives his presence to us with the gift of the earth. We call God's loving presence *grace*. This personal presence is so intimate and powerful that it gradually transforms us into being more like God, more like Christ.

We humans are granted our existence and are given dignity before God and others. We are allowed freedom to act and choose. We are made to interact with our universe, and are entrusted with the stewardship of all creation. Through the graciousness of God we are allowed to cooperate in the accomplishment of his plan.

If, then, God has indeed created a good world, and cares for all the creatures therein, why does evil exist? Evil is an unavoidable and painful mystery. The Catholic Church professes that only Christian faith as a whole can provide some response to the presence of evil in the world: the goodness of creation; the action of sin; the faithful and patient love of God; the Incarnation of Jesus Christ, the Son of God; God's gift of the Spirit; the gathering of the Church; the grace of the sacraments; freedom of choice; God's invitation to us to choose good and to live the blessed life.

Saint Francis of Assisi saw God's closeness to us in created things. This chapter, which helps the students realize that they are grace-filled, is an occasion for you to affirm their goodness. You can begin to build a classroom community that reflects the creative energy of God—a community that cares for others and God.

DAY 1
DOCTRINE

Objective

This lesson helps the students identify the good people and things in their lives.

Step 1 / INTRODUCTION

Learning About Our Lives

Introducing the Chapter

Direct attention to page 12 and have a volunteer read the chapter title and focus question aloud. Allow a few moments for the students to think about the people or things in their lives that they consider gifts. Then encourage each student to respond by answering the question.

Completing an Activity

Read aloud the directions to the activity on page 12 and have the students work independently to complete the activity. Move about the room, speaking individually with each student about their work. After they have had sufficient time to write the names of the good people and things in their lives and draw a picture of three of their favorite things, invite them to share one or more of these things with the class. Summarize by commenting on the good things the students have identified. Help them value goodness in their lives.

Step 2 / DEVELOPMENT

Learning About Our Faith

Reading About God's Gift of Goodness

Have the students read independently "God's Gift of Goodness" on page 13. Ask the following questions.

- Where do we read about the goodness we see in us and around us? (*In the Bible*)
- What do we know about everything that God creates? (*That it is good*)

Goodness from God

Who or what is the best gift in your life?

Activity

Write the names of some of the people, pets, foods, games, and places you see as good things in your life. Then draw in the space below a picture of one of your favorite things.

_____   _____

_____   _____

12 Doctrine

★ Enriching the Lesson ★

Conduct get-acquainted interviews among the students. Divide the class into pairs. As they interview each other, ask the students to record their partner's responses.

1. What is the most exciting thing that has ever happened to you?
2. What are your hobbies?
3. What is the most important thing you would like others to know about you?

When finished, have the students tell what they learned about each other.

🍎 Teaching Tips

If you have students with special needs in your class, keep the following general suggestions in mind. For the *visually impaired*, describe in detail the photographs that the students are to study. For the *hearing impaired*, write key words or discussion concepts on the chalkboard for them to read. For the *fine-motor impaired*, prepare in advance items that they would have difficulty manipulating and will need for creative activities.

12

God's Gift of Goodness

Our world is filled with good people. It is filled with many gifts of God's creation. In the Bible we read about the goodness we see in each other. This goodness is God's gift to us, just as it was a gift to the people of long ago.

The Bible tells us that God creates everything that is good and makes people in his own image. The world is the Creator's gift to us. God gives the world to us to enjoy, to care for, and to use with respect. We are responsible for all living beings and the environment.

Activity

We are made in God's own image. With words or pictures, describe what God sees when he looks at you.

Doctrine 13

Completing an Activity

Ask a volunteer to read aloud the directions for the activity on page 13. Have the students write a description or draw a picture of themselves in the mirror illustrated in their books. Respect the feelings of the shy child who may not want to share with the rest of the class his or her description or drawing.

Focus on

Grace According to the *Catechism of the Catholic Church* "grace is *favor,* the *free and undeserved help* that God gives us to respond to his call to become children of God . . . partakers of the divine nature and of eternal life" (# 1996).

🍎 Teaching Tips

Show the students the glossary in the back of their books, beginning on page 355. Explain that it contains all the words and definitions they will be learning. Encourage them to refer frequently to the glossary throughout the school year.

DAY 2
SCRIPTURE

Objective

This lesson helps the students appreciate that creation reflects God's goodness.

Step 1 / INTRODUCTION

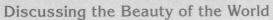

Learning About Our Lives

Discussing the Beauty of the World

Discuss the beautiful things in nature the students have seen on trips, in their community, in motion pictures, and in books and magazines.

Talking About the Beginning of the World

Invite the students to recall things that have caused them to wonder about the beginning of the world. Tell the students that people have always wondered about creation and told stories about how the world came to be. Explain that these people believed that all of the wonderful things in the universe are God's gift to us.

Step 2 / DEVELOPMENT

Learning About Our Faith

Reading and Discussing a Scripture Story

Direct the students to turn to pages 14 and 15 and give them a moment to look at the pictures in their books. Then ask the students to close their eyes and visualize the story as you read aloud "The Story of Creation."

Use the questions below to discuss the story.

- Before God created the earth, what was there? (*Darkness*)
- What did God think about the light? (*That it was good*)
- How did God create the man and the woman? (*In God's own image and likeness*)
- What did God ask the man and the woman to do with the earth? (*Care for it, use and enjoy it*)
- What did God do after creating the world, all the creatures, and the people? (*God rested.*)

The Story of Creation

In the beginning, God spoke into the darkness. God said, "Let there be light," and there was light. God saw how good the light was.

Then God made the dome of sky. God gathered the waters below the sky into seas and oceans. Dry land appeared. God called the dry land "earth," and God was pleased.

Then God said, "Let the earth bring forth plants and flowers and trees." And the earth was filled with life and colors, with fruits and grains. God saw how good it was.

Then God set the sun in the sky to give light by day, and the moon and stars to shine upon the earth by night. God saw how good it was.

14 Scripture

CURRICULUM CONNECTION

Art Encourage the students to work together to make a creation mural using colored chalk and white butcher paper, which you have taped to the floor or to a wall. Divide the story into five parts: sun, moon, stars; trees, flowers; birds, fish; animals; man and woman. Assign a few students to work on each part, creating five panels in all. Ask the students to write a caption for each panel. Display the completed mural in a high-visibility area of the parish or school.

Enriching the Lesson

You might want to clarify for the students what is meant by the phrase "made in God's own image and likeness." Tell the students that we believe that human beings most reflect God and his goodness because, unlike the rest of creation, we have the ability to make free choices and to love others and God even more than we love ourselves.

14

Then God said, "Let the waters be filled with living creatures and let birds fly in the sky." And so there were fish and birds of all kinds. God looked at them with great pleasure and blessed them all.

Then God said, "Let the earth be filled with every kind of animal." Animals both large and small, and tame and wild, began to move over the earth. And God saw how good it was.

And finally God said, "Let us make human beings in our own image and likeness to rule over the earth, the skies, and the seas." So God made a man and a woman who were very much like God.

God blessed the woman and man and said, "Have children who will live all over the earth. I am giving you and your children the whole world to care for, to use, and to enjoy."

God looked at everything and saw that it was all very good. So God stopped working and rested.

Based on Genesis 1:1—2:2

Activity

1. Name one part of God's creation that you think is most beautiful. Tell why.

_____

2. Name one animal for which you are particularly thankful. Tell why.

_____

3. God has given you some special people in your life. List as many as you can on the lines below.

_____   _____   _____
_____   _____   _____
_____   _____   _____

> ### Teaching Tips
>
> Display a copy of the Bible. Focus on the sacredness of the Scriptures. Explain to the class that the Scripture stories tell of God's goodness and how we are to live our lives.

■ What can we learn from the story of creation? (*Answers may vary. Help the students appreciate that the creation story tells us that the world God created was completely good. Emphasize that the story is not meant to be a scientific report.*)

Naming Ways to Care for the World

Invite the students to name ways in which they can care for the world. Discuss the environment; the importance of recycling and conservation; and caring for animals and pets. Point out that God wants us to rule over the world graciously.

Step 3 / CONCLUSION

Learning How to Live Our Faith

Writing About God's Gifts

Invite the students to complete the activity at the bottom of page 15. Be sure to give the students sufficient time to complete their answers. Afterward, invite sharing.

Reviewing the Lesson

Review the lesson by asking the following questions.

■ How are human beings like God? (*They are made in God's image and likeness.*)

■ What responsibilities do human beings have in ruling the earth? (*Caring for, using, and enjoying the world*)

Praying Together

Create a litany by having the students name, one at a time, some of the gifts of creation that they have identified in the writing activity. Use the litany below as a model.

Student: You give us the gift of the sun to warm us and brighten our world.

Class: Your creation is good, O God.

Student: You give us people who are made in your image.

Class: Your creation is good, O God.

15

DAY 3
MORALITY

Objective

This lesson helps the students understand that since they are created in God's image, like everything else created by God, they are good.

Step 1 / INTRODUCTION

Learning About Our Lives

Thinking About Good People

Direct the students' attention to the activity at the top of page 16. Give the students time to think about and complete the activity. When all have finished, divide the class into small groups of four or five students. Give each student in each group time to tell about the goodness of the persons named.

Step 2 / DEVELOPMENT

Learning About Our Faith

Reading about God's Grace

Choose a volunteer to read aloud "God's Grace" on page 16. Then ask the students to name some of God's gifts that benefit the world. Share everyday situations that show grace in our lives to help the students appreciate that each one of us is grace-filled. You might begin by describing events such as the following.

- Someone smiles at you.
- Your friend wants to play a game with you.
- Your puppy wags its tail at you.
- You help rake leaves.

Help the students appreciate that we are always surrounded by God's grace. Explain that when we act lovingly, God's grace works through us.

Presenting the Vocabulary

Write the word *grace* on the chalkboard. Point out the Vocabulary box. Ask the class to read aloud the definition. Encourage the students to memorize the definition by writing it or repeating it several times. Ask: What do we call God's loving presence in our lives? (*Grace*)

Activity

1. Name someone in your family who you think is a good person. _____

Give an example of his or her goodness.

_____

2. Name a friend who you think is a good person.

_____

Give an example of his or her goodness.

_____

God's Grace

Everything that God makes is good. In creation the mountains, the seas, the animals, and especially people remind us of the Lord's goodness, love, and presence with us. God gives us people and things to help us be happy. God is present here with us in our world through people and all creation.

Catholics call God's loving presence in our lives **grace.**

Grace is a very special gift from God. Grace helps us see human beings and all of creation as holy and good. Grace gives us the strength to say no to selfishness and to act as the good people God created us to be. God's loving presence helps us choose what is good.

16   Morality

CURRICULUM CONNECTION

Music   Teach the students the song "Amazing Grace" on page 128 of the THIS IS OUR FAITH *Hymnal.* When the students know the melody, have them sing along with the recording.

Activity

On the lines below, put a ✔ in front of the sentences below that show how you are a good person, filled with God's grace.

_____ I am generous.

_____ I get along well with others.

_____ I am cooperative in school.

_____ I am helpful at home.

_____ I tell the truth.

_____ I am a good friend.

_____ I respect people who are different from me.

_____ I remember to thank God in prayer.

_____ I invite others to be my friends.

_____ I encourage others when they need a kind word.

_____ I am kind to younger children.

_____ I respect my parents and teachers.

_____ I respect other people's property.

A Prayer to Our Creator

Loving God, Creator of all life, thank you for giving me life and making me in your image and likeness. Thank you for the many ways you make your presence known to me. Your love fills my life, and I am thankful. Amen.

Vocabulary

grace: God's loving presence in our lives

● ● ● ● ● ● ● ● ● ● ● ●

We Believe

All that God makes is good and shows his goodness, love, and presence with us. God gives us people and things to help us be happy. The Lord is present here with us in our world. We call God's loving presence *grace*.

Presenting the Doctrine

Present the doctrine in the We Believe statements. Explain that this section summarizes the important concepts in the lesson. Reinforce the students' understanding of the doctrine by asking them to paraphrase each sentence.

Step 3 / CONCLUSION

Learning How to Live Our Faith

Completing an Activity

Call attention to the activity on page 17. Explain the directions to the students. Give them sufficient time to complete the inventory. Help the students recognize that when their actions show their goodness, God's grace works through them to bring grace to the lives of others.

Writing a Wordgram

Ask the students to name qualities or attitudes that reflect God's grace in their lives. To get them started, give them a few suggestions, such as generosity, creativity, goodness, kindness, and love. Distribute lined paper and pencils. Instruct the students to write the word *grace* in a vertical column in the center of the page. Encourage them to write horizontally one quality for each letter of the word *grace*. Explain that the qualities do not need to begin with the letters. For example:

sharin**G**
c**R**eativity
be**A**uty
Care
lov**E**

Praying to God the Creator

Point out the prayer at the bottom of page 17. Give the students time to read the prayer silently. Then pray the prayer aloud together as a group.

Enriching the Lesson

Allow the students to interview each other to discover how God's grace fills their lives. Suggest questions such as the following.

■ What kinds of helpful things do you do for others?

■ What person in your life most helps you know that God is with you each day?

17

DAY 4
MORALITY

Objective

This lesson helps the students determine ways to be caretakers of God's creation.

Step 1 / INTRODUCTION

Learning About Our Lives

Identifying Signs of God's Love

Have the students talk about some things in their own lives and experiences that speak to them about God's love and goodness (*The love of a parent, pet, or friend; a special song, or a family project such as a garden*). Tell the students that today they will read about someone who saw God's goodness in the gifts of creation.

Step 2 / DEVELOPMENT

Learning About Our Faith

Reading and Discussing a Biography

To guide the students as they silently read the story "A Doer of Good Deeds" on page 18, write the following questions on the chalkboard. Encourage the students to look for the answers as they read.

- What was Francis like as a young man? (*Rich, ambitious*)
- How did Francis respond when he saw poor people? (*He gave them his money and clothes.*)
- Who did Francis want to be like? (*Jesus*)
- What are some of the things that Francis loved? (*Birds, animals, music, flowers, people*)
- What can we learn from the example of Saint Francis? (*To love God and his creation; to care for the poor; not to value material things*)

Have the class write a dramatization of the story of Saint Francis. Assign roles to a narrator, Francis, a poor man, and beggars. Use simple props and music to enhance the dramatization.

A Doer of Good Deeds

We can come to know God's love through the goodness of people and things in the world. A great Christian who saw the goodness of God in the people and things around him was Francis of Assisi.

Francis was born in Assisi, Italy, in 1182. Francis grew up to be a rich young man. He wanted to be a famous knight, who did great and noble deeds. One day, when Francis was dressed in a new uniform, he met a very poor man. Francis felt sorrow for the man, so he gave him his uniform.

On another day, Francis went to Rome, where he saw many beggars. He shared all his money with them. Soon Francis gave away everything— his money, his clothes, even his place in his father's house. Francis wanted only to do great and noble deeds for God. He wanted to be like Jesus.

Francis lived a simple, happy life, putting all his trust in God. He admired the simple life of the birds and other animals. He loved music and songs. He loved plants and flowers, so he had a beautiful garden.

Francis grew in his love for God. He also grew in his love for the goodness in people and things. Other people wanted to do great things for God, too. They began to follow Francis' example.

Today, Saint Francis of Assisi is one of the great saints of the Church. We celebrate his life and example on October 4.

18 Morality

Enriching the Lesson

Prepare a poster showing a picture of Saint Francis. Write the words *Doer of Good Deeds* across the top of the poster. List the students' names in a column on the left side. Assemble stickers of flowers, birds, stars, and other gifts of creation. Display the poster and invite the students to name a good deed they have done. As they respond, have them choose stickers and attach them to the poster next to their names.

Teaching Tips

Help the students appreciate the influence of Saint Francis of Assisi on Catholic Christians by displaying a variety of images of the saint. Statues, icons, holy cards, and other images of the saint are readily available. Display these items on your classroom prayer table or in another display area. Tell the students that Saint Francis is one of the most popular saints honored by the Church.

18

Following Francis' Example

Just like Francis, we are called to care for all that God has given to us.

When we care for our world, we care for God's gift of creation. When we respect all living creatures, and care for animals we remember that they too are gifts from God.

We take care of the environment by not wasting our natural resources.

We care for God's great gift of people by respecting all people. We are called to be kind to others and to help those in need, just as Francis did.

Learning about Saint Francis helps us to know what to do to live as followers of Jesus.

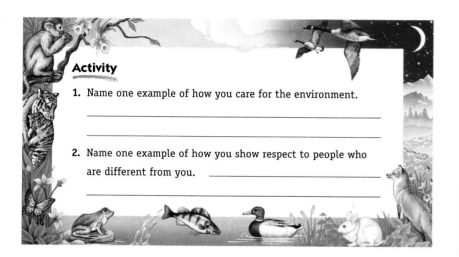

Activity

1. Name one example of how you care for the environment.

   _____

   _____

2. Name one example of how you show respect to people who are different from you. _____

   _____

Learning to Follow Francis' Example

Ask for volunteers to read aloud "Following Francis' Example" on page 19. Then ask them to name specific ways they can imitate Saint Francis. (*Responses may include picking up litter in the neighborhood; recycling paper, plastic, glass, and metal containers; caring for a plant or a pet; or playing with a younger brother or sister.*)

Step 3 / CONCLUSION

Learning How to Live Our Faith

Completing an Activity

Direct the students to the activity at the bottom of page 19. Have the students work together in groups of three or four to complete the activity. When all groups have finished, have one person from each group report their responses to the class.

Reviewing Previous Lessons

Have the students recite the definition of grace. Recall the responsibilities of human beings who are created in God's image and likeness: to care for, use, and enjoy the world.

CURRICULUM CONNECTION

Music   Have the class listen to the song "All Good Gifts" from *Godspell* by Stephen Schwartz. The recording is available on Arista, ARCD–8337. Afterwards, ask each student to name one thing for which he or she is thankful. Use the things the students name to create a class litany prayer. Invite the music specialist or choir director to teach the class effective but easy ways to improvise repetitive patterns, so as to sing the litany and accompany it on classroom instruments.

DAY 5
PRAYER/REVIEW

Objective

This lesson introduces students to prayers of praise and helps them pray a prayer of praise for the wonder of creation and the goodness of God.

Presenting Prayers of Praise

Explain the material about kinds of prayers and prayers of praise presented on page 20. Ask for volunteers to read aloud the paragraphs about prayers of praise. Tell the class they will be praying a prayer of praise to God and his creation based on "The Canticle of Brother Son and Sister Moon" by Saint Francis of Assisi.

Understanding "Canticle of the Sun"

Direct the students' attention to the prayer entitled "Canticle of the Sun" beginning in the middle of page 20. Read it aloud, then ask the class to reread it silently. Ask the students to name those lines that bring vivid images to their minds. Invite the students' responses.

Giving Thanks for God's Goodness

Set up a candle, a Bible, and a prayer cloth on the prayer table. Invite the students to gather around the prayer table with their books. Give them a few moments to put themselves in a prayerful state of mind. Then have the class pray Saint Francis of Assisi's prayer of praise.

Allow preparation time for the planning and rehearsal of gestures, dance steps, or music should the class want to pray this prayer of praise using these enhancements.

Praying Prayers of Praise

The Church teaches us many different ways of praying. One kind of prayer is called *praise*. To praise someone means to tell the person how wonderful he or she is. We praise God for being wonderful. When we pray a prayer of praise, we can use joyful words, gestures, song, or even dance.

Saint Francis of Assisi was a person who often praised God. Pray this prayer of praise in a way that is comfortable for you. You might want to add gestures, dance steps, or music to the prayer.

Canticle of the Sun

Praise to you, Lord,
for our brother the sun,
beautiful and radiant;
by him you give us light.

For our brother the wind,
for the air and for the clouds,
for the clear sky,
and for every kind of weather.

For our sister the water.
She is so useful,
so precious, and so pure.

For our brother the fire,
who makes us warm;
by him you light up the night.

For our mother the earth,
who carries us and feeds us.
She gives us her plants
and her colorful fruits.

Praise to you, Lord, for all creatures.
Saint Francis of Assisi

20   Prayer

CURRICULUM CONNECTION

Music   Your class may enjoy performing a musical setting of "Canticle of the Sun," found on page 26 in THIS IS OUR FAITH Music Program Director's Manual. Suggestions are also given for movement and use of instruments to accompany the performance of the song. The music can also be found on page 46 of the THIS IS OUR FAITH *Hymnal.* Teach the students the song. When they know the melody, add the movements and instrumental accompaniment.

Enriching the Lesson

Distribute drawing paper. Invite the students to create self-portraits for the bulletin board. Title the bulletin board display "We Are Made in God's Image and Likeness." While the students are working on their self-portraits, invite them to brainstorm qualities they have observed in one another that reflect God's goodness.

20

Chapter Review

Read each statement below. Then write **true** or **false** on the line in front of each statement.

False **1.** God looked at all of creation and called it evil.

True **2.** God gives us the world to enjoy, to care for, and to use with respect.

False **3.** Francis was born in Germany in 1182.

True **4.** Francis lived a simple life, putting all his trust in God.

False **5.** God's presence in our lives is called responsibility.

Write the answers to the first two questions.

1. What is meant by God's *grace*?

Grace is God's loving presence in our lives.

2. What does the story of creation tell us about ourselves, about the world, and about God?

From God we receive the gift of the world. We also

receive the gift of grace. God loves us and our world.

God is always here with us.

> **All that the Lord has made is good.**
> **Based on Sirach 39:33**

3. Discuss how we can show thanks to God for so many gifts.

CURRICULUM CONNECTION

Language Arts   Have the students write a profile about a person who has been an example of God's love and goodness to them. Give the students ample time to complete the profile. When they have finished writing, encourage volunteers to read their profiles to the class. If you wish, share with the class a profile about someone you know.

Identifying True or False Statements

Read the directions for completing the true or false section of the review at the top of page 21. Then give the class sufficient time to respond to each statement. Go over the correct answers with the class.

Completing the Chapter Review

Continue the review by having the students write their answers to the first two questions on the lines provided. Go through their responses, clarifying any misunderstandings or questions the students may have. Discuss item three. End the discussion by emphasizing that one of the best ways to show thanks to God for the gifts of creation is by caring for, using, and enjoying the world.

Reflecting on the Scripture Verse

Together, read aloud the Scripture verse at the bottom of the page. Direct the students to close their eyes and think about everything that God has created. Encourage them to memorize the verse.

2 Evil in the World

Objectives

To help the students

- Identify that both goodness and evil exist in the world.
- Understand that evil entered the world through original sin.
- Recognize how the Church community works to overcome evil in the world.
- Identify ways they can fight against evil.
- Learn how to pray spontaneously and review the chapter.

Chapter Outline

	Step 1 **Learning About Our Lives**	Step 2 **Learning About Our Faith**	Step 3 **Learning How to Live Our Faith**
Day 1	■ Review good deeds. ■ Introduce the chapter. ■ Study a photograph. ■ Understand feelings. *ABOUT 12 MINUTES*	■ Read about goodness and evil. ■ Complete an activity. *ABOUT 10 MINUTES*	■ Discuss and write about good and evil. *ABOUT 8 MINUTES*
Day 2	■ Introduce the Scripture story. *ABOUT 8 MINUTES*	■ Read the Scripture story. ■ Understand the existence of evil. ■ Learn the vocabulary. ■ Understand the doctrine. *ABOUT 14 MINUTES*	■ Pray together. *ABOUT 8 MINUTES*
Day 3	■ Recognize how our parish overcomes evil. *ABOUT 12 MINUTES*	■ Recognize groups that work against evil. *ABOUT 8 MINUTES*	■ Write solutions. *ABOUT 10 MINUTES*
Day 4	■ Share experiences of helplessness. *ABOUT 6 MINUTES*	■ Read and discuss the story. ■ Understand that one person can make a difference. *ABOUT 14 MINUTES*	■ Ease the hurt of others. *ABOUT 10 MINUTES*
Day 5	**Prayer** Introduce spontaneous prayer; read about spontaneous prayer; and pray spontaneously. **Review** Identify actions for combatting evil; complete the chapter review; and reflect on the Scripture verse.		

**Correlation
to the**

**Catechism of
the Catholic Church**

Paragraphs
**386–390, 397–410, 386, 389,
399, 412, 671, 1756**

Plan Ahead

Preparing Your Class

Day 1 Read through the entire lesson plan.

Day 2 Read the lesson plan. Prepare an example from your own life to help the students understand the doctrine in Step 2.

Day 3 Read through the lesson plan. If you choose to enrich the lesson, make all the necessary preparations. Remember to gather a collection of parish bulletins.

Day 4 Read through the lesson plan. If you choose to do the Enriching the Lesson activity, make all the necessary preparations.

Day 5 Read through the entire lesson plan. Look for song recording for the Curriculum Connection activity.

Materials Needed

Day 1
■ pencils or pens
■ stickers

Day 2
■ pencils or pens
■ writing paper

Day 3
■ pencils or pens
■ parish bulletins

Day 4
■ pencils or pens
■ newspapers and magazines
■ world map

Day 5
■ pencils or pens
■ prayer cloth
■ candle
■ Bible

Additional Resources

As you plan this chapter, consider using the following materials from The Resourceful Teacher Package.

■ *Classroom Activity Sheets 2* and *2a*

■ *Family Activity Sheets 2* and *2a*

■ *Chapter 2 Test*

■ *Prayers for Every Day*

■ *Projects: Grade 4*

You may also wish to refer to the following Big Book.

■ *We Celebrate God's Word,* page 2

In preparing the students for the Sunday readings, you may wish to use Silver Burdett Ginn's *Getting Ready for Sunday* student and teacher materials.

Books for the Journey

Tell Me the Bible. "Second Story of Creation," pp. 10–11. Joëlle Chabert and François Mourvillier. The Liturgical Press, 1991. The story of original sin.

Persephone and the Pomegranate. Kris Waldherr. Dial Books for Young Readers, 1993. A haunting Greek myth in which the eating of the seeds of a special fruit has serious consequences.

More Books for the Journey

Number the Stars. Lois Lowry. Houghton Mifflin, 1989. The story of a girl who becomes part of the Danish Resistance and helps make a difference against tremendous evil.

The Great Gilly Hopkins. Katherine Paterson. Thomas Y. Crowell, 1978. A child finally learns that she can live happily in a world where good and evil are mixed.

REDUCED CLASSROOM ACTIVITIES

NAME _____

EVIL IN THE WORLD

Good and evil coexist in our world. People can be helpful to one another, but they can also be hurtful. Look at the following list. Dump all the hurtful acts into the trash can and place all the helpful acts inside the treasure chest.

acting selfish
arguing
caring
complimenting
cooperating
encouraging
hitting
inviting
ignoring
respecting
saying mean things
telling lies

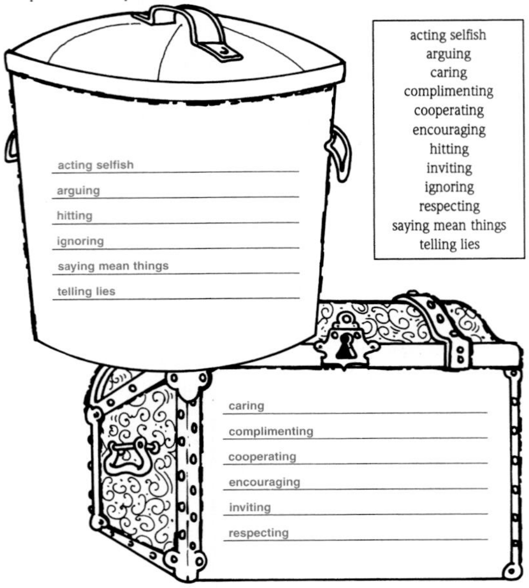

acting selfish
arguing
hitting
ignoring
saying mean things
telling lies

caring
complimenting
cooperating
encouraging
inviting
respecting

To the Teacher: This activity follows the story "Goodness and Evil."

Chapter 2 Evil in the World

THIS IS OUR FAITH 4 **2**

NAME _____

TURNING FROM EVIL

Write about a TV show or movie in which someone has fought against evil. Write the name of the TV show on the screen.

1. Who were the people who fought against evil?

_____

2. What evils did they fight against?

_____

3. How did they overcome evil?

_____

To the Teacher: This activity follows the story "What One Person Can Do."

2a THIS IS OUR FAITH 4

Chapter 2 Evil in the World

EVIL IN THE WORLD

In a most loving, marvelous act of creation, God makes us free, giving us the will to know, to love, and to serve him. But we do not always choose to love and serve God. Nine-year-olds know from their own inner struggles that they are sometimes drawn to evil acts. They have also been hurt by the selfish acts of others. They are aware of the moral evils of poverty, hunger, prejudice, and war.

This chapter confronts the reality of evil. The Genesis account states that God is not the cause of evil. Evil entered creation through the Tempter. The woman talks to the Tempter and God's word is distorted in the conversation. Evil begins with distortion of truth. Evil once yielded to spreads like a poison throughout creation. We have all inherited the effects of original sin, and thus the inclination to sin. Saint Paul wrote, "I cannot even understand my own actions. I do not do what I want to do but what I hate . . . This indicates that it is not I who do it but sin which resides in me . . . the desire to do right is there, but not the power" (based on Romans 7:15, 17–18). The Christian's journey takes us from creation in the image of God, through the fall, to "likeness" with him. It is the grace of God's continuing creative activity in us that enables us to undertake this journey. Saint Paul urges, "draw your strength from the Lord and from his mighty power. Put on the armor of God so that you may be able to stand firm against the tactics of the devil" (Ephesians 6:10–11).

Evil in the world is given even more power when we deny that it is evil. The journey toward sinfulness and alienation from God is usually rooted in the inability or unwillingness to recognize evil in the world.

Often, a child will articulate fear of evil by thinking, or saying, "If I am good and do everything God asks of me, nothing bad will happen." Sometimes a child may ask, "Why do bad things happen to good people?" The only honest response an adult can give is that we don't understand why evil or other bad things happen in life. But we do know that God loves us so much that no matter how bad something is, he is *always* with us, and cares for us.

Be sensitive to any students who may have been victims of evil. Your trust in God and your gentleness will help reassure them that his goodness can overcome troubles. Help the students focus on what they can do to bring justice. Explain that in praying together, we respond to God's call to united Christian moral action. As Catholics, we believe that evil has no power to overwhelm us, because Jesus Christ died for us and rose again.

Objective

This lesson helps the students identify that both goodness and evil exist in the world.

Step 1 / INTRODUCTION

Learning About Our Lives

Reviewing Good Deeds

Briefly review with the students the goodness of the people and the things around them as discussed in the previous chapter. If you opted to do the "Doers of Good Deeds" poster activity, use the poster for review. Ask the students to tell how they earned the stickers on the poster.

Introducing the Chapter

Ask the students to open their books to page 22. Read aloud the chapter title and chapter-focus questions. Elicit responses to the focus questions. Be sensitive to the hurts the students name. Help them appreciate that one of the things we can do when we are hurting is to reach out to those who love us.

Studying a Photograph

Direct attention to the photograph. Ask the students what they think the boy in the picture may be feeling. Responses may include: *loneliness, hurt, anger,* or *sadness.* Emphasize that hurt, sadness, and anger are universal feelings that everyone has experienced at one time or another.

Understanding Good and Bad Feelings

Ask for volunteers to read aloud the paragraphs about Jason under "I Don't Understand" on page 22.

Explain that bad things can happen to us, and we can choose to do bad things. We are not evil, but sometimes we act selfishly.

Invite student participation in the discussion question about their good and bad feelings.

2

Think of a time when you were hurting about something. How did you feel? What did you do to feel better?

Evil in the World

I Don't Understand

One day, Jason was thinking to himself, "I don't understand something. Why is it that I can do kind and loving things for others and feel happy one day and then another day I can be so unkind and feel like this—alone and sad? How can I have both good feelings and bad feelings in me?"

Jason continued thinking, "Then I look at our world. Lots of people are doing good, loving things for others, while other people are starting wars, selling drugs, and polluting our lakes and rivers. It seems that we live in a world that is good, but there is evil in it, too. Even in our hearts, goodness and sinfulness are mixed. We can love and hate, and help and hurt."

Discuss

Do you ever feel the same way that Jason feels?

 **Teaching Tips**

When students have hurt feelings, help them deal with these feelings by suggesting they consider doing the following.

- Talk to someone you trust about the way you feel.

- Seek the company of others when you feel hurt.

- Think about what you can do to stop feeling hurt and start feeling happy again.

 *Cultural Awareness*

Ask the students to name a group or an individual who may be experiencing the evils identified in the lesson. For example, anyone who is treated differently because of skin color, language, or appearance experiences prejudice. Emphasize that we are called to recognize and fight against evils that spoil the goodness of God's world and that all people have the right to share in the goodness of life.

Goodness and Evil

How do we know when something is evil? We can recognize evil in the world because evil is hurtful to others. Evil causes suffering and pain. Evil is always wrong and harmful. Evil tries to destroy what is good.

How do we know when something is good? Goodness causes happiness and peace. Goodness is choosing what is right and loving. All good people and good things can remind us of God.

Activity

Rearrange the letters in the words below to name different kinds of good and evil. The first letter of each word has been underlined for you.

KINDS OF GOOD

1. ove<u>l</u>   <u>love</u>
2. gessnor<u>f</u>ive   <u>forgiveness</u>
3. <u>p</u>hel   <u>help</u>
4. <u>s</u>coonmasip   <u>compassion</u>
5. ca<u>p</u>ee   <u>peace</u>
6. meli<u>s</u>   <u>smile</u>

KINDS OF EVIL

1. ar<u>w</u>   <u>war</u>
2. su<u>a</u>be   <u>abuse</u>
3. grune<u>h</u>   <u>hunger</u>
4. at<u>h</u>e   <u>hate</u>
5. <u>l</u>upintool   <u>pollution</u>
6. jd<u>p</u>eeicru   <u>prejudice</u>

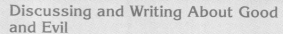

Morality   23

Focus on

Recognizing Evil Children may easily recognize the evil of the horrendous crimes of infamous individuals portrayed in the media. However, it is harder for children to see evil when many seemingly normal people in society participate in it; for example, the killing of the unborn; assisting suicides; ethnic-cleansing wars; physical, sexual, and verbal abuse; lack of concern for the needy; the death penalty; bigotry. Help the students recognize these kinds of evil whenever the opportunity arises.

Step 2 / DEVELOPMENT

Learning About Our Faith

Reading About Goodness and Evil

Call attention to the paragraphs at the top of page 23. Spend a few minutes discussing the questions and statements about goodness and evil in the two paragraphs to check for the students' understanding.

Completing an Activity

Explain the directions to the activity on page 23. When the students have finished, invite them to read aloud the unscrambled words. Discuss how each of the evils named can spoil happiness and how good deeds can bring happiness.

Step 3 / CONCLUSION

Learning How to Live Our Faith

Discussing and Writing About Good and Evil

Encourage the students to discuss why they think there is evil in the world. Ask: How can we overcome hate? Help the students appreciate that forgiveness and acceptance overcome hate. Do this with each of the evils named in the activity above. Emphasize that solving these problems requires great effort and cooperation. Recall that God created the world out of love. Assure them that God's love is greater than evil and that with his help we can overcome evil. Distribute writing paper. Then have the students write about ways in which evil can be overcome.

DAY 2

SCRIPTURE

Objective

This lesson helps the students understand that evil entered the world through original sin.

Step 1 / INTRODUCTION

Learning About Our Lives

Introducing the Scripture Story

Ask the students to recall the story of creation that they read in Chapter 1. Then ask if they can recall ever hearing or reading another story about Adam and Eve, the first people created by God. Elicit from the students what they can recall of this story.

Tell the students that they are going to read this story about Adam and Eve in the garden of Eden, as well as the explanation for the existence of evil in the world. Ask the students to open their books to page 24.

Step 2 / DEVELOPMENT

Learning About Our Faith

Reading and Discussing the Scripture Story

Invite the students to look at the pictures on pages 24 and 25. Then read aloud the title of the story. Ask for volunteers to read the story aloud.

Discuss the story and ask:

- Why did God make the world so good? (*God wanted to make the man and woman happy because he loved them.*)
- What happened to spoil the world's goodness? (*The man and woman disobeyed God.*)
- How is this story like your own life stories? (*When we are selfish and disobey God, we bring suffering on ourselves and others.*)
- What can we do to fight against evil? (*We can obey God.*)

Make sure the students understand that the man and woman disobeyed God. The woman and the man acted selfishly. God had given them everything they needed to be happy. God asked only that they be obedient. Because of their selfish disobedience, their lives changed for the worse.

A Beautiful Garden

God created man and woman and loved them. They lived in a beautiful garden. The woman and the man loved each other and were very happy. They loved the fish in the streams, the birds in the sky, and all the other animals. They loved and enjoyed the flowers and plants in God's garden. But there was one tree in the garden that God told the woman and man not to touch.

One day the Tempter appeared and asked the woman, "Did God really tell you not to eat the fruit of any of the trees in the garden?"

"No," the woman answered. "God told us not to eat the fruit of only one tree in the whole garden. God said that if we ate its fruit, we would die."

"You won't die," the Tempter said. "God knows that if you eat the fruit of that tree, you will be like gods. You will know good from evil."

The woman looked at the tree. It was beautiful and full of fruit. She took some of the fruit and ate it. She gave some fruit to the man, and he ate it, too. Suddenly the man and woman felt ashamed.

24 Scripture

CURRICULUM CONNECTION

Language Arts You might want to explore with the students how different life would be if Adam and Eve had not disobeyed God. Ask them to write a new ending to the story from the point where the Tempter tempts the woman. Divide the class into groups of three or four to do this activity, with one student in each group acting as the recorder. Distribute writing paper. Allow sufficient time for the students to rewrite the story. Have each group read aloud their new ending to the rewritten story.

24

That evening, God was moving about in the cool garden. The woman and man hid.

But God saw them and asked, "Why did you eat fruit from the tree?"

"The woman gave me some fruit, so I ate it," the man said.

"The Tempter tricked me, so I ate the fruit," the woman told the Lord.

"Because you disobeyed and did this evil thing," God said, "you will know suffering and pain. Your work will be hard, and you will become very tired. Thorns and weeds will grow from the earth. And you will die." Then God told the man and the woman that they must leave the garden.

Based on Genesis 2:8–3:23

Evil in the World

God made everyone and everything good. But we know from our experience that there is now evil mixed with good in all of creation. The Bible shows that evil comes not from God but from people's selfish choices. Sinful choices have **consequences**.

Sin spreads through the selfish actions of people. The Church calls the first selfish act **original sin**. It touches all of us who are born into a world hurt by evil.

Vocabulary

consequences: the things that follow from a choice or an action

original sin: the first selfish act of the first human beings, and the sinful condition into which we are born

We Believe

The goodness of the world is spoiled by sin. Sin is part of each one of us. It has been part of the world since God's first people began to act selfishly. This first selfish act is called *original sin*.

Teaching Tips

If a student asks, "Why does God allow evil to exist?" you might want to suggest that we don't completely understand God's plan for the world. Tell the student that we do believe, however, that in everything—even evil—God can make good come from it. Assure the student that we will have perfect understanding of God's entire plan when we see him face to face in heaven.

Assist the students in recognizing that we sometimes act selfishly like the man and the woman. You might remind the students that this story was written to help us understand something about our relationship with God and how sin spoils it. The story is not intended to be a scientific account.

Understanding the Existence of Evil

Read aloud "Evil in the World" on page 25. Help the students understand the twofold effect of evil: we can be hurt by the bad things that happen; and we can also act selfishly and hurt others by our actions. Explain that we always have a choice in how we respond when bad things happen. When we choose to be loving, we can help turn bad things to good.

Introducing the Vocabulary

Read aloud the new words in the vocabulary box. To check the students' understanding of original sin, ask them how original sin hurts each one of us. Encourage the students to name the consequences that came about from the first act of disobedience. Help the students memorize the definitions by repeating them aloud several times.

Presenting the Doctrine

Ask a student to read aloud the We Believe statements. Help the class understand that original sin affects each person. Ask the students if they can think of occasions when it seemed hard for them to do what was loving, and easier to do what was selfish. You might begin by sharing an incident from your own life. Explain that it is original sin that causes this difficulty in us.

Step 3 / CONCLUSION

Learning How to Live Our Faith

Praying Together

Ask the students to think of a prayer that mentions the word *evil*. When they have identified The Lord's Prayer, ask them who first prayed this prayer. Point out that Jesus recognized the evils in the world and asked his Father to protect and deliver us all from evil.

Suggest that the students pray "Deliver us from evil, O God" frequently during the day to ask God's help in overcoming the evils they named earlier in the chapter.

DAY 3
MORALITY

Objective

This lesson helps the students recognize how the Church community works to overcome evil in the world.

Step 1 / INTRODUCTION

Learning About Our Lives

Recognizing How Our Parish Overcomes Evil

Distribute a variety of parish bulletins to the class. Ask the students to find examples of how their home parish works to overcome evil. List all the examples the students find on the chalkboard. Tell the students that they are going to read about another parish and how it works to bring goodness and happiness into the world.

Step 2 / DEVELOPMENT

Learning About Our Faith

Recognizing Groups that Work Against Evil

Direct the students' attention to "A Parish Community Brings God's Goodness" on page 26. Ask for volunteers to read this section aloud. Guide the discussion using these questions.

- What do the preschool age children do to overcome evil? (*Donate juice to a hospice*)
- What project do the fourth graders organize? (*A winter coat collection*)
- In what type of service project do high school youths participate? (*Repairing and rebuilding homes for people in need*)
- What projects do your parish and Resurrection Parish have in common? Remember to refer to the list on the chalkboard from Step 1.
- In what projects would you like to be involved?

A Parish Community Brings God's Goodness

Resurrection Parish is a parish community in Oregon where all the parishioners of every age work together to overcome the evils that can be part of life today.

Adults at Resurrection Parish bring food and serve dinner to homeless people at a city shelter, and parish teenagers travel every summer to help repair and rebuild homes for families in need.

The fourth graders at Resurrection Parish have their own special project. They collect warm coats every year so that homeless and needy families will have warm clothing for the cold Oregon winters. One year the students collected more than 400 coats.

Every year the children of the parish gather school supplies and clothing to be taken to children in a mission parish in West Virginia. Even the very young children do their share of bringing goodness to God's people by bringing donated fruit juice to a local hospice.

By working together, the people of Resurrection Parish are fighting against evil in the world and bringing goodness to the people of God.

★ Enriching the Lesson ★

To help the hungry, the homeless, or the sick, plan a class project, such as a canned food or clothing drive or a bake sale after a parish Mass. Make flyers to advertise the project.

Donate the proceeds to the local soup kitchen or a shelter for the homeless.

🍎 Teaching Tips

Although this lesson stresses an awareness of the evils that surround us, spend some time discussing God's goodness and the goodness of human beings. Help the students realize that although we need to be aware of evil and its effects on us and on other people, we need to remember that God's loving goodness is stronger than even the worst evil we can experience.

Activity

The pictures show examples of evil that people can do something about. On the lines beside each picture, write what could be done to help.

_____

_____

_____

_____

_____

_____

_____

_____

_____

_____

_____

_____

_____

Writing Solutions

Have the students complete the activity on page 27 by writing solutions to the evils pictured on the page. Afterward, invite the students to offer their solutions to the class. You may want to vote on the best solution to each problem. If a solution emerges in which the entire class can participate, follow up on it. For instance, the class could write a letter to a state official or clean up the neighborhood or nearby park.

Enriching the Lesson

Invite a guest speaker from one of your parish's organizations to explain to the class how his or her group helps to overcome evil. Be sure that the guest speaks practically and concretely about the services offered by his or her group. You might want to invite several speakers from different parish groups to give a fuller view of your parish's services.

Objective

This lesson helps the students identify ways they can fight against evil.

Step 1 / INTRODUCTION

Learning About Our Lives

Sharing Experiences of Helplessness

Ask the students if they have ever felt helpless when something bad has happened. Give some examples from your own experience, for example, the Oklahoma Federal Building bombing, the serious illness of a relative or friend, or the divorce of parents. Tell the students that today they will learn about someone who decided to take action against the evil in the world. Have a student locate Lima, Peru on a globe or world map. Explain that the special person discussed in the lesson lived there.

Step 2 / DEVELOPMENT

Learning About Our Faith

Reading and Discussing the Story

Ask volunteers to read aloud "What One Person Can Do" on page 28. Explain that the Dominican order is a community of priests and religious brothers and sisters that was founded by Saint Dominic. Saint Martin de Porres was a brother in this order. Brothers promise to serve God and others. Discuss the story using the following questions.

- Where was Martin born? (*Lima, Peru*)
- How long ago did Martin live? (*400 years ago*)
- How did Martin treat poor people when he was young? (*Gave them money and food.*)
- What did Martin do as a Dominican? (*Gave medicine, food, and clothing to the poor.*)
- Why did Saint Martin become famous? (*He built a home and school for homeless children and took special care of slaves.*)
- What can we learn from this story? (*We can share with others and be concerned for the poor.*)

What One Person Can Do

God calls us to fight against all kinds of evil in ourselves and in our world. A great Christian who did just that was Saint Martin de Porres.

Martin was born in 1579. He lived in Lima, Peru, in South America. His father, a white Spaniard, did not want Martin because he was black like his mother. So Martin's mother took care of him by herself.

Even as a child, Martin could understand the sufferings of poor people. He gave them money and food.

As a teenager, Martin often cared for sick people. Later Martin joined a group of men called Dominican friars. Together they cared for sick priests and brothers. Rich people gave Martin medicine, food, and clothing, which he then gave to the poor.

Martin built a place for the poor children of Lima to live. He even built a school for them.

Martin took special care of the slaves who were brought to Peru. Martin became famous throughout Lima. About 300 years after Martin's death, Pope John XXIII named him a saint.

28 Morality

Enriching the Lesson

Distribute newspapers and news magazines. Have groups of three or four students look through these materials for photographs of people in today's world who need help. Instruct them to mount the images they choose onto a sheet of construction paper. Encourage the groups to write a caption for each photograph that tells why the people need help and how they can be helped. Arrange to display the students' work on a bulletin board in a public area of the parish.

Making a Difference

Most of the time we hear how groups of people are making a difference in our world. Yet often it is one person alone who takes the first step toward fighting evil. Saint Martin de Porres is a good example of what one person can do. Following Jesus' example, Martin began his work alone but was soon joined by others. Martin used the gifts and talents that God gave him to help others. His goodness helped overcome the hurt and suffering of many people.

Each of us has been given gifts and talents. Each of us can share our goodness with others. Alone or joined with others, we can each make a difference in the lives of people who are hurting.

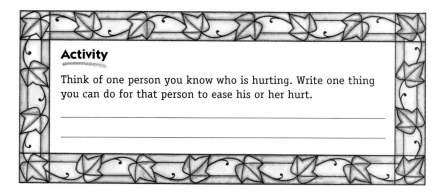

Activity

Think of one person you know who is hurting. Write one thing you can do for that person to ease his or her hurt.

_____

_____

Direct the students' attention to "Making a Difference" on page 29. Ask a volunteer to read these paragraphs aloud. Discuss how Saint Martin de Porres is a good example of what one person can do to fight against evil. Ask the students if they can think of anyone else who has made a difference. Allow all the students to share their ideas.

Step 3 / CONCLUSION

Learning How to Live Our Faith

Easing the Hurt of Others

Read the directions to the activity at the bottom of page 29. Give the students ample time to think about and write about a person they know who is hurting. Encourage the students to act on their ideas.

Enriching the Lesson

Prior to the session, write the following prayer on the chalkboard. Ask the students to copy it. Then pray the prayer aloud together.

God, our Creator, thank you for the example of selfless love we see in the life of Saint Martin de Porres. Help us to love others by sharing what we have and by bringing peace to this world in which we live. We ask this in the name of Jesus, our brother. Amen.

Focus on

Saint Martin de Porres Son of a black mother and Spanish father, Martin was born a victim of prejudice and poverty in an area wracked with hunger, disease, and slavery. Martin recognized the social dimension of sin and responded by aiding individuals. He acted as Jesus for the people of his day. In discussing Martin's story, point out that both the city of Lima and the country of Peru remain in dire need of Christian social action.

DAY 5

PRAYER/REVIEW

Objective

This lesson helps the students learn about spontaneous prayer and how to pray spontaneously.

Introducing Spontaneous Prayer

Ask if anyone knows the meaning of spontaneous. Give the class some examples of spontaneous actions. Explain that prayers can be prayed spontaneously also.

Reading About Spontaneous Prayer

Ask several volunteers to read aloud the text material on page 30. Ask questions to guide the students' understanding of the material.

Praying Spontaneously

Gather the class for prayer. Invite the students to pray a spontaneous prayer. Affirm all prayers prayed by the students.

Praying Spontaneously

One of the most wonderful things about prayer is that it can happen anywhere and at any time. We can pray at mealtimes and before going to sleep. We can gather with our families and with our school and parish communities for special times of prayer.

Spontaneous prayer is different. *Spontaneous* means "on the spur of the moment; without planning." By learning how to pray spontaneously, we can remember that God is always near us, in good times and in bad times. When we pray on the spur of the moment, we can have an ongoing conversation with God.

These fourth graders want to share with you how they pray spontaneously.

Teresa (Fairbanks, Alaska): Whenever I think about my dog Snowball and my cat Clancy while I'm at school I pray, "Thanks, God, for giving me Snowball and Clancy. Keep them safe and happy until I get home."

Ricardo (Brownsville, Texas): Sometimes I see homeless people on the streets. I pray, "God, it hurts me to see these people living on the streets. Please take care of them."

Kerry (Boston, Massachusetts): My mom taught me to say a little prayer each time I see an ambulance. I pray, "Dear God, please be with the person who is sick or injured, and be with those who are caring for the sick person."

If you could pray a spontaneous prayer right now, what would it be?

30   Prayer

CURRICULUM CONNECTION

Music   Play a recording of the song "Service" by Buddy Ceasar found in *Young People's Glory and Praise*, North American Liturgy Resources, available from OCP (Oregon Catholic Press), 5536 N.E. Hassalo, Portland, OR 97213. Have the students listen to the song and consider how it relates to the theme of Chapter 2. Emphasize that God calls each of us to do our part in fighting against evil.

Cultural Awareness

Often people who speak more than one language find it more meaningful to pray in their first language. If there are students in your class whose first language is not English, try to provide opportunities for them to pray the prayers in their native tongue. You may wish to give English-speaking students a chance to learn a prayer in another language by having them learn the Sign of the Cross in Spanish: *En el nombre del Padre, y del Hijo, y del Espíritu Santo. Amén.*

Chapter Review

On the lines below, list five evils that cause suffering in our world. Then on the lines next to each evil named, tell what could be done to fight against the evil.

1. _____   _____
                                _____

2. _____   _____
                                _____

3. _____   _____
                                _____

4. _____   _____
                                _____

5. _____   _____
                                _____

Write the answers to the first two questions.

1. What is meant by *original sin*?

   Original sin is the first selfish act of the first human

   beings and the sinful condition into which we

   are born.

2. When did evil in the world begin?

   Evil has been part of the world since God's first

   people began to act selfishly.

3. Discuss how evil in the world hurts each one of us and the world itself.

> **Turn from evil, and do good.**
> Psalm 34:15

★ ★★★ ★
Enriching the Lesson

Brainstorm ideas with the students for good deeds they can do during the week. Tell them that the good deeds they do need not be big things. Giving a smile to someone can be a good deed. If they ask themselves "How can I show love?" in each situation, then they will think of many good deeds they can perform.

Identifying Actions for Combatting Evil

Direct the students' attention to the top of page 31. Read aloud the directions to the activity. Have the students write several positive actions they can do to fight against five evils that cause suffering.

When the students have finished, invite them to share their ideas with the class. Stress how one person, with God's help, can combat evil in the world through personal action.

Completing the Chapter Review

Instruct the students to write answers to the first two questions. Check the students' responses. Clarify any misunderstandings the students may have. Encourage the entire class to participate in the discussion of item 3.

Reflecting on the Scripture Verse

Direct the class to read the Scripture verse on page 31. Write the word *evil* on the chalkboard. Ask the students to rearrange the letters to form a new word. Help them to discover that the letters also spell *live*. Emphasize that God wants all people to turn from evil and live good lives.

Encourage the students to memorize the Scripture verse.

Choices to Make

Objectives

To help the students

- Understand that we are all tempted.
- Identify ways in which Jesus was tempted.
- Understand temptation and realize that we sin only when we turn from God.
- Appreciate that, like Jesus, they can overcome temptation.
- Pray a psalm for strength to resist temptation and review the chapter.

Chapter Outline

	Step 1 — Learning About Our Lives	Step 2 — Learning About Our Faith	Step 3 — Learning How to Live Our Faith
Day 1	■ Talk about good deeds. ■ Introduce the chapter. *ABOUT 5 MINUTES*	■ Read and discuss the story and write a story ending. ■ Read about temptation. ■ Present the vocabulary. *ABOUT 17 MINUTES*	■ Discuss temptations. ■ Name temptations. *ABOUT 8 MINUTES*
Day 2	■ Play a choice game. ■ Discuss reactions to the game. *ABOUT 10 MINUTES*	■ Read the Scripture story. ■ Discuss the Scripture story. *ABOUT 12 MINUTES*	■ Complete a writing activity. ■ Compare temptations. *ABOUT 8 MINUTES*
Day 3	■ Study the photographs. ■ Analyze temptations. *ABOUT 8 MINUTES*	■ Read about sin and temptation. ■ Learn the vocabulary. ■ Understand the doctrine. *ABOUT 10 MINUTES*	■ Recognize the difference between sin and temptation. ■ Sing together. *ABOUT 12 MINUTES*
Day 4	■ Identify changing choices. *ABOUT 8 MINUTES*	■ Understand our freedom to make choices. *ABOUT 8 MINUTES*	■ Write story maps. ■ Review previous lessons. *ABOUT 14 MINUTES*

Day 5 **Prayer** Read about psalms as prayer; pray a psalm silently; sing together; and pray together.
Review Study the illustration; review the chapter; and reflect on the Scripture verse.

Plan Ahead ~~~~~~~~

Preparing Your Class	**Materials Needed**

Day 1 Read through the entire lesson plan. If you choose to have the students dramatize the story, be sure to give very specific directions.

- pencils or pens
- stickers
- lined paper

Day 2 Read the lesson plan. Make all necessary preparations for playing the game in Step 1.

- pencils or pens
- long and short straws
- one small prize for each student

Day 3 Read through the entire lesson plan. If you choose to do the Enriching the Lesson activity, make all the necessary preparations. Begin teaching "You Call Us to Live."

- pencils or pens
- THIS IS OUR FAITH hymnals

Day 4 Read through the lesson plan.

- pencils or pens
- THIS IS OUR FAITH hymnals

Day 5 Read through the entire lesson plan. Review the song "You Call Us to Live." Gather copies of the THIS IS OUR FAITH *Hymnal.*

- pencils or pens
- prayer cloth
- candle, Bible
- THIS IS OUR FAITH hymnals

Additional Resources

As you plan this chapter, consider using the following materials from The Resourceful Teacher Package.

- *Classroom Activity Sheets 3* and *3a*
- *Family Activity Sheets 3* and *3a*
- *Chapter 3 Test*
- *Prayers for Every Day*
- *Projects: Grade 4*

You may also wish to refer to the following Big Book.

- *We Celebrate God's Word,* page 23

In preparing the students for the Sunday readings, you may wish to use Silver Burdett Ginn's *Getting Ready for Sunday* student and teacher materials.

BOOKS FOR THE JOURNEY

The Children's Illustrated Bible. "The Temptations in the Wilderness," pp. 204–205. Retold by Selina Hastings. Dorling Kindersley, 1994. The story of Jesus' temptation in the desert with additional illustrations and information.

The Golden Carp. "The Ogre's Victim," pp. 29–49. Lynette Dyer Vuong. Lothrop, Lee & Shepard, 1993. A story about two young men—one consistently chooses what is wrong and the other chooses what is right, with consequences for both.

MORE BOOKS FOR THE JOURNEY

South and North East and West. "The Lion and the Hare," pp. 53–57. Edited by Michael Rosen. Candlewick Press, 1992. A fable about gullibility and trickery.

Hey World, Here I Am! "Maybe a Fight," pp. 11–12. Jean Little. Harper & Row, 1986. A delightful poem about wanting to fight but not wanting to deal with the consequences and being helped to make a friendly exchange of feelings.

REDUCED CLASSROOM ACTIVITIES

NAME _____

CHOICES TO MAKE

WANTED: Fourth-grade student to proofread story from Scripture. Must understand how the Tempter tempted Jesus as well as how Jesus responded. Must be able to find mistakes in text. Correct and rewrite each sample below and submit to teacher or parent for approval.

1. The Tempter appeared to Jesus after Jesus had been feasting for over a month.
   The Tempter appeared to Jesus after Jesus had been *fasting* for over a month.

2. Jesus said to the Tempter, "We don't live on dread alone, but on God's words."
   Jesus said to the Tempter, "We don't live on *bread* alone, but on God's words."

3. The Tempter wanted Jesus to change bread into stones, to Temple from the top of the jump, and to bow down and worship the Temple.
   The Tempter wanted Jesus to change bread into stones, to *jump* from the top of the *Temple*, and to bow down and worship the Tempter.

4. Jesus told the Tempter, "You will not tend the Lord your God."
   Jesus told the Tempter, "You will not *tempt* the Lord your God."

5. Jesus was tempted but he never sent. He never turned away from God.
   Jesus was tempted but he never *sinned*. He never turned away from God.

To the Teacher: This activity follows the Scripture story "Jesus Is Tempted."

Chapter 3 Choices to Make   THIS IS OUR FAITH 4 **3**

NAME _____

JESUS FIGHTS TEMPTATION

Use the words below to complete the poem. Then color the banner.

| heights | true | said | nights |
| bread | heard | too | word |

Jesus had been fasting
For forty days and _nights_
He suddenly saw the Tempter
Standing on the _heights_ .

The Tempter stood near Jesus,
And he quietly _said_ ,
"If you are the Son of God,
Change these stones into _bread_ ."

Jesus answered the Tempter
Loud enough to be _heard_ ,
"We don't live on bread alone,
But on God's _word_ ."

If we pray to Jesus,
When tempted not to be _true_ ,
He will surely help us,
For he was tempted, _too_ .

To the Teacher: This activity underscores the meaning of the Scripture story.

3a THIS IS OUR FAITH 4   Chapter 3 Choices to Make

Background for the Teacher

MAKING DECISIONS

Each day, fourth graders have choices to make. They can choose to help at home or ignore requests for help. They can help a classmate or laugh at his or her plight. At times they act hurtfully, with forethought or with little regard for the consequences of their actions. They feel the pull of temptation and sometimes yield to it or resist it. The story of Sarah will help them realize that to be tempted is not unusual, nor is it bad. Temptation is part of everyone's life. Jesus was tempted in the same way we all are. He relived the test of faith that the Israelites often underwent in the desert.

One of the greatest gifts that God has given us human beings is the ability to choose for ourselves. God does not move us around like chess pieces in the game of life, rather he loves us faithfully and cares for us patiently as we make our life choices. Even Mary, the mother of Jesus, was invited to make a choice. Her acceptance, "Be it done unto me according to your word," is a great example of the freedom to choose given so graciously by a generous God.

OVERCOMING TEMPTATION

After a conversion experience, we, like Jesus and the Israelites, often undergo temptation. The Holy Spirit led Jesus into the desert where he was tempted. The first temptation of Jesus after his forty-day fast involved food.

Here food represents the temptation to be satisfied by the material world. Jesus said, "Man does not live on bread alone." Jesus was emptying himself of all that could tie him to this world.

The next temptation—that Jesus cast himself down for the Father's rescue—was religious temptation. When we bargain with God, expecting him to fulfill our demands, saying things like, "If you help me pass this exam, I'll choose what is good," then we succumb to this temptation. The only question God asks at the end of our earthly days is, "How well did you love?"

The third temptation of Jesus was political. The Tempter promised Jesus everything if he would bow before him. Jesus replied that we worship only God. Jesus came to redeem us from the powers of darkness. He could have bowed to the Tempter, but he entertained no compromise measures. Unlike the Israelites and ourselves, Jesus never sinned. So we can confidently ask for his grace to strengthen us in times of temptation (see Hebrews 4:15–16).

Seeing Jesus tempted and overcoming temptation can help the students identify with him. His victory can help them draw on him for the strength to choose good. Be supportive of the students for the times they have resisted temptation. Your praise, coupled with hope of Jesus' help, will enable them to see that they can choose a life of love.

Objective

This lesson helps the students understand that we are all tempted.

Step 1 / INTRODUCTION

Learning About Our Lives

Talking About Good Deeds

If you have opted to do the "Doers of Good Deeds" activity, invite the students to talk about any good deed they may have done during the week. Supply stickers for them to place on the poster.

Introducing the Chapter

Ask the students to open their texts to page 32 and read the chapter title. Discuss the focus question. Help the class understand that making a choice between right and wrong is sometimes difficult.

Step 2 / DEVELOPMENT

Learning About Our Faith

Reading the Story and Writing a Story Ending

Select volunteers to read aloud the story "Sarah's Temptation" on pages 32 and 33. Encourage the students to work independently to write an ending for the story. When finished, encourage them to read what they have written to the class. Then focus a discussion on their reasons for ending the story the way they did.

Discussing the Story

Ask the students to think about Sarah's temptation. As you discuss the story, ask the class what we can learn from it. In this discussion, reaffirm why stealing is wrong. Emphasize that all people have certain rights with respect to their possessions. Ask:

- What was Sarah tempted to do? (*Steal a headband*)
- How was Sarah pulled toward something wrong? (*She wanted a headband and even though she knew it was wrong, she was tempted to steal it.*)
- Did Sarah sin? (*No*)

32

3

How do you choose between right and wrong?

Choices to Make

Sarah's Temptation

Sarah's mom asked Sarah to go with her to the mall. "You need new jeans," she said. "You can invite a friend if you want."

Sarah invited Jenny, who said she could be ready in fifteen minutes. It was always fun to go to the mall.

When they got to the mall, they looked at jeans and jackets, but Sarah's eyes were drawn to a headband in the next aisle. When her mom was not looking, Sarah whispered to Jenny, "I just love that headband! I want it, but I know my mom won't buy it for me."

Jenny glanced over at the headbands. She noticed that no one was working behind the counter. A couple of minutes later, she whispered back to Sarah, "While your mom is paying for your jeans, let's take a couple of headbands. They're cool. Nobody will see us."

🍎 Teaching Tips

Fourth graders do not yet have the moral development nor the life experience necessary for making some of the choices they may face. Assist their moral development by allowing them the opportunity to consider in advance, and in the security of their class setting, some of the choices which fourth graders must make.

★ Enriching the Lesson ★

Divide the class into groups of four. Have each group read the story quietly together and decide on an ending. Then invite each group to dramatize their version of the story. To keep the boys in your class involved, suggest that they change the story so that the central characters are male. Ask them to change the temptation from a headband to a video game.

Sarah's mom looked at her watch. "It's getting late," she said, "I'll pay for the jeans."

"We'll stay right here," Sarah said. "Jenny wants to look at more jeans."

Sarah's mom agreed, since the cash register was close by and the store was almost empty.

"Now's our chance," Jenny said, tugging on Sarah's arm. "Your mom has her back to us. In two seconds the headbands will be ours."

Sarah thought for a second longer and then she

_____

_____

_____

_____

Temptation in Our Lives

Everyone is tempted. We are tempted when something that we know is wrong looks very inviting to us. We may be drawn to act in a way that is wrong, or we may be tempted to say something we know is wrong. We may even find that we are attracted to people who always seem to get into trouble.

A **temptation** is an attraction to think, say, or do something we know is wrong. When we are tempted, we are *attracted* to do something wrong.

Everyone is tempted at some time to think, say, or do things that are wrong. Even Jesus was tempted. Jesus fought against his temptations. With his help, we can, too.

Vocabulary

temptation: an attraction to think, say, or do something we know is wrong

● ● ● ● ● ● ● ● ● ● ● ●

Morality 33

★ ★★★ ★
Enriching the Lesson ★

Invite the students to bow their heads and pray together. Have them repeat the following prayer after you. "O God, help me to overcome temptation. Help me to choose what is right. Stay close to me. Amen."

Reading About Temptation

Read through "Temptation in Our Lives" on page 33. Help the students understand that temptation happens when it is easier or more inviting for us to make a wrong choice than it is to make a right choice.

Presenting the Vocabulary

Present the definition of the word *temptation*. Have the class repeat it together.

Step 3 / CONCLUSION

Learning How to Live Our Faith

Discussing Temptations

Using the following questions to help the students understand that at times we have all been tempted to do something wrong.

■ When have you, like Sarah, felt torn between choosing to do what is right and what is wrong?

■ What influenced you to choose between right and wrong?

or . . .

On writing paper, ask the students to make a list of all the choices they have made that day. Encourage them to include the most simple choices, such as choosing one brand of cereal over another, as well as the more important choices they have made. Point out that making choices is something we do frequently and that sometimes we must choose between right and wrong. Help the class conclude that making moral decisions is more difficult than making everyday choices.

Naming Temptations

Ask the students to think of three different temptations that might be experienced by fourth graders. Poll the class and make a list of all the temptations. Discuss each temptation with the class, noting the most common responses. Explain that all the acts described are wrong. You might want to give specific examples of these acts to enable the students to appreciate that sometimes it can be difficult to choose what is right.

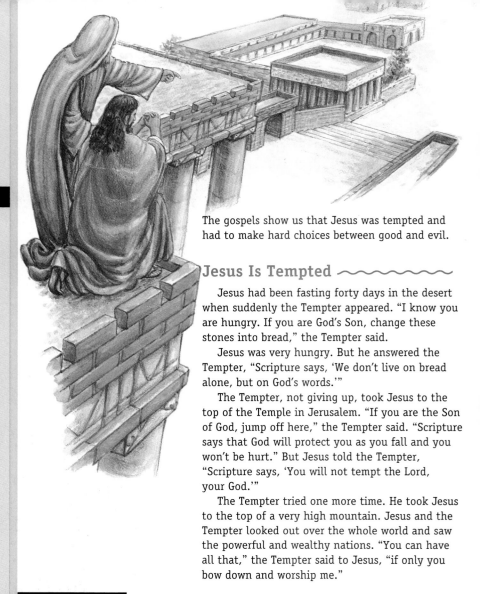

DAY 2
SCRIPTURE

Objective

This lesson helps the students identify ways in which Jesus was tempted.

Step 1 / INTRODUCTION

Learning About Our Lives

Playing a Choice Game

Distribute straws you prepared before class. Give each student one long straw and one short straw. Suggest that each student find a partner and take turns drawing straws. Tell the class that everyone who drew a long straw can come to your desk and receive a small prize.

Discussing Reactions to the Game

When the children have finished drawing straws and receiving prizes, discuss the game using the following questions.

■ How did you decide which straw to draw?

■ Were you happy with your choice?

■ Would you make the same choice again? Why or why not?

Ask the students if they can think of how this choice game fits in with the lesson. Help them recall the chapter title, "Choices to Make." Then give prizes to all the students who have not yet received any.

Step 2 / DEVELOPMENT

Learning About Our Faith

Reading the Scripture Story

Direct the students' attention to the Scripture story on pages 34 and 35. Explain that fasting means to go without food for a certain period of time. Jesus went to the desert for forty days and nights to pray and fast. He was preparing himself to tell people about God. Invite the volunteers to read aloud "Jesus Is Tempted."

Discussing the Scripture Story

Use the following questions to discuss the story.

■ What did the Tempter ask Jesus to do first? (*Change stones into bread*)

■ How did Jesus answer the Tempter? (*He said we don't live on bread alone.*)

34

The gospels show us that Jesus was tempted and had to make hard choices between good and evil.

Jesus Is Tempted

Jesus had been fasting forty days in the desert when suddenly the Tempter appeared. "I know you are hungry. If you are God's Son, change these stones into bread," the Tempter said.

Jesus was very hungry. But he answered the Tempter, "Scripture says, 'We don't live on bread alone, but on God's words.'"

The Tempter, not giving up, took Jesus to the top of the Temple in Jerusalem. "If you are the Son of God, jump off here," the Tempter said. "Scripture says that God will protect you as you fall and you won't be hurt." But Jesus told the Tempter, "Scripture says, 'You will not tempt the Lord, your God.'"

The Tempter tried one more time. He took Jesus to the top of a very high mountain. Jesus and the Tempter looked out over the whole world and saw the powerful and wealthy nations. "You can have all that," the Tempter said to Jesus, "if only you bow down and worship me."

34 Scripture

★ Enriching the Lesson ★

Have the students pray The Lord's Prayer silently to recall the line that speaks of temptation. Remind the class that Jesus taught his followers this prayer to pray to his Father. Help the students appreciate that Jesus recognized that everyone needs God's help in overcoming temptation. Conclude by inviting the students to pray the last two lines of The Lord's Prayer together.

Jesus answered, "Go away! Scripture says, 'You will only worship the Lord, your God.'"

The Tempter left as suddenly as he had come. Jesus had overcome the temptations.

Based on Matthew 4:1–11

Activity

The Tempter wanted Jesus to use his power in wrong ways. What were the three temptations that Jesus faced?

1. change stones into bread

2. jump off the Temple in Jerusalem

3. worship the Tempter

Jesus used strong words to answer the Tempter. Give an example of some words you might use when you are tempted.

_____

_____

Scripture 35

Focus on
★ ★ ★ ★

Tempting God The *Catechism of the Catholic Church* explains that tempting God is a sin of irreligion and goes against the first commandment. It consists of "putting his goodness and almighty power to the test by word or deed. Thus Satan tried to induce Jesus to throw himself down from the Temple and, by this gesture, force God to act. Jesus opposed Satan with the word of God . . . The challenge contained in such tempting of God wounds the respect and trust we owe our Creator and Lord" (# 2119).

Enriching the Lesson

Help the students recognize that Jesus overcame temptation. Help them understand why he was able to do so. The woman in the garden story presented in Chapter 2 chose to be selfish by giving in to temptation. Lead the class to see that if we acquire something through selfish actions, it will turn out badly for us. Emphasize that a temptation is not the same as a sin, or actual wrong-doing. Overcoming temptation makes us strong.

- What do the words of Jesus mean? (*To live as God wants us to; we obey God's word.*)
- Where did the Tempter take Jesus? (*To the top of the Temple in Jerusalem*)
- What did he want Jesus to do? (*Jump off*)
- How did Jesus answer him? (*He quoted Scripture: "You will not tempt the Lord, your God."*)
- What does that mean to you? (*Do not ask God to help you do stupid or dangerous things.*)
- What was the Tempter's last trick? (*He told Jesus he would give him everything in the world if Jesus would worship him.*)
- What did Jesus say? (*Told him to go away! We only worship the Lord, our God.*)
- What can we learn from this story? (*To keep saying "no" to temptation*)

Emphasize that Jesus was able to overcome the temptations because he had been praying to God. Ask the students to suggest other ways to overcome temptation. Ask them to think about this same story taking place in today's world. What would the Tempter offer Jesus? Where would he take Jesus?

Step 3 / CONCLUSION

Learning How to Live Our Faith

Completing an Activity

Give the students time to complete the activity. After they have finished, encourage sharing. Focus a discussion on the words the students might use when faced with temptation. Encourage them to use these words when tempted.

Comparing Temptations

Compare the temptations of Jesus with the temptation of the woman in the garden in Chapter 2. Help the students make the following points. Jesus prayed to God for forty days and forty nights before battling with the Tempter. He was prepared to be strong. The Tempter in the garden lied to the woman. The woman believed the lie. The Tempter lies, but Jesus does not pay attention to what he says. Jesus repeats the truth. The woman is tempted once and gives in. Jesus is tempted three times, about different things, but he does not give in. When the Tempter realizes Jesus will not give in, he goes away. If we say "no" to temptation, it goes away.

35

Objective

This lesson helps the students understand temptation and realize that we sin only when we choose to turn from God.

Step 1 / INTRODUCTION

Learning About Our Lives

Studying the Photographs

Call attention to the photograph on page 36 and have volunteers describe what is happening in the photograph. Discuss other situations in which people may be tempted to do something wrong. After the discussion, point out that the situations they described all present a choice. When we decide to do what is right, we usually feel good about the decision.

Analyzing Temptations

Read aloud the directions to the activity. After the students have finished the checklist, discuss each of the temptations with the class, having the students compare answers. Poll the students on which of these temptations are the most challenging. Emphasize that giving in to any one of these temptations would be wrong. Encourage the students to pray to God for strength to resist temptation, as Jesus did.

Step 2 / DEVELOPMENT

Learning About Our Faith

Understanding Sin and Temptation

Read aloud "Temptation and Sin" as the students follow along silently. Review the definition of *temptation* by writing it on the chalkboard. Ask the class to repeat its definition after you. Ask them to consider how we are made like God. Discuss what it means to feel the hurt of original sin. Lead the class to see how selfish actions can lead to harmful results. When we choose not to love God, we are also choosing not to love ourselves. Clarify the difference between sin, or actual wrong-doing, and temptation.

Reviewing the Vocabulary

Have the students repeat the definition for the word *sin*. Read the definition aloud with them. Then have the students memorize the definition.

36

Activity

Check the temptations that are real for you.

1. _____ To be mean to someone because I don't like him or her

2. _____ To refuse to do what my parents tell me to do

3. _____ To cheat on a test

4. _____ To lie so that I won't be punished

5. _____ To do something I know is wrong so that others will like me

Temptation and Sin

Our world is good, but evil hurts it. Though we are made like God, we feel the effects of original sin.

We are called to love God as we love ourselves and to love all people and things around us. But sometimes something can seem so good that we will do anything to get it. We become willing to do what we know is wrong, and we act selfishly. When we choose in this way to turn away from God, we **sin**. When we sin we are choosing not to love, or we are failing to do what we know we should do.

Temptation is not a sin. Jesus was tempted, as we are, but he never sinned. He chose never to turn away from God or God's way of life.

Teaching Tips

All children value choice. Even when neither of the choices presented to them is seen as particularly desirable, most children still prefer to have some voice in making a decision. Recognizing this, we can more appropriately address this chapter with the students in our classes.

Activity

Mark each of the following with a **T** if you think the person was only tempted. Mark each with an **S** if you think the person might have sinned.

____T____ Rebecca got an F on her report card. She thought about lying to her parents about it but changed her mind.

____S____ Roberto's teacher was sick at home with the flu. Roberto was extremely disruptive in class, making it very difficult for his classmates to learn or for the substitute teacher to teach.

____S____ At the store, Mark took some candy bars when the clerk wasn't looking.

____T____ A girl at school continued to make fun of Shamina. Shamina thought about calling the girl some bad names to get back at her. She decided to walk away.

____T____ Tong's brother accidentally gave him a bloody nose when they were fooling around. Tong was ready to hit him back to get even. Tong stopped for a minute and decided not to hit his brother.

Give one example of a temptation.

_____

_____

Give one example of a sin.

_____

_____

Doctrine **37**

Presenting the Doctrine

Present the We Believe statements. Discuss with the students how Jesus Christ can help us overcome temptation. Help them conclude that we can pray to Jesus to ask for the strength to say "no" to temptation. Point out that strength also comes from praying The Lord's Prayer.

Step 3 / CONCLUSION

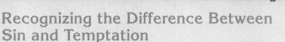

Learning How to Live Our Faith

Recognizing the Difference Between Sin and Temptation

Read aloud the directions to the activity on page 37. Give the students time to complete the activity individually. When the students have finished, ask them to share their answers in small groups of four or five. Check to see if there were any differences in opinion among group members. Review the activity with the entire class, to be sure that all students understand the difference between sin and temptation. Take time to answer any questions the students may have.

Singing Together

Distribute copies of the THIS IS OUR FAITH *Hymnal.* Begin teaching the song "You Call Us to Live," found on page 123 of the hymnal, so that the students will know it well by Day 5.

DAY 4
DOCTRINE

Objective

This lesson helps the students appreciate that, like Jesus, they can overcome temptation.

Step 1 / INTRODUCTION

Learning About Our Lives

Identifying Changing Choices

Ask the students to write how the kinds of choices they have had to make have changed as they have grown. Ask them to complete these sentences that you have written on the chalkboard: *When I was two years old I could make choices about . . . When I was six years old, I could make choices about . . .* and *As a fourth grader I can make choices about . . .* Then give the students time to write down all their ideas. Ask for volunteers to share their responses with the entire class. Help the students to see that as we grow older we are continually faced with challenging new choices to make and temptations to overcome.

Step 2 / DEVELOPMENT

Learning About Our Faith

Understanding Our Freedom to Make Choices

Call on volunteers to read aloud "Freedom to Choose" on page 38. Use the following questions to guide the discussion.

- What is one of the gifts that God has given us? (*The freedom to choose*)

- Why does our government enforce laws? (*To keep us safe in our communities*)

- Why do families set rules? (*To keep us safe and happy, and to help us make good choices*)

- What do you think the rules are that God gives us that you will be learning about in the chapters ahead? (*Answers may vary.*)

- Because of our freedom of choice, what will we always be faced with? (*Temptation*)

Freedom to Choose

One of the gifts God has given us is our freedom to choose. We can choose good instead of evil, and we can choose right instead of wrong. As we grow up, we will be able to make more and more choices for ourselves.

Even though God gives us freedom to choose, rules can guide our choices. For instance, our government gives us rules called laws. These laws are meant to keep us safe in our communities.

Our families also give us rules to live by because they love us. These rules are meant to keep us safe and happy and to help us make good choices.

Out of love for us, God also gives us rules that affect our freedom to choose. In the next weeks and months, we will learn more about God's rules.

Because we have the freedom to make choices, we can always be tempted to make the wrong choices. So as we grow and are able to make more choices for ourselves, we need to be ready to face temptations. When faced with temptation we can make good choices. We can choose to ask someone to help us. We can turn our attention away from the temptation and toward other things. We can also choose to remember that Jesus is with us.

38 Doctrine

★ ★★★ ★
Enriching the Lesson
★ ★

Discuss with the students what they can do when they are tempted to do something wrong. Three possible strategies are listed below.

- Think about something else.
- Ask a parent, friend, or sibling for help.
- Say a prayer, asking Jesus for help.

Activity

Look carefully at the photograph. Imagine yourself as the person being tempted. Think about how you feel, what you are drawn to, what you want, and what you could do. Then write two story maps, one in which you give in to temptation and the other in which you overcome it. In both story maps, write the outcomes of your choices and actions.

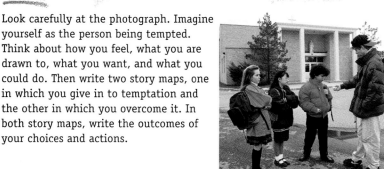

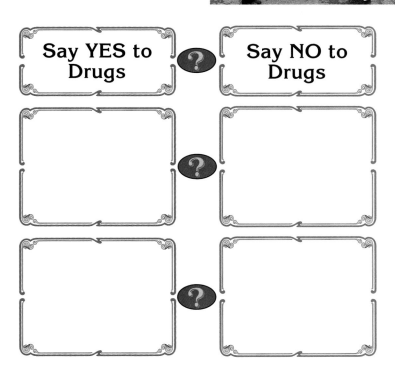

Say YES to Drugs

?

Say NO to Drugs

?

?

Learning How to Live Our Faith

Writing Story Maps

Remind the students that temptations are experienced by everyone. Assist them in understanding that Jesus can help us overcome the temptation to do what is wrong.

Read through the directions to the activity on page 39 with the class. Before having the students begin their story maps, make sure they have a full understanding of what is happening in the photograph. If there is any doubt, clarify that the teenager is trying to sell drugs to the younger children. Then have the students work independently to complete the activity by writing steps that tell the story for each choice. As they work, move around the room, commenting on their work and offering suggestions. When the students have finished, invite volunteers to share their story maps.

Reviewing Previous Lessons

Recall with the students that, like them, Jesus was tempted. Ask:

■ How did Jesus overcome temptation? (*He prayed.*)

■ How can you overcome temptation? (*Answers will vary.*)

Focus on

Overcoming Temptation The *Catechism of the Catholic Church* explains that "our sins result from our consenting to temptation." When we pray The Lord's Prayer we "ask our Father not to 'lead' us into temptation . . . 'God is faithful, and he will not let you be tempted beyond your strength, but with the temptation will also provide the way of escape, so that you may be able to endure it.'" The victory over temptation becomes "possible only through prayer" (#2846, 2848–2849).

Enriching the Lesson

Remind the students that as a class they are making a special effort to do good deeds this week. Encourage them to think of others first. Saying a kind word can be one way to be helpful.

Objective

This lesson helps the students learn that a psalm is another kind of prayer and helps them experience praying a psalm for strength to resist temptation.

Reading About the Psalms as Prayer

Ask for volunteers to read aloud "Praying the Psalms" on page 40. Guide the students' comprehension of this passage about the psalms as prayer by asking the following questions.

- According to tradition, who wrote the psalms? (*King David*)
- At Mass, when is a responsorial psalm sung? (*During the Liturgy of the Word*)
- What are some of the ways a psalm can be prayed? (*Singing the psalms; praying memorized lines over and over; reading aloud the psalms with others; choosing and praying a specific psalm for a specific reason*)

Praying a Psalm Silently

Have the class look at page 40 and pray silently the psalm that asks God's help in time of temptation. Point out that this prayer is based on Psalm 22:12, 20.

Singing Together

Review with the students "You Call Us to Live" on page 123 of the THIS IS OUR FAITH *Hymnal.*

Praying Together

Invite the students to bring their books and gather at the prayer table for prayer. Speak about the reality of temptation in our world. Remind them that God will always help them in times of temptation. Invite the class to pray aloud the psalm on page 40. Afterward, offer a brief prayer of thanks such as, "Thank you for being with us, Lord, to help us choose good over evil." Conclude by singing "You Call Us to Live," verses 3 and 4.

Praying the Psalms

People of the Jewish and Christian faiths have been praying the psalms for thousands of years. The psalms are prayer songs that were written for many different occasions and reasons. They were probably used most often when Jews gathered to pray at the Temple in Jerusalem.

We hear a psalm sung during the Liturgy of the Word each Sunday. We call it the Responsorial Psalm.

Singing the psalms is only one way psalms can be prayed. We can pray the psalms by

- memorizing a few lines of a favorite psalm and praying the words over and over.

- joining others and reading the psalm aloud; taking turns reading the verses.

- choosing a psalm to pray for a specific reason, such as Psalm 43: A Prayer to God in Time of Trouble.

The psalm below is a psalm that asks God's help in overcoming temptation. Pray it in a way that is most comfortable for you. You might want to copy the psalm onto a small index card and place it where you will see it often.

> Lord, be with me and help me,
> for I must choose.
> Be with me and help me.
>
> *Based on Psalm 22:11,19*

★ ★★★ ★
Enriching the Lesson

Refer back to the checklist on page 36. Ask the students to choose one of the temptations and to draw a story about someone their age experiencing this temptation. Suggest that they include a drawing of the decision that is made.

Chapter Review

Look at the picture. Write the answers to the questions below.

1. What is the person being tempted to do?

_____

2. How can this person overcome temptation?

_____

_____

Write the answers to the first two questions.

1. What is the difference between temptation and sin?

Temptation is not a sin. We sin only when we choose to give in to temptation

and turn away from God.

2. How can we know that we can overcome temptation?

Jesus was tempted just as we are, but he never sinned.

He overcame temptation. We believe that Jesus is

with us in our fight against temptation.

3. Discuss some ways in which we can fight against temptation.

> God says, "I give you a choice between good and evil. Choose to follow my ways."
> Based on Deuteronomy 30:19 – 20

Studying the Illustration

Have the students look at the illustration on page 41. Then have them write their answers to the two questions above it. Go over the answers with the class.

Reviewing the Chapter

Review the important content of this chapter by having the students fill in the answers to the two questions at the bottom of page 41. When the students have finished, check their responses. Clarify any questions they may have at this point. Discuss the third item and encourage all of the students to express their ideas.

Reflecting on the Scripture Verse

Ask a volunteer to read aloud the Scripture verse on page 41. Tell the class that in these words from the Bible, God is telling us how to be happy. Explain that when we love God and follow his ways, we are choosing good over evil. Encourage the students to memorize the Scripture verse.

Teaching Tips

To help any fine-motor impaired student that you may have in your class complete the Enriching the Lesson activity on this page, have both circles pre-cut before class. Pair the students, so that a buddy can assist the fine-motor impaired child to print the slogan on the circles and tape the safety pin to the back of the cardboard circle.

Enriching the Lesson

Have the students make buttons expressing the theme of Chapter 3. Provide cardboard, craft paper, several compasses, safety pins, glue, felt-tip markers, masking tape, and scissors. Have the students follow these directions: Use a compass to draw a circle on cardboard and one on craft paper; cut out both circles; write a slogan about Chapter 3 on the craft paper circle and glue it to the cardboard circle; tape the safety pin securely to the back of the cardboard circle.

4 Choosing What Is Good

Objectives ~~~~~~~~

To help the students

■ Learn that their conscience helps them choose between right and wrong.

■ Recognize that the Holy Spirit is with us to help us choose what is good.

■ Recognize that the Holy Spirit has guided Christians in the past.

■ Learn how to make a good choice.

■ Learn to pray a traditional prayer to the Holy Spirit and review the chapter.

Chapter Outline ~~~~~~~~~~

	Step 1 **Learning About Our Lives**	**Step 2** **Learning About Our Faith**	**Step 3** **Learning How to Live Our Faith**
Day 1	■ Report good deeds. ■ Review the previous lesson. ■ Introduce the chapter. ■ Study the illustration. *ABOUT 10 MINUTES*	■ Read and discuss the text. ■ Learn the vocabulary. *ABOUT 10 MINUTES*	■ Role-play and complete an activity. *ABOUT 10 MINUTES*
Day 2	■ Review Day 1. ■ Talk about fears. *ABOUT 8 MINUTES*	■ Read the Scripture story. ■ Discuss the Scripture story. ■ Recall the promise of Jesus. *ABOUT 12 MINUTES*	■ Find courage to do the right thing. ■ Pray together. *ABOUT 10 MINUTES*
Day 3	■ Find articles about bravery. ■ Share experiences of bravery. *ABOUT 12 MINUTES*	■ Read and discuss the story. ■ Identify signs of the Spirit. ■ Understand the doctrine. *ABOUT 12 MINUTES*	■ Analyze a photograph. *ABOUT 6 MINUTES*
Day 4	■ Share some choices that we have made. *ABOUT 8 MINUTES*	■ Learn how to make a good choice. *ABOUT 10 MINUTES*	■ Practice making good choices. *ABOUT 12 MINUTES*

Day 5 **Prayer** Read about traditional prayers; understand a traditional prayer; pray together; and listen to a song.

Review Review the chapter; order decision-making steps; answer the questions; and reflect on the Scripture verse.

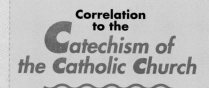

Plan Ahead ～～～～～～

	Preparing Your Class	**Materials Needed**
Day 1	Read through the entire lesson plan. If you choose to do the Enriching the Lesson activity, make all the necessary preparations.	■ pencils or pens ■ stickers
Day 2	Read the lesson plan. If you choose to use the Enriching the Lesson activity, make all the necessary preparations.	■ pencils or pens ■ lined paper ■ candle
Day 3	Read through the entire lesson plan. Review the song "Grow Strong" if you opt to do the Curriculum Connection activity.	■ pencils or pens ■ newspapers and magazines
Day 4	Read through the lesson plan. Review the song "Spirit, Move" if you opt to do the Curriculum Connection activity. Make necessary preparations if enriching the lesson.	■ pencils or pens
Day 5	Read through the entire lesson plan. Choose a song about the Holy Spirit that can be used with prayer or use "Pentecost Prayer" from THIS IS OUR FAITH *Hymnal.*	■ pencils or pens ■ prayer cloth ■ candle, Bible ■ copies of THIS IS OUR FAITH *Hymnal*

Additional Resources

As you plan this chapter, consider using the following materials from The Resourceful Teacher Package.

■ *Classroom Activity Sheets 4 and 4a*

■ *Family Activity Sheets 4 and 4a*

■ *Chapter 4 Test*

■ *Prayers for Every Day*

■ *Projects: Grade 4*

You may also wish to refer to the following Big Book.

■ *We Celebrate God's Word,* page 21

In preparing the students for the Sunday readings, you may wish to use Silver Burdett Ginn's *Getting Ready for Sunday* student and teacher materials.

BOOKS FOR THE JOURNEY

The Glory Field. Walter Dean Myers. Scholastic, Inc., 1994. A powerful story of a family making incredible choices for freedom and of one member making a profoundly unselfish choice for his cousin.

Tell Me the Bible. "A New Breath," pp. 100–101. Joëlle Chabert and François Mourvillier. The Liturgical Press, 1991. The story of Pentecost with fascinating illustrations.

MORE BOOKS FOR THE JOURNEY

Experience Jesus Today. "Pentecost," pp. 223–227. Charles Singer & Albert Hari. Oregon Catholic Press, 1993. The story of Pentecost with additional information, illustrations, and a prayer to the Holy Spirit.

Hand in Hand. "Martin Luther King," p. 119. Collected by Lee Bennett Hopkins. Simon & Schuster, 1994. A poem describing the choices a man made that continue to make a difference in American history.

REDUCED CLASSROOM ACTIVITIES

NAME _____

CHOOSING WHAT IS GOOD

Use the words on the flames to complete the paragraphs.

It is not always _easy_ to choose what we know is _good_. Our _consciences_ can help us judge between good and evil.

When Jesus had difficult _choices_ to make, he did not turn away from God's _love_. He _overcame_ temptation.

Jesus sends us the Holy Spirit to be our _helper_ and our guide. The Holy Spirit helps us fight _temptation_. We can _pray_ to the Holy Spirit to help us.

flames: choices, pray, good, easy, temptation, overcame, conscience, helper, love

To the Teacher: This activity follows the Scripture story "The Story of Pentecost."

Chapter 4 Choosing What Is Good

THIS IS OUR FAITH 4 **4**

NAME _____

A CHALLENGING GAME

With a classmate, play this game of tic-tac-toe. One player will use an **X** and the other will use an **O**. Put an **X** on all the true statements. Put an **O** on all the false statements.

X Our consciences help us judge between good and evil.	O The Bible lists three signs to help us recognize that the Holy Spirit is with us.	O After Jesus died, the Apostles were not afraid.
O Jesus did not pray to God when he had to make choices.	X The Holy Spirit helps us make good choices.	X Jesus sends us the Holy Spirit to be our helper.
X Jesus overcame temptation.	X Jesus' friends felt strong and brave after the Holy Spirit came to them.	X With the Holy Spirit, we can be caring with one another.

To the Teacher: This page reviews the content of the chapter and provides a cooperative learning situation.

4a THIS IS OUR FAITH 4

Chapter 4 Choosing What Is Good

CHRISTIAN MORALITY

In this chapter the worldly view, with its expectations of instant pleasures, is contrasted with the Christian vision of acting justly despite hardship. The students live in a world where the two views frequently clash. Often choosing to act justly is difficult. Jesus is with us in the Holy Spirit to help guide us. The Holy Spirit is at the heart of Christian moral life. In the sacraments of Baptism and Confirmation, the Spirit is poured out on us. The Spirit helps us discern what God wants us to do in specific situations. As we use the gifts of the Spirit, our lives begin to yield a harvest of good works marked by signs, or fruits, of the Spirit.

CONSCIENCE FORMATION

The development of one's conscience is affected by many factors, including education, the example of others, the companions we choose, the ability to know one's self, an awareness of right and wrong, and our power to judge our own actions and the actions of others. *The National Catechetical Directory* says, "The central factor in the formation of conscience and sound moral judgment should be Christ's role in one's life. His ideals, precepts, and examples are present and accessible in Scripture and the tradition of the Church. To have a truly Christian conscience, one must faithfully communicate with God in every phase of one's life, above all through personal prayer and through participation in the sacramental life and prayer of the Church. All other aspects of conscience formation are based on this" (190).

Moral development is a lifelong process. In his extensive studies, Dr. Lawrence Kohlberg found that many people may progress through six stages of moral growth. Students in fourth grade are, according to Kohlberg, at stage 3 or 4. In stage 3, the desire for approval and belonging leads the child to conform to the expectations of the family and the community in order to be accepted. In stage 4, a sense of justice and a need for fairness develop. People at this stage also begin to see the need for having and obeying rules.

When faced with a moral decision, one should (1) reflect upon it in light of the teachings of Jesus; (2) seek the counsel and guidance of appropriate people; and (3) pray for the wisdom and courage to make the right choice. These steps can be especially helpful when faced with a serious moral question.

As you teach this chapter, the students will come to recognize that making good decisions is sometimes difficult. However, you can assure them that Jesus and the Holy Spirit are with them, helping them to choose what is good.

Objective

This lesson helps the students learn that their conscience helps them choose between right and wrong.

Step 1 / INTRODUCTION

Learning About Our Lives

Reporting Good Deeds

Invite the students to talk about any good deeds they may have done during the week. If you have been doing the "Doers of Good Deeds" activity, allow time for the students to apply stickers representing these deeds on the poster.

Reviewing the Previous Lesson

Briefly review with the students what was learned in the last lesson by asking the following questions.

■ What is temptation?

■ What is sin?

■ How can we overcome temptation?

Introducing the Chapter

Direct attention to page 42. Read aloud the chapter title and focus question. Allow time for the students to reflect on the difficult decisions they have had to make. Encourage them to tell the class about the choices they made and whether or not they think that they made good decisions.

Studying the Illustration

Read the activity directions aloud. Discuss with the students the choices that are being made by each skater. Help the students decide who in the illustration is acting with love and who is acting selfishly. Help the students understand that excluding others is a selfish action.

Step 2 / DEVELOPMENT

Learning About Our Faith

Reading and Discussing the Text

Ask volunteers to read aloud "Our Conscience Can Help" on page 43. Explain that *conscience* means our power to judge whether something

42

4 Choosing What Is Good

What is one of the most difficult choices you have ever had to make?

Activity

The children skateboarding in the picture above are making choices about the girl who wants to join them. What kinds of choices are the children making? Label each child with a word that describes his or her choice.

Enriching the Lesson

Spend some time discussing the importance of developing our conscience. Tell the class that our conscience is a vital gift from God because it alerts us to situations and actions that could have serious consequences on our lives and on the lives of others. Listening to our conscience helps us speak and act in loving ways instead of hurtful, sinful ways.

Cultural Awareness

Discuss why the children in the illustration may have wanted to exclude the girl. Explain that they may have excluded her simply because she is different. Ask the students if it is fair to judge others without knowing them. Encourage the class to consider ways they can welcome people who are sometimes excluded because they are "different."

Our Conscience Can Help

Choosing can be difficult. But our **conscience,** or power to judge between good and bad, can help us. It is not always easy to choose what we know is good. We may be very sure of what we should do, but we still might find it hard to do. Sometimes we want to do what we know is wrong. In spite of our conscience, we decide that we don't want to choose what is good.

Activity

A TV reporter met people passing by on a busy street corner. The question she asked each person was this: "Why do you think people sometimes choose to do what is wrong?"

Here are some answers.

- "Probably they think their friends will laugh at them if they choose what is right."
- "Because they didn't think they would ever get caught."
- "People will do just about anything for money."
- "It feels good. It's fun."

Write your answer on the lines below.

_____

_____

_____

_____

_____

_____

_____

Vocabulary

conscience: our power to judge whether something is good or bad

• • • • • • • • • • • •

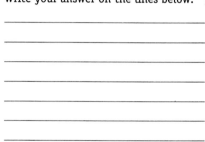

Enriching the Lesson

Distribute drawing paper and crayons or felt-tip markers. Invite the students to draw a two- or three-panel cartoon about someone making a choice with the help of their conscience. Afterward, invite sharing.

---

is good or bad. Discuss with the students situations in which they wanted to choose something they knew was not good. How did they make their decision? Read the following situations to the students and ask them to supply endings.

1. Ten-year-old Kevin had been told by his mother not to go to the glen because it is so dangerous. One day on his way home from school as he was passing the glen, he saw three of his friends playing ball in the glen with other boys. Kevin's mother would not get home until 5 o'clock. If he played ball for a while, his mother would never know.

2. Several boys were on their way to a Scout meeting. As they passed their friend Tim's house, they saw some objects shining on the ground. A closer look showed many silver dollars. They picked them up and rang the bell. There was no answer.

3. Susan did not finish her homework. She wanted to watch her favorite TV show. Her friend who was visiting finished all of Susan's homework for her.

Presenting the Vocabulary

Point out the Vocabulary box. Ask a volunteer to read the definition of *conscience* aloud. Answer any questions the students may have.

Step 3 / CONCLUSION ∿∿∿

Learning How to Live Our Faith

Role-playing and Completing an Activity

Ask the students if they have ever participated in an interview or if anyone has ever asked their opinion for a poll. Invite them to share the experiences they have had. Tell them that interviews and opinion polls help us learn what people feel about different things.

Ask the students to read silently the activity on page 43. Select eight volunteers to read it aloud, assigning one to narrate and four to take the first four parts. Have the remaining three students take turns answering orally for the role of the fourth grader. Then have all the students write their answers on the lines provided and then share their responses with the class.

Objective

This lesson helps the students recognize that the Holy Spirit is with us to help us know and choose what is good.

Step 1 / INTRODUCTION

Learning About Our Lives

Reviewing Day 1

Ask the students to identify their helper and guide in fighting against temptation. Recall that the Holy Spirit helps people choose good over evil.

Talking About Fears

Encourage the students to discuss times when they were frightened (for example: nightmares, being alone in the house, seeing a scary movie). Ask the students how they got over their fears. Explain that at one time or another, everyone is afraid. Tell the students that even the friends of Jesus were frightened.

Step 2 / DEVELOPMENT

Learning About Our Faith

Reading the Scripture Story

Direct the students to page 44 in their books. Ask them what they think is going on in the illustration. Invite three volunteers to read the story aloud, while the others read along silently.

Discussing the Scripture Story

When they have finished reading the Scripture story, discuss the story. Ask:

- What did the friends of Jesus want to do? (*Tell everyone about Jesus*)

- Why were they afraid to tell everyone about Jesus? (*They thought they would be killed.*)

- What kind of noise did they seem to hear? (*A strong wind*)

- What did they seem to see? (*Flames*)

- How did the friends of Jesus feel? (*Strong, brave, peaceful*)

- What did the friends of Jesus do? (*They told everyone about Jesus.*)

- Whom had Jesus sent? (*The Holy Spirit*)

44

The Story of Pentecost

It was a quiet morning in Jerusalem fifty days after Jesus died and was risen from the dead. Jesus' friends were together in a house. They locked the doors. They were afraid that if they went out into the streets they would be caught and killed, as Jesus had been. They prayed very hard.

Suddenly there was a noise. It sounded like a strong wind blowing all through the house. The friends saw flames that looked like tongues of fire moving around the room. The flames came to rest above each of Jesus' friends.

44   Scripture

 CURRICULUM CONNECTION

Language Arts   Have the students work in small groups of three or four to complete a creative writing activity. Direct them to think of a situation requiring that a moral choice be made and that a solution to the problem be suggested. Have each group write a skit that later will be acted out in the classroom.

Jesus' friends felt stronger and braver. Their fears seemed to disappear. They smiled as peace began to fill their hearts. Jesus' friends unlocked the doors. They went out to do what they had been afraid to do. They told everyone about Jesus. They knew that it was the Holy Spirit, promised by Jesus, who gave them their new courage, peace, and joy.

Based on Acts 2:1–4.

The Gift of the Holy Spirit

When Jesus had difficult choices to make, he did not turn away from God's love. Through the power of the Holy Spirit, Jesus overcame temptation. He promised to give us the Holy Spirit. The Holy Spirit comes to help and guide us in our fight against temptation, just as he first came to Jesus' followers on Pentecost.

Scripture 45

Focus on

The Gifts of the Spirit On the first Pentecost, the Holy Spirit gifted the disciples of Jesus with special gifts. These same gifts are given again to each of us in the sacrament of Confirmation. The gifts are *wisdom, understanding, knowledge, right judgment, courage, reverence,* and *wonder and awe.*

Recalling the Promise of Jesus

Help the students remember that Jesus promised to send the Holy Spirit to be with them always. Read to the class the promise Jesus made: "Do not be afraid. I will send you the Holy Spirit to be with you always" (based on John 14:16–18).

Ask a volunteer to read aloud "The Gift of the Holy Spirit" on page 45. Answer any questions the students may have.

Step 3 / CONCLUSION

Learning How to Live Our Faith

Finding Courage to Do the Right Thing

Distribute sheets of lined paper. Ask the students to give an example of a time someone their age was afraid to do the right thing. Ask: How could that person get the courage to do what is right? After the class has responded orally, give the students time to write their responses. When the students have finished, encourage them to share what they have written with the whole class.

Praying Together

Invite the students to form a prayer circle. If safety permits, light a candle. Tell the class that just as Jesus gave the Holy Spirit to his friends he also gives the Holy Spirit to all people to help in the fight against temptation. Note that just as the flames were a sign to the disciples that Jesus had kept his promise, the candle's flame is a sign that the Holy Spirit is present today. Encourage the students to carefully pass the candle around the circle. As the candle is passed from student to student, have each offer a brief prayer of thanksgiving for the Holy Spirit.

DAY 3
DOCTRINE

Objective

This lesson helps the students recognize that the Holy Spirit has guided Christians in the past.

Step 1 / INTRODUCTION

Learning About Our Lives

Finding Articles About Bravery

Divide the class into groups of three or four students. Give each group several newspapers and magazines. Have each group find one or two articles about bravery. Afterward, invite the groups to share their findings.

Sharing Experiences of Bravery

Discuss a time when the students were called upon to be strong or brave. Be supportive as the students relate their stories, emphasizing that bravery and strength have different meanings for each person.

Step 2 / DEVELOPMENT

Learning About Our Faith

Reading and Discussing the Story

Invite the students to read aloud "Two Brave Women" on page 46. Afterward, guide the students in a discussion using the following questions.

- Why were the women, Felicity and Perpetua, put in prison? (*They wanted to become Christians.*)
- Why were Felicity and Perpetua so afraid as they waited in the hot, dark prison? (*They were afraid that they would be beaten and killed.*)
- What temptation did the two women face? (*To turn away from Christ*)
- What happened to them because they said "no" to the temptation? (*They were killed.*)
- Why does the Church honor Perpetua and Felicity as saints? (*Because they were put to death because of their belief in Jesus Christ*)

Explain to the students that *martyrs* are people who die for their religious beliefs. Assist the students in understanding that the Holy Spirit helped Felicity and Perpetua avoid temptation.

46

Two Brave Women

It was the year 203 A.D. Two young women, Perpetua and Felicity, had a choice to make. And they had the Holy Spirit to help them make it.

Perpetua and Felicity were put in prison because they wanted to become Christians. The two women were afraid in the hot, dark prison. They feared they would be beaten and killed. They prayed for God's help.

Then Perpetua and Felicity were baptized. The Holy Spirit brought them great peace. They were no longer frightened.

Later the prison guards led Perpetua and Felicity outside to meet a judge. "Turn away from Jesus and worship our god," the judge ordered, "or I will have you killed."

The two women saw soldiers pacing back and forth, waiting to kill them with swords.

"No!" Perpetua said to the judge. "We will never turn away from Jesus."

"Let them die!" the judge ordered.

The two Christians hugged each other as the soldiers charged at them. Perpetua and Felicity were very brave as they faced death. The Church calls them saints and martyrs. We celebrate their feast on March 7.

Discuss

1. Why were the women in this story put in prison?
2. What temptation did the two women face?
3. What happened to them because of their decision?

46 Doctrine

Enriching the Lesson

Martyrdom can be a new and difficult concept for fourth graders. Tell the students that most Christians will never be asked to give up their lives because of their faith in Jesus. Yet, even today, there are certain circumstances which may ask a Christian to remain faithful to his or her belief in Jesus under the threat of death. You might want to tell the students about the El Salvador martyrs who were martyred in 1980.

CURRICULUM CONNECTION

Music Teach the class the song "Grow Strong" found in THIS IS OUR FAITH Music Program Director's Manual on page 67. Invite the choir director or parish minister of music to help teach the instrumental accompaniment parts. When the students know the melody well, the song can be performed as a two- three- or four-part round.

Signs of the Spirit

Jesus gives us the same Holy Spirit he gave to his friends on Pentecost and to Perpetua and Felicity. We celebrate this gift in each of the seven sacraments. The Holy Spirit is always with us to help us and guide us in our fight against temptation. With the Holy Spirit we can know what is good. We can choose good and turn away from what is evil. In this way we will love God and all the goodness around us.

Christians have come to recognize signs that remind us that the Holy Spirit is with us, guiding us to make good choices. The Bible names nine signs:

love	generosity
joy	faithfulness
peace	gentleness
patience	self-control
kindness	*Based on Galatians 5:22 – 23*

Activity

Study the photograph on this page. Then on the lines below, name the signs of the Holy Spirit that the photograph suggests.

_____
_____
_____
_____
_____
_____

We Believe

Jesus sends us the Holy Spirit to be our helper and guide in our fight against temptation. The Holy Spirit helps us know what is good for us. The Holy Spirit guides us in choosing good rather than evil.

Enriching the Lesson

Remind the students that they can pray to Jesus to send the Holy Spirit whenever they need help to be brave, to do the right thing, to be loving, or to be peaceful. Help them appreciate that when they are able to do what is right, they feel good about themselves and they can feel the love of Jesus. Every time they let the Holy Spirit help them, they become stronger.

Identifying Signs of the Spirit

Ask a volunteer to read aloud "Signs of the Spirit" on page 47. Explain that as we grow in holiness with the Spirit's help, we can see these signs of the Holy Spirit within us. Ask the class to enumerate together the nine signs of the Spirit. Tell them that the signs are also known as the fruits of the Holy Spirit.

Have the students name the sacraments they have received in celebration of the gift of the Holy Spirit.(*Baptism, Eucharist, Confirmation, Reconciliation*) Explain that at their Baptism, Jesus sent his Spirit upon them.

Presenting the Doctrine

Call attention to the We Believe statements and ask a volunteer to read them aloud. To help the students learn these statements, ask the following questions.

- Who does Jesus send? (*The Holy Spirit*)
- What does the Holy Spirit do? (*Helps us and guides us in our fight against temptation.*)
- What else does the Holy Spirit do? (*Helps us to know what is good and helps us choose good rather than evil.*)
- When does the Holy Spirit do this? (*When we are tempted*)

Step 3 / CONCLUSION

Learning How to Live Our Faith

Analyzing a Photograph

Invite the students to look at the photograph and identify the signs of the Holy Spirit in it.

DAY 4
MORALITY

Objective

This lesson helps the students learn how to make a good choice.

Step 1 / INTRODUCTION

Learning About Our Lives

Sharing Some Choices that We Have Made

Ask the students if they can remember a time when they made a decision and then afterward regretted making that decision. Encourage the students to share their stories. You might want to get them started by sharing an experience of your own first. Tell the students that today they are going to learn a technique that will help them to make good choices.

Step 2 / DEVELOPMENT

Learning About Our Faith

Learning How to Make a Good Choice

Read aloud the first sentence at the top of page 48. Discuss with the class how being wise, strong, and caring can help them make good decisions. Help the students appreciate that these qualities help us know what is right, give us the courage to choose good over evil, and help us to follow Jesus' example of love.

Ask volunteers to continue reading aloud "How to Make a Good Choice." Emphasize that these steps are a help to us when we are faced with a hard decision. As the students read through the text, point out how the photographs on this page illustrate each step. Help the students to practice using the steps by applying them to the situations below.

- Kendra steals two cigarettes from her mother. She gives one to Allie and wants Allie to smoke with her. Allie knows that smoking is wrong, but she doesn't want Kendra to call her a "chicken."

- Paul hears some of his classmates teasing a second grader. The child is standing in the center of the circle crying.

- In the cafeteria line at school, Shawn receives too much change from the cashier, who does not notice her mistake.

48

How to Make a Good Choice

The Holy Spirit helps us to be wise, strong, and caring so that we can make the right choices. Here are some steps to help you choose to do what is good when you feel drawn to do what is wrong.

▲1. **Stop** for a moment. Hold back from acting too quickly.

▲3. **Pray** and ask the Holy Spirit to help you make a good choice.

▲2. **Think** for a moment: Why do I want to do what I know is wrong? What will happen if I choose to do what I know is wrong? How will I feel? What would my parents and best friends think?

▲4. **Ask** someone you love and trust to tell you what he or she thinks is the right choice.

◄5. **Choose** to do what you think is the right thing to do.

CURRICULUM CONNECTION

Music You might want to teach the class to sing the chorus of the song "Spirit, Move." It is available on the record that accompanies the *Young People's Glory and Praise* hymnal, North American Liturgy Resources, available from OCP (Oregon Catholic Press), 5536 N.E. Hassalo, Portland, OR 97213. The printed music is number 66 in the hymnal. Play "Spirit, Move" and have the students join in on the chorus.

Focus on

Decision Making At times, making a decision will be easy. We know exactly what the right decision is, but it may exact some cost from us. We will need the strength to carry it out. At other times, making a decision may be difficult. We are unclear about what the greater good might be and, because of many complicating factors, it may seem impossible to predict the outcome of our decision. Following three steps—reflection, consultation, and prayer—before making a decision can be helpful.

Activity

Imagine that last summer you had a job doing yardwork for an elderly man. Each Saturday you rode your bike a mile to his house. The man could hardly walk and couldn't see very well. He always seemed to be in a bad mood and was never very nice to you. But you still liked the job because each week the man paid you six dollars.

Every Saturday the man would pay you with a $5 bill and a $1 bill. On the last Saturday of the summer, when you got home, you realized that the man had paid you with a $5 bill and a $20 bill by mistake. Instead of paying you six dollars, he paid you twenty-five dollars! What should you do? Complete the sentences below.

1. I would STOP and _____

2. I would THINK _____

3. I would PRAY. I would ask the Holy Spirit to _____

4. I would ASK _____

5. The CHOICE I would make would be to _____

Morality 49

Enriching the Lesson

Prepare a bulletin board. Post headings for the key concepts of this chapter. Have the students write statements on a sheet of colored paper and post them under the appropriate headings. Keep this bulletin board on display.

- Pat's older brother has begun to hang around with some kids in a gang. Pat is worried that her brother will join the gang and get into trouble. Pat loves her brother very much but she does not want to be a tattletale.

Step 3 / CONCLUSION

Learning How to Live Our Faith

Practicing Making Good Choices

Direct the students' attention to the activity on page 49. Invite two volunteers to read aloud the paragraphs describing the situation. Instruct the students to complete the activity independently. Afterwards, encourage the students to share what they have written. Be supportive of the ideas they share.

DAY 5
PRAYER/REVIEW

Objective

This lesson helps the students understand what a traditional prayer is and helps them to pray a traditional prayer about loving God.

Reading About Traditional Prayers

Ask a volunteer to read aloud "Praying a Traditional Prayer" on page 50. Answer any questions the students may have.

Understanding a Traditional Prayer

Read aloud together the Act of Love. Check to be sure that the students understand all of the words in the prayer. Then ask the students to briefly state what they think this prayer means. Help the students realize that loving God also means loving one's neighbor.

Praying Together

Gather the students in the prayer area. Give them a few moments to put themselves in a prayerful state of mind. Then pray together the Act of Love.

Listening to a Song

Conclude the prayer experience by having the students listen to or sing a song about loving God and our neighbor. "What We Need in This World Is" on page 116 of the THIS IS OUR FAITH *Hymnal* would be suitable.

Praying a Traditional Prayer

The Church has prayed certain prayers for hundreds of years. We call these prayers and other long-prayed prayers *traditional prayers*. Every generation of Catholics has learned and prayed these prayers. Your parents and grandparents have prayed them, and someday your children and grandchildren will pray the same prayers.

You already know some traditional prayers prayed by Catholics. The Lord's Prayer, the Hail Mary, and the Glory Be to the Father are traditional prayers.

Learn to pray this traditional prayer called the Act of Love.

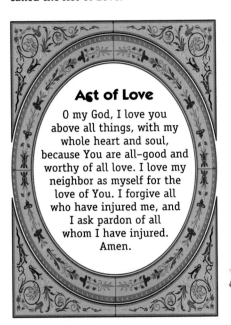

Act of Love

O my God, I love you above all things, with my whole heart and soul, because You are all–good and worthy of all love. I love my neighbor as myself for the love of You. I forgive all who have injured me, and I ask pardon of all whom I have injured. Amen.

50 Prayer

🍎 Teaching Tips

This might be a good time in the school year to review or teach other traditional prayers. Some of these prayers can be found in the student text on pages 1–6.

Chapter Review

Put the steps of decision making in the correct order by numbering the statements from 1 through 5.

___4___ Ask someone you love and trust to tell you what he or she thinks is the the right choice.

___2___ Think for a moment: What will happen if I choose to do what I know is wrong?

___1___ Stop for a moment. Hold back from acting too quickly.

___5___ Choose to do what you think is the right thing to do.

___3___ Pray. Ask the Holy Spirit to help you make a good choice.

Write the answers to the first two questions.

1. What is meant by *conscience?* _____

Conscience is our power to judge whether something

is good or bad.

2. How do we know that the Holy Spirit is with us to help us and guide us in making good choices?

Jesus promised to give us the Holy Spirit.

_____

3. Discuss how we can find help to choose good rather than evil.

> **The Spirit that God has given us makes us strong, loving, and wise.**
> **Based on 2 Timothy 1:7**

CURRICULUM CONNECTION

Language Arts Distribute writing paper and pencils. Invite the students to write and illustrate a fable about someone overcoming evil with the help of the Holy Spirit. Tell the class that the fable can take place in any time period or any land. Invite sharing.

Reviewing the Chapter

Recall with the students that the Holy Spirit is with them to help them overcome temptation. Ask:

■ How did the Spirit help the friends of Jesus? (*They felt stronger and braver.*)

■ What are some signs that the Holy Spirit is with you? (*We show love, joy, gentleness, faithfulness, kindness, generosity, self-control, patience, or have peace.*)

Ordering Decision-Making Steps

Read the directions to the activity on page 51 aloud. Give the students time to complete the activity while working independently. When all the students have finished, correct their answers.

Answering the Questions

Have the students write answers to the first and second review questions. Check their responses and clarify any questions they may have. Discuss the third item, encouraging all the students to participate. Stress the Holy Spirit's role in guiding a person's conscience.

Reflecting on the Scripture Verse

Read aloud together with the class the Scripture verse based on 2 Timothy. Encourage the students to memorize the verse.

End-of-unit pages include a Unit Organizer; Unit Review; Day to Day: Skills for Christian Living; and Opening Doors: A Take-Home Magazine.

Using the Unit Organizer

Completing a graphic organizer such as a chart or table can help the children organize information that has been presented in the unit. Organizers can enable the children to visualize their thinking and recognize relationships among ideas. This will give the children the opportunity to understand more completely the materials they have been studying.

Completing the Organizer

Have the students turn to page 52 in their books. Point out the four sections on the page. Explain to the students what they are expected to do in each section. Read aloud the directions to the first Unit Organizer activity as the students follow along. Then ask the students to complete the activity independently. Read the directions for the subsequent sections as the class finishes each section. If necessary, tell them that they may look back through the previous four chapters for help. When everyone has finished, have the students compare their responses with the class.

Looking Back: Self-Assessment

The critical reflection questions below give the students an opportunity to sharpen their thinking skills. The questions can be used as a class discussion or independent writing activity.

- What did you learn in this unit that could help you make good choices?
- Which Scripture story in this unit did you most enjoy? Why?
- Which picture in this unit did you like best? What did you like most about it?

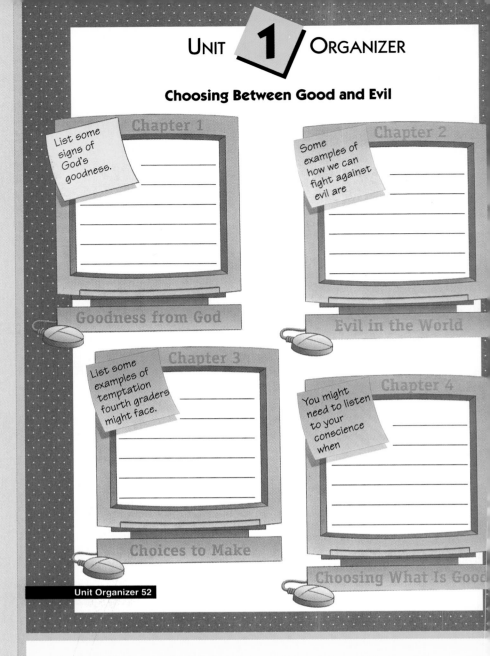

UNIT **1** ORGANIZER

Choosing Between Good and Evil

Chapter 1

List some signs of God's goodness.

Goodness from God

Chapter 2

Some examples of how we can fight against evil are

Evil in the World

Chapter 3

List some examples of temptation fourth graders might face.

Choices to Make

Chapter 4

You might need to listen to your conscience when

Choosing What Is Good

Unit Organizer 52

UNIT 1 REVIEW

Match the words in Column A with the definitions in Column B.

Column A

1. grace
2. original sin
3. temptation
4. sin
5. conscience

Column B

__4__ to choose to act selfishly; to turn away from God and choose not to love

__1__ God's gift of his own life and presence to people

__5__ our power to judge whether something is good or bad

__2__ the first selfish act and the sinful condition in which we are born

__3__ an attraction to think, say, or do something we know is sinful

Fill in the word(s) that best completes each sentence. You may use a word more than once.

evil	helper	love	Pentecost	God	Tempter
goodness	guide	unselfishness		people	temptation

1. All that God makes is good and shows God's __goodness__ and __evil__.

2. __Evil__ spreads through the selfish actions of __people__.

3. We sin only when we choose to give in to __temptation__ and turn away from __God__.

4. The Holy Spirit first came to Jesus' followers on __Pentecost__.

5. Jesus sends us the Holy Spirit to be our __helper__ and __guide__.

6. One of the signs of the Holy Spirit is __love__.

7. The __Tempter__ asked Jesus to bow down and worship him.

Reviewing the Unit

The purpose of the Unit Review is to reinforce concepts presented in the preceding four chapters and to check the students' understanding. After explaining the directions, give the students sufficient time to complete the two-page review. Answer any questions they may have as you check their work.

Testing

After the students have completed the Unit Review, you may wish to distribute copies of the Unit 1 Test from the Tests booklet.

Project

If time permits, you may wish to do the following project with the students.

Distribute writing paper and pens or pencils. Invite the students to write a story about someone who overcomes evil by showing one or more signs of the Holy Spirit. The story can take place in any area or land. If time permits, have the students illustrate their stories by drawing the main characters. Have the students read their stories.

UNIT 1 REVIEW

List the three temptations that Jesus faced.

1. Change stones into bread

2. Jump off the Temple

3. Worship the Tempter

Complete the word puzzle by filling in the blanks and then using the words to work the puzzle.

Across

3. _____ is one of the signs of the Holy Spirit.

4. Some _____ we make are good and some are bad.

7. Our _____ is the power to judge whether something is good or bad for us.

Down

1. A strong _____ seemed to blow through the house where Jesus' friends were.

2. The Holy Spirit first came to Jesus' friends on _____ .

3. On Pentecost, _____ that looked like tongues of fire seemed to come to rest above each of Jesus' friends.

5. Jesus gives us the Holy _____ to be our helper and our guide.

6. Like _____ we also have difficult choices to make.

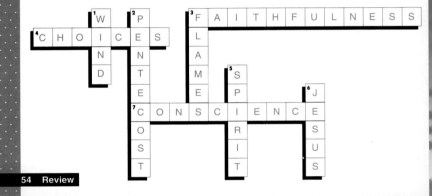

CELEBRATING MY CHRISTIAN IDENTITY

Jesus calls us to be his followers. As followers of Jesus we try to live our lives as Jesus lived his. We try to act in ways that are loving. We do this by being kind to others, treating others fairly, and by thinking of others' needs before our own.

Activity

For each of the stories that follow, tell if you think the main character is acting like a follower of Jesus.

Story #1

Tonya's little sister asks Tonya if she can play with Tonya and her friend. At first Tonya says no because she doesn't like having her sister tag along when she has a friend over after school. Then Tonya thinks about how unhappy her sister seems at having to play alone, and Tonya asks her friend if it's okay for her sister to play with them. Is Tonya acting like a follower of Jesus?

(Yes)   No

Story #2

Jim's brother's bike is in the shop for repairs. Jim's brother wants to go on a bike ride with his friends, and asks Jim if he can borrow his bike. Jim says no. Is Jim acting like a follower of Jesus?

Yes   (No)

Day to Day   55

Introducing Day to Day: Skills for Christian Living

A Guide for Moral Decision Making is presented in the five lessons of this special feature. The decision-making process includes awareness of what it means to be a follower of Jesus and how this special identity influences decision making; important questions to ask when making a moral choice; how to cope with decisions that make one unpopular with friends; and communication skills to use when asking for forgiveness, or responding to someone who asks to be forgiven.

Objective

To help the students become aware of qualities that are a part of a Christian identity and to clarify what it means to be a follower of Jesus.

Introducing the Lesson

Before the students open their books, ask if anyone knows what it means to be a follower of Jesus. You might write the students' suggestions on the board to compare with what is described in the book.

Have the students open their books to page 55. Read with them the opening paragraph. Draw comparisons with what students have just generated in the earlier discussion. Ask students to give examples of acting with kindness, treating others fairly, placing others' needs before their own, sharing with those less fortunate, being honest and forgiving.

Completing the Activity

Have students read each of the stories and decide whether or not the character in the story is acting like a follower of Jesus. Focus on each person's feelings and actions, then ask the following questions.

Lesson continues on page 56. ▶

55

(Note to the teacher: You may want to emphasize that sometimes it is difficult to put aside how we feel in the interest of treating someone lovingly. For example, if we are angry with someone, or have had our feelings hurt by another's words or actions, or feel that we want to have things our way, it may be difficult to act with kindness toward that person. This is part of the challenge of being a follower of Jesus.)

- Was Tonya considerate of her friend's feelings? (*Yes, she asked if allowing her sister to play was all right with her friend.*)

- Is Tonya acting like a follower of Jesus? How? (*Yes. She puts her sister's needs ahead of her own; she is being kind to her sister.*)

- Is Jim acting like a follower of Jesus? Why? (*No. Jim is being unkind by not letting his brother borrow his bike. Jim is not acting in a loving way toward his brother.*)

- What would be the more loving thing to do? (*Jim could let his brother borrow his bike.*)

- Is Jason acting like a follower of Jesus? How? (*Yes. He is trying to be honest and is considering his friend's need for help.*)

- Is Kate acting like a follower of Jesus? Why? (*No. She is not forgiving Jonna when Jonna tries to apologize.*)

- What would have been a more loving thing for Kate to have done? (*She could have accepted Jonna's apology and tried to mend their relationship.*)

Writing and Sharing Stories

Direct the students' attention to the writing activity on page 56. This may be completed as a homework assignment. When completed ask for volunteers to share their stories. Respect students who would prefer not to share. The content of their stories may be too personal.

Concluding the Lesson

Provide bulletin board space for students to create a display about what it means to be a follower of Jesus. Entitle the display "Christians in Action." Students may use magazine pictures and words to create the display, or you may choose to have them draw individual or group pictures that represent what it means to be a follower of Jesus. When completed, assemble the students and, as a closing prayer, offer a blessing for them and the things they do each day that show they are followers of Jesus.

56

Story #3

Jason's best friend asks to copy Jason's homework. Jason feels uncomfortable about giving it to him and says no. Jason offers to help his friend with the homework if there was something his friend didn't understand. Is Jason acting like a follower of Jesus?

(Yes)   No

Story #4

Kate is mad at Jonna because Jonna wouldn't play with her at recess. Jonna apologizes, but Kate turns her back and refuses to hear what Jonna has to say. Is Kate acting like a follower of Jesus?

Yes   (No)

Activity

Write a story that tells about a time when being a follower of Jesus was difficult for you.

_____
_____
_____
_____
_____
_____
_____
_____
_____
_____

PRAYER

Jesus, I want to live my life as you lived yours. Help me to be kind to others and to think of others" needs before my own. Amen.

OPENING DOORS
A Take-Home Magazine™

Growing Closer

MAKE A WEATHER-REPORT flip chart to display in your kitchen. The poster will chart what the communication climate is like in your home. You may want to use the illustrations on page 3 of this booklet. A sample illustration is provided.

Looking Ahead

Unit 2 will present the Christian way of love, mercy, and justice as formulated in the Great Commandment, the Beatitudes, and the Ten Commandments and as lived out by Jesus, the saints, and faithful Christians today. Your fourth grader will learn that these teachings of Jesus should be the guidelines for his or her life, too.

8

Opening Doors

A Take-Home Magazine

The five removable, family-directed supplements entitled *Opening Doors: A Take-Home Magazine* provide you, the teacher, with a unique opportunity to involve parents or guardians more fully in their child's catechetical program. Each magazine will include the following features.

A Closer Look
An article relating the unit theme in the text to a particular aspect of the Mass

Being Catholic
An article explaining a particular aspect of our Catholic heritage

Growing Closer
Suggested activities to help the family integrate faith into everyday life

Looking Ahead
A preview of the next unit in THIS IS OUR FAITH, Grade 4

Sending the Magazine Home

As you complete Unit 1 with your class, assist the children in carefully removing *Opening Doors: A Take-Home Magazine* (two pages) from their texts by separating them from the book along the perforations. Demonstrate how to fold the two pages, forming an eight-page booklet.

When the magazines are folded, take time to explain each section of the magazine to the children. Allow the children to ask any questions they may have. Ask the children to take the magazine home and encourage their families to read it with them and participate in the suggested activities. You may wish to attach a letter of your own, encouraging the family to use the magazine each time their child brings it home.

Follow the same procedure in sending home the remaining magazines for Units 2, 3, 4, and 5.

CLIMATE CONTROL

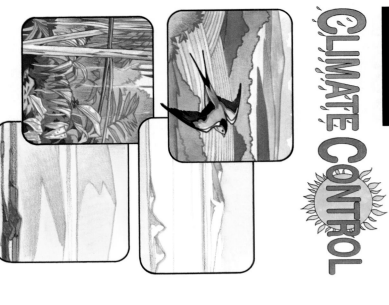

Some parishes offer family evening programs that focus on the family in its home setting. The family studies and discusses a designated topic, then completes a common activity.

• **Child-centered parish programs.** Most religion textbooks used today in parochial schools and in parish schools of religion contain suggested family activities. By completing these activities with your child, you can take an active part in your child's religious education. You can also further your own religious education.

• **Sunday liturgies.** Attending Mass with your child, reading together the Scripture readings before Mass, and discussing the homily after Mass can be excellent ways to share your faith as a family.

TRANSMITTING THE FAITH
TRANSMITTING THE FAITH
TRANSMITTING THE FAITH

Recent research reports about the religious formation of children emphasize the vital nurturing role of the family and supporting role of the Church community.

The National Catholic Educational Association (NCEA) study, *Toward Effective Parish Religious Education for Children and Young People* states, "Without faith-supporting activities at home, many youth fall prey to a religious skepticism that grows and festers. When parents are seen as mechanical religionists who practice the faith only at Mass, adolescents tend to learn that faith is an adult game that really has no important tie to work or family or life decisions. The family that practices faith models a mature faith, and the message does not escape our children."

Sharing the Light of Faith, National Catechetical Directory for Catholics of the United States states, "Within families there is need and opportunity for spouses to catechize each other and for parents to catechize children."

Most parishes are ready to support family efforts. The following ways describe how your family can transmit your faith to or catechize each other.

- **Parish family-centered programs.** Many parishes offer family-centered religious education programs. In some programs, the participants separate into age groups to discuss a scriptural topic or liturgical theme. Then everyone participates in a common activity and celebration.

At any given time, the climate of communication in your home may be like one or two listed below.

ARCTIC

People are barely speaking to each other. One person has decided to give everyone else the cold shoulder.

TROPICAL

People are listless. Everyone is exhausted. They do not have the energy or desire to improve the level of conversation.

DESERT

There are a few hot family issues that need to be discussed. However, someone is retreating to a little oasis.

TEMPERATE

Everyone is mellow. People are really expressing themselves calmly. Each person is participating in the conversation at the breakfast or dinner table.

- If you feel your family is experiencing an Arctic, tropical, or desert climate, what can you do to improve the atmosphere?

- If your family is experiencing a temperate climate, what can you do to maintain the pleasant atmosphere?

TURNING OFF and TUNING IN

What kind of energy does your family generate as you are getting ready for Mass each week? Take a few minutes to discuss this question with your family.

Sometimes your energy may be spent as you all rush about in a whirlwind getting dressed and piling into the car. During these times, you may feel like a tornado picked you up from your house and then plopped you into the middle of the church just as the entrance song begins. At other blessed times, you may have a few minutes of peace—a few minutes to turn off all sources of distraction from the previous week.

To help you turn off distracting waves of worry, planning, and the rehashing of situations, we pray together the Opening Prayer before the Liturgy of the Word begins. The priest invites us to pray, pauses for a few minutes of silence, and then begins the prayer, which is also known as the Collect.

The prayer below is the Alternative Opening Prayer for the Twenty-First Sunday in Ordinary Time. Find a few minutes to reflect on the meaning of the words during the coming week.

> **Lord our God,**
> **all truth is from you,**
> **and you alone bring oneness of heart.**
> **Give your people the joy**
> **of hearing your word in every sound**
> **and of longing for your presence more**
> **than for life itself.**
> **May all the attractions of a changing world**
> **serve only to bring us**
> **the peace of your kingdom which this**
> **world does not give.**

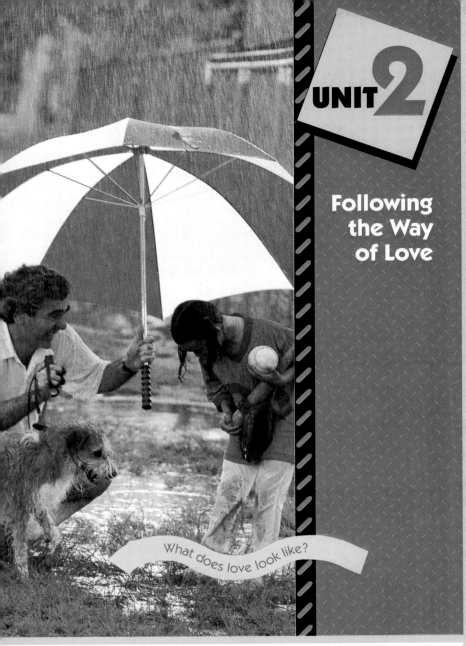

What does love look like?

UNIT 2

Following the Way of Love

To help the students learn the Great Commandment and begin to apply the Beatitudes and the Ten Commandments to their lives. The students will learn to identify these words as teachings of Jesus.

Doctrinal Summaries

CHAPTER 5

Jesus teaches us to love God above all else and to love our neighbor as we love ourselves. This is called the Great Commandment. We are called to care about others as the Good Samaritan did. We show our love for God when we help those who are in need.

CHAPTER 6

Christians believe that they will be happy if they live Jesus' Beatitudes. The Beatitudes are sayings of Jesus that teach us to love God and to love others.

CHAPTER 7

Jesus wants us to follow his example and his teachings so that we will be happy. The Beatitudes summarize Jesus' way to happiness, a way of love and caring.

CHAPTER 8

The Church teaches that the Ten Commandments are God's laws. They are ways of showing love for God and for other people. They are rules to help us live together in peace and happiness.

Note:
As you prepare this unit and the remaining units, you might wish to refer to the reference section, *Our Catholic Heritage*, beginning on page 327.

Additional resources for Unit 2 include: a Unit Test and a Family Letter as well as a video and selections from THIS IS OUR FAITH Music Program. You might also find it helpful to preview *Saints and Other Holy People* and *Prayer Celebrations* for possibilities to enhance the unit.

Introducing the UNIT

Invite the students to study the photograph on page 61. Ask a volunteer to read aloud the unit-focus question. After allowing time for all students to share their responses, tell them that in Unit 2 they will learn how Catholics are called to show their love for God, others, and themselves.

Vocabulary

neighbor
commandment
Temple
Samaritan
reign of God
justice
Beatitudes
disciples
mercy
peacemakers
shalom
wholeness
Ten Commandments
heaven

The Great Commandment

Objectives ~~~~~~~

To help the students

■ Learn the Great Commandment.
■ Witness how Christians can follow the Great Commandment.
■ Recognize that we show love for God by loving our neighbors.
■ Discover ways to keep the Great Commandment.
■ Learn what a prayer of petition is, pray it, and review the chapter.

Chapter Outline ~~~~~~~

	Step 1 **Learning About Our Lives**	**Step 2** **Learning About Our Faith**	**Step 3** **Learning How to Live Our Faith**
Day 1	■ Introduce the chapter. ■ Read the story. ■ Write a story ending. *ABOUT 16 MINUTES*	■ Learn about the Great Commandment. ■ Introduce the vocabulary. ■ Present the doctrine. *ABOUT 9 MINUTES*	■ Identify needs. *ABOUT 5 MINUTES*
Day 2	■ Think about Good Samaritans. *ABOUT 10 MINUTES*	■ Read about a modern day Good Samaritan. *ABOUT 10 MINUTES*	■ Complete stories. *ABOUT 10 MINUTES*
Day 3	■ Consider rules. *ABOUT 7 MINUTES*	■ Introduce the gospel story. ■ Read a Scripture story. ■ Discuss the story. ■ Introduce the vocabulary. *ABOUT 13 MINUTES*	■ Complete an activity. ■ Make a comparison. ■ Review the lesson. *ABOUT 10 MINUTES*
Day 4	■ Reflect on challenges. *ABOUT 10 MINUTES*	■ Read a story. *ABOUT 10 MINUTES*	■ Complete a drawing activity. ■ Review the lesson. *ABOUT 10 MINUTES*
Day 5	**Prayer** Introduce prayers of petition; write and pray prayers of petition. **Review** Review the chapter and read the Scripture verse.		

Plan Ahead

	Preparing Your Class	**Materials Needed**
Day 1	Read over the lesson. Plan now to invite a guest speaker to talk about parish organizations that help people.	■ pencils or pens ■ writing paper
Day 2	Read through the entire lesson plan. If you opt to enrich the lesson, gather materials for the collage.	■ pencils or pens
Day 3	Read the lesson plan. If you choose to use any of the additional activities, make all of the necessary arrangements.	■ pencils or pens
Day 4	Read through the lesson plan. Plan and prepare for the additional activities that you will have the students do.	■ pencils or pens ■ crayons or felt-tip markers ■ drawing paper
Day 5	Read over the lesson plan. If enriching the lesson, gather materials for making cards.	■ pencils or pens ■ Bible ■ prayer cloth ■ candle

Additional Resources

As you plan this chapter, consider using the following from The Resourceful Teacher Package.

■ *Classroom Activity Sheets 5 and 5a*

■ *Family Activity Sheets 5 and 5a*

■ *Chapter 5 Test*

■ *Prayers for Every Day*

■ *Projects: Grade 4*

You may also wish to refer to the following Big Book.

■ *We Celebrate God's Word,* page 9

In preparing the students for the Sunday readings, you may wish to use Silver Burdett Ginn's *Getting Ready for Sunday* student and teacher materials.

BOOKS FOR THE JOURNEY

The Children's Illustrated Bible. "The Good Samaritan," pp. 232–233. Retold by Selina Hastings. Dorling Kindersley, 1994. A version of the Good Samaritan story with additional information and illustrations.

Experience Jesus Today. "The Good Samaritan," pp. 127–131. Charles Singer & Albert Hari. Oregon Catholic Press, 1993. The Good Samaritan story with additional information, questions, and a prayer about the call that we have to be good samaritans.

MORE BOOKS FOR THE JOURNEY

On City Streets. "A Sad Song About Greenwich-Village," by Frances Park, p. 66. Selected by Nancy Larrick. M. Evans & Co., 1968. A powerful poem of someone alone and needy.

The Gift of the Sacred Dog. Paul Goble. Macmillan, 1984. The story of a courageous boy who knew that he had to do something for his people and set out to do it.

REDUCED CLASSROOM ACTIVITIES

NAME _____

THE GREAT COMMANDMENT

We should be proud when we show our love for God and others by following the Great Commandment. List special times when you can be proud.

I am proud of what I do about _____
_____

I am proud that even when my friends _____
_____

I _____

I am proud that I make my parents happy when I _____
_____

I am proud that I help make my classroom a happier place by
_____

To the Teacher: This activity follows "Jesus' Great Commandment" and encourages fourth graders to care for their neighbors.

Chapter 5 The Great Commandment

THIS IS OUR FAITH 4 **5**

NAME _____

FOLLOWING THE GOOD SAMARITAN'S EXAMPLE

You are a writer and an illustrator. Write your name in the space next to the word *By.* Think about a person you know who performs frequent acts of kindness. Write this person's name next to the word *Title.* In frames 2 and 3, draw a picture of your Good Samaritan and write in the blank speech balloons what you think each character would say. In the last frame, create your own ending about helping others more often. Be ready to share your results with the class.

Title: _____ *By:* _____

1. **I need HELP!**

2.

3.

4.

To the Teacher: This activity follows the Scripture story "The Good Samaritan."

5a THIS IS OUR FAITH 4

Chapter 5 The Great Commandment

61c Chapter Organizer

Background for the Teacher

THE LAW OF LOVE

The chapters of this unit show how to follow the way of love. At the heart of the Old Testament is the commandment to love God with all our heart, soul, and strength (Deuteronomy 6:5). The old covenant consisted of over 600 laws governing every aspect of life. Among them was the command to love one's neighbor as oneself. Jesus, the living embodiment of the law, elevated love of neighbor to an essential condition on which our love of God depends. He summed up the whole law in this double law of love. We show love for God in direct ways, such as worship, but if we do not love our neighbor, we do not love God. Love of neighbor is our response to the love of God for us. Jesus forged this covenant of love with his blood. In our love for others, God's love is made perfect in us, and we are brought to fulfillment in Jesus. Jesus sends his grace, his presence, the Holy Spirit, to be with us as we reach out in love (see 1 John 4:7–21).

WHO IS OUR NEIGHBOR?

In the old covenant, neighbor means one's fellow Jew. Jesus expanded the meaning to include anyone in need of love, even an enemy. Through our love of enemies, God's redemptive love reaches those in need. In the story of the Good Samaritan, Jesus challenged the religious thought of the time. The two who passed by the wounded man were devout men—a priest and a Levite. The man who assisted the traveler was one many Jewish people of the time hated—a Samaritan. The one who was thought to be outside God's law was closest to God. In addressing this parable to a lawyer, Jesus taught that love of neighbor fulfills the prescriptions of the old covenant (see Luke 10:25–37).

Nine- and ten-year old youngsters are curious about rules and moral principles. You can help them become more aware of the needs of others. You can help them grasp the fundamental law that underlies all other laws. There is much for children and adults today to learn from this parable. When Mother Teresa opened a soup kitchen in Newark, New Jersey, it was remarked that someone from one of the poorest nations had to come to the richest nation to show us how to care. In this chapter the students will be able to see how they can love both God and their neighbor.

DAY 1
DOCTRINE

Objective

This lesson helps the students learn the Great Commandment.

Step 1 / INTRODUCTION

Learning About Our Lives

Introducing the Chapter

Discuss the focus question on page 62 with the students. List the students' responses on the chalkboard. Help them appreciate that people make choices about helping others for many reasons. Then tell the students that they are going to read a story about someone who was faced with a choice about helping others.

or . . .

Invite the students to recall two personal experiences about a time when someone helped them or when they helped someone else.

Discuss with them if it is easier to help others or to be helped by others. Emphasize that we all need help at one time or another. Encourage the students to express how they feel when they are able to help someone else.

Reading the Story

Ask the students to look at the photograph on page 62 and describe what they think is happening. Direct their attention to the story title. Explain that when we feel two different ways about doing something, we say we have mixed feelings. Ask several volunteers each to read aloud a section of the story.

Writing a Story Ending

Distribute writing paper and instruct the students to write an ending to the story, telling what Jesse did and giving the reasons for his decision. When the students have finished writing, invite them to share their story endings with the whole group. Ask:

■ Why did Jesse's family go to the soup kitchen? (*To help poor people in need*)

■ Why didn't Jesse want to go? (*He wanted to stay in bed.*)

■ What are the consequences of the decision you had Jesse make? (*Answers will vary.*)

62

The Great Commandment

What are some reasons why people help those who are hurting?

Mixed Feelings

"Jesse! It's time to get up!"

Jesse rolled over. "I'm tired," he called back to his mother. He pulled the covers over his head.

Five minutes later, Jesse's sister came into his room. "Jesse," she said, "we have to hurry. It's our day to help out at the soup kitchen."

Jesse did not want to hear about poor people. He knew they would already be lined up in the cold outside the soup kitchen door. He wanted to stay in his warm, cozy bed.

"Let's go!" Jesse could hear his father say. "You're going to be late."

Jesse did not answer. "Those men and women lined up for food won't miss me," he thought. "Mom, Dad, and Kate can feed them. I'll just go back to sleep."

But he couldn't sleep. Jesse could hear his parents and sister packing boxes and getting ready. Restless, he wondered what it would be like not to have enough to eat.

"Well, it's not my fault if people are hungry," he thought to himself.

62   Doctrine

★ ★★★ ★ Enriching the Lesson ★

Distribute a Bible to each student. Explain that they will be looking up two different Scripture references that both define the Great Commandment: Mark 12:28–31 and Matthew 22:36–40. Once the students have located and read both passages, make a Venn diagram on the chalkboard and, as a class, list the similarities between the two passages.

Focus on

Soup Kitchens You might want to explain that a soup kitchen is a place where very poor or homeless people can come each day for meals. Volunteers of various service organizations cook the meals. Soup kitchens are usually found in large cities. These places are called soup kitchens because often they serve soup as well as other nourishing foods.

He was just dozing off when his dad came into his room and sat down on his bed. "Son, we have to leave in a few minutes. It's cold outside. Those people are already standing in the cold and are hungry. Your grandma is staying home. She has a bad cold. So you can stay in bed if you want, or you can go with us. If you decide to go, you have to be in the car in ten minutes."

His dad left the room. Jesse tossed and turned for a minute before deciding what to do.

Jesus' Great Commandment

Jesus teaches us to love God above all else and to love our **neighbor** as we love ourselves. This teaching is called Jesus' Great **Commandment**. For Jesus, our neighbor is the person who lives in our homes, in our neighborhoods, or in a country far away. Our neighbor is the person who sits next to us in school or who plays soccer on our team. Our neighbor is every man, woman, and child, especially anyone who is hurting and needs our love and care. Caring for our neighbor is how we best show our love for God.

Activity

List some things that people need in your home, in your school, and in your neighborhood.

_____

_____

_____

Doctrine 63

Vocabulary

neighbor: every man, woman, and child, especially someone who needs our love and care

commandment: a law given to us by God to help us live good lives by being loving people

////////////////////////

We Believe

Jesus teaches us to love God above all else and to love our neighbor as we love ourselves. This is called the Great Commandment. We are called to care about others. We show our love for God when we help those who are in need.

Enriching the Lesson

Invite the students to consider which needs they as fourth graders can help meet. Keep this discussion practical, helping the students to think of positive actions they can do. Encourage them to try to meet some of those needs before the next class session.

Teaching Tips

If you plan to invite a guest speaker to speak on Day 3, tell your speaker in advance that the theme of the chapter is the Great Commandment. Explain that you would like him or her to talk to the students about how the parish tries to live out the story of the Good Samaritan.

Help the students appreciate that Jesse had to make a decision between being selfish or being generous. Point out that sometimes we all feel lazy and that at other times, we find it inconvenient to do what is right. Explain that it is at these times especially that Jesus wants us to think about the needs of others.

Step 2 / DEVELOPMENT

Learning About Our Faith

Learning About the Great Commandment

Ask a volunteer to read aloud "Jesus' Great Commandment" on page 63. Guide a discussion using the following questions.

■ Who does Jesus say that our neighbor is? (*Every man, woman, and child, especially anyone who is hurting and needs our love and care.*)

■ How does Jesus teach us to treat our neighbor? (*To love our neighbor as we love ourselves*)

■ If Jesse follows Jesus' Great Commandment, what choice would he make? (*He would go with his family to help in the soup kitchen.*)

Introducing the Vocabulary

Ask a volunteer to read aloud the definitions of *neighbor* and *commandment* in the Vocabulary box on page 63. Encourage the students to memorize the definition by repeating it several times.

Presenting the Doctrine

Read aloud the We Believe statements as the students follow along. To check for understanding, ask volunteers to put the statements into their own words.

Step 3 / CONCLUSION

Learning How to Live Our Faith

Identifying Needs

Read aloud the directions to the activity on page 63. Discuss with the students what some needs of people in the home, school, and neighborhood might be. Write these needs on the chalkboard. Then ask the the students to complete the activity, using ideas from the chalkboard list or their own ideas.

DAY 2
MORALITY

Objective

This lesson helps the students witness how Christians can follow the Great Commandment.

Step 1 / INTRODUCTION

Learning About Our Lives

Thinking About Good Samaritans

Ask the students if they know any Good Samaritans. Give the students time to tell about the Good Samaritan they know and how this person follows the Great Commandment.

Step 2 / DEVELOPMENT

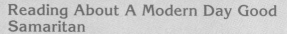
Learning About Our Faith

Reading About A Modern Day Good Samaritan

Ask for volunteers to read aloud "Keeping the Great Commandment" on page 64. Use the following questions to guide the discussion.

- Who are the two characters in this story? (*Jamesina, a fifteen-year-old high school freshman and Mrs. Tompkins, Jamesina's elderly neighbor*)
- What kinds of activities does Jamesina enjoy? (*Sports, music, reading, and being with people*)
- How does Jamesina live by the Great Commandment? (*By spending time with and reading to her elderly neighbor*)
- What does Jamesina remember about Mrs. Tompkins? (*That Mrs. Tompkins read aloud exciting stories to her and other neighborhood children*)

Keeping the Great Commandment

Christians are called to live by Jesus' Great Commandment of love. Some Christians care for people in their parishes. Some Christians help people who are alone. And some care for those who live right in their own neighborhoods.

This is a story about a Christian who lives out the Great Commandment.

James is a fifteen-year-old high-school freshman who lives in the busy city of Detroit. Besides his love for sports and music, James loves to read. Most of all, James loves people and enjoys being with others.

Mrs. Tompkins, who is elderly now, lives three houses down from James' family. Mrs. Tompkins is almost blind and has difficulty walking. She spends most of her time indoors, listening to the radio or TV.

James remembers when Mrs. Tompkins would sit on her front steps and read to him and the other neighborhood children. She always read wonderful, exciting stories, full of adventure and interesting characters. Story time with Mrs. Tompkins was always a special time for James.

Now James visits Mrs. Tompkins and reads to her. James brings books of poetry, short stories, and sometimes a long novel. The two neighbors continue to do what they have always enjoyed doing—reading a good story and just spending time together.

64 Morality

Enriching the Lesson

Talk with students about parish organizations or community services that try to live out the Great Commandment. If possible, arrange for a representative from a parish organization to tell the students what the parish group does to be Good Samaritans to others. Other possible guest speakers include a member of the Saint Vincent de Paul Society and volunteers from a ministry of care for shut-ins or outreach programs for the poor or homeless.

CURRICULUM CONNECTION

Music Play the recording of the song "Reach Out," found in *Young People's Glory and Praise*, NARL, available from OCP (Oregon Catholic Press), 5536 N.E. Hassalo, Portland, OR 97213. Have the students listen to the song and note the similarities between the words of the song and the Great Commandment.

64

Activity

Complete the following stories in a way that shows you understand the meaning of the Great Commandment.

1. Maria loved to go to Girl Scouts each Wednesday after school. One Tuesday evening Maria's mother told her she could not get a babysitter on Wednesday for Maria's little brother. Maria's mother asked Maria to give up Girl Scouts for one week and baby-sit for her little brother. Maria was very upset.

_____

_____

_____

2. Paul and his friend were in the middle of playing a video game. Paul's little sister was invited to go to a friend's house to play, but she was not allowed to walk there by herself. She pleaded with Paul to walk with her to her friend's house.

_____

_____

_____

3. Tom and Lisa were playing in the yard. They were having a great time until their next-door neighbor came over. He was locked out of his house. He asked them to help him find the house key that he had lost in the grass.

_____

_____

_____

_____

Learning How to Live Our Faith

Completing Stories

Call the students' attention to the writing activity on page 65. Have them finish the three stories, showing the Great Commandment being lived out. Afterward, invite sharing. Talk with the students about whether living by the Great Commandment is easy. Help them recognize that showing love and care for others may be difficult sometimes, but that is what Jesus asks. Then give the students time to write their own story about following the Great Commandment. Allow the students to share what they have written.

★ Enriching the Lesson ★

Distribute drawing paper, crayons or felt-tip markers, construction paper, fabric scraps, yarn, and glue to students. Invite them to create a collage showing adults and children from all over the world gathering as neighbors. Encourage the students to write the following Scripture verse on their collage:

God's law may be summed up in this: You will love your neighbor as you love yourself (Romans 13:9).

DAY 3
SCRIPTURE

Objective

This lesson helps the students recognize that we show love for God by loving our neighbors.

Step 1 / INTRODUCTION

Learning About Our Lives

Considering Rules

Introduce today's lesson by recalling the Great Commandment. Invite the students to suggest other rules that might bring happiness to the world. List their responses on the chalkboard. Vote to select the best rule. Leave the list on the chalkboard for later use.

Step 2 / DEVELOPMENT

Learning About Our Faith

Introducing the Gospel Story

Explain to the students that Jesus taught people how to act by telling stories. A parable is a story that helps us understand how God wants us to be. Print the word *parable* on the chalkboard and have the students repeat the word after you. Read aloud the title of the story on page 66. Explain that a Samaritan was someone from a land called Samaria. The Jewish people from Jesus' land regarded the Samaritans as their enemies.

Reading a Scripture Story

Begin reading the story aloud, stopping after the sentence "'Who is my neighbor?'" Ask the students who they think their neighbors are. What makes us neighbors to each other? Tell them that Jesus teaches us a special meaning for the word *neighbor*. Then continue reading the story.

Help the students understand that the two who passed by the wounded man did not actually sin when they didn't stop. But they were not as loving as Jesus wants his followers to be.

Discussing the Story

Use the questions below to discuss the story.

■ What does Scripture say we must do to live always in God's love and to inherit eternal life? (*Love God and our neighbor*)

The Good Samaritan

One day a young man saw Jesus and asked him a question. "Teacher," the man asked, "what do I have to do to live always in God's love?"

Jesus answered by saying, "What do you read in Scripture?"

"You will love the Lord, your God, with all your heart, with all your soul, with all your strength, and with all your mind; and you will love your neighbor as you love yourself," the young man answered.

"That's right," Jesus said. "Do that and you will live in God's love."

The young man realized that he had just answered his own question! So the young man asked another question, "Who is my neighbor?" Then Jesus told this story.

"One day a man was going on a trip from Jerusalem to Jericho. Robbers attacked him and stole his money. They left him almost dead.

"A little later a leader of the people walked by. He saw the man lying on the side of the road. But the leader just kept walking.

"Soon a man who worked in the **Temple** came down the road. He also saw the bleeding man but walked right past him.

"Then a **Samaritan** passed by. He saw how badly hurt the man was and felt sorry for him. He cleaned the man's wounds and bandaged them. He lifted the man onto his donkey and took him to a nearby inn.

"The Samaritan stayed with the man all day and cared for him. The next day the Samaritan gave money to the owner of the inn. 'Look after this man until I come back,' he said, 'If you need to spend more money, I'll pay you when I return.'"

66 Scripture

Enriching the Lesson

Ask the students to dramatize the Scripture story. Choose a narrator and select volunteers to take the parts of the robbers, the injured man, and other story characters. You might want to put the story in a contemporary setting. The story might take place in a big city; the Samaritan might be a truck or taxi driver; the passers-by might not help because of fear, being in a hurry, or assuming someone else would help; and the injured man might be taken to a hospital.

66

When the story was finished, Jesus looked at the young man and asked him, "Which of these three people acted like a neighbor to the man who was robbed?"

"The one who was kind to him," the young man answered.

Jesus said to him, "Then go and do the same."

Based on Luke 10:25–37

Activity

In the spaces below, list four words that could be used to complete the sentence.
A Good Samaritan is someone who

1. _____
2. _____
3. _____
4. _____

Vocabulary

Temple: the sacred house of worship for the Jewish people, which is located in Jerusalem

Samaritan: someone from Samaria, the land north of Jerusalem

//////////////////////

Scripture 67

- What was the last question a young man asked Jesus? (*Who is my neighbor?*)
- Who ignored the injured man? (*A leader of the people and a Temple worker*)
- What did the Samaritan do when he saw the man? (*Bandaged his wounds and took him to an inn.*)
- What did Jesus want us to learn from this story? (*All people are our neighbors and deserve love.*)

Introducing the Vocabulary

Point out the Vocabulary box to the students. Ask a volunteer to read the definitions aloud. Answer any questions the students may have.

Step 3 / CONCLUSION

Learning How to Live Our Faith

Completing an Activity

Have the students complete the activity on page 67. Afterward, discuss how the students can be Good Samaritans.

Making a Comparison

Call the students' attention to the list of rules on the chalkboard. Consider how these rules compare with the rule by which the Good Samaritan lived.

Reviewing the Lesson

Ask the following questions.

- How did the Good Samaritan live out the Great Commandment? (*He treated the man who was robbed just as he would want to be treated.*)
- What did Jesus want us to learn from the story of the Good Samaritan? (*To be kind and helpful*)
- Do you know any Good Samaritans? (*Answers will vary.*)

DAY 4
MORALITY

Objective

This lesson helps the students discover ways to keep the Great Commandment.

Step 1 / INTRODUCTION

Learning About Our Lives

Reflecting on Challenges

Help the students recall that James gave of his time and of himself as he lived the Great Commandment. Since he was a freshman in high school, he had homework to do. He probably had to spend time practicing music or a team sport. Yet he had time to share with an elderly neighbor. Ask the students for specific examples of challenges they face when trying to live the Great Commandment. (*Possible answers might include not having enough money, not being old enough, not having enough time, and so on.*)

Help the students understand that any one of the reasons that James had might have been enough to keep some people from following Jesus' teaching. However, James didn't use an excuse of lack of time to keep him from sharing his company with a needy neighbor. If we are going to live the Great Commandment, we too must be determined as we are faced with any variety of challenges.

Step 2 / DEVELOPMENT

Learning About Our Faith

Reading a Story

Direct the students' attention to "The Stranger on the Way" on page 68. Ask for volunteers to read the story aloud. Use the following questions to guide a discussion.

- What problem did the three friends come upon on their way to soccer practice? (*They came across an injured boy.*)

- What had happened to the boy before David, Jerry, and Andy arrived? (*He had fallen while skating and hurt his knees and hands very badly.*)

- Why didn't the boys recognize the stranger? (*Tony had just moved into town three weeks ago.*)

The Stranger on the Way

David, Andy, and Jerry were on their way to soccer practice. As they neared the playing field, they noticed someone crouched on the ground, holding his legs up to his chest. Quickly the boys hurried over to see who it was. Although the boy was a stranger to the three friends, it was easy to see what had happened. A brand new bike was on the ground and both of the stranger's knees were torn out of his jeans. And from the spots of blood on the ground, one could see that his knees were probably in worse shape than his jeans.

The three friends soon discovered that the stranger's name was Tony and that Tony and his family had just moved into town three weeks before. No wonder the boys hadn't recognized him.

Tony's knees were cut and bleeding, and the palms of his hands were badly scraped. Tony was in a lot of pain, and there were tears in his eyes.

68   Morality

Enriching the Lesson

Explain to the students that they will be comparing the parable of the Good Samaritan to the modern version they just read today. Distribute drawing paper. Instruct the students to make three columns on their paper. Have them label the columns 1) parable only, 2) modern story only, and 3) both stories. Then give the students time to write down the similarities and differences between the two stories.

68

"What should we do?" Andy asked his friends.

"We can't do anything," Jerry answered, "or we'll be late for soccer practice."

David nodded in agreement and added, "Besides, what could we do anyway? We better get going."

Andy thought for a moment and then spoke up. "You guys go ahead. Tell the coach that I'll get there as soon as I can. I'm going to help Tony get home."

Jerry and David shook their heads and then ran off in the direction of the soccer field.

As he watched his friends running off, Andy helped Tony to his feet. Then, with Tony leaning on Andy, and Andy walking Tony's bike, the two boys began the long slow walk to Tony's house.

Activity

Decide how you as a fourth grader could be a neighbor to these people in need.

1. There is an elderly man who lives on your street who seems to dislike children. Every time you and your friends walk past his house, he glares at you.

2. Your school bus driver is a young mother who must bring her toddler on the bus with her every morning and afternoon. Sometimes the little girl is cranky and wants her mother's attention. Mrs. Davis tries to quiet her daughter and drive the school bus. Mrs. Davis seems to be very upset.

★ ★ ★
Enriching the Lesson
★

After reading through the story, select volunteers to act out the story while it is read a second time. Ask the students what similarities they are able to see between the parable dramatization and this dramatization.

- What kind of help did the stranger need? (*He needed help to get home and medical attention.*)

- Why didn't Jerry and David offer to help Tony? (*They didn't want to be late for soccer practice.*)

- How did Andy help Tony? (*He helped him remove his in-line skates and walk home.*)

- Which of the three friends was a good neighbor to the injured stranger? (*Andy*)

- How was Andy living as a Good Samaritan? (*He treated Tony as he would have wanted to be treated.*)

- How do you think this experience will change the relationship between Tony and Andy? (*Answers may vary.*)

Step 3 / CONCLUSION

Learning How to Live Our Faith ✦

Completing an Activity

Read the directions to the activity on page 69. Ask volunteers to read aloud each story. Invite the students to share their ideas verbally with each other and encourage each other to carry out their ideas as well.

Reviewing the Lesson

Ask the students to repeat the words which summarize all of God's commandments: *You will love your neighbor as you love yourself.*

DAY 5
PRAYER/REVIEW

Objective

This lesson helps the students learn what a prayer of petition is and then pray a prayer of petition.

Introducing Prayers of Petition

Read aloud for the class "Praying Prayers of Petition" on page 70. Give them examples from the Prayer of the Faithful at Mass. Before asking the students to write prayers of petition, answer any questions they may have.

Writing and Praying Prayers of Petition

Encourage the class to give verbal examples of prayers of petition. Affirm their petitions. Then have them write their petitions. Gather the students for prayer and allow them a few moments to put themselves in a prayerful state. Invite the students to pray their prayers of petition silently or aloud with their class.

Praying Prayers of Petition

One kind of prayer that seems to come naturally to almost everyone is the prayer of petition. To *petition* means to ask or request. When we pray a prayer of petition, we ask God to give us what we need or to give to others what they need.

Young children first learn to pray by praying simple prayers of petition, such as "God, please make Grandma better," or "God, please give Daddy a new job."

We pray prayers of petition at Mass, too. The Prayer of the Faithful, or General Intercessions, is a prayer of petition in which we pray together for the world, our country, our Church leaders, and for those who are sick or in need.

What prayers of petition would you pray today? Write your petitions on the lines below. Then pray your prayers silently or aloud with your class.

> For _____,
> Lord, hear my prayer.
> For _____,
> Lord, hear my prayer.
> For _____,
> Lord, hear my prayer.

70 Prayer

★★★ Enriching the Lesson ★

Divide the class into groups of three or four. Invite each group to make a petitions poster. Have the students print their petitions and a response such as *We pray to the Lord*, or *Lord, hear our prayer.* Hang the posters around the classroom. Ask one student from each group to read the invocations and the entire class to join in with the response.

70

Chapter Review

Complete the sentences below with the correct words from the word box. You may use some words more than once.

ourselves	all else	Samaritan	commandment
love	neighbor	God	Great Commandment

1. Jesus teaches us to love ___God___ above ___all else___ .

2. We show our love for God by our ___love___ for others.

3. The ___Great Commandment___ teaches us to love our ___neighbor___ as we love ___ourselves___ .

4. In the Scripture story the person who stopped and helped the man who was robbed was a ___Samaritan___ .

5. A law given to us by God to help us live good lives by being loving people is a ___commandment___ .

Write the answers to the first two questions.

1. What does Jesus mean by the term *neighbor*?
   A neighbor is everyone, especially someone who needs our love and care.

2. What does Jesus' Great Commandment teach us?
   Jesus' Great Commandment teaches us to love God above all things and to love our neighbor as we love ourselves. We show our love for God when we help those who are in need.

3. Discuss what you can do to care for your neighbors.

All God's commandments may be summed up in this: You will love your neighbor as you love yourself.
Based on Romans 13:9

Reviewing the Chapter

Direct attention to the Chapter Review on page 71. Direct the students to fill in the blanks in the first section. Then have them write their answers to the first two questions on the lines provided. Check answers when the students have finished. For the discussion item, encourage all to participate. As the students suggest ways of caring for their neighbors, note the variety of ways in which people can live out the Great Commandment.

Reading the Scripture Verse

Ask the students to read aloud the verse on page 71. Encourage them to memorize the verse. Then ask:

■ What things would change in the world if all people loved their neighbors as much as they loved themselves? (*Crime, violence, hatred, prejudice, and so on*)

■ How would people act towards one another? (*Kindly, with consideration, and so on*)

★ Enriching the Lesson ★

Distribute construction paper and crayons or felt-tip markers. Have the students think of someone who has been a good neighbor to them. Instruct them to write a thank-you note to this person. Give the students time to decorate their cards. Encourage the students to give the thank-you notes to the persons to whom they are grateful.

Cultural Awareness

Write on the chalkboard:

No matter my color,
No matter my race,
No matter how different
Or alike my face,
All people I know
Are neighbors indeed,
And I'm called to help them
When they are in need.

Stress that Jesus teaches us that all people are our neighbors. Jesus treated all people equally and was not influenced by their color, religion, race, or nationality.

71

Happy Are Those . . .

Objectives

To help the students

- Appreciate that Jesus teaches the way to true happiness.
- Understand what it means to live out the Beatitudes.
- Understand the concept of justice and desire to seek it.
- Recognize that all Christians are called to live out the beatitudes.
- Understand meditation as one type of prayer and review the chapter.

Chapter Outline

	Step 1 Learning About Our Lives	**Step 2** Learning About Our Faith	**Step 3** Learning How to Live Our Faith
Day 1	■ Review the Great Commandment. ■ Introduce the chapter. ■ Complete a happiness survey. *About 12 minutes*	■ Read and discuss the Scripture story. ■ Learn about true happiness. ■ Present the vocabulary. *About 10 minutes*	■ Write about doing positive actions. *About 8 minutes*
Day 2	■ Wish for happiness. *About 5 minutes*	■ Understand the beatitudes of justice. ■ Review the vocabulary. ■ Understand the doctrine. *About 15 minutes*	■ Identify Beatitude people. ■ Review the lesson. *About 10 minutes*
Day 3	■ Stage a debate. *About 10 minutes*	■ Read about the first Christians. ■ Understand justice. *About 10 minutes*	■ Identify ways to work for justice. ■ Study the photographs. *About 10 minutes*
Day 4	■ Describe poverty. *About 5 minutes*	■ Read a biography. ■ Role-play. *About 20 minutes*	■ Complete an activity. *About 5 minutes*

Day 5   **Prayer**   Introduce meditation as prayer; prepare for meditation; pray and meditate about Jesus; and talk about the meditation.

            Review   Write about living the Beatitudes; review the chapter; and reflect on the Scripture verse.

Correlation
to the
Catechism of
the Catholic Church

Paragraphs
1716, 1717, 1725, 1726, 1728, 2723

Plan Ahead ~~~~~~~~

	Preparing Your Class	**Materials Needed**
Day 1	Read over the lesson. The students will need a wallet-size photograph of themselves for Day 1 in the next chapter. Tell them to bring in the photographs this week.	■ pencils or pens ■ writing paper
Day 2	Read the lesson plan. If you opt to do the Cultural Awareness activity, prepare a multiethnic picture collage prior to the session.	■ pencils or pens
Day 3	Read the lesson plan. If you plan to use the optional activities, review the song "What We Need In This World" and make the arrangements for a guest speaker.	■ pencils or pens
Day 4	Read the lesson plan. Decide how you want to direct the students in the role-playing activity in Step 2. If enriching the lesson, gather the necessary materials.	■ pencils or pens
Day 5	Read through the entire lesson plan. Plan for a place to have prayer and make all the necessary arrangements.	■ pencils or pens ■ prayer cloth ■ candle

Additional Resources

As you plan this chapter, consider using the following from The Resourceful Teacher Package.

■ *Classroom Activity Sheets 6* and *6a*

■ *Family Activity Sheets 6* and *6a*

■ *Chapter 6 Test*

■ *Prayers for Every Day*

■ *Projects: Grade 4*

You may also wish to refer to the following Big Book.

■ *We Celebrate God's Word,* page 11

In preparing the students for the Sunday readings, you may wish to use Silver Burdett Ginn's *Getting Ready for Sunday* student and teacher materials.

BOOKS FOR THE JOURNEY

The Story of Ruby Bridges. Robert Coles. Scholastic, 1995. A story of a child who acted courageously and prayerfully for justice.

The Doubleday Illustrated Children's Bible. "The Sermon on the Mount," pp. 256–261. Sandol Stoddard. Doubleday, 1983. A well-told version of what Jesus calls us to do to be happy.

MORE BOOKS FOR THE JOURNEY

The Jazz Man. Mary Hays Weik. Macmillan, 1993. The story of the things that made a small boy happy.

Happy Birthday to You. Dr. Seuss. Random House, 1987. The poetic telling of the great birthday bird fulfilling the most outlandish and unimagined wishes for a truly happy birthday.

REDUCED CLASSROOM ACTIVITIES

NAME _____

BEATITUDES OF JUSTICE

Use a green crayon to work through the maze. Unscramble the letters you find to complete Jesus' teaching.

"Happy are those who hunger and thirst for _justice_____.
They will be satisfied."

Based on Matthew 5:6

© Silver Burdett Ginn Inc.

I U J S C E T

To the Teacher: This activity follows the Scripture story "True Happiness."

Chapter 6 Beatitudes of Justice

THIS IS OUR FAITH 4 **6**

NAME _____

SEEKING HAPPINESS

Match the items in Column A with those in Column B by writing the correct numbers on the lines provided.

Column A

1. Happy are those who hunger and thirst for justice.
2. The gentle
3. Happy too are the sorrowing.
4. Happy are the poor in spirit.
5. People who hunger and thirst for justice
6. Happy are the gentle.
7. The sorrowing
8. The poor in spirit

Column B

4 The reign of God is theirs.

5 are people who want God's will to be done.

1 They will be satisfied.

2 believe love is the best way to fight evil.

3 They will be comforted.

6 They will receive all that God has promised.

7 are saddened by sin and evil.

8 are people who know they need God.

To the Teacher: This activity reviews the meaning of each beatitude presented in the lesson.

6a THIS IS OUR FAITH 4

Chapter 6 Beatitudes of Justice

© Silver Burdett Ginn Inc.

Background for the Teacher

THE CHALLENGE OF THE BEATITUDES

Nine- and ten-year-olds are increasingly aware of injustice in the world. They are ready to explore the challenging teachings of Jesus. In the Beatitudes, Jesus reverses the values of the world. He teaches that abiding spiritual happiness is most readily achieved by those who are meek. The poor who cling to God are rich. Those who do not assert themselves at the expense of others are the real successes.

THE FAITHFUL WHO LIVED THEM

The promises of the Beatitudes flesh out the Great Commandment. The Beatitudes teach that happiness comes to those who place their trust in God rather than in power, possessions, or pleasures. It comes in acting as God acts. The Beatitudes reflect the way Jesus lived. The latter part of the Sermon on the Mount gives examples for living the Beatitudes. In this discourse, Jesus speaks to the *anawim*, who were the numerous poor Jewish people who faithfully kept God's commands. The Beatitudes describe their way of life. The spirit of the Beatitudes is captured in Isaiah 61 and Psalm 37. The poor in spirit have no wealth or social status. In the time of Jesus, prosperous Jews considered poverty to be the lot of the sinner. The Lord teaches that the gentle will rule when God's reign is achieved fully. The words *hunger and thirst* are associated with Jesus who satisfies all who seek him. The lesson of those who mourn is that when we act mercifully, we will receive mercy.

BEATITUDE PEOPLE OF TODAY

The anawim prayed together. They loved one another as a family, and cared for the needy. In many ways they were similar to the *comunidades de base* so vital to the Church's life today in Latin America. These are Christians whose spirituality reflects solidarity with the poor because it signifies imitation of God, whose love embraces all. The historic roots of the anawim derive from the band of slaves in Pharaoh's Egypt who cried to God for deliverance. The Christians' spiritual roots, in turn, are found in the anawim.

Nine- and ten-year-old youngsters are attracted to the ideals of fairness and happiness described by the Beatitudes. Help them appreciate that their efforts can help bring peace, justice, and caring to their world.

Objective

This lesson helps the students appreciate that Jesus teaches the way to true happiness.

Step 1 / INTRODUCTION

Learning About Our Lives

Reviewing the Great Commandment

Review with the students the Great Commandment. Help the students recall that we best show our love for God when we love our neighbor as much as we love ourselves.

Introducing the Chapter

Direct the students to open their books to page 72 and silently read the chapter title and focus question. Invite the students to name the things that make them really happy. You may want to avoid having them discuss material possessions and focus more instead on people, events, and feelings that bring them joy.

Completing a Happiness Survey

Ask a volunteer to read aloud the directions to the survey on page 72. Give the students sufficient time to complete it. Invite the students to share their responses and explain their answers. Point out to the students that according to the survey results, both doing things for others and being the recipient of a good deed bring happiness to a person.

Step 2 / DEVELOPMENT

Learning About Our Faith +

Reading and Discussing the Scripture Story

Select several students to read aloud "True Happiness" on page 73. As the first beatitude is read, point out the definition of *reign of God*. Explain that these promises of Jesus are called the Beatitudes. Tell the students that the Beatitudes are a way of living that will bring us happiness, according to Jesus.

72

6

Happy Are Those...

Activity

Complete the survey by placing a ✔ in the column that best describes your level of happiness in each situation.

What does the word *happiness* mean to you?

	JUST OKAY	HAPPY	VERY HAPPY
Winning a game			
Receiving a gift			
Getting good grades in school			
Doing a favor for someone			
Giving someone a gift			
Being with friends			
Doing something nice for my family			
Getting new clothes or new toys			

Enriching the Lesson

Invite the students to close their eyes and imagine that they were seated in the crowd long ago when Jesus began to teach about true happiness. Slowly read the four beatitudes to the class. Conclude the lesson by praying: *Jesus, we want to learn how to be truly happy. Help us listen and understand your words. Amen.*

True Happiness

One day, crowds of people gathered to see Jesus. Near the top of a mountain, Jesus sat down and began to teach them how to find everlasting happiness.

> "Happy are the poor in spirit. The **reign of God** is theirs.
> "Happy, too, are the sorrowing. They will be comforted.
> "Happy are the gentle. They will receive all that God has promised.
> "Happy are those who hunger and thirst for **justice**. They will be satisfied."

Jesus stopped speaking. He had more to tell the people about finding everlasting happiness and the **kingdom of heaven** but he wanted to let the people think about what he had taught them.

Based on Matthew 5:1–6

Vocabulary

reign of God: the time when God's peace, love, and justice will begin to rule our lives in this world and be fulfilled when Christ comes again

justice: loving God and all people by treating everyone fairly

kingdom of heaven: another name for the reign of God

////////////////////

Scripture 73

★ ★ ★ ★ Enriching the Lesson ★ ★

Supply the students with magazines and newspapers. Instruct the students to look for stories that tell what makes people happy. When each student has found a relevant story, have the students read aloud the parts of the stories they selected. Have the students reflect on what they think brings happiness to most people.

Ask the students to circle in their books the kinds of people who Jesus says are happy. Help them identify the poor in spirit, the sorrowing, the gentle, and those who hunger and thirst for justice. Ask: Why do you think the people who first heard Jesus' teaching about finding happiness might have been confused or puzzled?

Lead the students to conclude that the people Jesus calls happy are not usually thought of by most people as examples of happiness. Ask the students to identify the things we often associate with happiness, such as money, a big house or car, an important job, and fancy clothes. Explain that Jesus taught that true happiness comes from giving love to others, especially to those who are in need.

Learning About True Happiness

Divide the class into two groups. Ask one group to read aloud the sentence that begins "Happy are . . ." Invite the other group to respond by reading aloud the sentence that follows. Repeat this procedure for each pair of sentences about happiness. Explore with the students what they think is meant by these words of Jesus.

Presenting the Vocabulary

Present the new vocabulary words and help the students learn the definitions by repeating them aloud several times. Answer any questions the students may have.

Step 3 / CONCLUSION

Learning How to Live Our Faith

Writing About Doing Positive Actions

Have the students circle all the words that are positive or happy in the four sets of sentences above. Distribute writing paper. Direct the students to use the words they circled in written sentences that show they are doing these positive actions. An example might be "I comfort my little brother when he falls and hurts his knee." Invite volunteers to share their sentences. Discuss how positive actions make students and others happy.

DAY 2
DOCTRINE

Objective
This lesson helps the students understand what it means to live out the Beatitudes.

Step 1 / INTRODUCTION
Learning About Our Lives

Wishing for Happiness
Read aloud the directions to the activity on page 74. Ask the students to write their wishes on the lines provided. Discuss the following questions.

- Do you think these will come true?
- What would happen if the wishes came true?
- What do you think you need to do to make your wishes come true?

Step 2 / DEVELOPMENT
Learning About Our Faith

Understanding the Beatitudes
Call attention to "Everlasting Happiness" on page 74 and ask a volunteer to begin reading. Ask volunteers to continue reading on page 75. Guide a discussion with the following questions.

- Who are the poor in spirit? Who are the sorrowing? and so on.
- What do these people do?

Help the students appreciate that Jesus wants us to live the Beatitudes. He wants us to know we need God's help. He wants us to comfort the sad people, and be gentle and patient with everyone.

Studying the Photograph
Ask the students to identify the person in the photograph on page 74. Clarify that it is a picture of Mother Teresa of Calcutta. Use the facts listed below to introduce the students to Mother Teresa.

- Mother Teresa was a high school teacher in India who decided to care for the poor and homeless.

Activity
List three wishes that if granted, you think would make you happy.

1. I wish _____
2. I wish _____
3. I wish _____

Lasting Happiness

Jesus was a happy man, and he taught his friends the way to everlasting happiness. The **Beatitudes** summarize how Jesus lived and how he calls us to live if we are to be truly happy in this world and the next.

Jesus promises that if we live the Beatitudes God's powerful love will change our hearts and our world. We will begin to see God's reign ruling our lives in this world. Yet the promises of the Beatitudes will only be fulfilled when Christ comes again.

74 Doctrine

Enriching the Lesson

Divide the class into four groups. Assign one of the Beatitudes to each group. Challenge each group to agree on two specific examples of a person or persons who live out the assigned beatitude. Tell the students that they can write about their examples, act them out, or use drawings to present them to the class. Provide all necessary materials.

Focus on

The Beatitudes The *Catechism of the Catholic Church* explains that the Beatitudes form the core of Jesus' preaching. "The Beatitudes fulfill the promises [made to the chosen people since Abraham] . . . The Beatitudes depict the countenance of Jesus Christ and portray his charity . . . The Beatitudes respond to the natural desire for happiness. This desire is of divine origin: God has placed it in the human heart in order to draw man to the One who alone can fulfill it . . ." (#1716–1718)

74

1. People who are *poor in spirit* know they need God. When we are poor in spirit, we trust in God's care for us, and are thankful for the good things we have been given.

2. People who are *sorrowing* are saddened by sin and evil. When we are sorrowing, we try hard to do what is good and to change what brings suffering to others.

3. People who are *gentle* believe love is the best way to overcome evil and heal what hurts others. When we are gentle, we treat ourselves and others kindly.

4. People who *hunger and thirst for justice* want everyone to be treated fairly and equally. When we hunger and thirst for justice, we share what we have and respect all people.

Activity

Choose one of the four beatitudes listed above and circle its number. Then on the lines below, write the name of someone you know who lives that beatitude. Finally, tell what he or she does to carry out that beatitude.

_____

_____

_____

_____

_____

_____

Vocabulary

Beatitudes: the teachings of Jesus on how to gain everlasting happiness; how Jesus lived

////////////////////////

We Believe

The eight Beatitudes are Jesus' sayings that teach us to love God and others, and promise us a place in the kingdom of heaven. Christians believe that they will be happy forever if they live Jesus' Beatitudes.

Teaching Tips

As you explain the meaning of each beatitude on page 75, have the students refer back to page 73 for the wording of each beatitude as based on the Gospel of Matthew. Encourage the students to learn the beatitudes of justice by heart.

Cultural Awareness

Show the class a picture collage you have made prior to the session that represents a variety of people of different ages, sexes, races, and interests. Have the students suggest one thing that might make everyone happy. Answers may include: *good health, a peaceful world, love, freedom, a home, happiness,* and so on. Help the students conclude that whatever our race, age, or sex, most people have the same basic desires for happiness.

- At first, Mother Teresa worked alone, teaching children in the slums who did not go to school. She spent the rest of each day walking the streets, comforting and helping the dying.

- Other women began to work with Mother Teresa. They began a community of Sisters called the Missionaries of Charity.

- Mother Teresa has won many awards for her work with the poor. She accepts the awards, not for herself or her nuns, but to help people begin to recognize the injustices that many people experience in life. Because of her work, Mother Teresa has been called a "living example of the Beatitudes."

Discuss with the students which beatitude is being shown in the photograph on the page. Then ask them to explain how Mother Teresa is a living example of the Beatitudes.

Reviewing the Vocabulary

Call attention to the Vocabulary box and ask a volunteer to read the definition of *Beatitudes* aloud. Ask the class to repeat the word and its definition aloud several times.

Understanding the Doctrine

Ask a volunteer to read aloud the We Believe statements. Ask the students to explain how this important doctrinal belief relates to the Great Commandment.

Step 3 / CONCLUSION

Learning How to Live Our Faith

Identifying Beatitude People

Direct the students' attention to the activity on page 75. Give them sufficient time to complete the activity. Invite the students to share what they have written.

Reviewing the Lesson

Briefly review the lesson by asking: Which beatitude would you like to grow in right now? (*Affirm all responses.*)

Objective

This lesson helps the students understand the concept of justice and the desire to seek justice.

Step 1 / INTRODUCTION

Learning About Our Lives

Staging a Debate

Write on the chalkboard the sentence "Money can't buy happiness." Divide the class into two teams and ask them to debate this issue. After the debate, point out that, in itself, money can't bring happiness but that money can permit people to help others to be happy.

Step 2 / DEVELOPMENT

Learning About Our Faith

Reading About the First Christians

Invite a volunteer to read on page 76 the introductory paragraph above the Scripture reading about how the first Christians tried to live the beatitudes. Then ask another student to continue reading the story of how the first Christians lived together and treated one another like members of a family. Ask and discuss the following questions.

- How did the early Christians live the Beatitudes? (*They shared everything. They sold possessions and gave money to those in need. They ate together. They prayed together and broke bread together.*)

- Look again at the beatitudes of justice on page 73. Give examples of how the early Christians lived out each of the Beatitudes.

Understanding Justice

Call attention to "Signs of Justice" on page 77. Ask volunteers to read this section aloud. Ask:

- What were some of the signs of justice that the first Christians lived out? (*They cared for the poor, the sick, the elderly, and treated one another equally.*)

- What do the Beatitudes remind us of? (*That today's followers of Jesus must also work for justice, respecting all human beings regardless of race, color, language, or religion.*)

As followers of Jesus, the early Christians tried to live the Beatitudes. The Acts of the Apostles tells us how they lived.

The First Christians

The first Christians treated one another like members of a family. They lived together and shared everything. They sold their possessions and gave the money to those who were in need. They ate their meals together. They prayed together and they broke bread together in memory of Jesus.

Based on Acts 2:42–47

76   Scripture

Enriching the Lesson

Invite a guest speaker to talk to the class about advocacy in working for justice. Possible guests might include: a social worker, a pastoral minister, a member of the Respect Life Committee, an attorney, or a health care worker. Prior to the visit, inform your guest of the topic you wish him or her to address. Encourage students to ask appropriate questions of the guest speaker.

Signs of Justice

The first Christians were concerned for one another. Their care for the poor, the sick, and the elderly, and their equal treatment of one another, were all signs that Jesus' Beatitudes were being lived out in their lives.

The Beatitudes remind us that today's followers of Jesus must also work for justice. People who work for justice share what they have with those who are in need. People of justice respect all human beings regardless of their race, color, language, or religion.

Activity

Listed below are actions that you can take to work for justice in your community. Add two more actions to the list. Then circle the action that you think is the most important.

1. I will treat all people fairly, even if they are younger than me.

2. I will believe that others are as good as I am, even if they look different.

3. I will respect those who speak a different language.

4. _____

    _____

5. _____

    _____

Learning How to Live Our Faith

Identifying Ways to Work for Justice

Read aloud the directions to the activity on page 77. Answer any questions the students may have. Brainstorm with the class possible actions that the students can do to work for justice. List their ideas on the chalkboard. Afterward, allow the students to choose two from the list or two new ideas to write in their texts. Ask the students to choose one from the list that they can commit to doing. Have the students share their commitment with a partner. Explain that the partners need to help each other remember this commitment and encourage each other to follow through with the action.

Studying the Photographs

Direct the students' attention to the photographs on page 77. Ask the students to identify what actions for justice are depicted or suggested by each photograph.

CURRICULUM CONNECTION

Music Teach the students "What We Need in This World Is," found on page 116 of the THIS IS OUR FAITH *Hymnal.* In the Teacher's Songbook, Grade 4, page 6, there are suggestions for movement, instrumentation, and tips for teaching the song.

77

Objective

This lesson helps the students recognize that all Christians are called to live out the beatitudes.

Step 1 / INTRODUCTION

Learning About Our Lives

Describing Poverty

Ask the students to describe what they think being poor means. Include in the discussion "being without food, housing, clothing, education, and entertainment." Brainstorm possible ways that the class can get involved in fighting poverty. (Possible activities include collecting canned foods, clothing, blankets, toys, or books for a parish or community pantry or shelter.) You might also broaden the students' understanding of poverty by talking about people who are lonely, ill, or sad. If possible, allow the students to make cards for parish shut-ins and arrange for a minister of care to distribute the cards. Help the students appreciate how these actions are practical ways of living out the Beatitudes.

Step 2 / DEVELOPMENT

Learning About Our Faith

Reading a Biography

Ask volunteers to take turns reading aloud "Saint Frances of Rome" on page 78. Then have the students discuss how Saint Frances lived the Beatitudes. After reading the story, talk with the class about how and where Saint Frances of Rome could live out the Beatitudes in our world today.

Role-Playing

Divide the class into groups of three or four students. Assign a beatitude to each group and have them imagine how Saint Frances might live that beatitude today. You might help the students clarify the distinction between charity (that is, a hand-out) and justice, which enables those who receive help to learn to improve the conditions of their lives. Then ask them to discuss and rehearse in their groups how to pantomime the beatitude assigned to their group.

78

Saint Frances of Rome

Frances, born in 1384, grew up to have had everything she wanted. Her husband, Lorenzo, loved her, and she loved him. They had three beautiful children. The family was rich, and Frances had many fine things.

She prayed every day, thanking God for so many gifts. But she felt sad for people who did not have all the good things she had. So she sold her fine clothes and used the money to buy food and medicine for the poor. She even turned part of her home into a hospital.

Then there was a war. Enemies sent Frances' husband into exile and ruined their home. One son was taken prisoner. Frances' daughter and her other son died. Frances was now poor herself, but she continued to trust in God's care.

Placing her life in God's hands, Frances prayed and worked even harder for those who were sick or poor. She set up a soup kitchen and begged for food to feed the hungry.

At the end of the war, Frances' husband and son were able to return home. For the next twenty years, Frances cared for her family and continued her work for the poor and the sick. She organized a community of women to help the people of Rome.

Then Frances' husband died. Frances missed him very much. She spent even more time praying and working with her community of women to help the poor of Rome.

Frances died in 1440, four years after her husband died. The people of Rome loved her so much that they named the church where she was buried the Church of Saint Frances of Rome. Catholics celebrate the feast of Saint Frances on March 9.

78 Morality

CURRICULUM CONNECTION

Language Arts Encourage the students to think about what makes people happy. Ask them to write about the many different reasons people have for being happy, focusing especially on those people who keep God's law to love others. Invite the students to read aloud what they have written.

Teaching Tips

The students may have some confusion as to the spelling and usage of the name Frances. Explain that Frances—spelled with an *e*—is a name for a female (Saint Frances of Rome) and that Francis—spelled with an *i*—is a name for a male (Saint Francis of Assisi).

Activity

Complete the Venn diagram by naming ways in which Saint Frances helped others find happiness and ways in which you help others find happiness. Are any ways the same? Write those ways in the overlapping part of the circle.

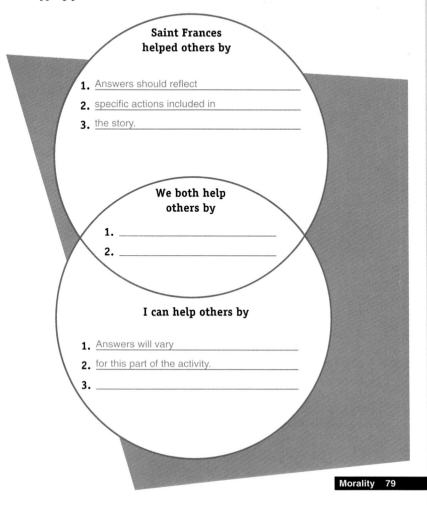

Saint Frances helped others by

1. Answers should reflect
2. specific actions included in
3. the story.

We both help others by

1. _____
2. _____

I can help others by

1. Answers will vary
2. for this part of the activity.
3. _____

Allow time for the groups to take turns pantomiming the Beatitudes while the other students guess each beatitude. Assist the students in appreciating that Saint Frances is an example to us and that we can carry on her work.

Step 3 / CONCLUSION

Learning How to Live Our Faith

Completing an Activity

Read aloud the directions to the activity on page 79. Give the students sufficient time to complete the activity, working independently. When the students have finished, ask volunteers to share their answers. Answer any questions the students may have.

Enriching the Lesson

Invite the students to make Beatitude booklets. Distribute drawing paper, pencils, and felt-tip markers. Ask them to write their favorite beatitude across the top of the paper and then draw a picture that shows someone living out that beatitude. Collect the drawings for use in the next chapter.

DAY 5
PRAYER/REVIEW

Objective

This lesson helps the students understand that meditation is a special kind of prayer and helps them to pray by meditating.

Introducing Meditation as Prayer

Invite a volunteer to read aloud "Praying and Meditating" on page 80. Outline on the chalkboard the four steps for one way to meditate. Ask the students to repeat and think about the four steps.

Preparing for Meditation

Gather the students for prayer. You can gather in the prayer area in your classroom or, if possible, have the students sit on a large carpeted area. Encourage them to sit in a comfortable position on the floor and close their eyes. Explain to the students that they will be asked to be very quiet and still. They will talk to Jesus silently and listen to Jesus speaking to them in their minds and hearts.

Praying and Meditating About Jesus

Begin the meditation experience. Allow sufficient time for the prayer experience to be meaningful. Read the following meditation slowly.

Picture yourself in a large crowd. . . . Everyone around you is silent. . . . They are listening to a gentle, deep voice. . . . You look toward where the voice is coming from. . . . A man is speaking. . . . His voice is kind and loving. . . . You recognize that this man is Jesus. . . . You listen to him answer a question. . . . Then Jesus notices you in the crowd. . . . He smiles at you. . . . "Follow me," Jesus says. "Will you follow me?". . . You want to answer Jesus. . . . Speak to Jesus now in your heart. . . . Tell him how much you want to be his follower. . . . After you are finished answering Jesus . . . leave the crowd . . . come back to our room . . . and open your eyes.

Talking About the Meditation

Encourage the students to talk about their meditation experience. Ask them how well they were able to picture the scenes in the meditation. Stress that they can talk and listen to God when they meditate.

Praying and Meditating

Meditation is a special kind of prayer. When we meditate, we turn all of our attention to God. We think about God. We wonder about God. We imagine ourselves in the presence of God.

There are different ways to meditate. Here is one of those ways.

1. *Prepare*: Find a quiet place. Sit comfortably. Breathe slowly and deeply until you feel peaceful.
2. *Picture*: Read a gospel story slowly. Picture the scene in your mind. Hear the words of Jesus. Imagine how it feels to be with Jesus.
3. *Pray*: When you are ready, talk to Jesus. Tell him how you feel about his words and his presence. Tell him what you are thinking. Ask him questions. Listen as Jesus speaks to you.
4. *Practice*: Decide how you will live what Jesus told you in prayer.

Focus on

Meditation Some of the purposes and results of meditation are to use the imagination and reason in deep, mental prayer; examine one's conscience and resolve to change motives and intentions; be receptive and listen to God; become part of the Christian mysteries; focus entirely on the presence of the Holy Spirit; receive God's grace and help more fully; and give God glory and praise.

Chapter Review

Think of one way you and others can live each of the first four beatitudes. Write your answers on the lines provided.

1. Happy are the poor in spirit. _____
   _____
   _____

2. Happy are the sorrowing. _____
   _____
   _____

3. Happy are the gentle. _____
   _____
   _____

4. Happy are those who hunger and thirst for justice.
   _____
   _____

Write the answers to the first two questions.

1. What are the Beatitudes?

   The Beatitudes are the teachings of Jesus on how to gain everlasting
   happiness. The Beatitudes teach us how Jesus lived.

2. How does Jesus say we can be happy?

   Jesus says we can be happy if we live his Beatitudes.
   They teach us how Jesus lived. Jesus gives us the
   Holy Spirit to help us live the Beatitudes.

3. Discuss what we can do to bring more justice into the world.

Those who are kind to the poor will be happy.
Based on Proverbs 14:21

Writing About Living the Beatitudes

Direct the students' attention to the first activity in the Chapter Review on page 81. Explain the directions and have the students write about ways for living out the four beatitudes. Encourage them to put their ideas into action during the coming week.

Reviewing the Chapter

Direct the students to write answers to the first two review questions on the lines provided. For the discussion item, encourage all to participate.

Reflecting on the Scripture Verse

Together, read aloud the Scripture verse at the bottom of the page. Encourage the students to think about the meaning of true happiness. Encourage the class to memorize the verse.

CURRICULUM CONNECTION

Music Invite the students to bring in song recordings of contemporary music that teach a positive justice message. Provide the audio equipment to play the music for the class. Point out that writing and performing songs with a message is one way to work for justice. The performers heighten the awareness of their listeners to the social problems presented in the lyrics.

... The Reign of God Is Theirs

Objectives

To help the students

■ Appreciate that Jesus teaches about true peace and happiness.
■ Understand the meaning of the remaining Beatitudes.
■ Understand peace and desire to seek peace.
■ Recognize ways that they can live out the Beatitudes.
■ Learn to pray the Jesus Prayer and review the chapter.

Chapter Outline

	Step 1 Learning About Our Lives	**Step 2** Learning About Our Faith	**Step 3** Learning How to Live Our Faith
Day 1	■ Recall good actions. ■ Introduce the chapter. ■ Identify peaceful actions. ■ Study the photograph. *ABOUT 10 MINUTES*	■ Introduce the Scripture story. ■ Read the Scripture story. ■ Present the vocabulary. *ABOUT 10 MINUTES*	■ Talk about discipleship. ■ Make a photo poster. *ABOUT 10 MINUTES*
Day 2	■ Identify peacemakers. *ABOUT 7 MINUTES*	■ Understand the remaining Beatitudes. ■ Review the vocabulary. ■ Present the doctrine. *ABOUT 13 MINUTES*	■ Complete an activity. ■ Review the lesson. *ABOUT 10 MINUTES*
Day 3	■ Dramatize an interview. ■ Discuss questions. *ABOUT 10 MINUTES*	■ Understand peace. ■ Present the vocabulary. *ABOUT 10 MINUTES*	■ Identify actions of peace. *ABOUT 10 MINUTES*
Day 4	■ Complete an activity. ■ Learn about El Salvador. *ABOUT 8 MINUTES*	■ Read and discuss a biography. ■ Recall El Salvador. ■ Complete an activity. *ABOUT 12 MINUTES*	■ Identify the remaining Beatitudes. *ABOUT 10 MINUTES*
Day 5	**Prayer** Introduce the Jesus Prayer and pray the Jesus Prayer. **Review** Write about living the Beatitudes; review the chapter; and read the Scripture verse.		

Plan Ahead

	Preparing Your Class	**Materials Needed**

Day 1 — Read the lesson plan. Gather the students' wallet-sized pictures for Step 3. Begin search for news articles about El Salvador with school librarian's assistance.

- pencils or pens
- photos of each student
- 4" construction paper squares
- posterboard, glue
- crayons or felt-tip markers

Day 2 — Read the lesson plan. If enriching the lesson, gather newspapers and news magazines.

- pencils or pens

Day 3 — Read through the lesson plan. If enriching the lesson, gather all the necessary materials.

- pencils or pens

Day 4 — Read through the lesson plan. Gather a collection of news clippings about El Salvador. If enriching the lesson, have addresses of important leaders on hand.

- pencils or pens
- newspaper and magazine articles about El Salvador
- globe or world map

Day 5 — Read through the entire lesson plan. If enriching the lesson, gather materials for making posters or murals.

- pencils or pens

Additional Resources

As you plan this chapter, consider using the following from The Resourceful Teacher Package.

- *Classroom Activity Sheets* 7 and 7a
- *Family Activity Sheets* 7 and 7a
- *Chapter 7 Test*
- *Prayers for Every Day*
- *Projects: Grade 4*

You may also wish to refer to the following Big Book.

- *We Celebrate God's Word,* page 11

In preparing the students for the Sunday readings, you may wish to use Silver Burdett Ginn's *Getting Ready for Sunday* student and teacher materials.

BOOKS FOR THE JOURNEY

Experience Jesus Today. "Open," p. 171. Charles Singer & Albert Hari. Oregon Catholic Press, 1993. A prayer asking for help to recognize the face of God in the needy and to work for peace and justice.

The Table Where Rich People Sit. Byrd Baylor. Charles Scribner's Songs, 1994. A poetic narrative in which a child learns what real happiness and riches are for her family.

MORE BOOKS FOR THE JOURNEY

The Cherry Tree. Daisaku Ikeda. Alfred A. Knopf, 1991. The story of two children who have lost their home and father to a war, helping an old man care for a tree which, when it blooms, brings happiness, healing, and hope to their mother and the village.

Hey World, Here I Am! "Mrs. Thurstone," pp. 82–85. Jean Little. Harper & Row, 1986. A poetic narrative of a child visiting and loving an elderly hospitalized woman.

REDUCED CLASSROOM ACTIVITIES

NAME _____

BEATITUDES OF PEACE

Read the sentences below. Each set of sentences contains a symbol that needs to be decoded. Write the solution on the line provided below each set.

Set 1

****** are those who show mercy to others. They will receive mercy.

****** are the single-hearted. They will see God.

****** are those who are treated unfairly for doing what is right. The reign of God is theirs.

Solution: ****** = Happy

Set 2

People who show mercy are kind to all ⌇⌇⌇'s creatures.

People who are single-hearted keep ⌇⌇⌇ and ⌇⌇⌇'s way of love first in their hearts.

People who are treated unfairly do what ⌇⌇⌇ wants, even when others threaten to hurt them.

Solution: ⌇⌇⌇ = God

Set 3

Happy are the ☐☐☐☐☐☐. They will be called children of God.

People who are ☐☐☐☐☐☐ try to bring peace where there is none.

When we help others stop fighting and find ways to solve problems, we are ☐☐☐☐☐☐.

Solution: ☐☐☐☐☐☐ = peacemakers

To the Teacher: This activity follows the Scripture story "Words of Peace and Happiness."

Chapter 7 Beatitudes of Peace   THIS IS OUR FAITH 4 **7**

NAME _____

A PRAYER FOR PEACE

Jesus helped his disciples find happiness by teaching them to be peacemakers. As a disciple of Jesus, you too can be a peacemaker by praying for peace. Write your own prayer for peace on the lines below. Begin each line with the letter given.

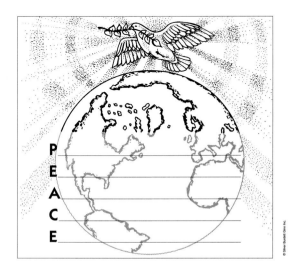

7a THIS IS OUR FAITH 4   **Chapter 7** Beautitudes of Peace

JUSTICE AND MERCY

All eight Beatitudes express the core attitudes of justice, mercy, and good faith that Jesus named as the more important matters of the law in Matthew 23:23. These profound orientations of the heart echo what God reveals as all that is required of us: to do right, to love goodness, and to walk humbly with our God (Micah 6:8). Mercy, love, and humility are the essential Christian values. To do right implies the goal of Christian love—to work to assure each person's God-given rights.

The Beatitudes proclaim a unique message in that they announce a religious happiness for the *anawim*—those who lack material goods and stand in need of the spiritual blessings promised by God. The Beatitudes promise the fulfillment of this happiness through Christ. The recognition of the anawim contrasts with the religious thought of the time which regarded human affliction and sorrow as the punishment for personal sin, or the sins of the parents. This is a message of good news for the poor and afflicted.

The kingdom of God is brought about through the graciousness of God. But this will not happen without human collaboration (See Chapter 1.) God's Kingdom exists wherever his will is at work. The kingdom of God is a kingdom of justice and peace, equality for all, consolation for the afflicted. The kingdom of God, begun on earth by Jesus Christ, will be fully realized at the end of time.

THE REMAINING FOUR BEATITUDES

In Scripture, peace is always seen as a gift from God. But, as with all of God's goodness to us, we must collaborate with him in bringing about the peaceable kingdom.

The Church interprets the Beatitudes at both a personal and social level. Archbishop Oscar Romero decried the cycle of poverty, suffering, and death that enslaves the people of El Salvador. He labored to change these injustices through peaceful means. The harvest that the Archbishop's martyrdom yields is the conversion of many in El Salvador to desire peace in the spirit of the Beatitudes. Archbishop Romero lives on as the patron of a Church that labors for justice on behalf of the poor all over the world.

Fourth graders are at the ideal age to become aware gradually of the social dimensions of Christian morality. Working to change laws that keep people poor is as much an application of the Beatitudes as providing a meal for one person in need. In this chapter you can help the students continue to develop principles of justice and peace that are expressed in action.

...The Reign of God Is Theirs

DAY 1
SCRIPTURE

Objective

This lesson helps the students appreciate that Jesus teaches about true peace and happiness.

Step 1 / INTRODUCTION

Learning About Our Lives

Recalling Good Actions

Ask the students if they had opportunities to live out the beatitudes that they studied in Chapter 5. Encourage them to share their experiences. Share any of your own. Invite the students to discuss any good actions they might have accomplished from the activities on pages 79 and 81 in their books.

Introducing the Chapter

Direct the students to page 82 and ask a volunteer to read aloud the chapter title and focus question. List the students' responses on the chalkboard. Tell them that in this chapter they will learn how the Beatitudes call us to be peacemakers.

Identifying Peaceful Actions

Ask a volunteer to read aloud the directions to the activity on page 82. After the students complete the activity independently, have them share their ideas with the class.

Studying the Photograph

Point out the photograph on page 82. Ask the students to identify how the people in the photograph are acting as peacemakers.

Step 2 / DEVELOPMENT

Learning About Our Faith

Introducing the Scripture Story

Help the students recall the four beatitudes studied in Chapter 6.

- Happy are the poor in spirit. The reign of God is theirs.
- Happy, too, are the sorrowing. They will be comforted.
- Happy are the gentle. They will receive all that God has promised.

82

What are some things that help you and your classmates live peacefully and happily together instead of fighting and hurting one another?

82   Scripture

Activity

Fill in the blanks to complete the sentences below, using your own words.

1. When I hear the word *peace*, I think of

   _____ .

2. The opposite of peace is _____ .

3. A peacemaker is someone who _____ .

4. The most peaceful person I know is

   _____ .

   because _____ .

Enriching the Lesson

Read aloud the following poem.

Showing Our Love

If people would hug more
It just seems to me
That all of us might live
more peacefully.
If people would hug more,
And try to be friends,
There's a good chance that all
of our wars would end.
Perhaps that's too simple,
But we'll never know
Until people hug more,
And let their love show.

Focus on

Peacemaking "The Challenge of Peace: God's Promise and Our Response," a pastoral letter by the United States bishops, states: "Peacemaking is not an optional commitment. It is a requirement of our faith. We are called to be peacemakers . . . by our Lord Jesus. Respecting our freedom, he does not solve our problems, but sustains us as we take responsibility for his work of creation and try to shape it in the ways of the Kingdom. We believe his grace will never fail us."

Words of Peace and Happiness

Jesus had been telling his **disciples** and many other people how to live happy lives. He had already shared with them four ways to find everlasting happiness. Now Jesus wanted to teach them more. So he began to speak again.

"Happy also are those who show **mercy** to others. They will receive mercy.

Happy are the single-hearted. They will see God.

Happy are the **peacemakers**. They will be called children of God.

Happy are those who are treated unfairly for doing what is right. The reign of God is theirs."

Jesus looked around. He could see that the people were trying to understand what he had said.

Based on Matthew 5:7–10

Vocabulary

disciples: followers of Jesus

mercy: loving care, or compassion

peacemakers: people who try to bring peace and friendship where these things are needed

//////////////////

Scripture **83**

Teaching Tips

Explore with the students the causes of war and of peace. Help the students compare fighting between individuals and fighting between nations. Talk about ways in which peace is restored between people. Ask the students to suggest ways that peace can be restored between nations. Help the students understand that anything individuals do to bring peace in their own lives helps bring peace to the world community.

■ Happy are those who hunger and thirst for justice. They will be satisfied.

As each beatitude is repeated aloud, print it on the chalkboard. Remind the students that Jesus wants us to be happy, loving people.

Reading the Scripture Story

Invite several students to read aloud "Words of Peace and Happiness" on page 83. Briefly explore with the students what they think each beatitude means. Help them understand that anything we, as individuals, do to promote peace helps to bring peace to the world. Point out that the same is true of our own efforts to live the Beatitudes, for each of us can help make the world a better place in which to live.

Presenting the Vocabulary

Present the vocabulary words *disciples, mercy,* and *peacemakers.* Have the students repeat the definitions several times.

Step 3 / CONCLUSION

Learning How to Live Our Faith

Talking About Discipleship

Talk about the meaning of the word *disciple.* Ask the students if they consider themselves disciples of Jesus. Have them explain their answers. Encourage them to be specific in terms of how they follow Jesus.

Making a Photo Poster

Distribute to each student a 4" square of construction paper, crayons or felt-tip markers, and glue. Give the students the wallet-size picture of themselves that you collected last week. Have them glue their pictures to their construction paper squares and decorate the frames around the pictures with their names and symbols that represent that they are disciples. While they are doing this, letter the words "We Are Disciples of Jesus" on a sheet of posterboard. When everyone has finished, have the students come forward individually to glue or tape their pictures to the poster. As they do so, encourage them to say, "I am (*Name*). I am a friend and follower of Jesus."

83

DAY 2
DOCTRINE

Objective

This lesson helps the students understand the meaning of the remaining Beatitudes.

Step 1 / INTRODUCTION

Learning About Our Lives

Identifying Peacemakers

Point out the activity on page 84. Give the students time to complete the activity. Afterward, invite the students to share their ideas. Help the students to appreciate that peacemaking is not the responsibility of politicians and people in the news. Even fourth graders are capable peacemakers. More importantly, we are all called to live as peacemakers in the world.

Step 2 / DEVELOPMENT

Learning About Our Faith

Understanding the Beatitudes of Peace

Ask several volunteers to each read a portion of "Ways to Everlasting Happiness" on pages 84 and 85. Help the students appreciate that the Beatitudes work together to help us live in awareness of the presence of God. Jesus sends the Holy Spirit to help us trust in God's love for us. You may want to have the students review the meaning of the eight Beatitudes by studying the charts on pages 75 and 85.

Brainstorming

Divide the class into groups of four. Distribute writing paper. Assign one of the beatitudes presented in the lesson to each group. Invite the students in each group to brainstorm ways in which they can live that beatitude. Ask one student in each group to make a list of the group's ideas and then read the list aloud. Invite each student to choose an idea to put into practice, and write it down.

Reviewing the Vocabulary

Review the vocabulary presented in the last session. Ask them to repeat the definitions aloud several times.

84

Activity

World leaders are often peacemakers. What advice would you give the President of the United States that might help him bring peace to the world?

_____
_____
_____
_____
_____
_____

Ways to Everlasting Happiness

The word *beatitude* means "blessed" or "happy." The Beatitudes show us Jesus' way to eternal happiness. They let us see how Jesus lived and how he wants us to choose to live. If we live the Beatitudes, Jesus promises that we will be happy forever in the kingdom of heaven.

We learned about the first four beatitudes in Chapter 6. Now we will learn about the last four. In these four beatitudes, Jesus invites us to live as people of peace.

84 Doctrine

CURRICULUM CONNECTION

Music Invite the parish music director or minister of music to teach the class "Prayer of Saint Francis" by Sebastian Temple. The music is published by Franciscan Communications Center, © 1967. Invite older students who can play the guitar to accompany the class in a performance of this well-known song.

Cultural Awareness

Discuss with the class how the command, "Do unto others as you would have them do unto you" is a reminder to live the Beatitudes. You might point out that in some parts of the world, people are prevented from worshiping God in their own way and that there are individuals who are treated unfairly because of their religious beliefs. Help the students appreciate that we are called to respect the religious beliefs of all people.

5. People who *show mercy* care for people who are hurting and forgive those who hurt them. When we try to understand how others feel, accept their faults, forgive them, and ease their pain, we show mercy.

6. People who are *single-hearted* keep God and his way of love first in their hearts. When what God wants us to do is more important to us than what anyone tempts us to do, we are single-hearted.

7. People who are *peacemakers* try to bring peace where there is none. When we help others stop fighting and find ways to solve problems, we are peacemakers.

8. People who are *treated unfairly* do what God wants, even when others threaten to hurt them. When we do what is right and others laugh and make fun of us, or exclude us, we are treated unfairly.

Activity

The words below describe some of the qualities found in the Beatitudes. The sentences are examples of those qualities. Match the word to the sentence by writing the correct numbers on the lines below.

1. peacefulness
2. understanding
3. mercy
4. care
5. trust
6. forgiveness

_5_ I believe in you.

_1_ I'm happy when we get along.

_2_ I know how you feel.

_6_ It's okay. I forgive you.

_3_ I won't punish you unjustly.

_4_ I'd like to help you.

We Believe

Jesus wants us to follow his example and his teachings so that we will be happy in this world and the next. The Beatitudes summarize Jesus' way to happiness, a way of loving and caring.

Doctrine 85

Enriching the Lesson

Distribute newspapers and news magazines to the students. Give them sufficient time to locate an article on the topic of injustice or strife. Ask the students to pray silently for those suffering from injustice and violence. Move about the room so that if students have any questions, they can ask without disrupting the prayer of their classmates.

Presenting the Doctrine

Present the We Believe statements to the students. Ask them which beatitude teaches us kindness, which beatitude teaches us to care about others, and which one teaches us to be merciful.

Step 3 / CONCLUSION

Learning How to Live Our Faith

Completing an Activity

Point out the activity on page 85. Direct the students to complete the activity. When the students have finished, go over the answers and have the students make any corrections.

Reviewing the Lesson

Have the students close their books. Read through the We Believe statements, omitting key words. Invite the students to orally supply the missing words to show they understand the important concepts presented in today's lesson. (*Teachings, happy, happiness, love*)

DAY 3
MORALITY

Objective

This lesson helps the students understand peace and helps them want to seek peace.

Step 1 / INTRODUCTION

Learning About Our Lives

Dramatizing an Interview

Select students to take the parts of the TV anchor, the boy, the girl, Olga, and Mr. Harrison in the interview "Person of the Week." Allow a few minutes for the students to become familiar with their parts. Then invite them to come to the front of the room with their books and read the interview aloud.

Discussing Questions

Discuss the following questions.

- What makes people fight? (*Help the students understand that selfishness, discrimination, unfairness, hate, and anger are some things that keep people from living together in peace.*)

- What are some things you feel help young people get along together more peacefully and happily? (*Lead the students to conclude that care, love, trust, forgiveness, patience, kindness, and understanding are qualities that help us live together more peacefully.*)

Step 2 / DEVELOPMENT

Learning About Our Faith +

Understanding Peace

Ask for volunteers to read aloud "Signs of Peace" on page 87. Ask: What did the disciples teach about seeking peace? (*Seek faith, and love, and peace. Do not be quarrelsome. Be kind to all.*)

Help the students appreciate that seeking peace is not only working against violence, it is also working actively for peace. Ask: What are some of the meanings of *shalom*? (*Freedom from violence or misfortune, wholeness, well-being, and peace*)

Person of the Week

TV anchor: Now our *Person of the Week*. In her troubled East Side neighborhood, this young girl took a risk that paid off. She called it *Project Peace*. Her name is Olga Frascati. Here is what she did.

Boy: There were fights all the time. I was afraid to walk down the street.

Girl: I was looking forward to moving and getting out of here. Kids sold drugs everywhere.

TV anchor: Olga decided to do something about this sad situation. With the help of people in the community, she began *Project Peace*. Olga, what is *Project Peace*?

Olga: *Project Peace* brings people together to talk about problems instead of fighting over them. We also plan fun ways for kids from different backgrounds to get to know and understand one another. We made up posters and slogans, such as "Open Your Hands to Help, Not Hurt." A group of kids wrote and recorded a great rap song, which they call "Melting Down Hearts."

Enriching the Lesson

Distribute crayons or felt-tip markers and construction paper. Direct the students to create bumper stickers that express the need to live together more peacefully. As the students work, move about the room, affirming their efforts and commenting on their ideas. When they have finished, allow time for them to show their bumper stickers to the group. Display the bumper stickers in a prominent area of the parish or school.

Chapter Review

Think of one way you can live each of the last four beatitudes. Write your answers on the lines after each beatitude.

Happy are those who show mercy.

_____

_____

Happy are the single-hearted.

_____

_____

Happy are the peacemakers.

_____

_____

Happy are those who are unjustly treated for doing what is right.

_____

_____

Write your answers to the first two questions on the lines provided.

1. What is meant by *disciples*?

Disciples are friends and followers of Jesus.

2. What does Jesus teach us in the last four beatitudes?

Jesus teaches us how to act as he did. He wants us

to be kind to all God's creatures. He wants us to be

fair to others and show love for them. Jesus teaches

us how to forgive and have mercy on others.

_____

3. Discuss how you can be a peacemaker.

Jesus says, "Treat others the way you would have them treat you."
Based on Matthew 7:12

★ ★★★ ★
Enriching the Lesson

Challenge the students to create posters or murals as the students involved in Project Peace did. Ask them to use the titles suggested in the interview: "Open Your Hands to Help, Not Hurt" and "Melting Down Hearts." Divide the class into groups of three or four to work on their projects. Have appropriate materials on hand for the students to use, including butcher paper, posterboard, lined paper, crayons, and felt-tip markers. When the projects are completed, arrange to display them in a public area of the school.

Writing About Living the Beatitudes

Read the directions at the top of page 91 for ways to live out the Beatitudes. Ask the students to write their answers on the lines provided. Afterward, invite the students to share their ideas. Encourage the students to act on their ideas to live the Beatitudes.

Reviewing the Chapter

Read aloud the first two questions and ask the students to write the answers to the questions. For the discussion item, encourage all to participate.

Reading the Scripture Verse

Read together the verse at the bottom of the page. Ask the students to give examples of how they would like to be treated by their friends, teachers, and parents. Ask: What familiar "rule" is a rewording of this verse? (*The Golden Rule: Do unto others as you would have them do unto you.*)

8 God's Commandments

Objectives ~~~~~

To help the students

- Connect the Great Commandment to the Ten Commandments.
- Understand that Jesus calls us to share with others and helps us to do so.
- Appreciate that the Commandments help us to live in peace and justice.
- Apply the Ten Commandments to their own lives.
- Pray for peace and justice and review the chapter.

Chapter Outline ~~~~~~~~~~~~

	Step 1 Learning About Our Lives	**Step 2** Learning About Our Faith	**Step 3** Learning How to Live Our Faith
Day 1	■ Introduce the chapter. ■ Read the story. ■ Write rules. ■ Discuss living without rules. *ABOUT 15 MINUTES*	■ Read about the Ten Commandments. ■ Understand the Ten Commandments. *ABOUT 10 MINUTES*	■ Apply the Ten Commandments to life. *ABOUT 5 MINUTES*
Day 2	■ Consider special rules. *ABOUT 8 MINUTES*	■ Read and discuss a Scripture story. ■ Go beyond the law. ■ Present the vocabulary. *ABOUT 12 MINUTES*	■ Complete an activity. ■ Review the lesson. *ABOUT 10 MINUTES*
Day 3	■ Identify rules that help us. *ABOUT 10 MINUTES*	■ Become people of peace and justice. *ABOUT 10 MINUTES*	■ Complete an activity. *ABOUT 10 MINUTES*
Day 4	■ Reflect on rules. *ABOUT 8 MINUTES*	■ Interpreting the commandments. *ABOUT 10 MINUTES*	■ Read letters to the editor. ■ Complete an activity. ■ Write an editorial response. ■ Follow God's commandments. *ABOUT 12 MINUTES*
Day 5	**Prayer** Explain the prayer celebration; prepare the prayer celebration; pray for peace and justice; and sing together. **Review** Identify commandments; review the chapter; and read the Scripture verse.		

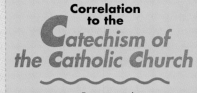

Plan Ahead

	Preparing Your Class	**Materials Needed**
Day 1	Read through the entire lesson plan.	■ pencils or pens
Day 2	Read the lesson plan. If you choose to enrich the lesson, make all necessary preparations.	■ pencils or pens
Day 3	Read through the entire lesson plan. If you opt to do the music activity, obtain the song "Love Life."	■ pencils or pens ■ worksheets
Day 4	Read through the lesson plan. Obtain an editorial page from a newspaper.	■ pencils or pens ■ editorial page from newspaper
Day 5	Read through the entire lesson plan.	■ pencils or pens ■ candle ■ prayer cloth

Additional Resources

As you plan this chapter, consider using the following from The Resourceful Teacher Package.

■ *Classroom Activity Sheets 8* and *8a*
■ *Family Activity Sheets 8* and *8a*
■ *Chapter 8 Test*
■ *Prayers for Every Day*
■ *Projects: Grade 4*

You may also wish to refer to the following Big Book.

■ *We Celebrate God's Word,* page 3

In preparing the students for the Sunday readings, you may wish to use Silver Burdett Ginn's *Getting Ready for Sunday* student and teacher materials.

BOOKS FOR THE JOURNEY

Experience Jesus Today. "The Rich Young Man," pp. 142–145. Charles Singer & Albert Hari. Oregon Catholic Press, 1993. The story of a rich young man with additional information, illustrations, questions, and a prayer.

Hand in Hand. "The Gettysburg Address," pp. 63–65; "The Battle Hymn of the Republic," p. 75. Collected by Lee Bennet Hopkins. Simon & Schuster, 1994. Writings that reflect the spiritual rules and laws that are part of the inner fabric of America.

MORE BOOKS FOR THE JOURNEY

The Orphan Boy. Tolowa M. Mollel. Clarion Books, 1990. An African folktale about an old man who cannot keep the only rule of the boy who has brought him companionship and good fortune.

Afternoon of the Elves. Janet Taylor Lisle. Scholastic, Inc., 1989. A story of coping, of friendship, and of showing love for others.

REDUCED CLASSROOM ACTIVITIES

NAME _____

GOD'S COMMANDMENTS

Imagine that you live in a place where nobody follows any of God's commandments. Write a story to describe what it might be like to live without rules. Then write a title for your story.

To the Teacher: This activity reviews the Ten Commandments. Encourage the class to include several commandments. The completed projects can be cut out and displayed by commandment number.

Chapter 8 God's Commandments

THIS IS OUR FAITH 4 **8**

NAME _____

LIVING THE GREAT COMMANDMENT

Think about the talk Jesus had with the rich young man. If Jesus asked you to give something to the poor, what would you give? Draw or briefly describe that item on the moving cart below.

That probably wasn't a very difficult decision for you to make. But what if Jesus asked you to give something that is one of the most cherished things you own? Now draw or briefly describe *that* item on the moving cart.

Jesus didn't ask the rich young man to give up just one or two items; he asked him to give up *everything* and follow him. What possessions would be almost impossible for you to give up? Draw or describe them now.

To the Teacher: This activity follows the Scripture story "The Rich Young Man."

8a THIS IS OUR FAITH 4

Chapter 8 God's Commandments

Background for the Teacher

THE TEN COMMANDMENTS

In this chapter, the Ten Commandments of the earlier covenant are set within the framework of the later covenant. An overview of the Ten Commandments is presented in the context of Jesus' message and what he requires of his followers.

Remember that the Ten Commandments do not constitute the covenant, rather, they flow from it. We may think that morality, or the keeping of the Commandments, must come first, and only then will God's love follow. But in fact, the opposite is true. Out of love for the Chosen People, God offered the covenant first. In response, out of love for God, the people keep the Commandments. The connection becomes even clearer when we compare the words of the covenant with the Ten Commandments: "I will be your God" seeks response in the first three commandments. "You shall be my people" seeks response in the next seven commandments.

THE LAW OF LOVE

The Ten Commandments given to Moses are God's revelation for living the covenant of love God established with his people. For today's faithful Christians and Jews, the Ten Commandments continue to help us live peacefully and justly in sight of God and with our neighbor. Jesus illuminates the meaning of the Ten Commandments by showing that their real meaning derives from the law of love. Jesus calls us to an interior life of deeper holiness, to a radical conversion. External actions are not enough. The Lord has come to claim our hearts.

THE SPIRIT OF POVERTY

In the Scripture story, the rich young man asks Jesus how to share in everlasting life. Jesus tells him that he must keep the commandments. The man says he has always obeyed these and would like to do more. Jesus tells him that if he wishes to be perfect he should sell his riches, give to the poor, and follow him.

In this story, Jesus emphasizes the spirit of poverty as a dimension of all Christian lives. Some are called to give up literally all they own as a witness to the love of Christ. We see this example in the lives of men and women who take the vow of poverty. All Christians, however, are called to care in their own way for the needy. Living with our eyes open to the needs of others, especially the poor, is required of all followers of Jesus.

Our love for God cannot be separated from our love for others, because Jesus identifies himself with the lowliest of humans. Jesus teaches us that ultimately we will be judged by how well we have loved and served others (Matthew 25:31–46). Help your students begin to memorize the Ten Commandments.

DAY 1
MORALITY/DOCTRINE

Objective

This lesson helps the students see the relationship between the Great Commandment and the Ten Commandments.

Step 1 / INTRODUCTION

Learning About Our Lives

Introducing the Chapter

Ask the students to open their books to page 92 and read the focus questions. On the chalkboard, make a list of the rules the students must observe on a daily basis. After each student has had an opportunity to add to this list, ask the class to order the list by numbering each rule according to its importance. Then talk with the students about why rules and laws are important. Help them conclude that rules help us live together peacefully, keep us safe, and help us make good decisions.

Reading the Story

Ask the students to read silently "A Computer Game." Then ask two volunteers to take the parts of Stephanie and Jim and read the story aloud.

Writing Rules

Ask each student to write five rules that are important for the boys and girls in the video game to survive and be happy on the planet where they have landed. When the students have finished, divide the class into groups of three or four students. Ask them to compare their list of rules with the other students in the group. Instruct them to work together to come up with their five best rules. Then write the five best rules of one group on the chalkboard. Put check marks on the chalkboard after any rules that are the same. Add new rules to the list. Invite the students to talk about the rules that are most often stated, and discuss why these rules are especially important.

Discuss Living Without Rules

Discuss with the class what would happen if the children in the story tried to live on the new planet without any rules. Help the students appreciate that all people need rules to live together happily.

92

8

God's Commandments

A Computer Game

"What are you doing on the computer?" Jim asked Stephanie.

"I'm trying to play a new game," Stephanie answered. "Do you want to play?"

"Okay. Is it like a trivia game?" Jim asked.

"No," said Stephanie. "It's about rules, all kinds of rules. Here's how it works."

"Six boys and girls get into a spaceship. They blast off and go through space for a few days. Then the boys and girls see a planet that looks like Earth, but it's much smaller. They get closer to the planet. They can see water, plants, and even animals on the planet. But there are no people. They land their spaceship."

"Sounds like fun!" Jim said. "How do you play?"

"We decide which rules the boys and girls will need to live on the planet," Stephanie explained. "The winner of the game is the player who chooses the most important rules."

What are some rules and laws that are part of your daily life? Why are laws and rules important?

Focus on

The Ten Commandments The Ten Commandments are referred to as the *Decalogue*. Literally, this is translated to mean "ten words," the ten words which God gave to God's people out of love for them. References to the ten words begin in the Old Testament. In the context of the Exodus, God speaks ten words, conditions for the life to which the people were called. The Decalogue provides a path for life.

Rules to Live By

We can read in the Bible about the special rules that God has given to us. These rules are called the **Ten Commandments.** The Ten Commandments are rules that God has given us to help us live good lives.

Jesus taught the Great Commandment of love and the Beatitudes. They show us how to live like Jesus. But Jesus says that keeping the Ten Commandments is also important. If we do all these things, we can follow Jesus and live as he lived.

The Ten Commandments

1. I, the Lord, am your God. You shall not have other gods besides me.

2. You shall not take the name of the Lord, your God, in vain.

3. Remember to keep holy the Sabbath.

4. Honor your father and your mother.

5. You shall not kill.

6. You shall not commit adultery.

7. You shall not steal.

8. You shall not bear false witness against your neighbor.

9. You shall not covet your neighbor's wife.

10. You shall not covet anything that belongs to your neighbor.

Based on Exodus 20:2–17 and Deuteronomy 5:6–21

Vocabulary

Ten Commandments: the ten special rules given to us by God to help us live good lives

////////////////////

We Believe

The Church teaches that the Ten Commandments are God's laws. They are ways of showing love for God and for other people. The Ten Commandments are laws that help us live together in peace and happiness.

Doctrine 93

Focus on

Teaching Tips

Briefly review the lesson by having the students orally respond to the following questions.

■ How are the Ten Commandments like the Great Commandment? (*The first three commandments teach us how to love God; the remaining commandments teach us how to love others.*)

■ How do the Ten Commandments help us? (*They help teach us how to live together in peace and happiness.*)

Learning About Our Faith

Reading About the Commandments

Read "Rules to Live By" on page 93. Explain to the students that God gave us the Ten Commandments to help us remain close to one another. Read the Ten Commandments aloud together. Afterwards, define the following words: *in vain* (without respect), *Sabbath* (a day set aside for worshiping God and resting), *adultery* (unfaithfulness in marriage), *false witness* (lying), and *covet* (want or desire).

Understanding the Commandments

Point out that the first three commandments teach us how to love God.

1. We understand God is above all things and we are to pray and worship him.
2. We speak God's name with reverence.
3. We keep Sundays special for worshiping God at Mass and by resting from work.

The next commandments teach us how to love our neighbor as ourselves.

4. God wants us to respect our parents.
5. God wants us to take care of our bodies and respect others' bodies.
6. Married people should be faithful to each other.
7–8. We should not lie, cheat, or take things that do not belong to us.
9–10. God wants us not to be jealous of another person's friends or possessions.

Learning the Vocabulary

Present the definition of the term *Ten Commandments.*

Presenting the Doctrine

Read the We Believe summary with the students. Assist them in memorizing it.

Step 3 / CONCLUSION

Learning How to Live Our Faith

Applying the Commandments to Life

Ask the students to recite the first part of the Great Commandment and look at the Ten Commandments to find the commandments that help us know how to love God above all things. Follow this same procedure with the second part of the Great Commandment.

DAY 2
SCRIPTURE

Objective

This lesson helps the students understand that Jesus calls us to share with others and helps us to do so.

Step 1 / INTRODUCTION

Learning About Our Lives

Considering Special Rules

Make three columns on the chalkboard. Label them *City*, *School*, and *Playground*. Have the students call out rules for each category. Talk about the necessity for each rule. Tell the students that many of the rules in society are difficult to follow.

Step 2 / DEVELOPMENT

Learning About Our Faith

Reading and Discussing a Scripture Story

Have the students silently read "A Rich Young Man" on pages 94 and 95. Select volunteers to read the parts of Jesus and the young man. Also choose a narrator and instruct this student to pause when the text calls for Jesus or the young man to speak. Read the story again. Discuss the story.

- What did the young man ask Jesus? (*What he must do to live always in God's love*)

- What did Jesus tell the young man? (*To keep the Commandments*)

- What else did Jesus tell the young man? (*Sell what he had and give the money to the poor*)

- Why is this hard to do? (*Answers will vary.*)

Impress upon the students that Jesus was teaching that our possessions should not be more important to us than God and Jesus, and that we can show this by sharing what we have with others.

Going Beyond the Law

Ask a volunteer to read "Beyond the Law" on page 95. Answer any questions the students may have.

The Rich Young Man

One day, Jesus was walking from one town to another. Along the way a rich young man ran up to him. He bowed to Jesus and asked him a question.

"Good Teacher, what must I do to live always in God's love?"

Reminding the man of God's laws, Jesus answered, "You know the commandments:
You shall not kill;
You shall not commit adultery;
You shall not steal;
You shall not cheat;
Honor your father and your mother.'"

The young man smiled happily. "But, Teacher," he said to Jesus, "I have kept all these laws since I was a child."

Jesus looked at the man and smiled. "There is one more thing you should do," Jesus told him. "Go and sell what you have and give to the poor; then you will be rich in **heaven**. After that, come and follow me."

94 Scripture

Enriching the Lesson

Instruct the students to write a prayer asking for Jesus' help at times when it is difficult to follow God's law of love. Afterward, gather the class for prayer. Light a candle and pray briefly in silence. Then invite each student to offer their written prayer. Conclude by praying: *Be with us, Jesus, as we try to live always in God's love.*

The smile left the man's face as he listened to Jesus speak. Sadness filled the man's eyes. He did not want to give his money away. He turned around and sadly walked away, for he was very rich.

Based on Mark 10:17–22

Beyond the Law

Jesus reminded the young man in the Scripture story of God's commandments. Jesus told him then and tells us today that keeping the Ten Commandments is an important part of being disciples and necessary for being truly happy. The Ten Commandments are ways of showing love for God and for other people. The commandments are laws that help us live together in peace and happiness.

But Jesus didn't stop there. He taught that there is more to being one of his friends and followers than keeping the Ten Commandments. Jesus' Great Commandment and the Beatitudes ask us to go beyond simple obedience to God's laws.

Activity

On the lines below, name an action that goes beyond the law. The first one is done for you.

1. **Law:** Do not steal.

   Beyond the law: Always ask your brother's or sister's permission before borrowing his or her possessions.

2. **Law:** Tell the truth.

   Beyond the law: _____

   _____

3. **Law:** Don't be mean to others.

   Beyond the law: _____

> **Vocabulary**
>
> **heaven:** being with God forever
>
> ////////////////////

Scripture 95

Focus on

Heaven *The Catechism of the Catholic Church* states that "Those who die in God's grace and friendship . . . live for ever with Christ. They are like God for ever, for they 'see him as he is,' face to face . . . This perfect life with the Most Holy Trinity—this communion of life and love with the Trinity, with the Virgin Mary, the angels and all the blessed— is called 'heaven.' Heaven is the ultimate end and fulfillment of the deepest human longings, the state of supreme, definitive happiness" (#1023–1024).

Presenting the Vocabulary

Ask the students to read aloud and memorize the definition of *heaven*.

Step 3 / CONCLUSION

Learning How to Live Our Faith

Completing an Activity

Explain the directions to the activity on page 95. Give the students time to write their answers. Afterward, invite sharing. Discuss and affirm appropriate responses.

Reviewing the Lesson

Briefly review with the students what they have learned so far by having them discuss how the Ten Commandments help them.

DAY 3
MORALITY

Objective

This lesson helps the students appreciate that the Ten Commandments help us to live in peace, freedom, and justice.

Step 1 / INTRODUCTION

Learning About Our Lives

Identifying Rules That Help Us

Direct the students to the activity on page 96. Give the students time to complete the activity. Afterward, invite sharing.

or . . .

Before class begins, prepare a two-column worksheet, with four boxes in each column. Label the boxes on the left side *school rules, team rules, family rules,* and *citizen rules.* Leave the boxes on the right side blank. Distribute copies of the worksheet to the students and ask them to write two rules for each category in the appropriate box. Allow time for sharing. Then discuss the value of the rules they named.

Step 2 / DEVELOPMENT

Learning About Our Faith

Becoming People of Peace and Justice

Call attention to "Toward Justice and Peace" on pages 96 and 97. Ask volunteers to read aloud these paragraphs. Discuss with the students how different the world would be if everyone kept the Ten Commandments.

96

Activity

Name one rule that makes each of the communities listed below work better. Then explain why each rule works.

PLACE	RULE	WHY RULE WORKS
HOME		
SCHOOL		
CLUB OR TEAM		

Toward Justice and Peace

The New Testament gives us many examples of how important the commandments of God are to every Christian. Here is one example taken from the Second Letter of John.

I make this request of you, although it is a commandment we have had from the start: Let us love one another.
To love one another means that we must live according to the commandments.

Based on 2 John 5–6

The Ten Commandments guide us in living our lives as people of peace and justice. We can bring peace and justice into our families and classroom by the way we show our love for God and for one another.

96   Morality

 CURRICULUM CONNECTION

Music To reinforce that the Commandments and the Beatitudes help us to live happy, full lives, invite the students to listen to the recording of the song "Love Life" found in *Young People's Glory and Praise.*

Focus on

The International Peace Clubs The aim of the Peace Clubs is to introduce children around the world to the concepts of peaceful living that they can carry into adult life. According to the founder of Children As The Peacemakers Foundation, the goal is to "rear the first worldwide generation committed to peace and possessing the skills to achieve it." For more information write to the Foundation at 1591 Shrader Street, San Francisco, CA 94117.

We work for peace and justice each time we play a game fairly, allowing every one to have his or her turn.

We work for peace and justice each time we stand up for someone who is falsely accused or treated unkindly, even if our friends don't support us.

We work for peace and justice each time we pray for people around our country and around our world who don't have enough to eat because others have too much.

We show our love for God by keeping the commandments. The first three commandments teach us how to love and serve God. The remaining seven commandments teach us how to love and serve one another.

Activity

Put a ✓ in front of the sentences below that tell how you can bring peace and justice to your family and classroom.

_____ **1.** I can try not to argue with my brothers and sisters.

_____ **2.** I can play fairly on the playground.

_____ **3.** I can do my chores without reminders.

_____ **4.** I can cooperate with my teachers and principal.

_____ **5.** I can obey school rules.

Completing an Activity

Direct the students' attention to the activity on page 97. Ask a volunteer to read the directions aloud. Then give the students time to check off their answers.

★ ★ ★ ★ ★
Enriching the Lesson

Have the class make up an acrostic puzzle. Explain that the class is to write words down through the boldface letters of the word **COMMANDMENTS** that you have written across the chalkboard. The number in parentheses is the number of letters in the word. The first word tells what God is (4). The second word is something we all seek (9). The third word is very important for our world today (5). The fourth word is what we can work toward bringing to the world (7).
(*Love, happiness, peace, justice*)

97

Day 4
MORALITY

Objective

This lesson helps the students apply the Ten Commandments to their own lives.

Step 1 / INTRODUCTION

Learning About Our Lives

Reflecting on Rules

Distribute writing paper. Ask the students to think about and write answers to the following questions.

■ Which two commandments are the easiest for you to remember and follow? (*Answers will vary.*)

■ Which two commandments are the most difficult for you to remember and follow?

Give the students time to respond to both questions. When the students have finished writing, invite them to share their ideas. Help the students to appreciate that rules are set to help us live good lives and make good decisions. Ask the students to offer what their family life or school environment might be like without any rules.

Step 2 / DEVELOPMENT

Learning About Our Faith

Interpreting the Ten Commandments

Ask a volunteer to read aloud the text on page 98. Help the students see that the statements are ways of keeping God's commandments that apply to the life of a fourth grader.

What Do the Commandments Mean?

The laws of God that we know as the Ten Commandments are meant to help people of all ages live lives of justice and peace. Here are some ways in which fourth graders can live God's laws.

First Commandment
I remember to pray.
Second Commandment
I speak God's name only in prayer or in conversation about God.
Third Commandment
I attend Mass each Sunday.
Fourth Commandment
I respect and obey my parents.
Fifth Commandment
I am careful not to say mean or hurtful things to others.

Sixth Commandment
I respect my body and the bodies of others.
Seventh Commandment
I treat other people's property with care.
Eighth Commandment
I always try to tell the whole truth.
Ninth Commandment
I respect the promises that married people have made to each other.
Tenth Commandment
I try not to be greedy or jealous.

98 Morality

★ ★ ★ ★ Enriching the Lesson ★

Ask each student to consider one commandment that he or she desires to keep. Distribute writing paper. Ask the students to describe in one or two sentences how they will strive to follow the commandment better during the coming week. Then invite the students to read aloud what they have written.

Activity

You are the editor of your school newspaper. You have just received two Letters to the Editor. Write a short response to each letter.

Page 4

School Newspaper of Saint Michael the Archangel Elementary School

Dear Editor,

Recently a girl from your school came to deliver cookies that your school is selling. When I paid for the cookies, I gave her too much money. She quickly showed me my mistake and made sure that she was paid only the correct amount.

We are lucky to have such an honest girl in our neighborhood. And Saint Michael's should feel proud to have such an honest student in its fourth-grade class.

Sincerely,
Mr. Roger Brown

_____
_____
_____
_____
_____
_____
_____
_____
_____
_____

Dear Editor,

The other day I left my new jacket out on the playground when I went into school. Luckily for me, the person who found it brought the jacket to the principal's office and I got it back.

I would just like to thank the person who returned my jacket.

Sincerely,
Amy Anderson
Grade 4

_____
_____
_____
_____
_____
_____
_____
_____
_____
_____

Morality 99

Enriching the Lesson

In order to add depth to the activity on page 99 that deals with letters to the editor, ask the students to identify which commandments are being lived out in each editorial story.

Challenge the students to consider more closely how the everyday events in their lives can be faith-filled moments.

Learning How to Live Our Faith

Reading Letters to the Editor

Explain to the students that "Letters to the Editor" is a place in the newspaper for people to air their feelings, raise issues, and talk about how news affects the average person. Show an editorial page from a local newspaper to the students and share a few of the letters with them.

Completing an Activity

Read aloud the activity on page 99. Ask the students how they think the editor should respond.

Writing an Editorial Response

Have the students write their responses to the letters in the space provided. Afterward encourage sharing.

Committing to Follow God's Commandments

Direct the students' attention once again to the examples of living the commandments on page 98. Ask the students to choose one or two of these examples that they will try to keep. Ask the students to share their intentions with a classmate. Encourage the students to help each other keep God's commandments.

DAY 5
PRAYER/REVIEW

Objective
This lesson helps the students pray for peace and justice.

Explaining the Prayer Celebration
Tell the students that today they will pray for peace and justice and that they will learn a prayer written by Saint Francis of Assisi known as "The Prayer of Saint Francis." Explain that each class member is encouraged to live for peace and justice as well as pray for these things.

Preparing the Prayer Celebration
Assign two students to take the parts of **Leader** and **Reader**. The rest of the class will pray the part of **All**. Allow sufficient time for the students to become familiar with the prayer celebration by having them first read it silently. Have the reader prepare the reading from the Bible.

Praying for Peace and Justice
Invite the students to put themselves into a prayerful state of mind. Then pray the prayer celebration aloud.

Singing Together
Play a recording of "The Prayer of Saint Francis" to review the melody. Invite the class to join in the singing of this well-known song to conclude the prayer service.

100 Prayer

Praying for Peace and Justice

Leader: Today we bring our desire for true peace and justice before the Lord. We ask the Lord to create new hearts in us so that we may not only *pray* for peace and justice but rather, that we may *live* for peace and justice.

Reader: Let us listen carefully to a reading from the Gospel of Mark.
(Read Mark 10:17-22.)

All: Praise to you, Lord Jesus Christ.

Leader: Let us turn our thoughts to thoughts of peace by praying together the following prayer of Saint Francis of Assisi.

All: Lord, make me an instrument of your peace.
Where there is hatred, let me sow love;
where there is injury, pardon;
where there is doubt, faith;
where there is despair, hope;
where there is darkness, light.
O divine master, grant that I may not so much seek to be consoled as to console;
to be understood as to understand;
to be loved as to love;
for it is in giving that we receive;
it is in pardoning that we are pardoned;
and it is in dying that we are born to eternal life.

Leader: Let us end our prayer as people of peace and justice.

All: Amen.

🍎 Teaching Tips
Now would be a good time to review the life of Saint Francis of Assisi. Refer the students to page 18 in their books.

100

Chapter Review

Read these news headlines. Beside each one, write the name of a commandment the headline relates to.

Police Make Arrest in Murder Case

Police Investigate Credit Card Cheats

President Attends Church in Tennessee

25¢

Teenager Admits Selling Drugs in School Hallway

Union Leader Accused of Lying About Mob

25¢

Child Injured in Fall; Ignored Mother's Warnings

Wife of Attorney Says Husband Was Unfaithful

Department Store Prices Up Due to Rise in Thefts

Write the answers to the first two questions.

1. What is meant by *heaven*?

Heaven is being with God and with those he
loves forever.

2. What do the Ten Commandments help us to do?

The Ten Commandments help us to show love for God
and for other people. They help us live together in
peace and happiness. If we keep the Ten
Commandments, we can follow Jesus and be his
friends.

3. Discuss what you can do to be a better disciple of Jesus.

> **Those who live by the Lord's commandments will be happy.**
> **Based on Psalm 119:1–2**

★ ★ ★ Enriching the Lesson ★

Choose four key sentences from each chapter. Post the sentences as incomplete statements on a classroom bulletin board. Have the students complete the statements by writing their responses on strips of colored paper and posting them under the appropriate statements. Refer to the bulletin board often.

Identifying Commandments

Explain the directions to the headline activity on page 101. Ask the students to work independently to complete it. Then review the students' answers. Point out that, sadly, we see examples of people breaking the Ten Commandments every day.

Reviewing the Chapter

Read aloud the first review question and allow a volunteer to give the answer. Direct the students to write the answer on the lines provided. Repeat the process for the second question. Encourage all students to participate in the discussion of the third item.

Reading the Scripture Verse

Read aloud the verse from the Book of Psalms with the students. Explain that God loves us so much that God tells us the many ways that we can find happiness: through living the Ten Commandments, the Beatitudes, and the Great Commandment.

Using the Unit Organizer

Completing a graphic organizer such as a chart or table can help the children to organize information that has been presented in the unit. Organizers can enable the children to visualize their thinking and recognize relationships among ideas. This will give the children the opportunity to understand more completely the materials they have been studying.

Completing the Organizer

Have the students turn to page 102 in their books. Read aloud the directions to the Unit Organizer activity. Then ask the students to complete the activity independently. If necessary, tell them that they may look back through the previous four chapters for help. When everyone has finished, have the students compare their responses with the class.

Looking Back: Self-Assessment

The critical reflection questions below give the students an opportunity to sharpen their thinking skills. The questions can be used as a class discussion or independent writing activity.

- Which activity in this unit did you most enjoy? Why?
- Which was your favorite story in this unit? What did you like most about it?
- What did you learn in this unit that you think you will always remember?

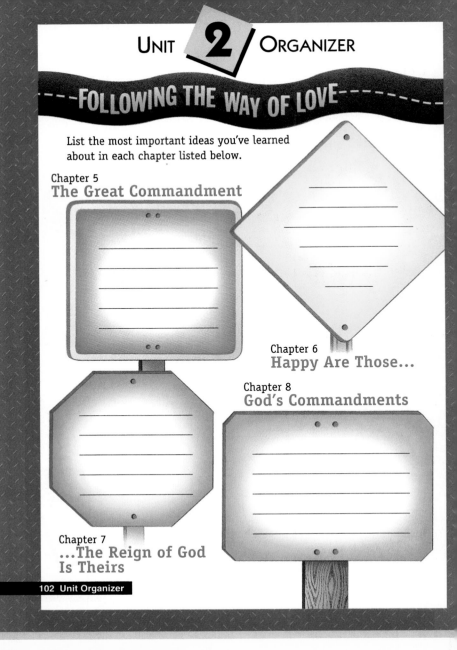

UNIT **2** ORGANIZER

FOLLOWING THE WAY OF LOVE

List the most important ideas you've learned about in each chapter listed below.

Chapter 5
The Great Commandment

Chapter 6
Happy Are Those...

Chapter 8
God's Commandments

Chapter 7
...The Reign of God Is Theirs

102 Unit Organizer

UNIT 2 REVIEW

Circle the word(s) to complete each sentence.

1. Jesus taught the Beatitudes to show us how to be _____ .
   rich   selfish   (happy)

2. Jesus wants us to act as he did and _____ people who have hurt us.
   ignore   (forgive)   fight with

3. God's love will bring freedom, justice, and peace to _____ .

   only the single-hearted   only the merciful   (everyone)

4. _____ worked for justice and peace in El Salvador.

   Francis of Assisi   (Archbishop Romero)   Martin de Porres

Match the first part of each commandment in Column A with its second part in Column B.

Column A

1. I, the Lord, am your God. You shall not have

2. You shall not take the name of

3. Remember to keep holy

4. Honor

5. You shall not

6. You shall not commit

7. You shall not

8. You shall not bear false witness against

9. You shall not covet

10. You shall not covet

Column B

___6___ adultery.

___10___ anything that belongs to your neighbor.

___8___ your neighbor.

___7___ steal.

___1___ other gods besides me.

___4___ your father and your mother.

___2___ the Lord, your God, in vain.

___3___ the Sabbath day.

___5___ kill.

___9___ your neighbor's wife.

Reviewing the Unit

The purpose of the Unit Review is to reinforce the concepts presented in the previous four chapters and to check the students' understanding. After explaining the directions, give the students sufficient time to complete the two-page review. Answer any questions they may have as you check their work.

Testing

After the students have completed the Unit Review, you may wish to distribute copies of the Unit 2 Test from the Tests booklets.

Project

Celebrate with a prayer experience. Before the class meets, cut a sheet of construction paper into four rectangles for each student. Ask the students to think of the Ten Commandments, the Beatitudes, and the Great Commandment as gifts we have been given to help us love, help, and care for others.

Distribute the paper rectangles and crayons. Ask the students to write on the rectangles the names of the people they love. Encourage them to decorate the rectangles to resemble gifts. Place the Bible on a small table. Invite the students to gather around the table, bringing with them their books and gift rectangles. If available, play verses 1 and 2 of the song "This Is My Commandment," found on the recording that accompanies *Young People's Glory and Praise*.

Ask a student to read "The Good Samaritan" on page 64 in Chapter 5. Now ask the students to place their gifts on the prayer table. Trace the Sign of the Cross on each student's forehead, saying, *"Care for others in the name of the Father, and of the Son, and of the Holy Spirit."* Lead the group in singing the song "Reach Out," found on the same album.

UNIT **2** REVIEW

Write **True** if the sentence is true, and **False** is the sentence is false.

1. ___False___ A neighbor is just the person who lives next door.

2. ___True___ The reign of God will be present in its fullness when Christ comes again.

3. ___True___ Justice means loving all our neighbors and treating everyone fairly.

4. ___False___ A beatitude is one of the signs of the Holy Spirit.

5. ___False___ The disciples were friends and followers of the Good Samaritan.

6. ___False___ Peacemakers are those who try to bring peace and friendship only in times of war.

Fill in the missing word(s) to complete each sentence.

1. Jesus' teaching to love God above all things and to love our neighbor as we love ourselves is called the ___Great Commandment___ .

2. The ___poor in spirit___ are people who know they need God.

3. We are called to care about others as the ___Good Samaritan___ did.

4. The Ten Commandments are God's ___laws___ .

5. The ___single-hearted___ will be with God forever.

6. ___Heaven___ is being with God and those he loves 1forever.

7. The Ten Commandments are ways of showing love for ___God___ and for ___other people___ .

DECIDING WHAT'S RIGHT and WHAT'S WRONG

A choice between what is right and wrong is called a *moral choice*. We use our conscience to help us decide the right thing to do. Sometimes we are tempted to do things that are wrong and we know clearly that they are wrong. At other times we may be unsure about what is right and what is wrong. We call these times of uncertainty *moral dilemmas*. The following guide can be helpful at these times of uncertainty.

GUIDE for MAKING GOOD CHOICES

Step One: I can think about what I want to do and why I want to do it.

Step Two: I can think about the possible consequences of my choice.

Step Three: I can ask for advice from someone I trust.

Step Four: I can pray for guidance.

Step Five: I can ask myself if this choice shows that I am a follower of Jesus.

Help Juanita do the right thing by reading the story and answering the questions below.

Lucy is a new girl in school this year. No one really likes Lucy. She is bossy and always wants her own way. Because of how she treats others, Lucy has no friends. Juanita feels sorry for Lucy. She thinks that Lucy probably feels lonely and wants to have friends. Some of Juanita's friends are finding ways to get back at Lucy for the way she acts toward them. Juanita disagrees with how her friends are acting, but she is unsure about what to do. Juanita considers all the possible ways she could act.

- She could continue to ignore the situation and let Lucy deal with the problem.
- She could go along with her friends and begin to treat Lucy in the same way.
- She could try to help her friends and Lucy get along better.

Day to Day 105

Day to Day

Objective

This lesson introduces students to a five-step guide for moral decision making.

Introducing the Lesson

Begin by asking students if they know what it means to make a moral decision. After a few suggestions from the students, if they have not defined a moral decision as making a choice between what is right and wrong, ask them how a moral choice might be different from a choice about what to wear on a Saturday morning. Allow a few minutes for discussion, and then ask the students to open their books to page 105.

Read with the students the opening paragraph. Ask students to provide examples of choices they might make that are moral choices. Explain that sometimes knowing the right thing to do is very easy, but at other times a person might not be so sure. Invite a volunteer to read aloud the five steps listed in the guide for making moral choices. Be sure that the students understand the terminology in the guide before reading about Juanita and Lucy in the first story. Clarify that *consequences* means what might happen as a result of your choice and that *advice* means to seek help.

Completing the Activity

Have students read aloud the story about Juanita and Lucy and then respond to the four questions on page 106. Have students write their answers before discussing as a group. Discuss the following questions.

- What do you think Juanita should do? Why? (*One possible response might be: if Juanita is worried about her own popularity and is insecure with her friends, she might want to stay uninvolved. She may worry that by becoming Lucy's friend her other friends might like her less.*) **Note:** This is a fairly typical worry of students who are not feeling secure in their own peer relationships. It might be helpful to review those qualities of a true friend who would not think less of you for befriending someone who is not well-liked.

Lesson continues on page 106.

- If Juanita chooses to do this, what might be some of the consequences of her choice? (*Again, answers will vary.*) **Note:** Listen for authenticity in the students' responses. Are they thinking of both short-term and long-term consequences? Be sure that students consider Lucy's hurt feelings as a consequence, if they think Juanita would not intervene to help Lucy. Have students share instances when they have had their feelings hurt by someone else's actions.

- Does this choice show Juanita to be a follower of Jesus? Why or Why not? (*Again, answers will vary depending upon previous responses. Have students recall the characteristics of a follower of Jesus that were introduced in the previous lesson, as well as in material found in the lessons of* THIS IS OUR FAITH. *Help students to see that this is an important question to help guide moral decision making. If your choice does not show you to be a follower of Jesus, it is a good indication that the choice might not be the right thing to do.*)

Turning to Others for Advice

Continue having the class read the next paragraph. Have the students write in their books the two people Juanita could turn to for advice. Then discuss with the students those helpful people in their lives to whom they might turn for advice. Ask the students to share why they would choose the persons they suggested.

Writing a Prayer

Have the students write a prayer that Juanita might use when asking Jesus to help her decide the right thing to do. Allow time for students to share what they have written. Make sharing voluntary, since some students may feel that what they have written is too personal to share.

Following Jesus

Read together the Following Jesus section. Ask students to think about friendship choices they have made recently. Have them consider silently whether or not their choices and actions brought Jesus' love to the other person.

Concluding the Lesson

Pray together the prayer in the Prayer box at the end of the lesson.

106

What do you think Juanita should do?

_____

Why do you think Juanita should do this?

_____

If Juanita chooses to do this, what might be a consequence of her choice?

_____

Does this choice show Juanita to be a follower of Jesus? Why or why not?

_____

Figuring out the right thing to do isn't always easy. Sometimes it is helpful to seek advice from someone who is older and more experienced. Even though Juanita has considered her various options and their consequences, she's still uncertain about what to do. List two people Juanita might ask for advice.

_____   _____

Jesus is always available to help us when we are trying to make decisions between right and wrong actions. Through prayer we can ask Jesus for his help. Use the space below to write a prayer that Juanita might use when seeking Jesus' help.

_____

_____

_____

Following Jesus

Jesus calls us to love one another as he has loved us. When faced with difficult choices, it is important to consider whether or not our decision is a loving one. Could someone be physically hurt by what we choose to do? Could feelings be hurt? Or, do our actions spread Jesus' love by bringing peace and justice?

PRAYER

Jesus, I know you are always with me. Help me to know right from wrong. Help me to act in ways that show I am your follower. Amen.

OPENING DOORS
A Take-Home Magazine™

GRADE 4/UNIT 2

THIS IS OUR FAITH

Growing Closer

WRITE FAMILY COMMANDMENTS to nurture and remind each other about the importance of family sharing. Use the two commandments below as models for writing.

Write your list of commandments on construction paper. Display the commandments where family members will read them often. Check yourself regularly to see how you are doing at implementing them.

Do not steal precious time from being with each other; time passes too quickly to waste.

Do not wish for anyone else's life; no one else possesses the gift of each person in our family.

Looking Ahead

Unit 3 will take a closer look at the commandments that help us show respect for God, ourselves, other people, and all God's creation. Your fourth grader will learn that we are called to express love by worshiping God, honoring our parents, respecting life, and being faithful in marriage.

© Silver Burdett Ginn Inc.

8

Opening Doors

Sending the Magazine Home

As you complete this unit with your class, assist the students in carefully removing *Opening Doors: A Take-Home Magazine* (two pages) from their books by separating them from the book along the perforations. Demonstrate how to fold the two pages, forming an eight-page booklet. Ask the students to take the magazine home and encourage their families to read it with them and participate in the suggested activities.

108

Loving Frames of Mind

One of the subtle ways you can reinforce Jesus' teaching about the Christian ways of love, justice, and peace is by sharing stories with your child. You may choose to read aloud with your child. Or, each of you may want to read separately and then discuss the story when you have the opportunity.

Happy are the poor in spirit...

Other Bells for Us to Ring. Robert Cormier. Dell, 1992.

Frederick. Leo Lionni. Knopf Books, 1967.

Happy are they who mourn...

The Big Wave. Pearl S. Buck. HarperCollins, 1986.

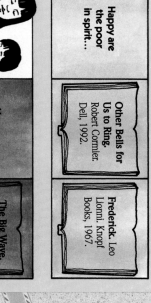

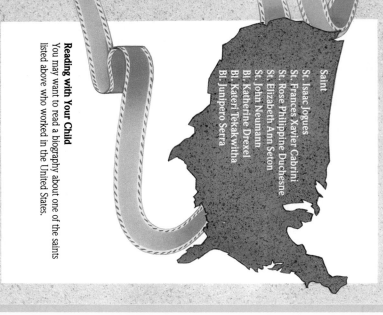

Saint

- St. Isaac Jogues
- St. Frances Xavier Cabrini
- St. Rose Philippine Duchesne
- St. Elizabeth Ann Seton
- St. John Neumann
- Bl. Katherine Drexel
- Bl. Kateri Tekakwitha
- Bl. Junipero Serra

Reading with Your Child

You may want to read a biography about one of the saints listed above who worked in the United States.

6

7

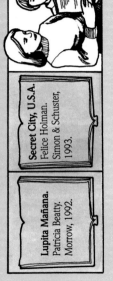

My Shalom, My Peace. Jacob Zim. McGraw-Hill, 1975.

A Taste of Blackberries. Doris B. Smith. HarperCollins, 1992.

Happy are the peace-makers…

The War with Grandpa. Robert Kimmel Smith. Dell, 1984.

Happy are those who hunger and thirst for justice…

Secret City, U.S.A. Felice Holman. Simon & Schuster, 1993.

Lupita Mañana. Patricia Beatty. Morrow, 1992.

3

Being Catholic

The Communion of Saints

Many Christians reflect Christ's presence and way of life in both ordinary and extraordinary ways. They can be models for us as we struggle to follow Jesus in our everyday lives. Some of these Christians may be in our own families, neighborhoods, or parishes.

The Church canonizes some exceptional followers of Jesus and calls them saints. All Christians, both living and dead, are part of the communion of saints. Mary, the mother of Jesus, is the greatest of all saints. The process of canonization includes the following three steps:

1. If it can be proved that a deceased Church member has led a life of extraordinary holiness and heroic virtue, then he or she is nominated to receive the title, "venerable."

2. If, after this title is conferred, a miracle is worked in this person's name, then the person receives the title "blessed." He or she is given a special feast day on the Church calendar.

3. If a second miracle is performed in this person's name, the Church declares him or her a "saint."

6

You Are Invited

"Happy are those who are called to his supper." These words are spoken by the priest at Mass shortly before we receive Communion. Similar words in Scripture give us an insight into the meaning and use of the words in the Mass.

When Jesus was a dinner guest at the home of one of the Pharisees, he began telling the other guests parables. One of these parables which you can read in Luke 14:16–24 is about a man planning a great feast. The point of the parable is that the invited guests made excuses and refused to come. Therefore, the host ordered his servants to go out into the streets and alleys to bring in the poor and the crippled, the blind and the lame, and anyone they could find who was willing to share in the feast.

It is important for us to remember that we are invited not only to share in the Eucharist but also to partake of the heavenly banquet. We have been gathered from the East and the West. We come as we are to become the people of God, to be shaped by the law and the beatitudes, to become poor in spirit, gentle, merciful, just and loving.

We come to the Eucharist in response to God's invitation. We come not only in response to the commandments to love and worship God but also to become the people who can truly love others. The Eucharist gives us the strength to obey God's law and to realize that the reign of God is within us.

UNIT 3

Respecting God and People

Who makes you feel important?

Unit Aim ～～～～～～

To help the students understand and be able to honor the first three commandments and the fourth, fifth, sixth, and ninth commandments.

Doctrinal Summaries

CHAPTER 9
The first three commandments teach us to place God first in our lives. We learn to use God's name with respect and we learn to honor God in a special way each Sunday and holy day.

CHAPTER 10
The fourth commandment teaches us to love, honor, and obey our parents and others who are responsible for us.

CHAPTER 11
The fifth commandment teaches us to respect and care for all living things. It teaches us that all life is special.

CHAPTER 12
The sixth and ninth commandments call married people to love each other and live together faithfully. They call all of us to respect our own and others' bodies.

Note:
As you prepare this unit and the remaining units, you might wish to refer to the reference section, *Our Catholic Heritage*, beginning on page 327.

Additional resources for Unit 3 include: a Unit Test and a Family Letter as well as a video and selections from THIS IS OUR FAITH Music Program. You might also find it helpful to preview *Saints and Other Holy People* and *Prayer Celebrations* for possibilities to enhance the unit.

Introducing the UNIT

Ask a volunteer to read aloud the unit-focus question on page 111. Invite the students to respond with an example from their own lives. Tell the class that in Unit 3 they will learn that when we keep the commandments, we are showing our love for God and others.

Vocabulary

values
in vain
Sabbath
reverence
respect
obey
honor
sacred
violence
abuse
faithful
adultery
covet

9 Worshiping God

Objectives

To help the students

- Understand the importance of God in their lives.
- Learn the first three commandments.
- Find ways of showing respect and reverence for God.
- Identify ways that they can follow the first three commandments.
- Pray to God in the sacred dwelling place of their hearts and review the chapter.

Chapter Outline

	Step 1 Learning About Our Lives	Step 2 Learning About Our Faith	Step 3 Learning How to Live Our Faith
Day 1	■ Introduce the chapter. ■ Write about people. *ABOUT 15 MINUTES*	■ Read about the importance of God. *ABOUT 7 MINUTES*	■ Write about the importance of God. *ABOUT 8 MINUTES*
Day 2	■ Choose values. ■ List what is important. *ABOUT 12 MINUTES*	■ Learn about and review the first three commandments. ■ Review the vocabulary. ■ Present the doctrine. *ABOUT 12 MINUTES*	■ Restate the commandments. *ABOUT 6 MINUTES*
Day 3	■ Discuss actions. *ABOUT 8 MINUTES*	■ Read and discuss the Scripture story. ■ Present the vocabulary. *ABOUT 12 MINUTES*	■ Discover ways to show respect for God. ■ Complete an activity. *ABOUT 10 MINUTES*
Day 4	■ Discuss decisions. *ABOUT 6 MINUTES*	■ Read and discuss a story. *ABOUT 12 MINUTES*	■ Complete an activity. ■ Review the commandments. *ABOUT 12 MINUTES*

Day 5   **Prayer**   Prepare for prayer; pray together; read the Bible; and sing together.
               Review   Review the chapter; answer the review questions; and read the Scripture verse.

Correlation
to the
**Catechism of
the Catholic Church**

Paragraphs
**398, 593, 2084–2195,
2084, 2096, 2110, 2160,
2161, 2162, 2168, 2173,
2176, 2177, 2190, 2193,
2194, 2709, 2711**

Plan Ahead

	Preparing Your Class	Materials Needed
Day 1	Read through the lesson plan.	■ pencils or pens
Day 2	Read the lesson plan.	■ pencils or pens ■ writing paper
Day 3	Read the lesson plan. If you opt to enrich the lesson, make all the necessary preparations prior to the church visit.	■ pencils or pens
Day 4	Read through the lesson plan. If you plan to teach "Joyful, Joyful, We Adore Thee," review the song ahead of time.	■ pencils or pens
Day 5	Read through the entire lesson plan. Talk to your parish liturgist or choir director about accompanying the singing of "Here I Am."	■ pencils or pens ■ Bibles, one per student ■ prayer cloth ■ candle ■ THIS IS OUR FAITH *Hymnal*

Additional Resources

As you plan this chapter, consider using the following materials from The Resourceful Teacher Package.

■ *Classroom Activity Sheets 9 and 9a*

■ *Family Activity Sheets 9 and 9a*

■ *Chapter 9 Test*

■ *Prayers for Every Day*

■ *Projects: Grade 4*

You may also wish to refer to the following Big Book.

■ *We Celebrate God's Word,* pages 3, 6, 11, 23

In preparing the students for the Sunday readings, you may wish to use Silver Burdett Ginn's *Getting Ready for Sunday* student and teacher materials.

BOOKS FOR THE JOURNEY

The Seeing Stick. Jane Yolen. Thomas Y. Crowell, 1977. An old man helps a blind princess to use the sense of touch to replace her sense of sight.

Talking with Artists. "Tom Feelings," pp. 48–53. Compiled and edited by Pat Cummings. Bradbury Press, 1992. A personal story by an artist in which he names another black artist who encouraged and inspired him.

MORE BOOKS FOR THE JOURNEY

The Barn. Avi. Orchard Books, 1994. The story of a boy who changes the course of his own life to care for his seriously ill father.

Experience Jesus Today. "When Jesus Was Twelve," pp. 38–41. Charles Singer & Albert Hari. Oregon Catholic Press, 1993. The story of Jesus in the Temple with additional illustrations, information, questions, and a prayer.

REDUCED CLASSROOM ACTIVITIES

NAME _____

WORSHIPING GOD

Read the paragraphs below. Each paragraph explains one of the first three commandments. Write the correct commandment on the lines below the paragraph.

1. We show respect through words and actions. We are to use God's name only with love and reverence.

   You shall not take the name of the Lord, your God, in vain.
   _____

2. No person or thing is to be more important to us than God. No person or thing is to come between God and us. We should remember to talk with God because God is always with us.

   I, the Lord, am your God. You shall not have other gods beside me.
   _____

3. Sunday is the Christian Sabbath. We celebrate the Eucharist each Sunday. Sunday is a day of rest and prayer.

   Remember to keep holy the sabbath day.
   _____

To the Teacher: This activity reviews the first three commandments.

Chapter 9 Worshiping God   THIS IS OUR FAITH 4   **9**

NAME _____

A MONTH OF SUNDAYS

Plan your Sundays for one month. Write ways that you can keep Sunday as a day of rest and prayer. Some possibilities might include reading, praying at mealtime, sharing a special family blessing as you wake up, and taking a family walk.

Sunday, _____
        (month)   *(day)*

Sunday, _____
        (month)   *(day)*

Sunday, _____
        (month)   *(day)*

Sunday, _____
        (month)   *(day)*

PARENTS: Choose one of the four suggestions above for keeping Sunday as a day of rest and prayer. Please sign and return the following agreement.

I, _____, will follow my fourth grader's suggestions for
        (signature)

Sunday, _____, to honor the Sabbath as a day of rest and prayer.
        (month)   *(day)*

To the Teacher: This activity encourages the entire family to practice the third commandment. To mark each of the four Sundays, post selected suggestions in a special place in the classroom.

9a THIS IS OUR FAITH 4   *Chapter 9* Worshiping God

Background for the Teacher

THE FIRST COMMANDMENT

The Lord delivered the Israelites from slavery under the Egyptians only to find them falling into the self-induced slavery of idolatry. In our society, idolatry is perhaps best described as the worship of self. By the first commandment, God brings us out of the slavery of self-worship. In keeping our gaze focused on God, we turn away from slavish desires and turn toward him, who is the true source of our satisfaction. We are to have no gods except the Almighty, for what is the human but a creature of God. Our freedom lies in recognizing our position in God's scheme: we are little less than the angels, given rule over the work of God's hands (based on Psalm 8). The response which the first commandment evokes from us is to put God before all else.

Love of God, in the Great Commandment of Jesus, comes before love of self. Love of God is deeply related to the love of life; we are of God in a way so basic and profound that we can never be outside of him. Jesus tells us our command is this—to love God above all and in all. Fourth graders, with their limited experience, will not yet embrace the full understanding of this. The richness of this truth unfolds over time.

BIBLICAL MORALITY

The first three commandments form the core of biblical morality. They call forth a response of love and commitment to God, who consistently demonstrated love and commitment to his Chosen People. The people of Israel saw the commandments as a great gift from God, and a sign of their intimate relationship with him. Obviously, if the people believed in other gods, Yahweh would no longer be their God, and the covenant would be meaningless. The people of the new covenant have received Christ, who sends the Spirit to impart the inner grace necessary to observe the commandments.

Fourth graders want to do what is right, and they need our assistance and direction in discovering ways to show love, respect, and honor for God. In discussing the first commandment, encourage a daily prayer time. In discussing the second commandment, make the students aware that casual, irreverent use of God's name violates the commandment.

As you discuss the third commandment, "Observe the Sabbath, keeping it throughout their generations as a perpetual covenant . . . an everlasting token" (Exodus 31:16–17), do be sensitive to those youngsters whose parents must work on Sundays.

Objective

This lesson helps the students understand the importance of God in their lives.

Step 1 / INTRODUCTION

Learning About Our Lives

Introducing the Chapter

Divide the class into groups of three or four. Ask one student in each group to be a discussion leader. Direct the groups to discuss the two chapter-focus questions on page 112. Direct the discussion leaders to make a list of reasons why the people named by the students are important to them. After allowing sufficient time for the groups to respond, invite the discussion leaders to read aloud their lists.

Writing About People

Call attention to the photographs on page 112 and explain the directions to the activity. Direct the students to write a sentence or two of dialogue for each picture.

When the students have finished writing, encourage them to share their answers. Although the students' responses may vary slightly, they should express that in the first picture the boy and his grandfather may be talking about what they enjoy doing together, sharing about their lives, or just enjoying being together.

In the second picture, the grandmother and child may be talking about the art of quilting, family traditions, and the joy of helping one another.

or...

List the following words on the chalkboard: *grandmother, dad, best friend, teacher, sister or brother,* and *mom.* Invite the students to choose one of the people from the list and tell how they show that person that he or she is important to them. To involve the students more fully in this activity, you may want to have them pair off and role-play a situation. Help the students appreciate that our words and actions show others how important they are to us.

112

9 Worshiping God

Who are some of the important people in your life? Why are these people important to you?

112   Morality

Activity

How can you tell that the people in the photographs are important to one another? On the lines below, write what you think they might be saying to each other.

1. _____

   _____

   _____

   _____

2. _____

   _____

   _____

   _____

Enriching the Lesson

Distribute construction paper, felt-tip markers, and scissors. Direct the students to make a thank-you card for one of the people they named in Step 1 of this lesson. Encourage the students to list specific reasons why the people named are important to them.

Focus on

Worship The Catechism of the Catholic Church states, "Adoration is the first act of the virtue of religion. To adore God is to acknowledge him as God, as the Creator and Savior, the Lord and Master of everything that exists, as infinite and merciful Love. 'You shall worship the Lord your God, and him only shall you serve,' says Jesus, citing Deuteronomy" (#2096).

Jesus Gives Us an Example

Jesus loved the good things God created. In the gospel stories, we read that Jesus enjoyed the gifts of creation. He walked by the sea. He taught on the mountainside.

Jesus taught that people are more important than things. People are the most important part of God's creation. The gospels tell us how Jesus showed his love for people. He cared for the poor. He forgave sinners. He healed the sick. He cared for and taught his disciples.

Yet there was Someone more important than people or things. God was the most important of all. Jesus' Great Commandment teaches us to love God above all else. It reminds us of the first three commandments.

Activity

Think about why God is important to you. Complete each sentence by writing your reasons on the lines.

1. God is important to me because

_____

2. God is important to me because

_____

3. God is important to me because

_____

4. God is important to me because

_____

Focus on

The Great Commandment Jesus teaches the Great Commandment in the parable of the Good Samaritan (Luke 10:25–37). Have the students read the Great Commandment in the Bible. You might like to review the story of the Good Samaritan with the students. This Scripture story can be found on pages 64-65 in the student text. Then have the class read the story from the Bible.

Step 2 / DEVELOPMENT

Learning About Our Faith

Reading About the Importance of God

Direct the students' attention to "Jesus Gives Us an Example" on page 113. Ask a volunteer to read this section aloud. Use the following questions for discussion.

- How do we know that Jesus enjoyed the gifts of creation? (*Jesus walked by the sea, and taught on mountainsides.*)
- What did Jesus teach about people? (*That they were the most important part of God's creation*)
- How did Jesus show his love for people? (*He cared for the poor, forgave sinners, healed the sick, and cared for his disciples.*)
- What was more important than the things of creation or people? (*God*)
- What does the Great Commandment teach us? (*To love God above all else*)

Step 3 / CONCLUSION

Learning How to Live Our Faith

Writing About the Importance of God

Point out the activity on page 113. Give the students a few examples of your own, and then direct the students to complete the activity. When the students have finished, invite them to share their ideas with the rest of the class.

113

DOCTRINE

Objective

This lesson helps the students learn the first three commandments.

Step 1 / INTRODUCTION

Learning About Our Lives

Choosing Values

Read aloud the first paragraph on page 114. Explain that *values* are what people consider important. Tell the students that our values are our most important beliefs and ideas. Then read aloud the second paragraph with the class and ask the students to complete the activity.

When the students have finished, call on volunteers to read aloud the completed sentences. Explore with the students how the first statement is erroneous and how always seeking to have fun can be a selfish value.

Repeat with each of the other three statements. Assist the students in understanding that these things are not wrong or harmful to us unless they become so important in our lives that they are more important than anyone or anything else. When that happens, we are like slaves to these things.

Listing What Is Important

Distribute writing paper. Ask the students to list things and people who are important to them. Tell them to include the words *God* and *myself* on the list. Instruct them to rank the items on their lists, placing a *1* before the most important, *2* before the second most important, and so on. When the students have completed ranking their lists, ask the students to compare their lists with those of the person sitting closest to them. Ask them to discuss why the first few items are so important to them.

Step 2 / DEVELOPMENT

Learning About Our Faith

Learning About the First Three Commandments

Invite volunteers to read aloud the paragraphs on pages 114 and 115. As each commandment is presented, invite all the students to repeat it.

114

Activity

People see certain things in their lives as more important than other things. The important things become the **values** that direct their lives and for which they live and sometimes die.

Look at the Wheel of Values below. Start with the **F** at the top of the wheel and then skip every other letter. Use the letters to write a word in the blank spaces, completing the sentences below. The sentences tell you about the selfish values some people have.

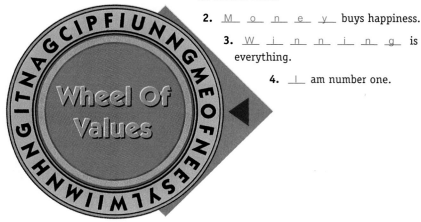

1. Life is short, so have <u>f</u> <u>u</u> <u>n</u>, no matter what.
2. <u>M</u> <u>o</u> <u>n</u> <u>e</u> <u>y</u> buys happiness.
3. <u>W</u> <u>i</u> <u>n</u> <u>n</u> <u>i</u> <u>n</u> <u>g</u> is everything.
4. <u>I</u> am number one.

Understanding the Commandments

Because of God's great love for us, he gives us the Ten Commandments to live by. These laws, or rules, are given by God to help us learn the values that will guide us in living good lives.

The first three commandments teach us how to love and serve God.

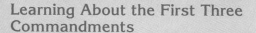

Enriching the Lesson

To review the first three commandments, ask:

- Which commandment teaches us to honor God in a special way on Sundays and holy days? (*Third*)
- Which commandment teaches us to keep God first in our lives? (*First*)
- Which commandment teaches us to show respect for God through our words and actions? (*Second*)

Focus on

The Ten Commandments The Council of Trent teaches that the Ten Commandments are obligatory for Christians to follow. The Second Vatican Council confirms: "As successors of the apostles, bishops receive from Him the mission to teach all nations and to preach the gospel to every creature, so that all men may attain to salvation by faith, baptism, and the fulfillment of the commandments." (*Dogmatic Constitution on the Church*, #24)

1. The first commandment is *I, the Lord, am your God. You shall not have other gods besides me.* It teaches us to keep God first in our lives. No person or thing is to be more important to us than God is. No person or thing is to come between God and us. We remember God's goodness, and we talk and listen to God in prayer.

2. The second commandment is *You shall not take the name of the Lord, your God, in vain.* It teaches us to show respect for God. We show respect through words and actions. We use the names of God, Jesus, and all holy persons with respect and love. We treat holy places and things with reverence. We never say God's or Jesus' name without care, or use their names to express anger.

3. The third commandment is *Remember to keep holy the Sabbath.* It teaches us to honor God in a special way on Sundays and holy days. Sunday is the Christian Sabbath. We worship God by celebrating the Eucharist together each Sunday. Sunday is also a day for rest and prayer. We relax and do special things on Sunday in honor of God.

Vocabulary

values: what people consider important

in vain: in a disrespectful way

Sabbath: the weekly day of prayer and rest: Sunday for Christians, Saturday for Jews, and Friday for Muslims

We Believe

The first three commandments teach us to place God first in our lives. We learn to use God's name with respect. And we learn to honor God in a special way each Sunday.

Doctrine 115

Ask the students to discuss ways in which they can keep the first commandment. Help them appreciate that when someone is important to us, we like to be with them. When we seek and listen to God every day, we are happy because we cooperate with God, who helps us become the person God made us to be.

For the second commandment, clarify the meaning of the phrase *in vain*. Refer to the definition in the Vocabulary box. Ask the students how they feel when their names are spoken nicely, or spoken in anger, or made fun of. Help them appreciate that when our names are honored, we are honored. When we honor God's name, we honor God. We sin if we use God's name to curse, to express anger, or when we use it pointlessly in casual speech.

As you present the third commandment, explain that when God created the world, God rested on the seventh day. God wants us to rest one day a week to spend special time with God. This day of rest is called the *Sabbath*. Direct attention to the definition in the Vocabulary box. Clarify that Christians keep the Sabbath on Sunday to remember the day Jesus rose from the dead. By celebrating Mass, Catholics keep holy the Sabbath.

Reviewing the Vocabulary

Refer to the Vocabulary box on page 115. Ask volunteers to each read a definition aloud to review the meaning of the new words.

Presenting the Doctrine

Present the We Believe statements on page 115. Help the students learn the meaning of the first three commandments by reading this section aloud several times.

Step 3 / CONCLUSION

Learning How to Live Our Faith

Restating the Commandments

Direct the students to turn over their papers on which they wrote their lists. Encourage the students to rewrite the first three commandments in their own words. Afterward, invite sharing.

115

Objective

This lesson helps the students find ways of showing respect and reverence for God.

Step 1 / INTRODUCTION

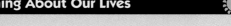

Learning About Our Lives

Discussing Actions

Help the students recall the people they named earlier in the chapter as people who are important in their lives. Give the students a few moments to remember the people and why they are so important. Ask: What are some ways in which you show people how important they are to you? Encourage the students to share their answers as you write them on the chalkboard.

Help the students understand that their words and actions indicate whether a person is important to them or not. Explain that in this lesson they are going to read a story about a time when Jesus' words and actions showed the importance of God.

Step 2 / DEVELOPMENT

Learning About Our Faith

Reading and Discussing the Scripture Story

Invite volunteers to read aloud the Scripture story on page 116. When they have finished, explain that the Temple was very large, that it was the largest house of worship, and it was in Jerusalem. The Jewish people traveled to it to celebrate some of the Jewish feasts, especially Passover. On this feast they commemorated how God saved them from slavery in Egypt. To honor God on the Passover, the Jewish people offered sacrifices of doves or other animals. Doves were the least costly to buy; they were what the poorest people offered as their sacrifice. The birds were sold in the court of the Temple so that people who came from afar would not have to bring them from home, which could be difficult and costly. People came from all over with different kinds of money. So men at the Temple exchanged the different kinds of money into the kind of money that could be used at the Temple in Jerusalem.

116

Jesus teaches us that God is more important than anyone or anything in life.

Jesus Goes to the Temple

One day Jesus went to the Temple with his disciples to pray.

Jesus saw that the Temple court, or entrance, was very crowded. People were selling doves and shouting out their sale prices. Others were pushing people out of their way. Money changers sat at tables with stacks of coins, exchanging money for customers.

Jesus became very angry. He saw that the people were not putting God first even in the holy Temple. Jesus knew that people needed to exchange their money. He knew that they needed to buy doves. Jesus was not against buying or selling. But it seemed to him that business in the Temple had become more important to people than prayer.

Jesus felt that this was wrong. He turned over the tables of the money changers. Coins rolled all over the floor. Then Jesus called out to the surprised crowd. He reminded the people of God's laws, saying, "My house will be called a house of prayer for all people. But you have turned it into a den of thieves."

Based on Mark 11:15–17

★ ★ ★ Enriching the Lesson ★

Take the students to the church. Point out the tabernacle and the lighted candle, a symbol of the reverence we show for God's presence. Talk with them about the ways people show reverence or respect for God's house: genuflecting before the altar, receiving Communion reverently, males removing hats, talking and behaving quietly. Conclude by asking the students to pray that they will always treat God's house as a house of prayer.

Focus on

Superstition Somewhat related to the worship of idols, which is forbidden by the first commandment, can be superstition, divination, or spiritism. Superstition attributes godlike power to ordinary things, such as numbers, black cats, broken mirrors. Divination seeks to learn the future from horoscopes, palm readers, or fortune tellers. Spiritism attempts to communicate with the dead through seances and mediums.

Respect for God

Jesus became angry when he saw that people did not show respect for God and for God's house. As Catholics we show a special respect for God's sacred dwelling place, the church, for we know that God is present there in a special way. We also treat other holy places and things with respect and **reverence**. We try to act in ways that show that God is first in our lives.

Activity

Complete the following statements.

1. I show respect for my parish church by

_____.

2. When I receive the Eucharist, I show reverence by

_____.

3. When I am at Mass, I show respect for God by

_____.

4. I show respect for the Bible by

_____.

5. When I pray, I show respect for God by

_____.

Vocabulary

reverence: an attitude of respect and care

Scripture 117

Jesus was upset because the sellers and the crowd seemed to think buying and selling were more important than worshiping God.

Discuss the story with the students. Ask:

- Why did Jesus go to the Temple? (*To pray*)
- What was being sold in the Temple? (*Doves*)
- What were the money changers doing? (*Exchanging people's money so that they would have the correct currency to buy doves*)
- Why was Jesus angry? (*He felt doing business had become more important than praying.*)
- What did Jesus do? (*He turned over the money changers' tables.*)
- What did Jesus tell the people? (*My house should be a house of prayer, not a den of thieves.*)
- What do you think Jesus meant when he told the people that his home should be a house of prayer? (*Answers may vary.*)
- What can we learn from the story? (*To put worship of God above all else, especially on the Sabbath*)
- Which two commandments is Jesus asking us to keep? (*First and third*)

Presenting the Vocabulary

Point out the Vocabulary box and ask a volunteer to read the definition aloud. Answer any questions the students may have.

Step 3 / CONCLUSION

Learning How to Live Our Faith

Discovering Ways to Show Respect for God

Ask a volunteer to read aloud "Respect for God" on page 117. Ask: How is God present in church in a special way? (*In the Blessed Sacrament; in the Eucharist; and when two or more are gathered together in God's name to pray, God is there.*)

Completing an Activity

Direct the students to complete the activity. When all have finished, encourage the students to share their ideas with someone sitting close to them. Afterward, elicit a few responses for each statement from the whole class.

DAY 4
MORALITY

Objective

This lesson helps the students identify ways that they can follow the first three commandments.

Step 1 / INTRODUCTION

Learning About Our Lives

Discussing Decisions

Ask the students to consider difficult things they have done for someone important to them. Invite them to relate their personal examples. Share some of the hard decisions you have made. Tell the students that today they will learn about someone who made a hard decision to show that God was first in his life.

Step 2 / DEVELOPMENT

Learning About Our Faith

Reading and Discussing a Story

Introduce the story of Saint Thomas More by reading aloud the first sentence at the top of page 118. Then have volunteers take turns reading the story aloud. Discuss the story, using the questions that follow.

- Why was Thomas happy? (*Thomas loved God and his family.*)
- What was Thomas' job? (*Thomas was Lord Chancellor of England.*) (Explain that this position is similar to the vice president's job in the United States.)
- What did King Henry decide to do? (*Make himself head of the Church*)
- Why did Thomas disagree with the king? (*Yes. He knew the pope was the leader of the Church.*)
- How did King Henry punish Thomas? (*He put Thomas in prison; then the king put him to death.*)
- Why couldn't Thomas do what the king wanted? (*Because he loved God above all*)
- What does this story teach us? (*Love of God is the most important thing.*)

118

It is not always easy to keep God first in one's life, but the Holy Spirit and the example of others can help us. Thomas More is a good example of someone who always kept God first in his life.

Thomas More

Thomas More enjoyed life. He loved his wife and their four children. They lived in a beautiful home just outside London, England. Thomas was very happy when he was at home with his family.

Thomas liked everything in his life, but he loved God most of all. "Praise God and be merry," Thomas used to say.

Thomas was well-liked by everyone. When Henry VIII became king, he named Thomas More the Lord Chancellor of England, the second most powerful man in the country.

Then King Henry decided to make himself the head of the Church. But Thomas knew that the pope was the leader of the Church, so Thomas disapproved of what the king was doing.

This made the king very angry. The king decided to put Thomas in prison. Thomas' family begged him to honor the king as head of the Church. Thomas loved his family very much, but he knew that he could not put his love for them before his love for God.

The king then ordered that Thomas More be put to death. Before his death in 1535, Thomas said, "I die the king's good servant, but God's first." The Church honors Thomas More as a saint on June 22.

Discuss

Why did Thomas More not do what the king asked of him?

118 Morality

Enriching the Lesson

Ask volunteers to portray Saint Thomas More, his wife, their four children, and a few of their friends in an improvised skit. Have the friends and family members try to convince Thomas More to honor King Henry as the head of the Church. What would they, as friends and family members, say to Thomas? How would Thomas respond? How would they feel about his decision?

CURRICULUM CONNECTION

Music Teach the students "Joyful, Joyful, We Adore Thee," found on page 133 of THIS OUR FAITH *Hymnal*. Help the students recognize that this song praises God. Explain that singing songs of praise is one way we can show the importance of God in our lives.

Activity

Complete each of the stories. Then write in the box the number of the commandment that matches the story.

1. The Sabbath is a special day at the Diaz house. On Sunday morning everyone gets ready to

_____ .

While they are there, they _____

_____ .

At the end of the day, they remember God's

goodness by _____

_____

_____ .

Which commandment does this story match? ☐

2. Maureen is an altar server at Saint Ann Parish. Father Charles thinks Maureen is one of the best altar servers because of the way

_____

_____ .

Some of Maureen's friends swear and curse a

lot, but Maureen says _____

_____ .

Which commandment does this story match? ☐

3. Karim's oldest brother believes that the most important thing in life is to have lots of money. Karim told him that he thinks

_____

_____ .

Which commandment does this story match? ☐

Help the students value the courage and faithfulness of Saint Thomas More. Explain that few of us will ever be called to make the same decisions that Thomas did, but that all of us will have the opportunity to put God first in our lives through our words and actions.

Step 3 / CONCLUSION

Learning How to Live Our Faith

Completing an Activity

Read aloud the directions to the activity on page 119. Direct the students to complete the stories and match the commandments to the stories independently. When the students have finished, encourage them to share their responses.

Reviewing the Commandments

Have the students recite the first three commandments from memory. Affirm those who are able to do this and encourage those who had difficulty to study the commandments so they will know them by heart.

Focus on

The First Three Commandments From these commandments we learn the first part of God's covenant with God's people, "I will be your God." The Israelites saw the commandments as a great gift from God. The psalmist speaks of God's special love for them, and their love for God's law.

Your word, O Lord, will last forever. How I love your law. The taste of your commands is sweeter than honey. Your word is a lamp to guide me and a light for my path (based on Psalm 119).

Objective

This lesson helps the students pray to God who dwells within the sacred space of the human heart.

Preparing for Prayer

Ask a volunteer to read aloud page 120. Go over with the class the four steps to pray to God who dwells within each person.

Praying Together

Create a prayerful environment and gather the students for prayer. Give them a few moments to quiet themselves and put themselves in a prayerful mood. Allow sufficient time for the students to meet God dwelling within them in silent prayer.

Reading the Bible

Distribute Bibles to each student. Ask them to open their Bibles and read aloud together this passage from Ephesians 3:14–19: "For this reason I kneel before the Father, from whom every family in heaven and on earth is named, that he may grant you in accord with the riches of his glory to be strengthened with power through his Spirit in the inner self, and that Christ may dwell in your hearts through faith; that you, rooted and grounded in love, may have strength to comprehend with all the holy ones what is the breadth and length and height and depth, and to know the love of Christ that surpasses knowledge, so that you may be filled with all the fullness of God."

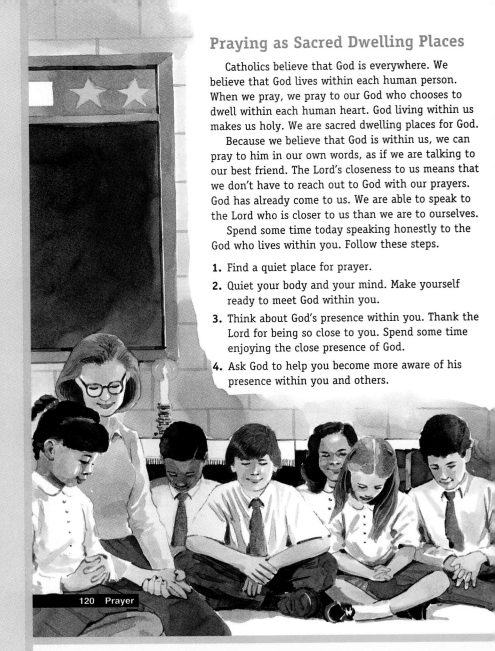

Praying as Sacred Dwelling Places

Catholics believe that God is everywhere. We believe that God lives within each human person. When we pray, we pray to our God who chooses to dwell within each human heart. God living within us makes us holy. We are sacred dwelling places for God.

Because we believe that God is within us, we can pray to him in our own words, as if we are talking to our best friend. The Lord's closeness to us means that we don't have to reach out to God with our prayers. God has already come to us. We are able to speak to the Lord who is closer to us than we are to ourselves.

Spend some time today speaking honestly to the God who lives within you. Follow these steps.

1. Find a quiet place for prayer.
2. Quiet your body and your mind. Make yourself ready to meet God within you.
3. Think about God's presence within you. Thank the Lord for being so close to you. Spend some time enjoying the close presence of God.
4. Ask God to help you become more aware of his presence within you and others.

120 Prayer

CURRICULUM CONNECTION

Music Read with the class the words of the responsorial psalm "Here I Am," found on page 25 of THIS IS OUR FAITH *Hymnal*. Point out verse 2 which tells of listening to the Lord in our hearts as the Lord calls our name. Then teach the melody. When the class knows the music well, select a soloist for the verses and have the rest of the class join in with the response.

Chapter Review

Read each statement below. Then write **True** or **False** on the line in front of each statement.

<u>True</u> **1.** Jesus' Great Commandment to love God above all else reminds us of the first three commandments.

<u>False</u> **2.** The money changers had great respect and reverence for God's holy Temple.

<u>True</u> **3.** Thomas More disapproved of King Henry VIII's action in making himself head of the Church.

<u>True</u> **4.** Thomas More was put in prison and then put to death for his beliefs.

<u>False</u> **5.** Thomas More put his love of family before his love for God.

On the lines provided, write your answers to the first two questions.

1. What is meant by *in vain*?

   In vain means in a disrespectful way.

2. What do the first three commandments teach us?

   1. To keep God first in our lives

   2. To show respect for God

   3. To honor God in a special way on Sunday

3. Discuss how we can place God first in our lives.

My trust is in you,
O Lord; I say,
"You are my God."
Based on Psalm 31:15

CHAPTER REVIEW

Reviewing the Chapter

Read the directions for the true and false statements at the top of the page. When the students have completed this section, correct the answers with them.

Answering the Review Questions

Then read aloud the review questions. Direct the students to write the answers on the lines provided. Encourage all to participate in the discussion of item 3.

Reading the Scripture Verse

Read aloud the Scripture verse with the students. Write the following example of trust on the chalkboard. *I trust you, God, because you have given me loving parents to care for me.* Ask the students why they trust God. Add their comments to the list on the chalkboard.

Teaching Tips

There may be children in your class whose families do not attend Mass on a regular basis. Some of these children may feel guilty about not attending Mass. Help the students understand that they are not breaking a commandment when they cannot get to church on their own, but rather need to rely on their parents for transportation. Encourage the children to spend time in prayer with God on the Sabbath, even when they are able to attend Mass.

Honoring Our Parents

Objectives

To help the students
- Understand the fourth commandment.
- Learn about the Holy Family and consider how their family can be like it.
- Identify ways in which they have honored their parents.
- Recognize their responsibilities toward their parents.
- Discover ways to pray a family blessing and review the chapter.

Chapter Outline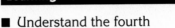

	Step 1 Learning About Our Lives	**Step 2** Learning About Our Faith	**Step 3** Learning How to Live Our Faith
Day 1	■ Review the first three commandments. ■ Introduce the chapter. ■ Write about families. *ABOUT 10 MINUTES*	■ Understand the fourth commandment. ■ Review the vocabulary. ■ Present the doctrine. *ABOUT 12 MINUTES*	■ Live the fourth commandment. *ABOUT 8 MINUTES*
Day 2	■ Study and write about photographs. *ABOUT 10 MINUTES*	■ Read the Scripture story. ■ Discuss the Scripture story. *ABOUT 10 MINUTES*	■ Discuss ways of being like the Holy Family. ■ Pray together. *ABOUT 10 MINUTES*
Day 3	■ Read the story. ■ Discuss the story. ■ Relate the story to our lives. ■ Write about obeying parents. *ABOUT 15 MINUTES*	■ Understand the fourth commandment. *ABOUT 5 MINUTES*	■ Write ways to follow the fourth commandment. *ABOUT 10 MINUTES*
Day 4	■ Study the photographs. *ABOUT 7 MINUTES*	■ Read about parents. ■ Complete statements. *ABOUT 8 MINUTES*	■ Complete an activity. ■ Review the lesson. *ABOUT 15 MINUTES*

Day 5   **Prayer**   Talk about blessings; read a blessing; write a family blessing; and pray together.
            Review   Review the chapter; answer the questions; and read the Scripture verse.

Correlation to the

Catechism of the **C**atholic **C**hurch

Paragraphs
**531, 532, 2196–2257, 2197,
2198, 2199, 2200, 2205,
2215, 2222, 2822**

Plan Ahead ～～～～～～～

	Preparing Your Class	**Materials Needed**
Day 1	Read through the lesson plan.	■ pencils or pens ■ writing paper
Day 2	Read through the lesson plan. Gather visual representations of the Holy Family.	■ pencils or pens ■ various visual representations of the Holy Family
Day 3	Read the lesson plan. If you opt to invite a guest speaker, be sure to make all the necessary preparations. If you assign the interview, schedule time for sharing the results.	■ pencils or pens ■ writing paper
Day 4	Read through the lesson plan.	■ pencils or pens ■ writing paper
Day 5	Read through the lesson plan.	■ pencils or pens ■ Bible ■ prayer cloth ■ candle ■ small bowl of holy water

Additional Resources

As you plan this chapter, consider using the following materials from The Resourceful Teacher Package.

■ *Classroom Activity Sheets 10* and *10a*

■ *Family Activity Sheets 10* and *10a*

■ *Chapter 10 Test*

■ *Prayers for Every Day*

■ *Projects: Grade 4*

You may wish to refer to the following Big Book.

■ *We Celebrate God's Word,* pages 6, 10, 11

In preparing the students for the Sunday readings, you may wish to use Silver Burdett Ginn's *Getting Ready for Sunday* student and teacher materials.

BOOKS FOR THE JOURNEY

Always My Dad. Sharon Dennis Wyeth. Alfred A. Knopf, 1995. The story of a parent doing what he can to love his children and of a girl who realizes that no matter where her dad is, he loves her and is always her dad.

Emmet Otter's Jug Band Christmas. Russell Hoban. Buccaneer Books, 1992. A delightful story of an otter and his mother who are very poor but are still secretly determined to give each other something special for Christmas.

MORE BOOKS FOR THE JOURNEY

Stone Fox. John Reynolds Gardiner. HarperCollins, 1983. The story of a boy who decided to do something to give his ailing grandfather a reason to live.

The War with Grandpa. Robert Kimmel Smith. Delacorte, 1984. The story of how a boy and his grandfather work out a room problem after the grandfather comes to live with the boy's family.

REDUCED CLASSROOM ACTIVITIES

NAME _____

HONORING OUR PARENTS

Read the list of phrases below. Then make two lists by writing each phrase under the correct heading.

asking questions politely

listening quietly

making faces

saying "please" and "thank you"

talking back

turning your back on someone

doing something the first time you're asked

making fun of someone

screaming

Showing Respect

asking questions politely

listening quietly

saying "please" and "thank you"

doing something the first time you're asked

Being Disrespectful

making faces

talking back

turning your back on someone

making fun of someone

screaming

To the Teacher: This activity contrasts respectful and disrespectful behaviors as they pertain to the fourth commandment.

Chapter 10 Honoring Our Parents

THIS IS OUR FAITH 4   **10**

NAME _____

THE FOURTH COMMANDMENT

You have just turned on the time machine and ZAP!—you are now a parent. Write the name of your fourth-grade son or daughter here.

_____

Keeping the fourth commandment in mind, what advice would you give your child about being a better Christian? Write your ideas on the lines below.

_____
_____
_____
_____
_____

The time machine has brought you back to the present. Now underline the part of the advice you wrote that might help you the most right now. Find a partner in your class and compare his or her advice with yours. Are there similarities? Write them here.

_____
_____
_____
_____

Would you like to add to or change your advice? If so, write your changes here.

_____
_____
_____
_____

To the Teacher: This activity will help fourth graders verbalize their understanding of the fourth commandment. Allow time for partners to engage in follow-up discussion.

10a THIS IS OUR FAITH 4

Chapter 10 Honoring Our Parents

121c Chapter Organizer

RELATING TO PARENTS

A constant reality in the lives of most children is their relationship with their parents. Fourth graders can recognize that their parents love and care for them. They are also becoming increasingly aware of their parents' authority, as they strive, in many small ways, for independence. Most children experience some tension in response to the authority of their parents and others who have responsibility for them.

DIMENSIONS OF THE FOURTH COMMANDMENT

Yahweh gave the fourth commandment to the people of Israel to urge them to have respect for the elders of their society. In ancient Israel, as in our own time, parents were responsible for the training of the children. It was, and is, in the home where children learn to respect themselves and others. No community can survive for long without love, care, and respect for all the members. The fourth commandment reminds us that we are communal and social beings.

The key moral imperative for children is to respect, love, and obey their parents and others in authority. Parents are called to love, respect, and act responsibly toward their children and toward their own parents. The fourth commandment has special relevance today when modern stresses can make family life difficult.

Although we tend to think of this commandment as being directed toward children and teenagers, it particularly speaks to adults. The fourth commandment becomes more and more relevant for adult children as they see their parents living into their eighties and nineties. In adulthood we must assure the physical and emotional care of our elderly parents. We must respect their life experience and value their hard-earned wisdom. We are called to support them in the most trivial requests as well as in the crisis of illness.

The fourth commandment defines very clearly the relationship between parents and children based on mutual respect. This respect is a sign of gratitude to God, for the family is one of his greatest blessings. In response we are obliged to contribute to family stability and to treat one another with honor and respect throughout our lives.

GROWING IN THE FOURTH COMMANDMENT

Be sensitive to varied family situations such as two parents who work outside the home, remarried parents, single parents, and parents who do not live with their children.

Respect for parents does not stop because parents divorce. Parents in any situation can love their children and children can love and respect their parents.

In presenting this chapter, help the students appreciate that as they honor their parents, they also honor God.

Objective

This lesson helps the students understand the fourth commandment.

Step 1 / INTRODUCTION

Learning About Our Lives

Reviewing the First Three Commandments

Ask for volunteers to recite the first three commandments from memory. Praise the students who have learned the first three commandments and encourage the others to learn them.

Introducing the Chapter

Direct attention to page 122. Ask a volunteer to read aloud the chapter title and focus question. Invite the students' responses. Be sensitive to those class members who may live in single parent homes. Help the students recognize that there are many different kinds of families.

Writing About Families

Ask a volunteer to read the directions to the activity on page 122. Have the students work independently as they describe their families. Afterward, encourage the students to share their completed sentences.

Step 2 / DEVELOPMENT

Learning About Our Faith

Understanding the Fourth Commandment

Ask volunteers to read aloud "The Fourth Commandment" on page 123. Lead the students in repeating the fourth commandment after it is read. As each vocabulary word is introduced, refer to the definition in the Vocabulary box.

Honoring Our Parents

Think of how your parents show their love for you. How do you show your love for them?

Activity

Some families are large, and some are small. Some have many members, and some have only two or three. Complete the following sentences to help you describe your family.

1. There are _____ people in our family.

2. We live at _____.

3. I have _____ sisters and _____ brothers.

4. One thing our family likes to do together is

_____.

5. You can tell we are a family by the way we

_____

_____.

Enriching the Lesson

Distribute construction paper, felt-tip markers or crayons, and scissors. Invite the students to make cards for their parents, grandparents, or guardians expressing the ways in which these adults are special. Encourage the students to make the cards personal, listing specific examples of why they consider their parents special and mentioning why they are thankful for their parents.

Focus on

The Fourth Commandment
The fourth commandment is intended to nurture a healthy relationship between parents and children. Children will best learn to be respectful in a home where adults show respect for each other and for the children.

Children will learn to obey when they grow up with adults who themselves show obedience for those in authority. Children will learn to love their parents in response to their parents' love of them and others.

The Fourth Commandment

People who love and care for one another and live together make up a family. Some families have two parents and their children. Some families are made up of a mother and her children. Others have a father and his children. Sometimes families include grandparents who live with them.

Jesus wants us to respect our parents and our grandparents as Jesus respected Mary and Joseph.

The fourth commandment calls us to love our parents and to show our love in what we say and do. We are to **respect** our parents and others who are responsible for us and who care for us. We are to **obey** them unless they tell us to do something that is not good. We are also to pray for them and help them.

Throughout his life, Jesus honored his mother and his foster father. By doing this he was obeying the fourth commandment. The fourth commandment is ***Honor** your father and your mother*. When we honor our parents, we are following Jesus' example.

Vocabulary

respect: to act with care toward someone or something

obey: to do what someone who is responsible for you tells you to do

honor: to treat with respect

We Believe

The fourth commandment teaches us to love, honor, and obey our parents and others who are responsible for us.

Doctrine 123

Teaching Tips

When teaching students about the fourth commandment, it is important to point out that God does not require obedience when parents or lawful authority figures ask a child to commit harmful or illegal acts. Be sure to emphasize the clause from the sentence about obedience to parents, found in the student text on page 123: "We are to obey them *unless they tell us to do something that is not good.*"

Studying the Picture

Use the picture of the family on page 123 to discuss ways to follow the fourth commandment. Invite the students to share specific instances in which they obeyed, helped, respected, and loved their parents. Ask them to think of times when they prayed for their parents.

Reviewing the Vocabulary

Clarify the meaning of the word *respect* by presenting the definition. Invite the students to give examples of occasions when they respected someone. Review the other two new words in the same way.

Presenting the Doctrine

Assist the students in learning the We Believe statements by asking them to repeat the statements a few times. Ask the students to explain what the fourth commandment teaches us.

Step 3 / CONCLUSION

Learning How to Live Our Faith

Living the Fourth Commandment

Distribute writing paper. Ask the students to write three sentences showing how the fourth commandment can be lived. Instruct them to use one of the vocabulary words in each sentence. For example: I show respect for my mother when I listen to what she says.

DAY 2
SCRIPTURE

Objective

This lesson helps the students learn about the Holy Family and consider how their family can be like the Holy Family.

Step 1 / INTRODUCTION

Learning About Our Lives

Studying and Writing About Photographs

Direct the students' attention to the photographs on page 124. Discuss what is happening in each picture. Have the students write how people are showing concern for each other. Invite the students to share their ideas.

Invite the students to share some of the things that their parents or other family members do to show their love and care for them. Tell the class that Jesus, too, had a family who loved and cared for him.

Step 2 / DEVELOPMENT

Learning About Our Faith

Reading the Scripture Story

Ask a volunteer to read aloud the story "Jesus at Home" on page 125. Encourage the class to comment on what is shown in the illustration on page 125. (*Jesus is learning how to be a carpenter. Joseph is teaching him.*)

Discussing the Scripture Story

Discuss the story, using the questions below.

■ Where did Jesus grow up? (*In a small town called Nazareth*)

■ With whom did Jesus live? (*Mary and Joseph*)

■ How did Mary and Joseph take care of Jesus? (*They taught Jesus how and when to pray; they taught him about life and God. Joseph showed Jesus how to be a carpenter.*)

■ In what ways did the family show their love for God? (*They praised and thanked God at mealtimes. They worshiped God on the Sabbath at home and in the synagogue.*)

124

Activity

Talk about the family in each photograph. On the lines near the photographs, tell how the people are showing respect and care for each other.

CURRICULUM CONNECTION

Art Engage the assistance of the art teacher or librarian in helping you find reproductions of fine arts pieces that depict the Holy Family. Jesus, Mary, and Joseph are often shown in such scenes entitled *The Adoration of the Magi, The Nativity, The Presentation in the Temple, The Flight into Egypt,* primarily by painters of the 14th, 15th, 16th, and 17th centuries. Modern depictions can sometimes be found in the religious art calendars distributed by parishes.

Focus on

Jesus We know very little about Jesus' early life. His public life began when he was about thirty years old. The very limited number of stories about Jesus' childhood tell us about his obedience to his parents and the finding of Jesus in the Temple. During the greater part of his life, Jesus probably shared the condition of most people of his time: a daily life spent without evident greatness. Have the students read Chapter 2 of Luke's Gospel for the scriptural account of Jesus' life from his birth to his twelfth year.

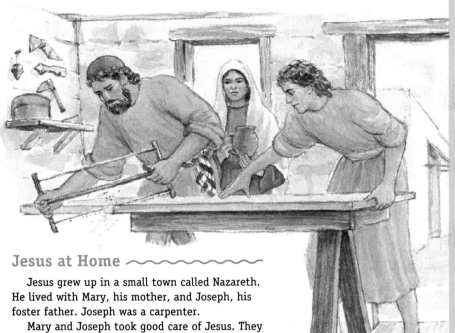

Jesus at Home

Jesus grew up in a small town called Nazareth. He lived with Mary, his mother, and Joseph, his foster father. Joseph was a carpenter.

Mary and Joseph took good care of Jesus. They worked hard so that Jesus would have what he needed to grow up happy and healthy. They taught Jesus about life and about God. They brought him to the synagogue to learn more from the rabbis.

Mary and Joseph taught Jesus to pray. The family prayed together in the morning, afternoon, and evening. They praised and thanked God at mealtimes. They celebrated the Sabbath at home and in the synagogue.

Jesus loved his parents. He obeyed them and helped them. He learned to be a carpenter in Joseph's shop. Under Mary's and Joseph's care, Jesus grew in wisdom, age, and grace.

Based on Luke 2:39–40, 51–52

Scripture 125

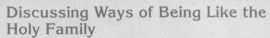

Enriching the Lesson

Discuss with the students the different types of families that are portrayed on television or in the movies. List the families on the chalkboard. Talk about the qualities that these families might have in common with the Holy Family. Note specifically how family members show love, care, and respect for one another.

- How did Jesus show love for his parents? (*He obeyed and helped them.*)
- How did God and others feel about Jesus? (*They loved him.*)

Explain that God loves all people, even those who do not love God. When people welcome God's love, they do what God asks of them. Then they can feel God's love. Jesus loved God so much that he was able to use God's grace to do whatever God expected of him.

Step 3 / CONCLUSION

Learning How to Live Our Faith

Discussing Ways of Being Like the Holy Family

Help the students recall that the family of Jesus is called the Holy Family. Show the students the various visual representations of the Holy Family that you gathered prior to the session. Discuss with the students how their family can be like the Holy Family; for example, praying and worshiping together, learning from each other, helping one another, taking care of each other, being happy together, and loving all the good things that God made.

Praying Together

Invite the students to offer brief prayers asking God to help their families become more like the Holy Family. Conclude by praying, *God, you gave us the Holy Family as an example of family life. Keep our families always in your heart. Help us to grow in wisdom and love. Amen.*

Objective

This lesson helps the students identify ways in which they have honored their parents.

Step 1 / INTRODUCTION

Learning About Our Lives

Reading the Story

Ask for volunteers to read aloud "Caring for Grandma" on pages 126 and 127. You may want to choose specific students to read the parts of Grandma, Mrs. Anderson, and Michael.

Discussing the Story

Discuss the story with the students, using the following questions.

- Why does Mrs. Anderson want to take care of her mother? (*Her mother took good care of her when she was growing up.*)

- What is Mrs. Anderson doing to show how much she cares? (*She is taking good care of her mother who is elderly, sick, and needs her help.*)

- Why should Michael obey his mother? (*Children are to obey their parents so as to live out the fourth commandment. His mother wants him to be good to his grandmother also.*)

Help the students appreciate Mrs. Anderson's love and concern for her mother and Michael's sorrow and his willingness to make up for not obeying his mother.

Relating the Story to Our Lives

Help the students relate this story to their own lives by asking them the following questions.

- Have you ever felt like Michael did?

- What happened to make you feel that way?

Writing About Obeying Parents

Distribute writing paper, pens, or pencils. Read the following to the students.

Your parents or other people who take care of you may want you to act in a certain way. Sometimes you may find it very hard to do what they want you to do even though it is right to do. Write about a time when this happened.

126

Caring for Grandma

Mrs. Anderson's mother was sick in bed. Mrs. Anderson called out, "Hi, Mom! Sorry I'm late. We had a long meeting at the office."

"I'm glad you're home," Mrs. Anderson's mother said softly. "I'm hungry."

"Didn't Michael bring you your lunch?" Mrs. Anderson asked. "I called Michael from work and told him to be sure that you got something to eat. I'll get dinner started right away."

Just then Michael came in from outside. "Hi, Mom!" he said with a big smile on his face.

"Michael, Grandma is hungry and very upset. I asked you to make lunch for her. Why didn't you do it?"

"I was going to," Michael explained. "But Chrissy and Peter asked me to play ball with them. I ran out to play and forgot all about Grandma's lunch."

Then Mrs. Anderson asked Michael to sit down. "Grandma is my mother," she told him. "She took good care of me when I was growing up. Now she needs my care. I want you to be good to her, too."

"I'm sorry, Mom," Michael answered with his head down.

Enriching the Lesson

Invite a guest speaker to talk to the students about taking care of elderly relatives. Ask the guest specifically to mention both the rewards and frustrations of taking care of aging relatives.

Focus on

The Christian Family The *Catechism of the Catholic Church* states, "The Christian family is a communion of persons, a sign and image of the communion of the Father and the Son in the Holy Spirit. In the procreation and education of children it reflects the Father's work of creation. . . Daily prayer and the reading of the Word of God strengthen it in charity. The Christian family has an evangelizing and missionary task" (#2205).

"You can bring Grandma her dinner in a little while," Mrs. Anderson said. "And please tell her you're sorry and you'll never forget her lunch again."

We Honor Our Parents

We do not come into the world alone. We do not grow up by ourselves. The fourth commandment reminds us that parents are a great gift to us. We show that we appreciate the gift of parents by following the fourth commandment.

We honor our parents by helping at home, by listening to their advice, and by obeying their rules. We treat them with respect in all we say and do. Even when we are grown, we continue to help them, care for them, and treat them with love and respect.

Activity

Think of what it means to honor your father and mother throughout your life. Then answer these questions.

1. How did I follow the fourth commandment when I was in first grade?

_____

2. How do I honor my father and mother now as a fourth grader?

_____

3. How might I follow the fourth commandment when I am sixteen?

_____

4. How might I follow the fourth commandment when I am my parents' age?

_____

Then ask volunteers to read aloud to the others what they wrote.

Step 2 / DEVELOPMENT

Learning About Our Faith

Understanding the Fourth Commandment

Ask a volunteer to read aloud "We Honor Our Parents" on page 127. Explain to the students that we are called to honor our parents all of our lives, not just when we are young children. We honor, respect, and care for our parents in thanksgiving for the gift of our parents and the gift of life that they gave to us.

Step 3 / CONCLUSION

Learning How to Live Our Faith

Writing Ways to Follow the Fourth Commandment

Read aloud the directions to the activity on page 127. Ask the students to answer the questions independently. Give the students sufficient time to complete the activity. Help the students imagine how they might follow the fourth commandment as they grow older. Invite the students to share their ideas.

Enriching the Lesson

Direct the students to interview an adult family member about that person's growing-up years. Tell the students to ask the person specifically how he or she showed respect for his or her parents as a young child, then as he or she grew older, and finally, as an adult. You might want to brainstorm interview questions together as a class to help the students prepare for the interview.

DAY 4
MORALITY

Objective

This lesson helps the students recognize their responsibilities toward their parents.

Step 1 / INTRODUCTION

Learning About Our Lives

Studying the Photographs

Direct the students' attention to the pictures on page 128. Discuss how the fourth commandment is being lived in each picture. Help the students appreciate that spending time together, participating in family activities, and having fun are some of the ways people can show their love for those who care for them.

Step 2 / DEVELOPMENT

Learning About Our Faith

Reading About Parents

Ask volunteers to read aloud "Parents Are People, Too" on page 128. Discuss the students' responsibilities to their parents and the other adults who work hard to help them. Explain that, like children, parents also feel tired, angry, unhappy, or are preoccupied at times. Emphasize that God helps parents and children show love for one another.

Completing Statements

Distribute writing paper to the students. Print the following statements on the chalkboard.

■ *The best part of being a parent is _____ .*

■ *The hardest part of being a parent is*

_____ .

Have the students copy and complete the statements. Afterward, discuss the joys and difficulties of being a parent that the students have identified. Ask them how they can help their parents. Assist them in understanding that they can best help their parents by keeping the fourth commandment.

128

Parents Are People, Too

Being a parent is not always easy. Parents and other adults who care for us work hard to help us. They want us to grow up to be good people. They try to make our lives safe, comfortable, and happy. Sometimes they feel worried, angry, or sad about us.

There are many ways to show love and respect for our parents and other caring adults. We may not always feel like doing this. We may feel tired, angry, or unhappy, or we may have other important things to think about. But God calls us to show love and respect for all those people who care for us.

128   Morality

★ ★ ★ ★
Enriching
the Lesson ★

Invite the students to brainstorm ways of keeping the fourth commandment. List their ideas on the chalkboard. Have each student silently choose a specific way to honor his or her parents during the upcoming week and encourage them to follow through on their commitment.

Activity

Read these stories. Then write endings that show how the child in each story followed the fourth commandment.

1. One afternoon Alex waited and waited for his mother to pick him up at the bus stop. He felt angrier with each passing minute. When his mother finally arrived, Alex screamed at her for making him wait so long. He got in the car and slammed the door. Neither one said a word all the way home. Alex went straight to his room. Before supper he went to his mother and

_____

_____

_____

2. "You are not to cross the street except when the light is green," Joan's father ordered. "Do you understand?" Joan nodded her head. The next day, Joan was in a hurry coming home from a science fair at school. She was on her bicycle. She did not want to stop at a very busy corner. The light was red and Joan could see cars coming. But she thought that she would have plenty of time to cross the street if she pedaled faster. Then Joan remembered what her father had told her. Joan decided to

_____

_____

_____

Morality   129

Learning How to Live Our Faith

Completing an Activity

Explain the directions to the activity on page 129. Read the stories aloud with the students. Give them sufficient time to write a conclusion to each story.

Have the students read aloud their story endings. Although the students' responses may vary, they should all illustrate ways of following the fourth commandment.

Afterward, give the students time to write their own story that shows how a child followed the fourth commandment. Give the students an opportunity to share their stories with the class.

Reviewing the Lesson

Ask the students to recite the fourth commandment from memory. Praise those who have learned it and encourage others to memorize it. Have the students recall three ways in which we keep this commandment: *We love, obey, and respect our parents and those who care for us.*

Objective

This lesson helps the students discover ways to pray a family blessing.

Talking About Blessings

Discuss the word *blessing*. Help the students understand that a blessing can be both a prayer and an action. Point out that the priest blesses us at the end of the Mass and that parents sometimes trace the sign of the cross on our foreheads to bless us.

Reading a Blessing

Have the students look at the painting of the Holy Family on page 130 and then close their eyes. Invite them to imagine the scene as you read aloud "A Family Blessing."

Writing a Family Blessing

Ask the students to consider the blessings they would like their family to receive from God. Have them think about any special needs their families may have. Then, instruct them to write a blessing for their family in the space provided. Afterward, invite each student to pray his or her blessing for the class. Suggest that they take their books home and pray their blessings with their families.

You may want to have the students copy their blessing on notebook paper, decorate it, and display it in a prominent place at home.

Praying Together

Gather the students around a table on which you have placed an open Bible and a small bowl of holy water. Call each student forward by name. Say, "(*Name*), obey your parents." Then have the students bless themselves with the holy water as each one says, "May God bless me as I try to follow the fourth commandment."

Praying a Family Blessing

Blessings are an important part of our faith as Catholics. We have blessings for people and pets. We have blessings for meals, objects, and places. Our blessings praise God and ask that certain gifts such as faith and trust be given to us.

Read the blessing for families below. Then on the lines provided, write a prayer of blessing for your family.

A Family Blessing

May the Lord Jesus,
who lived with his holy family in Nazareth,
dwell also with our family,
keep it from all evil,
and make all of us one in heart and mind.
Amen.

My Family Blessing

_____

_____

_____

_____

_____

The Fourth Commandment
This commandment speaks to parents as well as to their children. Parents are obliged to take seriously their responsibility to their children, and must be worthy of their respect. Paul begins by admonishing children in Ephesians 6:1–2. He goes on to give words of advice to parents in Ephesians 6:4.

Cultural Awareness

In certain cultures such as those of Spanish-speaking peoples, it is often a custom for children to ask a blessing from their mother or father before going to sleep. The child would ask, for instance, "Bendición, mamá" (*A blessing, Mother*), and the mother would answer, "Dios lo (or la) bendiga" (*God bless you*).

Chapter Review

Fill in the blanks to find the missing words. Then write these words in the puzzle below. You will find one word that sums up the fourth commandment.

1. When our parents are in need, we should _H_ _E_ _L_ _P_ them.

2. We should _O_ _B_ _E_ _Y_ our parents.

3. We should pray for our _P_ _A_ _R_ _E_ _N_ _T_ _S_ .

4. Giving gifts is one way of showing _L_ _O_ _V_ _E_ for our parents.

5. We show _R_ _E_ _S_ _P_ _E_ _C_ _T_ for our parents by speaking kindly to them.

Answer the first two questions on the lines provided.

1. What is meant by *honor*?

   To treat with respect

2. What does the fourth commandment teach us?

   To love, honor, and obey our parents and others

   who are responsible for us

Children, obey your parents.
Based on Ephesians 6:1

3. Discuss how we can obey the fourth commandment.

Reviewing the Chapter

Direct the students' attention to the puzzle activity at the top of page 131. Read the directions aloud. Have the students complete the activity. To check their answers, have them read through the sentences together and correct their own work.

Answering the Questions

Go through the first two questions on page 131. Have the students write the answers to the questions on the lines provided. Encourage all to participate in the discussion of item 3.

Reading the Scripture Verse

Ask the students to read aloud together the Scripture verse. Encourage the class to memorize the verse.

Teaching Tips

As an incentive to help the students learn the Ten Commandments, make a commandments poster. Print a title at the top of the poster. Draw horizontal rules across the poster, one line for each student's name. Draw vertical lines to make ten columns. As the students master each commandment, place a star or a sticker next to the students' names. Continue this activity as you teach the next four chapters until all the remaining commandments are presented.

131

Respecting Life

Objectives

To help the students
- Understand the fifth commandment.
- Understand that Jesus taught against violence through both actions and words.
- Recognize violence in our world and ways to cope with it.
- Consider ways of living out the fifth commandment.
- Pray the Way of the Cross and review the chapter.

Chapter Outline

	Step 1 Learning About Our Lives	**Step 2** Learning About Our Faith	**Step 3** Learning How to Live Our Faith
Day 1	■ Review the commandments. ■ Study a cartoon. ■ Decide what to do. ■ Write answers to questions. *ABOUT 15 MINUTES*	■ Read about the fifth commandment. ■ Understand the vocabulary. ■ Review the doctrine. *ABOUT 10 MINUTES*	■ Draw a picture. ■ Review the lesson. *ABOUT 5 MINUTES*
Day 2	■ Listen to and discuss a story. *ABOUT 5 MINUTES*	■ Read a Scripture story. ■ Complete an activity. ■ Learn that Jesus is a model of nonviolence. *ABOUT 15 MINUTES*	■ Participate in a discussion. *ABOUT 10 MINUTES*
Day 3	■ Read and discuss a story. ■ Write a story ending. *ABOUT 15 MINUTES*	■ Read about the fifth commandment. *ABOUT 5 MINUTES*	■ Write about coping with violence. ■ Make a continuum from disrespect to violence. *ABOUT 10 MINUTES*
Day 4	■ Complete an activity. *ABOUT 5 MINUTES*	■ Read a Scripture story. ■ Study how violence happens. ■ Review the vocabulary. *ABOUT 15 MINUTES*	■ Consider how to work for nonviolence. ■ Review the fifth commandment. ■ Complete an activity. *ABOUT 10 MINUTES*

Day 5   **Prayer**   Recall the Way of the Cross; read about praying the Way of the Cross; pray the Way of the Cross; invoke God's help; and sing together.

            Review   Review the fifth commandment; review the chapter; and read the Scripture verse.

Correlation to the Catechism of the Catholic Church

Paragraphs
356, 2258–2330, 2262, 2302, 2303, 2304, 2305, 2306, 2319, 2669

Plan Ahead

	Preparing Your Class	**Materials Needed**
Day 1	Read through the lesson plan.	■ pencils or pens
Day 2	Read the lesson plan.	■ pencils or pens ■ news magazines ■ Bibles, one per student
Day 3	Read the lesson plan.	■ pencils or pens
Day 4	Read the lesson plan. If making the curriculum connection, review the song "World Peace Prayer" in THIS IS OUR FAITH *Hymnal*.	■ pencils or pens ■ writing paper
Day 5	Read the lesson plan. If you plan to hold the prayer service at the church, make all the necessary arrangements.	■ pencils or pens ■ Bible, cross ■ candle ■ copies of THIS IS OUR FAITH *Hymnal*

Additional Resources

As you plan this chapter, consider using the following materials from The Resourceful Teacher Package.

■ *Classroom Activity Sheets 11* and *11a*

■ *Family Activity Sheets 11* and *11a*

■ *Chapter 11 Test*

■ *Prayers for Every Day*

■ *Projects: Grade 4*

You may also wish to refer to the following Big Book.

■ *We Celebrate God's Word*, pages 12, 18

In preparing the students for the Sunday readings, you may wish to use Silver Burdett Ginn's *Getting Ready for Sunday* student and teacher materials.

BOOKS FOR THE JOURNEY

Chernowitz. Fran Arrick. Bradbury Press, 1981. A story of prejudice in which a student is rejected by his schoolmates and treated in a very hurtful way.

Frederick's Fables. "Cornelius," pp. 61–70. Leo Lionni. Knopf, 1993. A story of rejection by one's own and being helped by another.

MORE BOOKS FOR THE JOURNEY

The Real Thief. William Steig. Farrar, Straus, and Giroux, 1984. A story about suffering caused by misjudgment and disloyalty.

The Children's Illustrated Bible. "The Garden of Gethsemane," pp. 266–267. Retold by Selina Hastings. Dorling Kindersely, 1994. The story of Judas' and Peter's actions in the Garden of Gethsemane and Jesus' response.

REDUCED CLASSROOM ACTIVITIES

NAME _____

RESPECTING LIFE

Write a prayer to Jesus. In Part 1, praise Jesus and express your love. In Part 2, tell Jesus about the fears you have of violence. In Part 3, ask Jesus for peace in your heart and respect for all life.

Part 1

Jesus, _____

Part 2

Jesus, _____

Part 3

Jesus, _____

To the Teacher: Use this activity after you have presented the Scripture story "Put Away Your Sword."

Chapter 11 Respecting Life   THIS IS OUR FAITH 4   **11**

NAME _____

KEEPING THE COMMANDMENTS

Thinking about the order Jesus gave to his disciple. Then follow the directions below.

1. Name the fifth commandment. Then tell why the fifth commandment is important to you.
   Fifth commandment: You shall not kill. _____

   Why it is important _____

2. Explain how obeying the fifth commandment means that followers of Jesus must respect all living things.

   _____

3. If Jesus were to ask you to put away your sword, what violent words and actions would you have to get rid of? Explain you answer.

   _____

To the Teacher: Use this activity after you have presented the Scripture story "Put Away Your Sword."

11a THIS IS OUR FAITH 4   **Chapter 11** Respecting Life

131c Chapter Organizer

Background for the Teacher

YOU SHALL NOT KILL

Children are full of zest for living. They are curious about living things; animals and insects fascinate them. They feel a kinship with their pets. They prefer companionship to being alone. Children, however, like all humans, can at times exhibit a lack of compassion, even cruelty, toward others. It is from this context of mixed experiences that the students will approach the fifth commandment.

Whenever human life is hurt or destroyed, or the quality of life is so diminished that human rights are denied, the fifth commandment is violated. By this commandment we are called to revere, care for, and protect life as a sacred gift from the Creator. Sin against the fifth commandment, therefore, has been defined as a denial of human rights and a refusal to see life as a gift from God.

Originally, the fifth commandment was a prohibition against murder. For the people of Israel, capital punishment was justified, but the taking of innocent life was not acceptable. The taking of a life was seen as denying God's gift of life, and Yahweh's dominion over all life. Today, we realize that the fifth commandment reaches beyond murder into all the areas of respect for life.

Current teaching of respect for life has its roots in the Church's teachings regarding life: as persons created by God, we are all made in the image and likeness of God.

Therefore, there is an intrinsic dignity to the human person. Any action or attitude which diminishes the dignity of the human person is wrong.

THE PEACE OF JESUS

Jesus loved and respected all life. He sought out those whose lives were fractured and those who were viewed as castaways. In a society embroiled in violence, Jesus asserted the rights of all in a peaceful manner. Faced with a violent attack on himself, he refused to take up the sword and condemned the use of violence. The gospel accounts of the agonized Jesus in the garden, followed by his arrest, reveal him as strengthened by prayer. He greeted his enemies in full control of the situation. He was protective of the Apostles and allowed himself to be taken captive.

TODAY'S PROBLEMS

Jesus' example and teaching are of particular relevance in today's world. Civil wars rage in different parts of the world. People continue to suffer from prejudice and discrimination. The crime of abortion stands in direct opposition to the fifth commandment. Environmental issues facing all of us today are also the concerns of the fifth commandment.

DAY 1
MORALITY/DOCTRINE

Objective

This lesson helps the students understand the fifth commandment.

Step 1 / INTRODUCTION

Learning About Our Lives

Reviewing the Commandments

Invite the students to recite the commandments they have learned. Encourage them to continue memorizing the commandments.

Introducing the Chapter

Read aloud the chapter title and focus question on page 132. Elicit the students' responses. If the students are uncomfortable sharing their own experiences, encourage them to give examples of someone who has been hurt by the words or actions of others. Help the students appreciate that when we are treated cruelly we may feel many emotions, including sadness, anger, embarrassment, or loneliness.

Studying a Cartoon

Direct attention to the cartoon. Ask the students to read the cartoon silently. Then ask them to choose the statement that most closely matches how they would respond if they knew that one of their classmates had no friends.

Completing an Activity

Read aloud the text beneath the cartoon. Ask the students to answer the questions and explain their comments. Encourage the students to act out the following situations.

■ A group of fourth graders gets together to plan an activity, but refuses to include a student whom they think has no friends. How does the excluded student react?

■ Some fourth graders want to exclude a classmate from a group activity. Another student convinces the group to change their behavior toward the left-out student. How do they all react?

Writing Answers to Questions

Give the students time to write their answers to the questions at the top of page 133. Then discuss their responses.

132

Respecting Life

"I don't want to lose my friends just because that kid doesn't have any."

"I don't feel sorry for him. If he wasn't so weird, he'd have lots of friends."

"He's not cool enough to hang around with us. Don't get involved with him."

"I feel sorry for him, but I don't want to start hanging around with him."

"I don't care what the teacher says. I'm not going to be caught dead eating lunch with that kid."

How do you feel when someone does not treat you well and hurts you with their words or actions?

Activity

The cartoon above tells a story about what happened one day in school when some fourth graders were asked by their teacher to be kind to a student who didn't have any friends.

132   Morality

Focus on

The Fifth Commandment Recognizing that all human life is sacred, we know that the taking of a life is one of the gravest sins a person can commit. Any action which brings about the death of another, whether directly or indirectly, is forbidden by the fifth commandment. This would include putting someone in grave danger; the unwillingness to give aid and assistance to a person who is in danger; any negligent behavior which causes death or injury to another; abortion; euthanasia; or suicide.

Enriching the Lesson

Discuss with the students why some people avoid people who have AIDS or cancer and people who are blind or deaf. Explain that fear and ignorance keep some people from reaching out to others. Tell the students about a class of junior high boys who shaved their heads as a sign of support for a classmate who was losing his hair from cancer treatments. People who are ill or challenged by physical problems need and deserve our love and support.

1. If you had been a part of the conversation in the cartoon, what comment would you make?

_____

_____

_____

2. Would you change your behavior toward the boy, or would you let others worry about him?

_____

_____

_____

Understanding the Fifth Commandment

Jesus lived nonviolently all his life. He had great respect and love for all living things. Most of all, he loved people and respected human life. He healed people instead of hurting them. He became angry at evil and injustice, but he did not fight or kill. He took the side of the weak and helped those whom others avoided and looked down on.

The fifth commandment is *You shall not kill.* Jesus lived by the fifth commandment. He wants us to live by it, too.

The fifth commandment calls us to respect all living beings. It teaches us that all life is **sacred**. We are to care for ourselves and our health. We must work against **violence** and help those who have been hurt. If we follow the fifth commandment, we will work to protect all life.

Vocabulary

sacred: entitled to respect; holy

violence: rough or harmful actions or words

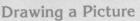

We Believe

The fifth commandment teaches us to respect and care for all living things. It teaches us that all life is sacred.

Doctrine **133**

Step 2 / DEVELOPMENT

Learning About Our Faith

Reading About the Fifth Commandment

Ask volunteers to read aloud "Understanding the Fifth Commandment" on page 133. Ask the students to underline in their texts the answers to the following questions.

- What actions of Jesus showed that he lived by the fifth commandment? (*He healed instead of hurt. He became angry at evil and injustice, but he did not fight or kill. He took the side of the weak and helped those whom others avoided and looked down on.*)
- What does the fifth commandment teach us? (*All life is sacred.*)
- If we follow the fifth commandment, what will we do? (*We will work to protect all life.*)

Understanding the Vocabulary

Point out the Vocabulary box. Ask a volunteer to read the definitions aloud. Discuss the definition of *violence* with the students, helping them to understand that violence is anything rough or harmful, not just involving fighting or guns. Bullying, name-calling, and teasing are acts of violence.

Reviewing the Doctrine

Call attention to the We Believe statements. Ask the students to read the statements to themselves. Answer any questions.

Step 3 / CONCLUSION

Learning How to Live Our Faith

Drawing a Picture

Distribute drawing paper, and felt-tip markers or crayons. Instruct the students to draw a picture of themselves protecting or showing respect for themselves, for others, or for something in nature. Afterward, invite the students to share their pictures with the rest of the class.

Reviewing the Lesson

Ask the following questions.

- What is the fifth commandment? (*You shall not kill.*)
- What does the fifth commandment teach us? (*To respect and care for all living things*)

DAY 2
SCRIPTURE

Objective
This helps the students understand that Jesus taught against violence through both his actions and his words.

Step 1 / INTRODUCTION

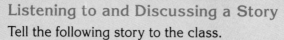
Learning About Our Lives

Listening to and Discussing a Story
Tell the following story to the class.

You and Robin are best friends. You walk to school together and play together. One day you hear some other children talking about Robin. "Robin is so dumb," says one boy. Then he tells them about a mistake that Robin made in school. Everyone laughs. Finally one of the girls says, "Let's not be friends with Robin anymore."

Ask the students to consider what they would do as Robin's best friend.

■ Will you tell Robin what the children are saying?

■ If so, what can you say that will make Robin feel better?

■ What do you think Robin should do?

Tell the students that today they will learn how Jesus felt about people hurting one another.

Step 2 / DEVELOPMENT

Learning About Our Faith

Reading and Discussing a Scripture Story

Ask for volunteers to read aloud the Scripture story on page 134. Invite them to look at the illustration and identify each of the persons named in the story. Discuss the story using the questions below.

■ What was Jesus doing in the garden of Gethsemane? (*Praying*)

■ Whom was Jesus with? (*Peter, James, and John*)

■ What did Jesus and his friends hear and see? (*Angry voices and a crowd of men*)

■ How did they feel? (*Surprised and afraid*)

■ Which disciple of Jesus was in the crowd? (*Judas*)

134

Put Away Your Sword

It was dark in the garden of Gethsemane. Jesus went there to pray. Peter, James, and John were with him.

Suddenly Jesus and his disciples heard people walking. They heard angry voices coming closer. A crowd of men rushed into the garden. They carried swords and clubs. Jesus' friends were surprised and afraid.

Judas, one of Jesus' disciples, was part of the mob. He walked up to Jesus and hugged him. This was a sign to the others that Jesus was the man they wanted.

Some men grabbed Jesus and held his arms. One of the disciples had a sword. He pulled it out and struck at one of the men who held Jesus. He cut off the man's ear.

But Jesus said to his disciple, "Put your sword back where it belongs. Those who use the sword will be destroyed by it."

The mob then took Jesus off into the darkness.

Based on Matthew 26:36–37; 47–52

134 Scripture

Enriching the Lesson

Supply the students with news magazines to find examples of violence. Explore with the students the underlying causes for the violence reported in the news stories, such as, poverty, racism, politics, selfishness. Explain that violence hurts others and does not solve problems and that Jesus wants us to live peacefully. As each picture is displayed and explained, pray this short prayer with the students: *Teach us respect for one another, Lord.*

Teaching Tips

The students have a right to become aware of global issues and their moral implications. They need models of nonviolence, of gentle strength. Try to be aware of and respond with a sensitivity to any students who may have been subject to cruelty or hurt. The child who has been rejected by classmates or who feels like an outsider also needs you to model Christ's compassionate protection of them.

Activity

Think about the meaning of Jesus' words in the Scripture story you just read. On the lines below, write why you think Jesus told his disciple to put his sword away.

_____

_____

_____

What might you have done if you had been in Jesus' place?

_____

_____

Jesus, Our Model of Nonviolence

The disciples had seen many other examples of Jesus' nonviolence. Later, after Jesus died and had risen from the dead, they understood even more.

The Bible tells us of a time when a crowd of people attacked a woman. They were going to kill her by throwing stones at her. Jesus stopped them.

Even throughout his suffering and death, Jesus remained nonviolent. He never fought back. He never called for his followers to come and fight for him.

Jesus' message of nonviolence is the same message we hear today. Jesus calls us to settle our differences peacefully, to avoid fighting and other forms of violence, and to treat all people with gentleness and kindness.

Scripture 135

★ ★★★ ★
Enriching the Lesson ★

Distribute Bibles. Have the students locate and read the following Scripture references, which describe Jesus' teachings of nonviolence.

- John 8:1–11
- Matthew 5:38–42
- Matthew 26:51–52
- Luke 6:27–36

- What did the embrace of Judas mean? (*That Jesus was the one the angry men wanted*)
- What did the men do to Jesus? (*They grabbed him and held his arms.*)
- How did one of the disciples of Jesus respond? (*He cut one of the men from the crowd very badly with his sword.*)
- What did Jesus say? (*Put your sword back. Those who use the sword will be destroyed by it.*)
- What can we learn from this story? (*Answers will vary. Accept any reasonable answer such as we can learn to live peacefully, or we can learn not to use violence.*)

Help the students appreciate that Jesus hated violence. He taught that violent actions, such as using the sword, would cause more violence.

Completing an Activity

Invite the students to think about the meaning of Jesus' words in the story. Have them work independently to complete the activity on page 135. Afterward, ask the students to share what they wrote.

Learning that Jesus Is a Model of Nonviolence

Ask volunteers to read aloud "Jesus, Our Model of Nonviolence" on page 135. Help the students to see that Jesus taught about nonviolence by never acting in a violent way even when people treated him and others with violence. Not even his own crucifixion evoked a violent response from Jesus.

Step 3 / CONCLUSION

Learning How to Live Our Faith

Participating in a Discussion

Read to the class the following Scripture verse about Jesus: "A bruised reed he will not break" (Matthew 12:20). Explain the quotation, telling the students that reeds were hollow grass stems that grew in the land where Jesus lived. Invite the students to participate in a discussion of how this quotation reveals Jesus' love of nonviolence. Help them understand the message that Jesus was such a peaceful man that he would not damage or cause harm to any part of God's creation. Invite students to cite examples of how they can be peaceful individuals, respecting the environment, themselves, their family members, other people, and animals.

DAY 3
MORALITY

Objective

This lesson helps students consider ways of living out the fifth commandment.

Step 1/INTRODUCTION

Learning About Our Lives

Reading and Discussing a Story

Ask volunteers to read aloud "Rahjid's Dilemma" on page 136. Explain that when people move to the United States from other countries it can be very scary. They are in an unfamiliar land where they do not know the language and cannot communicate their needs to others. The food is strange and often makes them ill. Also, many have left loved ones behind that they miss dearly.

Discuss the story using the following questions.

- Why were Rahjid and his younger brother teased and made fun of? (*Because of the way they spoke; their clothes were different*)

- Why didn't Rahjid react to the violent words and actions? (*His parents had taught him that violence was never the way to solve a problem.*)

- How did Rahjid feel when he saw the boys bullying his younger brother? (*He was furious!*)

Discuss with the students the possible story endings.

Writing a Story Ending

Distribute writing paper and ask the students to write an ending to the story that shows Rahjid following the fifth commandment. Afterward, invite the students to share their story endings, explaining how Rahjid followed the fifth commandment.

Rahjid's Dilemma

Rahjid came to the United States from India when he was eleven years old. At his new school, the principal put him in the third grade because she knew it would be difficult for him to keep up with his own class. There were so many new things to learn, especially English! Because he was older and bigger than his classmates, Rahjid found it hard to make friends. His younger brother was having problems being accepted by his classmates, too.

Children in school made fun of the way Rahjid and his brother dressed and the way they spoke. Children in their neighborhood called them bad names. But Rahjid's parents had taught the boys never to use violence to solve a problem. So, even when Rahjid felt angry and hurt, he never reacted with violent words or actions.

On the playground one day, two boys began teasing and shoving Rahjid's younger brother. They were going to take his new jacket from him. By the time Rahjid rushed to his brother's side, the boys had already pushed the young boy down. Rahjid's brother was frightened and crying. Rahjid was furious! Rahjid was bigger and stronger than the boys who were bullying his brother. He could easily shove them around and hurt them. He thought for a moment about what to do.

Discuss

What do you think Rahjid did?
Why do you think Rahjid made this decision?

Teaching Tips

Many schools today teach conflict resolution skills. Some schools also have peer mediation programs. If your school has instituted either of these programs, ask the students to explain how learning conflict resolution skills or going through peer mediation helps them to live out the fifth commandment.

Called to Respect All Life

The fifth commandment *You shall not kill* means much more than not taking someone's life. It means showing respect for human life. When we care about our health, we are keeping the fifth commandment. When we avoid hitting or pushing others, we are also keeping the fifth commandment.

When we stop being respectful of people and other living things, we move toward violent words and actions. Violent words and actions are hurtful and disrespectful of others.

We are called to keep the fifth commandment as Jesus did. Jesus always respected people because he knew that all people are made in God's image.

Activity

Some violent actions are listed below. For each violent action, write an opposite, peaceful action.

Making fun of others _____

Lying about someone _____

Using hurtful words _____

Pushing or shoving others _____

Starting fights _____

Trying to injure someone _____

Taking someone's life _____

Morality 137

★ ★★★ ★
Enriching the Lesson

Distribute drawing paper. Instruct the students to make a continuum similar to the continuum in Step 3 of this lesson. Explain to them that instead of writing examples of violence, they are to graph their continuum with nonviolent and peaceful actions, such as helping to resolve conflicts in a peaceful manner. Afterward, encourage the students to share their graphed continuums with the class.

Step 2 / DEVELOPMENT

Learning About Our Faith

Reading About the Fifth Commandment

Ask volunteers to read aloud "Called to Respect All Life" on page 137. Discuss with the students the meaning of the fifth commandment. Ask them to repeat together the fifth commandment and then to list the ways of keeping this commandment.

Step 3 / CONCLUSION

Learning How to Live Our Faith

Writing About Coping with Violence

Direct the students' attention to the activity at the bottom of page 137. Read the directions aloud to the class and instruct them to work independently to complete the activity. Afterward, encourage the students to share their ideas.

Making a Continuum from Disrespect to Violence

Ask the students to make a continuum of violence on a horizontal line. Have them list the following behaviors as a continuum, from the least violent to the most violent: making fun of others, using hurtful words, calling people names, lying about someone, being a bully, pushing/shoving others, hitting, starting fights, injuring someone, taking someone's life. Then ask the students if there are any violent actions that they would add to the continuum. List their ideas on the chalkboard.

137

DAY 4
SCRIPTURE/MORALITY

Objective

This lesson helps the students recognize violence in our world and ways to cope with it.

Step 1 / INTRODUCTION

Learning About Our Lives

Completing an Activity

Read and explain the directions for rating TV shows in the activity at the top of the page. Recall the definition of *violence* as *rough or harmful actions or words*. Point out the definition of *abuse* in the Vocabulary box and ask a volunteer to read the definition aloud. Ask the students to complete the activity. List the students' favorite TV shows on the chalkboard and keep a tally of which shows are most popular.

Then allow the students to rate the shows for violence. Encourage the students to make conclusions about their selections. Do the students prefer violent or nonviolent shows? Do they prefer action shows or comedies? Talk with the students about how violence on TV can affect us. Help them recognize that seeing so much violence on TV can make us think it is all right to hurt others.

Step 2 / DEVELOPMENT

Learning About Our Faith

Reading a Scripture Story

Ask volunteers to read aloud "Love Your Enemies" on page 138. Have students make a list of those actions that show how a follower of Jesus can respond in loving ways to the hurtful actions of an enemy.

Studying How Violence Happens

Direct the students' attention to the photographs on page 139. Ask volunteers to read "Violence in Our World." Take time after each picture to discuss the type of violence being described and talk with the students about how these words or actions hurt others.

138

Activity

Various kinds of violence and abuse are shown on TV. What are your three favorite TV programs? List the shows' titles below. Then check the box next to each show title to rate how often you think violence and abuse are shown on that show.

TV Violence

	Never	Sometimes	A lot
Show Number **1** _____	☐	☐	☐
Show Number **2** _____	☐	☐	☐
Show Number **3** _____	☐	☐	☐

138   Scripture

Love Your Enemies

One day while Jesus was teaching a large group of people, he said something that was very surprising.

"I tell you this, love your enemies. Do good to those who dislike you. Use only words of blessing on those who curse you. Pray for those who treat you badly.

"If a person slaps you on one cheek, offer the person your other cheek also. And if a person steals your coat, give that person your shirt as well. Share everything you have with those who ask you. And if a person wrongfully takes what belongs to you, don't ask for it back.

"Do to other people what you would want other people to do to you."

Based on Luke 6:27–31

CURRICULUM CONNECTION

Music Teach the students "World Peace Prayer," found in THIS IS OUR FAITH *Hymnal,* page 120, or in THIS IS OUR FAITH *Teacher's Songbook,* Grade 4, page 8.

Focus on

Peace According to the *Catechism of the Catholic Church,* "Respect for and development of human life require *peace.* Peace is not merely the absence of war, and it is not limited to maintaining a balance of powers between adversaries. Peace cannot be attained on earth without safeguarding the goods of persons, free communication among men, respect for the dignity of persons and peoples, and the assiduous practice of fraternity" (#2304).

Violence in Our World

Even in our everyday lives, violence and **abuse** occur all around us. Rough and dangerous actions can hurt us physically. Hateful and unkind words can hurt us emotionally.

People are violent when they
※ use words like "shut up!" or "I hate you!"
※ call other people names or hurt the feelings of others.
※ ignore someone or keep someone out of the group.

※ say that a person is not as good as he or she is only because the person may be different from him or her.
※ tell lies about others.
※ threaten and bully others.
※ try to cause physical harm to others or to the property of others.

Activity

Name the violent actions that you think most fourth graders struggle with.

1. _____

2. _____

Now name one way you can avoid violence in your life.

_____

_____

Vocabulary

abuse: violence toward someone or something

Morality   139

Ask the class to repeat aloud the term *abuse* and its definition. Ask the students to give some examples of abuse, as in the seven statements in their books on page 139.

Step 3 / CONCLUSION

Learning How to Live Our Faith

Considering How to Work for Nonviolence

Refer once again to the photographs on page 139. Discuss with the students possibilities for working for nonviolence in each of the examples of violence. Remind the students that sometimes they can teach others to live nonviolently by acting as an example to others. Other times they may need to speak out against violence.

Reviewing the Fifth Commandment

Talk with the students about ways to obey the fifth commandment. To help them be specific, encourage them to focus on one topic at a time, such as health, family members, friends, other people, pets, or the environment we live in.

Completing an Activity

Ask the students to read the directions to the activity at the bottom of page 139. Have them complete the activity independently. Invite volunteers to share their responses with the class.

Enriching the Lesson

Distribute Bibles and have the students find Matthew 5:9: "Blessed are the peacemakers, for they will be called children of God." Tell the class that the first word of the Beatitudes is translated as *Blessed* or *Happy*. Ask the students if they remember this verse from Chapter 7, "The Beatitudes of Peace." Ask them to define the term *peacemakers* in their own words.

139

DAY 5

PRAYER/REVIEW

Objective

This lesson helps the students pray the Way of the Cross.

Recalling the Way of the Cross

Help the students recall learning the Way of the Cross last year as a third grader. Remind them that the Way of the Cross is a prayer recalling the passion of Jesus, his suffering, death, and resurrection.

Reading About Praying the Way of the Cross

Ask for volunteers to read silently the explanatory paragraph and the titles of the fifteen Stations of the Cross. Then discuss and decide with the class how each station will be prayed.

Praying the Way of the Cross

Gather the students for prayer. If possible, pray the Way of the Cross in the church, following each Station of the Cross. Otherwise, display a Bible, a cross, and a candle. Begin with a brief opening prayer and then pray the Way of the Cross as decided by you and the class. Invite the students to respond appropriately.

Invoking God's Help

Continue by praying: *Loving God, thank you for creating all living things. Help us always to respect life. Teach us to be gentle. Help us to learn from Jesus' example.* Invite the students to pray for anyone they know who has been a victim of violence. Ask the students to share a sign of peace with one another.

Singing Together

Conclude by singing together the "World Peace Prayer" on page 120 of the THIS IS OUR FAITH *Hymnal.*

140

Praying the Way of the Cross

The Way (or Stations) of the Cross is a traditional devotion most often prayed during the season of Lent. It recalls the suffering, death, and resurrection of Jesus. There are many different ways we can pray the Way of the Cross. We can pray this devotion alone or with others. Decide with your teacher and classmates how your class can pray the Way of the Cross.

1. Jesus is condemned to death.
2. Jesus accepts the cross.
3. Jesus falls the first time.
4. Jesus meets his mother.
5. Simon helps Jesus carry the cross.
6. Veronica wipes the face of Jesus.
7. Jesus falls the second time.
8. Jesus meets the women of Jerusalem.
9. Jesus falls the third time.
10. Jesus is stripped of his clothes.
11. Jesus is nailed to the cross.
12. Jesus dies on the cross.
13. Jesus is taken down from the cross.
14. Jesus is buried in the tomb.
15. Jesus rises from the dead.

140 Prayer

★ Enriching the Lesson ★

Make a collage of people respecting life. Display a large sheet of posterboard at the front of the classroom. Using magazines and newspapers, have the students find pictures of people who are showing respect for the lives of others. Instruct them to cut these out and glue them to the posterboard. Ask for suggestions for a slogan to write at the top of the collage. Display the collage in a prominent place in the school or classroom.

Cultural Awareness

Remind the students of other people they have already learned about who also worked for justice. Those people would include Archbishop Romero (Chapter 7), Saint Frances of Rome and Mother Teresa (Chapter 6), of Calcutta. These individuals belonged to different ethnic and cultural groups and lived in different geographical areas, yet they all shared something in common. Encourage the students to discover that these people all shared a deep belief in the teachings of Jesus.

Chapter Review

Check **Yes** if the fifth commandment is being followed. Check **No** if it is not.

Yes No

1. ☐ ☑ Mr. Harris speeds through a red light to get to work on time.

2. ☑ ☐ Lee Ann keeps her body healthy. She eats foods that are good for her.

3. ☐ ☑ Henry hits someone whom he doesn't like.

4. ☐ ☑ A country starts a war to take over another country.

5. ☑ ☐ Amy is kind to someone who has no friends.

6. ☐ ☑ Doug and Tom take drugs that can hurt them.

7. ☐ ☑ Keneisha and her friends make fun of Margarita because she speaks with an accent.

On the lines provided, write your answers to the first two questions.

1. What is *violence*?

   rough or harmful words or actions

   _____

2. What does the fifth commandment teach us?

   It teaches us to respect and care for all human beings.

   It teaches us that all life is sacred.

   _____

   _____

3. Discuss how we can obey the fifth commandment.

Jesus says, "Learn from me for I am gentle."
Based on Matthew 11:29

Reviewing the Fifth Commandment

Explain the directions to the activity. Ask the students to explain their answers after they have completed the activity.

Reviewing the Chapter

Invite the students to answer the two questions on the lines provided. Encourage and support every student to participate in the discussion of the third item.

Reading the Scripture Verse

Read aloud the verse from Matthew's Gospel. Ask the students to give you examples of the gentleness of Jesus.

🍎 Teaching Tips

Name for the students some organizations and groups that work to protect the life of people and other living things; for example, the animal rights groups, world peace advocates, agencies that care for the handicapped or elderly, the American Cancer Society. Share some ways for the students to learn more about these groups: by listening to a guest speaker; researching and writing a brief report about such a group; writing for information and literature; or by making a bulletin board display.

Being Faithful in Marriage

Objectives

To help the students

■ Reflect on their experience of friendship.

■ Appreciate the sixth and ninth commandments as a help to married couples.

■ Understand the promises of marriage.

■ Learn that married couples are called to a love that reaches out to others.

■ Pray for faithfulness and review the chapter.

Chapter Outline

	Step 1 **Learning About Our Lives**	Step 2 **Learning About Our Faith**	Step 3 **Learning How to Live Our Faith**
Day 1	■ Review the Ten Commandments. ■ Introduce the chapter. ■ Study a photograph. ■ Complete an activity. *ABOUT 12 MINUTES*	■ Read about and discuss friendship. ■ Present the vocabulary. *ABOUT 10 MINUTES*	■ Complete an activity. *ABOUT 8 MINUTES*
Day 2	■ Complete an activity. ■ Study the photograph. *ABOUT 10 MINUTES*	■ Understand the commandments. ■ Present the vocabulary. ■ Review the doctrine. *ABOUT 10 MINUTES*	■ Complete an activity. ■ Name promises. *ABOUT 10 MINUTES*
Day 3	■ Reflect on promises. *ABOUT 7 MINUTES*	■ Read about and discuss marriage. ■ Talk about the photograph. *ABOUT 10 MINUTES*	■ Unscramble words. ■ Complete an activity. ■ Write about a married couple. ■ Pray a litany. *ABOUT 13 MINUTES*
Day 4	■ Talk about family times. ■ Complete an activity. ■ Read about and discuss reaching out to others. *ABOUT 12 MINUTES*	■ Read and discuss a story. *ABOUT 12 MINUTES*	■ Participate in a discussion. *ABOUT 6 MINUTES*
Day 5	**Prayer** Read about faithfulness; write petitions for faithfulness; and pray together. **Review** Complete an activity; solve a puzzle; answer the review questions; and discuss the Scripture verse.		

Correlation
to the
**Catechism of
the Catholic Church**

Paragraphs
**1604, 1621, 1646,
2331–2400, 2332, 2336,
2347, 2360, 2364, 2365,
2380, 2533**

Plan Ahead

	Preparing Your Class	**Materials Needed**
Day 1	Read through the lesson plan.	■ pencils or pens ■ markers or crayons ■ Ten Commandments poster
Day 2	Read through the lesson plan.	■ pencils or pens
Day 3	Read through the lesson plan.	■ pencils or pens ■ writing paper
Day 4	Read the lesson plan. If you plan to invite guest speakers, make all the necessary arrangements.	■ pencils or pens
Day 5	Read through the lesson plan.	■ pencils or pens ■ prayer cloth ■ candle ■ Bible

Additional Resources

As you plan this chapter, consider using the following materials from The Resourceful Teacher Package.

■ *Classroom Activity Sheets 12* and *12a*

■ *Family Activity Sheets 12* and *12a*

■ *Chapter 12 Test*

■ *Prayers for Every Day*

■ *Projects: Grade 4*

You may also wish to refer to the following Big Book.

■ *We Celebrate the Sacraments,* page 22

In preparing the students for the Sunday readings, you may wish to use Silver Burdett Ginn's *Getting Ready for Sunday* student and teacher materials.

Chapter Organizer 141b

BOOKS FOR THE JOURNEY

Hey World, Here I Am! "Not Enough Emilys," pp. 13–16. Jean Little. Harper & Row, 1986. A poem about a friendship and how important a friend is.

Grandfather Tang's Story. Ann Tompert. Crown Publishers, 1990. A friendship, almost destroyed by playful challenging, is saved when the friends finally put it before their pride.

MORE BOOKS FOR THE JOURNEY

The Blessing Cup. "In Honor of Marriage," pp. 36–37. Rock Travniker. St. Anthony Messenger Press, 1979. A simple rite for celebrating the sacrament of marriage.

The Big Wave. Pearl S. Buck. HarperCollins, 1986. The story of how a family became a strong shelter for Jiya after a tidal wave destroyed his home and family.

REDUCED CLASSROOM ACTIVITIES

NAME _____

BEING FAITHFUL IN MARRIAGE

You're a contestant on the TV game show *Two Truths and a Lie*. You've chosen the category "Friendship and Marriage" because you know a lot about being a faithful friend. Three guests appear for each question and tell something about faithfulness in friendship or marriage. But only two of the guests will be telling the truth.

Read the three statements for Round 1 and circle the two truths. Continue with Round 2. Each truth is worth 1,000 points. No points are given for the lie. You'll find Rounds 3, 4, 5, and 6 on the next page. When you're finished, compare answers with a partner and decide how many points you've earned in each round. In case of disagreement, your teacher will be the final judge. Total your points at the bottom of page 12a. The highest score possible is 12,000 points for six rounds of play.

ROUND 1
- (Faithful friends stand up for each other.)
- (Faithful friends are honest with each other.)
- Faithful friends embarrass each other.

ROUND 2
- Faithful married friends give the special love promised in marriage to someone other than their husbands or wives.
- (Faithful married friends respect each other's differences.)
- (Faithful married friends listen to each other.)

To the Teacher: This two-page activity will reinforce the meanings of the sixth and ninth commandments.

Chapter 12 Being Faithful in Marriage   THIS IS OUR FAITH 4   **12**

NAME _____

ROUND 3
- (Faithful friends are patient with each other.)
- Faithful friends break promises.
- (Faithful friends try to understand each other's feelings.)

ROUND 4
- (Faithful married friends enjoy spending time together.)
- (Faithful married friends encourage each other to keep trying.)
- Faithful married friends neglect their husbands or wives.

ROUND 5
- (Faithful friends are comfortable being with each other.)
- (Faithful friends stay with each other in hard times.)
- Faithful friends constantly point out each other's faults.

ROUND 6
- (Faithful married friends trust each other.)
- Faithful married friends care more for themselves than for the other person.
- (Faithful married friends help each other.)

My score is: _____

12a THIS IS OUR FAITH 4   *Chapter 12 Being Faithful in Marriage*

Background for the Teacher ~~~~~~

LOVE AND FIDELITY

God created marriage and family life as sacred. When men and women marry, they imitate the love of Christ for his Church. In Ephesians 5:25–33, Paul compares spousal love to the love of God for Israel, and to the love which Christ has for the Church. This passage can enlighten our appreciation of the import of the sixth and ninth commandments.

The *Catechism of the Catholic Church* discusses fidelity in these terms: "Fidelity expresses constancy in keeping one's given word. God is faithful. The Sacrament of Matrimony enables man and woman to enter into Christ's fidelity for his Church. Through conjugal chastity, they bear witness to this mystery before the world" (#2365).

THE SIXTH AND NINTH COMMANDMENTS

In this chapter, the sixth and ninth commandments are presented as safeguards so that couples may honor their matrimonial vows. God commands that the personal faithfulness of couples should reflect his permanent faithfulness to us.

When married couples have children, they reflect the life of the Trinity. God protects families so that the sacred covenant made between spouses—to meet both their basic need for loving partnership and to cooperate with God's creative activity—can be fulfilled.

Children follow the sixth and ninth commandments by respecting the dignity of their bodies and the bodies of others and liking themselves as boys or girls. Pope John Paul II upholds the human right to dignity so that all may be allowed to reach their God-given potential.

TODAY'S PRESSURES

After God created man and woman, they suffered the fall from grace that left their union weakened. Married couples are prey to temptation. In the contemporary world, where economic and emotional stress upon family is severe, marriages are as likely to be torn down as to be cherished and protected. The challenge in this lesson is to present the Christian ideal, and at the same time, to be compassionate toward those children whose family life does not represent the ideal. Children have a right to know that God created man and woman to be faithful, loving partners and that God wants children to receive the love of their parents. Children should be able to feel love and respect from both parents.

Objective

This lesson helps the students reflect on their experience of friendship.

Step 1 / INTRODUCTION

Learning About Our Lives

Reviewing the Ten Commandments

Have the students recite the commandments they have memorized. Be sure to mark the students' progress on the Ten Commandments poster.

Introducing the Chapter

Direct attention to the focus questions on page 142. Invite the students to respond. As they answer, list their responses on the chalkboard. Help the students appreciate that there are many ways of showing friendship.

Studying the Photograph

Ask the students how the individuals in the photograph are showing friendship for one another. Then invite them to name some of the things they enjoy doing with their friends.

Completing an Activity

Read the directions to the activity on page 142 and then read through the list slowly, giving the students a moment to consider each item. Allow the students to work independently as they add one more statement to complete the list. When they have finished, encourage them to read their statements aloud. Then poll the group to determine what they think are the most and least important items.

Step 2 / DEVELOPMENT

Learning About Our Faith

Reading About and Discussing Friendship

Ask a volunteer to read aloud "A Faithful Friend" on page 143. Ask the students to describe a strong shelter. Discuss the following questions.

---

12 Being Faithful in Marriage

 What makes someone a good friend? What do friends do for one another?

142   Morality

Activity

Think of your friends. Then read each of the following statements that show how people are friends with others. Add one more statement you think is also important.

- We have fun together.
- We share secrets.
- We are important to each other.
- We help each other.
- We trust each other.
- We are honest with each other.
- We stand up for each other.

- We _____.

★ Enriching the Lesson ★

The qualities of a friend are described in Scripture. Distribute Bibles and have the students find the scriptural references to these important qualities. Ask the students to share what they find with the rest of the class in the following.

- Proverbs 17:17
- Ecclessiastes 4:9f
- Job 6:14
- Sirach 6:5–6
- Sirach 9:10

A Faithful Friend

The Bible tells us in the Book of Genesis that people are not meant to be lonely. We read that God created people so that no one would be alone.

The Bible also tells us how important friends are. We read,

"A faithful friend is a strong shelter; whoever finds one finds a treasure."

"A faithful friend is more valuable than anything; no money can equal what a friend is worth" (based on Sirach 6:14–15).

Activity

Think about one of your best friends. Design a friendship T-shirt for him or her. Use words and symbols to show on it what friendship means to you. Use the extra space on the right for any extra symbols or words.

Vocabulary

faithful: able to be trusted and depended upon

■ How is a faithful friend like a treasure? (*A true friend is precious, has worth greater than gold or silver or expensive jewels.*)

Encourage the students to think of specific friends or situations. Continue with the following questions.

■ When has a friend sheltered or protected you?

■ What do you treasure about your friends?

■ How do you treat someone you treasure?

Explain to the students that in this chapter they will learn that many of the qualities that make friendship strong and good are also important in marriage.

Presenting the Vocabulary

Assist the students in learning the definition of *faithful* by repeating it together aloud several times.

Step 3 / CONCLUSION

Learning How to Live Our Faith

Completing an Activity

Direct attention to the drawing activity on page 143. Explain that a symbol is a drawing that stands for something else. Ask the students to think about what kinds of symbols they could draw that represent friendship, or that show someone doing something that represents friendship, or that could represent the faithfulness of a friend. Give out felt-tip markers or crayons. After the students have completed their T-shirt designs, encourage them to share, explaining either the action shown, or why a faithful friend is like the symbol shown. Help the students appreciate that God wants us to have friends and to be faithful friends to others.

Teaching Tips

Share the following quotes with the class. Discuss the quotations with the students and ask what they think each person meant by what he said.

"Friendship is like money, easier made than kept." *Samuel Butler*

"A friend is one who walks in when others walk out." *Walter Winchell*

143

DAY 2
DOCTRINE

Objective

This lesson helps the students appreciate the sixth and ninth commandments as a help to married couples.

Step 1 / INTRODUCTION

Learning About Our Lives

Completing an Activity

Direct the students' attention to the activity at the top of page 144. Read the directions aloud and have the students work independently to complete the sentences. Afterward, invite the students to share what they wrote about faithfulness.

Studying the Photographs

Call attention to the photographs on page 144. Ask the students to explain how the people in the pictures are showing their faithfulness for each other.

Step 2 / DEVELOPMENT

Learning About Our Faith

Understanding the Commandments

Ask volunteers to read aloud "Called to Faithfulness and Respect" on pages 144 and 145. Explain that Catholics receive the sacrament of Matrimony when they marry. When Catholics receive any sacrament, they receive a special grace. When a man and a woman marry, they are symbols of Christ's love for us. They promise to share their lives as Jesus shares his life with us. Explain the meaning of the sixth commandment as a husband and wife keeping their special love only for each other. The ninth commandment teaches that they not desire to be married to anyone else. God gave married couples these commandments to help their love for each other grow strong.

Be sensitive to any children from separated or divorced families. Be sure this discussion does not make these children feel as if their parents have broken the sixth and ninth commandments.

144

Activity

Answer the following question about faithfulness, and then complete the sentences.

1. What does faithfulness mean to you?

   _____

   _____

2. A parent shows faithfulness to a child by

   _____

3. A teacher shows faithfulness to a student by

   _____

4. A friend shows faithfulness to a friend by

   _____

5. A child shows faithfulness to a parent by

   _____

Called to Faithfulness and Respect

The sacrament of Matrimony celebrates the love between a man and a woman. Love in marriage is a sharing between two people. As married people, they promise to love each other and to share their lives together.

God gives us two commandments to teach us about the love between a husband and a wife. They are the sixth and ninth commandments.

144 Doctrine

★ ★★★ ★ Enriching the Lesson ★

Show the students a wedding album, pointing out the various traditions; for example, family pictures, the exchange of vows, the reception line, the wedding toast. Then invite the students to talk about weddings that they have attended or participated in. Have them share what the weddings were like and how the people celebrated. If any of the students have had special roles in a wedding, ask them to tell the class what they were called upon to do.

The sixth commandment is *You shall not commit **adultery**.*
The ninth commandment is *You shall not **covet** your neighbor's wife.*

Through the sixth and ninth commandments we learn that two married people are to be faithful to each other. They are to love and respect each other.

These two commandments call all of us to respect the gift of our sexuality. Our bodies and our sexuality are gifts from God that help us express our love for others and to feel their love for us.

Activity

We can show respect for each other and for ourselves in many ways. Name some of the ways you show respect for others and yourself every day.

_____
_____
_____
_____
_____
_____
_____
_____
_____
_____
_____

Vocabulary

adultery: being unfaithful to one's husband or wife by giving to someone else the special love promised in marriage

covet: to want something someone else has

We Believe

The sixth and ninth commandments call married people to love each other and live together faithfully.

Doctrine   145

Enriching the Lesson

Help the students understand that the sacrament of Matrimony calls couples to love each other with the perfect, unconditional love that Jesus Christ has for the Church. Distribute Bibles. Ask the students to find Ephesians 5:25–32. Ask the students to explain what Saint Paul meant by these words.

Focus on

The Commandments   The listing of the ninth and tenth commandments in Deuteronomy 5 distinguishes between a man's wife and his other property. This allows for a school of thought which suggests that these last two commandments deal with immoral attitude, whereas the first eight commandments specify immoral action. The sixth commandment forbids the immoral action of adultery. The ninth commandment forbids the immoral attitude of desiring another's spouse.

Discuss how we can show respect for our bodies and the bodies of others. The discussion can include good health habits, being modest, avoiding movies and TV shows that emphasize sex, not making jokes about our body parts, and not allowing others to touch the private parts of our bodies.

Presenting the Vocabulary

Present the new vocabulary words to the students, and ask them to repeat the words and definitions.

Reviewing the Doctrine

Point out the We Believe statement. Ask the students to repeat this important statement aloud. Answer any questions the students may have.

Step 3 / CONCLUSION

Learning How to Live Our Faith

Completing an Activity

Instruct the students to complete the activity at the bottom of page 145. Have them work independently. Afterward, review each of the items listed and discuss the students' answers. Ask the students if they can think of any additional ways that they can show respect for their bodies. Write their responses on the chalkboard.

Naming Promises

Have the students brainstorm promises that married couples make to one another. Help the students appreciate that married couples promise to be faithful, to love, to respect, and to help each other. They promise to work together and enjoy good times, too.

145

DAY 3

MORALITY

Objective

This lesson helps the students understand the promises of marriage.

Step 1 / INTRODUCTION

Learning About Our Lives

Reflecting on Promises

Direct the students to write a list of some of the promises fourth graders might make to classmates and friends; to parents; and to God. Give the students time to write their lists of promises as they work independently. Afterward, invite the students to share their responses.

Explain that in marriage, the couple makes special promises to each other. The couple commits to these promises forever.

Step 2 / DEVELOPMENT

Learning About Our Faith

Reading About and Discussing Marriage

Select one or more students to read aloud "A Special Love" on pages 146 and 147. Explain that Catholics are often married at Mass. Discuss the text, using the following questions.

- Why do a man and a woman decide to marry? (*They decide to marry because they are in love and want to spend their lives together.*)

- What promises do the couples make to one another? (*To be faithful to each other for the rest of their lives, to love one another*)

- What is the ring a symbol of? (*Their love and promises of faithfulness*)

- What does the priest ask God to do? (*Help them to be faithful friends and examples of Christ's love for the Church*)

Talking About the Photograph

Point out the photograph on page 147 of the couple celebrating their fiftieth wedding anniversary. Explain that often when two people marry, they are young adults. People change as they grow older. Being faithful to the marriage promises is not always easy. People who have

146

A Special Love

Sometimes a man and a woman are in love and want to spend their lives together.

They decide to marry and invite their families and friends to their wedding.

At the wedding, they promise to be faithful to one another for the rest of their lives. They promise to love one another.

As they hold hands, they each say, "I promise to be true to you in good times and in bad, in sickness and in health. I will love you and honor you all the days of my life" (Consent, *Rite of Marriage*). The man and woman are now married. They are husband and wife.

Cultural Awareness

Explain to the class that every culture has unique ways of celebrating weddings. Point out that at a Jewish wedding the couple stands under a special covering called a canopy. The canopy is a sign of the home they will share together. Other traditions you might share are the practice of throwing rice or bird seed at the bride and groom as a sign that they will be blessed with children and good luck. Mention the custom of the bride wearing a veil, which is a sign of the bride's purity.

Teaching Tips

Fourth graders know about divorce from their own experience, or that of their schoolmates. Children of divorced parents sometimes experience guilt and low self-esteem. Help these children develop healthy ways to cope. They can be responsible and can often show compassion toward those who suffer. God's grace also abounds in divorced families. The Church, the Body of Christ, can help divorced families begin to rebuild their lives.

They each place a ring on the other's finger and say, "Take this ring as a sign of my love and fidelity" (Blessing of Rings, *Rite of Marriage*).

The priest blesses them. The priest prays that they will always live together in love. He asks God to help them be faithful friends and marriage partners.

"Father," the priest prays, "keep them always true to your commandments. Keep them faithful in marriage and let them be living examples of Christian life" (Nuptial Blessing, *Rite of Marriage*).

Activity

Complete the sentences below with examples of how the married couples can show love, faithfulness, and respect.

1. José and Elena have been married for twelve years. José has just lost his job and doesn't know how he will support his family.

   Elena could ____

   ____

   ____.

2. Sean and Sarah are newlyweds. Sean is often out of town on business. Sarah goes to her job each day and takes care of her elderly mother. Sean could ______________________________

   ____

   ____.

Enriching the Lesson

Ask the students to share any experiences they have had of wedding anniversary celebrations. Talk with the students about the importance of celebrating anniversaries. Help the students understand that a couple needs the loving support of friends and family members to help them stay faithful in marriage through the difficult times as well as the happy times.

been married for many years would probably say that at first it was easy to keep their promises. But when life is hard, that can be difficult. We celebrate the faithfulness of people who have weathered hard times and have shared special joys.

Step 3 / Conclusion

Learning How to Live Our Faith

Unscrambling Words

Write **v o l e** and **n s t h u f l i a f e s** on the chalkboard. Ask the class to look at the scrambled words. Tell the students they name what a man and a woman promise to each other when they marry. Have the class unscramble the words. Then write the words on the chalkboard (*Love, faithfulness*)

Completing an Activity

Read aloud the directions for the activity on page 147. After the students have completed the sentences, have them share their ideas with the class.

Writing About a Married Couple

Have the students write the names of a loving, married couple. Then distribute writing paper and have the students write why they think this is a special marriage. Invite the students to read their responses to the class.

Praying a Litany

Using the names the students have written, pray a litany with the class. Have each student read their names, saying "For (*Name*) and (*Name*)." Encourage the class to respond, "May God bless their love and faithfulness."

DAY 4
MORALITY

Objective

This lesson helps the students learn that married couples are called to a love that reaches out to others.

Step 1 / INTRODUCTION

Learning About Our Lives

Talking About Family Times

Invite the students to talk about some of the activities they enjoy doing with their families. Ask them to relate family traditions that are especially meaningful to them. Help the students appreciate the many ways in which parents' love has been shared with them. Be sensitive to students not living in two-parent homes.

Completing an Activity

Invite the class to look at the photographs on page 148. Have the students write what the parents in the pictures above are sharing with family and friends.

Reading About and Discussing Reaching Out to Others

Have one of the students read aloud "Reaching Out to Others" on page 148. Stress that married people make a commitment to share their lives, not just with each other, but with their children and other people. Explain that Jesus gives married couples special grace to help them share their lives.

Step 2 / DEVELOPMENT

Learning About Our Faith +

Reading and Discussing a Story

Introduce the story "A Loving Marriage" on page 149. Then ask volunteers to take turns reading aloud. Ask the following questions.

- Why did Margaret have to leave England? (*England was at war.*)
- Who invited Margaret to stay in his palace? (*King Malcolm of Scotland*)
- What happened to Margaret and Malcolm? (*They loved each other and married.*)

148

Activity

Examine these photographs. Write one thing the husbands and wives are sharing with each other and with others.

▲ _____
_____

▲_____
_____

◄_____
_____

Reaching Out to Others

Married people are called to live out their promises of faithfulness. In doing so, they share many things together. God also asks married people to reach out to others. They are expected to share their belongings and their time with others. The more that married couples and all good friends care about each other, the more they tend to reach out to others.

Enriching the Lesson

Invite a married couple to visit your class and talk about how they share their lives with one another, their children, and the parish community. Ask them to bring their wedding album if possible. Before they arrive, you might work with the students to prepare a list of interview questions.

Focus on

Vocation to Love The *Catechism of the Catholic Church* states, "God who created man out of love also calls him to love—the fundamental and innate vocation of every human being. For man is created in the image and likeness of God who is himself love. Since God created him man and woman, their mutual love becomes an image of the absolute and unfailing love with which God loves man. It is good, very good, in the Creator's eyes" (#1604).

A Loving Marriage

Margaret was a beautiful princess. But her beauty was no protection in time of war. When the armies of William the Conqueror invaded England, Margaret and her brother tried to leave, but they became shipwrecked. They both survived and were taken to the palace of King Malcolm of Scotland.

The king immediately fell in love with the beautiful princess. Margaret soon came to love the king, and agreed to marry him.

In the years that followed, Malcolm and Margaret had a large family—six sons and two daughters—whom they loved very much. The king and queen loved each other, too. They traveled together. They often prayed together. They did many good things for the people of Scotland.

Malcolm and Margaret often left their palace to visit the poor and to care for the sick. During Advent and Lent, hundreds of needy people went to the palace for help. Malcolm and Margaret gave them food, money, and medicine.

The king and queen had been happily married for twenty-three years at their deaths, just a few days apart, in A.D. 1093.

Catholics honor Margaret as a saint and patroness of Scotland. November 16 is the feast day of Saint Margaret.

Discuss

What were two of the ways Margaret and Malcolm reached out to others?

Morality 149

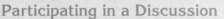

- How did Margaret and Malcolm spend their time together? (*They traveled; they helped the poor of Scotland.*)
- What did the king and queen do for the poor? (*They gave them money, clothing, and food; they took care of the sick.*)
- Why is Margaret a saint? (*Because of her generosity to the poor of Scotland*)
- What can we learn from this true story? (*Answers may vary. Accept any reasonable answers, such as the following: When married people love each other, they have much love to give others; when two people help others, there is much good they can do.*)

You might tell the students that Queen Margaret and King Malcolm had eight children—six boys and two girls.

Step 3 / CONCLUSION

Learning How to Live Our Faith

Participating in a Discussion

Have the students reread the story before having them participate in the discussion activity with their books closed.

CURRICULUM CONNECTION

Social Studies Have the students locate England and Scotland on a map. With the help of the social studies teacher, have the class locate the city in England where Margaret lived before going to Scotland and where in Scotland King Malcolm's palace was located.

149

Objective

This lesson helps the students pray for faithfulness.

Reading About Faithfulness

Call attention to "Praying for Faithfulness" on page 150 and invite volunteers to read the text aloud. Ask the following questions to discuss the scriptural reading about love and faithfulness.

What are some of the attributes of love? (*Love is patient, kind, not jealous, not proud, not self-centered; polite; unselfish; not quick-tempered*)

Writing Petitions for Faithfulness

Then instruct the students to finish writing the prayers that petition God for faithfulness.

Praying Together

Create a prayerful environment and gather the class for prayer. Ask the students to bring their books with them to prayer. Begin with a brief opening prayer and continue with a student reading the verses from 1 Corinthians 13:4–8.

Ask the students to pray their prayers of petition silently to themselves. Conclude with a brief closing prayer, such as, *May God bless our love and faithfulness in all of our relationships. And May God bless us all in the name of the Father, the Son, and the Holy Spirit. Amen.*

150

Praying for Faithfulness

When a man and a woman celebrate the sacrament of Matrimony, their family and friends come to the wedding to pray with them. Together they listen to Scripture and pray for God's gift of faithfulness for themselves and for the newly married couple. They might listen to the Scripture reading below about love and faithfulness.

> Love is patient, love is kind. It is not jealous. Love is not proud or self-centered. It is not rude or selfish. Love is not quick-tempered, it does not dwell on injury. Love does not rejoice over wrongdoing, but rejoices with goodness. Love bears all things, believes all things, hopes all things, endures all things. Love never fails.
>
> *Based on 1 Corinthians 13:4–8*

Activity

Complete the prayer below, asking God to help you be a more loving and faithful person.

Faithfulness ♥ Faithfulness ♥ Faithfulness

Dear God,
Help me be a loving and faithful son/daughter by _____
_____.

Help me be a faithful friend by _____
_____.

Help me show my love and faithfulness to you by _____
_____.

I ask your help through Jesus, your Son. Amen.

Enriching the Lesson

Select key sentences from each chapter in this unit. Leave off the concluding words of each sentence, for example: In the gospel stories we read that Jesus . . . (Possible responses are *taught that people were more important than things; walked by the sea; enjoyed the gifts of creation.*) Post the incomplete statements on a bulletin board in the classroom. Ask the students to complete each statement on strips of colored paper and post them under the appropriate statements. Keep the bulletin board on display.

SONGS for Christ's Followers

The Book of Psalms in the Old Testament, also called the Hebrew Scriptures, contains prayers and songs from the time of King David and after (1000 B.C. to 400 B.C.). Priests and scribes put the psalms together to use in the Temple in Jerusalem after their time of exile.

There are different types of psalms, including the following: hymns of praise and thanksgiving, psalms of wisdom that chart ways to happiness, songs to honor the king, and prayers to petition God's help in time of sickness, war, and death.

In many of the psalms, the writers used journey or traveling images. Some of these poetic words are on page 7. You and your family may want to think about and pray these words on your faith journey. You may also want to read the entire psalm in the Bible.

The LORD is my shepherd; I shall not want
In verdant pastures he gives me repose;
Beside restful waters he leads me;
he refreshes my soul.
He guides me in right paths
for his name's sake.

Psalm 23:1-3

Excess Baggage

Product developers are constantly researching ways to make luggage lighter and easier to carry. Wrinkle-free clothing has been discovered and travel irons and alarm clocks have been sold for a long time. The business of travel is so popular and extensive that now even special instructors teach people how to pack.

In your role as guide for your family's journey of faith, you may need to teach the younger members how to pack. Use the story of the rich young man (Mark 10:17–22) to illustrate your points about possessions and priorities. In light of that story and the Beatitudes (Matthew 5:1–6), discuss what your family considers excess baggage.

3

CHRIST OUR LIGHT

Our journey of faith begins at Baptism. After a child has been baptized, someone in the family lights a small candle from the flame of the Easter candle and the celebrant prays the following prayer:

"Parents and godparents, this light is entrusted to you to be kept burning brightly. This child of yours has been enlightened by Christ. He (she) is to walk always as a child of light. May he (she) keep the flame of faith alive in his (her) heart. When the Lord comes, may he (she) go out to meet him with all the saints in the heavenly kingdom."

The Rite of Baptism

4

To help us continue to walk as children of light and to keep the flame of faith alive in our hearts, the Church reminds us during the liturgical year of Christ's light. This happens particularly during the service of light at the Easter Vigil.

The priest blesses the new fire, which is started outside.

Father,
we share in the light of your glory
through your son, the light of the world.
Make this new fire ✦ holy, and inflame us with new hope.
Purify our minds by this Easter celebration
and bring us one day to the feast of eternal light.

After the Easter candle is lit from the new fire, the priest then prays the following words:

May the light of Christ, rising in glory,
dispel the darkness of our hearts and minds.

Daily, you help to dispel the darkness by teaching and guiding as a parent and chasing away gloom and depression with a smile, a hug, or words of comfort and cheer.

5

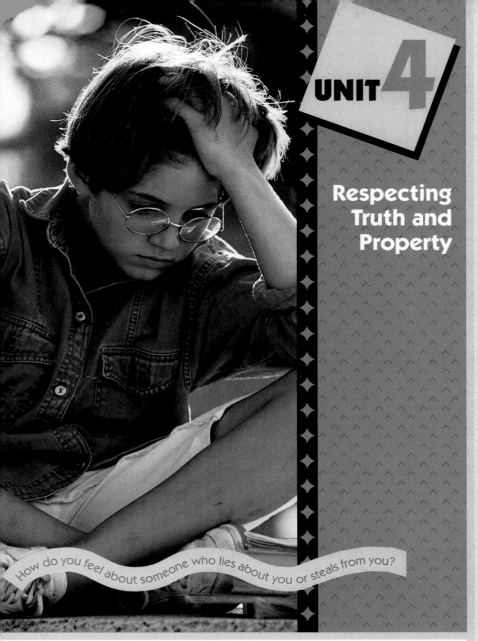

UNIT **4**

**Respecting
Truth and
Property**

How do you feel about someone who lies about you or steals from you?

To help the students obey the seventh, eighth, and tenth commandments and seek forgiveness of God through Jesus Christ when they sin.

Doctrinal Summaries

CHAPTER 13
God makes the world for all people. Everyone has the right to a share of the good things of life. We should not harm or steal anything that belongs to others.

CHAPTER 14
God calls us to respect the truth. When we lie, we hurt ourselves and others.

CHAPTER 15
God is merciful and forgiving. God keeps on loving us when we sin. God is always ready to forgive us when we show that we are sorry.

CHAPTER 16
Jesus came to bring God's mercy to everyone. He continues to bring God's forgiveness to those who show that they are sorry for their sins.

Note:
As you prepare this unit and the remaining units, you might wish to refer to the reference section, *Our Catholic Heritage*, beginning on page 327.

Additional resources for Unit 3 include: a Unit Test and a Family Letter as well as a video and selections from THIS IS OUR FAITH Music Program. You might also find it helpful to preview *Saints and Other Holy People* and *Prayer Celebrations* for possibilities to enhance the unit.

Introducing the UNIT

Ask the students to describe what is happening in the photograph on page 161. Give each student an opportunity to respond to the unit-focus question. Then read aloud the Unit 4 title. Help the class understand that in this unit, they will learn more about the commandments and how they are called to ask forgiveness when they sin.

Vocabulary

greed
envy
cheat
high priest
bear false witness
reconciliation
inheritance
Galilean
compassion

13 Respecting What Belongs to Others

Objectives

To help the students

- Understand the reality of greed and selfishness in the world and in our own lives.
- Learn the seventh and tenth commandments.
- Identify ways of keeping the seventh and tenth commandments.
- Recognize that Jesus calls us to fight against selfishness and to share with others.
- Pray with gratitude for God's gifts and review the chapter.

Chapter Outline

	Step 1 **Learning About Our Lives**	**Step 2** **Learning About Our Faith**	**Step 3** **Learning How to Live Our Faith**
Day 1	■ Introduce the chapter. ■ Read the story. ■ Discuss the story. *ABOUT 15 MINUTES*	■ Understand greed. ■ Learn the vocabulary. *ABOUT 10 MINUTES*	■ Discuss sharing. *ABOUT 5 MINUTES*
Day 2	■ Review Day 1. ■ Study a picture. *ABOUT 7 MINUTES*	■ Learn the commandments. ■ Understand the doctrine. ■ Learn the vocabulary. *ABOUT 15 MINUTES*	■ Complete an activity. ■ Review the lesson. *ABOUT 8 MINUTES*
Day 3	■ Study pictures. *ABOUT 5 MINUTES*	■ Reflect on our actions. *ABOUT 10 MINUTES*	■ Discuss difficulties. ■ Complete an activity. *ABOUT 15 MINUTES*
Day 4	■ Write about sharing. *ABOUT 7 MINUTES*	■ Read and discuss a Scripture story. ■ Reflect on Jesus' message. *ABOUT 15 MINUTES*	■ Identify reasons for sharing. ■ Pray together. *ABOUT 8 MINUTES*

Day 5 **Prayer** Make flowers of praise; prepare for praying with gratitude; pray with gratitude; and sing together.

Review Name ways to follow the seventh and tenth commandments; review the chapter; and read the Scripture verse.

Correlation to the

Catechism of the Catholic Church

Paragraphs
**2401–2463, 2402, 2407,
2408, 2462, 2463, 2534,
2536, 2538, 2557, 2637**

Plan Ahead

	Preparing Your Class	**Materials Needed**
Day 1	Read through the entire lesson plan.	■ pencils or pens ■ writing paper
Day 2	Read the lesson plan. If using the curriculum connection, review the song "You Are the Way."	■ pencils or pens ■ copies of THIS IS OUR FAITH *Hymnal*
Day 3	Read the lesson plan. Gather pictures that show people choosing whether or not to follow the seventh and tenth commandments.	■ pencils or pens ■ newspaper and magazine pictures
Day 4	Read the lesson plan. Think about how you want the students to dramatize the Scripture story. Make all the necessary preparations.	■ pencils or pens
Day 5	Read the lesson plan. Make a sample praise flower to show the students.	■ paper plate ■ construction paper ■ scissors, glue ■ crayons or markers ■ hymnals

Additional Resources

As you plan this chapter, consider using the following materials from The Resourceful Teacher Package.

■ *Classroom Activity Sheets 13* and *13a*

■ *Family Activity Sheets 13* and *13a*

■ *Chapter 13 Test*

■ *Prayers for Every Day*

■ *Projects: Grade 4*

You may also wish to refer to the following Big Book.

■ *We Celebrate God's Word*, page 3

In preparing the students for the Sunday readings, you may wish to use Silver Burdett Ginn's *Getting Ready for Sunday* student and teacher materials.

Books for the Journey

The Crane Wife. Sumiko Yagawa. William Morrow, 1987. A story of how greed and curiosity destroy a happy relationship.

The Pied Piper of Hamelin. Retold by Val Biro. Silver Burdett & Ginn, 1985. A new version of a traditional story.

More Books for the Journey

The Fables of Aesop. "The Goose that Laid the Golden Eggs," p. 15; "The Dog and the Bone," p. 66. Selected and edited by Ruth Spriggs. Rand McNally, 1975. Two fables about being greedy.

The Children's Illustrated Bible. "Lazarus and the Rich Man," p. 244. Retold by Selina Hastings. Dorling Kindersley, 1994. The story of the rich man and Lazarus with additional illustrations.

REDUCED CLASSROOM ACTIVITIES

NAME _____

RESPECTING WHAT BELONGS TO OTHERS

Think about the difference between what we need to live a good life and what we want but do not really need. Then make a chart by listing each item below under the appropriate heading.

expensive jeans

clean clothes for school

gold chains

warm jacket for winter

books for school

money to spend on video games

computer

enough money for lunch

pencils and paper for school

many pens with different colors of ink

Needs	Wants
pencils and paper for school	many pens with different colors of ink
clean clothes for school	expensive jeans
warm jacket for winter	gold chains
books for school	money to spend on video games
enough money for lunch	computer

To the Teacher: This activity will help students distinguish between needs and wants. Encourage students to suggest additional items for both lists.

Chapter 13 Respecting What Belongs to Others   THIS IS OUR FAITH 4   **13**

NAME _____

THE RICH MAN AND LAZARUS

Reread the story of the rich man and Lazarus in Luke's Gospel, Chapter 16, verses 19–23. Then imagine that the story took place this month in your town. Now rewrite the story, following these rules.

1. Keep the lesson that Jesus was teaching in this story the same.
2. Change the characters' names, genders, and ages.
3. Change the storyline so that the characters do not die; write a new ending.

Once there was _____
_____
_____
_____
_____
_____
_____
_____
_____
_____
_____
_____
_____
_____
_____
_____
_____
_____

To the Teacher: This activity will allow students the opportunity to reexamine the message of this Scripture story.

13a   THIS IS OUR FAITH 4   **Chapter 13** Respecting What Belongs to Others

THE SEVENTH AND TENTH COMMANDMENTS

Fourth graders have been exposed to attitudes of disrespect for what belongs to others. They know that stealing, damaging property, and wasting resources occur. Most fourth graders may recall a situation in which an object was stolen from a classmate's desk or locker. They can all identify with the feeling of wanting something they do not have.

They are growing up in a culture in which a person's worth is often determined by his or her possessions. They are constantly exposed to values of consumerism, which are marked by greed and envy.

The seventh and tenth commandments protect the basic rights of people to what they legitimately possess. These two commandments strike at greed and envy as well as at actions like stealing, damaging property, and being wasteful.

The seventh commandment appears to focus on particular actions, and the tenth commandment seems to deal with attitude. The tenth commandment as written in the Hebrew Scriptures is as follows: "You shall not covet your neighbor's wife. You shall not desire your neighbor's house or field, nor his male or female slave, nor his ox or ass, nor anything that belongs to him. (Deuteronomy 5:21)."

SOCIAL DIMENSIONS

In recent years the Christian community has reemphasized respect for the rights of others to the basic necessities of life. The Church has taken a stand with the poor and insists that everyone has the God-given right to share in the goods essential to living decently. It is thievery for wealthy individuals or nations to neglect the needs of millions of people for the essentials of food, housing, land, and health care. God created a world rich in resources to provide for all humans. Yet the world's resources are now so unevenly distributed that the majority of people live in poverty, disease, malnutrition, and even starvation.

The seventh and tenth commandments challenge this global inequity. The students can be made aware of the realities of the world and of the fundamental imperatives of Christian morality. God offers us an opportunity to love and serve him by serving our brothers and sisters. Help the students learn to share. Challenge them to be charitable and just. Today, we can readily see that the loss of respect for the rights and property of others can lead to a "siege mentality." We must be ever alert to threats to ourselves and our property. We cannot leave doors unlocked nor move about freely without some risk. Although we may not be held in slavery in Egypt as were the Israelites, most of us know what it is to have our freedom restricted out of fear.

Objective

This lesson helps the students understand the reality of greed and selfishness in the world and in their own lives.

Step 1 / INTRODUCTION

Learning About Our Lives

Introducing the Chapter

Ask the students to open their books to page 162. Read aloud the chapter-focus paragraph and invite the students' responses. Ask them to be specific in identifying the things they desired but could not have. Discuss why they could not have the things they wanted and how they felt. Tell the students that they will now read about a boy who wanted something that belonged to someone else.

or . . .

Distribute writing paper and pens or pencils. Direct the students to answer the following questions.

- What is your favorite commercial?
- Do you want what is advertised? Why?
- Do commercials make you want more and more things? Explain your answer.

Invite volunteers to share their responses with the group. Discuss the power of advertising, explaining that commercials often make people want things that they do not really need.

Reading the Story

Focus attention on the story "Andy's Greed." Ask the students to define the word *greed*. Tell them that they will have a clearer understanding of what the word means after they read the story. Ask volunteers to read aloud the story on pages 162 and 163.

13 Respecting What Belongs to Others

Think of the last time you wanted something you couldn't have. How did you feel?

Andy's Greed

Andy and Nicole were neighbors. They were also good friends. Nicole and Andy often played in Nicole's house.

Andy's parents bought Andy some hand-held computer games for his birthday, but they did not get the one that Andy really wanted. The game he liked best was the one that Nicole had.

"I wish I had Nicole's computer game," Andy thought to himself. "It's the most fun."

CURRICULUM CONNECTION

Language Arts Ask the students to brainstorm endings to the story in Step 1 of this lesson. Encourage them to write endings that show the right thing to do. Invite the students to read their story endings aloud. Condense their statements, for example, "Andy should tell Nicole the truth" or "Andy should go to his parents for help." Write these statements on the chalkboard and keep a tally of the various story endings suggested.

Focus on

The Seventh Commandment The *Catechism of the Catholic Church* states, "The seventh commandmant forbids unjustly taking or keeping the goods of one's neighbor and wronging him in any way with respect to his goods. It commands justice and charity in the care of earthly goods and the fruits of men's labor. For the sake of the common good, it requires respect for the universal destination of goods and respect for the right to private property" (#2401).

Andy dreamed about having Nicole's computer game. He thought about how he could get one just like it. He could not ask his parents for it, because they had just given him some games. So Andy decided to take Nicole's game the next time he went to her house.

The next day Andy was at Nicole's house. Nicole's mother called her out of the room. While Nicole was with her mother, Andy took Nicole's game. Then Andy yelled to Nicole that he had to go home. Andy was in such a hurry to leave that he fell as he ran down the front sidewalk, dropping the computer game. He picked both himself and the game up quickly and ran to his house.

Andy's mother and father were not home from work yet, so Andy sat down to play the game. He tried and tried, but it did not work. Something was wrong. Andy looked carefully at the game. It must have been damaged when he dropped it.

"What will I do now?" Andy wondered.

Greed in Our Lives

All that God has created in the world is good. Through God's generosity we have been given many gifts. But sometimes we want more and more things. Sometimes we want more than we need. This is called **greed**.

Though we may have what we need, we may sometimes want what someone else has. We may even want it so much that we take it from the other person. Wanting something that belongs to another is called **envy**.

When we are not willing to share what we have with others, we are being selfish. Wanting to keep everything for ourselves is never right.

Vocabulary

greed: wanting more and more things when they are not needed

envy: wanting something that belongs to another

✦ ✦ ✦ ✦ ✦ ✦ ✦ ✦ ✦ ✦ ✦

Morality   163

★ ★ ★ ★ Enriching the Lesson ★

Challenge   Ask the students to think of examples of greed. Then ask the students to share their examples with the rest of the class. Be sure to help the students understand that at times we are all greedy. Encourage the students to be more aware of greed in their own lives. As you discuss greed with the students, help them to see that true greed is destructive. Challenge the class to give examples of how greed can be destructive.

Discussing the Story

Discuss the story with the students. Ask:

■ What did Andy do that was wrong? (*Andy took Nicole's computer game.*)

■ What should Andy have done instead? (*Answers may vary.*)

■ Why do some people take things that belong to others? (*Answers may vary.*)

Assist the students in recognizing that people take things that belong to others for a variety of reasons. In Andy's case the reason was greed. Another possible motive might be jealousy.

Help the children appreciate that we are called to respect the property of others. Taking things that belong to others or using things without permission are two ways in which we do not show respect for the property of others.

Step 2 / DEVELOPMENT

Learning About Our Faith

Understanding Greed

Ask a volunteer to read aloud "Greed in Our Lives" on page 163. Help the students to understand the meaning of *greed*.

Learning the Vocabulary

Point out the Vocabulary box. Ask volunteers to read and repeat the definitions aloud.

Step 3 / CONCLUSION

Learning How to Live Our Faith

Discussing Sharing

Ask the students to think of things other than possessions that can be shared (for example, themselves and their time). Have them suggest ways of sharing themselves with others (for instance, playing a game with a younger sibling or writing a letter to a grandparent). Help them appreciate the many opportunities they have to share with others.

DAY 2
DOCTRINE

Objective

This lesson helps the students learn the seventh and tenth commandments.

Step 1 / INTRODUCTION

Learning About Our Lives

Reviewing Day 1

Ask the students to recall what they learned in Day 1 of this chapter. Assist them in remembering that we can share ourselves as well as our possessions.

Studying a Picture

Direct the students to look at the picture on page 164. Have the students study the picture and make up a story to go along with it.

Step 2 / DEVELOPMENT

Learning About Our Faith

Learning the Commandments

Ask volunteers to take turns reading aloud "The Commandments of Sharing" on pages 164 and 165. Have the students repeat the seventh and tenth commandments. Reinforce that if we are to keep these commandments, there are things we must do and things we must not do. Invite the students to assist you in making two lists on the chalkboard, such as the lists below. Write down the "Must Do" list for use on Day 5.

Must Do

- share
- be happy with what we have
- care for what God has created
- fight against feelings of envy and greed

Must Not Do

- steal
- cheat
- waste what God has given us
- be selfish
- desire what others have

Read aloud once again the first sentence on page 165. Explain that God wants us to not only give what is extra, but also to do without something in order to give to others.

164

The Commandments of Sharing

When Jesus was teaching, he knew that some people were filled with greed. They wanted more than they already had. They would **cheat**, or trick, other people to get what they wanted. Jesus also knew that some people were full of envy. They wanted the good things that belonged to others. And Jesus knew that sometimes people did not share what they had with the poor.

God gives us two rules, or commandments, to teach us that everyone has a right to the things they need to live happy, healthy lives. They are the seventh and tenth commandments.

The seventh commandment is *You shall not steal.*

The tenth commandment is *You shall not covet anything that belongs to your neighbor.*

Enriching the Lesson

Play charades with the students, using the following scenarios.

- Your little brother broke his favorite toy.
- Your friend forgot lunch.
- A storm destroyed your neighbor's house.

For each scenario, invite the students to pantomime possible solutions that demonstrate keeping the seventh and tenth commandments.

Focus on

The Seventh Commandment
Some scholars believe that the original intent of the seventh commandment was to prohibit kidnapping for the purposes of slavery. It warned the Israelites not to hold another in slavery because Yahweh had freed them from slavery in Egypt. At first, this commandment was a mandate for the people to respect one another's freedom. Later, the people understood the commandment to prohibit the stealing of any property that belonged to another.

All of God's gifts are meant for everyone. We are called to show that we are grateful for God's gifts by caring for what we have and sharing our gifts with others. We should not take what belongs to others. We should not cheat others out of what is theirs or waste anything that God has made. We are asked to fight against envy and greed in our hearts. We should be thankful for the good things we have been given.

Activity

| steal | selfishness | envy | greed | cheat |

Write the correct word on each line.

1. Wanting more and more things

   greed
2. To get something from someone in a dishonest way

   cheat
3. Wanting to keep everything for yourself

   selfishness
4. Wanting something that belongs to another

   envy
5. To take something that belongs to another

   steal

Vocabulary

cheat: to get something from someone in a dishonest way

✦ ✦ ✦ ✦ ✦ ✦ ✦ ✦ ✦ ✦ ✦ ✦

We Believe

God makes the world for all people. Everyone has the right to a share of the good things of life. We should not purposely damage or steal anything that belongs to others.

CURRICULUM CONNECTION

Music With the help of the music specialist or choir director, teach the students to sing verse 1 of "You Are the Way," found in THIS IS OUR FAITH *Hymnal,* page 122. The song can also be found in THIS IS OUR FAITH *Teacher's Songbook,* Grade 4, page 12.

Understanding the Doctrine

Present the We Believe statements and have the students repeat them several times. Conclude by reading aloud the We Believe statements, omitting key words. Have the students orally fill in the missing words.

Learning the Vocabulary

Have the students read aloud the definition of *cheat* in the vocabulary box. Answer any questions the students may have.

Step 3 / CONCLUSION

Learning How to Live Our Faith

Completing an Activity

Direct the students' attention to the activity on page 165. Read the directions aloud. Have the students complete the activity independently. Afterward, review the answers with the students, having them change any incorrect answers.

Reviewing the Lesson

Instruct the students to close their books. Ask them to recite the seventh and tenth commandments from memory.

Objective

This lesson helps the students identify ways of keeping the seventh and tenth commandments.

Step 1 / INTRODUCTION

Learning About Our Lives

Studying Pictures

Bring in a collection of newspaper and magazine pictures that show people choosing to follow or not to follow the seventh and tenth commandments. Show each picture to the class, asking the students to tell whether or not the people in the pictures are following the seventh and tenth commandments. Have the students explain their answers.

Step 2 / DEVELOPMENT

Learning About Our Faith

Reflecting on Our Actions

Direct the students' attention to "Do I Respect the Property of Others?" on page 166. Ask volunteers to take turns reading aloud each paragraph. After each paragraph is read, ask the students to reread the paragraph silently and reflect on their own behavior in regard to the seventh and tenth commandments.

Afterward, have the students brainstorm ways in which they can follow the seventh and tenth commandments as you write their responses on the chalkboard.

166

Do I Respect the Property of Others?

The seventh and tenth commandments tell us that we must respect the property of others. Ask yourself the following questions to discover what kinds of actions go against these commandments.

1. *We do not respect the property of others if we are wasteful.* Do I waste paper or school supplies? Do I waste food or other things that belong to my family?

2. *We do not respect the property of others if we are careless.* Am I careless with things others allow me to use? Am I careless with materials I use at school?

3. *We do not respect the property of others if we purposely cause harm or damage to something.* Do I write on walls or desks? Do I write in books or tear the pages? Do I ruin something that belongs to another because I am envious or angry?

4. *We do not respect the property of others if we try to cheat others.* Do I try to trick younger children into giving me their things? Do I try to cheat others out of their belongings?

5. *We do not respect the property of others if we take what belongs to someone else.* Do I take things that belong to others without permission? Do I cheat on tests? Do I keep things I find without trying to find the owner? Do I take anything in a store without paying for it? Do I copy homework from other students?

Enriching the Lesson

Divide the class into five groups. Assign each group one of the following Scripture passages to look up in the Bible.

Luke 21:1–4
Matthew 5:40–42
Acts 4:32, 34–35
Sirach 29:8–11
Luke 6:29–38

Give help where needed. Ask the students to read their verses and explain what the verses mean and what is being shared in each passage.

Activity

Write what the person in each story can do to follow the seventh and tenth commandments.

1. Dolores is with her mother and little brother in the grocery store. Dolores likes cherries. While her mother's back is turned, Dolores goes to the fruit section to find the cherries. She could take some and eat them.

Dolores should _____

_____

_____.

2. Peter's mother always makes a lunch for him to take to school. He doesn't want the apple that his mother put in his lunch. He could just throw it out.

Or Peter could _____

_____

_____.

3. Mrs. Williams works in an office. There is a closet filled with office supplies. Her children always need paper, pens, and pencils for school. She can remove the supplies from the office supply closet and then take them home. No one will know that they are missing. But Mrs. Williams knows that this is wrong.

Mrs. Williams should _____

_____.

Morality   167

Discussing Difficulties

Discuss with the students the fact that it is sometimes difficult to share our things, fight against envy, or be satisfied with what we have. Help the students appreciate that we are not alone in this struggle because Jesus has given us the Holy Spirit to help us keep the commandments.

Completing an Activity

Explain the directions to the activity. Ask the students to write endings that show ways in which the seventh and tenth commandments can be followed. When the students have finished, invite them to read their answers aloud. The students' responses may vary a great deal. This will give you an opportunity to reinforce the many ways in which we can choose to follow God's commandments.

Focus on

Respect for Human Dignity
The *Catechism of the Catholic Church* states, "In economic matters, respect for human dignity requires the practice of the virtue of *temperance*. . . the practice of the virtue of *justice*. . . and the practice of *solidarity*, in accordance with the golden rule and in keeping with the generosity of the Lord, who 'though he was rich, yet for your sake. . . became poor so that by his poverty, you might become rich'" (#2407).

CURRICULUM CONNECTION

Art   Distribute drawing paper and crayons or felt-tip markers. Ask the students to recall the seventh and tenth commandments. Ask them to think of a choice a fourth grader might have to make about these two commandments. Direct them to draw their choice on the paper. Later, invite sharing. Display the pictures in a prominent place in the parish hall or school.

167

Day 4

SCRIPTURE/MORALITY

Objective

This lesson helps the students recognize that Jesus calls us to fight against selfishness and to share with others.

Step 1 / INTRODUCTION

Learning About Our Lives

Writing About Sharing

Direct the students' attention to the top of page 168. Read the paragraph aloud and have the students work independently to complete the sentences. Afterward, invite the students to explain what they have written.

Step 2 / DEVELOPMENT

Learning About Our Faith

Reading and Discussing a Scripture Story

Read aloud the title of the Scripture story. Then select volunteers to read the story aloud. Discuss the story with the students. Ask:

- How do you know the man was rich? (*He lived in a big house, wore the finest clothes, and ate the best food.*)
- Who was Lazarus? (*A beggar who was sick and very hungry*)
- What did Lazarus want? (*The scraps of food left over from the rich man's table*)
- What did the rich man do? (*He refused to give Lazarus anything.*)
- Where did Lazarus go when he died? (*He went to be with God.*)
- Where did the rich man go when he died? (*To a place of suffering*)
- What can we learn from the story Jesus told? (*When we refuse to share what we have with others, we sin.*)
- In what way was the rich man selfish? (*He never gave Lazarus anything or even noticed him.*)
- What could the rich man have shared? (*Clothing, food, shelter, companionship, or compassion*)

168

Activity

Sometimes it is difficult to share what we have with others. Complete the sentences to find out what you think about sharing.

1. The three things that are the most difficult for me to share are

   _____

   _____

   _____.

2. The three things that are the easiest for me to share are _____

   _____

   _____.

The Rich Man and Lazarus

One day, Jesus told this story.

"Once there was a rich man. He lived in a big house, and he dressed in the finest clothes. He and his family ate the best food every day.

"At the rich man's door," Jesus went on, "lay a man named Lazarus. He was sick and covered with sores. He was so hungry that he wanted to eat the scraps that fell from the rich man's table. Dogs even came to lick his sores.

"The rich man hardly noticed Lazarus and never gave him anything," Jesus said. "The beggar died and went to live with God. The rich man died, too, but he went to a place of suffering. When the rich man looked up in his pain, he could see Lazarus happy with God."

Based on Luke 16:19–23

168 Scripture

CURRICULUM CONNECTION

Music As a continuation of the Curriculum Connection activity presented on Day 2, teach the students the rest of the song "You Are the Way," found in THIS IS OUR FAITH *Hymnal,* page 122; or in THIS IS OUR FAITH *Teacher's Songbook,* Grade 4, page 12.

Teaching Tips

To assist the hearing impaired, consider making a cassette recording of the Scripture story and the discussion questions prior to the session. Make the cassette available to those students who would benefit from listening to the story and questions at a comfortable volume level. Also, as the questions are discussed, be sure that key phrases and concepts are written on the chalkboard for the students to read.

Jesus Teaches Us About Sharing

Jesus' story tells us that those who have the good things of life must share them with those who are in real need. Even if we do not have much, we are still expected to share what we have with others. God created the world and all that is in it for the good of everyone.

Activity

Below are ten reasons or excuses why people are either willing or unwilling to share what they have. Read each sentence and then put a ✓ in the appropriate column.

	WILLING	UNWILLING
1. People won't appreciate what I give them.	☐	✓
2. God has made all things for the good of everyone.	✓	☐
3. Jesus tells us that we must share what we have with others.	✓	☐
4. I won't have enough for myself.	☐	✓
5. God has been good to me, so I will share what I have.	✓	☐
6. Other people don't really need anything from me.	☐	✓
7. They won't take care of what I give them.	☐	✓
8. I deserve what I have; others don't.	☐	✓
9. I don't really need as much as I have.	✓	☐
10. I don't have much, but you can have some.	✓	☐

★ ★ ★ ★
Enriching the Lesson
★ ★ ★

Select students to dramatize the Scripture story of the rich man and Lazarus. Ask for volunteers to play the roles of God, Lazarus, the rich man, and the rich man's family. Reread the story as the students act it out.

Reflecting on Jesus' Message

Continue reading "Jesus Teaches Us About Sharing" on page 169. Guide the students to appreciate how important it is to share what we have with others, especially those less fortunate than ourselves.

Step 3 / CONCLUSION

Learning How to Live Our Faith

Identifying Reasons for Sharing

Call attention to the activity on page 169. Ask a volunteer to read the directions aloud. Ask the students to complete the activity independently. Afterward, invite the students to share their responses. Help the students appreciate that at times it seems as though we have good reasons for not sharing, but we are called to fight against selfishness. We need to work at learning how to share. This means sharing with others as well as respecting what others have when they share with us.

Praying Together

Conclude this lesson by praying, *Jesus, help us to fight against selfishness. Help us to share with others.*

DAY 5

PRAYER/REVIEW

Objective

This lesson helps the students pray with gratitude for the gifts that God has given them.

Making Flowers of Praise

Distribute a small paper plate, a sheet of construction paper, scissors, glue, and crayons or felt-tip markers to each student. Ask the students to think of the gifts they have been given by God in their lives. For each gift they think of, have them cut a flower petal out of the construction paper. Encourage them to draw a picture or write the name of the gift on each petal. Have them glue the petals to the paper plate, leaving a space in the center to write their names. Allow time for the students to show and explain their flowers of praise to the class.

Preparing for Praying with Gratitude

Ask a volunteer to read aloud "Praying with Gratitude" on page 170. Have each student write a list of ten people, places or things for which he or she is thankful.

Praying with Gratitude

Ask the students to make a circle. Establish a prayerful atmosphere. Then ask each student to thank God for one item on their lists. Keep the prayers of gratitude moving around the circle several times until each student has had the opportunity to thank God for at least three items on their lists. Conclude with a spontaneous prayer thanking God for helping us keep the commandments and live as Jesus lived.

Singing Together

Have the students return to their seats. Conclude by singing together "You Are the Way" on page 122 of the THIS IS OUR FAITH *Hymnal* or page 12 of the THIS IS OUR FAITH *Teacher's Songbook*, Grade 4.

170

Praying with Gratitude

God has given each of us so much for which we can be thankful. Prayers of thanks or gratitude are important prayers because these prayers remind us that it is *God* who is responsible for all the good things in our lives. We remember God's goodness and give thanks.

Make a list of ten people, places, or things for which you are thankful. Then use your list to join your class in praying a prayer of gratitude.

God, our Creator, I thank you for

_____

_____

_____

_____

_____

_____

_____

_____

170 Prayer

★ ★★★ ★
Enriching the Lesson
★ ★ ★

Begin by copying onto the chalkboard the "Must Do" list you saved from Day 2. Create a prayerful environment after gathering the students for prayer. Invite volunteers to read the items on the list, inserting the words *When we* before each item. Have the class complete each phrase in the manner of a responsorial prayer by praying *we are following the commandments* after each item.

Chapter Review

Six words in the list below relate to keeping the seventh and tenth commandments. Write these words on the lines provided.

waste	share	envy	care	steal	respect	greedy	harm	lie
unselfish	cheat	generous	truthful	fight	covet	gossip		

_____ share _____	_____ unselfish _____
_____ care _____	_____ generous _____
_____ respect _____	_____ truthful _____

Write your answers to the first two questions on the lines provided.

1. What is meant by *greed*?

Greed is wanting more and more things when they are not needed.

2. Why are the seventh and tenth commandments so important?

The seventh and tenth commandments teach us that God wants us to share some of what we have with others who are in need and that we should not purposely damage or steal what belongs to others.

You must not steal or cheat.
Based on Leviticus 19:11–13

3. Discuss how we can better follow the seventh commandment.

Naming Ways to Follow the Seventh and Tenth Commandments

Direct the students to the activity at the top of page 171. Direct the students to cross out the words that do not follow the seventh and tenth commandments and write the words that name ways to follow the seventh and tenth commandments. Afterward, review the answers to check the students' understanding of these two commandments. Ask the students to correct their work.

Reviewing the Chapter

Invite the students to answer the two questions that follow. Direct the students to write their answers on the lines provided. Encourage all to participate in the discussion of the third review item.

Reading the Scripture Verse

Read aloud the verse from Leviticus with the students. Explain that God gave this law to the people even before Jesus came into the world. Help the students understand that stealing and cheating are wrong and keep us from living the way God wants us to live. Point out that if we hurt or damage someone's property, we must make up for that damage by replacing the item or having it repaired.

14 Respecting the Truth

Objectives

To help the students
- Understand that telling lies hurts people.
- Learn the eighth commandment.
- Identify what it means to live out the eighth commandment.
- Appreciate that God's gift of the Holy Spirit helps us to live in truth.
- Pray with honesty and review the chapter.

Chapter Outline

	Step 1 Learning About Our Lives	Step 2 Learning About Our Faith	Step 3 Learning How to Live Our Faith
Day 1	■ Introduce the chapter. ■ Review the commandments. ■ Read the stories. *ABOUT 10 MINUTES*	■ Discuss lying. *ABOUT 10 MINUTES*	■ Read a haiku poem. ■ Write haiku poems. ■ Sing together. *ABOUT 10 MINUTES*
Day 2	■ Write about experiences of dishonesty. *ABOUT 10 MINUTES*	■ Read a Scripture story. ■ Understand the eighth commandment. ■ Review the doctrine. ■ Learn the vocabulary. *ABOUT 12 MINUTES*	■ Identify trustworthy people. ■ Complete an activity. *ABOUT 8 MINUTES*
Day 3	■ Listen to and discuss a story. ■ Read and discuss a biography. *ABOUT 15 MINUTES*	■ Read about and discuss honesty. *ABOUT 5 MINUTES*	■ Write advertisements. *ABOUT 10 MINUTES*
Day 4	■ Complete an honesty survey. *ABOUT 5 MINUTES*	■ Read about the Holy Spirit. ■ Recognize the Holy Spirit. *ABOUT 10 MINUTES*	■ Complete an activity. ■ Review the lesson. ■ Pray together. *ABOUT 15 MINUTES*
Day 5	**Prayer** Read about praying honestly to God; write a prayer; pray together; and sing together. **Review** Review how lying hurts; rebuild trust; review the chapter; and read the Scripture verse.		

Plan Ahead ～～～～～

	Preparing Your Class	**Materials Needed**
Day 1	Read through the lesson plan. Obtain the story of Pinocchio.	■ pencils or pens ■ Pinocchio story, condensed version ■ copies of THIS IS OUR FAITH *Hymnal*
Day 2	Read the lesson plan.	■ pencils or pens ■ writing paper ■ hymnals
Day 3	Read through the lesson plan. If enriching the lesson, talk to the school librarian about gathering resources on martyrs.	■ pencils or pens ■ crayons or markers
Day 4	Read through the lesson plan. If using the curriculum connection, review the song "Pentecost Prayer."	■ pencils or pens ■ construction paper ■ crayons or markers
Day 5	Read through the lesson plan.	■ pencils or pens ■ Bible, candle ■ prayer cloth ■ writing paper ■ hymnals

Additional Resources

As you plan this chapter, consider using the following materials from The Resourceful Teacher Package.

- *Classroom Activity Sheets 14* and *14a*
- *Family Activity Sheets 14* and *14a*
- *Chapter 14 Test*
- *Prayers for Every Day*
- *Projects: Grade 4*

You may also wish to refer to the following Big Book.

- *We Celebrate God's Word,* page 16

In preparing the students for the Sunday readings, you may wish to use Silver Burdett Ginn's *Getting Ready for Sunday* student and teacher materials.

BOOKS FOR THE JOURNEY

Experiencing Jesus Today. "Before Pilate," pp. 185–189. Charles Singer & Albert Hari. Oregon Catholic Press, 1993. The story of Jesus before the high priest with additional information, illustrations, questions, and a prayer.

Hey World, Here I Am! "Five Dollars," p. 38. Jean Little. Harper & Row, 1986. A narrative poem of a child wanting to be honest about some money she has taken.

MORE BOOKS FOR THE JOURNEY

Tread Softly. Corinne Gerson. Dial, 1979. A story of a girl who gets caught in a web of lies.

The Stories of Hans Andersen. "The Emperor's New Clothes," pp. 72–76. Retold by Robert Mathias. Silver Burdett & Ginn, 1985. Everyone in the kingdom lies about the Emperor's nakedness, except one small boy.

REDUCED CLASSROOM ACTIVITIES

NAME _____

RESPECTING THE TRUTH

Lies can hurt us and other people. When we hurt someone with our lies, we are bearing false witness against them. These are sinful lies.

But sometimes our truthful words can hurt someone's feelings, too. We're not sinning against the eighth commandment when we choose our words carefully to avoid hurting someone.

Read each "Truth" statement below and decide if the statement next to it is a sinful lie or not. In the space provided, write *Yes* if the statement is a sinful lie, or *No* if it is not. When you've finished, discuss your decisions with a partner.

TRUTH		SINFUL LIE?
1. I'm mad at Josh.	Yes	"Josh, Gerardo said he's not your best friend anymore."
2. I wrapped this tie for my dad's birthday.	No	"No, Dad, I can't tell you what's in that package."
3. Teresa hurt my feelings.	Yes	"Everyone in the class is mad at you, Teresa!"
4. The story Leon wrote isn't very interesting.	No	"I liked the way you described the main character, Leon."
5. I lost my library book.	Yes	"I returned it last week, Mr. Ward."
6. The phone call is for my parents, but they're not home.	No	"My parents can't come to the phone right now, may I take a message?"
7. The ball I threw hit Zach in the head.	Yes	"I never threw any ball, Ms. Root. He's lying."

To the Teacher: This activity will encourage students to evaluate respect for truth in concrete situations.

Chapter 14 Respecting the Truth   THIS IS OUR FAITH 4 **14**

NAME _____

THE EIGHTH COMMANDMENT

Choose one of the words in the box to complete each sentence.

eighth	high priest	truth	occupied	death
evil	teaching	farmer	false	lie

1. A __high priest__ was a powerful leader of the people at the time of Jesus.

2. To bear false witness means to tell a __lie__.

3. The __eighth__ commandment tells us not to bear false witness against our neighbor.

4. Franz Jaegerstaetter was a __farmer__ in Austria.

5. Austria was later __occupied__ by the Nazis.

6. The Nazi movement was __evil__. Franz Jaegerstaetter said so openly.

7. Franz was condemned to __death__ because he would not lie.

8. Jesus tells us that the __truth__ will set us free.

9. If we live by the __teaching__ of Jesus, we will know the truth.

10. You bear false witness against your neighbors when you spread __false__ rumors about them.

To the Teacher: This activity reviews chapter vocabulary and the biography of Franz Jaegerstaetter.

14a THIS IS OUR FAITH 4   **Chapter 14** Respecting the Truth

Background for the Teacher

THE EIGHTH COMMANDMENT

Fourth graders know the difference between telling the truth and telling a lie. They have experienced falsehood in their encounters with peers and adults. They have been hurt by the dishonesty of others. Yet they may have been tempted to lie themselves. At times this might reflect an attitude of dishonesty that infects our society. Children may have heard from parents and other adults that our governmental leaders lie because they are "politicians." They may have observed in their own homes and schools instances when people say one thing but do another.

Children of this age have a deep sense of honesty and fairness. Fourth graders appreciate the value of truth and respect people's right to truth. The eighth commandment can be seen as a law protecting a basic human right to the truth. Without respect for truth, without basic honesty, relationships crumble, bonds of life in society are weakened, and nations can fall.

We find the eighth commandment in the Hebrew Scriptures in Exodus 20 and in Deuteronomy 5. In both places the commandment is presented in the same words which we use today in our traditional catechetical formula: "You shall not bear false witness against your neighbor." This should leave little room for any misinterpretation of this commandment.

THE WAY, THE TRUTH, AND THE LIFE

A superficial observance of the eighth commandment is to avoid lying. Beyond that, Jesus came to tell us to seek the truth. In the Gospel of John, Jesus, on trial before Pilate, said, "The reason I was born, the reason why I came into the world, is to testify to the truth. Anyone committed to the truth hears my voice." "Truth?" said Pilate. "What does that mean?" (based on John 18:37–38). Pilate's response reflects the cynicism that permeated not only the God-less Roman world of his time, but of our contemporary world as well.

TRUTH FREES US

Jesus is the light of the world, the life-giving truth that dispels the darkness of lies, disintegration, and death. Jesus says he is the way, the truth, and the life. No one comes to the Father except through him (see John 14:6). Jesus is the Word of God. The Word is the double-edged sword that cuts deeply, even to where bone meets marrow, to reveal our deepest longings that Christ desires to satisfy.

Jesus' truth makes us whole, heals us, frees us from the lies that bind us, even the psychological lies we might believe about ourselves. All that he requires is that we live according to his teaching. Then we are truly his disciples. We will know the truth and the truth will set us free (see John 8:31–32).

Objective

This lesson helps the students understand that telling lies is wrong and hurts people.

Step 1 / INTRODUCTION

Learning About Our Lives

Introducing the Chapter

Instruct the students to open their books to page 172. Ask a volunteer to read aloud the chapter title and focus questions. Elicit responses to the focus questions. If the students are reluctant to share a story about a lie that they told, invite them to discuss lies that they are aware of that were told about other people. Then ask them to consider how the person who was lied about must have felt. Help the students understand that lies hurt people, damage people's good names, and may cause others to turn against the victim of the lie.

or . . .

Read or tell the class a condensed version of the story of Pinocchio, the stringed puppet who came alive through a wish made by the carpenter Geppetto. In the story, Pinocchio does not become a real boy until he stops lying and begins to love Geppetto. Help the class understand that the story teaches us that until we accept the truth and behave and act in the truth, we are not acting like ourselves, like the real persons God made us to be.

Reviewing the Commandments

If you are charting the students' progress in memorizing the Ten Commandments, invite volunteers to recite the commandments they have mastered. Give them stickers or stars to place in the appropriate columns on the Ten Commandments poster.

Reading the Stories

Direct attention to the activity on page 172 and ask the students to read silently the two stories. Then ask the students to explain how each story shows an example of lying. Discuss with the class who acted dishonestly in each story and what made their actions dishonest.

172

Respecting the Truth

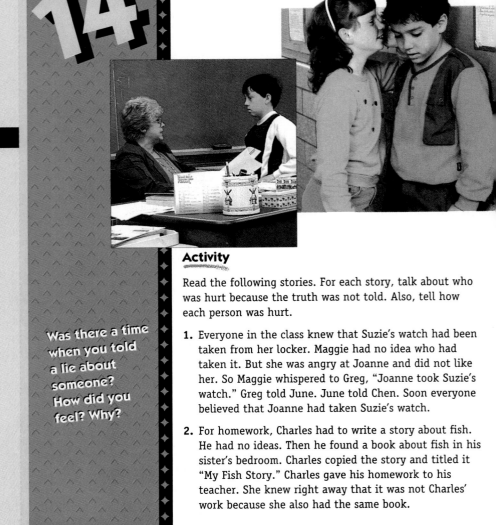

Was there a time when you told a lie about someone? How did you feel? Why?

172 Morality

Activity

Read the following stories. For each story, talk about who was hurt because the truth was not told. Also, tell how each person was hurt.

1. Everyone in the class knew that Suzie's watch had been taken from her locker. Maggie had no idea who had taken it. But she was angry at Joanne and did not like her. So Maggie whispered to Greg, "Joanne took Suzie's watch." Greg told June. June told Chen. Soon everyone believed that Joanne had taken Suzie's watch.

2. For homework, Charles had to write a story about fish. He had no ideas. Then he found a book about fish in his sister's bedroom. Charles copied the story and titled it "My Fish Story." Charles gave his homework to his teacher. She knew right away that it was not Charles' work because she also had the same book.

🌐 Cultural Awareness

Help the students value the contribution of all cultures to our world. Point out that the Japanese have shared poetry such as the haiku with us. Ask the students to name contributions that other nations or peoples have made to enrich the world. Emphasize that everyone benefits when nations share with one another.

Focus on

The Eighth Commandment
This commandment addresses one of the essential cornerstones for any community: honesty. Whether in the family, or in impersonal organizations, everyone has a right to expect justice and honesty. Widespread acceptance of lying, cheating, stealing, and other forms of dishonesty tear at the fabric of communal existence on all levels. All ten commandments are meant to assure the community's welfare, and support the continued strength of the family system.

Lying Hurts Others

Lying always hurts someone. When we tell lies about another person, the person gets hurt. Sometimes even the family or the friends of the person can be hurt by our lies.

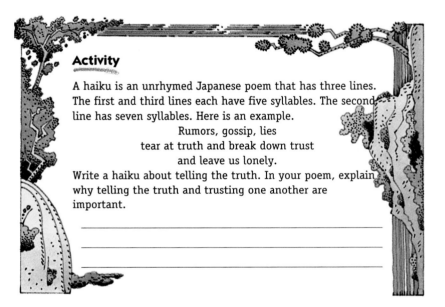

When we lie, we hurt ourselves by doing something that is wrong and we lose the trust of our friends and families. Afterward, they may no longer believe us, even when we tell the truth. We may begin with one lie, but soon we may be telling more lies.

Jesus teaches us to be truthful. We need to be truly honest. Others need to know that we can be trusted. They want to know that they can believe what we say.

Activity

A haiku is an unrhymed Japanese poem that has three lines. The first and third lines each have five syllables. The second line has seven syllables. Here is an example.

Rumors, gossip, lies
tear at truth and break down trust
and leave us lonely.

Write a haiku about telling the truth. In your poem, explain why telling the truth and trusting one another are important.

_____

_____

_____

Ask the students to list the names of the people who were hurt in the stories because the truth was not told. (*Joanne and Charles*)

Step 2 / DEVELOPMENT

Learning About Our Faith

Discussing Lying

Point out "Lying Hurts Others" on page 173. Ask volunteers to read this section aloud. Then divide the class into small groups. Ask each group to choose a leader. Then instruct the groups to discuss why people lie and whether or not anyone wins or profits by not telling the truth. Visit each discussion group. Then invite the leaders to summarize the groups' conclusions. Help the students understand that lying is wrong and always hurts ourselves and others.

Step 3 / CONCLUSION

Learning How to Live Our Faith

Reading a Haiku Poem

Direct attention to the activity on page 173. Ask volunteers to read about haiku. Read the poem aloud together. Then analyze the structure of the poem, explaining the number of syllables in each line. Make sure the students understand the structure before they begin writing their own poems.

Writing Haiku Poems

Work together to compose a haiku on the chalkboard. Then help the students write haiku poems about telling the truth. As they work, move about the room, offering assistance. Allow time for sharing. Reinforce the importance of telling the truth and trusting others.

Singing Together

Sing with the students verse 2 of "You Are the Way," found on page 122 of the THIS IS OUR FAITH *Hymnal* or on page 12 of the THIS IS OUR FAITH *Teacher's Songbook,* Grade 4.

Enriching the Lesson

Have the students copy their haiku poems on writing paper and illustrate them, using crayons or felt-tip markers. Use these illustrated poems as a bulletin board display in the church's gathering space or parish hall.

Objective

This lesson helps the students learn the eighth commandment.

Step 1 / INTRODUCTION

Learning About Our Lives

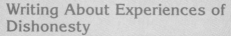

Writing About Experiences of Dishonesty

Distribute writing paper. Invite the students to write a story about an experience they have had in which someone did not tell the truth. Afterward, invite sharing. Encourage the students to identify (not by name, however) who was dishonest in the story and how that individual acted dishonestly.

Step 2 / DEVELOPMENT

Learning About Our Faith

Reading and Discussing a Scripture Story

Tell the students that the story they will read continues the gospel story "Put Away Your Sword," which they read in Chapter 11. Select one or more volunteers to read "False Witnesses" aloud, as the other students follow along in their books. Discuss the story, using the following questions.

- Where was Jesus taken? (*He was taken to the home of the high priest.*)

- What were some of the leaders trying to find? (*A reason to put Jesus to death*)

- How were some of the leaders false witnesses? (*They told lies about Jesus and hurt him.*)

- What did the high priest ask Jesus? (*"Do you think you are God's messiah and so have the right to criticize us in front of the people?"*)

- How did Jesus answer? (*"I am."*)

- What did Jesus know would happen because of his honest answer? (*He would be put to death.*)

- What decision did the leaders make? (*To put Jesus to death because they decided he was guilty.*)

174

False Witnesses

Jesus told the truth even when people lied about him. Jesus told the truth even when he knew it would lead to his death.

It was night. The men had taken Jesus from the Garden of Gethsemane. They led him to the home of the **high priest**, a powerful leader of the Temple.

Some other Temple leaders were gathered at the high priest's house. They were trying to find a reason to put Jesus to death, but they could not agree. Some people told lies about Jesus, but their stories did not agree.

Finally, the high priest stood up before everyone. He questioned Jesus.

"Have you no answer to what these men say about you?" the high priest asked.

Jesus did not answer. Then the high priest became angry. He asked Jesus, "Do you think you are God's messiah and so have the right to criticize us in front of the people?"

"I am," Jesus said. Jesus knew that his honest answer would lead to his death.

The high priest turned to all those gathered before him. "What more do you need to hear?" he asked. "What is your decision?"

"Jesus is guilty!" they all shouted.

Based on Mark 14:53–64

174 Scripture

CURRICULUM CONNECTION

Drama Instead of reading the Scripture story aloud, direct the students to dramatize the story as if it were a play. Choose volunteers to act out the parts of the narrator, the high priest, and Jesus. Invite the rest of the class to take the part of the crowd. You may want to use props and costumes. Instruct the students to gather in an open area of the room to dramatize the story.

Focus on

The Eighth Commandment We are required to respect the honor and reputation of others. Our words must be truthful, and our deeds must be true. We must guard against hypocrisy. To deceive a neighbor intentionally is wrong. We, as a holy people, are obliged to bear witness to our God who is all Truth. When we sin against this commandment, we refuse to commit ourselves to moral uprightness. This basic infidelity to God undermines the foundations of the covenant.

Chapter Review

1. Think about a time when someone told a lie about you. What could you do so that you and that person could make peace with each other?

I could

forgive the person and tell him or her that

God wants us to respect the truth.

2. We hurt others when we lie to them or about them. Think about a time when you may have hurt someone in this way. Write about what you will do to make up for the hurt.

I will

tell the person that I am sorry and try to live

the way that Jesus wants me to.

On the lines provided, write your answers to the first two questions.

1. What is meant by *bear false witness*?

To bear false witness is to tell a lie.

_____

2. Why should we respect the truth?

God wants us to respect the truth by not lying to others

or about others. When we lie, we hurt ourselves.

We hurt others too because we break down trust.

_____

3. Discuss what the world would be like if no one followed the eighth commandment.

Speak the truth in love.
Based on Ephesians 4:15

★ ★ ★ ★ ★
Enriching the Lesson

Invite the students to write resolutions about making up for hurts caused by fictitious people. (*Their answers might include admitting to what was done, resolving not to do it again, confessing to the priest and to God, asking forgiveness, and making amends by telling the truth.*) Encourage the students to share their resolutions with the class. Summarize by naming the four steps: admitting, resolving, confessing, and making amends.

Reviewing How Lying Hurts

Ask the students to read silently the paragraphs about lying at the top of page 181. Instruct them to think about what they could do to rekindle trust or how they can make up for hurts they have caused others because the truth was not told. Have them write their ideas on the lines provided. Have the students read aloud what they wrote.

Rebuilding Trust

Explore with the students the ways in which trust can be rebuilt when a lie has hurt them. (*Answers might include receiving an apology, forgiving the person, having the person make amends by telling the truth.*)

Reviewing the Chapter

Take time to go through the review questions at the bottom of the page. Direct the students to write the answers to the two questions on the lines provided. For the third item, encourage all to participate in the discussion. Be supportive of each student who contributes his or her ideas to the discussion.

Reading the Scripture Verse

Direct attention to the Scripture verse at the bottom of the page. Help the students learn the verse by heart, repeating it aloud with them several times. Help the students understand that we show our love for God and others when we speak the truth.

181

Our Merciful God

Objectives

To help the students
- Understand that God is merciful.
- Learn a story about God's mercy.
- Consider the difficulties of asking for and giving forgiveness.
- Understand that we are called to forgive others.
- Pray a prayer of mercy and review the chapter.

Chapter Outline

	Step 1 Learning About Our Lives	**Step 2** Learning About Our Faith	**Step 3** Learning How to Live Our Faith
Day 1	■ Review the Ten Commandments. ■ Introduce the chapter. ■ Discuss family rules. ■ Read and discuss the story. *ABOUT 10 MINUTES*	■ See God as a forgiving Father. ■ Review the doctrine. ■ Learn the vocabulary. *ABOUT 5 MINUTES*	■ Act out forgiveness skits. ■ Review the lesson. *ABOUT 15 MINUTES*
Day 2	■ Discuss mistakes. *ABOUT 6 MINUTES*	■ Read the Scripture story. ■ Discuss the Scripture story. ■ Participate in a discussion. ■ Understand God's forgiveness. *ABOUT 12 MINUTES*	■ Meditate. *ABOUT 12 MINUTES*
Day 3	■ Read and discuss a story. *ABOUT 11 MINUTES*	■ Learn the way to forgiveness. *ABOUT 5 MINUTES*	■ Write an ending to a story. *ABOUT 14 MINUTES*
Day 4	■ Reflect on forgiving others. *ABOUT 8 MINUTES*	■ Read and discuss a Scripture story. ■ Understand the call to forgive. *ABOUT 12 MINUTES*	■ Give advice. *ABOUT 10 MINUTES*
Day 5	**Prayer** Talk about forgiveness; complete an acrostic; introduce a prayer of mercy; and pray together. **Review** Review forgiveness and reconciliation; review the chapter; and read the Scripture verse.		

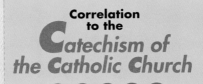

Plan Ahead ~~~~~~~~~~~

	Preparing Your Class	**Materials Needed**
Day 1	Read through the lesson plan. Bring stickers if you have opted to make a commandments poster.	■ pencils or pens
Day 2	Read the lesson plan. If enriching the lesson, bring the personal ad section from a newspaper.	■ pencils or pens
Day 3	Read through the entire lesson plan.	■ pencils or pens ■ Copies of THIS IS OUR FAITH *Hymnal*
Day 4	Read through the lesson plan. If using the curriculum connection, obtain the recording of "The Prodigal Son."	■ pencils or pens ■ recording of "The Prodigal Son"
Day 5	Read through the lesson plan.	■ pencils or pens ■ writing paper ■ Bible ■ candle ■ prayer cloth

Additional Resources

As you plan this chapter, consider using the following materials from The Resourceful Teacher Package.

■ *Classroom Activity Sheets 15* and *15a*

■ *Family Activity Sheets 15* and *15a*

■ *Chapter 15 Test*

■ *Prayers for Every Day*

■ *Projects: Grade 4*

You may also wish to refer to the following Big Books.

■ *We Celebrate God's Word,* page 8

■ *We Celebrate the Sacraments,* pages 13–15

In preparing the students for the Sunday readings, you may wish to use Silver Burdett Ginn's *Getting Ready for Sunday* student and teacher materials.

BOOKS FOR THE JOURNEY

Experience Jesus Today. "The Prodigal Son," pp. 134–137. Charles Singer & Albert Hari. Oregon Catholic Press, 1993. The story of the merciful father with additional illustrations, information, a prayer, and questions.

The House of Wings. Betsy Byars. Puffin, 1982. The story of how a boy who is left with his grandfather matures through compassion.

MORE BOOKS FOR THE JOURNEY

Renfroe's Christmas. Robert Burch. Brown Thrasher Books, 1993. The story of how a boy deals with his own selfishness and shows compassion toward another.

The In-Between Days. Eve Bunting. HarperCollins, 1994. The story of a boy who does something that hurts others, repents, and helps to bring about a good ending.

REDUCED CLASSROOM ACTIVITIES

NAME _____

OUR MERCIFUL GOD

Reread the story about the merciful father. Then choose two items from each category below to help you write a modern version of the story. Write your story in the space provided on page 15a.

Time	Place
evening	desert
summer	lake
autumn	office
morning	field
noon	seashore
dawn	mountain
supper	large city
a winter night	farming town

People	Ways of Reconciliation
mother	hugging
father	having a party
friends	giving a gift
brother	talking on the phone
sister	crying
young daughter	shaking hands
grandparent	sharing a meal
young son	making an agreement

© Silver Burdett Ginn Inc.

To the Teacher: This two-page activity follows the Scripture story "A Merciful Father."

Chapter 15 *Our Merciful God*

THIS IS OUR FAITH 4 **15**

NAME _____

MY STORY

❀RECONCILIATION ♥ forgiveness ❀

_____

© Silver Burdett Ginn Inc.

15a THIS IS OUR FAITH 4

Chapter 15 *Our Merciful God*

Background for the Teacher

CHRISTIAN IDEALS

The students have reviewed the major Christian principles of moral living: the Great Commandment of love that Jesus gave us, his Golden Rule, his Beatitudes, and the Ten Commandments. These texts set forth both the highest ideals of the moral teachings of Jesus as well as the minimal standards for living according to God's will. The challenge to Christians is to live in a way that is often at variance with the dominant values and lifestyles of our culture. The command to love God and each other constantly challenges us to rise above our innate selfishness and to strive at all times to live up to these ideals.

GOD'S MERCY

The most reassuring feature of our God, who is infinite love, is his merciful forgiveness. For without forgiveness, love would not be infinite. As Christians we must recognize that God is both compassionate and just.

THE FORGIVING FATHER

The parable of the two brothers is often referred to as the story of the prodigal son or the story of the forgiving father. Fourth graders usually relate to the elder brother who remained at home and obeyed the father, although as they move into adolescence, they begin to see themselves reflected in the prodigal son. It is not until adulthood that most of us recognize this as a story of a forgiving father, a story of our merciful God.

The prophets, psalmists, and sages all praise God as slow to anger and governing with mercy, a mercy that endures forever (see Wisdom 15:1; Psalms 118 and 136). The history of God's people is the story of human infidelity and divine mercy. Jesus lives this biblical portrait of a forgiving God, showing us a love beyond human imagining. In his parable of the Prodigal Son, Jesus reveals a father extravagant with welcoming love for his son who returned to him. Each of us is that younger son; or we are the older one, whose self-righteousness and hardness of heart are more subtle sins. God looks for our return as eagerly as the father in the parable waited for his son. God forgives those who are sorry for their sins as quickly and completely as that father did.

As your students learn the demanding ways of living as a follower of Jesus, their faith must be founded on the certainty of God's readiness to forgive. Impart the image of a tender and merciful father who understands us better than we understand ourselves, who longs for us when we stray, and seeks to welcome us with open arms. That image will help the students seek reconciliation whenever they fail to live up to Christ's ideals. It will encourage them to extend the hand of forgiveness to others.

DAY 1
MORALITY/DOCTRINE

Objective

This lesson helps the students understand that God is merciful.

Step 1 / INTRODUCTION

Learning About Our Lives

Reviewing the Ten Commandments

Give the students an opportunity to recite the Ten Commandments from memory. Emphasize the importance of knowing and living the Ten Commandments. Give the students stickers to update their column on the Ten Commandments poster, if you have opted to make one.

Introducing the Chapter

Direct attention to the focus question on page 182. Invite the students to name different ways they have been forgiven when they have done something wrong. Ask them to discuss how they feel when they have been forgiven. Tell the students that in today's lesson they will learn about God's forgiveness.

Discussing Family Rules

Ask the students to name things they are not allowed to do or touch at home without supervision. Use the questions below to guide discussion.

- Why did your parents make these rules?
- Have you ever broken one of these rules?
- What happened when you broke the rule?

Reading and Discussing the Story

Ask volunteers to take turns reading aloud the story "A Forgiving Mother." Help the students realize that both Ellen and her mother felt sorrow. Ask:

- Why did Ellen's mother get angry? (*Ellen did something that she knew she should not do.*)
- Why did both Ellen and her mother feel sorry? (*Ellen felt sorry for disobeying her mother. Ellen's mother felt sorry for yelling at Ellen and sending her friend home.*)
- Who was forgiving in the story? (*Both Ellen and her mother were forgiving. They both accepted each other's apologies.*)

182

Our Merciful God

When you have said or done wrong and hurtful things, what are some ways that you have been forgiven?

182 Morality

A Forgiving Mother

School ended early because of snow. Ellen invited Linda to go home with her. "Let's go to my house and do our homework together," Ellen suggested. "My mother is still at work."

Linda liked the idea, so the girls went to Ellen's house. Linda noticed a VCR and said, "Let's watch a movie instead of doing our homework. It looks like your mom has some good ones."

"We can't," Ellen answered. "My mother told me not to play any of her movies when she's not here."

"But your mother is at work," Linda said. "She'll never know."

Ellen thought for a minute, and then she shrugged her shoulders. "Okay," she agreed. "Let's watch a movie."

CURRICULUM CONNECTION

Art Distribute drawing paper and crayons or markers. Explain to the students that sometimes we can show our feelings on paper. Instruct the students to show by using color and lines how it feels when we sin and hurt someone. Then ask the students to show how it feels when we feel sorrow for that hurt. Finally, challenge the students to show how it feels when the person whom we've hurt forgives us. Label the first drawing *sin*, the second *sorrow*, and the third *forgiveness*.

Focus on

God's Mercy The *Catechism of the Catholic Church* states, "Jesus invites sinners to the table of the kingdom: 'I came not to call the righteous, but sinners.' He invites them to that conversion without which one cannot enter the kingdom, but shows them in word and deed his Father's boundless mercy for them and the vast 'joy in heaven over one sinner who repents.' The supreme proof of his love will be the sacrifice of his own life 'for the forgiveness of sins' " (#545).

They were enjoying the movie when Ellen's mother unexpectedly came home an hour early.

"Ellen!" her mother said sternly. "Didn't I tell you not to play any movies when I'm not with you? Now go to your room! And Linda, I think you should go home."

Linda left quickly, and Ellen ran to her room, crying.

Ellen's mother hung up her coat, and then she went upstairs to speak to Ellen.

"I'm sorry, Ellen, but you shouldn't have touched the VCR and my movies when I had told you not to," she said.

Ellen put her arms around her mother. "I'm sorry," Ellen said. "I know I was wrong. But we didn't have much homework, and Linda wanted to watch a movie."

"Let's go downstairs and make dinner," Ellen's mother said. "Then maybe we can watch a movie together."

God Is a Forgiving Father

Even when we are very young, we make mistakes. As we grow older, we may choose to do wrong. But no matter how many times we choose to do wrong, our parents will always love us and forgive us.

God is a merciful father. The Lord always loves us and is eager to show us mercy. Like a loving father, God is ready to forgive us when we show that we are sorry. Our sorrow for sin and God's forgiveness lead to **reconciliation**.

Vocabulary

reconciliation: making up through sorrow and forgiveness

✦ ✦ ✦ ✦ ✦ ✦ ✦ ✦ ✦ ✦ ✦ ✦

We Believe

God the Father is merciful and forgiving. God keeps on loving us when we sin. The Lord is always ready to forgive us when we show that we are sorry.

Doctrine **183**

★ ★★★ ★
Enriching the Lesson
★   ★

Distribute Bibles and have the students find and read Matthew 18:21–35. Discuss the Scripture story with the students. Ask them what Jesus wants us to learn from this story.

■ How did they show their forgiveness? (*They went downstairs to make dinner and planned to watch a movie together.*)

■ Have you ever felt the way Ellen felt?

Step 2 / DEVELOPMENT

Learning About Our Faith

Seeing God as a Forgiving Father

Read "God Is a Forgiving Father" on page 183 with the class. Make comparisons between God's willingness to forgive us and the willingness of Ellen's mother to forgive Ellen.

Reviewing the Doctrine

Call attention to the We Believe statements. Ask a volunteer to read this section aloud. Stress the importance of this belief.

Learning the Vocabulary

Have the students learn the meaning of the word *reconciliation* by repeating its definition several times. Answer any questions the students may have.

Step 3 / CONCLUSION

Learning How to Live Our Faith

Acting Out Forgiveness Skits

Divide the class into groups of three or four students. Ask each group to think of a situation that involves sin, sorrow, and forgiveness. Encourage the students to think of stories that involve both adults and fourth graders. Then ask each group to prepare a skit to present to the class. Give the students time to prepare. Visit each group while they are rehearsing their skit, offering assistance where needed. Afterward, invite each group to perform its skit for the class.

Help the students understand that we can both forgive and be forgiven.

Reviewing the Lesson

To check that they understand the meaning of the new vocabulary word, ask the students to use the word *reconciliation* in a sentence. Read through the We Believe statements omitting key words. Have the students fill in the missing words.

Objective

This lesson helps the students learn a story about God's mercy.

Step 1 / INTRODUCTION

Learning About Our Lives

Discussing Mistakes

Encourage the students to think about what happens when they make a serious mistake and have to tell someone about it. Ask:

- How did you feel?
- What makes admitting mistakes hard?
- What helps make admitting a mistake easier?

Assist the students in understanding that admitting mistakes is easier for us when we know we will be forgiven.

Step 2 / DEVELOPMENT

Learning About Our Faith

Reading the Scripture Story

Read aloud the title and first paragraph introducing the gospel story on page 184. Guide the students in understanding that God gives us merciful and forgiving people like our parents so that we can learn of God's mercy. Read the story with the class.

Discussing the Scripture Story

Discuss the story, using the questions below.

- What did the younger son want? (*His inheritance, his share of the family's money*)
- Where did he go when he got the money? (*To another country*)
- Why did he have to go to work? (*He spent all his money.*)
- What kind of work did he do? (*Took care of pigs*)
- What did the son think about? (*How everyone had enough to eat at his father's home*)
- What did he decide to do? (*Ask his father to take him back as a servant*)
- How did the father feel toward his son? (*Loving and forgiving*)

184

In the following Scripture story, we learn that when people forgive each other they are imitating God, who is always ready to forgive. We also learn that we will be forgiven by God every time we ask.

A Merciful Father

One day, Jesus told this story about a merciful father. A man had two sons. One day his younger son came to him. "Father," the young man said, "please give me my share of the **inheritance**."

The father gave him his share. The younger son gathered up his belongings and left home to start a new life in a foreign country. There he lived a wild life and wasted all his money, until he had nothing left.

So the young man went to work for a farmer. The farmer put him to work caring for the pigs. The young man worked hard but did not make much money. Sometimes he was so hungry that he wanted to eat the pigs' food. Finally, the young man thought about his home. "Even my father's servants have enough to eat," he thought to himself, "and here I am starving. I'll go back to

184   Scripture

Enriching the Lesson

Distribute lined paper. Show the students the personal ad section of a newspaper. Read a few ads aloud to the class. Emphasize that in "A Merciful Father" the father and son did not know how to get in touch with one another. Tell the students that we have learned that God is always willing to forgive us when we are sorry. Invite the students to write two personal ads: one expressing God's willingness to forgive them when they sin and another expressing their desire to be forgiven. Invite sharing.

Teaching Tips

The parable of the Prodigal Son is found only in the Gospel of Luke, although there is a parallel theology found in Ephesians 2:1-22. The passage in Ephesians assures us of the generosity of God's plan.

my father and tell him that I'm sorry. I do not deserve to be his son. I'll ask my father to take me back as one of his servants."

The next morning the young man set out for home. He was down the road from his father's house when his father saw him. His father's heart was filled with love and forgiveness. The father ran down the road to meet his son. He hugged and kissed him.

The young man began to say that he was sorry. "Father, I have sinned against God and against you. I no longer deserve to be your son."

But the father stopped him. He called to his servants, "Hurry! Bring my son some clean clothes. Put a ring on his finger and shoes on his feet. And prepare a grand celebration. My son, who was lost, is now found." Then the father took his son into the house.

Based on Luke 15:11–24

Discuss

Why do you think the young man thought he did not deserve to be treated as a son when he returned home?

Jesus Teaches About Reconciliation

The story that Jesus told about a son who is sorry and a father who forgives is really a story about God and us. We are like the son. When we sin and are sorry for our sins, we can ask the Father's forgiveness.

God is like the father in the Scripture story. God loves us no matter what we do and is eager to show us mercy. Like a loving father, God always forgives us when we are sorry for our sins.

We imitate God when we forgive people who hurt us, just as the father in the Scripture story forgave his son. We experience the Lord's forgiveness through people who forgive us.

Vocabulary

inheritance: the money and property received from someone who has died

◆ ◆ ◆ ◆ ◆ ◆ ◆ ◆ ◆ ◆ ◆

Scripture   185

Teaching Tips

Often, some students come up with the idea that committing a sin is something of little importance or consequence since God is so willing to forgive. They reason that if they sin, they can just ask God to forgive them over and over again. Help the students understand that being truly sorry for their actions includes a resolution to do better.

■ What did the father do? (*He took his son home; asked for clean clothes, a ring, and shoes for his son; and called for a celebration.*)

Discuss the phrase, "My son, who was lost, is now found." Help them understand that the son was "lost" to the father because they were separated from one another. The father did not know where the son was. He couldn't talk to his son or show his love for him. When the son came back home, it was like finding something that was lost. The father was happy.

Participating in a Discussion

Have the students discuss the question on page 185. Encourage all students to share their ideas.

Understanding God's Forgiveness

Tell the students that Jesus wants us to discover something about ourselves and about God when we read this story. Ask for volunteers to read aloud "Jesus Teaches About Reconciliation" on page 185. Emphasize that God is always willing to welcome us back when we express sorrow for our sins.

Step 3 / CONCLUSION

Learning How to Live Our Faith

Meditating

Invite the students to think of a time when they needed forgiveness. Then have the students choose a partner and sit side by side. If a student is without a partner, have them do this meditation exercise with you. Explain that the students will have a chance to imagine that they are the son and also the father in the story. Ask all the students on the right of their partner to raise their hands.

Tell the students on the right to close their eyes and imagine being the "son." Invite them to think of how much they have hurt the father and want to be forgiven. The students can assume a posture that expresses their need for forgiveness, such as bending their heads. Tell their partners to imagine being the "father," who feels great love, joy, and forgiveness toward the "son." Allow the students a few moments to meditate like this, and then direct them to reverse roles so that they have the opportunity to feel the need for forgiveness and be forgiven.

DAY 3
MORALITY

Objective

This lesson helps the students consider the difficulties of asking for and giving forgiveness.

Step 1 / INTRODUCTION

Learning About Our Lives

Reading and Discussing a Story

Direct the students' attention to "Maria's Birthday Present" on page 186. Ask volunteers to take turns reading the story aloud. Ask:

- What did Maria want for a long time? (*A pair of in-line skates*)

- When did Maria get the skates? (*Her parents bought them for her tenth birthday.*)

- What was the one rule Maria's parents expected her to follow? (*No skating in the street.*)

- What did Maria promise? (*Never to skate in the street.*)

- Why did Maria skate in the street? (*She was becoming more skilled and the sidewalk seemed too confining.*)

- What happened while Maria was skating in the street? (*A car had to skid to a stop to avoid hitting her.*)

- Why did Maria need courage as she headed for home? (*She knew that her parents already knew about the incident. She also knew that her parents would be angry and disappointed.*)

Ask the students if they have had similar experiences. Give the students the opportunity to exchange stories with a partner.

Step 2 / DEVELOPMENT

Learning About Our Faith

Learning the Way to Forgiveness

Ask a volunteer to read aloud "The Way to Forgiveness" on page 187. Emphasize the importance of both being sincerely sorry for what we have done and making a decision never to do it again when we ask for forgiveness. Ask the students to recall a

186

Maria's Birthday Present

Ever since she was in the second grade, Maria had wanted a pair of in-line skates. So, for her tenth birthday, Maria's parents took her shopping to buy the long-desired skates and the necessary safety equipment.

On the way home, Maria's parents made it clear: No skating in the street! EVER!

"Oh, no!" Maria promised, "I will never, never go in the street."

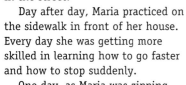

Day after day, Maria practiced on the sidewalk in front of her house. Every day she was getting more skilled in learning how to go faster and how to stop suddenly.

One day, as Maria was zipping down the sidewalk, instead of stopping where the sidewalk ended, she continued on the street. She looked at the wide street in front of her. This was really going to be exciting!

She was proud of how skillfully she skated down the hill. Suddenly, there was a car in front of her! The driver skidded to a screeching stop, leaving long black marks on the street. Maria glided on past the car, her heart pounding like a hammer.

It was a long time before Maria finally worked up her courage and headed for home. She knew that her parents would already know of the dangerously close call she had just had. After all, the driver of the car was their next door neighbor.

186 Morality

CURRICULUM CONNECTION

Music   Sing with the students verses three and four of "You Are the Way" on page 122 of THIS IS OUR FAITH *Hymnal* or page 12 of THIS IS OUR FAITH *Teacher's Songbook*, Grade 4.

The Way to Forgiveness

When we want forgiveness, three things are necessary.

1. We must be sincerely sorry for what we have done.
2. We must say that we are sorry and ask forgiveness.
3. We must make a firm decision never to do it again.

We make these three promises to ourselves and to the person who forgives us. The promises are necessary when we ask forgiveness from God as well.

Activity

On the lines below, finish the story about Maria and her in-line skates. Tell what happened when she went into the house. Tell about Maria's need for forgiveness and reconciliation.

_____

_____

_____

_____

_____

_____

_____

_____

Morality 187

time when they were forced by a teacher or a parent to apologize to someone for something they had done. Help the students understand that in these situations, there usually is not a sincere desire for forgiveness.

Step 3 / CONCLUSION

Learning How to Live Our Faith

Writing an Ending to the Story

Point out the writing activity on page 187. Ask a volunteer to read the directions aloud. Give the students sufficient time to write their story endings, working independently. Afterward, invite the students to share their endings. Do not let the students forget that a reconciliation also needs to happen between Maria and the neighbor.

Objective

This lesson helps the students understand that we are called to forgive others.

Step 1 / INTRODUCTION

Learning About Our Lives

Reflecting on Forgiving Others

Ask the students to think of three reasons why it is sometimes difficult to forgive others. Invite the students to share their ideas as you list them on the chalkboard. Help the students understand that we are called to be forgiving always, not just when it is easy. Tell the students that they are going to read about a young man who has a difficult time forgiving his father and brother. Ask the students to try to figure out why he is having such a difficult time being forgiving.

Step 2 / DEVELOPMENT

Learning About Our Faith +

Reading and Discussing a Scripture Story

Ask volunteers to take turns reading aloud the Scripture story on page 188. Then ask:

- Where was the older son when his brother returned home? (*He was out working in the field.*)
- What did the older brother hear on his way home from the field? (*The sounds of a party*)
- What did the servant tell the older brother when he asked about the reason for the party? (*"Your brother has returned home. Your father is so happy that he is having a great feast."*)
- How did the older son react? (*He was angry and refused to go to the party.*)
- Why was the older brother so angry? (*He had always worked hard, obeyed his father, and the father had never given him a party.*)

 or . . .

Dramatize the story. Choose students to play the roles of a narrator, the father, the two sons, the servant, and the people at the party. Give the students a few minutes to rehearse and then have them perform the dramatization.

Continue reading the story that Jesus told about the merciful father.

A Merciful Father 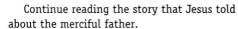 *(continued from pages 184, 185)*

While the father had been greeting his returning son, the older son was still out working in the field. As he was returning home from his day's labor, he heard the sounds of a party. He called to one of the servants and asked the reason for the party.

The servant answered, "Your brother has returned home. Your father is so happy that he is having a great feast."

The older son grew angry when he heard this and he would not join the festivities. But his father came out and began to plead with him.

The son said to his father, "For years I have stayed and worked for you. I never disobeyed one of your orders. Yet you never even let me have a party for my friends. Now, when my brother returns after wasting your money, you welcome him home with a celebration."

"My son," replied the father, "you are with me always. Everything I have is yours. But we have to celebrate and rejoice! Your brother was lost and now he is found."

Based on Luke 15:25–32

188 Scripture

 **CURRICULUM CONNECTION**

Music   Play the song "The Prodigal Son" from the record or cassette *Show Me Your Smile* (Joe Wise, NALR, available from Oregon Catholic Press, 5536 N.E. Hassalo St., Portland, OR 97213). Emphasize the father's joy at his son's return. Talk with the students about how the father might have acted if he were not a forgiving, merciful person. Remind the students that the father's mercy and love are examples of God's mercy and love.

Focus on

Forgiveness of Sins   When we say the Creed, we state our belief in the forgiveness of sins, faith in the Holy Spirit, in the Church, and in the communion of saints. "Baptism is the . . . chief sacrament of forgiveness of sins." Christ gave the disciples the power to forgive sins, and our sins are forgiven through the blood of Jesus and the action of the Holy Spirit, "normally in the sacrament of Penance" (*Catechism of the Catholic Church*, 981, 984–986). As God forgives us, so must we forgive others.

Called to Forgive Others

Just as God is merciful with us, we must be merciful with one another. In the Scripture story, "A Merciful Father," it wasn't enough for the father to forgive his son and welcome him home. The boy's father urged the older son to do the same.

We are like the older son. Jesus calls us to forgive our brothers and sisters, neighbors, friends, parents, and any one else who asks our forgiveness.

Even though it is often difficult to forgive others, many people in our lives give us wonderful examples. Each time our families forgive us, they show us how to forgive. Each time our friends and classmates are merciful with us, we learn how to be merciful with others.

Jesus is our greatest teacher of mercy and forgiveness. In many gospel stories, we can read about Jesus forgiving others. Even as Jesus was dying on the cross, he forgave the people who put him there.

Activity

Read the story below. Then on the lines below the story, write the advice you would offer to each person.

Jessica was very helpful at home last week. But Dad asked Jessica's brother to go to the soccer game instead of inviting her. Jessica stormed up the steps and slammed the door of her bedroom when she found out.

Dad looked at Joe and asked, "What should we do now?" Joe didn't know what to say.

My advice to Jessica is _____.

My advice to Jessica's dad is _____.

My advice to Joe is _____.

Scripture 189

189

Objective

This lesson helps the students to pray a prayer of mercy.

Talking About Forgiveness

Help the students appreciate that God forgives us in many ways. God's forgiveness can come to us when we are alone. Tell the students that we can also experience God's mercy through others. Invite them to discuss times when they experienced God's mercy when they were alone or through the forgiveness of others.

Completing an Acrostic

Recall that God is merciful. On the chalkboard write vertically the word *MERCY* in capital letters. Encourage the class to use this word to make an acrostic. Stress that this acrostic has many answers. Note the following example.

When you com**M**it a sin,

rem**E**mber God's love.

Say you are so**R**ry.

Celebrate.

You are forgiven.

Encourage each student to write a mercy acrostic and copy it on the chalkboard for all to see.

Introducing a Prayer of Mercy

Invite a volunteer to read aloud the first paragraph of "Praying a Prayer of Mercy" on page 190. Have the entire class repeat the words *Kyrie eleison* and *Christe eleison* after you. Ask the class the meaning of these words.

Praying Together

Create a prayerful environment, and invite the students to bring their books with them as they gather for prayer. Pray together the prayer of mercy as outlined on page 190. You might like to conclude by singing together "You Are the Way" on page 90 of the THIS IS OUR FAITH *Hymnal* or page 12 of the THIS IS OUR FAITH *Teacher's Songbook*, Grade 4.

190

Praying a Prayer of Mercy

Kyrie Eleison is a prayer that we often pray at Mass. The Greek words *Kyrie eleison* mean, "Lord, have mercy." For hundreds of years, the Church used the Greek words to pray this prayer. Now it is usually prayed in the language of the people. Kyrie Eleison is a prayer praising the Lord's great kindness and merciful love.

Teacher: Let us pray.

All: In the name of the Father, and of the Son, and of the Holy Spirit. Amen.

Teacher: Let us ask the Lord's mercy on us all. Kyrie eleison.

Students: Kyrie eleison. Lord, have mercy.

Teacher: Christe eleison.

Students: Christe eleison. Christ, have mercy.

Teacher: Kyrie eleison.

Students Kyrie eleison. Lord, have mercy.

Teacher: Let us pray together a psalm in praise of God's mercy.

All: The Lord is merciful and loving,
slow to become angry and full of kindness.
As high as the sky is above the earth,
so great is God's love for those who love the Lord.
As far as the east is from the west,
so far does God put our sins from us.
As a father understands his children,
so God understands those who honor the Lord.

Based on Psalm 103:8–13

190 Prayer

Cultural Awareness

Point out to the students that the language of origin of *Kyrie Eleison* is Greek. Help the students appreciate the richness of praying in different languages. If you or your students are fluent in languages other than English, pray the Prayer of Mercy aloud in those languages as well.

Chapter Review

Name three things that are necessary for forgiveness.

1. <u>to be sincerely sorry</u>

2. <u>to ask forgiveness</u>

3. <u>to promise not to do it again</u>

In this chapter you have read three stories about forgiveness and reconciliation. Fill in the blanks to complete the sentences.

1. <u>Jesus</u> teaches us about reconciliation in the Scripture story about a merciful father.

2. _____ is always willing to forgive us. We can learn how to be forgiving people by following our <u>parents'</u> example when they forgive us.

On the lines provided, write your answers to the first two questions.

1. What is meant by *reconciliation*?

<u>Reconciliation means making up through sorrow</u>
<u>and forgiveness.</u>

2. When does God forgive us?

<u>God is merciful and forgiving. God keeps on</u>
<u>loving us when we sin. The Lord is eager to forgive</u>
<u>us when we show that we are sorry for our sins.</u>

3. Discuss ways that people experience God's mercy and forgiveness.

> **The Lord is kind and merciful. God forgives our sins.**
> Based on Sirach 2:11

★ ★★★ ★
Enriching the Lesson

Distribute writing paper. Invite the students to consider if it is more difficult to forgive someone who has hurt us, or to ask forgiveness from someone we have hurt. Ask them to copy and complete the following sentences: "It's easier to forgive when . . . " "It's easier to ask forgiveness when . . . " Emphasize that God calls us always to forgive those who ask for our forgiveness.

Reviewing Forgiveness and Reconciliation

Direct the students to write the three things necessary for forgiveness. Have them continue with the fill in exercise based on the stories read in the chapter.

Reviewing the Chapter

Call attention to the two review questions at the bottom of the page. Direct the students to write their answers on the lines provided. Afterward, invite the students to share their responses with the class. Encourage all to participate in the discussion of the third item.

Reading the Scripture Verse

Read aloud the verse from Sirach. Help the students understand that God forgives our sins because he is kind and merciful. Encourage the class to memorize the Scripture verse.

16 Bringing God's Forgiveness

Objectives

To help the students

- Understand that Jesus was forgiving.
- Appreciate Jesus' mercy and his willingness to forgive everyone.
- Understand that Jesus brings us God's forgiveness through his teaching.
- Recognize that Jesus brings us God's forgiveness through the sacraments.
- Pray with Mass prayers and review the chapter.

Chapter Outline

	Step 1 **Learning About Our Lives**	**Step 2** **Learning About Our Faith**	**Step 3** **Learning How to Live Our Faith**
Day 1	■ Introduce the chapter. ■ Understand and discuss a picture story. *ABOUT 15 MINUTES*	■ Introduce the Scripture story. ■ Read and discuss the Scripture story. ■ Learn the vocabulary. *ABOUT 10 MINUTES*	■ Answer the discussion questions. *ABOUT 5 MINUTES*
Day 2	■ Talk about forgiving. ■ Write and share stories. ■ Describe models of forgiveness. *ABOUT 12 MINUTES*	■ Study the illustration. ■ Read about Jesus' forgiveness. ■ Review the doctrine. ■ Learn the vocabulary. *ABOUT 6 MINUTES*	■ Locate passages from Scripture. ■ Complete an activity. *ABOUT 12 MINUTES*
Day 3	■ Express sorrow and forgiveness. *ABOUT 7 MINUTES*	■ Understand Jesus' message. ■ Pray The Lord's Prayer. *ABOUT 8 MINUTES*	■ Study The Lord's Prayer. *ABOUT 15 MINUTES*
Day 4	■ Recognize signs of forgiveness. *ABOUT 10 MINUTES*	■ Read about and discuss the sacraments. *ABOUT 15 MINUTES*	■ Identify sacraments. *ABOUT 5 MINUTES*
Day 5	**Prayer** Prepare to pray with Mass prayers and pray together. **Review** Complete the sentences; review the chapter; discuss ways to forgive; and read the Scripture verse.		

Correlation to the Catechism of the Catholic Church

Paragraphs
587–591, 594, 1279, 1393, 1446, 2227, 2845, 2862

Plan Ahead

	Preparing Your Class	**Materials Needed**
Day 1	Read through the lesson plan.	■ pencils or pens ■ magazines and newspapers
Day 2	Read the lesson plan. If using the curriculum connection, find examples of artwork that illustrate Jesus' compassion.	■ pencils or pens ■ lined paper
Day 3	Read through the lesson plan. You might want to obtain a recording of a musical setting of The Lord's Prayer.	■ pencils or pens ■ recording of The Lord's Prayer
Day 4	Read through the lesson plan.	■ pencils or pens
Day 5	Read through the lesson plan.	■ pencils or pens ■ Bible, candle ■ prayer cloth

Additional Resources

As you plan this chapter, consider using the following materials from The Resourceful Teacher Package.

■ *Classroom Activity Sheets 16* and *16a*

■ *Family Activity Sheets 16* and *16a*

■ *Chapter 16 Test*

■ *Prayers for Every Day*

■ *Projects: Grade 4*

You may also wish to refer to the following Big Book

■ *We Celebrate God's Word,* pages 11–14

■ *We Celebrate the Sacraments,* pages 2, 3, 4, 7, 13, 16

In preparing the students for the Sunday readings, you may wish to use Silver Burdett Ginn's *Getting Ready for Sunday* student and teacher materials.

BOOKS FOR THE JOURNEY

The Children's Illustrated Bible. "Peter's Denial," pp. 268–269. Retold by Selina Hastings. Dorling Kindersley, 1994. The story of Peter denying Jesus with additional information and illustrations.

The Golden Carp. "The Ogre's Victim," pp. 29–49. Lynette Dyer Vuong. Lothrop, Lee & Shepard, 1993. A magical story of being wronged and yet being completely forgiving.

MORE BOOKS FOR THE JOURNEY

Hey World, Here I Am! "Growing Pains," pp. 8–9. Jean Little. Harper & Row, 1986. A special poem about how complicated the feelings can be when someone says, "I'm sorry."

Somewhere in the Darkness. Walter Dean Myers. Scholastic, Inc., 1992. The story of a father who wants to be understood, accepted, and forgiven by his son.

REDUCED CLASSROOM ACTIVITIES

NAME _____

BRINGING GOD'S FORGIVENESS

In groups of six, dramatize the story "Jesus Forgave His Friend."

Narrator 1: The enemies of Jesus had taken him to the home of the high priest to be put on trial.

Narrator 2: While this was going on, Jesus' enemies waited outside.

Rebecca: You were with Jesus, weren't you, Peter?

Peter: No, I don't even know this man.

Narrator 1: Peter was so afraid. He hoped that no one would remember that he was a friend of Jesus.

Samuel: You are one of the friends of Jesus. I can remember seeing you with him many, many times.

Peter: No, I tell you, no! You are very much mistaken. I am not one of them.

Narrator 2: An hour later a man seemed sure that Peter was one of the friends of Jesus. He began to speak to the crowd.

Josh: I am certain that this man was with Jesus. Can't you see that he is a Galilean?

Peter: I don't know what you are talking about, my friend.

Narrator 1: The soldiers then led Jesus out of the high priest's house. Jesus saw Peter and looked at him with great sadness.

Peter: *(sadly)* My heart is full of sadness. I am so sorry for what I have done. I know, Jesus, that you will forgive me if I just ask you.

Narrator 2: Peter ran out of the yard. He sat down beside the road and cried for a long time.

To the Teacher: This activity follows the story "Jesus Forgave His Friend."

Chapter 16 *Bringing God's Forgiveness*   THIS IS OUR FAITH 4   **16**

NAME _____

A PERSONAL INTERVIEW

Imagine that you are interviewing Jesus after he saw that Peter had denied knowing him. Write the questions you would ask and the answers you think Jesus would give you.

1. Question: _____
   _____

   Jesus' answer: _____
   _____
   _____
   _____

2. Question: _____
   _____

   Jesus' answer: _____
   _____
   _____

3. Question: _____
   _____

   Jesus' answer: _____
   _____
   _____

To the Teacher: This activity will help students personalize this Scripture story.

16a THIS IS OUR FAITH 4   **Chapter 16** *Bringing God's Forgiveness*

FORGIVENESS

The students have experienced moments of hurt and healing in their daily lives. They know what it is to be forgiven and to forgive. Through these experiences they can understand the mercy of Jesus, who extends God's forgiveness to them and the people around them. Story after story in the Gospels reveal the compassion of Jesus. Familiar names are those of forgiven sinners: Zacchaeus, Magdalene, Peter, and the Good Thief. From the cross, Jesus forgave even the people who caused him such humiliation, torture, and death. In the Gospels, Jesus only spoke harshly to those who refused to repent their sins or to show mercy to others.

THE HIGH PRIEST

Jesus knew from personal experience about human weakness. He knew well that all of us, at times do what we know to be wrong. Paul's letter to the Hebrews calls Jesus the high priest who is able to sympathize with our weaknesses . . . who was tempted in every way that we are, yet never sinned (based on Hebrews 4:15). Jesus wants us to extend his mercy to others. He tells us, when he speaks of the penitent woman who washed his feet with her tears and dried them with her hair, that her many sins were forgiven because of her great love (see Luke 7:47).

Jesus is not interested in our worshipful acts if we do not love and forgive other people. In Matthew's Gospel, he said, "Go and learn the meaning of the words, 'I desire mercy, not sacrifice.' I did not come to call the righteous but sinners." (Matthew 9:13).

The risen Christ brings God's forgiveness to those who turn away from sin and come back to him. When we think of forgiveness, the sacrament of Reconciliation comes to mind. Saint Augustine had said that when the priest absolves, it is Christ who absolves. Even though the sacrament of Reconciliation is the clearest means of God's forgiveness, each of the sacraments in its own way is also a sign of penance and reconciliation. In Baptism, our sins are first washed away. In Eucharist, we have Christ's great sign of community reconciliation. In the ritual of Anointing of the Sick, forgiveness is also experienced.

The sacraments celebrate Christ's forgiveness in the daily round of life. We encounter God's forgiveness in the ebb and flow of contrition and forgiveness in our family lives and in our friendships. You can help the students value the responsibility to be forgiving.

Objective

This lesson helps the students understand that Jesus was forgiving.

Step 1 / INTRODUCTION

Learning About Our Lives

Introducing the Chapter

Instruct the students to open their books to page 192 and silently read the chapter title and focus statements. Elicit the students' responses. Tell the class that in this session they will learn that Jesus brings us God's mercy and forgiveness.

or...

Instruct the students to look through news magazines and newspapers that you have brought to class. Ask them to find pictures and stories about people in need of God's forgiveness. Then have them show and tell about their pictures or stories and explain why they chose them. Remind the class that God always loves us and that God wants us to recognize our sins, be sorry for them, and seek reconciliation.

Understanding and Discussing a Picture Story

Direct attention to the picture story. Ask volunteers to describe what is happening in each frame.

Direct the students to write their own endings to the story. Emphasize that Melissa enjoyed listening and is disappointed that the player is broken. You might also explain that it takes humility to admit when we have done something wrong. If Jake can say he is sorry and accept Melissa's forgiveness, then they can be friends again.

Discuss the students' endings. Recall that God wants us to live together in peace. You might explain that God always forgives us and that he expects us to forgive others.

192

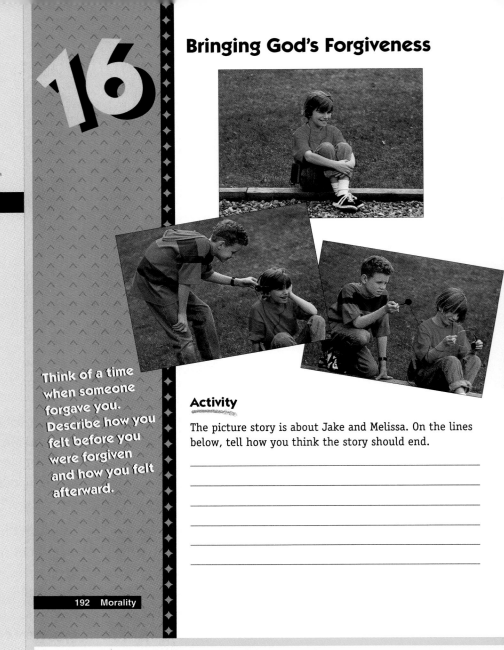

16 Bringing God's Forgiveness

Think of a time when someone forgave you. Describe how you felt before you were forgiven and how you felt afterward.

Activity

The picture story is about Jake and Melissa. On the lines below, tell how you think the story should end.

_____

_____

_____

_____

_____

_____

192   Morality

⭐ Enriching the Lesson ⭐

Select students to play the parts of Peter, Jesus, the three accusers, and the crowd. Have the students act out the Scripture story as you read it aloud. Or, you might like to ask a volunteer to read the story aloud.

CURRICULUM CONNECTION

Social Studies   Have the students turn to the map of the Holy Land on page 329 in their books. Help them to find Galilee. Explain that the story "Jesus Forgave His Friend" took place in Jerusalem, which is many miles away from Galilee.

Jesus Forgives His Friend

The enemies of Jesus had taken him to the home of the high priest. Jesus was questioned there. While this was going on, Jesus' enemies waited outside.

It was a cool night so they lit a fire in the yard to keep warm. One of Jesus' disciples, Peter, sat with them. He was afraid. Peter hoped that no one would remember that he was a friend of Jesus.

A servant girl noticed Peter. She stared at him for a while. Then she pointed to Peter and said, "This man was with Jesus."

"You're wrong," Peter answered. "I don't even know Jesus."

A few minutes later a man looked carefully at Peter. "You are one of Jesus' friends," he said.

Peter answered, "No, I am not one of them."

About an hour later another person was sure that Peter was one of Jesus' friends. "This man was certainly with Jesus, for he is a **Galilean**," the person said to those around the fire.

Again Peter said, "Woman, I don't know what you are talking about."

Just then soldiers led Jesus out of the high priest's house. Peter looked at Jesus. Jesus saw Peter and knew that Peter's heart was filled with sadness. Peter was sorry for what he had done. He knew that Jesus forgave him.

Peter ran out of the yard. He sat down beside the road and cried for a long time.

Based on Luke 22:54–62

Vocabulary

Galilean: someone from Galilee, the land north of Samaria

✦ ✦ ✦ ✦ ✦ ✦ ✦ ✦ ✦ ✦ ✦

Scripture **193**

★ ★★★ ★ Enriching the Lesson ★

Explain to the students that in the Scripture story Peter was trying to be brave, but without Jesus being there to help him, it was difficult to be brave. It was out of fear that Peter denied knowing Jesus. But one look from Jesus filled Peter with sorrow for being disloyal, because Peter remembered how much Jesus loved him.

Learning About Our Faith

Introducing the Scripture Story

Explain that the story "Jesus Forgives His Friend" is a continuation of the Scripture story the students read in Chapter 14. Jesus had been arrested and taken to the home of the high priest. Peter was outside in the yard. He had followed at a distance because he was worried about his friend, Jesus, but he was also frightened.

Reading and Discussing the Scripture Story

Read the story along with the students. Then ask:

- Why was Peter afraid? (*Because Jesus was arrested, Peter thought he might be, too.*)
- Who noticed Peter first? (*A servant girl*)
- What did she say? (*"This man was with Jesus."*)
- How did Peter answer her? (*"I don't even know Jesus."*)
- Who else noticed Peter? (*A man*)
- What did Peter say when the man accused him of being a friend of Jesus? (*"I am not one of them."*)
- What was Peter's answer when the third person said he was with Jesus? (*Peter said, "I don't know what you are talking about."*)
- Why did Peter keep denying that he knew Jesus? (*He was afraid; he didn't want to be caught by the enemies of Jesus.*)
- How did Peter feel when he saw Jesus? (*Very, very sad*)
- Despite his sadness, what did he know? (*That Jesus forgave him*)
- What did Peter do? (*He cried for a long time.*)

Step 3 / CONCLUSION

Learning How to Live Our Faith

Answering the Discussion Questions

Discuss the following questions.

- Have you ever been afraid to defend a friend? Why were you afraid? (Have the students relate positive and negative experiences of defending friends, parents, siblings, or teachers.)
- Have you ever been embarassed that someone would know you are a friend of Jesus? (*Answers will vary.*)

193

DAY 2
SCRIPTURE

Objective

This lesson helps the students appreciate the mercy of Jesus and his willingness to forgive everyone.

Step 1 / INTRODUCTION

Learning About Our Lives

Talking About Forgiving

Invite the students to close their eyes and think about a time when someone did something to hurt someone else and how the person was forgiven. The students might think of the following situations: someone breaking a toy, borrowing something and not returning it, or not letting someone join in a game or activity.

Writing and Sharing Stories

Distribute lined paper. Have the students write a story about their memory of forgiving. Afterward, invite sharing. Ask the students the following questions.

- Was forgiving the person who hurt you difficult?
- Why did you choose to forgive?
- How did you feel after you made up?

Compliment the students on being able to forgive.

Describing Models of Forgiveness

Call attention to the activity on page 194. Read the directions aloud and have the students complete the activity independently. Afterward, ask the students to share their responses and explain their reasons for choosing them.

Step 2 / DEVELOPMENT

Learning About Our Faith

Studying the Illustration

Direct attention to the illustration on page 194. Ask the students to describe what is happening in the illustration.

194

Activity

Complete the following sentences with ideas of your own.

1. To be a good parent, a person needs to be _____.
2. To be a good son or daughter, a person needs to be _____.
3. To be a good Christian, a person needs to be _____.

Peter. Peter cried not only because he was sorry for what he had done but also because he felt Jesus' forgiveness.

Jesus spent much of his life bringing God's mercy to people who had sinned. The gospels tell us that Jesus went from town to town, looking for people who needed human **compassion** and God's forgiveness. Jesus forgave people whom the Temple priests said could not be forgiven, even by God.

Jesus forgave Judas, who had betrayed him. Even as Jesus hung on the cross, he asked God to forgive those who were responsible for his death.

194 Scripture

 **CURRICULUM CONNECTION**

Art Show the students other pictures that illustrate Jesus' compassion. Your parish library and the local public library may be excellent sources for traditional Christian art. Tell the class that Jesus' life has inspired artists throughout history to create great works of art in his honor. Afterward, distribute drawing paper and crayons or felt-tip markers. Invite the students to draw a picture of Jesus bringing forgiveness to today's world.

 **Teaching Tips**

To assist any visually impaired students in your class, be sure to describe the illustration in detail.

When looking up a Scripture passage, follow these steps.

Example: **Matthew 9:35-37**

STEP 1: **Matthew** Find *The Gospel According to Matthew*, located in the second half of the Bible.

STEP 2: **9** Look at the tops of the pages and find *Matthew 9*. This means Matthew's Gospel, Chapter 9. Look at the pages of Matthew 9 to find the beginning of the chapter.

STEP 3: **35–37** Notice that the first sentence in Chapter 9 has been marked with a small **1**. Scan the story until you find a small verse **35**. Now read verses 35–37.

Activity

Using a Bible, locate the following gospel stories that give examples of how Jesus showed compassion for others. Then, on the lines provided, tell who received Jesus' loving compassion.

Matthew 20: 29–34

_____

Mark 1: 40–41

_____

Luke 15: 11–32

_____

Vocabulary

compassion: feeling another's pain and wanting to relieve it

◆ ◆ ◆ ◆ ◆ ◆ ◆ ◆ ◆ ◆ ◆

We Believe

Jesus came to bring God's mercy to everyone. He continues to bring God's forgiveness to those who show that they are sorry for their sins.

Reading About Jesus' Forgiveness

Ask volunteers to read aloud "Jesus Brings God's Forgiveness" on page 194. Help the students appreciate the mercy of Jesus and his willingness to forgive everyone.

Reviewing the Doctrine

Point out the We Believe statements. Ask a volunteer to read the statements aloud. Answer any questions the students may have.

Learning the Vocabulary

Call attention to the Vocabulary box. Read the definition aloud. To check the students' understanding, ask the students to write a sentence using the word *compassion*.

Step 3 / CONCLUSION

Learning How to Live Our Faith ✞

Locating Passages from Scripture

Read the explanation of how to locate passages from Scripture with the class. Distribute Bibles. Guide the students through the three steps to help them locate Matthew 9:35–37.

Completing an Activity

Read aloud the directions to the activity on page 195 and ask the class to complete it independently. Afterward, invite the students to share what they wrote.

Cultural Awareness

Remind the students that Jesus has compassion for all people, especially those who are poor, sick, or treated unfairly. Ask them to name people or groups in our world today who are in need of Jesus' compassion. List their responses on the chalkboard. Emphasize that Jesus calls us to work to ease the pain of others. Challenge the students to suggest practical actions that can help the people they named.

DAY 3
SCRIPTURE

Objective

This lesson helps the students understand that Jesus brings us God's forgiveness through his teaching.

Step 1 / INTRODUCTION

Learning About Our Lives

Expressing Sorrow and Forgiveness

Make two lists on the chalkboard. Title one list *Expressing Sorrow* and the other *Expressing Forgiveness*. Invite the students to brainstorm words and phrases that express sorrow and forgiveness.

Step 2 / DEVELOPMENT

Learning About Our Faith

Understanding Jesus' Message

Direct the students' attention to "Jesus Teaches About Forgiveness" on page 196. Ask volunteers to take turns reading aloud this section. Afterward, ask the following questions.

■ What are some examples of times that Jesus taught about forgiveness through his own example? (*Forgiving Peter, forgiving those who crucified him, and the Zaccheus story*)

■ Why did people begin asking Jesus what was expected of them? (*They saw Jesus' examples of forgiveness.*)

■ How often does Jesus say we must forgive someone? (*Seventy times seven times*)

■ What do you think Jesus means by his answer? (*Jesus asks us to have no limits to our willingness to forgive others.*)

Praying The Lord's Prayer

Invite the students to prayerfully read The Lord's Prayer on page 197. Then if possible, play a recorded musical version of this prayer for the students to listen to as they follow along in their books.

196

Jesus Teaches About Forgiveness

As Jesus went about Galilee preaching, he often taught about forgiveness. We read in the Bible about the many times Jesus taught about forgiveness by his example. We have just read about Jesus forgiving Peter. We know that even as Jesus was dying on the cross, he forgave those who crucified him. We know the story of Zacchaeus. Jesus brought God's mercy through his example and his teaching.

As the people and the disciples saw these examples of forgiveness, many began to ask Jesus what was expected of them. In the Gospel of Matthew we read about one of the times Jesus taught about forgiveness with words rather than by example.

Peter came up to Jesus and asked him this question. "Lord, when my brother does something against me, how often must I forgive him? Seven times?"

"No," Jesus replied, "not seven times. I say seventy times seven times."

Based on Matthew 18:21–22

196 Scripture

Enriching the Lesson

Explain that Jesus teaches us about forgiveness in many ways. Jesus taught about forgiveness through his example, through parables, and through his words. Distribute Bibles and ask the students to find the following passages where Jesus teaches us about forgiveness through his words.

Matthew 5:23–24
Luke 6:37
Luke 23:34
Luke 17:3–4

Teaching Tips

This might be a good time to refer the students to the section Let Us Pray in the front of the students' texts. Have them turn to page 1 and read The Lord's Prayer in English and Spanish.

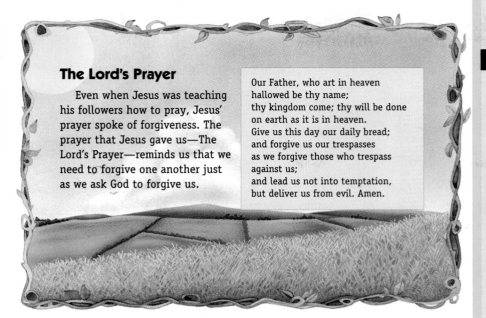

The Lord's Prayer

Even when Jesus was teaching his followers how to pray, Jesus' prayer spoke of forgiveness. The prayer that Jesus gave us—The Lord's Prayer—reminds us that we need to forgive one another just as we ask God to forgive us.

Our Father, who art in heaven
hallowed be thy name;
thy kingdom come; thy will be done
on earth as it is in heaven.
Give us this day our daily bread;
and forgive us our trespasses
as we forgive those who trespass
against us;
and lead us not into temptation,
but deliver us from evil. Amen.

Activity

Prayerfully read and think about the meaning of The Lord's Prayer. Then write the answers to the following questions.

1. With which words of the prayer do we bless God's name?

   Hallowed be thy name.

2. With which words of the prayer do we ask God's forgiveness?

   Forgive us our trespasses.

3. Which words express our promise to God that we will be forgiving?

   As we forgive those who trespass against us.

4. With which words do we ask God to keep us from the temptations and evils in the world?

   Lead us not into temptation, but deliver us from evil.

Learning How to Live Our Faith

Studying The Lord's Prayer

Have the students answer the questions at the bottom of page 197. Afterward, check their answers. Help the students appreciate that Jesus taught us The Lord's Prayer so we could learn how to praise God, thank God, and ask God for the things we need and help us forgive as we are forgiven.

Enriching the Lesson

Read the following story to the class. *You promised your mother that you would take care of your little brother while she ran an errand for Mr. Jenkins. Instead, you watched TV. When your mother got home, she discovered that your brother had gotten into her lipstick and used it to color the bedroom wall. Your mother is angry and upset. What do you do now?* Invite the students to suggest ways they could express sorrow and make up for what happened.

DAY 4
DOCTRINE

Objective

This lesson helps the students recognize that Jesus brings us God's forgiveness through the sacraments.

Step 1 / INTRODUCTION

Learning About Our Lives

Recognizing Signs of Forgiveness

Read aloud the directions to the activity on page 198. Have the class study the pictures, then write how each picture shows a sign of forgiveness. Explain that saying we are sorry is often difficult. Stress that a hug or a handshake often expresses what we mean and makes admitting what we did or offering forgiveness easier.

Step 2 / DEVELOPMENT

Learning About Our Faith

Reading About and Discussing the Sacraments

Ask volunteers to take turns reading "Forgiveness Through the Sacraments." Tell the students that when Jesus healed people, he also forgave their sins. Today, Jesus uses the sacraments to bring us very powerful forgiveness. Talk with the students about Baptism, Eucharist, Reconciliation, and Anointing of the Sick. Highlight the following points.

1. In the sacrament of Baptism, the first sacrament that we receive, Jesus welcomes us as a brother or sister; original sin is forgiven; and we begin a new life as a Christian. The Holy Spirit is given to us to help us stay close to Jesus by living the way he wants us to live.

2. When we come to Mass, we express sorrow for any sins we have committed and ask God's forgiveness. In the sacrament of the Eucharist, which we can receive when we come to Mass, Jesus forgives us. He welcomes us in love and actually shares his life with us. The Eucharist gives us the strength to be loving as Jesus is loving.

198

Activity

Words are only one sign that expresses forgiveness. On the line next to each photograph, name the sign of forgiveness being offered.

Forgiveness Through the Sacraments

God invites us to be forgiven and to be forgiving people. God's forgiveness comes to us through the many ways people forgive each other. Catholics believe that Jesus also brings us God's forgiveness through the Church's sacraments.

In the sacrament of Baptism we become a part of a people who are both forgiven and forgiving. Through Baptism, original sin and all other sins are forgiven.

In the sacrament of the Eucharist, we share in the peace that Jesus won for us by his death and resurrection. The Church teaches that the Eucharist is an important source of reconciliation.

Doctrine 198

★ Enriching the Lesson ★

Distribute writing paper. Have the students write a prayer thanking Jesus for the sacraments of forgiveness. Afterward, invite the students to pray aloud the prayers they have written. Conclude by praying together The Lord's Prayer.

Focus on

Reconciliation and the Eucharist The Church teaches that the Eucharist is the *primary* source of reconciliation in the Church. Within our Eucharistic assembly reconciliation begins with the Penitential Rite. As we pray the Our Father, we ask forgiveness and promise to forgive others. Then to give action to our words, we share a sign of peace with one another. We continue to petition forgiveness during the breaking of the bread as we pray, *Lamb of God, you take away the sins of the world, have mercy on us . . .*

In the sacrament of Reconciliation, we celebrate forgiveness and peace. When we celebrate this sacrament, we celebrate God's faithful mercy and forgiveness.

When we are sick, the sacrament of Anointing of the Sick brings us Jesus' forgiveness, healing, and peace.

Activity

The photographs below show the four sacraments through which Jesus brings us God's forgiveness. Write the names of the sacraments shown to complete the sentences.

1. Jesus forgives through

_____.

2. Jesus forgives through

_____.

3. Jesus forgives through

_____.

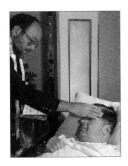

4. Jesus forgives through

_____.

Doctrine 199

3. In the sacrament of Reconciliation, we confess what we have done wrong to offend God and others. When we speak to the priest, we are also speaking to Jesus who forgives the sins we have confessed and any other sins in our lives for which we are sorry. We are freed of the guilt. In God's eyes it is as though we never sinned.

4. In the sacrament of Anointing of the Sick, the priest anoints with holy oil to bring us forgiveness of sin and strength for body and mind.

Step 3 / CONCLUSION

Learning How to Live Our Faith

Identifying Sacraments

Ask a volunteer to read the directions to the activity on page 199. Direct the students to identify the sacrament shown in each photograph. Check the students' responses.

DAY 5
PRAYER/REVIEW

Objective

This lesson helps the students pray with Mass prayers.

Preparing to Pray with Mass Prayers

Ask volunteers to take turns reading aloud the Mass prayer on page 200 taken from the *Eucharistic Prayer for Masses with Children II*. Give the students a few minutes to read the prayer over a few times to help them become familiar with the words.

Praying Together

Create a prayerful environment and gather the students for prayer. Explain to the students that they are going to echo the prayer phrase by phrase as you pray it aloud. Then ask the class to pray together with you the sections marked All, while you pray the section marked Teacher.

Praying the Eucharistic Prayer

The Eucharistic Prayer is the great prayer of thanks prayed at Mass during the Liturgy of the Eucharist. In this prayer the priest thanks God for all the gifts of creation and especially for God's greatest gift, Jesus.

During the Eucharistic Prayer, we remember Jesus' sacrifice on the cross. We hear the priest pray the same words that Jesus used at the Last Supper.

At the end of the Eucharistic Prayer, we join the priest in praying together the Great Amen. Our Amen says that we add our consent to the great prayer of thanks the priest just prayed. We are indeed grateful for all God's gifts to us, especially Jesus.

Join your teacher and classmates in praying the following prayer, taken from the Eucharistic Prayer for Masses with Children II.

All: Blessed be Jesus, whom you sent
to be the friend of children and of the poor.

Teacher: He came to show us
how we can love you, Father,
by loving one another.
He came to take away sin,
which keeps us from being friends,
and hate, which makes us all unhappy.

He promised to send the Holy Spirit
to be with us always
so that we can live as your children.

All: Blessed is he who comes in the name of the Lord.
Hosanna in the highest.

200   Prayer

★ ★★★ ★ Enriching the Lesson ★

Allow the students to meditate silently. When it seems as though the students have had enough time, pray the following prayer. Invite the students to respond *Thank you, Jesus.*

Jesus, you forgive and nourish us in the sacrament of the Eucharist.

Jesus, you forgive and welcome us back in the sacrament of Reconciliation.

Jesus, you forgive us through others.

Focus on

Reconciliation and the Eucharist The Church is very clear in its teaching regarding the reconciling nature of the sacrament of the Eucharist. The words we say in prayer that ask for forgiveness occur at the start of the Communion Rite. We again acknowledge our sinfulness and we petition God's mercy in these words: *Lord, I am not worthy to receive you, but only say the word and I shall be healed.*

200

Chapter Review

Place the words in the box below into the correct sentences.

Judas   Peter   Baptism   Reconciliation   peace

1. Jesus forgave __Peter__ when he said he didn't know Jesus.

2. Jesus forgave __Judas__ even after he betrayed Jesus.

3. The sacrament of __Baptism__ forgives original sin and all other sins..

4. The sacrament of __Reconciliation__ celebrates God's faithful mercy and forgiveness.

5. In the sacrament of the Eucharist, we share in the __peace__ Jesus won for us.

Write your answers to the first two questions on the lines provided.

1. What is meant by *compassion*?

   Compassion is feeling another's pain and
   wanting to relieve it.

2. How does Jesus bring God's forgiveness to people today?

   Jesus brings God's forgiveness today to all who
   show that they are sorry for their sins. He brings
   God's forgiveness through the sacraments.

3. Discuss how we can act like Jesus and be forgiving.

Forgive as the Lord forgives you.
Colossians 3:13

Review   201

★ ★ ★ ★
Enriching the Lesson ★

Review with the students the Penitential Rite that is prayed at Mass. It can be read aloud from the parish missalette.

Completing the Sentences

Call attention to the review activity at the top of page 201. Read the directions aloud and give the students time to complete the activity independently. Afterward, check the students' answers.

Reviewing the Chapter

Direct attention to the review questions at the bottom of page 201. Instruct the students to write the answers on the lines provided.

Discussing Ways to Forgive

Remind the students that Jesus forgives us through other people. Ask them to discuss ways to show forgiveness.

Reading the Scripture Verse

Read aloud the Scripture verse. Ask the students to consider times when they were forgiven by God. Encourage them to memorize the verse.

Using the Unit Organizer

Completing a graphic organizer such as a chart or table can help the students to organize information that has been presented in the unit. Organizers can enable the students to visualize their thinking and recognize relationships among ideas. This will give the students the opportunity to understand more completely the materials they have been studying.

Completing the Organizer

Have the students turn to page 202 in their books. Read aloud the directions to the Unit Organizer activity. Then ask the students to complete the activity independently. If necessary, tell them that they may look back through the previous four chapters for help. When everyone has finished, have the students compare their responses with the class.

Looking Back: Self-Assessment

The critical reflection questions below give the students an opportunity to sharpen their thinking skills. The questions can be used as a class discussion or independent writing activity.

- Which activity in this unit did you most enjoy? Why?
- What did you learn in this unit that you think you will always remember?
- Which prayer was your favorite prayer in this unit? Why?

UNIT 4 ORGANIZER

Chapter 13: Respecting What Belongs to Others

Chapter 14: Respecting the Truth

Summarize the main ideas of each chapter in this unit.

Chapter 15: Our Merciful God

Chapter 16: Bringing God's Forgiveness

202   Unit Organizer

UNIT 4 REVIEW

Read each statement below. Then write **True** or **False** on the line in front of each statement.

1. __T__ Greed is wanting more and more things when they are not needed.

2. __F__ Cheating is one way of showing love for our neighbor.

3. __T__ When we lie, we bear false witness.

4. __T__ Reconciliation is making up through sorrow and forgiveness.

5. __T__ Envy is wanting something that belongs to another person.

6. __F__ Sometimes lying doesn't hurt anyone.

Each statement describes an action that shows we are following a certain commandment. Write the number of that commandment in the blank next to the statement.

1. __7th__ We do not take from others what belongs to them.

2. __10th__ We fight against feelings of envy in our hearts.

3. __8th__ We respect the truth.

4. __7th__ We share what we have with others.

5. __7th__ We do not cause deliberate harm to another's property.

6. __7th__ We are not careless or wasteful.

7. __8th__ We do not spread rumors or gossip about others.

8. __10th__ We give thanks for all that God has given us.

Reviewing the Unit

The purpose of the Unit Review is to reinforce the concepts presented in the previous four chapters and to check the students' understanding. After explaining the directions, give the students sufficient time to complete the two-page review. Answer any questions they may have as you check their work.

Testing

After the students have completed the Unit Review, you may wish to distribute copies of the Unit 4 Test from the Tests booklets.

Project

Have the students make buttons or stickers on the themes of this unit. Before class, trace one or more circles for each student from sheets of light-colored construction paper. Make each circle approximately 4 inches in diameter.

In class, direct the students to cut out the circles. On the chalkboard, list the themes for Unit 4.

- Respect truth.
- Respect property.
- Share good things.
- God is merciful.
- Jesus forgives.

Give out felt-tip markers. Invite the students to select one of these themes and create a sticker or button with their paper disks. Have them use pictures, words, and symbols to express how they can live these values.

UNIT **4** REVIEW

Circle the letter of the word needed to complete each sentence correctly.

1. God is always ready to _____ us when we show that we are sorry.

   (a)   punish   **(b)** forgive   **(c)**   forget

2. In the story of the merciful father, we are like the _____.

   (a)   servants   **(b)** father   **(c)** lost son

3. Jesus came to bring God's forgiveness to _____.

   (a)   everyone   **(b)** saints   **(c)** Peter

4. When we lie, we hurt _____.

   (a) ourselves   **(b)** others   **(c)** ourselves and others

5. In reconciliation, we make up through _____.

   (a) forgiveness   **(b)** sorrow   **(c)** sorrow and forgiveness

6. Jesus taught that we must forgive each other _____ times.

   (a)7   **(b)** 70   **(c)** 70 times 7

Finish the sentences below by giving one example of a sin against the commandment.

1. We sin against the seventh commandment when we

_____

2. We sin against the eighth commandment when we

_____

3. We sin against the tenth commandment when we

_____

WHEN SAYING YES SOMETIMES MEANS SAYING NO

By choosing to do what we know is right we say yes to Jesus' call to be his followers. Sometimes doing the right thing can be an unpopular choice. It may mean saying no to what our friends want us to do. We may experience doubt about our choice and worry that others might think we aren't cool. Doing the loving thing isn't always the popular thing to do. Sometimes being a follower of Jesus means risking others' disapproval.

What Should David Do?

David and two of his friends walk home from school together every day. They usually stop at the convenience store for a soft drink. Lately David's friends have been sneaking candy bars out of the store in their pockets. This has gone on for a week or two, and now they are pressuring David to do the same. They tell David that taking the candy is no big deal. The candy costs less than a dollar, and besides, it's the store owners' fault for not watching their customers. They call David "chicken".

How do you think David is feeling?

What do his friends want him to do?

What do you think David wants to do?

What do you think is the right thing for David to do?

What choice does David need to make to show that he is a follower of Jesus?

Day to Day 205

Day to Day

Objective

This lesson helps the students explore how saying *yes* to what is right might be an unpopular choice, and learn how to cope with the social ramifications of one's choice.

Introducing the Lesson

Read with the students the opening paragraph on page 205. Ask students to share how someone might feel who knows doing the right thing is going to put them at odds with what their friends want to do. (*Might feel lonely, worried, insecure, or confident, yet sad*)

Completing the Activity

Have the class read the story about David and use the questions that follow the story to guide discussion.

■ How do you think David is feeling? (*Pressured, unsure, afraid*)

■ What do his friends want him to do? (*Steal candy bars*)

■ What do you think David wants to do? (*David doesn't want to take the candy; wants his friends to stop asking him to take the candy; and wants his friends to stop taking the candy.*)

■ What do you think is the right thing for David to do? Why? (*David should tell his friends "no," and not take the candy.*)

Use this question as a way of exploring the wrongfulness of stealing, which is the larger moral issue in this dilemma. Ask students to consider whether or not David should report the stealing. Reporting the stealing puts David in a sensitive position with his peers, and could in some cases jeopardize his safety. Allow discussion on this point. Encourage students to seek advice from an adult when they are faced with situations of uncertainty such as this.

■ What choice does David need to make to show that he is a follower of Jesus? (*Not take the candy*)

Lesson continues on page 206.

Continue reading the story on page 206. Emphasize that David is again faced with a decision about the right thing to do. Ask:

■ How is David feeling when the teasing continues? (*Angry and hurt*)

■ What is David tempted to do? (*Hit his friends to get them to stop the teasing*)

■ What keeps David from hitting? (*Knowing that hurting someone, even if they have hurt you first, is not a solution that a follower of Jesus would choose.*)

Have the students write in their books their responses to the question about what David might do to help himself feel better. Allow time for students to share their answers.

Read with the students that "one of the things David decides to do is tell his friends how he feels about their teasing." Ask the students if "telling how you feel" is an easy or hard thing to do. Have them explain why. (Most students will agree that sharing feelings is a hard thing to do. There is a certain amount of risk involved in sharing something this personal— risk that the other person might not care about your feelings. Emphasize that they can show they are followers of Jesus by caring about and respecting each other's feelings.)

Review with the students what David needs to remember when telling about his feelings. Have the students write their responses on the lines provided.

Role-playing

Invite the students to role-play David telling his friends how he feels. Craft an "I feel" statement as a class before doing the role-play. (*I feel angry when you keep teasing me about stealing the candy bar. I wish you would stop.*) Call on volunteers to take the various parts. Ask class members to observe voice tone, eye contact, and body posture. Upon completion of the role-play, discuss observations. Ask the person playing David to explain how easy or difficult it was to say the I-statement.

Concluding the Lesson

Read with the class the Following Jesus section. Ask the students if they think David's decision moved him closer to who Jesus is calling him to be, or further away? Conclude by praying the prayer together with the class.

206

Let's suppose that David believes that stealing is wrong and chooses not to steal the candy. His friends continue to pressure him. They call him names and make fun of him. Even when they are away from the store, his friends still taunt him. David feels angry and hurt by their behavior.

David is unsure about what to do. David is tempted to strike out at his friends, yet he knows that fighting is a hurtful response and goes against what it means to be a follower of Jesus.

Can you think of some things David might do to help himself feel better without hurting someone else? List your ideas on the lines below.

_____

_____

_____

One of the things David decides to do is to tell his friends how he feels about their teasing. When telling how he feels, David needs to remember to

• use "I"-language. Begin by saying "I feel_____,

  when you _____."

• use a firm voice tone.

• look at the other person when speaking to them. This is called eye contact.

• stand tall. Lean your body slightly toward the other person.

Following Jesus

Just like David, we are involved in lots of different situations where we have to make decisions about how we are going to act. The choices we make can lead us closer to Jesus and the type of persons he calls us to be as his followers, or can move us farther away.

PRAYER

Jesus, wrap your love around me. Help me share your love through my words and actions. Help me follow you even when the path is difficult. Amen.

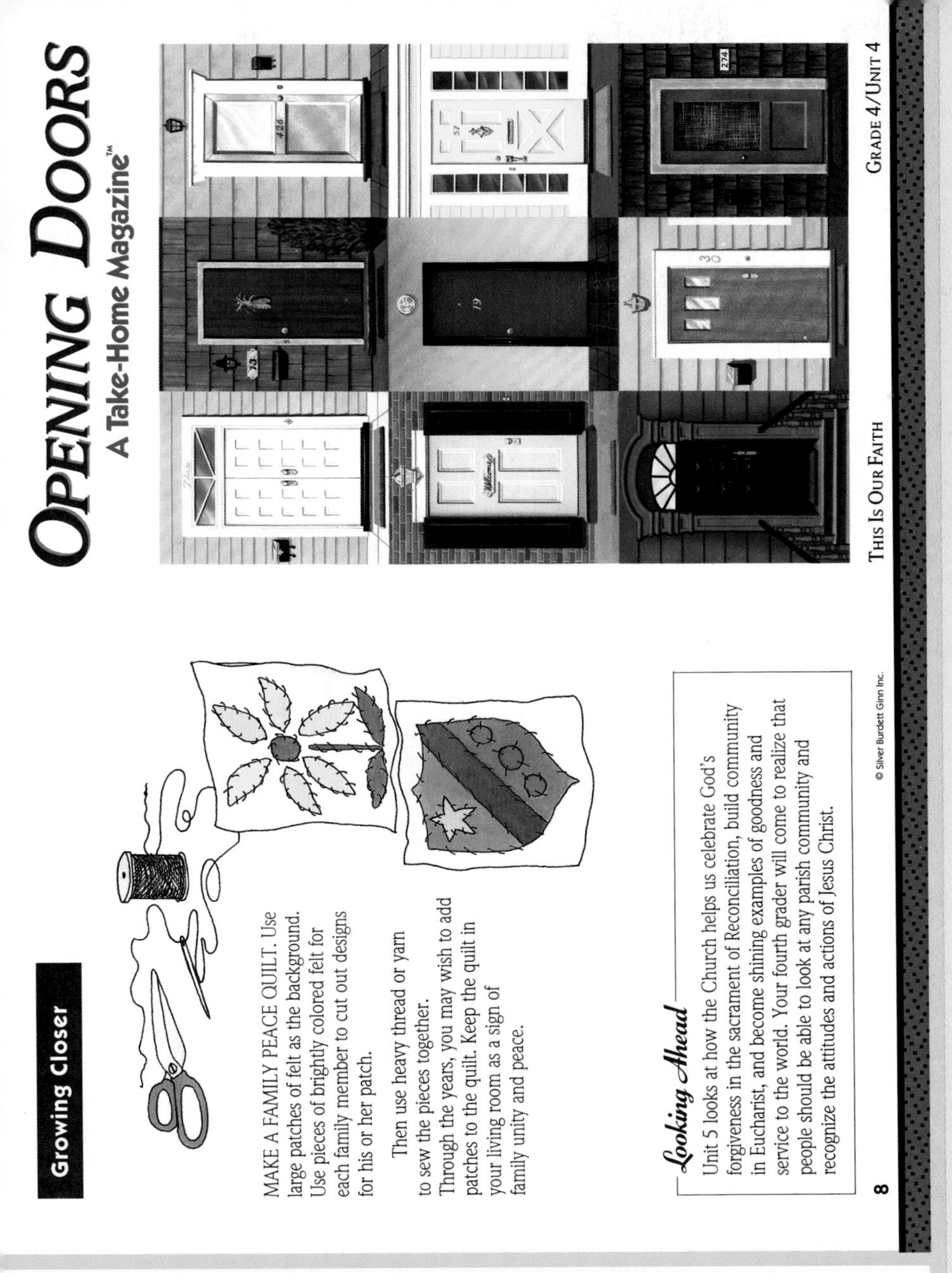

Growing Closer

MAKE A FAMILY PEACE QUILT. Use large patches of felt as the background. Use pieces of brightly colored felt for each family member to cut out designs for his or her patch.

Then use heavy thread or yarn to sew the pieces together. Through the years, you may wish to add patches to the quilt. Keep the quilt in your living room as a sign of family unity and peace.

Looking Ahead

Unit 5 looks at how the Church helps us celebrate God's forgiveness in the sacrament of Reconciliation, build community in Eucharist, and become shining examples of goodness and service to the world. Your fourth grader will come to realize that people should be able to look at any parish community and recognize the attitudes and actions of Jesus Christ.

8

OPENING DOORS

A Take-Home Magazine™

THIS IS OUR FAITH GRADE 4/UNIT 4

Opening Doors

Sending the Magazine Home

As you complete Unit 4 with your class, assist the students in carefully removing *Opening Doors: A Take-Home Magazine* (two pages) from their books by separating them from the book along the perforations. Demonstrate how to fold the two pages, forming an eight-page booklet. Ask the students to take the magazine home and encourage their families to read it with them and participate in the suggested activities.

UNMASKING PROBLEMS

The rapid rate of growth and maturation in your child may lead you to forget how fragile his or her feelings may be. You may not always be able to read your child's faces, moods, verbal or nonverbal responses to your questions, corrections, or statements.

As your child continues to mature, each choice or decision he or she makes holds more faces. And even though your child may send out messages of independence, he or she still wants clear and consistent adult direction and honesty.

When there are problems or conflicts of family life, masks of indifference or escape may be worn. To prevent this from happening, invite your child to participate with the entire family in problem solving. You may find the conflict-resolution process on page 3 helpful.

Procession to honor
Virgin del Carmen
Paucartambo, Peru

A musical procession
Qoyllur Rit'i
Cusco, Peru

Pilgrimage to the Virgin
of Copacabana, Bolivia

2

208

FACING THE ISSUES

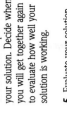

1. State the problem or conflict clearly. Sometimes you may have to weed out side issues to discover the main problem.

2. Brainstorm possible solutions to the problem. List everyone's suggestions even though you think some are far-fetched.

3. Take turns crossing off suggestions that are not acceptable. When just a few ideas remain, stop, and discuss each one carefully. Then agree on one idea or a combination of ideas.

4. Set a trial run period for your solution. Decide when you will get together again to evaluate how well your solution is working.

5. Evaluate your solution. Make adjustments if necessary. In some cases, you may have to scrap your solution because it is not working at all. You may agree then to try another idea that was first rejected.

3

Mary, a Sign of Hope

Nativity, Serigraph, Sadao Watanabe, Japan, 1970.

. . . Mary shines forth on earth, until the day of the Lord shall come as a sign of sure hope and solace for the pilgrim People of God.
(Dogmatic Constitution on the Church No. 68)

6

Facing Our Humanity

The most basic kind of honesty is being honest with ourselves before God. To help you understand this truth, Jesus told the following parable.

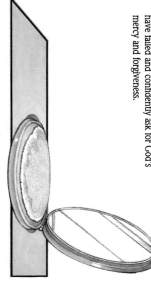

"Two people went up to the temple area to pray; one was a Pharisee and the other was a tax collector. The Pharisee took up his position and spoke this prayer to himself, 'O God, I thank you that I am not like the rest of humanity—greedy, dishonest, adulterous—or even like this tax collector. I fast twice a week, and I pay tithes on my whole income.' But the tax collector stood off at a distance and would not even raise his eyes to heaven but beat his breast and prayed, 'O God, be merciful to me a sinner.' I tell you, the latter went home justified, not the former."

Luke 18:10-14

4

During the Penitential Rite at Mass, we each have a chance to turn to God and admit our failures and sins. The priest invites us to do this in one of the following ways.

As we prepare to celebrate the mystery of Christ's love, let us acknowledge our failures and ask the Lord for pardon and strength.

Coming together as God's family, with confidence let us ask the Father's forgiveness, for he is full of gentleness and compassion.

My brothers and sisters, to prepare ourselves to celebrate the sacred mysteries, let us call to mind our sins.

We respond by honestly admitting that we have failed and confidently ask for God's mercy and forgiveness.

5

UNIT 5

Celebrating and Serving

What can we do to make the world a better place?

To help the students appreciate how the Church's celebration of Reconciliation and Eucharist fulfills our needs for forgiveness and unity. To appreciate the Church's mission to teach and serve.

Doctrinal Summaries

CHAPTER 17

In the sacrament of Reconciliation, the Church celebrates God's forgiveness.

CHAPTER 18

The Church is called to be a community. We gather at the Eucharist to celebrate our unity and to help it grow.

CHAPTER 19

The community of the Church is a light to the world. Every member of the Church is called to live a good life. In this way all people can see the true way to God and happiness.

CHAPTER 20

The Church is a servant Church. Jesus Christ calls the Church community to care for those in need and to work with those who want to build a better world.

Note:

As you prepare this unit, you may wish to refer to the reference section, *Our Catholic Heritage,* beginning on page 327.

Additional resources for Unit 5 include: a Unit Test and a Family Letter as well as a video and selections from THIS IS OUR FAITH Music Program. You might also find it helpful to preview *Saints and Other Holy People* and *Prayer Celebrations* for possibilities to enhance the unit.

Introducing the UNIT

Direct attention to the unit-focus question on page 211. Elicit the students' responses. Lead them to conclude that people can make the world a better place through kindness, caring, cooperation, and acting with love. Tell the class that in Unit 5 they will learn how the Church helps us to become better persons.

Vocabulary

examination of
  conscience
absolution
Church
Corinthians
light of the world
service

17 The Sacrament of Reconciliation

Objectives ~~~~~~

To help the students

- Learn the process of reconciliation: admit sins, ask forgiveness, and celebrate.
- Examine their conscience for the sacrament of Reconciliation.
- Learn about the sacrament of Reconciliation.
- Appreciate God's forgiveness through the sacrament of Reconciliation.
- Express sorrow for their sins and review the chapter.

Chapter Outline ~~~~~~

	Step 1 Learning About Our Lives	**Step 2** Learning About Our Faith	**Step 3** Learning How to Live Our Faith
Day 1	■ Review the previous chapter. ■ Introduce the chapter. ■ Introduce the story. ■ Read and discuss the story. *ABOUT 15 MINUTES*	■ Read about God's forgiveness. *ABOUT 5 MINUTES*	■ Write stories. ■ Pray spontaneously. *ABOUT 10 MINUTES*
Day 2	■ Talk about remembering. *ABOUT 5 MINUTES*	■ Read about examination of conscience. *ABOUT 10 MINUTES*	■ Examine our conscience. *ABOUT 15 MINUTES*
Day 3	■ Identify people. *ABOUT 7 MINUTES*	■ Read about individual and communal reconciliation. ■ Learn the vocabulary. ■ Review the doctrine. *ABOUT 15 MINUTES*	■ Read Scripture. *ABOUT 8 MINUTES*
Day 4	■ Write about celebrations. *ABOUT 10 MINUTES*	■ Read a Scripture story. ■ Discuss the meaning of the Scripture story. ■ Understand reasons to celebrate. *ABOUT 15 MINUTES*	■ Ask for God's help. *ABOUT 5 MINUTES*

Day 5 **Prayer** Understand the Act of Contrition; pray an act of contrition; and memorize the Act of Contrition.

  Review Name the four steps of reconciliation; name two ways to celebrate reconciliation; review the chapter; and read the Scripture verse.

Plan Ahead ~~~~~~~~~~~~~~

	Preparing Your Class	Materials Needed

Day 1 — Read through the entire lesson plan. Have a story about your own experience of reconciliation to share with the students.
- pencils or pens
- lined paper

Day 2 — Read through the entire lesson plan. If enriching the lesson, have one Bible for each student on hand.
- pencils or pens

Day 3 — Read through the lesson plan. If you plan to invite a priest to go through the four steps of reconciliation, make all the necessary arrangements.
- pencils or pens
- Bibles, one per student

Day 4 — Read through the lesson plan. If using the Curriculum Connection, have all the necessary art materials on hand.
- lined paper
- pencils or pens

Day 5 — Read through the lesson plan. If using the Curriculum Connection, obtain a recording of "Peace Time" by Carey Landry.
- pencils or pens
- Bible, candle
- prayer cloth
- lined paper

Additional Resources

As you plan this chapter, consider using the following materials from The Resourceful Teacher Package.

- *Classroom Activity Sheets 17* and *17a*
- *Family Activity Sheets 17* and *17a*
- *Chapter 17 Test*
- *Prayers for Every Day*
- *Projects: Grade 4*

You may also wish to refer to the following Big Book.

- *We Celebrate the Sacraments,* page 13

In preparing the students for the Sunday readings, you may wish to use Silver Burdett Ginn's *Getting Ready for Sunday* student and teacher materials.

BOOKS FOR THE JOURNEY

Frederick's Fables. "Theodore and the Talking Mushroom," pp. 93–104. Leo Lionni. Knopf, 1993. The story of a little mouse who fooled his friends, ran away, and was never reconciled with them.

The Seven Ravens. By the Brothers Grimm. Adapted by Laura Geringer. HarperCollins, 1994. How a little girl, inspired by love, by faith in forgiveness, and by the powerful desire for a family that is whole, rescued her seven brothers.

MORE BOOKS FOR THE JOURNEY

South & North East & West. "The Four Brothers," pp. 58–63. Edited by Michael Rosen. Candlewick Press, 1992. A reconciliation story of four brothers and their wives.

The Miracle Tree. Christobel Mattingley. Harcourt, Brace, Jovanovich, 1986. The story of three people, each missing one another, eventually being reunited one Christmas by a very special tree.

REDUCED CLASSROOM ACTIVITIES

NAME _____

THE SACRAMENT OF RECONCILIATION

For pages 17 and 17a, cut along the heavy black lines and fold along the dotted lines. Your teacher will use tape or glue to help you put the pages back together to make a booklet.

I say an act of contrition.

My God,
I am sorry for my sins
with all my heart.

In choosing to do wrong
and failing to do good,
I have sinned against you
whom I should love
above all things.

I firmly intend, with your
help, to do penance,
to sin no more, and to
avoid whatever leads me
to sin.

Rite of Penance

6

The priest reads a story from the Bible.
The story is about God's forgiveness.

3

The priest says, **"Go in peace."**
I answer,
"Amen."

The Sacrament of Reconciliation

✝

The priest and I thank God for being forgiving.

Name _____

8   1

To the Teacher: This two-page activity will help familiarize students with the Rite for Reconciliation of Individual Penitents. The assembled booklet can be used when students celebrate the sacrament.

Chapter 17 The Sacrament of Reconciliation   THIS IS OUR FAITH 4   **17**

NAME _____

I confess my sins.

The priest listens as I talk about how I have turned away from God and hurt myself and others.

4

The priest gives me a penance.

The priest asks me to say a prayer or do a good act. This will show God that I am sorry and want to be more caring.

5

Before I celebrate the sacrament of Reconciliation, I examine my conscience.

I think about things I have said or done to hurt God.

2

The priest gives me absolution.

The priest says,

"I absolve you from your sins in the name of the Father, and of the Son, and of the Holy Spirit."

7

17a THIS IS OUR FAITH 4   **Chapter 17** The Sacrament of Reconciliation

SIN

As we learn in the Genesis account of the first man and woman, personal sin never remains an isolated act. The effects of sin ripple outward. Pope John Paul II talks about the social effects of personal sin as well as the effects of social sin upon the individual.

In Paul's letter to the Romans we read that Christ, the second Adam, through sacrifice, reconciled us with God. After his resurrection, Christ breathed the Holy Spirit upon the disciples, thereby giving us a way to mend rifts in our relationships with God and with others.

RECONCILIATION

Human beings have a need to confess wrongful acts. The process of confessing is a challenging one. Much healing takes place in loving dialogue between friends. Jesus Christ has given us the sacrament of Reconciliation, the sanctified opportunity to repent with all our hearts. When we renounce our wrongful acts, we can be forgiven. To receive the absolving grace of the sacrament, certain conditions must be met. We must express sorrow, confess to a priest, promise to amend, or do better, and receive the Lord's forgiveness.

The priest to whom we confess represents God and the Church. The divine grace we receive frees us from the guilt of sin. As we approach the sacrament, we can pray that Jesus will speak a healing word to us through the priest. The sacrament can be received individually or communally. When we celebrate communally, we acknowledge that our sin causes rupture in the Body of Christ. We seek forgiveness both from God and from the community gathered in Christ's name.

Sin starts from the inside. It is a mixture of pride, an attitude of resentment, and willingness to reject God's offer of life and love. But when we act responsibly and repent, God always forgives. Then Christ's work of suffering, Christ's offer of healing and life is received. The truth is this: if we only have love, then there is always hope. Reconciliation involves the discovery of love. Encourage the students to participate in the celebration of this sacrament often. If at all possible, arrange for the students to receive the sacrament as part of this chapter.

There are three forms (or rites) for the celebration of the sacrament of Reconciliation: individual, or private, confession; communal penance; and communal penance with general absolution. The latter is usually celebrated when the number of penitents is disproportionately large for the number of priests present.

DAY 1
MORALITY

Objective

This lesson helps the students learn the process of reconciliation: admitting our sins, asking forgiveness, and celebrating.

Step 1 / INTRODUCTION

Learning About Our Lives

Reviewing the Previous Chapter

Remind the students that in the last chapter they learned that Jesus brings God's forgiveness. Help them recall that Peter sinned and was forgiven. Invite them to share any forgiving experiences that may have taken place in their lives since the last session. Then share a story about your reconciliation to share with the students.

Introducing the Chapter

Ask the students to turn to page 212 in their books. Invite them to read the chapter-focus question silently and spend a few moments reflecting on the different ways that they have made up with someone. Invite them to share their experiences with a partner. Then ask the students to describe how they felt after having made up with someone they have hurt. Tell them that in Chapter 17 they will learn how to make up for their sins and to begin again to lead loving lives.

Introducing the Story

Have the students think of a time when they discovered an important piece was missing from a toy, a game, or a puzzle. Ask:

■ Could you play the game with the piece missing?

■ How did you feel when you discovered the piece was missing?

Explain that in today's lesson the students will read about how a missing piece caused problems between two friends.

Reading and Discussing the Story

Read aloud the chapter title. Direct the students to read silently "The Missing Pieces." Write the following questions on the chalkboard.

■ Have you ever hurt someone you love?

212

17

The Sacrament of Reconciliation

What are some things you have done to make up with someone you have wronged or hurt?

212 Morality

The Missing Pieces

"I have a board game that I'm tired of," Becky told her best friend, Kate. "And you have two trivia games. I'll trade you my board game for one of your trivia games."

"Okay," Kate agreed. "That's a fair trade."

Becky was happy to be rid of her board game because she knew that it was missing some pieces.

That night, Kate and her grandfather decided to play the board game. After a few minutes, they realized that some of the pieces were missing. Kate was angry.

The next morning, Kate went to Becky's house. "Give back my trivia game, you cheater!" Kate shouted. "You knew there were pieces missing from the board game."

Enriching the Lesson

Invite the students to dramatize the story "The Missing Pieces." Select volunteers to act out the parts of Kate, Becky, and Becky's mother. Have another student take the part of the narrator.

For three weeks the two friends did not talk to each other. Then one Saturday morning, Becky's mother asked her daughter, "What's wrong between you and Kate?"

"We're mad at each other," Becky said. "Kate thinks I knew that the board game I traded for her trivia game was missing some pieces."

"Did you?" Becky's mother asked. When Becky did not answer, her mother said, "Becky, if you did try to cheat your friend, you need to tell Kate you are sorry. If she forgives you, then you can be friends again."

Becky thought about what her mother had said. The next day she went to Kate's house. "Kate," Becky said, "it's my fault. I did try to cheat you, and I'm sorry. I would really like to be your friend again."

"It's okay," Kate answered.

"I'll give back your trivia game," Becky promised. "Let's do something special to celebrate making up and being friends again."

Being Reconciled

Sometimes we hurt others. Then often we are sorry and want to be forgiven. We want to be reconciled. When this happens, we need to go to the person we have hurt and admit that we have done something wrong. We need to ask forgiveness.

We are unhappy when we are separated from one another. When we forgive and make up, we celebrate because we are happy to be united and forgiven.

Catholics have a very special way of celebrating God's forgiveness and expressing sorrow for sins. We call this sacramental celebration *Reconciliation* or *Penance*.

CURRICULUM CONNECTION

Art Discuss what symbols the class could draw to represent reconciliation, for example, a rainbow. Explain that a rainbow appears after a rain shower and reminds us that the gloomy skies are gone. Flowers, too, can be a symbol of reconciliation because they show new life. Invite the students to name other symbols such as a heart, two people holding hands, a cross, a dove, or a happy face. Distribute drawing materials and have the class draw their own symbols of reconciliation.

- Have you ever been hurt by a friend?
- How did you and that person make up?
- How did it feel to be at peace again?

Ask the students to think about one of the first three questions. Tell them to close their eyes as they recall what was said and done. Then have the students open their eyes. Read aloud the fourth question and invite the students to give their answers. Help them conclude that once they have made up with their friend, they feel much better. The hurt feeling is gone. Help the students focus on the positive feelings of peace, happiness, and love that come with reconciliation.

Step 2 / DEVELOPMENT

Learning About Our Faith

Reading About God's Forgiveness

Ask a volunteer to read aloud "Being Reconciled" on page 213. Emphasize the process of reconciliation: admitting our sins, asking forgiveness, and celebrating reconciliation. Help the students understand that asking for forgiveness is often difficult. Explain that if we ask God's help, he will give us strength to do this. Point out that when we have been hurt by another person, forgiving this person is sometimes difficult. Stress that prayer can help us become more forgiving.

Step 3 / CONCLUSION

Learning How to Live Our Faith

Writing Stories

Distribute lined paper. Invite the students to write original stories about reconciliation, incorporating the steps of admitting sin, asking forgiveness, and celebrating reconciliation. Afterward, invite sharing.

Praying Spontaneously

Invite the students to offer spontaneous prayers thanking God for the opportunity to restore our relationship through reconciliation. Conclude by praying, "We trust you, O Lord. Help us remember your love and forgiveness when we have sinned."

DAY 2
MORALITY

Objective

This lesson helps the students learn to examine their conscience for the sacrament of Reconciliation.

Step 1 / INTRODUCTION

Learning About Our Lives

Talking About Remembering

Discuss what helps the students remember things. Explain that today the students will learn how to prepare for reconciliation by remembering.

Step 2 / DEVELOPMENT

Learning About Our Faith

Reading About Examination of Conscience

Ask volunteers to read aloud "Recognizing Our Sins" on page 214. Use the following questions to check the students' understanding.

- Who are some people that can help us know right from wrong? (*Our families and teachers*)

- What is our conscience? (*Our power to judge between good and evil*)

- How do we know when our conscience is telling us something is wrong? (*We might feel ashamed or guilty.*)

- How do we do an examination of conscience? (*We think about Jesus' Great Commandment, the Beatitudes, the Ten Commandments, and ask ourselves if we have been following these laws.*)

Presenting the Vocabulary

Assist the students in learning the new vocabulary term and its definition. Suggest that the students repeat aloud the definition several times.

214

Recognizing Our Sins

We know that God is always ready to forgive us. Because God is merciful, we can honestly admit our sins and express our sorrow. But how can we recognize our sins?

Sometimes our families or teachers tell us when we have done something wrong. They can help us know right from wrong.

At other times we know that we have done something wrong by the way we feel. We feel guilty about what we have done. We hope that nobody finds out about it. We may even be afraid that we will be punished.

When we experience these feelings, our conscience is helping us recognize that we have sinned. Our conscience is our power to judge between good and evil.

At these times we can think about Jesus' Great Commandment, the Beatitudes, and the Ten Commandments. We can ask ourselves if we have been following these laws. When we ask ourselves these questions, we are making an **examination of conscience.**

★★★★★ Enriching the Lesson

Distribute Bibles and direct the students to locate the following verses from Scripture.
1 John 1:9
James 5:15–16

Ask the students to name the words related to forgiveness in each verse as you write them on the chalkboard. Discuss how we are cleansed and healed when we admit our sins and ask forgiveness. Recall that when we are reconciled, God forgives our sins as if we had never sinned.

Activity

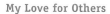

Read these questions and think about each one. What are some other questions you can ask yourself? Write those questions on the lines provided.

My Love for God

- Do I use God's name respectfully?
- Do I pray? Do I worship God on Sunday?

_____

_____

My Love for Myself

- Do I care for my health?
- Do I improve my talents by study and practice?
- Do I respect my body?

_____

_____

My Love for Others

- Do I treat others fairly and with respect?
- Do I obey my parents and those responsible for me?
- Do I tell the truth?
- Do I respect others' bodies and belongings?

_____

_____

My Love for the World

- Do I use things with care? Do I respect the environment?
- Do I respect things that belong to others?
- Do I share what I have with those who have less?

_____

_____

Vocabulary

examination of conscience: thinking about what we have said and done and how we may have sinned

✖ ✖ ✖ ✖ ✖ ✖ ✖ ✖ ✖ ✖ ✖ ✖

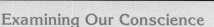

Learning How to Live Our Faith

Examining Our Conscience

Direct the students' attention to the activity on page 215. Read the directions aloud. On the lines provided, ask the students to write additional questions they might ask themselves, about the following topics.

My Love for God
Do I thank God for all God has given me?
My Love for Myself
Am I careful about what I do?
Do I think before I act?
My Love for Others
Do I care for people who are in need?
Am I peaceful with others?
My Love for the World
Do I waste things?
Am I satisfied with all I have?

CURRICULUM CONNECTION

Music   Teach the students the song "You Forgive All Wrong," found on page 22 of the THIS IS OUR FAITH *Hymnal*.

DAY 3
DOCTRINE

Objective

This lesson helps the students learn about the sacrament of Reconciliation.

Step 1 / INTRODUCTION

Learning About Our Lives

Identifying People

Recall the process of reconciliation in the story "The Missing Pieces" on page 212. Explain that talking to another person or asking advice helps when we have hurt another person. Remind the students that in the story Becky's mother helped Becky think of ways in which she and Kate could become friends again. Invite the students to share examples from their own lives of people who helped them find ways to be reconciled.

Step 2 / DEVELOPMENT

Learning About Our Faith

Reading About the Sacrament of Reconciliation

Tell the students that there is a special way to make up with God for things that we do that offend God and others. Ask the students to read aloud the title and the first three paragraphs on page 216. Emphasize that there are two ways to celebrate this sacrament. Ask:

- What are the two ways the sacrament of Reconciliation can be celebrated? (*Individually or communally*)
- What is an examination of conscience? (*We think about how we may have sinned.*)
- When do we do this? (*Before going to the priest to confess our sins*)

Reading About Individual Reconciliation

Read aloud the section "Individual Reconciliation" on pages 216 and 217. Discuss each of the four steps for individual reconciliation. Explain that when a penitent goes into the reconciliation room he or she can either sit or kneel. The priest usually greets the penitent. He or she can make the Sign of the Cross, saying the words aloud.

216

The Sacrament of Reconciliation

Sometimes we do not live lovingly and responsibly, as Jesus wants us to live. We sin, but we want to make up for our sin. We celebrate God's forgiveness in the sacrament of Reconciliation.

There are two ways we normally celebrate this sacrament. One way is together as a community. This is called *communal* reconciliation. When we celebrate the sacrament without the community gathered, it is called *individual* reconciliation.

In both ways of celebrating reconciliation, we need to pray and make an examination of conscience before going to the priest to confess our sins. We think about how we have lived since our last celebration of this sacrament. We think about any sins we may have committed. Then we go to the priest and do four important things.

Individual Reconciliation

When we celebrate this sacrament we do four important things.

1. We confess our sins to the priest.

We go to the priest in the reconciliation room. We can sit in a chair, facing the priest, or we can kneel behind a screen that separates the priest from us.

2. We accept a penance.

The priest talks to us about our sins and gives us a penance. The penance can be a prayer that we pray or a task that we do, such as helping the poor. Doing the penance will help us avoid sinning in the future.

216 Doctrine

Focus on

Communal Reconciliation A form of reconciliation that is particularly effective in helping people see that sin is not just between "me and God" is communal reconciliation. The experience of reconciliation in a communal setting helps people understand the communal dimension of sin, and that we all share in the human condition of sinfulness.

Enriching the Lesson

Have the students role-play the four steps of individual reconciliation. Ask for a volunteer to act as penitent. Invite the student to join you in the prayer area, where you have set up two chairs. Go through the remaining steps. The student should not actually confess. Explain that the priest talks to the child about his or her sins, suggesting ways the penitent can improve. Explain that the priest then asks the penitent to express sorrow for sins.

3. We express our sorrow.

We tell God and the priest that we are sorry for our sins. We ask forgiveness. We can use our own words, or we can pray an act of contrition, a prayer of sorrow.

4. We receive **absolution** from the priest.

The priest stretches out his hands over us. He prays the words of absolution. He asks God to forgive our sins. Jesus acts through the Church to bring us God's forgiveness. When the priest absolves us, the risen Christ absolves us.

Communal Reconciliation

When a group of Catholics celebrates this sacrament together, it is called communal reconciliation. Several priests are present. Usually there are Scripture readings, songs, and prayers. In the communal celebration a priest leads everyone through the sacrament together. But the confession of sins, the acceptance of a penance, and the receiving of the priest's absolution are still done individually.

Vocabulary

absolution: the prayer of forgiveness prayed by the priest in the sacrament of Reconciliation

✖ ✖ ✖ ✖ ✖ ✖ ✖ ✖ ✖ ✖ ✖ ✖ ✖

We Believe

In the sacrament of Reconciliation, the Church celebrates God's forgiveness.

Doctrine 217

The priest may say a prayer. When he finishes, the response is, "Amen." The priest may read about God's forgiveness in a story from the Bible. Then the penitent confesses his or her sins to the priest. This sacrament is sometimes called *confession*, because sins are confessed.

Explain that after receiving absolution, the penitent spends time in prayer, thanking God for the gift of the sacrament of Reconciliation and for the priest who celebrated the sacrament. Then the penitent prays the prayers of penance and asks God's help to overcome sinfulness.

Learning About Communal Reconciliation

Read aloud the section "Communal Reconciliation." Assist the students in recalling any communal reconciliation celebrations they may have celebrated. Point out that these services are often held during Advent and Lent. Tell the students that communal celebrations help us remember that everyone sins. They remind us that we not only need to receive God's forgiveness through Jesus but that we also need to be forgiven by our Christian community, whom we have hurt by our sins.

Learning the Vocabulary

Assist the students in learning the new vocabulary word and its definition. Suggest that the students work in teams to prompt and encourage one another.

Reviewing the Doctrine

Ask a volunteer to read the We Believe statement aloud. Answer any questions the students may have.

Step 3 / CONCLUSION

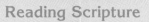

Learning How to Live Our Faith

Reading Scripture

Tell the students that Jesus brings us God's forgiveness and that after Jesus rose from the dead, he came to his disciples, who were gathered in a room together. Distribute Bibles and have the students look up John 20:21–23. Ask a volunteer to read the verses aloud. Explain that Jesus gives priests the power to forgive sins by the power of the Holy Spirit.

Objective

This lesson helps the students appreciate the celebration of God's forgiveness through the sacrament of Reconciliation.

Step 1 / INTRODUCTION

Learning About Our Lives

Writing About Celebrations

Distribute lined paper and ask the students to write about some celebrations they have experienced. Give the students sufficient time to complete the writing activity individually. Afterward, invite the students to share their experiences.

Step 2 / DEVELOPMENT

Learning About Our Faith

Reading a Scripture Story

Ask volunteers to take turns reading aloud "The Lost Sheep" on page 218. Use the following questions to help the students understand the story.

- How many sheep did the shepherd have? (*One hundred*)
- How many sheep did he lose? (*One*)
- Why was the shepherd upset? (*Because he loved his sheep*)
- What did the shepherd do then? (*He went in search of the lost sheep.*)
- Did he find the lost sheep? (*Yes*)
- How did he respond? (*With rejoicing*)
- To what does Jesus compare this story? (*To the greater rejoicing there will be in heaven over one sinner who returns to God and asks forgiveness than for ninety-nine persons who have no need of forgiveness*)

Discussing the Meaning of the Scripture Story

Lead the class in the discussion of the two questions in the students' books on page 219.

Understanding Reasons to Celebrate

Invite a volunteer to read aloud "Celebrating God's Forgiveness" on page 219. Ask:

218

The Lost Sheep

One day, Jesus told his friends this parable: "There once was a shepherd who had one hundred sheep. One day the shepherd noticed that one of the sheep had wandered away. The shepherd loved his sheep and was very upset to have lost even one of them.

"The shepherd decided that he must leave the ninety-nine sheep grazing on the mountainside and go in search of the lost sheep. And when he found his lost sheep, he picked up the sheep and carried it home on his shoulders, rejoicing.

"So it is with God. There is greater rejoicing and celebrating in heaven over one sinner who returns and asks forgiveness than over ninety-nine persons who have no need of forgiveness."

Based on Luke 15: 1–7

218 Scripture

 Focus on

Communal Penance Reconciliation may be celebrated communally by people who are seeking sacramental forgiveness of their sins. The faithful pray together and express their sorrow for sin. They individually confess their sins to the priest and receive absolution.

In this rite, the priest may give the same penance to all who desire absolution rather than giving individual penances.

 **CURRICULUM CONNECTION**

Art Distribute art materials and direct the students to make party decorations. Have the students print phrases on them that celebrate reconciliation. Instruct the class to print sayings such as *Begin Anew* or *Turn Back to God* on the decorations.

Discuss

1. Why was the shepherd so worried about losing one of his sheep when he still had ninety-nine others?

2. If you were the shepherd, would you do what the shepherd in this Scripture story did? Why or why not?

Celebrating God's Forgiveness

The sacrament of Reconciliation gives us many reasons to rejoice and celebrate. We celebrate because the sacrament gives us an opportunity to admit our sins, ask forgiveness, and experience reconciliation with God and with those we've hurt. We know that God has forgiven us and has taken away all our guilt. We are no longer separated from one another. Instead, we are friends, once more united in peace and love. We can begin again to follow Jesus more closely and faithfully.

Activity

Put a ✔ in front of the occasions listed below in which forgiveness and reconciliation were a real celebration in your life.

_____ After a family argument

_____ After a fight with a friend

_____ After celebrating the sacrament of Reconciliation

_____ After saying hurtful words to a classmate

_____ After having a serious talk with a parent

_____ After getting in trouble in school

_____ Other _____

Morality 219

Teaching Tips

Take the class to the reconciliation area in the parish church. Point out the screened kneeler and the chairs used for face-to-face reconciliation. If this is a new experience for the students, have them take turns kneeling at the screen or sitting in the chairs. Discuss any questions they may have about receiving the sacrament of Reconciliation.

Enriching the Lesson

Distribute Bibles and have the students read the story of the Forgiving Father, or the Prodigal Son, found in Luke 15:11–32. Help the students understand that the party that the father gave for the son who returned home was a celebration of forgiveness.

- What do we celebrate in the sacrament of Reconciliation? (*That God has forgiven our sins*)

- Why do we celebrate? (*Because the sacrament gives us an opportunity to admit our sins, ask forgiveness, and experience reconciliation with God and those we have hurt.*)

- How does reconciliation affect our relationship with God? (*We know that God has forgiven us and has taken away our guilt.*)

Step 3 / CONCLUSION

Learning How to Live Our Faith

Completing an Activity

Direct the students' attention to the activity on page 219. Give the students sufficient time to think about the situations listed before they check off their answers. Afterward, invite sharing.

DAY 5

PRAYER/REVIEW

Objective

This lesson helps the students express sorrow for their sins.

Understanding the Act of Contrition

Invite a volunteer to read aloud "Praying an Act of Contrition" on page 220. Ask the following questions to check the students' understanding.

- What is an act of contrition? (*A special prayer that allows us to tell God that we are sorry for our sins*)
- What does *contrition* mean? (*Sincere sorrow*)
- When is a good time to say this prayer? (*As part of the celebration of the sacrament of Reconciliation; following an examination of conscience in preparation for the sacrament; at bedtime, as we look back on our actions throughout the day*)

Praying An Act of Contrition

Invite the students to read silently "An Act of Contrition," found on page 220. Then ask volunteers to reread aloud slowly and prayerfully each of the four sections of the examination of conscience on pages 216 and 217. Encourage the class to reflect on each step as it is read. Allow a brief period of silence. Then invite the students to stand and pray the act of contrition aloud together.

or . . .

Distribute lined paper. Invite the students to write their own personal acts of contrition. Encourage them to use "An Act of Contrition" on page 220 as a model. Encourage the students to read their prayers aloud.

Memorizing the Act of Contrition

Close the lesson by encouraging the students to memorize the act of contrition and pray it frequently.

220

Praying an Act of Contrition

The Act of Contrition is a special prayer that allows us to tell God that we are sorry for our sins. The word *contrition* means "sincere sorrow." When we pray this prayer, we are expressing sincere sorrow for our sins.

A prayer of contrition is often prayed as part of our celebration of the sacrament of Reconciliation. It can also be prayed when we examine our conscience before celebrating the sacrament.

As we get ready for bed each night, it is good for us to recall our words and actions of the day. It can also be a time for us to pray a prayer of contrition. Memorize the Act of Contrition below or another prayer of sorrow used in your school or parish.

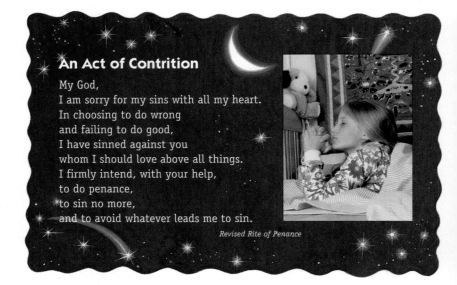

An Act of Contrition

My God,
I am sorry for my sins with all my heart.
In choosing to do wrong
and failing to do good,
I have sinned against you
whom I should love above all things.
I firmly intend, with your help,
to do penance,
to sin no more,
and to avoid whatever leads me to sin.

Revised Rite of Penance

220 Prayer

CURRICULUM CONNECTION

Music   Have the students listen to a recording of "Peace Time" by Carey Landry, found in *Young People's Glory and Praise,* North American Liturgy Resources, available from OCP (Oregon Catholic Press), 5536 N.E. Hassalo St., Portland, OR 97213.

Then discuss how forgiving those who have hurt us is sometimes difficult. Invite sharing. Help the class recognize that when we forgive others as God forgives us, we are, as the song says, "close to God's heart."

Chapter Review

What are the four steps of the sacrament of Reconciliation?

1. <u>We confess our sins to the priest.</u>

2. <u>We accept a penance.</u>

3. <u>We express our sorrow.</u>

4. <u>We receive absolution.</u>

In what two ways can we celebrate the sacrament?

1. <u>Individual reconciliation</u>

2. <u>Communal reconciliation</u>

1. Why is there a sacrament of Reconciliation?

<u>Sometimes we do not live the way that Jesus wants us to live. We sin, but we</u>

<u>want to make up for that sin. There is a sacrament of Reconciliation so that</u>

<u>we can express our sorrow for sin and celebrate God's forgiveness.</u>

_____

_____

2. What is an examination of conscience?

<u>An examination of conscience is thinking about what we</u>

<u>have said and done and how we may have sinned.</u>

_____

_____

3. Discuss how we can be reconcilers, helping people make up through sorrow and forgiveness.

> **Through our Lord Jesus Christ, we have received reconciliation with God.**
> **Based on Romans 5:11**

Naming the Four Steps of Reconciliation

Direct the students' attention to the writing activity at the top of page 221. Ask the students to complete the activity. Afterward, review the answers with the students. Have the students correct any incorrect answers.

Naming Two Ways to Celebrate Reconciliation

Ask the students to write on the lines provided the two ways to celebrate the sacrament of Reconciliation.

Reviewing the Chapter

Read the two review questions aloud. Instruct the students to write their answers on the lines provided. Invite students to share their responses. For the discussion item, encourage all to participate.

Reading the Scripture Verse

Read the verse aloud with the students. Explain that Jesus brings us God's forgiveness. Encourage the class to memorize the verse.

🍎 Teaching Tips

Arrange ahead of time for the students to receive the sacrament of Reconciliation by inviting the pastor or another parish priest to celebrate the sacrament with your class. You may wish to provide a simple snack in the classroom when the sacrament is completed as a way of celebrating God's forgiveness and peace.

18 Unity Through the Eucharist

Objectives

To help the students

- Learn about the Christian call to unity.
- Recognize that they are members of one body.
- Understand that the Eucharist is a sign of our unity.
- Appreciate the difficulty of living in unity.
- Value Eucharist as a celebration of unity and review the chapter.

Chapter Outline

	Step 1 Learning About Our Lives	Step 2 Learning About Our Faith	Step 3 Learning How to Live Our Faith 
Day 1	■ Pray the Act of Contrition. ■ Introduce the chapter. ■ Introduce the story. ■ Read and discuss the story. *ABOUT 15 MINUTES*	■ Introducing the vocabulary. ■ Read about community. ■ Review the doctrine. *ABOUT 8 MINUTES*	■ Write and pray a class litany. *ABOUT 7 MINUTES*
Day 2	■ Name things made up of many parts. ■ Discuss sharing. *ABOUT 10 MINUTES*	■ Read the Scripture story. ■ Discuss the Scripture story. ■ Read Scripture. ■ Learn the vocabulary. *ABOUT 12 MINUTES*	■ Discuss Paul's example. ■ Complete an activity. *ABOUT 8 MINUTES*
Day 3	■ Share a snack. *ABOUT 10 MINUTES*	■ Recognize signs of unity. ■ Review the doctrine. *ABOUT 12 MINUTES*	■ Pray together. ■ Sing together *ABOUT 8 MINUTES*
Day 4	■ Express signs of unity. *ABOUT 15 MINUTES*	■ Work for unity. *ABOUT 7 MINUTES*	■ Complete an activity. *ABOUT 8 MINUTES*
Day 5	**Prayer** Learn a prayer for unity; sing together; and share a sign of peace. **Review** Complete an activity; review the chapter; and pray the Scripture verse.		

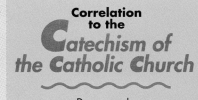
Plan Ahead

	Preparing Your Class	**Materials Needed**
Day 1	Read through the entire lesson plan. Have markers and butcher paper available if enriching the lesson.	■ pencils or pens
Day 2	Read the lesson plan. Review the song "Jesus, You Are Bread For Us" if you plan to use the Curriculum Connection.	■ pencils or pens ■ copies of THIS IS OUR FAITH *Hymnal*
Day 3	Read through the entire lesson plan. Remember to bring a treat for the class today.	■ pencils or pens ■ a snack to share ■ music and recording of "One Bread, One Body"
Day 4	Read through the lesson plan. Prepare song sheets if using the Curriculum Connection.	■ pencils or pens
Day 5	Read through the entire lesson plan.	■ pencils or pens ■ prayer cloth, candle ■ Bible ■ copies of THIS IS OUR FAITH *Hymnal*

Additional Resources

As you plan this chapter, consider using the following materials from The Resourceful Teacher Package.

■ *Classroom Activity Sheets 18* and *18a*

■ *Family Activity Sheets 18* and *18a*

■ *Chapter 18 Test*

■ *Prayers for Every Day*

■ *Projects: Grade 4*

You may also wish to refer to the following Big Book.

■ *We Celebrate the Sacraments,* page 7

In preparing the students for the Sunday readings, you may wish to use Silver Burdett Ginn's *Getting Ready for Sunday* student and teacher materials.

BOOKS FOR THE JOURNEY

Bless This Food. "Make us worthy, Lord . . ." prayer 77. Mother Teresa of Calcutta. Adrian Butash. Delacorte Press, 1993. A prayer to live for others, especially the poor.

Christians. "A World Family," Chapter 12. John Drane. Lion Publishing, 1994. Information on what it means for a Church to be a family, a community.

MORE BOOKS FOR THE JOURNEY

Praise for the Singing. "We Gather Together," PP. 60–61. Edwin T. Buehrer and Adrian Valerius. Collected by Madelaine Gill. Little, Brown, 1993. A song of community.

The Fables of Aesop. "The Father and His Sons," p. 48. Retold by Frances Barnes-Murphy. Lothrop, Lee & Shepard, 1994. A fable in which a father helps his sons appreciate how much they need each other.

REDUCED CLASSROOM ACTIVITIES

NAME _____

UNITY THROUGH THE EUCHARIST

Choose words from the box to complete the sentences. Then look at the circled letters of your answer. Unscramble these letters and write the correct word in the Scripture passage below.

Body	divided	Greece	died
blessing	Corinthians	unity	

1. Corinth is a city in G (r) e e c (e).

2. Paul was called to be an apostle after Jesus (d) i e d.

3. The Eucharist is a source of u n i t y and love.

4. Each member of the B o d y of Christ has a special job to do.

5. The cup of (b) l e s s i n g that we thank God for at Mass is shared in the blood of Christ.

6. Paul told the C o r i n t h i (a) n s all about Jesus.

7. Some of the early Christian groups were d i v i d e d.

"And the __bread__ that we break at the Eucharist is a sharing in the body of Christ."

Based on 1 Corinthians 10:17

To the Teacher: This activity follows the Scripture story "One Bread, One Body."

Chapter 18 Unity Through the Eucharist   THIS IS OUR FAITH 4 **18**

NAME _____

LIVING IN UNITY

Look at the scene on this page. It is missing people working in unity. Draw yourself and other people living the unity you celebrate at the Eucharist.

To the Teacher: This activity will help students understand their roles in creating unity.

18a THIS IS OUR FAITH 4   **Chapter 18** Unity Through the Eucharist

UNITY

In this chapter we examine the goal of reconciliation, which is unity. We, as Church, are a community called to be both the vertical and horizontal axes of unity that shape the symbol of the cross. We are called to unity with God through Christ, and also to a real unity with its members.

Fourth graders feel a need for unity. They express this in their desire to be accepted and be part of the group. Sometimes this desire to belong leads to the exclusion of children who may be perceived as not fitting in. The children's experience is not unlike the problems that the Christian community at Corinth experienced. That early Christian community began to focus on their differences rather than on their oneness.

The unity to which Christ calls the Church fulfills a basic human need. Christian unity includes respect for differences, understanding, trust, and genuine caring. Community is built up and nurtured by thinking of others' needs first.

THE EUCHARIST

The Eucharist has always been at the heart of the Church's strivings to become a united community of believers. The earliest accounts of the life of the first Christian communities record how these followers of Jesus met regularly in homes to "break bread." Saint Paul's teaching, which is recalled in this chapter, sets forth the ideals of Christian unity with the celebration of the Eucharist. A prayer of the early Christians emphasized the unifying role of the Eucharist:

As the elements of this broken bread, once scattered over the mountains, were gathered together and made one, so may your Church be built up from the ends of the earth and gathered in your kingdom.

Saint Paul points out that the Body of Christ is one, just as the human body is one, regardless of the diversity and number of its members. Through Baptism, we have all been incorporated into the one body of Christ. Therefore, the Church, the assembly of the baptized, is the manifestation of the Lord's one body in the world. The Eucharist is the expression of that unity, and it is the source of our becoming one.

Saint Augustine linked the Body of Christ given in Eucharist with the growth of the Body of Christ that is the Church. That is why we can respond "Amen" to the priest's words "the Body of Christ," as he gives us communion. We are to become what we receive. In our own times Vatican Council II affirmed the link between Eucharist and unity. The Eucharist celebrates and fosters unity. Encourage the students to develop their functions as members of Christ's Body in harmony with the greatest gift of the Spirit—love.

DAY 1
DOCTRINE

Objective

This lesson helps the students learn about the Christian call to unity.

Step 1 / INTRODUCTION

Learning About Our Lives

Praying the Act of Contrition

Open the lesson by allowing the students a moment of silence to recollect any of their wrongdoings of the previous week. Then have them pray aloud together the Act of Contrition they learned in the last session.

Introducing the Chapter

Ask the students to open their books to page 222. Read the chapter title and focus question aloud. Invite the students' responses to the question. Explain that *unity* means cooperating with others so that the same goals are shared.

Introducing the Story

Engage the students in a discussion about activities they enjoy, using the following questions.

- What do you like to do on Saturday mornings?
- What activities, games, or hobbies are you good at?
- If your class could plan an all-day outing or field trip, where would you choose to go?
- What kinds of things would you do there?

Tell the students that today's lesson talks about a field trip that a group of fourth graders enjoyed.

Reading and Discussing the Story

Read aloud the story on pages 222 and 223 with the students and discuss it. Write the students' responses to the questions on the chalkboard.

- What different types of activities did the children enjoy on the class picnic? (*They played tennis, volleyball, soccer; put together a puzzle.*)
- Why didn't Mrs. Garcia make the children play all together? (*Because they had different likes and talents*)

222

Unity Through the Eucharist

What are some things that are more fun to do with others rather than alone?

Around the Campfire

Mrs. Garcia's class went on a picnic. Mrs. Garcia watched as groups of children went off to play.

"Let's go and play tennis," she heard Jeff suggest.

"That's a good idea," Luke agreed. "Nobody can play tennis like us."

So Jeff, Luke, and two other friends found a place to play tennis.

About the same time, Lucy said to Denise, "Why don't we play volleyball?"

Denise liked the idea. She invited six other friends to join her and Lucy.

Vincent brought a soccer ball with him to the picnic. He and his friends were the best soccer players in the class. He called Mario. Mario called Doug. Doug called his sister, Gina. Then they went off to practice together.

222   Doctrine

Enriching the Lesson

Remind the students that Jesus shared meals with others like Zacchaeus and the disciples. Tell them that Jesus felt closer to people when he ate with them. Explain that Jesus wants us to cooperate with him so that we not only share the same goals, but become one in mind and heart. Jesus wants us to become one people.

CURRICULUM CONNECTION

Art   Help the students make a mural that identifies the special gifts each of them contributes to the class. Place a large sheet of butcher paper on a table or floor. Distribute crayons or markers. Invite the students to print boldly their first names. Then invite them to list the gifts they share with the class community. Title the mural "Our Community Has Unity." Display the mural in a public area of the school or in the parish hall.

Another group of children formed at one of the picnic tables. They were having a good time putting together a huge jigsaw puzzle.

Mrs. Garcia knew that it was good for the children to have different likes and talents. But she thought to herself, "After the children play their favorite games, we should eat together around the campfire. Then they will feel how good it is to be with all the others."

As evening came, Mrs. Garcia lit the campfire. Everyone gathered around it. There were large jugs of juice. The children filled their cups from the jugs. They all roasted their hot dogs over the campfire. They passed a tray of rolls around so that each child could take a roll.

Mrs. Garcia and the class laughed and talked together as they ate by the campfire. "This is great!" Juan said. "We are a terrific class!"

Discuss

1. Why did Mrs. Garcia want the children to come together for their meal?

2. Why do you think that eating together helps people feel closer to one another?

Christians Share in Community

Like the people in Mrs. Garcia's class, each person has special interests, gifts, and talents to bring to his or her school community. In the same way, each Catholic has special gifts to bring to the Catholic community we know as the Church. The **Catholic Church** is the Christian community which celebrates the seven sacraments and recognizes the pope and bishops as its leaders.

Vocabulary

Catholic Church: the Christian community which celebrates the seven sacraments and recognizes the pope and bishops as its leaders

✗ ✗ ✗ ✗ ✗ ✗ ✗ ✗ ✗ ✗ ✗ ✗

Doctrine 223

CURRICULUM CONNECTION

Music Have the students listen to a recording of "We Are One Body" by Dana available on *Say Yes*, Heartbeat Records, PO Box 20, Donnellson, Iowa 52625. Tell the students that this song was written specifically for the visit of Pope John Paul II at the World Youth Day in Denver, Colorado.

■ What did Mrs. Garcia decide to do after the games were finished? (*Have everyone eat together*)

■ Why did Mrs. Garcia want the children to come together for their meal? (*Answers will vary.*)

■ Why do you think eating together helps people feel closer to one another? (*Answers will vary.*)

Help the students appreciate that the class in the story felt united because of the food, laughter, singing, and talking that they shared around the campfire. Emphasize that the children had different activities that they enjoyed participating in, but they were all able to become one because of what they shared.

■ What groups do you belong to in your school or your neighborhood? (*Answers will vary.*)

■ Have you shared food with others in your groups? (*Answers will vary.*)

Step 2 / DEVELOPMENT

Learning About Our Faith

Introducing the Vocabulary

Write the word *Church* (with a capital C) on the chalkboard. Ask the students to give the definition found on page 223. Have the class repeat it several times.

Reading About Community

Read aloud "Christians Share in Community." Ask: What is another name for the Church? (*The Body of Christ*)

Step 3 / CONCLUSION

Learning How to Live Our Faith

Writing and Praying a Class Litany

Invite the students to help you write a class litany on the chalkboard, mentioning the gifts that each student brings to the class; for example: *For Mary, who gives us the gift of music . . . For David, who gives us the gift of leadership . . . For Jennifer, who gives us the gift of enthusiasm . . .* Encourage the class to respond, "Unite us, Lord" to each petition.

223

Objective

This lesson helps the students recognize that they are members of one body.

Step 1 / INTRODUCTION

Learning About Our Lives

Naming Things Made Up of Many Parts

Direct the students to think of examples of things that are made up of many different parts. Have the students work in pairs as they jot down their ideas. Afterward, discuss the students' examples, which might include a team, a house, a car, a community park, a shopping mall. Help the students appreciate how essential each part or element is to the whole. Stress that if one part or element is missing, everything is affected. Emphasize that the students are an important part of the Catholic Christian community.

Discussing Sharing

Invite the students to share recent experiences when sharing or joining together in activities was difficult. Point out that adults often have these same difficulties. Explain that today they will learn that some of the first Christian communities had trouble being united.

Step 2 / DEVELOPMENT

Learning About Our Faith

Reading the Scripture Story

Read aloud the story on page 224 while the students follow along silently. As you read, explain that Greece is a country in Europe. It is located on the Mediterranean Sea. If possible, locate Greece on a globe or map for the students. Tell the class that ancient Greece was a center for learning and the arts.

Discussing the Scripture Story

Use the questions below to talk about the story.

■ Who organized a Christian community in Corinth? (*The apostle Paul*)

■ What happened to the Corinthians after a while? (*They divided into separate groups.*)

One Bread, One Body

After Jesus died and rose from the dead, he invited Paul to be an apostle. Paul learned to love Jesus and to follow his ways.

Paul became a great Christian leader. He was the first to tell the **Corinthians**, the people of Corinth, a city in Greece, about Jesus. He organized the Christian community there.

But after a time, the Corinthians broke up into a number of separate groups. Each group felt that the members of their group were better Christians than the members of the other groups.

Paul heard about how the groups had divided. He was very sad. He wrote a long letter to all the Christians in Corinth. He told them that differences were good but that all Christians should be united. He told them that the Eucharist is a source of unity and love. Part of Paul's letter to the Corinthians is on the next page.

224   Scripture

 **Cultural Awareness**

Recall that the Corinthians divided into separate groups because each group felt that they were better than the others. Ask: Why do some people look down on or discriminate against others? Help the class recognize that people often discriminate against those who look, act, or speak differently, or have different ideas or ways of doing things. Discuss why some people think they are better than others. Emphasize that Jesus calls us to work together in unity.

 *Focus on*

Union with Jesus In Chapters 10, 11, and 12 of Paul's first letter to the people of Corinth, he addresses the Corinthians regarding divisions which have arisen among their Christian communities. At the time that Paul was writing, there were at least three, perhaps four, different factions within the Church of Corinth. Paul reminds the Corinthians that God has called them to an ultimate and essential union with Jesus through the gift of faith.

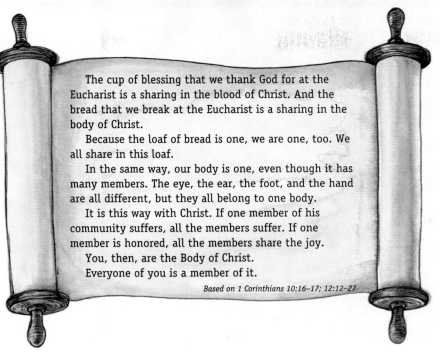

The cup of blessing that we thank God for at the Eucharist is a sharing in the blood of Christ. And the bread that we break at the Eucharist is a sharing in the body of Christ.

Because the loaf of bread is one, we are one, too. We all share in this loaf.

In the same way, our body is one, even though it has many members. The eye, the ear, the foot, and the hand are all different, but they all belong to one body.

It is this way with Christ. If one member of his community suffers, all the members suffer. If one member is honored, all the members share the joy.

You, then, are the Body of Christ. Everyone of you is a member of it.

Based on 1 Corinthians 10:16–17; 12:12–27

Activity

1. Name one gift or talent that you share for the good of your class.

   _____

2. Name someone in your class who shares his or her gifts for the good of the whole class.

   _____

3. Name some ways your class shows that it is a community.

   _____

   _____

   _____

Vocabulary

Corinthians: The people who lived in Corinth, a city in Greece

Scripture 225

CURRICULUM CONNECTION

Music Teach the students "Jesus, You Are Bread for Us," found on page 74 of the THIS IS OUR FAITH *Hymnal.*

- What did Paul do when he heard what had happened? (*He wrote a letter to these people.*)
- What did Paul tell the Corinthians? (*All Christians should be united.*)
- What did he say should be their source of unity and love? (*The Eucharist*)

Explore with the students what happens when a group divides into smaller groups. Have them think of school groups, clubs, or civic organizations. Ask them to consider what would happen to these groups if they began to break apart into smaller, separate groups, with each one thinking it was better than the others. Help the class appreciate that when one small part of a group thinks it is more important than the whole group, then unity of the group is damaged.

Reading Scripture

Ask volunteers to read from the scroll pictured on page 225. Explain that when we share the bread and wine at Mass, we are sharing the body and blood of Jesus. Jesus offered his life to the Father who blessed the sacrifice. He raised Jesus from the dead, enabling Jesus to share his life and love with us. Paul was reminding these Christians that it was their love of Jesus and the Eucharist that made them a community.

Learning the Vocabulary

Ask the students to learn the new vocabulary word by repeating the word and its definition several times.

Step 3 / CONCLUSION

Learning How to Live Our Faith

Discussing Paul's Letter

Help the students understand the meaning of "because the loaf of bread is one, we are one" with the following example. Explain the process of milling wheat. Wheat grows on stalks. Each stalk yields fifty or more grains. The grain is ground up and sifted until it becomes flour. The flour, with other ingredients, is used to make bread. The Corinthians shared a loaf of bread that had been made from many grains of wheat. By sharing together, they became one.

Completing an Activity

Direct the students to complete the activity on page 225. Afterward, discuss the students' responses.

Unity in the Eucharist

The Catholic Church celebrates its unity at the Eucharist. Even though Catholics come from many different places and have many different gifts, in the Eucharist we are one. We eat and drink from the same table as a family. Sharing the body of Christ helps us to become the Body of Christ. We may be many parts, but we are all one body, the Body of Christ.

As Catholics we share special signs of our unity. The Church celebrates and deepens its unity at the Eucharist. We experience our unity through a variety of signs and actions.

1. As we gather to celebrate the Eucharist, we come together from many families and neighborhoods. We bring different gifts and the experiences of our lives. Still, we are one community that is gathered. We stand together. We sing together. We pray together. We are one family, the family of Jesus.

2. During the penitential rite, we ask forgiveness for any actions that may have separated us from one another and threatened our unity.

DAY 3
DOCTRINE

Objective

This lesson helps the students understand that the Eucharist is a sign of our unity.

Step 1 / INTRODUCTION

Learning About Our Lives

Sharing a Snack

You may want to begin this step of the lesson by sharing a treat, such as juice, or apples and cheese, with the students. As they eat you can talk about how you have seen them grow in unity during this past year. Give specific examples that you have observed. Encourage the students to share how they have come to feel that they are a part of the group.

Step 2 / DEVELOPMENT

Learning About Our Faith

Recognizing Signs of Unity

Direct the students' attention to "Unity in the Eucharist" on pages 226 and 227. Ask volunteers to take turns reading aloud. Use the following questions for discussion.

- What is the significance of the community gathering to celebrate the Eucharist? (*The members come from different places, but in celebrating the Eucharist, are united as one family, the family of Jesus Christ.*)

- Why do we need to ask forgiveness? (*We need to ask forgiveness for any actions that may have threatened our unity.*)

- What do we learn from the stories of Jesus? (*The word of God calls all Christians to unity.*)

- What is the significance of the profession of faith? (*We say that we are all one because we all believe the same thing.*)

- What is a common physical sign of unity as people pray The Lord's Prayer? (*Holding hands*)

- How do we become one body, the body of Jesus Christ? (*By sharing in the Eucharist*)

- What are we sent forth to do at the end of Mass? (*To live as the Body of Jesus Christ in the world*)

Teaching Tips

This would be an appropriate time to review the parts of the Mass with the students. Ask the students to turn to page 336 in their books and read "About the Mass."

3. We tell the story of Jesus. As we hear the gospel proclaimed, we all stand as a sign of our respect for Jesus. The gospel message calls all Christians to unity.

4. We profess our faith. Together we say that we all believe in one God. We believe in God's only Son, Jesus. We share one faith. We are one because we all believe in Jesus and the Church.

5. We pray The Lord's Prayer together because it is the prayer given to us by Jesus and is prayed by all Christians. In some parishes, the people hold hands while they pray The Lord's Prayer as a physical sign of their unity.

6. We share the greeting of peace with one another as a reminder of our unity as brothers and sisters of Jesus.

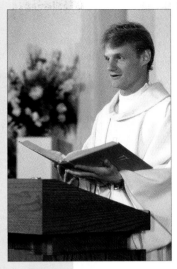

7. We share a meal. As a family, we are all fed at the same table. As we share in the one body and blood of Jesus, we are strengthened in our unity with Jesus and with one another.

8. As the Mass ends, we are sent forth to live united as the Body of Christ in the world.

We Believe

The Church is called to be a community. We gather at the Eucharist to celebrate our unity and to help it grow.

Doctrine 227

CURRICULUM CONNECTION

Art Distribute art materials and help the students make a banner. Have the students print the word *EUCHARIST* vertically down the center of a large sheet of construction paper. Intersect the *I* of *EUCHARIST* with the word *UNITY*. Around the edges of the banner, have the students draw signs of unity as found in their parish and in their families.

■ How does the Catholic Church celebrate its unity? (*In the Eucharist, eating and drinking from the same table, like a family*)

Reviewing the Doctrine

Have the students read aloud the We Believe statements. Do this several times to assist the class in memorizing the doctrine.

Step 3 / CONCLUSION

Learning How to Live Our Faith

Praying Together

Gather the students for prayer. Establish a prayerful environment. Pray aloud, *Lord, we ask you to help us appreciate our unity in you through the Eucharist. We are grateful for your many gifts. Help us always to keep us united as the body of Christ in the World. Amen.*

Singing Together

Read aloud the words to the refrain of the song "One Bread, One Body" by John Foley, S.J., to reinforce the idea of our oneness in the Eucharist and our unity in Jesus, the Lord. Have the class repeat the words after you. Then play a recording so that the students may sing along.

DAY 4
MORALITY

Objective

This lesson helps the students appreciate the difficulty of living in unity.

Step 1 / INTRODUCTION

Learning About Our Lives

Expressing Signs of Unity

Direct the students' attention to the writing activity at the top of page 228. Read the directions aloud and have the students complete the activity, working independently. Afterward, invite the students to share their ideas, which might include: eating together; sharing the responsibility of chores; praying together; going to church; celebrating birthdays, anniversaries, and holidays; and living together.

Step 2 / DEVELOPMENT

Learning About Our Faith

Working for Unity

Ask volunteers to take turns reading "Working for Unity" on pages 228 and 229. Ask:

■ What do we have to do in order to live in unity? (*Learn to respect our differences and overlook each other's faults*)

■ What can help us live in unity in our families? (*Learning to appreciate the gifts of each family member*)

■ How can the world become a better place? (*If each of us works to live in unity*)

Activity

The photographs below show some ways that people live in unity. Next to each photograph, write how the people are expressing their unity.

◀ _____
_____
_____
_____

_____
_____ ▶
_____
_____

◀ _____
_____
_____
_____

Working for Unity

Living together in unity is not always easy. We have to work hard at being together in peace. To live in unity means that we learn to respect our differences and overlook each other's faults. We need to forgive one another and care about what is best for the entire Christian community.

It is easy to take one another for granted in our families. We must learn to appreciate the gifts of each family member. It may not be easy for everyone to live in harmony and unity, but we can work at it.

Enriching the Lesson

Divide the class into groups of three or four students. Assign to each group one of the following communities: *home, neighborhood, school,* or *church.* Ask the groups to create a skit about their community working together in unity to solve a problem. Allow sufficient time for the students to prepare and practice their skits. Visit the groups as they work, offering suggestions and encouraging their efforts. Then invite each group to come to the front of the room and perform the group's skit for the class.

CURRICULUM CONNECTION

Music Distribute song sheets of the song "Friends All Gather 'Round" from *Young People's Glory and Praise,* North American Liturgy Resources, available from Oregon Catholic Press. Play the recording and encourage the students to sing along.

We have many different kinds of people in our classroom. We have different interests and talents. We have different ideas and opinions. Sometimes it is hard to agree, but we can work at it.

In our neighborhoods and towns, we have people of many different ages, ethnic backgrounds, and religions. We look different from one another, and we may even speak different languages. Although it may not always be easy to live in unity, we can work at it.

In all of these communities, our lives can show the unity that we celebrate in the Eucharist.

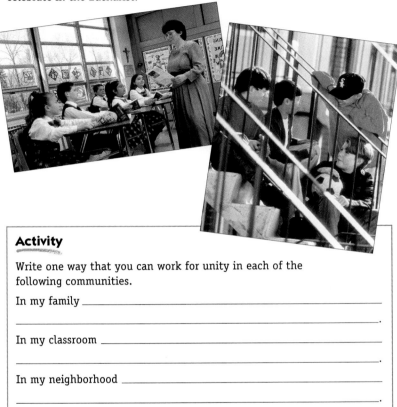

Activity

Write one way that you can work for unity in each of the following communities.

In my family _____

_____.

In my classroom _____

_____.

In my neighborhood _____

_____.

Learning How to Live Our Faith

Completing an Activity

Direct the students to the activity on page 229. Give the students sufficient time to complete the activity independently. Afterward, invite the students to share their ideas with the rest of the class.

★ ★★★ ★
Enriching
the Lesson ★

Discuss how children in a school work together and do their best to bring unity to the school community. Emphasize that not everyone has to do the same thing. People may have different responsibilities, but each is an important part of the class or team.

DAY 5
PRAYER/REVIEW

Objective

This lesson helps the students value Eucharist and the Sign of Peace as a celebration of unity.

Learning a Prayer for Unity

Ask volunteers to read aloud the first three paragraphs of "Praying a Sign of Peace and Unity" on page 230. Point out that God's kingdom is a place of peace and unity. Stress that we are called to work toward these goals in our daily lives. Then talk with the students about their experiences of the Sign of Peace at Mass.

Singing Together

Create a prayerful environment and gather the students for prayer. Begin by singing "World Peace Prayer" on page 120 of the THIS IS OUR FAITH *Hymnal* or page 8 of the THIS IS OUR FAITH Grade 4 *Teacher's Songbook*.

Sharing a Sign of Peace

Provide sufficient time for the students and you to exchange a sign of peace.

Complete the prayer experience by singing another song of peace that the students are familiar with.

Praying a Sign of Peace and Unity

When we gather at the Eucharist, we are a united community of believers in Jesus Christ. As one body, the Body of Christ, we praise God and hear his word proclaimed in the Scriptures. As one community of Catholics, we offer our gifts and our lives to God in praise. We are one as we share in Jesus' Body and Blood in the Eucharist. We are no longer only individuals. We are now a united community of people who believe in Jesus.

One sign of unity that we share at Mass is called the Sign of Peace. At the Sign of Peace, we wish one another the peace of Christ and are reminded again that we are one family of believers, united in Jesus.

Share a sign of peace with your teacher and classmates.

Enriching the Lesson

Ask a volunteer to locate 1 Corinthians 13:4–7 in the Bible and read it aloud prayerfully, while the others listen. Remind the students that every time we share in the Eucharist, we come to a deeper understanding of what it means to love others.

Chapter Review

Eight signs of unity that we share in the Eucharist are listed below, but not in the correct order. Put them in the correct order by numbering them as they happen at Mass.

___8___   We are sent forth.

___4___   We profess our faith.

___7___   We share a meal.

___1___   We gather.

___3___   We tell the story of Jesus.

___2___   We ask forgiveness.

___5___   We pray The Lord's Prayer.

___6___   We share the greeting of peace.

1. Who were the Corinthians?

The Corinthians were the people who lived in Corinth,

a city in Greece.

2. What does the Church celebrate at the Eucharist?

The Church celebrates its unity at the Eucharist. We

gather as a community. We eat and drink from the same

table, like a family. Sharing the body of Christ in the

Eucharist helps our unity grow.

3. Discuss what we can do to help build unity in the groups we belong to.

> **All who eat the bread of life are one.**
> Based on
> 1 Corinthians 10:17

CURRICULUM CONNECTION

Art Give each student a fist-sized ball of clay and some newspaper to protect the work area. Invite the students to make clay unity symbols, such as a loaf of bread, the number one, a circle, or a clay person. Set the completed symbols aside to dry. Later, have the students paint them with tempera. Have them show and explain their painted symbols to the class. Encourage the students to take their clay symbols home to be used as a centerpiece to promote family unity.

Enriching the Lesson

Distribute newspapers, magazines, or parish bulletins. Direct the students to find a picture or article that shows people working together. Ask each student to tell the class how working together is a sign of unity. Ask them to describe how they can live out the unity they celebrate at the Eucharist.

Completing an Activity

Call attention to the activity at the top of page 231. Direct the students to complete the activity. Afterward, review the correct answers with the class. Instruct the students to change any incorrect answers.

Reviewing the Chapter

Read aloud the two review questions at the bottom of page 231. Direct the students to write the answer to each question on the lines provided. For the discussion item, encourage all to participate.

Praying the Scripture Verse

Gather the students in a circle. Invite them to join hands. Read aloud the Scripture verse and have them repeat it after you. On the last word, *one*, direct all the students to raise their arms with hands still joined together.

A Light to the World

Objectives

To help the students

- Understand that Jesus calls his followers to be a light for the world.
- Learn that Jesus teaches us what it means to be a light for the world.
- Identify ways in which others are a light to them.
- Respond to the call to be a light to the world.
- Pray about being a light to the world and review the chapter.

Chapter Outline

	Step 1 Learning About Our Lives	Step 2 Learning About Our Faith	Step 3 Learning How to Live Our Faith
Day 1	■ Introduce the chapter. ■ Study the picture. ■ Complete an activity. *ABOUT 8 MINUTES*	■ Read about being light. ■ Review the doctrine. *ABOUT 7 MINUTES*	■ Write a poem. *ABOUT 15 MINUTES*
Day 2	■ Brainstorm ways to live. *ABOUT 8 MINUTES*	■ Read and discuss the story. ■ Learn the vocabulary. *ABOUT 12 MINUTES*	■ Talk about images of light. *ABOUT 10 MINUTES*
Day 3	■ Introduce the story. ■ Read and discuss the story. *ABOUT 10 MINUTES*	■ Read and write about being light. *ABOUT 8 MINUTES*	■ Identify people of light. ■ Make certificates. *ABOUT 12 MINUTES*
Day 4	■ Identify qualities. *ABOUT 5 MINUTES*	■ Read about the day of Pentecost. ■ Read about and discuss the Holy Spirit. *ABOUT 15 MINUTES*	■ Complete an inventory. ■ Pray together. *ABOUT 10 MINUTES*
Day 5	**Prayer** Read about the symbol of light and pray together. **Review** Answer three review questions; review the chapter; and pray the Scripture verse.		

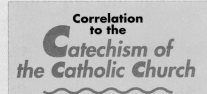

Correlation
to the
**Catechism of
the Catholic Church**

Paragraphs
774–776; 1088

Plan Ahead ~~~~~~~~~~

	Preparing Your Class	**Materials Needed**
Day 1	Read through the entire lesson plan. Make arrangements to have several thesauruses on hand.	■ pencils or pens ■ thesauruses
Day 2	Read through the entire lesson plan.	■ pencils or pens
Day 3	Read through the lesson plan. Arrange for presenting the certificates to the award winners in person.	■ pencils or pens ■ parchment-like paper ■ crayons or felt-tip markers
Day 4	Read through the entire lesson plan.	■ pencils or pens
Day 5	Read through the lesson plan. If you plan to bring the class to the parish church for prayer, make all the necessary arrangements.	■ pencils or pens ■ small candles, one per student ■ Bible, prayer cloth ■ large candle ■ lined paper

Additional Resources

As you plan this chapter, consider using the following materials from The Resourceful Teacher Package.

■ *Classroom Activity Sheets 19* and *19a*

■ *Family Activity Sheets 19* and *19a*

■ *Chapter 19 Test*

■ *Prayers for Every Day*

■ *Projects: Grade 4*

You may also wish to refer to the following Big Book.

■ *We Celebrate God's Word,* page 21

In preparing the students for the Sunday readings, you may wish to use Silver Burdett Ginn's *Getting Ready for Sunday* student and teacher materials.

Books for the Journey

Why the Sun and the Moon Live in the Sky. Elphinstone Dayrell. Houghton Mifflin, 1990. The source of light is playfully and imaginatively woven into a story that tells of the origins of the world.

Praise for the Singing. "This Little Light," pp. 46–47. Collected by Madelaine Gill. Little, Brown, 1993. A song in which the ones who are singing declare their intention to be a light to the world.

More Books for the Journey

Children of Promise. "Daybreak in Alabama," by Langston Hughes, p. 68. Edited by Charles Sullivan. Harry N. Abrams, Inc., 1991. A poem in which the moment of daybreak symbolizes a more enlightened and caring human family.

Hand in Hand. "Child of the Sun," by Lillian M. Fisher, p. 48. Collected by Lee Bennett Hopkins, Simon & Schuster, 1994. The sun is one of the symbols in this poem that expresses courage, hope, pride, and oneness of a people.

Reduced Classroom Activities

NAME _____

A Light to the World

Use the code in the light bulb to decipher Jesus' special message for all people. Write the message on the lines provided.

"You are the light of the world." *Matthew 5:14*

To the Teacher: This activity follows the Scripture story "Jesus and Light."

Chapter 19 A Light to the World

This Is Our Faith 4 **19**

NAME _____

Being a Light to Others

Jesus told his followers to go out and be a light to all people, so they could live in his love. To help you become a light, find a partner and play "connect the stars." Here are the directions.

1. Player 1: Draw a line connecting two adjacent stars. (Diagonal lines are not allowed.)
2. Player 2: Do the same; you may continue your partner's line or begin in a new place.
3. Continue to take turns, connecting only two stars at a time.
4. The player who draws the fourth line to close a box writes his or her initials in the box.
5. The game continues until all the stars are connected.
6. As partners, decide on one thing you will do to "light up" the class this week and then write it on the lines provided.

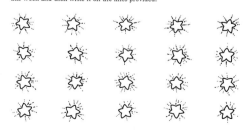

"Together, let's do this to light up our class this week: _____
_____."

Signed: _____   Signed: _____

To the Teacher: This activity will help students plan a strategy for being a light to others.

19a This Is Our Faith 4

Chapter 19 A Light to the World

DARKNESS

Children typically do not like the dark. Many youngsters have had frightening experiences related to darkness. They often associate darkness with "wild things"—ghosts, monsters, and bad dreams. As adults we often have a sense of darkness when we cannot discern God's will, or have difficulty making the "right" decision. Our vision may be clouded by selfishness or ulterior motives. Children, too, can experience this kind of darkness as they try to make good decisions and choices in their lives. At times like these, we may be enlightened by another person's words or example.

LIGHT

Into the realms of both external and interior darkness light can fall, removing the danger and easing our fears. The light may be physical like the light from a flashlight or light bulb, or emotional, such as a touch, a word, a song. Light of both kinds brings feelings of warmth, joy, security, and confidence.

The symbols of darkness and light are used throughout Scripture. Light represents spiritual vision, salvation, and God's revelation—indicating spiritual life for humanity in God. His light brings life as surely as the sunlight coaxes life from the soil. God promised that in the fullness of time the people who walk in darkness of sin, death, and confusion will see a great light (Isaiah 9:1).

THE LIGHT OF CHRIST

Jesus of the New Testament is that great light. He identifies himself as the light of the world. Those who follow him walk in his light and live by his light. That symbolism is expressed in the words of Jesus, "You are the light of the world" (Matthew 5:14a). In this passage from Scripture, the important role of the disciples is illustrated by the metaphor of a lamp. A lengthy passage follows, instructing the disciples how to become a light to the world. Just as the metaphor of the lamp illustrated the function of the disciples then, it is meant to do the same for followers of Jesus Christ today.

God's light, aflame in the life and words of Jesus, burns on in his disciples and followers. The Easter Vigil dramatizes this each year as we light our individual candles from the Easter candle that represents the risen Christ. Vatican Council II developed the biblical symbolism of light. The Council's central document on the Church, *Lumen Gentium*, begins with "Christ is the light of all nations." That light of Christ "Brightens the countenance of the Church." Just as Christ is our light, so are we called to be light to one another. We are light through our words, our example, and our witness.

DAY 1
DOCTRINE

Objective
This lesson helps the students understand that Jesus calls his followers to be a light for the world.

Step 1 / INTRODUCTION

Learning About Our Lives

Introducing the Chapter
Ask the students to keep their books closed. Explain that you want them to respond to the question you are about to ask with the first thought that pops into their minds. Ask them to close their eyes. Then read aloud the focus question. Invite the students' responses. Tell the class that this chapter is about light.

or . . .
Ask the students to close their eyes and imagine a world without light. Talk with them about how different our world would be without light. Help them appreciate that light is part of God's creation. Explain that without light, life could not exist.

Studying the Picture
Direct the students to page 232 of their books. Read the chapter title aloud. Ask the students to look at the photograph on the page. Invite comments. Recall that at the creation of the world, God first created light.

Completing an Activity
Emphasize how essential light is in our lives. Explain the directions to the activity. Encourage the students to work independently to complete it. When they are finished, invite them to compare their responses with one another. In the last sentence, ask the students to name the source of light before reading aloud their sentences.

Step 2 / DEVELOPMENT

Learning About Our Faith

Reading About Being Light
Select a volunteer to read aloud "Shining Examples" on page 233. Ask the students to

A Light to the World

19

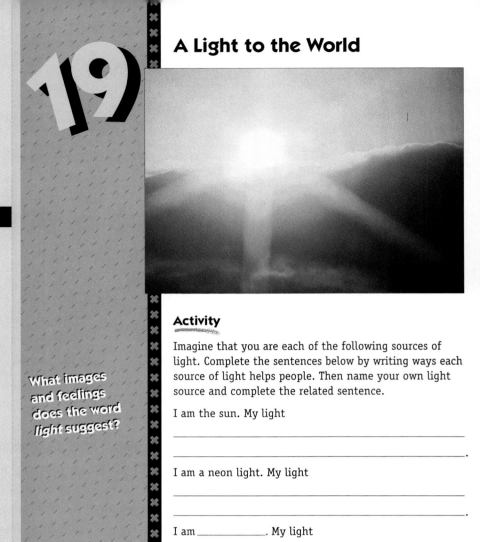

What images and feelings does the word light suggest?

Activity
Imagine that you are each of the following sources of light. Complete the sentences below by writing ways each source of light helps people. Then name your own light source and complete the related sentence.

I am the sun. My light

_____

_____.

I am a neon light. My light

_____

_____.

I am _____. My light

_____

_____

232 Doctrine

Cultural Awareness

Ask the students if they know anyone who is blind or has great difficulty seeing, even in the brightest light. Discuss the problems a sightless person may have. Explain that new technology (voice-controlled computers, books on tape, large print books, and machines that scan text and translate into sound, and so on) helps those with vision problems. Help the class understand that blind people do not want pity; they want to be treated like everyone else.

Focus on

Light In the Old Testament, light accompanies God's presence. In Genesis, God's creative initiative called forth light from the primordial darkness. Later, God's presence guided the Hebrews escaping from slavery in Egypt in the form of a pillar of fire that lit their night journey. Psalm 104:2a describes God as "robed in light."

Shining Examples

Light helps us in many ways. It helps us when we cannot find our way, and it helps us see things more clearly.

Jesus' teachings and actions were a light to all who listened because they helped people see what God is like. Jesus' followers today come to know who God is by listening to the teachings of Jesus, the Light of the World.

Jesus draws on people's experience of light and its importance in their lives to describe the Church's task in the world. The Church is to be such a caring, happy, hopeful community of people that all people will be moved to live more caring, happy, hopeful lives. Jesus calls each of us in the Church to be a light to others. Our lives should be examples to everyone we meet. The Church is to be a light to the world. Those who see us should be able to learn about God by what we do and what we say.

Activity

Write a poem about light that suggests how light makes you feel or why light is important to you. Use any kind of poetry you like. Be sure to give your poem a title.

_____

_____

_____

_____

_____

_____

We Believe

The community of the Church is a light to the world. Every member of the Church is called to live a good life. In this way all people can see the true way to God and happiness.

Doctrine 233

name specific actions and teachings of Jesus that helped others see what God's life is like; for example, Jesus healing the sick; Jesus forgiving Peter; Jesus telling stories of the Good Shepherd; the Merciful Father; the Good Samaritan. Emphasize that through his example and teachings, Jesus was telling us about God's love and how God wants us to live.

Reviewing the Doctrine

Have the students read aloud the We Believe statements several times. Recall the unity theme of Chapter 18 and Paul's words, "If one member of Christ's community suffers, all the members suffer. If one member is honored, all the members share joy." (Based on 1 Corinthians 12:26) Help the students recognize that being a light to others by living good lives also helps us grow in unity.

Step 3 / CONCLUSION

Learning How to Live Our Faith

Writing a Poem

Read the directions to the activity on page 233. The students may use any form for their poems—free verse or any rhyme scheme. You may wish to suggest the cinquain form, a poem with five lines. The first line is one word that names the subject of the poem. The second line names two things that describe the subject. The third line is made up of three words that tell what the subject does. These words end in -ing. In the fourth line, four words are used to tell how the subject makes us feel. The fifth line is one word describing the poem's subject. A sample cinquain is found below. Write it on the chalkboard and read it with the class. Have several thesauruses available for the students' use while they write.

Light
bright, sunny
warming, inviting, guiding
shows me the way
Illumination.

At the time of Christ, most Palestinian peasants lived in a one-room house that was lighted by a single lamp, and the followers of Jesus knew the importance of this single source of light. Matthew uses the metaphor of the lamp to describe the role of the disciples.

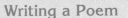

Have the students think of individuals who act as a light to them. Stress that these people, because of their good example, inspire us to live good lives. Invite the students to share who these people are and describe what they do. Afterward, invite the students to bow their heads in prayer. Ask them to offer a silent prayer thanking God for the people in their lives who are like a light to them. Encourage them to ask God's help in being an example to the people they meet.

233

DAY 2
SCRIPTURE

Objective

This lesson helps the students learn that Jesus teaches us what it means to be a light for the world.

Step 1 / INTRODUCTION

Learning About Our Lives

Brainstorming Ways to Live

Brainstorm the following questions.

- What are some of the ways Jesus asked his followers to live?
- What does Jesus want us to do?

On the chalkboard, list the students' responses. Tell the students that the story they are going to read is an example Jesus gave about how to live.

Step 2 / DEVELOPMENT

Learning About Our Faith

Reading and Discussing the Story

Invite one or more volunteers to read aloud the story beginning on page 234. Then discuss the story using the following questions.

- Who does Jesus say is the light of the world? (*People who follow him*)
- What do you think Jesus means? (*Answers will vary*)
- How can people be a light to other people? (*Answers will vary*)
- How does Jesus want his followers to live? (*Answers will vary*)
- What does Jesus say will happen when other people see our light? (*They will praise and thank God for his goodness.*)

When discussing the last question with the students, help them appreciate that their example is a sign to others of God's presence in the world. Our example leads others to see the true way to God and to being happy.

Learning the Vocabulary

Refer the students to the new vocabulary term *light of the world*. Assist them in recognizing that the way we live our lives is a light to

Jesus and Light

A large crowd of people sat on the side of the mountain where Jesus had been teaching his disciples. Jesus sat where everyone could see and hear him. He had just finished talking about his way to be happy.

After a few moments, Jesus began to speak again. All the people became silent and listened to him.

"You are the (light of the world)," Jesus said to his disciples. "A city set on a hill cannot be hidden."

The people in the crowd had all seen cities and towns built high up on hills. Anyone could find a city on a hill.

"People do not (light a lamp) and then put it under a bushel basket," Jesus went on. "They set it on a stand where it (gives light) to everyone in the house."

Enriching the Lesson

Encourage the students to identify times when their example has helped others. Invite the students to share their experiences with the class.

Again the people could understand what Jesus was saying. They all used candles and oil lamps to light their homes.

"In the same way," Jesus told his disciples, "your light must shine before people. Let your good deeds show for all to see. Then all will praise God, your heavenly Father."

Based on Matthew 5:14–16

Activity

Read the Scripture story again. Circle all the words about light. Talk about the meanings of these images.

Vocabulary

light of the world: the lives of Jesus and his followers shining before others and lighting the way to God and happiness

✖ ✖ ✖ ✖ ✖ ✖ ✖ ✖ ✖ ✖ ✖ ✖

Scripture 235

---

others and shows them the way to happiness. Help the students consider how they can be a light to others. Encourage them to name specific good deeds and actions that can help other people see how to live good lives.

Step 3 / CONCLUSION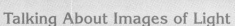

Learning How to Live Our Faith ✠

Talking About Images of Light

Direct the students' attention to the activity on page 235. Have the students circle all the terms of light in "Jesus and Light" (*Light of the world, glowing lights, light a lamp, gives light, candles, oil lamps,* and *shine*). Ask the students to complete the activity independently. Help the students understand that our actions, words, and example should brighten the world and lead the way for others to God. Afterward, encourage the students to share what they wrote.

📖 **CURRICULUM CONNECTION**

Art Distribute scissors, glue, crayons, and one black and one yellow sheet of craft paper to each student. Tell the students to draw various sizes and shapes of windows on the black sheet. Have them cut out the windows and glue the black sheet on top of the yellow paper, which represents light shining from within a home. In the window spaces, have the students write words that show how Jesus wants us to live and treat others; for instance, *kindness, love, care, sharing, generosity, listening,* and *help.*

DAY 3
MORALITY

Objective

This lesson helps the students identify ways in which others are a light to them.

Step 1 / INTRODUCTION

Learning About Our Lives

Introducing the Story

Ask the students if they have older brothers or sisters. Then ask how many of them look up to their older brothers and sisters as examples of how to live a good life. Explain to the students that today they are going to read about a boy who has an older brother who is a light for him.

Reading and Discussing a Story

Invite volunteers to read aloud "A Light in My Life" on page 236. Use the following questions for discussion.

- How does Manuel show his care for José? (*He shoots baskets with José, helps him with homework, and buys him presents.*)

- What does José admire about Manuel? (*He is a good basketball player. He does well in school and plans to go to college. He has a job.*)

- What does José try to do, in following his brother's example? (*He studies hard, tries not to get into trouble, and helps his mom whenever he can.*)

Step 2 / DEVELOPMENT

Learning About Our Faith

Reading and Writing About Being Light

Read through "Lights to the World" on page 237 with the class. You may ask each student to read one sentence aloud. Emphasize that there are many ways of bringing the light of hope, caring, and happiness to others.

Direct the students to work in pairs to find other ways of being light to the world. Instruct each pair to create two "When someone . . ." statements. Encourage them to be specific. When everyone has finished, invite the students to read their responses to the class.

236

A Light in My Life

Hi! I'm José and I'm eleven years old. I live in Brooklyn with my mom and my older brother, whose name is Manuel.

You would really like Manuel. He's a cool guy. He's one of the best players on the high school basketball team. Sometimes he shoots baskets with me after school.

Some of Manuel's friends have quit school, but not Manuel. He studies hard so that he'll be able to go to college next year. He even helps me with my school work when I'm having a hard time.

Manuel has a job at a neighborhood grocery store on weekends. He doesn't make much money, but he often buys Mom and me presents.

I know that I can't be exactly like Manuel, but I study hard and try not to get into trouble. I try to help Mom out whenever I can.

Mom says that Manuel is a good example for me and my friends. I agree, but mostly I just think he is a great brother!

When I pray, I always thank God for Mom and for Manuel and I ask the Lord to help me follow Manuel's good example.

236 Morality

 **CURRICULUM CONNECTION**

Music Teach the students to sing "This Little Light of Mine," Grade 5, p. 22, Silver Burdett Ginn's WORLD OF MUSIC. The song is recorded on the accompanying CD 1-10.

 *Focus on*

The Works of Mercy The *Catechism of the Catholic Church* states: "The *works of mercy* are charitable actions by which we come to the aid of our neighbor in his spiritual and bodily necessities. Instructing, advising, consoling, comforting are spiritual works of mercy . . . The corporal works of mercy consist especially in feeding the hungry, sheltering the homeless, clothing the naked, visiting the sick; . . . giving alms to the poor is . . . a work of justice pleasing to God." (#2447)

Lights to the World

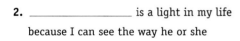

Jesus calls each of us to be a light to others by the way we live.

When someone stands up for those who are not treated fairly, he or she is a light to the world.

When someone teaches others what they do not know, he or she is a light to the world.

When someone tells the truth and not a lie, he or she is a light to the world.

When someone is honest and refuses to cheat, he or she is a light to the world.

When someone cares when others are sad, he or she is a light to the world.

When someone reaches out to help others who are hurting, he or she is a light to the world.

When someone helps a friend with homework, he or she is a light to the world.

Activity

Tell about two different people who are lights in your life by completing the following sentences. Be sure to mention specific things that you see these persons doing.

1. _____ is a light in my life
   because I can see the way he or she

   _____ .

2. _____ is a light in my life
   because I can see the way he or she

   _____

   _____ .

Step 3 / CONCLUSION

Learning How to Live Our Faith

Identifying People of Light

Call attention to the activity at the bottom of page 237. Read the directions aloud and have the students work independently to complete the activity. When all have finished, invite the students to tell about the people they chose to write about. Encourage the students to personally thank these people for being examples for them.

Making Certificates

Distribute a sheet of parchment-like paper and crayons or markers to each student. Invite the students to think of people in the parish or in the community who have served as examples to others. List their suggestions on the chalkboard; for example, parish priests; catechists; teachers; the Director of Religious Education, parents. Invite the students to make award certificates entitled "You Are a Light to the World" for each of the people they have named. As the students make the certificates, encourage them to write about how the named person has been a light to others. Decide with the class how the certificates will be presented. If possible, invite the award winners to visit your class and receive their awards.

CURRICULUM CONNECTION

Art Distribute drawing paper and crayons or markers. Instruct the students to draw pictures that show what people are doing to make your parish a light to others. After the students draw their pictures, invite them to share their drawings with the class.

Enriching the Lesson

As a way of doing a work of mercy, and thereby being a light to the world, encourage the students to share with the poor some of the money that they would normally spend on themselves. Suggest that they make a contribution to the poor box or arrange to collect nonperishible food items for the parish pantry to be distributed to the poor.

237

DAY 4

SCRIPTURE

Objective

This lesson helps the students recognize that the Holy Spirit helps us respond to the call to be a light to the world.

Step 1 / INTRODUCTION

Learning About Our Lives

Identifying Qualities

Help the students recall the people they named in the previous lesson as lights in their lives. Then ask the students to name the qualities they think it takes to be a light for others. List the students ideas on the chalkboard. Possible qualities might include: *caring, generous, kind, helping, loving, and faithful.* Tell the students that in today's lesson, they are going learn how the Holy Spirit can help them to have these same qualities and be a light to others.

Step 2 / DEVELOPMENT

Learning About Our Faith

Reading About the Day of Pentecost

Read aloud with the class the paragraph about the day of Pentecost on page 238. Ask: What came upon the followers of Jesus with the sound of the rush of a violent wind? (*The Holy Spirit*)

Reading About and Discussing the Holy Spirit

Invite volunteers to take turns reading aloud "The Power of the Holy Spirit." Direct the students to underline in their books what the followers of Jesus were able to do with the power of the Holy Spirit. (*They preached about Jesus; lived in communities and shared everything; tried not to be selfish; cared for one another and helped strangers.*) Ask: How did the number of Christians grow? (*When people saw the example of Jesus' followers, they wanted to hear about Jesus and his teachings.*)

238

The Day of Pentecost

When the day of Pentecost came, the followers of Jesus were all together in one place. Suddenly from heaven there came a sound like the rush of a violent wind. It filled the whole house where they were sitting. Tongues, as of fire, appeared among them, and came to rest on each of them. All of them were filled with the Holy Spirit.

Based on Acts of the Apostles 2:1–4

The Power of the Holy Spirit

Since the day of Pentecost, through the power of the Holy Spirit, the followers of Jesus were able to go out and preach about Jesus. They lived in communities where they shared everything in common. They tried not to be selfish. They cared for one another and helped strangers. They lived as Jesus had told them. Together they were an example to others and a light to the world.

When other people saw how the followers of Jesus lived together in kindness and generosity, they became curious. They wanted to hear about Jesus and his teachings. The number of Christians grew.

238 Scripture

CURRICULUM CONNECTION

Music Read to the students the words of the song "We Are the Light of the World" by Jean Anthony Greif, in *Breaking Bread* or the current *Music Issue,* available from OCP (Oregon Catholic Press), 5536 N.E. Hassalo St., Portland, OR 97213. Teach the students to sing the refrain: *We are the light of the world, may our light shine before all, that they may see the good that we do, and give glory to God.*

The Holy Spirit gave the early followers of Jesus the courage to let their light shine before others. In the same way, the Holy Spirit can give us the strength and courage we need to be a light for others. Jesus has called each of us to be a light for the world by what we say and do.

Activity

In many ways, the Holy Spirit is already helping you to be a light to the world. The inventory below will help you see how well you are doing. It can also give you some ideas on how you can do better. Place an **X** in the column that best describes you.

	I already do this.	I am going to start doing this.
1. I am kind to others.		
2. I can be trusted.		
3. I treat my parents and teachers with respect.		
4. I pray every day.		
5. I am a friend to those who don't have many friends.		
6. I'm a peacemaker, not a troublemaker.		
7. I don't say mean things to others, or lie about them.		
8. I am a good example to my friends.		

Enriching the Lesson

Distribute Bibles and have the students locate and read aloud the following references to being children of light.

John 12:36
1 Thessalonians 5:5
Ephesians 5:8

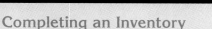

Learning How to Live Our Faith

Completing an Inventory

Ask a volunteer to read aloud the introductory paragraph on page 239. Then ask another volunteer to read the directions to the activity aloud. Give the students sufficient time to complete the inventory independently.

Praying Together

Invite the students to bow their heads in prayer and silently thank God for sending them the Holy Spirit to help them be a light to the world. Afterward, help the students understand that prayer helps us to know God better and teaches us how God wants us to live.

DAY 5
PRAYER/REVIEW

Objective

This lesson helps the students pray about and celebrate their call to be a light to the world.

Reading About the Symbol of Light

Ask a volunteer to read aloud "Praying About Light" on page 240. Be sure that the students know where the candle near the tabernacle is in their parish church. Explain that this candle is called a *sanctuary lamp*. Also explain the significance of lighting a candle for prayer: that it is a sign of Christ's presence as well as a reminder that we are to be light to the world.

Praying Together

If possible, take the students to the church for this prayer service, and gather near the Easter candle or the sanctuary lamp. Otherwise, create a prayerful environment and gather around a large candle in the classroom. You may want the students to bring their books with them to prayer.

Select three students to each read one of the verses from Scripture. Have the rest of the class join in on the response. Then begin the prayer. After the third reading and response, pray the concluding paragraph. Then call each student by name and distribute small candles to light from the large candle. When all the students have a lighted candle, continue praying the closing prayer together. Direct the students to extinguish their candles immediately following the prayer. For safety, it may be better to use small electric candles.

Praying About Light

Light has been a religious symbol for people since ancient times. The Jews of Jesus' time always kept a light burning in the Temple in Jerusalem, as a reminder to them that God was present there in a special way. In the same way, Catholics keep a light burning near the tabernacles in our churches as a reminder that Jesus is present there in a special way. And when we gather for prayer, we often light a candle as a sign of Christ's presence among us.

Pray the prayer below with your class.

Reader: The people who walked in darkness have seen a great light.

Isaiah 9:1

Response: Christ is our light.

Reader: The light shines in the darkness, and the darkness has not overcome it.

John 1:5

Response: Christ is our light.

Reader: I am the light of the world. No follower of mine shall ever walk in darkness.

Based on John 8:12

Response: Christ is our light.

Teacher: Loving God, we are filled with the light of your Son, Jesus Christ. May the light of Christ shine forth in our words and in our actions. We ask this through Jesus Christ, your Son. Amen.

240 Prayer

Enriching the Lesson

Distribute Bibles. Have the students locate in the Book of Genesis the references to the light that God created in the beginning when God created the heavens and the earth. The students should find *light (Day)*, *lights in the dome of the sky [sun, stars, and planets] to separate the day from the night . . . and to give light upon the earth; two great lights—the greater light . . . and the lesser light [the sun and moon] and the stars.*

CURRICULUM CONNECTION

Music A musical representation of somber darkness and God's creation of light can be heard in the oratorio *The Creation* composed by Franz Joseph Haydn. Play a recording of the opening of this great musical work. In the Introduction, the students will hear "The Representation of Chaos," followed by the brilliant choral sound of "Let there be light!" A version sung in English, conducted by Robert Shaw, is available on Telarc 2 CD 80298.

240

Chapter Review

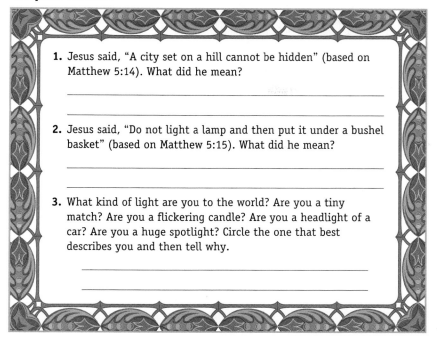

1. Jesus said, "A city set on a hill cannot be hidden" (based on Matthew 5:14). What did he mean?

   _____

   _____

2. Jesus said, "Do not light a lamp and then put it under a bushel basket" (based on Matthew 5:15). What did he mean?

   _____

   _____

3. What kind of light are you to the world? Are you a tiny match? Are you a flickering candle? Are you a headlight of a car? Are you a huge spotlight? Circle the one that best describes you and then tell why.

   _____

   _____

1. Why is light important in our lives?

   Light can give us the courage to find our way in the darkness and
   to help others find their ways, too.

2. Why were the disciples a light to the world?

   The disciples were a light to the world because they
   followed Jesus. Their lives shined before others
   and lighted the way to God and happiness.

   _____

3. Discuss how the community of the Church can become a brighter light for people today.

Go out and be
a light to all
people so they
can live in my
love.
Based on Acts 13:47

CURRICULUM CONNECTION

Science   Explain that light is a form of energy that can be seen. Have the class discover what happens when white light (sunlight) passes through a prism. White light appears to be colorless, but it is really a mixture of different colors. Make the comparison of the many colors of refracted light to the many different actions of goodness, kindness, caring, helpfulness, and so on that we bring to the world by being light to the world.

Answering Three Review Questions

Direct the students' attention to the three questions at the top of page 241. Direct the students to complete the activity, working independently. Afterward, invite the students to share their responses.

Reviewing the Chapter

Read aloud the two review questions. Ask the students to write the answers on the lines provided. Encourage all to participate in the discussion of item 3.

Praying with the Scripture Verse

On lined paper, invite the students to write prayers asking Jesus to help them be more of a light to others. Ask them to bring their prayers to the prayer area. Light a large candle. Read aloud the verse from the Acts of the Apostles at the bottom of page 241. Invite the students to pray what they wrote. Encourage the class to memorize the Scripture verse.

20 A Servant to the World

Objectives

To help the students

- Understand that Christians are called to serve others.
- Appreciate the example of Jesus in serving others.
- Understand that the Church is called to serve and build a better world.
- Identify ways they can build a better world.
- Pray with gestures and review the chapter.

Chapter Outline

Day	Step 1 Learning About Our Lives	Step 2 Learning About Our Faith	Step 3 Learning How to Live Our Faith 
Day 1	■ Talk about being light. ■ Introduce the chapter. ■ Study the pictures. *ABOUT 15 MINUTES*	■ Read about and discuss service. ■ Learn the vocabulary. *ABOUT 7 MINUTES*	■ Write about people who serve. *ABOUT 8 MINUTES*
Day 2	■ Imagine a better world. *ABOUT 10 MINUTES*	■ Read and discuss the Scripture story. ■ Remember Holy Thursday. *ABOUT 10 MINUTES*	■ Read about then and now. ■ Discuss service. *ABOUT 10 MINUTES*
Day 3	■ Review parish bulletins. *ABOUT 10 MINUTES*	■ Read about and discuss the servant Church. ■ Review the doctrine. *ABOUT 10 MINUTES*	■ Write about parish service. *ABOUT 10 MINUTES*
Day 4	■ Imagine a perfect world. *ABOUT 10 MINUTES*	■ Understand Jesus' call to build a better world. *ABOUT 8 MINUTES*	■ Write ways to serve. ■ Discuss vocations. *ABOUT 12 MINUTES*

Day 5 **Prayer** Understand praying with gestures and pray together.

Review Identify examples of the servant Church; review the chapter; and learn the Scripture verse.

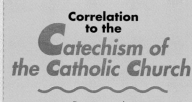

Correlation
to the
Catechism of
the **C**atholic **C**hurch

Paragraphs
876, 1551, 2420

Plan Ahead ~~~~~~~

	Preparing Your Class	Materials Needed
Day 1	Read through the lesson plan.	■ pencils or pens
Day 2	Read through the lesson plan.	■ pencils or pens ■ lined paper
Day 3	Read through the lesson plan. Gather recent parish bulletins for use in Step 1. If you plan to invite a guest speaker, make all the necessary arrangements.	■ pencils or pens ■ parish bulletins ■ lined paper
Day 4	Read through the lesson plan.	■ pencils or pens
Day 5	Read through the lesson plan.	■ pencils or pens ■ Bible, candle ■ prayer cloth ■ copies of THIS IS OUR FAITH *Hymnal*

Additional Resources

As you plan this chapter, consider using the following materials from The Resourceful Teacher Package.

■ *Classroom Activity Sheets 20* and *20a*

■ *Family Activity Sheets 20* and *20a*

■ *Chapter 20 Test*

■ *Prayers for Every Day*

■ *Projects: Grade 4*

You may also wish to refer to the following Big Book.

■ *We Celebrate God's Word,* pages 16–17

In preparing the students for the Sunday readings, you may wish to use Silver Burdett Ginn's *Getting Ready for Sunday* student and teacher materials.

BOOKS FOR THE JOURNEY

The Story of Jumping Mouse. John Steptoe. Morrow, 1989. An exceptionally fine story of caring and using one's gifts to help another.

The Ch'i-lin Purse. "The Ch'i Lin Purse," pp. 3–15. Retold by Linda Fang. Farrar Straus Giroux, 1995. A story of a young woman who helped another and who believed that if you have a chance to do something good, be sure to do it.

MORE BOOKS FOR THE JOURNEY

Guests. Michael Dorris. Hyperion Books for Children, 1994. A story about extending hospitality to people who are in need even when it isn't easy and learning some of what it means to be who you are.

Hand in Hand. "Harriet Tubman," on a tablet in Auburn, New York, p. 61; from "Song of Myself," by Walt Whitman, p. 70. Collected by Lee Bennett Hopkins. Simon & Schuster, 1994. Poems of people who made the world a better place.

REDUCED CLASSROOM ACTIVITIES

NAME _____

A SERVANT TO THE WORLD

Choose words from the box to complete the sentences.

Jesus	service	community	better	gifts
need	servant	serve	Church	

The Church community is to be of service to the entire world. We can do this by helping people who are in need . We also can serve by working with those people who are trying to build a better world.

The Church is a servant Church. Jesus calls the Church community to respond to the world's needs. Everyone has special gifts and talents. We must use them to do the work of the Church on earth.

To the Teacher: In this activity, students identify their call to be members of a servant Church.

Chapter 20   A Servant to the World   THIS IS OUR FAITH 4   **20**

NAME _____

WHAT IF?

1. What would you do if you had a lot of money to share with others? _____
_____
_____
_____

2. What problem would you try to solve if you were a renowned scientist or medical doctor? _____
_____
_____

3. What steps would you take if you were put in charge of a class project entitled "Service to the Elderly"? _____
_____
_____
_____
_____

To the Teacher: This activity can be used to encourage students to undertake a service project.

20a   THIS IS OUR FAITH 4   Chapter 20   A Servant to the World

Background for the Teacher

LIGHT TO THE WORLD

The Church as light to the nations is a traditional symbol. God's people praised him with thanksgiving for the special gifts he gave them, but they recognized that with their gifts came responsibility. They were called to let their light shine on all—so all might discover the Light. Such a view gave rise to great and creative missionary work. The Church was motivated by the awareness that the world might be lost if it could not hear the gospel.

SERVANT TO THE WORLD

In recent times the Catholic Church has given renewed emphasis to the servant dimension of its identity and mission. Pope John XXIII exemplified and taught the servant nature of the Church. He taught with authority, but listened as well. He joined hands with those of other faiths, and praised their efforts to bring goodness, justice, and peace in the world.

The mission of the whole Church is articulated in the Documents on Vatican Council II as follows: (1) proclamation of the gospel; (2) celebration of the sacraments; (3) witnessing to the gospel through a life-style that is marked by humility, compassion, respect for human rights, and so forth; and (4) witnessing to the gospel through a life of service to those in need, both inside and outside the Church.

The idea of the Church as "servant to the world" is not something that Catholics can ignore. It is integral to who we are as the Body of Christ; it is essential to the very mission of the Church. As a Church, we have both corporate and individual responsibility. Both the institution and individual Catholics recognize that to be a servant to the world reaches beyond the confines of the Church, and calls us to serve all people. We are mandated to work to build a better world.

The Church, then, not only illuminates the dark world with the light of Christ, but it also serves the bright and hopeful struggles of all people to better the world. The Church is servant to all who strive to build a more humane world. So the Church needs to listen, observe, respect, and work with others, as well as teach and direct.

As a teacher you can help the students recognize that they make a difference in other people's lives. Their acts of service motivated by love to others can make the world in which they live—home, school, and Church—a better place. You can impress upon them that no opportunity to serve others is unimportant and that each is a challenge to live out the example of Jesus.

Objective

This lesson helps the students understand that Christians are called to serve others in making a better world.

Step 1 / INTRODUCTION

Learning About Our Lives

Talking About Being Light

Ask the students to describe how they have tried to be a light to others since the last session. Encourage their efforts to show others the way to God and true happiness.

Introducing the Chapter

Emphasize that every day people are presented with opportunities to make the world better. Invite the students to open their books to page 242 to discover how ordinary people do this. Read the chapter title. Ask them to define the word *servant* (someone who is hired to perform certain tasks).

Direct attention to the chapter-focus question. Use the students' answers to make two lists on the chalkboard. Then ask them to rank order the lists, identifying the five things they like best about the world and the five things they most want to change.

Studying the Pictures

Read aloud the Discuss paragraph. Direct the students to look at the three photographs on page 242 and then discuss one picture at a time. Help them to recognize how each person enriches the world. Ask the students to explain how those pictured are serving others.

Discuss the first picture. Explore with the class how construction workers serve others. Emphasize that safety standards are an important part of building a house.

Discuss the picture of the scientist. Ask the students to name how the scientist is being a servant. Explain that she might be inventing a new medicine to help others, developing a new way of testing for a disease, or studying the results of people's tests. She is serving others by working in the lab.

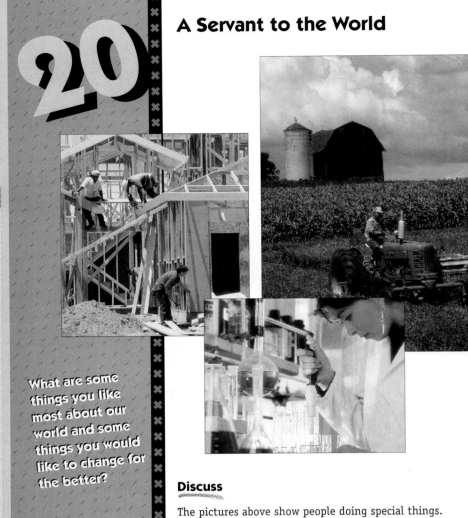

20 A Servant to the World

What are some things you like most about our world and some things you would like to change for the better?

Discuss

The pictures above show people doing special things. Think about what they are doing. How can their work help make the world a better place for people to live happily together?

242 Morality

★ Enriching the Lesson ★

Distribute newspapers and periodicals. Ask the students to use these to find articles about people or groups who are trying to make the world a better place. Have the class summarize the articles by answering the questions below.

- How did the person (people) make the world a better place?

- What made the person in the article do what he or she did?

- How would you have acted in the same situation?

Chapter Review

Look at the photographs. On the lines provided, tell how the people in each photograph are examples of the Servant Church.

_____   _____
_____   _____
_____   _____
                                 _____

1. What is meant by *service*?

   <u>Service is work that helps others who need our care.</u>

2. How can we serve others as Jesus did?

   <u>We can serve others as Jesus did by caring for our neighbors. We</u>
   <u>can work with people who want to build a better world. We</u>
   <u>can use our special gifts and talents to work for justice and</u>
   <u>peace. And we can serve others by praying for them.</u>

   _____

3. Discuss how Catholics can serve the world today.

> **Serve one another out of love.**
> Based on
> Galatians 5:13

Identifying Examples of the Servant Church

Direct the students' attention to the photographs at the top of page 251. Ask the students to write their answers on the lines provided. When the students have finished, invite class members to share their ideas. List the responses on the chalkboard.

Reviewing the Chapter

Go through the two review questions at the bottom of page 251. Have the students suggest at least four ways of serving others in question 2. For the discussion, encourage all to participate. Affirm the verbal contributions of all participants.

Learning the Scripture Verse

Summarize the lesson by pointing out the Scripture verse in the box on page 251. Invite the students to read it aloud together. Emphasize that all our acts of service should be motivated by love.

Focus on

Service The Medical Missionaries of Mary have opened a mission in a refugee camp in Cyanika, Rwanda. "We serve a great, great need," explained Sister Jude Walsh. "We see some 1,000 patients a day." Many people live in makeshift huts; they find hope in the Eucharist; there are about 150,000 orphans. For materials to help your class understand the global needs of the poor, contact the Propagation of the Faith, 366 Fifth Avenue, New York, NY 10001, or your diocesan mission office.

Enriching the Lesson

You might want to encourage the class to show gratitude to those who serve in your parish. Distribute lined paper to the students so that they can write thank-you notes to some of the parishioners who serve in your parish. You can find the names of these people in your parish bulletin. Arrange with the pastor or another member of the parish staff to distribute the notes to the appropriate persons.

251

End-of-unit pages include a Unit Organizer; Unit Review; Day to Day: Skills for Christian Living; and *Opening Doors: A Take-Home Magazine.*

Using the Unit Organizer

Completing a graphic organizer such as a chart or table can help the students to organize information that has been presented in the unit. Organizers can enable the students to visualize their thinking and recognize relationships among ideas. This will give the students the opportunity to understand more completely the materials they have been studying.

Completing the Organizer

Have the students turn to page 252 in their books. Ask the students to write their responses to the statements in the Unit Organizer activity independently. If necessary, tell them that they may look back through the previous four chapters for help. When everyone has finished, have the students compare their responses with the class.

Looking Back: Self-Assessment

The critical reflection questions below give the students an opportunity to sharpen their thinking skills. The questions can be used as a class discussion or independent writing activity.

■ Which was your favorite Scripture story in this unit? What did you like most about it?

■ Which picture or illustration in this unit did you like best? What did you like about it?

■ Which prayer was your favorite prayer in this unit? Why?

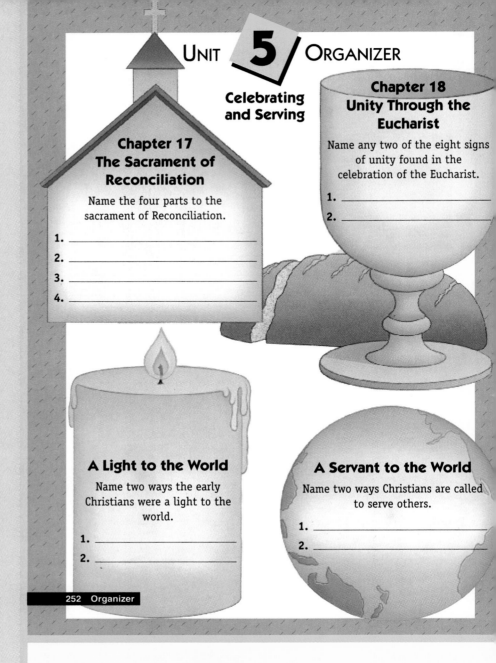

UNIT **5** ORGANIZER

Celebrating and Serving

**Chapter 17
The Sacrament of Reconciliation**

Name the four parts to the sacrament of Reconciliation.

1. _____
2. _____
3. _____
4. _____

**Chapter 18
Unity Through the Eucharist**

Name any two of the eight signs of unity found in the celebration of the Eucharist.

1. _____
2. _____

A Light to the World

Name two ways the early Christians were a light to the world.

1. _____
2. _____

A Servant to the World

Name two ways Christians are called to serve others.

1. _____
2. _____

252 Organizer

252

UNIT 5 REVIEW

Match the words in Column A with the definitions in Column B.

Column A

1. examination of conscience
2. absolution
3. Corinthians
4. Penance
5. service

Column B

___3___ the people who lived in Corinth, a city in Greece

___1___ thinking about what we have said and done and how we may have sinned

___5___ work that helps others who need our care

___2___ a prayer of forgiveness for sins prayed by the priest in the sacrament of Reconciliation

___4___ another name for the sacrament of Reconciliation

Fill in the missing words to complete each sentence.

1. When we celebrate Reconciliation, we p _r_ _a_ _y_ and make an examination of conscience, we c _o_ _n_ _f_ _e_ _s_ _s_ our sins to the p _r_ _i_ _e_ _s_ _t_, we accept a p _e_ _n_ _a_ _n_ _c_ _e_, we express our s _o_ _r_ _r_ _o_ _w_, and we r _e_ _c_ _e_ _i_ _v_ _e_ absolution from the priest.

2. Saint Paul called the Church the B _o_ _d_ _y_ of C _h_ _r_ _i_ _s_ _t_.

3. We gather at the E _u_ _c_ _h_ _a_ _r_ _i_ _s_ _t_ to celebrate our u _n_ _i_ _t_ _y_ and to help it grow.

Review 253

Reviewing the Unit

The purpose of the Unit Review is to reinforce the concepts presented in the previous four chapters and to check the students' understanding. After explaining the directions, give the students sufficient time to complete the two-page review. Answer any questions they may have as you check their work.

Testing

After the students have completed the Unit Review, you may wish to distribute copies of the Unit 5 Test from the Tests booklets.

Project

Tell the students they will work together to write a class newspaper on the themes of Unit 5. Have them suggest a name for their newspaper. Divide the class into several small groups and give the reporters their assignments for the articles they will write for the newspaper.

■ *Current News:* Ask a group of students to write stories that tell about people who help the Church celebrate God's forgiveness and unity.

■ *Historical News:* Using books about the lives of the saints, challenge other students to report about saints who have shown us how to serve others.

■ *Artwork:* Other students can illustrate the news.

When the students have finished their assignments and have written or drawn them neatly, instruct the students to glue their assignments to posterboard on which you have lettered the title.

4. The community of the Church is a l <u>i</u> <u>g</u> <u>h</u> <u>t</u> to the
w <u>o</u> <u>r</u> <u>l</u> <u>d</u>'. Every member of the Church is called to live a
g <u>o</u> <u>o</u> <u>d</u> l <u>i</u> <u>f</u> <u>e</u> .

5. All C <u>h</u> <u>r</u> <u>i</u> <u>s</u> <u>t</u> <u>i</u> <u>a</u> <u>n</u> <u>s</u> belong to the one
Body of Christ the C <u>h</u> <u>u</u> <u>r</u> <u>c</u> <u>h</u> .

Write an X next to the correct examples of how the Church serves people
and tries to build a better world.

____x____ sending missionaries to teach people about Jesus

_____ inventing larger airplanes

____x____ opening health clinics in poor countries

____x____ sending clothing to poor areas

____x____ providing shelter for homeless children

_____ opening more grocery stores

____x____ teaching people how to grow better crops

Use the words below to complete the following sentence.

followers	God	Jesus	Light of the World	happiness

__Jesus__ , the __Light of the World__ , and the lives of his
__followers__ shine before others, lighting the way to __God__
and __happiness__ .

LEARNING to SAY "I'M SORRY" RESPONDING with FORGIVENESS

Conflict or disagreements occur in all relationships. Feelings are often hurt by what is said or done. As followers of Jesus, we are called to be forgiving of those who have hurt us, and to ask forgiveness of those whom we have hurt. Saying "I'm sorry" and "It's okay, I forgive you" are important words of forgiveness and reconciliation. These words are not always easy to say, especially when the hurt feeling still exists. Jesus promises that he will be with us. Jesus will help heal the hurt we feel. Jesus will give us the strength to be forgiving even when it is difficult.

APOLOGIZING

What you say and how you say it are both very important parts of an apology. A helpful apology begins with "I'm sorry," followed by what it is you are sorry about. For example: "I'm sorry I hurt your feelings when I called you a name." The tone of voice is also important. A sincere voice tone suggests that the person really means what he or she is saying.

Apologies mean very little if the words of forgiveness are not followed by a change in what is said and done. If we continue to do the things that are hurtful, our apology is of little value in bringing healing to the relationship.

When someone apologizes, he or she is asking for our forgiveness. When we accept someone's apology, we are telling the other person that we do forgive him or her. The words we choose might sound like these:

"It's okay." I forgive you."

"I forgive you."

"Let's be friends again."

I'M SORRY I TALKED BACK TO YOU, MOM..

I FORGIVE YOU, LISA. I KNOW YOU DIDN'T MEAN WHAT YOU SAID.

I'M SORRY I PUSHED IN FRONT OF YOU IN LINE.

THAT'S OKAY I FORGIVE YOU.

Day to Day 255

Objective

This lesson helps the students increase their ability to apologize sincerely and respond positively when asked to be forgiving.

Introducing the Lesson

Ask the students to tell about a time when they had a disagreement with a friend. What was the disagreement about? How did they feel? How did they make up? Was making up an easy or hard thing to do? Why?

Have the students open their books to page 255 and read aloud the lesson title and the opening paragraph. Ask if anyone has had the experience of wanting to forgive, yet still felt the hurt of the conflict or disagreement.

Invite volunteers to read aloud the paragraphs under "Apologizing." Have students demonstrate what it means to use a sincere tone of voice when apologizing. Emphasize that a change in behavior—what is said or done—also signifies that the person who has apologized is sincere. Explore with the class how a person feels when his or her apology is not accepted. Note that the hurt continues and reconciliation can't take place.

Completing the Activity

Have students read silently the story about Lisa and Melanie. Then ask the following questions to guide the discussion.

■ Who needs to apologize in this story? (*Both Lisa and Melanie. Lisa needs to apologize for trying to get the others not to like Melanie. Melanie needs to apologize for excluding Lisa from the game. Help students understand that it is OK to make new friends, but that it is important to "be friendly" with everyone. Being "inclusive" rather than "exclusive" brings us closer to being a true follower of Jesus.*)

■ Does it matter who apologizes first? (*Not really. Some may think that the first person to start the disagreement should apologize first. Such a rule might impede the process of reconciliation. Being able to admit you were wrong and are sorry regardless of who started the disagreement is what is most important.*)

Lesson continues on page 256.

Have the students write words of apology and forgiveness for Lisa and Melanie in the speech balloons. Ask the students to share their responses.

After the students have shared their responses, invite volunteers to role-play Lisa and Melanie apologizing and forgiving one another. Have the other members of the class observe voice tone and level of sincerity. Ask the role-players to comment on whether it was easy or difficult to apologize and forgive the other person. (Similar to using I-feel talk, there is a certain amount of risk involved in offering an apology—risk that the other person won't accept what we are saying. By offering an apology we open ourselves to the other person with the hope that the relationship will be restored.)

Conclude this activity by having the students tell what Lisa and Melanie need to do after they have apologized and forgiven each other. (*Lisa needs to stop trying to get the others to not like Melanie; Melanie needs to include Lisa in the recess games with her new friend.*)

Concluding the Lesson

Lead the class through the prayer on page 256. Ask the students to get very quiet, close their eyes, and think for a minute about a relationship they might have right now that is in need of healing. Perhaps someone has fought with a friend, or someone isn't being treated fairly, or there's been a disagreement with a family member. Ask the students to silently ask Jesus to bring his healing touch to the hurt they feel and to the relationship that is under strain from this hurt. Conclude by praying, "Jesus, we know you are with us now. Please listen as we ask you to bring your peace and healing to all who suffer the pain and hurt of relationships that are in conflict. Amen."

256

Can You Help Lisa and Melanie?

Lisa and Melanie have been good friends for a long time. Lately they have not been getting along very well. Melanie has been playing with someone else at recess and Lisa feels left out. Whenever Lisa asks to play, Melanie tells her that only two people can play what she and her other friend are playing. Lisa's feelings are hurt. She tries to get back at Melanie by getting her other friends to dislike Melanie. Both Lisa and Melanie end up being angry at each other.

Let's suppose that Lisa is sorry and wants to apologize to Melanie. Use the speech balloons below to tell what Lisa could say and how Melanie might respond.

Apologizing is an important first step in reconciling. What else needs to happen between the girls for healing to occur?

_____

_____

_____

256   Day to Day

PRAYER

Close your eyes and think about a relationship you may have that is in need of healing. You may have tried to resolve the problem but may have not been successful.

Silently ask Jesus to bring his healing touch to the hurt you feel and to the relationship that is broken.

OPENING DOORS
A Take-Home Magazine™

Growing Closer

AS A SIGN OF FAMILY UNITY and sense of Christian mission, plan an act of service for others. Everyone in the family should participate. The following are suggestions.

• Write notes or send greeting cards to someone who needs words of comfort or cheer.

• Do without a special treat. Donate the money to a shelter for the homeless or other charitable organization.

• Volunteer the family to help serve a meal at a shelter.

• Invite someone who is lonely as a guest for a family meal. Make this a special occasion by sharing your family's blessing cup.

Looking Ahead

Take advantage of the leisure days of summer to share with your child the hopes and dreams you have for each other. May you walk safely in the light and warmth of the summer sun.

© Silver Burdett Ginn Inc.

8

Opening Doors

Sending the Magazine Home

As you complete Unit 5 with your class, assist the students in carefully removing *Opening Doors: A Take-Home Magazine* (two pages) from their books by separating them from the book along the perforations. Demonstrate how to fold the two pages, forming an eight-page booklet. Ask the students to take the magazine home and encourage their families to read it with them and participate in the suggested activities.

Opening Doors

Family Gathering

After the resurrection, Jesus appeared to his followers often at mealtime. The story of Emmaus (Luke 24:13-35), when Jesus walked with two disciples and broke bread with them reminds us of Jesus' presence when we celebrate the Eucharist.

It also reminds us that Jesus, the risen Lord, is with us always and everywhere.

The gathering and sharing of the family meal symbolize and remind us of Christ's presence with us in our weekly routine. To help your family make at least one meal a month a sacramental occasion, you may want to adopt the sharing of the blessing cup described on page 3. Some families have adopted this ritual and have adapted prayers and types of sharing to fit their family needs.

Review with your child the names and uses of the vessels used during the Mass.

- The cruets are bottles which hold the wine and water brought to the altar during the Offertory procession.

- The chalice is the sacred cup in which wine is consecrated.

- The paten is the plate which holds the bread that is consecrated.

- The ciborium is a container used to hold hosts for communion distribution and for reservation in the tabernacle.

Cruets

Chalice

Paten

Ciborium

During prayer at mealtime, each person in the family drinks from a cup that your family has designated as the family blessing cup. The cup can be shared at every family meal or reserved for birthdays, anniversaries, holidays, or other occasions that your family considers special: when a visitor is dining with you, when someone brings home good news, when you want to welcome the first day of vacation.

Your family may also choose to share the blessing cup when family peace has been disturbed by quarrels, tension, bad news, or sickness. As you say a traditional or spontaneous prayer, each person drinks from the cup. Through this ritual your family will be reminded of bonds of love, unity, and peace.

Blessing cups are sold in religious goods stores or you may wish to use a family heirloom. Any glass, cup, or drinking vessel can be used. The cup should be set aside in a special place. Any beverage may be used, but fruit juice, water, or milk may be the most symbolic because of their nourishing and nurturing qualities.

Sacred Vessels

The next time you are in church draw your child's attention to the tabernacle. Explain that in this safe-like box is the Blessed Sacrament.

Tell your child we genuflect when we enter the pews in church as a sign of respect and reverence of Christ's presence with us.

Go in Peace

The sacrament of the Eucharist calls us to unity and peace. The sacramental ritual symbolizes and renews the unity for which Jesus prayed at the Last Supper. The Eucharist is also the sacrament of Christ's total self-giving. We share in the Eucharist and are called to service of others.

The Mass concludes with the Blessing and the Dismissal. We are blessed and sent out to be a blessing to others. It may be a simple or solemn blessing or a prayer over the people.

The following words are one of the solemn blessings during Ordinary Time. It is from the Blessing of Aaron in the Old Testament, the Hebrew Scriptures.

May the Lord bless you and keep you.   R/Amen.

May his face shine upon you,
and be gracious to you.   R/Amen.

May he look upon you with kindness,
and give you his peace.   R/Amen.

May almighty God bless you,
the Father, and the Son, and the Holy Spirit.   R/Amen.

4

To Love and Serve

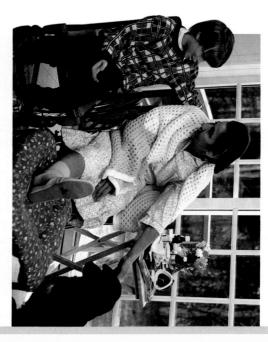

When Latin was used in the Mass, the priest dismissed the people with the words *Ite missa est*. The word Mass is derived from the word *missa*. It is interesting that the English word "mission" comes from the same root.

At the Dismissal of Mass we are given the mission to love and serve the Lord faithfully as we do the work of Christ in the world.

5

260

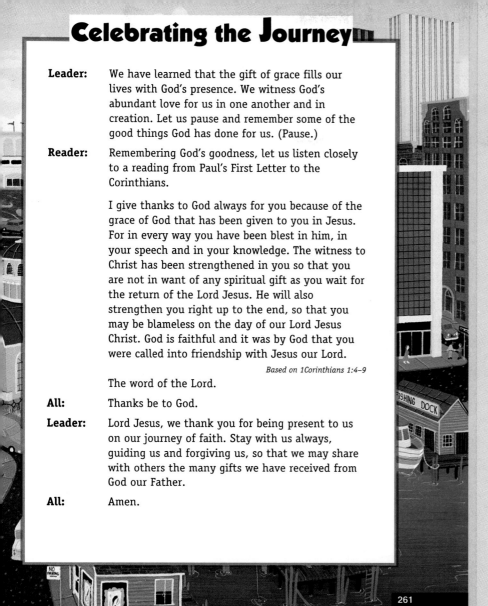

Celebrating the Journey

Leader: We have learned that the gift of grace fills our lives with God's presence. We witness God's abundant love for us in one another and in creation. Let us pause and remember some of the good things God has done for us. (Pause.)

Reader: Remembering God's goodness, let us listen closely to a reading from Paul's First Letter to the Corinthians.

I give thanks to God always for you because of the grace of God that has been given to you in Jesus. For in every way you have been blest in him, in your speech and in your knowledge. The witness to Christ has been strengthened in you so that you are not in want of any spiritual gift as you wait for the return of the Lord Jesus. He will also strengthen you right up to the end, so that you may be blameless on the day of our Lord Jesus Christ. God is faithful and it was by God that you were called into friendship with Jesus our Lord.

Based on 1Corinthians 1:4–9

The word of the Lord.

All: Thanks be to God.

Leader: Lord Jesus, we thank you for being present to us on our journey of faith. Stay with us always, guiding us and forgiving us, so that we may share with others the many gifts we have received from God our Father.

All: Amen.

261

Introducing "Celebrating the Journey"

A vital dimension of our Catholic Christian faith is the experience of celebration at all the important moments of our lives. Celebrating the Journey is a special feature designed to help celebrate the completion of another important phase of the faith journey.

Using "Celebrating the Journey"

Plan a special time at the end of the year to use this prayer service with your class. Select a volunteer to read the suggested reading from Scripture. Choose a few of the students' favorite songs to sing at various times during the celebration. You may wish to choose a song or acclamation from the THIS IS OUR FAITH *Hymnal.* Allow the students to participate as fully as possible. You may wish to invite others, such as the Director of Religious Education, the principal, the pastor, or the students' families, to the celebration. End the celebration with a simple snack.

AMEN TOC (TK)

Our Church Celebrates Advent   264
Our Church Celebrates Christmas   272
Our Church Celebrates Lent   280
Our Church Celebrates Holy Week   290
Our Church Celebrates Easter   294

262

Our Church Honors Saints   302

Our Church Honors Mary   310

Our Church Celebrates Holy Days   316

In the Spirit of Jesus   322

263

Our Church Celebrates Advent

Objectives ～～～～

- **LESSON 1:** To help the students recognize Advent as a season of preparation for Christmas.
- **LESSON 2:** To help the students participate in the Church's celebration of Advent.
- **LESSON 3:** To help the students understand that we wait in hope for the coming of the Savior.
- **LESSON 4:** To help the students enter into the prayerful spirit of the Advent season.

Lesson Outlines ～～～～

	Step 1 Learning About Our Lives	**Step 2** Learning About Our Faith	**Step 3** Learning How to Live Our Faith
Lesson 1	■ Discuss travel plans. *ABOUT 5 MINUTES*	■ Read a story. ■ Look at a map. ■ Journeying Toward Jesus. *ABOUT 12 MINUTES*	■ Complete a writing activity. ■ Discuss choices. ■ Pray together. *ABOUT 13 MINUTES*
Lesson 2	■ Discuss how colors affect us. *ABOUT 7 MINUTES*	■ Read about and discuss the Advent season. *ABOUT 5 MINUTES*	■ Make an Advent banner. *ABOUT 18 MINUTES*
Lesson 3	■ Discuss holiday visitors. *ABOUT 5 MINUTES*	■ Read a story. ■ Learn about God's promise. *ABOUT 8 MINUTES*	■ Write about Christmas preparations. ■ Pray together. *ABOUT 17 MINUTES*
Lesson 4	**Project** Read about Advent wreaths; make an Advent wreath; and write an Advent prayer. **Prayer** Review the Advent season; create signs that show welcome; and pray together.		

Plan Ahead

	Preparing Your Class	**Materials Needed**
Lesson 1	Read through the entire lesson plan. Have a backpack available in the classroom or bring a small suitcase.	■ pencils ■ backpack or small suitcase
Lesson 2	Read through the lesson plan. Gather examples of colorful and colorless items. Gather art materials for banner-making activity.	■ art materials, scissors ■ lightweight fabric ■ glue or thread and needles ■ sleigh bells (optional) ■ vestment in Advent color
Lesson 3	Read through the lesson plan. Practice teaching the signs in Step 3.	■ pencils
Lesson 4	Read the lesson plan. Make a wreath using students' materials. Cut strips and small squares for paper candles. Choose reflective music for the prayer service.	■ candles, four for each student ■ plastic foam rings, cut evergreens ■ scissors, florist's wire, glue ■ purple paper strips (1" × 4") and 1" yellow squares, four per student

Additional Resources

As you plan these lessons, consider using the following material from The Resourceful Teacher Package.

- *Classroom Activity Sheets* for Advent
- *Family Activity Sheets* for Advent
- *Prayers for Every Day*

You may also wish to refer to the following Big Book.

- *We Celebrate God's Word,* page 4

In preparing the students for the Sunday readings, you may wish to use Silver Burdett Ginn's *Getting Ready for Sunday* student and teacher materials.

REDUCED CLASSROOM ACTIVITIES

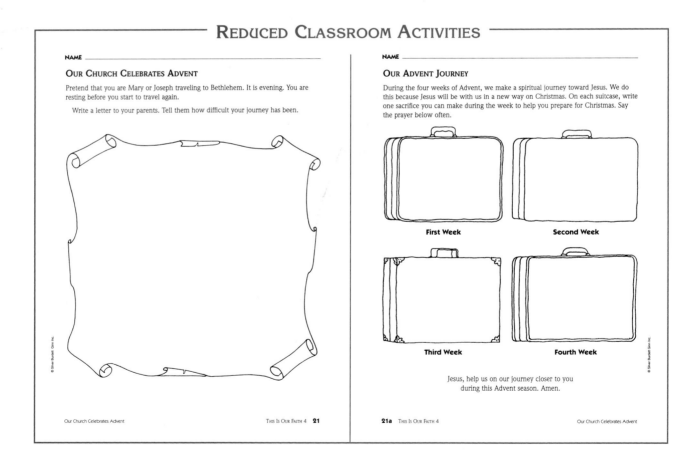

NAME _____

OUR CHURCH CELEBRATES ADVENT

Pretend that you are Mary or Joseph traveling to Bethlehem. It is evening. You are resting before you start to travel again.

Write a letter to your parents. Tell them how difficult your journey has been.

NAME _____

OUR ADVENT JOURNEY

During the four weeks of Advent, we make a spiritual journey toward Jesus. We do this because Jesus will be with us in a new way on Christmas. On each suitcase, write one sacrifice you can make during the week to help you prepare for Christmas. Say the prayer below often.

First Week   **Second Week**

Third Week   **Fourth Week**

Jesus, help us on our journey closer to you
during this Advent season. Amen.

THE MEANING OF ADVENT

The word *advent* is derived from the Latin word *adventus,* meaning "coming." During the liturgical season of Advent, the Church focuses on the threefold coming of the Lord Jesus: We prepare to welcome the Lord in a new way at Christmas. We think about his coming in history. We rejoice in his presence among us now in the circumstances and graced moments of our daily lives. We refer to this as the coming of Jesus in mystery. And during Advent, we look forward to the time when we will greet the Lord at his final coming at the end of time. We can call this his coming in majesty.

PREPARE HIS WAY

Advent is a time to make it possible for the Lord to come to us and for us to move toward him on the way. John the Baptizer urges us to "prepare the way of the Lord, make straight his paths" (Matthew 3:3). John echoes the prophet Isaiah when he proclaims, "Every valley shall be filled and every mountain and hill shall be leveled. The windings shall be made straight and the rough ways smooth" (Luke 3:5–6).

During Advent we are invited to recognize the clutter and obstacles in our lives, to acknowledge the roughness that needs smoothing and the valleys and hills that require leveling. Unlike Lent, Advent is a joyful time—four weeks of excitement and anticipation of the Lord's renewed presence in our lives. As we prepare for his coming, we pray, *Come, Lord Jesus.*

In these lessons, the students will be called to identify with the human concerns of Mary and Joseph, understand the signs and symbols of the Advent season, and recognize how different cultures prepare to celebrate the birth of Christ. Fourth graders are growing in their ability to reflect upon their own lives. Advent can be for them, then, an opportunity for new growth and an awareness of filling in the valleys and leveling the hills of their own growth as loving children of God. It can also be a time of great hope and joy in the coming of our Savior and a chance to feel a sense of unity with Christians throughout the ages who have waited for the coming of the Lord.

LESSON 1

Objective

This lesson helps the students recognize Advent as a season of preparation for Christmas.

Step 1 / INTRODUCTION

Learning About Our Lives

Discussing Travel Plans

Talk about the upcoming holidays. Ask how many of the students will be having family members come to celebrate or how many of them will be traveling to spend the holidays elsewhere. Discuss what advance plans must be made. Talk about packing and show the small suitcase or backpack you have brought to class. Share examples of your own experience of traveling. Encourage the students to share their experiences of trips or overnight stays with friends.

Step 2 / DEVELOPMENT

Learning About Our Faith

Reading a Story

Give the students an opportunity to study the illustration on page 264 of Mary and Joseph. Review with them that Mary and Joseph traveled from their hometown of Nazareth to the town of Bethlehem. Ask volunteers to read aloud "The Journey to Bethlehem."

Looking at a Map

Have the students look at the map of the Holy Land on page 329 in their books. Help them trace a route from Nazareth to Bethlehem. Point out how difficult such a journey would have been since the distance traveled was about seventy miles over uphill terrain and the journey was made on foot or by riding on a donkey. Ask:

- What special things for the new baby may Mary have had to leave behind? (*Clothes, toys, blankets*)
- What things might Joseph have made for the child that he could not have brought along? (*A cradle, a chair, a crib*)

264

Our Church Celebrates Advent

The Journey to Bethlehem

During Advent, we get ready for Jesus to come into our lives at Christmas. Part of the Advent story is the journey of Mary and Joseph to Bethlehem.

At that time the ruler of their land ordered all people to return to their hometowns to be counted in a census of the whole country. Bethlehem was Joseph's hometown, so Mary and Joseph had to travel there.

Mary would soon give birth to her baby. Joseph was worried about Mary, because he loved her very much, and knew the trip to Bethlehem would be hard for her. Joseph felt sad about the trip, but he believed that God would watch over them and help take care of Mary.

Mary was worried about Joseph, too, because she loved him very much. She knew the trip would be tiring for him. Mary also felt sad that she and Joseph would have to travel to Bethlehem.

Focus on

Census Remind the students that Mary and Joseph returned to Bethlehem to be officially counted. Explain that this counting is called a census. The word *census* comes from a Latin phrase that means "to tax." Census takers prepared lists of people and property so that the government could tax the people for services and enforce military service requirements. The United States conducts a census every ten years.

But she, too, believed that God would watch over them. Mary knew that God would help her take care of Joseph.

Based on Luke 2:1–5

Journeying Toward Jesus

When Mary and Joseph traveled to Bethlehem, they probably took only what they really needed. Bringing a lot of things would have made the trip more difficult.

During the season of Advent, we make a spiritual journey toward Jesus, who will be with us in a new way on Christmas. Like Joseph and Mary, we, too, must decide what will help us on our way. We can ask, "What must I take with me if I want to journey toward Jesus? What must I leave behind?"

Activity

Travel along the road above. It leads to Jesus. Read each word along your way. Decide if you will take it with you as you travel or leave it behind. Then fill in the blanks below with the words.

Take it along	Leave it behind
1. _____	1. _____
2. _____	2. _____
3. _____	3. _____
4. _____	4. _____

CURRICULUM CONNECTION

Math   Have the students turn to the map of the Holy Land on page 329 and recall the distance Mary and Joseph had to travel from Nazareth to Bethlehem (*about 75 miles*). Tell the students that the average person can walk one mile in approximately 20 minutes. Have the students calculate the minimum number of hours it might have taken Mary and Joseph to walk to Bethlehem (*25 hours*). Explain that Mary and Joseph probably covered this distance over several days.

Journeying Toward Jesus

Direct the students to read "Journeying Toward Jesus" on page 265. Stress that we prepare for the celebration of Christmas during Advent and that we journey toward Jesus.

Step 3 / CONCLUSION

Learning How to Live Our Faith

Completing a Writing Activity

Ask the students to do the activity at the bottom of page 265. Note that as they travel to Bethlehem they should decide which words describe an attribute that they want to bring along or leave behind on their journey to Jesus.

Discussing Choices

Discuss the students' choices. Encourage each student to select a good quality that he or she will develop or a negative quality that he or she will try to eliminate during the first week of Advent.

Praying Together

Invite the students to join you in prayer. Introduce the prayer by saying something like the following.

"During Advent we recall Jesus' birth long ago. We are reminded of Jesus' presence with us today. During Advent we journey toward Jesus. We seek him in our daily lives. Some of our thoughts and actions help us welcome Jesus. Some of our thoughts and actions do not help us. We want to leave these behind." (Allow silent time. Then pray aloud.) *"Jesus, help us to grow in* (pause) *during the first week in Advent."* (Pause.) *"Dear Jesus, help us to journey closer to you during this Advent season. Amen."*

265

LESSON 2

Objective

This lesson helps the students participate in the Church's celebration of Advent.

Step 1 / INTRODUCTION

Learning About Our Lives

Discussing How Colors Affect Us

Recall briefly that during Advent we prepare for and wait for the coming of Christ. Have the students think about and write down their three favorite colors and why these colors are their favorites. Then tally their choices. Discuss the individual and shared reasons why the students like the colors they do. Show an array (construction paper, jars of tempera paint, articles of clothing) of colorful and colorless items. Ask volunteers to share what moods the colors evoke and how the colors make them feel. Ask:

- What do the colors red, white, and blue remind Americans of? (*The flag, our country*)

- What are our school colors?

- What does green remind us of? (*Life, growth*)

Point out that some color choices reflect individual taste while other colors have meaning because everyone understands the color's meaning. (Be aware of students from other cultures for whom colors may have other meanings.)

Step 2 / DEVELOPMENT

Learning About Our Faith

Reading About and Discussing the Advent Season

Read aloud "The Advent Season" on page 266. As part of the discussion of the text, show the students a stole or some other article that is used in church during the Advent season. If purple vestments are used in your parish, take a little extra time to talk about the joyful penitence that precedes Christmas. Recall that during Lesson 1 the students learned that we journey to Jesus in Advent. Note that this four-week journey entails performing kind acts and praying daily in preparation for Jesus' coming.

The Advent Season

Colors are important to us. Some colors make us feel joyful and happy. Other colors seem quiet and peaceful.

The Church uses a different color during each of its special seasons. The colors tell us something about the meaning of each season.

The season of Advent is a prayerful time. It is a time of waiting and hopefulness. We look forward eagerly to the new coming of Jesus at Christmastime. We also prepare our hearts for the coming of Jesus when he returns in glory.

During Advent, the priest wears purple vestments. The Advent wreath in church has three purple candles and one pink candle. Purple is a sign of preparation and change. Pink is a sign of hope and joy. These colors help us remember that Advent is a time to prepare for Jesus by showing our love for others and having hope in God's promises. As we prepare for God's gift of Jesus at Christmas, we give the gift of ourselves to others during Advent.

Enriching the Lesson

Work with the class to prepare an Advent bulletin board in the classroom, the main hall of the school, or the church vestibule. The students might recreate the illustration on page 265 on the bulletin board, urging others to leave behind selfishness, laziness, jealousy, anger, and other qualities as they journey toward Christmas. Or they might make a large Advent wreath or small reproductions of the banners they made in today's lesson.

Activity

Design an Advent banner. Imagine that your banner will hang in church. What color or colors will you use? What symbols or words will you choose to help the people of your parish celebrate this Advent season?

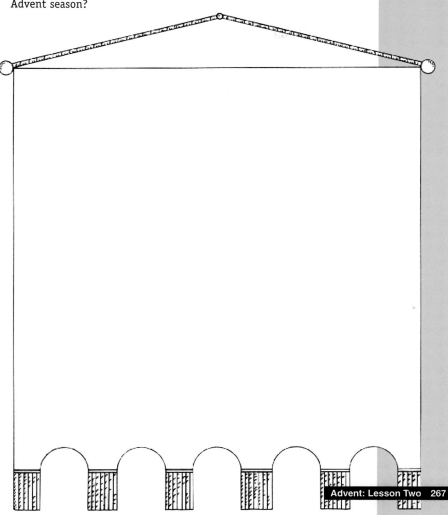

Also point out that the Advent season calls us to have faith that God's promises will come to pass.

Step 3 / CONCLUSION

Learning How to Live Our Faith

Making an Advent Banner

Have the students design a banner on page 267. Discuss the use of banners. Point out that banners, like colors, call up certain feelings and create or set moods, much like kites or balloons or flights of birds do. Afterward, invite the students to make real banners. Provide lightweight materials that move easily in the slightest breeze. If possible, provide small sleigh bells that are readily available in stores before Christmas. Suggest that the students hang these on slender ribbons or at the ends of their banners, so that they will be "ear"-catching as well as eye-catching. Urge the students to use one simple, clear design element in each banner. As they finish their work, suspend the banners around the classroom. Enlist the permission and help of appropriate members of the parish to select a place where the banners can be seen and enjoyed during this happy, contemplative season.

LESSON 3

Objective

This lesson helps the students understand that we wait in hope for the coming of the Savior.

Step 1 / INTRODUCTION

Learning About Our Lives

Discussing Holiday Visitors

Ask the students if they have ever had overnight guests visit their homes during the Christmas season. Invite them to identify who these visitors were and how long they stayed. Then encourage the students to share their experiences of getting ready for holiday visitors. Ask:

- What kinds of things need to be done to welcome guests?
- Who is responsible for making these preparations?

Tell the students that in this lesson they will read a story about a family preparing for guests.

Step 2 / DEVELOPMENT

Learning About Our Faith

Reading a Story

Call on volunteers to read aloud "Visitors for Christmas" on pages 268 and 269. Then use the following questions for discussion.

- Who was coming to visit the Ramírez family? (*Tina's and Carlos' grandparents*)
- What did Tina remember about her family's visit to Mexico three years before? (*The neighborhood procession, called* las posadas, *and the manger scene, called* nacimiento)
- Why was Tina disappointed when she heard when her grandparents were coming? (*She thought it was too long to wait.*)

Learning About God's Promise

Read through "The Coming of the Savior" on page 269 with the class. Help the students appreciate that people throughout history had hope in God's promise to send a savior for all people.

268

Visitors for Christmas

Tina and Carlos heard their mother talking excitedly on the phone in Spanish. Although the children knew many words in Spanish, their mother was talking too quickly for them to understand what she was saying. They knew that something important was going on.

Finally, Mrs. Ramírez hung up the phone and clapped her hands, "*Los abuelitos vienen para las Navidades!*" Then she repeated the good news in English, "Your grandparents are coming for Christmas!"

Tina and Carlos were surprised. They had not seen their grandparents in three years. Carlos was too young to remember visiting them at Christmas in Mexico City when Tina was in first grade. But Tina remembered every minute of the exciting trip. She remembered helping her Mexican cousins set up the *nacimiento*, the Christmas scene of the manger where Jesus was born.

Enriching the Lesson

Decorate a box to look like a manger. Place the box on a table, along with thin strips of yellow construction paper and markers. Tell the students that each time they do a good deed, they can write it on a strip of paper and place it in the manger. Explain that the paper strips represent straw and that the students' good deeds help prepare Jesus' crib.

"Now we can show Grandma and Grandpa how we get ready for Christmas!" said Tina. "When are they coming?"

Mrs. Ramírez circled December 20 on the calendar with red ink. Tina counted the days. "Fourteen days until they come?" she complained. "That's too long to wait!"

The Coming of the Age of Peace

Long before Jesus was born, God promised that one day the world would be a place of peace and justice. The prophet Isaiah spoke of the day when "The Lord will judge between the nations, and shall settle the disagreements of many peoples; they shall beat their swords into shovels and their spears into gardening tools. Nation shall not lift up sword against nation, neither shall they learn war anymore.

(Based on Isaiah 2:4).

Christians celebrate the birth of Jesus as the beginning of the Age of Peace expected by the prophets.

Activity

In the space below, write about the special ways your family prepares for Christmas.

THINGS TO DO BEFORE CHRISTMAS

_____
_____
_____
_____
_____

Learning How to Live Our Faith

Writing About Christmas Preparations

Ask a volunteer to read aloud the directions to the activity on page 269. Allow sufficient time for the students to write about their family Christmas preparations. When all have finished, invite the students to share their responses with the class. Emphasize that all our preparations for Christmas, when done with hope and joy, show our happiness and gratitude for God's gift of Jesus.

Teaching Tips

During Advent, make a special effort to notice the students' attempts to prepare for Jesus' coming at Christmas. As much as possible, ignore negative behavior and reinforce Christian attitudes and actions by commenting on the good things you see and hear. Praise the students publicly each time you "catch" them doing a good deed or acting with love.

Lesson 4

PROJECT

Objective

This lesson helps the students enter into the prayerful spirit of the Advent season.

Reading About Advent Wreaths

Drawing on the students' experience of previous Advents and on their response to the illustration on page 270, elicit the students' ideas about the Advent wreath's circular shape, the color and use of evergreens, and the four candles and their colors. Have the students read the explanation at the bottom of the page. Note the similarities and differences between the students' ideas and the explanation in the text.

Making an Advent Wreath

Distribute all the art materials for making the Advent wreath. Work with the class as a whole, proceeding step by step. Encourage the students to help one another. *Option:* If you are unable to procure the materials suggested on page 270, create construction-paper wreaths. Pre-cut and distribute large (12") white circles. Have the students cut (using a pattern or creating their own) paper holly leaves or paper pine branches. Have the students arrange these around the circle as they would arrange real holly or pine boughs and glue them in place. Have the students cut out purple paper bows for their wreaths. Provide purple and pink votive candles. Point out that the students can set these on their wreaths or they can hang the wreath on a wall and then place the candles in front of the wreath at a safe distance.

Writing an Advent Prayer

Have the students create a prayer or copy the prayer at the bottom of page 271. Encourage them to take this prayer home with their Advent wreaths.

270

An Advent Wreath

To make an Advent wreath for your family, you will need these materials.

- three purple candles and one pink candle
- a plastic foam ring about 12" in diameter
- some fresh evergreens

1. Make four holes in the plastic foam ring.

2. Put the candles in the holes.

3. Cover the plastic foam ring with the evergreens. Sprinkle water on them to keep them fresh. Change the branches when they become dry.

4. Take the Advent wreath home. Talk with your family about what the Advent wreath means.

The Meaning of the Advent Wreath

The circular shape of the wreath reminds us that God's love is without end. The evergreens show us that Jesus lives forever. We light one more candle each week of Advent to remind us to prepare for the new coming of Jesus, the Light of the World, at Christmastime. We light the pink candle the third week because Christmas is coming closer and we are joyful. As we begin the fourth week of Advent, we light all four candles. Use the Advent wreath each day when you pray.

Cultural Awareness

The custom of the Advent wreath began in Germany in the sixteenth century. Long ago, it was common for people to have festivals during December honoring the sun god. Huge bonfires were lighted during these festivals. The Advent wreath brought a Christian dimension to this pagan custom. In recent years, it has become popular for people to place a large white candle in the center of the Advent wreath on Christmas Eve. The candle represents Jesus, whose light now shines forth in the world.

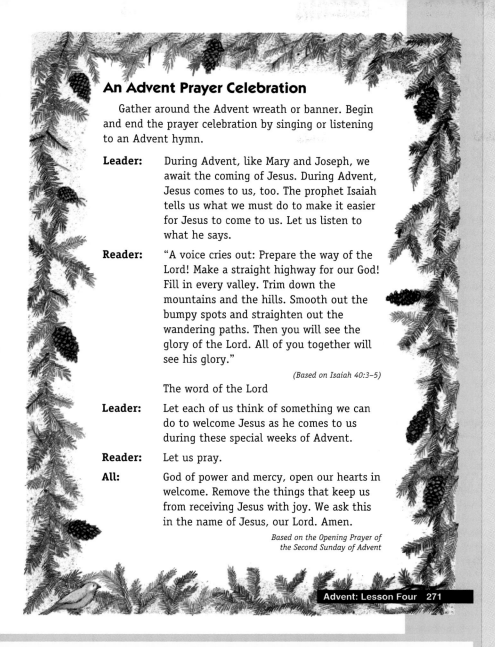

An Advent Prayer Celebration

Gather around the Advent wreath or banner. Begin and end the prayer celebration by singing or listening to an Advent hymn.

Leader: During Advent, like Mary and Joseph, we await the coming of Jesus. During Advent, Jesus comes to us, too. The prophet Isaiah tells us what we must do to make it easier for Jesus to come to us. Let us listen to what he says.

Reader: "A voice cries out: Prepare the way of the Lord! Make a straight highway for our God! Fill in every valley. Trim down the mountains and the hills. Smooth out the bumpy spots and straighten out the wandering paths. Then you will see the glory of the Lord. All of you together will see his glory."

(Based on Isaiah 40:3–5)

The word of the Lord

Leader: Let each of us think of something we can do to welcome Jesus as he comes to us during these special weeks of Advent.

Reader: Let us pray.

All: God of power and mercy, open our hearts in welcome. Remove the things that keep us from receiving Jesus with joy. We ask this in the name of Jesus, our Lord. Amen.

Based on the Opening Prayer of the Second Sunday of Advent

Advent: Lesson Four 271

Focus on

Isaiah, the Prophet In preparing for the prayer service, point out the words based on Isaiah on page 271. Explain to the students that Isaiah was a prophet, someone called by God to speak in God's name. Tell the students that Isaiah was called by God to announce the coming of Jesus almost 700 years before Jesus was born.

Reviewing the Advent Season

Briefly recall that during Advent, a time of joyful preparation, we remember Jesus' birth long ago and try to prepare our hearts by setting aside selfish ways and welcoming Christ into our everyday lives.

Creating Signs that Show Welcome

Distribute four purple strips, four yellow squares (to be cut into flames), scissors, and glue. Read aloud the verses from Isaiah ("A voice . . .") in the prayer service. Help the students understand that Isaiah is urging us to prepare to welcome the Lord. Recall with the students ways they can prepare their hearts by giving to others during Advent. List their ideas on the chalkboard. Have the students make paper candles, one for each week of Advent. Afterward, tell the students that during the service they will be asked to write on each candle one thing they will do each week in Advent to welcome Christ. Remind them that they can choose to do one single thing four times. (For example: They can volunteer each week to look after a brother or sister.)

Praying Together

Have the students read "An Advent Prayer Celebration" on page 271. Help them select appropriate Advent songs for the celebration. Select students to take the Reader and the Leader roles. When all is ready, begin the prayer celebration. Before you play the reflective music, remind the students that at this time they will write down the four actions they will do during Advent. You might want to provide envelopes for the paper candles. At the end of the day, check to see that the students have their envelopes as they leave for home.

Our Church Celebrates Christmas

Objectives

- **LESSON 1:** To help the students learn the Christmas image of Jesus as the Light of the World.
- **LESSON 2:** To help the students understand that we are called to make our light shine by imitating Jesus' example.
- **LESSON 3:** To help the students recognize that Christ is present in those around them.
- **LESSON 4:** To help the students dramatize Christ's presence in others and celebrate Christ as the Light of the World.

Lesson Outlines

	Step 1 **Learning About Our Lives**	Step 2 **Learning About Our Faith**	Step 3 **Learning How to Live Our Faith**
Lesson 1	■ Experience light and darkness. *ABOUT 8 MINUTES*	■ Read and discuss Scripture. ■ Identify Jesus as light. *ABOUT 7 MINUTES*	■ Write about ourselves as light. ■ Sing together. *ABOUT 15 MINUTES*
Lesson 2	■ Discuss Christmas decorations. *ABOUT 7 MINUTES*	■ Read the text. *ABOUT 8 MINUTES*	■ Write about being an example. ■ Pray with light. *ABOUT 15 MINUTES*
Lesson 3	■ Review Christ as the Light of the World. *ABOUT 5 MINUTES*	■ Read and discuss a story. ■ Identify Christ among us. *ABOUT 13 MINUTES*	■ Write a diary entry. *ABOUT 12 MINUTES*
Lesson 4	**Project** Review Christ's presence with us; prepare a dramatization; and present a dramatization. **Prayer** Review the chapter; prepare a prayer celebration; and pray together.		

Plan Ahead

	Preparing Your Class	**Materials Needed**

Lesson 1
Read over the entire lesson. Note that Step 3 suggests an exchange of names and offers a way for the students to be aware of and responsive to others in the classroom.

- pencils
- a small treat for the students
- candles or flashlights
- construction paper, scissors, paper slips with students' names (optional)

Lesson 2
Read through the lesson plan. Assemble the materials needed for the prayer in Step 3.

- pencils
- votive candle in decorative container

Lesson 3
Read through the lesson plan.

- pencils

Lesson 4
Read through the lesson plan. Gather simple props and costumes. Make arrangements for others to see the play.

- props and costumes
- Bibles
- table with a Bible and four candles

Additional Resources

As you plan these lessons, consider using the following material from The Resourceful Teacher Package.

- *Classroom Activity Sheets* for Christmas
- *Family Activity Sheets* for Christmas
- *Prayers for Every Day*

You may also wish to refer to the following Big Book.

- *We Celebrate God's Word,* page 5

In preparing the students for the Sunday readings, you may wish to use Silver Burdett Ginn's *Getting Ready for Sunday* student and teacher materials.

REDUCED CLASSROOM ACTIVITIES

OUR CHURCH CELEBRATES CHRISTMAS

Reread the story "Our Savior Is Born." Then write something about each person who was present when Jesus was presented in the Temple.

Mary
_____
_____

Joseph
_____
_____

Anna
_____
_____

Simeon
_____
_____

OUR CHURCH CELEBRATES CHRISTMAS

Draw a picture that illustrates the sentence in each box. Then on the lines provided, write ways you can bring the light of Jesus to others. All the words are from the Book of Isaiah.

The people who walked in darkness have seen a great light. *Based on Isaiah 9:1*	The light shines on those who live in sadness. *Based on Isaiah 9:1*	For a child is born who will save us and lead us. *Based on Isaiah 9:5,6*

_____
_____
_____
_____
_____
_____
_____
_____
_____

A Lenten Prayer Celebration

Teacher: Lent is a time to grow and change. It is a time to ask ourselves how we can follow Jesus more closely. During Lent, the Church encourages us to find ways to pray, to make sacrifices, and to do good works. Let us listen to what Jesus tells us in the Gospel of Matthew.

Reader 1: Jesus says, "When you pray, don't act like showoffs who just want people to notice them. Instead, when you pray, go to your room or a quiet place and pray to your Father in private" (based on Matthew 6:5–6).

All: Jesus, help us find time to pray this Lent.

Reader 2: Jesus says, "When you make sacrifices, don't look sad and gloomy. Showoffs do that so everyone will know they are making a sacrifice. Instead, be pleasant and cheerful so that no one but you and God will know" (based on Matthew 6:16–18).

All: Jesus, help us to have the courage this Lent to give up some of the things we want so that others can have what they need.

Reader 3: Jesus says, "When you do kind deeds, be careful you are not doing them so that other people will praise you. No, when you do works of mercy, don't even let your left hand know what your right hand is doing. This will please your heavenly Father and God will reward you for all you do" (based on Matthew 6:1–4).

All: Jesus, help us find ways this Lent to care for and serve others.

Lent: Lesson Five 289

★ ★ ★ ★ Enriching the Lesson ★

The readings in today's prayer celebration call to mind the Church's three most traditional Lenten practices: prayer, fasting, and almsgiving. Almsgiving is the gift of one's time, money, presence, or possessions to someone in need. Plan a Lenten service project with the students that will help them appreciate Jesus' call to serve others through the works of mercy.

Discussing Ways to Follow Jesus

Tell the students that today they will learn about Jesus' words about praying, fasting (doing penance), and giving alms (giving goods and services to help others). Turn to "A Lenten Prayer Celebration" on page 289. Read with the students the parts designated *Reader 1, 2,* and *3.* In the discussion, be clear that Jesus wants his followers to center their prayer and good works on God, not on getting the attention of other people. Ask the students to pair off. Invite them to think up mimes (or to act out) opposite situations such as the following: a person praying in private to God and a person making a great deal of his or her prayer in public, a person quietly helping another or quietly passing up a dessert or treat and a person doing and calling everyone's attention to his or her sacrifice, a person quietly helping another or sending an anonymous gift or contribution and another rendering a service while being sure everyone notices. After a number of pairs have volunteered their mimes, summarize that Jesus wants us to think about God and follow God's will and wishes for us, rather than think about the praise of friends and family.

Assign readers to take the three reader roles. As they practice separately, go through the parts labeled *All* with the class so that the students can easily read in unison.

Praying Together

When all is ready and the students are quiet and reflective, begin the prayer celebration. After the prayer celebration, you might want to lead the students in a song that expresses the mood of this shared observance of the Lenten season.

Our Church Celebrates Holy Week

Objectives ~~~

- LESSON 1: To help the students recognize that on Passion Sunday we celebrate Jesus as our king.
- LESSON 2: To help the students understand the liturgies of the Triduum.

Lesson Outlines ~~~~~

	Step 1 Learning About Our Lives	**Step 2** Learning About Our Faith	**Step 3** Learning How to Live Our Faith
Lesson 1	■ Discuss greetings. *ABOUT 5 MINUTES*	■ Read and discuss Scripture. ■ Learn about Passion Sunday. *ABOUT 12 MINUTES*	■ Fill in the missing words. ■ Pray together. *ABOUT 13 MINUTES*
Lesson 2	■ Name meaningful liturgies. *ABOUT 5 MINUTES*	■ Read about the Triduum. *ABOUT 7 MINUTES*	■ Complete a true/false activity. ■ Make Triduum booklets. *ABOUT 18 MINUTES*

Plan Ahead

	Preparing Your Class	**Materials Needed**
Lesson 1	Read through the lesson plan for this class.	■ pencils
Lesson 2	Read through the lesson plan. For Step 1, be prepared to discuss liturgies you find meaningful.	■ pencils ■ crayons ■ scraps of construction paper ■ glue ■ white drawing paper

Additional Resources

As you plan these lessons, consider using the following material from The Resourceful Teacher Package.

■ *Classroom Activity Sheets* for Holy Week

■ *Family Activity Sheets* for Holy Week

■ *Prayers for Every Day*

You may also wish to refer to the following Big Book.

■ *We Celebrate God's Word,* pages 15–18

In preparing the students for the Sunday readings, you may wish to use Silver Burdett Ginn's *Getting Ready for Sunday* student and teacher materials.

REDUCED CLASSROOM ACTIVITIES

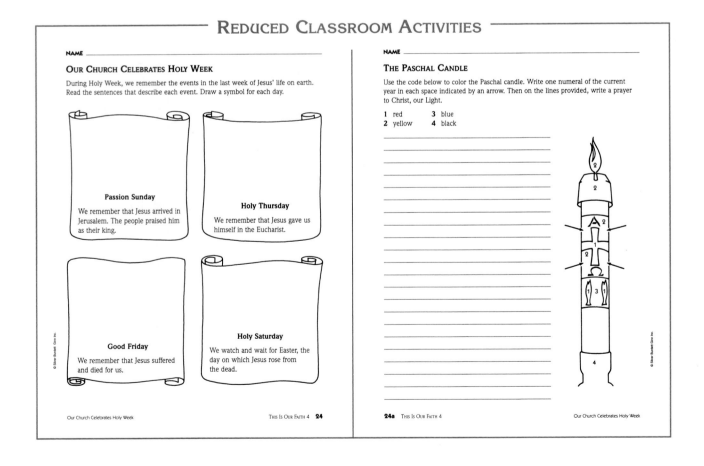

NAME _____

OUR CHURCH CELEBRATES HOLY WEEK

During Holy Week, we remember the events in the last week of Jesus' life on earth. Read the sentences that describe each event. Draw a symbol for each day.

Passion Sunday

We remember that Jesus arrived in Jerusalem. The people praised him as their king.

Holy Thursday

We remember that Jesus gave us himself in the Eucharist.

Good Friday

We remember that Jesus suffered and died for us.

Holy Saturday

We watch and wait for Easter, the day on which Jesus rose from the dead.

NAME _____

THE PASCHAL CANDLE

Use the code below to color the Paschal candle. Write one numeral of the current year in each space indicated by an arrow. Then on the lines provided, write a prayer to Christ, our Light.

1 red   **3** blue
2 yellow   **4** black

Background for the Teacher

PASSION SUNDAY

Holy Week, the most solemn week of the Church year, begins with Passion Sunday. On Passion Sunday, we celebrate the triumphal entry of Jesus into the city of Jerusalem. Throughout Lent, we have been journeying with Jesus toward this holy city. Today, carrying palms and shouting praise, we hail Jesus' arrival and greet him as a king and hero.

Our joyful greeting of Christ on Passion Sunday is bittersweet, for we know that it will soon be followed by his arrest, suffering, and crucifixion. Jesus' recognition of what he was about to endure and his acceptance of God's will is seen clearly throughout Mark's Gospel. Passion Sunday also carries an unmistakable message for all who follow Jesus—suffering and death are part of our journey to eternal life.

As you teach Lesson 1, help the students understand the excitement of the crowds that greeted Jesus. Encourage them to add their own prayers of praise to the Lord, who comes in glory to save us from sin and death.

THE TRIDUUM

Holy Week culminates in the celebration of the Easter Triduum, the three most sacred days of the year. The Triduum celebrates the Passover of the Lord, Jesus' passage through death to new life. During these three days, the Church community gathers together for the Evening Mass of the Lord's Supper, the Celebration of the Lord's Passion, and the Easter Vigil.

On Holy Thursday night, when the Triduum begins, we recall Christ's example of service in the washing of the feet and his gift of self in the institution of the Eucharist. On Good Friday, we remember Jesus' suffering, death, and burial. During the liturgy, we venerate the cross "on which hung the Savior of the world." On Holy Saturday, we wait and keep watch at the tomb, anticipating the resurrection. During the Vigil, we rejoice in the light of Christ "rising in glory." We celebrate the baptism of new members and renew our baptismal commitment, mindful that through Baptism, we too are invited to share in the promise of everlasting life.

Lesson 2 presents you with the opportunity to help the students grow in their awareness of God's saving love in the life, death, and resurrection of Jesus. The rituals and prayers of the Triduum invite us to enter fully into the mystery of God's love and experience anew our own rebirth.

LESSON 1

Objective

This lesson helps the students recognize that on Passion Sunday we celebrate Jesus as our king.

Step 1 / INTRODUCTION

Learning About Our Lives

Discussing Greetings

Have the students demonstrate or explain how they would greet each of the following people: the president of the United States, a current sports hero, the pope, a popular rock star, Mother Teresa, and the school principal. Then ask the students to discuss why they might greet these people in different ways. Help the class recognize that our greetings show a variety of feelings—respect, admiration, acceptance, and approval. Explain that in today's lesson, the students will learn how the people of Jesus' time greeted him when he came to Jerusalem.

Step 2 / DEVELOPMENT

Learning About Our Faith

Reading and Discussing Scripture

Ask volunteers to read aloud the Scripture story from Mark, beginning on page 290. Then ask:

- Why did Jesus send two of his disciples ahead of him? (*To find a donkey for him to ride*)

- What happened when Jesus rode into Jerusalem? (*People spread their coats and leafy branches on the ground; they waved the branches in the air; they shouted greetings to him.*)

Learning About Passion Sunday

Read through the text at the top of page 291 with the class. Help the students understand that Jesus was greeted as a king and hero. Explain that word of Jesus' teachings and miracles had spread throughout the city. Emphasize that only four days after this kingly greeting, Jesus was arrested. Note that the

290

Our Church Celebrates Holy Week

Passion Sunday

Jesus and his disciples journeyed to Jerusalem. When they got near the city, Jesus sent two of his disciples ahead of him. He said, "Go into the next village, where you will find a donkey that has never been ridden. Untie the donkey and bring it to me. If anyone asks what you are doing, tell them that the Lord needs the donkey."

The disciples went off and found a donkey tied to a gate. While they were untying it, some people asked, "What are you doing?" They answered just as Jesus had told them to do.

They led the donkey to Jesus. They put their cloaks on its back and helped Jesus get on. As Jesus rode along, the people spread their coats on the road in front of him. Others cut leafy branches from the trees. They laid them in front of Jesus and waved them in the air shouting, "Hosanna! Blessed is the one who comes in the name of the Lord! Hosanna to God in heaven!"

Based on Mark 11:1–10

Passion Sunday is the first day of Holy Week. On Passion

Focus on

Passion Sunday   Passion Sunday is also called "Palm Sunday" because we are given blessed palms to take home in commemoration of the reaction of the crowds that greeted Jesus. The palms are sacramentals, objects that remind us of Jesus' presence. We call this day Passion Sunday because the gospel account of Jesus' suffering and death—or passion—is read.

Holy Saturday

On Holy Saturday, we prepare to welcome the risen Jesus. There are no Masses until night, when we celebrate the Easter Vigil. During the Easter Vigil, we light the Easter candle, which is a sign that Jesus is risen and gives light to the whole world. We listen to stories about God's love for his people since the time of Creation. We baptize and confirm new members of the Catholic community and renew our own Baptism promises. Finally, we welcome our new members to the Lord's table for the first time and we receive Eucharist with them.

Activity

Write **True** if the sentence is true. Write **False** if the sentence is false.

1. __False__ The word *triduum* means "holy days."

2. __True__ Jesus washed his disciples' feet to give them an example of service.

3. __False__ Jesus gave us the Eucharist for the first time on Good Friday.

4. __True__ We show respect for the cross on Good Friday.

5. __False__ New members are baptized on Holy Thursday.

6. __True__ We share the Eucharist in memory of Jesus.

7. __True__ We baptize and confirm new members of the Catholic community at the Easter Vigil.

Help the students recognize that through the Church celebration of the Triduum, we experience again Jesus' suffering, death, and resurrection. Explain that these liturgies show us how God's plan for the world and God's promises to us are fulfilled.

Step 3 / CONCLUSION

Learning How to Live Our Faith

Completing a True/False Activity

Explain the directions to the activity on the bottom of page 293 and have the students work independently to complete it. In checking the students' answers, have them correct each false statement by rephrasing the sentence.

Making Triduum Booklets

Pass out crayons, scraps of construction paper, glue, and white drawing paper. Ask the students to fold the drawing paper in half twice to create a four-page booklet. Have them use the scraps of paper to create a symbol representing the Triduum on the cover of their booklets. On the inside pages, instruct them to write what each of the Triduum liturgies means to them. Urge the students to join their families in celebrating the Triduum.

> ### 🍎 Teaching Tips
>
> Explain to the students that the events of the Triduum were originally celebrated by the first Christian communities in one liturgy, which began at sundown on Holy Saturday and ended at dawn on Easter Sunday. In time, Church leaders decided to celebrate Jesus' Last Supper, death, and resurrection as Jesus experienced them, over three days.

Our Church Celebrates Easter

Objectives ~~~~~~~~

- ■ LESSON 1: To help the students understand the story of the first Easter.
- ■ LESSON 2: To help the students recognize that they live by faith in the risen Lord.
- ■ LESSON 3: To help the students recognize that faith is based on trust in the goodness of God.
- ■ LESSON 4: To help the students participate in the Church's celebration of Easter.

Lesson Outlines ~~~~~~~~~~~

	Step 1 Learning About Our Lives	Step 2 Learning About Our Faith	Step 3 Learning How to Live Our Faith
Lesson 1	■ Recall the first Easter. *ABOUT 5 MINUTES*	■ Act out an Easter play. *ABOUT 12 MINUTES*	■ Respond to Mary's message. ■ Decode an Easter message. *ABOUT 13 MINUTES*
Lesson 2	■ Play a guessing game. *ABOUT 5 MINUTES*	■ Read and role-play a story. ■ Discuss Christ's presence. *ABOUT 15 MINUTES*	■ Decode a prayer. ■ Pray together. *ABOUT 10 MINUTES*
Lesson 3	■ Review the story of Thomas. *ABOUT 5 MINUTES*	■ Read and discuss a story. ■ Write a letter. *ABOUT 10 MINUTES*	■ Study the Act of Faith. ■ Create a symbol of faith. *ABOUT 15 MINUTES*
Lesson 4	**Project** Discuss the risen Lord; decorate an Easter candle; and pray together. **Prayer** Prepare for the prayer celebration; and pray together.		

Plan Ahead

	Preparing Your Class	**Materials Needed**
Lesson 1	Prepare for class by reading the lesson plan.	■ a large empty box or carton ■ pencils
Lesson 2	Read through the lesson plan. For Step 1, prepare and pack a gift box containing Easter treats to share with the students.	■ gift box containing Easter treats ■ pencils
Lesson 3	Read through the lesson plan. Make an anchor out of pipe cleaners as a sample for the students to see.	■ pipe cleaners, two for each student ■ pencils
Lesson 4	Read through the lesson plan. Locate two or three cardboard boxes and a cutting tool to make temporary candleholders for the students. Be sure to use artist's tissue, which is colorfast.	■ artist's tissue ■ an ample supply of mixed water and glue ■ pillar or taper candles, one for each student

Additional Resources

As you plan these lessons, consider using the following material from The Resourceful Teacher Package.

■ *Classroom Activity Sheets* for Easter

■ *Family Activity Sheets* for Easter

■ *Prayers for Every Day*

You may also wish to refer to the following Big Book.

■ *We Celebrate God's Word,* page 19

In preparing the students for the Sunday readings, you may wish to use Silver Burdett Ginn's *Getting Ready for Sunday* student and teacher materials.

REDUCED CLASSROOM ACTIVITIES

NAME _____

OUR CHURCH CELEBRATES EASTER

Imagine that you are in the room with the disciples on the first Easter night. Write an eyewitness account of what happened when Jesus stood before his followers.

_____
_____
_____
_____
_____
_____
_____
_____
_____

NAME _____

AN EASTER MESSAGE

Find the words hidden in the picture. On the line provided, write Jesus' Easter message to us.

Peace be with you. _____

John 20:26

293c Organizer

Background for the Teacher

BELIEF IN THE RISEN LORD

The celebration of Easter provides us with an opportunity to examine and express what we believe. The death and resurrection of Jesus are at the core of Catholic Christian faith. The accounts of the appearances of Jesus to his friends and followers are proclaimed to us each year. As we reflect on the meaning of these events, we are strengthened in our faith. The first two lessons in this section contrast the belief and faith of Mary of Magdala, Peter, and John with the doubting faith of Thomas. When we remember the difficulty with which the apostles came to believe in the risen Lord, we are heartened in our own struggles to grow in faith. As Jesus tells us, "Blessed are those who have not seen me, but still believe" (John 20:29).

What is the nature of faith? Faith is the gift from the Holy Spirit, given at Baptism, that enables us to say, "I believe." Faith means taking God's word for something even when we cannot prove it for ourselves. Through faith we respond to an unseen level of meaning in our lives.

GROWTH IN FAITH

Faith is a dynamic virtue, nurtured by the Christian life. As with all living things, there is change and growth, even death and new life. Sometimes believers are frightened when they experience doubts. They become anxious when questions surface in their minds and hearts regarding matters of faith.

However, it is safe to expect that in the mature believer, doubt will sometimes exist alongside faith. This conflict can be an opportunity to deepen one's faith. The sincere believer will seek out and welcome opportunities to grow in faith by Christian reading, study, prayer, and committed Christian service.

By fourth grade, most students no longer believe in Santa Claus, the Easter Bunny, or the Tooth Fairy. What sometimes happens, then, is that stories of Jesus and other religious truths and practices are called into question as well. Significant adults can be most helpful in assisting youngsters as they sort out truth and fantasy. As a teacher, you have an opportunity to use these lessons to assure the students as they share their questions with you. Point out that even those who had been closest to Jesus sometimes found it hard to believe. Jesus understood that. But he also praised those who had never seen him and yet had faith.

LESSON 1

Objective

This lesson helps the students understand the story of the first Easter.

Step 1 / INTRODUCTION

Learning About Our Lives

Recalling the First Easter

Invite the students to recall details about Jesus' resurrection by asking questions such as the following.

- How did the disciples learn that Jesus had risen?
- What happened on the first Easter?
- Who first saw the risen Jesus?

After allowing the students to discuss what they remember, explain that each of the four gospels tells us about the resurrection. Explain that the Gospels of Matthew, Mark, Luke, and John give us different details about how Jesus' followers learned that he had risen. Tell the students that in today's lesson, they will learn John's story of the resurrection.

Step 2 / DEVELOPMENT

Learning About Our Faith

Acting Out an Easter Play

Choose volunteers for the speaking parts of the Easter play on pages 294 and 295: the seven readers, Mary of Magdala, the angel, and Jesus. Assign the various roles to these students and have them find and mark their lines in the text. Also select two students to take the two non-speaking parts of John and Peter. Tell the remaining students that they will portray the disciples gathered together in Jerusalem.

Clear a large area in which to act out the play. Have the students portraying the disciples (including Mary, John, and Peter) bring their books and sit or kneel as a group off to the right. Place a large empty box in the center of the "stage" to represent Jesus' tomb. Tell the readers and the students taking the parts of Jesus and the angel to remain "off-stage" on the left of the area. Walk the students through

294

Our Church Celebrates Easter

An Easter Play

Reader 1: On the first day of the week, when it was still dark, Mary of Magdala went to the place where Jesus was buried. She saw that the stone had been rolled back from the entrance of the tomb. Mary ran to tell Peter and the other disciples.

Mary: They have taken Jesus from the tomb and I don't know where they have put him.

Reader 2: Peter and another disciple ran to the tomb. The other disciple looked in. He saw the cloths that had covered Jesus' body lying there. When Peter arrived, he went into the tomb and saw that the cloth that had covered Jesus' head was in a different place from the other cloths.

Reader 3: Then the other disciple followed his friend into the tomb. They saw the burial cloths and were amazed at what had happened. Then both disciples returned home.

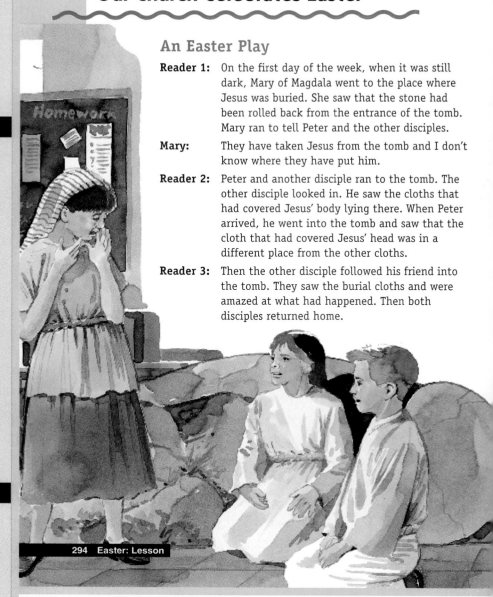

294 Easter: Lesson

★ Enriching the Lesson ★

Have the students make construction paper Easter eggs for a bulletin board display. Explain that eggs are an Easter symbol because the shell is a symbol of Jesus' tomb. Jesus emerged from the tomb to new life. Direct the students to write a message on the eggs that expresses their belief in Jesus' resurrection and then to decorate the eggs, using felt-tip markers.

Reader 4: But Mary stayed outside the tomb crying. She looked into the tomb and saw two angels sitting in the place where Jesus' body had been. One of the angels spoke to her.

Angel: Woman, why are you crying?

Mary: Someone has taken my Lord and I do not know where they have put him.

Reader 5: Mary turned around and saw Jesus, but she did not recognize him. She thought he was the gardener. Mary talked to the man.

Mary: Sir, if you carried Jesus away, tell me where you have laid him and I will go and get him.

Reader 6: Just then Jesus called out Mary's name. At once, she recognized him. Mary was filled with joy! She reached out to touch Jesus and called him by name.

Mary: Teacher!

Jesus: Go to my disciples, Mary, and tell them that I have risen and that I will soon return to my Father and your Father who is in heaven.

Reader 7: Mary went to the disciples as Jesus asked.

Mary: I have seen the Lord!

Based on John 20:1–18

Activity

To discover what we celebrate on Easter, write the letter in the alphabet that comes AFTER each letter in the puzzle.

I J<u>d</u>e<u>r</u>s<u>t</u>u<u>r</u>s h<u>i</u>r<u>s</u>

q<u>r</u>h<u>i</u>r<u>s</u>d<u>e</u>m<u>n</u> e<u>f</u>q<u>r</u>n<u>o</u>l<u>m</u>

s<u>t</u>g<u>h</u>d<u>e</u> c<u>d</u>d<u>e</u>z<u>a</u>c<u>d</u> z<u>a</u>m<u>n</u>c<u>d</u>

r<u>s</u>g<u>h</u>z<u>a</u>q<u>r</u>d<u>e</u>r<u>s</u> g<u>h</u>h<u>i</u>r<u>s</u>

m<u>n</u>d<u>e</u>v<u>w</u> k<u>l</u>h<u>i</u>e<u>f</u>d<u>e</u>

v<u>w</u>h<u>i</u>s<u>t</u>g<u>h</u> t<u>u</u>r<u>s</u>.

---

the play, having them read their parts as you direct them where to stand as they recite their lines. After this rehearsal, have the students dramatize the play.

Step 3 / CONCLUSION

Learning How to Live Our Faith

Responding to Mary's Message

Invite the students to imagine that they were among the disciples gathered in Jerusalem after Jesus' death and burial. Have the student who took the part of Mary stand before the group and recite her last line. Elicit responses to the following questions.

- What might the disciples have said?
- What might the disciples have felt?
- What might they have done?

Invite the students to respond spontaneously to Mary's message.

Decoding an Easter Message

Call on a volunteer to read aloud the directions to the activity at the bottom of page 295. Have the students work on their own to complete the activity. Afterward, recite the Easter message aloud together.

Focus on

Easter Explain to the class that Easter does not occur on the same date each year. Easter is always celebrated on the first Sunday following the first full moon after the first day of spring. Show the students a calendar displaying the phases of the moon. Locate the first day of Spring, have them find the next full moon, and then note the following Sunday, which is Easter.

295

LESSON 2

Objective

This lesson helps the students recognize that they live by faith in the risen Lord.

Step 1 / INTRODUCTION

Learning About Our Lives

Playing a Guessing Game

Before class begins, select one student and tell him or her what is in a gift box that you have prepared before class time. When class begins, show the class the gift box and invite the students to guess what is in it. After the students have made a few guesses, have the appointed student tell the others what is in the box. Point out that the students have to trust the student and you about what they cannot yet see. The student is a witness to what is in the box. Ask for a show of hands of those who believe that what you told the student is true. Assure the students that you will open the box later.

Step 2 / DEVELOPMENT

Learning About Our Faith

Reading and Role-Playing a Story

Look at the illustration of the risen Lord and the apostles on page 296. Identify the apostle Thomas. Read "The Story of Thomas." Ask:

- Why were the disciples afraid on the first Easter night? (*Jesus had risen but the apostles had not seen him yet.*)

- How did Jesus assure them that he was alive? (*He appeared to them and spoke to them.*)

- Why do you think Thomas doubted the disciples' words about the risen Jesus? (*He was sad that he didn't see Jesus. Or he thought the news was too good to be true.*)

- What did Thomas say that confirmed his belief in the risen Lord? (*"My Lord and my God."*)

- Whom do you think Jesus was referring to when he said those who believe but do not see are blessed? (*Christians*)

This gospel account lends itself to dramatization. Review the sequence of events and assign the roles; include both boys and girls.

The Story of Thomas

After Jesus died on the cross, his friends were confused. They had trouble believing that Jesus had risen from the dead and lives in a new way. Jesus visited them to help them believe. Here is a story of a time when the risen Jesus came to be with his followers.

On the night when Jesus rose from the dead, his disciples were together in a locked room. They were afraid because of what had happened to Jesus. Jesus came and stood before them. "Peace be with you," he said. Then Jesus showed his disciples his hands where he had been nailed to the cross. He showed them his side where he had been speared.

"It really is you, Jesus," they cried. They started talking with him all at once.

Thomas was not in the room with the other disciples. Later, when the disciples saw Thomas, they said, "Jesus is really alive! He was with us and we talked with him. He showed us his hands and his side. It really was Jesus!"

But Thomas shook his head. "I'll never believe that," he said, "unless I touch the wounds in his hands and his side."

A week later the disciples were together in the room again. This time Thomas was there, too. Again Jesus came and stood before them. "Peace be with you," he said.

Teaching Tips

Call attention to Jesus' first words to his followers on Easter Sunday: "Peace be with you." Ask the students to name a time when we hear words similar to these. Help them recall that during the greeting at Mass, the priest says, "The grace and peace of God our Father and the Lord Jesus Christ be with you." Review the response with the class: "And also with you." Remind the students that at the end of the Mass, the priest says, "The Lord be with you" and we respond, "And also with you."

296

Then he said to Thomas, "Come, touch my hands and my side. Believe what the others told you. I am alive."

Thomas prayed, "My Lord and my God."

Then Jesus said, "Thomas, you became a believer because you saw me. Blessed are those who have not seen me, but still believe."

Based on John 20:19–29

Activity

Use the secret code to find the words. The words make up a prayer to say when you find it hard to believe.

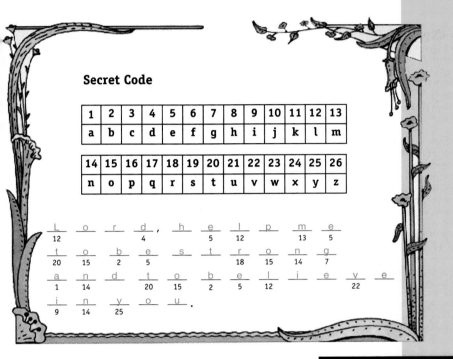

Secret Code

1	2	3	4	5	6	7	8	9	10	11	12	13
a	b	c	d	e	f	g	h	i	j	k	l	m

14	15	16	17	18	19	20	21	22	23	24	25	26
n	o	p	q	r	s	t	u	v	w	x	y	z

L o r d , h e l p m e
12   4   5 12 13 5

t o b e s t r o n g
20 15 2 5   18 15 14 7

a n d t o b e l i e v e
1 14 20 15 2 5 12   9   22

i n y o u .
9 14 25 15 21

Discussing Christ's Presence

Point out that Jesus knew that his followers, because they would not have seen him as the Apostles had, would need to live by faith. Make clear to the students that we are given the gift of faith at our Baptism and that the whole Catholic community supports and helps us to grow in the gift of faith. Have the students name people they know who help them grow in their faith. They might suggest you, the priest, their parents, older friends, or people they admire.

Step 3 / CONCLUSION

Learning How to Live Our Faith

Decoding a Prayer

Have the students decode the message on page 297. Invite a volunteer to read the prayer aloud.

Praying Together

Tell the students that they can pray as Thomas prayed. Read again the prayer the students have just decoded. Lead the students in adding spontaneous prayers to ask the Holy Spirit to help them grow strong in their faith in the risen Lord.

As you bring this class to a close, open the gift box and enjoy the Easter treats together.

★ Enriching the Lesson ★

Distribute Bibles to the class and write the following Scripture passages on the chalkboard: Matthew 28:1–10; Mark 16:1–8; Luke 24:1–12; Luke 24:13–35; and John 21:1–14. Explain to the students that these are different gospel stories about Jesus' appearances after his resurrection. Divide the class into five groups and assign one of the readings to each group. Have the students read their assigned passage and report back to the class on the circumstances of Jesus' appearance.

297

LESSON 3

Objective

This lesson helps the students recognize that faith is based on trust in the goodness of God.

Step 1 / INTRODUCTION

Learning About Our Lives

Reviewing the Story of Thomas

Recall that Thomas, who doubted, came to believe when he saw the risen Lord. Ask:

- Who helps you grow in your faith? (*Priests, parents, friends, teachers*)

Step 2 / DEVELOPMENT

Learning About Our Faith

Reading and Discussing a Story

Have the students turn to page 298 and read aloud "A Chance to Trust." Ask:

- What was Tim afraid of? (*Going to camp alone*)

- Do you think he doubted his parents' word that he'd enjoy his time at camp? Why or why not?

Use the discussion questions at the bottom of the page to explore Tim's doubts and the students' experiences.

Writing a Letter

Direct the students to page 299 and read the opening of the letter with the students. To check the students' understanding that Tim's doubts had been resolved, ask:

- Which did Tim doubt—his own ability to make new friends or his parents' words? Why?

- Who was Tim's new friend? (*Sam*)

- What do you imagine Tim enjoyed doing at camp?

Have the students complete the letter that Tim might have written from camp. Then have the students read their letters to one another or to the entire class.

298

A Chance to Trust

"But I won't know anybody," Tim said as he plopped his backpack into the backseat of the car.

"You'll make new friends," his mother said.

"What if it's no fun?" Tim continued.

"You'll have a great time, Tim," said his father as he wedged the sleeping bag into the already crowded car. "Trust us," he added.

Tim was worried. At first, going to camp seemed like a good idea. His best friend, Jeff, was going, too, and they had talked for hours about all the fun they would have together. Canoeing and archery were the activities that sounded like the most fun.

Then Jeff's grandmother got sick, and the whole Thompson family had to change their summer plans. Jeff would have to miss camp.

"I'm just not sure I want to go to camp," Tim tried for the final time.

"Don't be such a doubting Thomas," his mother said with a smile. "By this time next week, you probably won't even want to come home."

Discuss

1. Why did Tim's mother call him a doubting Thomas?

2. Have you ever been a doubting Thomas? When?

Focus on

Faith *The Catechism of the Catholic Church* states: " . . . faith is not an isolated act. No one can believe alone, just as no one can live alone. You have not given yourself faith as you have not given yourself life. The believer has received faith from others and should hand it on to others . . . Each believer is thus a link in the great chain of believers. I cannot believe without being carried by the faith of others, and by my faith I help support others in the faith" (#166).

Activity

Tim had to trust his parents about going to camp. Finish the letter below that Tim wrote to his family from camp.

Dear Mom and Dad,

    Camp is great! Yesterday my new friend Sam and I

_____

_____

_____

_____

_____

_____

_____

_____

_____

_____

_____

_____

                   Love,
                   Tim

Step 3 / CONCLUSION

Learning How to Live Our Faith

Studying the Act of Faith

Recite the Act of Faith to the students.

Act of Faith
O my God,
I firmly believe that you are one God in three Divine Persons,
the Father, the Son, and the Holy Spirit.
I believe in Jesus Christ, Your Son,
who became man and died for our sins,
and who will come to judge the living and the dead.
I believe these and all the truths
which the Holy Catholic Church teaches,
because You have revealed them,
who can neither deceive nor be deceived.
Amen.

For emphasis, write on the chalkboard the last four lines, which tell that the person's faith is based on trust in God. Make the connection between our faith in adults, who try to be trustworthy, and faith in God, who never fails us. In discussing the Act of Faith, help the students understand each phrase.

Creating a Symbol of Faith

Show to the students pictures of an anchor or draw a sample one on the chalkboard. Talk to the students about the function of anchors—as stabilizers in stormy or calm seas. Ask the students why an anchor is often a symbol of our trust or faith in God. Give each student two pipe cleaners and show them how to make a simple anchor by following these directions: Bend one pipe cleaner in half to make the long shank and twist the top to make a small, open hole. Bend the second pipe cleaner in half and twist it around the shank directly beneath the hole at the top, making a crossbar. Twist the first pipe cleaner near the bottom and then bend each end up toward the crossbar to make the bottom of the anchor. Have the students take their anchors home at the end of the day to remind them of their faith in God.

LESSON 4

PROJECT

Objective

This lesson helps the students participate in the celebration of Easter.

Discussing the Risen Lord

Refer to the picture of the Easter (Paschal) candle on page 293. Review the meaning of each symbol on the candle as well as the service of light at the Easter Vigil.

Decorating an Easter Candle

Provide art materials to decorate an Easter candle. Discuss each step given on page 300. Encourage the students to help one another so that the class can proceed together. Have on hand enough cardboard boxes so that you can cut out a cardboard square for each student. Using a cutting tool, cut an "x" through the middle of each square. Then each student can push his or her candle through the "x" to make a temporary candleholder. After all the candles are decorated and propped securely in their temporary holders, collect them for use in a simple prayer service.

Praying Together

Light your own candle. Tell the students that the candle reminds them of their risen Lord, the Lord in whom Thomas professed his belief, the Lord in whom we profess our belief. Then call each student forward to receive his or her candle. When all have received their candles, close by praying: *"You have been enlightened by the light of Christ. Walk always as God's dear children. Keep the light of faith burning in your heart. When the Lord comes, you will enjoy God and all the saints forever. Amen."*

An Easter Candle

For Catholic's, candles are a reminder of the presence of the risen Christ in our midst. The Easter candle in your parish church will be lighted each time the parish community gathers to worship during the Easter season and at every Baptism and funeral Mass throughout the year.

You will need these materials to make an Easter candle for your family.
- a white candle, any diameter
- scraps of different colored tissue paper
- a dish with equal amounts of glue and water

1. Tear the tissue paper into pieces of different shapes and sizes.

2. Dip the tissue paper, one piece at a time, into the glue mixture, soaking it well.

3. Put the wet pieces of tissue paper on your candle. Overlap different colors. Leave the upper 1/4 of your candle undecorated so that the paper will not burn when you light the candle.

4. When the tissue paper has dried thoroughly, take your candle home. Ask your family to light the candle at one meal each day during the Easter season. Let the light and colors remind you of the risen Jesus.

300   Easter: Lesson Four

Enriching the Lesson

Have the class visit the church to examine the Easter candle. Point out the first and last letters of the Greek alphabet—*Alpha* and *Omega*. Explain that these letters are signs that Jesus is the beginning and end of our lives as his followers. Note the five grains of incense that represent Jesus' wounds. Teach the students to pray the prayer that is said as the Easter candle is lighted: *May the light of Christ, rising in glory, dispel the darkness of our hearts and minds.*

An Easter Prayer Celebration

Teacher: Thomas found it hard to believe that Jesus had risen from the dead. Jesus knew the disciples would need time to see him and talk with him. Let us listen to two gospel stories about Jesus' appearances to his disciples after his resurrection.

Reader 1: Mary of Magdala, a friend of Jesus, was weeping beside the empty tomb. She turned and saw Jesus, but Mary thought he was the gardener. Then Jesus said, "Mary." When she heard him call her name, Mary recognized Jesus. She was filled with joy. Jesus told her to tell the other disciples that she had seen him. So off she went to share the good news.

Based on John 20:11–18

All: Jesus, we believe you are with us. You call each of us by name. Help us to share the good news.

Reader 2: One evening Peter and some of the other disciples decided to go fishing. All night they caught nothing. At dawn, a man standing on the shore called out to them. "Friends, have you caught anything?" They answered, "Not a thing!" He told them to throw the net over the other side of the boat. The net was soon filled with so many fish they could hardly haul it in. Then one of the disciples shouted, "It is the Lord!" Peter jumped into the water and swam ashore. When they all arrived on shore, Jesus shared with them a meal of bread and fish.

Based on John 21:1–14

All: Jesus, we believe you are with us. Help us to share your love with one another.

Focus on

The Risen Jesus The students may wonder why Mary of Magdala and Peter failed to recognize the risen Jesus. Although we cannot explain exactly how Jesus looked after his resurrection, the Church teaches that Jesus possessed the "new properties of a glorious body" and that he enjoyed the "sovereign freedom of appearing as he wishes: in the guise of a gardener or in other forms familiar to his disciples, precisely to awaken their faith" (*Catechism of the Catholic Church*, #645).

PRAYER

Preparing for the Prayer Celebration

Review pages 296–297, which tell the story of Jesus' post-Resurrection appearance to the disciples and to Thomas. Tell the students that John's Gospel tells us of other times when Jesus appeared to his friends after his resurrection. Have the students turn to page 301 and read with them the sections labeled *Reader 1* and *Reader 2*. In reading the story of Mary of Magdala, point out that Mary and the women were the first witnesses of the resurrection, the first to share the good news of the risen Lord. Then read the second story about Jesus with the Apostles at the seashore. Because these stories both lend themselves to dramatic presentation, invite the students to act the stories out. Select students to play the roles of Mary, Jesus, and those who heard Mary's good news. For the second story, select students to play Jesus, Peter, John, and the other disciples. While these groups are rehearsing, take time to read the parts labeled *All* so that the class can read them in unison during the prayer celebration.

Finally, invite the students' suggestions as you select an Easter song to open the prayer service.

Praying Together

Have the students assemble in the area where you will have the prayer service. Decide ahead of time whether you want the students to act out the Reader 1 and Reader 2 parts or simply to read them. When all is ready, begin the prayer service. After the celebration, talk briefly with the students about ways they can carry the good news to others and be loving to one another for the rest of this day.

301

Our Church Honors Saints

Objectives

- **LESSON 1:** To help the students recognize that we are all called to holiness.
- **LESSON 2:** To help the students explore how work fulfills their vocation to follow Christ.
- **LESSON 3:** To help the students want to serve others as Saint Vincent de Paul did.
- **LESSON 4:** To help the students learn about their favorite saint and reflect on the Christian vocation to be saints.

Lesson Outlines

	Step 1 Learning About Our Lives	Step 2 Learning About Our Faith	Step 3 Learning How to Live Our Faith
Lesson 1	■ Discuss saints. *ABOUT 8 MINUTES*	■ Read about a saint. ■ Complete an activity. *ABOUT 10 MINUTES*	■ Discuss the communion of saints. ■ Research favorite saints. ■ Pray a litany together. *ABOUT 12 MINUTES*
Lesson 2	■ Review the call to be saints. *ABOUT 5 MINUTES*	■ Read and discuss a story. ■ Write about our vocation. *ABOUT 7 MINUTES*	■ Create a patron saint quilt. *ABOUT 18 MINUTES*
Lesson 3	■ Discuss the value of education. *ABOUT 5 MINUTES*	■ Read and discuss a story. *ABOUT 8 MINUTES*	■ Research parish organizations. ■ Listen to a guest speaker. ■ Pray together. *ABOUT 17 MINUTES*
Lesson 4	**Project** Review vocations to holiness; read and discuss a story; and present saint stories. **Prayer** Prepare a prayer celebration; and participate in a prayer celebration.		

Plan Ahead

	Preparing Your Class	**Materials Needed**
Lesson 1	Read over the entire lesson plan as you prepare for class. Have available an ample supply of books on the lives of the saints.	■ books on the lives of the saints ■ pencils
Lesson 2	Read through the entire lesson plan.	■ 8" squares of drawing paper, one for each student ■ crayons or felt-tip markers ■ pencils
Lesson 3	Prepare for class by studying the lesson plan. Invite a guest speaker to visit your class as suggested in Step 3.	■ pencils ■ copies of parish bulletins
Lesson 4	Read through the lesson plan. Have on display the class "quilt," the class saint-book, and other objects that have to do with saints.	■ crayons or felt-tip markers ■ holy cards (optional)

Additional Resources

As you plan these lessons, consider using the following material from The Resourceful Teacher Package.

■ *Classroom Activity Sheets* for Saints

■ *Family Activity Sheets* for Saints

■ *Prayers for Every Day*

In preparing the students for the Sunday readings, you may wish to use Silver Burdett Ginn's *Getting Ready for Sunday* student and teacher materials.

REDUCED CLASSROOM ACTIVITIES

NAME _____

OUR CHURCH HONORS SAINTS

The Catholic Church honors many people who give us examples of how to live holy, unselfish lives. You have learned about some of these people.

On the lines below, write about your favorite saint. Tell how he or she showed us how to follow Jesus' teachings.

_____
_____
_____
_____
_____
_____
_____
_____
_____
_____
_____
_____
_____
_____
_____
_____

NAME _____

TEACHING OTHERS

The family that Elizabeth Ann Seton stayed with in Italy taught her about the Catholic faith. On the lines below, write two things that you might teach others about Jesus and the Church.

Jesus

1. _____
   _____
   _____

2. _____
   _____
   _____

The Church

1. _____
   _____
   _____

2. _____
   _____
   _____

301c Organizer

Plan Ahead

	Preparing Your Class	Materials Needed
Lesson 1	Read through the lesson plan. Write biblical references on slips of paper, one for each pair of students. Consult Step 3 and select appropriate hymns about Mary.	■ Bibles, pencils ■ slips of paper with biblical references ■ missalettes or hymnals ■ song recording
Lesson 2	Read through the lesson plan. Have available current magazines.	■ magazines ■ pencils
Lesson 3	Read through the lesson plan.	■ scrap paper ■ Bibles ■ pencils

Additional Resources

As you plan these lessons, consider using the following material from The Resourceful Teacher Package.

■ *Classroom Activity Sheets* for Mary

■ *Family Activity Sheets* for Mary

■ *Prayers for Every Day*

You may also wish to refer to the following Big Book.

■ *We Celebrate God's Word,* page 4

In preparing the students for the Sunday readings, you may wish to use Silver Burdett Ginn's *Getting Ready for Sunday* student and teacher materials.

REDUCED CLASSROOM ACTIVITIES

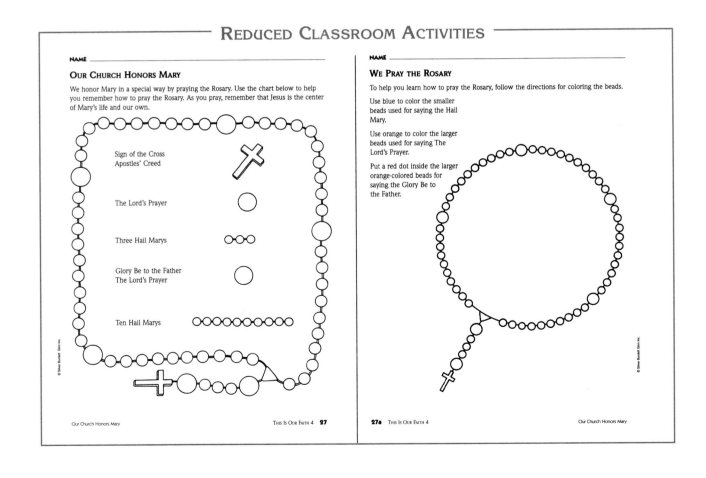

OUR CHURCH HONORS MARY

We honor Mary in a special way by praying the Rosary. Use the chart below to help you remember how to pray the Rosary. As you pray, remember that Jesus is the center of Mary's life and our own.

Sign of the Cross
Apostles' Creed

The Lord's Prayer

Three Hail Marys

Glory Be to the Father
The Lord's Prayer

Ten Hail Marys

© Silver Burdett Ginn Inc.

Our Church Honors Mary

THIS IS OUR FAITH 4 **27**

WE PRAY THE ROSARY

To help you learn how to pray the Rosary, follow the directions for coloring the beads.

Use blue to color the smaller beads used for saying the Hail Mary.

Use orange to color the larger beads used for saying The Lord's Prayer.

Put a red dot inside the larger orange-colored beads for saying the Glory Be to the Father.

© Silver Burdett Ginn Inc.

27a THIS IS OUR FAITH 4

Our Church Honors Mary

309c Organizer

Background for the Teacher

THE ASSUMPTION AND THE IMMACULATE CONCEPTION

In 1854, Pope Pius IX solemnly proclaimed the doctrine of Mary's Immaculate Conception, stating that Mary was free from actual and original sin, full of grace and all holy. When Pope Pius XII, on November 1, 1950, defined the dogma of Mary's assumption into heaven, he stated clearly what had been a traditional belief for centuries. Mary, the mother of Jesus, was assumed, body and soul, into heaven. The official statement reads as follows: "The Immaculate Mother of God, the ever-Virgin Mary, having completed the course of her earthly life, was assumed body and soul into heavenly glory"(*Munificentissimus Deus*).

HONORING MARY

Mary is given the place of honor she enjoys in Catholic tradition for two reasons: She became the mother of Jesus, the son of God, because of her wholehearted response as a woman of faith. She is also a model to the Church of what each of us is called to be—a person for whom the will of God comes first. Mary's assumption is the crowning event of a life lived in union with God. She offers us a glimpse of what we too will experience.

In presenting Mary, emphasize that Mary's holiness lay in her following the will of God for her, which is exactly where our holiness lies. In this we can imitate Mary. Remind your students that Mary is a powerful intercessor for us. She is our heavenly mother who comforts us in times of need and brings us close to her son.

The devotions of the Rosary and the Angelus are a part of Catholic tradition. Lesson 1 provides you with the opportunity to review the mysteries of the Rosary and how to pray this ancient prayer. In Lesson 3, the students are introduced to the Angelus, which you can pray daily with your class at noon. In this way, the students will become familiar with this scriptural prayer and incorporate it into their personal treasury of prayer.

LESSON 1

Objective

This lesson helps the students understand that at the end of her earthly life Mary was taken up into heaven.

Step 1 / INTRODUCTION

Learning About Our Lives

Discussing Mary

Show the students a picture of a woman you respect and love—your mother, a teacher, a mentor. Tell the students why this person means so much to you. Elicit names from the students of women they particularly admire and love. Show the students a picture or a statue of Mary. Ask them to share everything they know about Mary's life. List their responses on the chalkboard. Then arrange the events of Mary's life in chronological order. Label the great events in Mary's life, using the traditional titles such as the Annunciation, the Visitation, Nativity.

Step 2 / DEVELOPMENT

Learning About Our Faith

Researching Biblical References to Mary

Have the students pair off. Give each pair a Bible and a slip of paper containing one of the following references from the Gospel of Luke: 1:28; 1:30; 1:31 and 33; 1:35; 1:37; and 1:45. Have the students look up and write the verse assigned to them. (See the directions for looking up the verses on page 328 in their texts.) Then invite the students to take turns reading their verses aloud in sequence.

Reading About the Rosary

Have the students turn to page 352 and read the information about the rosary. Recall the events in Mary's life that the students discussed in Step 1. Point out that many of these events are included in the rosary as the joyful mysteries. Share these mysteries with the students, as presented in the rosary. The titles of the joyful mysteries follow on page 311.

310

Our Church Honors Mary

Feast of the Assumption

During the year, Catholics think about Mary, the mother of Jesus. They remember the important things that happened to her.

Even before Mary was born, she had already been chosen to be the mother of God's Son. When Mary was a young woman, God sent a special messenger to ask her if she would be the mother of Jesus. Mary was free to choose between saying yes or no to God's messenger. Mary was surprised that God had chosen her for something so wonderful. Mary said, "I am the servant of the Lord. I will do what God wants me to do." These words show how much Mary loved and trusted God.

Based on Luke 1:26–38

Being the mother of Jesus was not always easy. Luke's Gospel tells us that before Jesus was born, Mary and Joseph traveled to Bethlehem. The trip was hard for Mary. Then, when Jesus was twelve years old, Joseph and Mary took him to the Temple in Jerusalem. He was lost there for three

---

Focus on

Holy Days Remind the students that the Feast of the Assumption is a holy day of obligation, one of six special days (in addition to Sunday) in which Catholics come together to celebrate the Eucharist. Review the other holy days with the class: the Solemnity of Mary, Mother of God (January 1); Ascension Thursday (40 days after Easter); All Saints' Day (November 1); Solemnity of the Immaculate Conception (December 8); and Christmas (December 25).

Background for the Teacher

THE ASCENSION OF THE LORD

Forty days after Easter, the Church celebrates the ascension of the Lord. This is a joyous feast, not a day of sad farewells. We know this because of Jesus' final promise to us in the Gospel of Matthew: "Behold, I am with you always, until the end of the age" (Matthew 28:20). The Feast of the Ascension celebrates Jesus' continued presence among us.

The Church began to celebrate Jesus' ascension as a separate feast during the fourth century. It is important to celebrate this feast in light of Jesus' resurrection at Easter and the coming of the Holy Spirit on Pentecost, ten days after the ascension. Jesus' ascension prefigures the day when, we too will be raised up. Then we will see Christ face to face.

As you teach Lesson 1, help the students appreciate the promise of everlasting life that is inherent in Jesus' return to his Father in heaven. Urge them to continue building the kingdom of peace, love, and justice in anticipation of the day when Jesus will bring us all home.

PENTECOST SUNDAY

On Pentecost, we celebrate the generous outpouring of Jesus' Spirit on the disciples, transforming them from a disparate group of believers into the Church. In the Opening Prayer on Pentecost, we pray: "God, our Father, let the Spirit you sent on your Church to begin the teaching of the gospel continue to work in the world through the hearts of all who believe."

In Lesson 2, the students recall that they first received the Holy Spirit at Baptism. With a growing awareness of their ability to make decisions, they are led to the recognition that the Holy Spirit guides and informs their conscience to help them choose good over evil. In teaching this lesson, encourage the students to allow the Spirit to work through them as they take on the mission of living and sharing the good news of Jesus.

UNLIKELY SAINTS

It has been remarked that God writes straight with crooked lines. God's choice of Peter and Paul and the remarkable impact each had on the early Church bears out the truth of that statement. A look at the early life of each man might have raised questions about their suitability for Christian leadership. Jesus gave Peter his name, which means "rock." Yet Peter proved himself unworthy of his new name. Before his conversion, Paul was an ardent persecutor of Christians. Yet the Lord was able to use each of these men to accomplish great work in spreading the gospel.

In introducing your students to Saint Peter and Saint Paul in Lesson 3, emphasize that God wants each of us to use our gifts to spread the good news.

Lesson 1

Objective

This lesson helps the students understand that on the Feast of the Ascension we celebrate Jesus' return to his Father in heaven.

Step 1 / INTRODUCTION

Learning About Our Lives

Discussing Farewells

Have the students name experiences of saying good-bye to a friend who is moving away or to a parent who is going on a long business trip. Discuss how these experiences are similar and how they are different and what kind of promises people make in these situations. Explain that when people say good-bye, they often promise to stay in touch. Tell the students that in this lesson, they will learn about a promise Jesus made to his disciples before he left them.

Step 2 / DEVELOPMENT

Learning About Our Faith

Reading a Scripture Story

Direct attention to the story from Acts on page 316. Ask volunteers to read the story aloud. Explain that a witness is someone who tells what he or she has seen and heard. Then discuss the following questions.

- How long did Jesus stay with the disciples after his resurrection? (*Forty days*)

- Who did Jesus promise to send to be with his followers? (*The Holy Spirit*)

- Where did the two men tell the disciples that Jesus had gone? (*To heaven*)

Understanding the Message

Read through the text at the bottom of page 316 and the top of page 317 with the class. Write the word *ascension* on the board and have the students repeat it after you. Help the students understand that the ascension celebrates Jesus being taken up to heaven to share in his Father's kingdom. Discuss with the class why the ascension is a source of hope and joy to all who believe in Jesus and try to follow his example. Emphasize that we

316

Our Church Celebrates Holy Days

The Ascension of the Lord

After rising from the dead, Jesus appeared to his disciples for forty days. Jesus spoke to them about the kingdom of God. He told them to stay in Jerusalem to wait for the Spirit whom the Father promised to send. He said, "You will receive power when the Holy Spirit comes upon you. You will be my witnesses all over the earth."

After Jesus said this, and while they were watching, he was lifted up. A cloud took him out of their sight. The disciples could not see him, but as he went up, they kept looking up into the sky.

Suddenly, two men dressed in white clothing stood before them. They said, "Why are you standing there looking up into the sky? Jesus has been taken up into heaven. But he will return to you in the same way that you have seen him go."

Based on Acts of the Apostles 1:3–5, 8–11

316   Holy Days: Lesson One

⭐ ⭐⭐⭐ ⭐
Enriching the Lesson ⭐

Make witness pins with the class. Give out tag board, scissors, and crayons. Instruct the students to cut a 3" circle from tag board. Ask them to write on the circle one thing that they have learned about Jesus that they want to share with others and decorate the circle. Use straight pins to allow the students to wear their witness pins.

Plan Ahead

	Preparing Your Class	**Materials Needed**
Lesson 1	Study the lesson plan for this class. Practice reading Matthew 16:13–19 for Step 2.	■ pencils
Lesson 2	Read through the lesson plan. Be prepared to teach the song "We Shall Overcome" in Step 3.	■ pencils ■ music or recording of a song

Additional Resources

As you plan these lessons, consider using the following material from The Resourceful Teacher Package.

■ *Classroom Activity Sheets* for In the Spirit of Jesus

■ *Family Activity Sheets* for In the Spirit of Jesus

■ *Prayers for Every Day*

In preparing the students for the Sunday readings, you may wish to use Silver Burdett Ginn's *Getting Ready for Sunday* student and teacher materials.

REDUCED CLASSROOM ACTIVITIES

NAME _____

IN THE SPIRIT OF JESUS

Sister Thea Bowman taught all Americans to break down the walls that separate them and to see each person as a special gift from God. Write a letter to Sister Thea, describing how the lessons she taught are being lived out in your home, neighborhood, and school.

Dear Sister Thea,

_____
_____
_____
_____
_____
_____
_____
_____
_____
_____

Your friend,

_____

NAME _____

IN THE SPIRIT OF JESUS

Think about the people, near and far, who do not believe, as Sister Thea did, that there is a place for people of every color in God's kingdom. Then think how you might convince them that Sister Thea's message is true. Write your convincing message on the lines below.

_____
_____
_____
_____
_____
_____
_____
_____
_____
_____

321c Organizer

Background for the Teacher

POPE JOHN PAUL II

Karol Wojtyla was born in Wadowice, Poland, on May 18, 1920. His mother died when he was a young child and he was raised by his father. Karol excelled academically and socially. He was interested in art, drama, and athletics. He was an accomplished skier and even traveled for a time with a theatrical company.

Karol's carefree student life came to an abrupt end when Poland was invaded by the Nazis during World War II. The injustices he saw during the war—the denial of food to those displaced from their homes and the unfair treatment of workers—awakened in him the desire to serve God through the ministry of the priesthood. As a priest, he felt that he would be able to share with his people Christ's message of equality and the inherent dignity of all people.

AN EXAMPLE OF JESUS

Lesson 1 focuses on Pope John Paul II's life as priest and pope. In this lesson, you have the opportunity to help the students recognize that John Paul is a modern-day example of the values and qualities that Jesus calls us to emulate. He does not just preach gospel values; they are clearly lived and visible in his life. This is especially true in the pope's response to the failed assassination attempt on his life that occurred in 1981. Like Christ, who forgave those who crucified him as he hung on the cross, John Paul II, speaking from his hospital bed, publicly forgave the man who shot him.

Sister Thea Bowman Lesson 2 introduces the students to Thea Bowman, a vibrant, African American nun. (She was a member of the Franciscan Sisters of Perpetual Adoration.) Named Bertha when she was born, she chose the name "Thea" as her religious name, after her father, Theon. Bertha converted to the Catholic faith during the latter years of grammar school, having been influenced by the nuns who taught her. Their caring and compassion had such a lasting impact on Bertha that after finishing high school, she left Mississippi for the first time to travel to LaCrosse, Wisconsin, to join their order. She became the only black member of the order.

Over the next thirty-seven years, Sister Thea became known as a teacher, artist, evangelist, gospel singer, and instrument of change. She founded the Institute of Black Catholic Studies at Xavier University in New Orleans. She helped organize the 1987 Black Catholic Congress, in addition to directing Intercultural Awareness for the Diocese of Jackson, Mississippi. She helped people begin to understand the experience of being black and Catholic and she worked to incorporate African rituals and African American spirituals into eucharistic celebrations.

In 1990, Thea died from bone cancer.

Organizer 321d

LESSON 1

Objective

This lesson helps the students recognize Pope John Paul II as an example of peace and reconciliation.

Step 1 / INTRODUCTION

Learning About Our Lives

Studying a Photograph

Direct attention to page 322 and have the students identify the person in the photograph. After the students have named Pope John Paul II, invite them to discuss what they know about the pope, including where John Paul II lives and some of his accomplishments and duties.

Step 2 / DEVELOPMENT

Learning About Our Faith

Listening to a Scripture Story

Tell or read the story of Peter's commissioning as leader of the Church (Matthew 16:13–19) to the students. Help them understand that Jesus gave Peter the authority to teach and lead the Church in his name. Emphasize that this power has been passed down from Jesus through Peter to every pope since the beginning of the Church. Tell the students that the Holy Spirit guides the pope to teach as Jesus did. We believe that the pope of the Catholic Church helps the Church remain faithful to the teachings of Jesus.

Reading About Pope John Paul II

Call on volunteers to take turns reading aloud "Pope John Paul II" on pages 322 and 323. Use the following questions to guide discussion.

- What was Karol Wojtyla's native land? (*Poland*)
- Why did Karol decide to become a priest? (*He felt that God was calling him to a life of service.*)
- Why did some people hate Cardinal Wojtyla? (*Because he spoke out for freedom, justice, and the rights of people*)
- What happened to Pope John Paul in May of 1981? (*He was shot.*)

322

In the Spirit of Jesus

Pope John Paul II

When Karol Wojtyla was in college, the people of his country were living in fear. The German army had attacked Poland. Schools were closed and Karol had to go to work. During the war, Karol became angry at the injustices he saw. He wanted to speak out against the way people were being treated. Karol felt that God was calling him to a life of service. He decided to become a priest.

Karol was ordained a year after the war ended. Father Wojtyla loved being a parish priest. He was a wonderful preacher who shared Jesus' message of hope and love with his people. When he was only thirty-eight, he became a bishop. Soon after, he was named Cardinal of Krakow, Poland. He spoke out for freedom and justice. He fought against Communism, which did not permit people to celebrate their faith. Some people hated Cardinal Wojtyla for talking about the rights of people. They warned him to stop.

Enriching the Lesson

Divide the class into cooperative groups and distribute recent issues of your diocesan newspaper. Direct the students to look through the papers for articles and pictures about Pope John Paul II to discover new information about him. After the students complete this research activity, have each group report on the pope's recent activities.

In 1978, Karol Wojtyla became Pope John Paul II, the leader of the Catholic Church. John Paul II traveled all over the world, more than any other pope. He spoke out for equality. He repeated Jesus' message everywhere he went: "Love one another. We are all brothers and sisters. We must live in peace."

On May 13, 1981, while blessing the people in St. Peter's Square in Rome, Pope John Paul II was shot. He was rushed to the hospital for surgery. Four days later, the pope broadcast a message from his bed to the crowds in St. Peter's Square. He said that he was praying for the man who shot him. He called the man "his brother." After he had recovered, John Paul II visited the jail where the would-be assassin was being held. He prayed with the man who tried to kill him. The pope forgave him and blessed him.

Pope John Paul II is a living example of the peace and reconciliation Jesus came to bring. His life reminds us to treat every human being with love and respect and to forgive those who have hurt us.

Activity

If Pope John Paul II came to your city or town today, what do you think he would speak out against? What message would he have for you and your family? Write your ideas on the lines below.

_____

_____

_____

_____

_____

_____

_____

_____

_____

- How did Pope John Paul II treat the man who had shot him? (*He prayed for the man, visited him in jail, heard his confession, and forgave him.*)
- How does Pope John Paul II live in the spirit of Jesus? (*Like Jesus, John Paul II calls us to respect all people and to forgive those who have hurt us.*)

Step 3 / CONCLUSION

Learning How to Live Our Faith

Completing an Activity

Read aloud the directions to the activity at the bottom of page 323 and have the students work independently to complete it. When all have finished, invite volunteers to share their responses with the class.

Praying a Litany Prayer

Use the words and teachings of Pope John Paul II to compose a litany prayer asking Jesus to help us live in his spirit. For example: *Jesus, you call us to forgive on another* or *Jesus, you call us to live in peace.* Have the students respond, "Help us to love and serve you always."

Focus on

The Pope   The pope has many titles, including Bishop of Rome, Vicar of Jesus Christ, Successor of Saint Peter, and the Prince of the Apostles. The word *pope* is taken from the Latin and Greek words which mean "father." It is for this reason that we refer to the pope as the "Holy Father." Since Saint Peter, there have been 262 popes.

LESSON 2

Objective

This lesson helps the students understand that Sister Thea Bowman called the Church to be one in Christ.

Step 1 / INTRODUCTION

Learning About Our Lives

Talking About Discrimination

Write the word *discrimination* on the chalkboard and have the students define it. Elicit from the class that discrimination means treating others differently because of the way they look, act, speak, or behave. Have the students identify people they feel are discriminated against in today's society. Responses might include: *the handicapped, people of color, the elderly, people who do not speak English, the homeless, people with AIDS,* and so on. Explain that in today's lesson, they will read about a woman who worked to help all people recognize that every person is a child of God. As you teach this lesson, you can help the students celebrate their faith with joy and strive to treat all others as brothers and sisters in Christ.

Step 2 / DEVELOPMENT

Learning About Our Faith

Reading and Discussing a Biography

Read with the class "Sister Thea Bowman" on page 324. Then discuss the following questions.

- How did Thea's father experience discrimination? (*The hospital in Canton did not allow African American doctors or patients.*)

- Why did Thea become a Catholic? (*She saw how the nuns and priests in her town loved Jesus and their work.*)

- What was Sister Thea's prayer? (*"Use me, Lord."*)

- What did Sister Thea tell people of different nationalities? (*To be one in Christ*)

- Why did Sister Thea describe death as "going home?" (*Answers will vary. Help the students understand that Sister Thea saw death as the beginning of a new life of happiness with God.*)

324

Sister Thea Bowman

Thea Bowman was born in Yazuu City, Mississippi in 1937. She was the granddaughter of a slave and the daughter of a doctor. Doctor Bowman, Thea's father, was not allowed to care for patients in the local hospital because the hospital was not open to African Americans.

Thea became a Catholic when she was twelve years old. She made this decision because she saw how much the nuns and priests loved Jesus and witnessed their work with the poor families in Thea's hometown. She was so impressed by their faith that Thea joined the convent when she was fifteen. She became a Franciscan Sister of Perpetual Adoration.

Sister Thea's life was a celebration. She shared the good news with children, teenagers, and college students. She sang, danced, told stories, and read poetry to help people of all ages understand God's love. She often prayed a simple three-word prayer: "Use me, Lord." Thea wanted God to help her use her gifts to bring more peace, love, and justice to the world. She wanted everyone to know that there was a place for people of every color in God's kingdom.

In 1984, Sister Thea became very ill. Although she was in pain, she continued to give speeches all over the country. She also recorded gospel songs, in which she shared her African American music with the world. Thea called on people to break down the walls that separated them and to see each person as a special gift from God. "Be Irish American, be Italian American, be Native American, be African American," Thea said, "but be one in Christ."

Before Thea died, a friend asked her what he should say at her funeral. Thea said, "Tell them that I'm going home like a shooting star." Sister Thea Bowman went home to God on March 30, 1990.

Teaching Tips

As the students work on the gifts and talents activity on page 325, take the time to point out the gifts and qualities you have noticed in the students as individuals and as a group. Affirm the students and help them recognize that each of them is a special, unique creation of God.

Focus on

Sister Thea Bowman Although diagnosed with bone cancer and weak from treatment and rapidly failing health, Sister Thea continued writing, singing, and preaching. When asked about dying, she quoted Sojourner Truth: "I'm not going to die. I'm going home like a shooting star." Sister Thea Bowman died on March 30, 1990. Posthumously, she was awarded the prestigious Laetare Medal from Notre Dame for enriching the arts, the Church, and humanity.

Learning How to Live Our Faith

Writing About Gifts

Have a student read the directions to the writing activity on page 325. Allow ample time for the students to write about their gifts and how they can be used to build God's kingdom. Afterward, invite sharing.

Singing Together

Explain that in 1989, Sister Thea spoke to the United States bishops. Thea said that the Church must reach out to all cultures and be more aware of the needs of minorities. Thea ended her talk by asking the 225 bishops to stand, join hands, and sing a song of hope, a song African Americans have sung in their struggle for equality. Teach the students "We Shall Overcome" and have them sing it with you.

The words of the song are:

We shall overcome; we shall overcome;
We shall overcome some day.
Oh, deep in my soul, I do believe:
We shall overcome some day.

Then discuss with the class the problems that need to be overcome in our world.

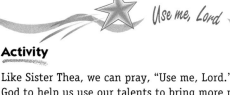

Use me, Lord

Activity

Like Sister Thea, we can pray, "Use me, Lord." We can ask God to help us use our talents to bring more peace, love, and justice to the world. On the lines below, write two talents or gifts that you have been given. Tell how these gifts can be used to help God's kingdom grow in the world.

_____

_____

_____

_____

Use me, Lord   Use me, Lord

Cultural Awareness

Explore with the students their cultural heritage. Invite them to share family traditions that reflect their heritage. These might include holiday customs, foods, ways of praying, music and clothing, and so on. Emphasize that honoring the traditions of other cultures helps make our Church and world a better sign of God's kingdom.

325

OUR CATHOLIC HERITAGE

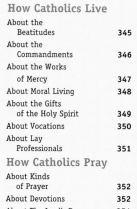

What Catholics Believe

About the Bible	328
About the Trinity	330
About the Catholic Church	332
About Mary and the Saints	332
About Life Everlasting	333

How Catholics Worship

About the Sacraments	334
About the Mass	338
About Reconciliation	342
About the Liturgical Year	344

How Catholics Live

About the Beatitudes	345
About the Commandments	346
About the Works of Mercy	347
About Moral Living	348
About the Gifts of the Holy Spirit	349
About Vocations	350
About Lay Professionals	351

How Catholics Pray

About Kinds of Prayer	352
About Devotions	352
About The Lord's Prayer	354

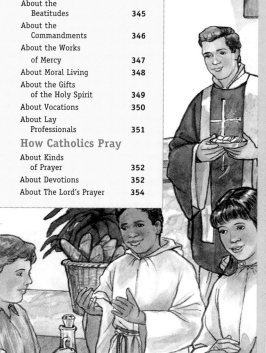

Our Catholic Heritage

In June 1994 the *Catechism of the Catholic Church* was published in English and widely distributed throughout the United States. Bishops, pastors, and educators have used the *Catechism* as a basic resource in summarizing Catholic doctrine and for a better understanding of the theological background of the Church's teaching.

In this section, *Our Catholic Heritage,* there is a summary of Catholic belief, organized in the same way as the *Catechism.* It is meant as a ready reference for both you and your students to provide in summary fashion the basic teachings of the Catholic Church.

Over the course of the THIS IS OUR FAITH program, the *Our Catholic Heritage* section of each grade level is developmental in nature and planned to complement the information presented in the lesson plans. These pages are most effectively used in conjunction with the student book pages that cover the topics in question.

You may want to read the Apostolic Constitution *Fidei Depositum* and the *Prologue* (paragraphs 1–25). These introduce the *Catechism* and provide a better understanding of its purpose in religious education.

What Catholics Believe

The *Catechism of the Catholic Church,* published in 1994, provides a clear and extensive statement of Catholic doctrine, divided into four parts, or pillars, of our faith. The first, "The Profession of Faith," develops the foundations of our creed, based on sacred Scripture and the tradition of the Church throughout the ages. As a Catholic Christian community, we renew our dedication to these beliefs each week at Sunday Mass, at Baptism and Confirmation, and during the Easter Vigil. Our recitation of the creed reminds us of our unity in faith with Catholic Christians throughout the world.

About the Bible

TEACHER REFLECTION

Sacred Scripture is a source of nourishment and strength for the Church. The Church has accepted throughout history that certain books of both the Old Testament and the New Testament were written under the inspiration of the Holy Spirit. The Church has recognized the importance of biblical scholarship for understanding the Scriptures. We are encouraged to study the Bible continually to be able to appreciate more deeply the word of God.

You may want to review for yourself the teachings of the Church about the Bible in paragraphs 101–133 in the *Catechism of the Catholic Church.*

STUDENT REVIEW

Ask volunteers to read "About the Bible" on page 328 in their books. This describes the structure of the Bible according to books, chapters, and verses. Distribute Bibles to the class. Check the students' understanding of what they have read by asking them to locate the Old Testament and the New Testament. Make sure each student is aware of this division in the Bible. If you have time, ask the students to begin at the Book of Genesis and name each book of the Old Testament. Do the same for the New Testament.

We can come to know and understand our faith in many ways.

ABOUT The Bible

The **Bible** is the story of God and God's people. It is the written word of God. The word *Bible* means "books." In the Bible there are seventy-three books of stories, laws, history, poetry, and prayers.

The Bible was the first book ever printed by machine. Today millions of Bibles are printed and read by people throughout the

world. The Bibles may have a different number of pages and may be written in different languages. However, all Bibles give us the same message of God.

To read the Bible more easily, we need to know how to find the parts or passages that are indicated in Bible references. Each time there is a passage from the Bible in your book, there is a Bible reference at the end. Finding passages in the Bible is not like finding something in a story book or a textbook. Remember, the Bible is made up of many books. Each book has a name. Each book is divided into chapters, and each chapter has a number. The chapters are divided into verses, which may contain one or more sentences. Verses also have numbers.

There is a Bible passage in this book on page 93. To find this passage in the Bible, you will need to find Sirach 6:14. Use the key to help you. Begin by finding the Book of Sirach (it is in the Old Testament). Then find Chapter 6. Finally, find verse 14.

Sirach	6:	14
Book	Chapter	Verse

Sometimes the Bible passage contains more than one verse. For example, in Matthew 9:1–8, you are reading verses one through eight.

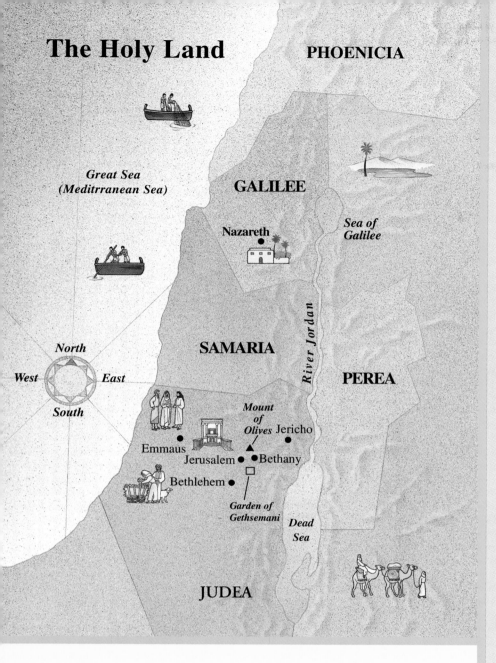

The Holy Land

PHOENICIA

Great Sea
(Meditrranean Sea)

GALILEE

Nazareth

*Sea of
Galilee*

North

West   *East*

South

SAMARIA

River Jordan

PEREA

*Mount
of
Olives*   Jericho

Emmaus

Jerusalem   Bethany

Bethlehem

*Garden of
Gethsemani*

*Dead
Sea*

JUDEA

Ask the students to find the passage from Sirach and verses 1–8 in Matthew 9 in the Bible, following the directions in their books on page 328. Then have them read the passages aloud. Ask the class to give the names and places found in each passage. Then direct the students to study the map on page 329. Help the students locate on the map the places named in the Scripture passages.

Continue using the map to help the students identify the various places described in the gospels. Recall with the students that Jesus was born in Bethlehem and grew up in Nazareth. Jesus went to Jerusalem with Joseph and Mary at special times. He traveled to that city with his disciples during his ministry. The story of the Good Samaritan takes place on the road from Jerusalem to Jericho.

Help the students understand map directions. Direct them to note the letters *N, E, S, W* in the shape of a cross on the left-hand side of the map. Tell them that this is called a direction finder. Explain that its purpose is to help locate the direction of one point on the map from another. Make sure the students understand that the letters *N, E, S,* and *W* stand for the directions north, east, south, and west. Test their understanding with the following questions.

- Is Galilee north or south of Jerusalem? (*North*)
- Which direction is the Sea of Galilee from Nazareth? (*East*)
- If Jesus walked from Jerusalem to Bethlehem, in what direction would he have walked? (*South*)

About the Trinity

TEACHER REFLECTION

Over the centuries the Church has come to an "understanding" of the Trinity as a result of reflection on the action of God on our lives. We have come to know God as love, creative and redemptive. This revelation of God, in whose image we are made, helps us understand both the meaning of our humanity and our calling to be part of a community. We believe that God reveals the work of the Trinity in the mystery of creation.

You may want to review for yourself the teachings of the Church about creation in paragraphs 279–412 in the *Catechism of the Catholic Church.*

STUDENT REVIEW

Ask volunteers to read "About the Trinity" on pages 330–331 in their books.

Explain that these paragraphs summarize the basic Catholic beliefs about God, the Father, Son, and Holy Spirit. Ask the students to name the three persons of the Blessed Trinity. Elicit from the students the attributes of God (*One God in three persons, all-good, all-holy, and all-knowing, just, and merciful*).

Review with the students the Catholic beliefs about Jesus Christ, the Second Person of the Trinity (*Jesus is both human and divine. Jesus is the Messiah, our Savior, who rose to new life.*)

Ask:

■ What does the resurrection of Jesus teach us? (*That death is not an ending, but rather a new beginning that leads us to new and everlasting life.*)

■ What is the ascension? (*Jesus' return to God the Father after he rose from the dead.*)

Review with the students the Catholic teaching about the Holy Spirit, the Third Person of the Trinity. Emphasize that the Holy Spirit inspired the authors of the Bible to write God's word and is still with us today, helping us to be followers of Jesus. Ask: What happened at Pentecost? (*The Holy Spirit came down upon the disciples and filled them with courage to share Jesus' good news with the world.*)

ABOUT The Trinity

We Believe in God

There is only one God. We know God as three Persons: God the Father, God the Son, and God the Holy Spirit. We believe that there is one God in three Persons, whom we call the **Blessed Trinity.**

God is all-good, all-holy, and all-knowing. God is always just and merciful.

We believe that God speaks to us in many ways. God is made known to us especially through Jesus, the Bible, and the Church.

God created all things out of goodness and love. Human beings are made in the image and likeness of God. We share the gift of God's life and loving presence as well as the responsibility to help care for the world.

We Believe in Jesus

Jesus, God's own Son, is the Second Person of the Blessed Trinity. Jesus is both God and man. Our belief that God became human in Jesus while remaining God is called the **Incarnation.** Jesus is both human and divine.

Jesus is the **Messiah**, sent by God. Jesus' mission was to announce the good news about God's reign of peace, love, and justice, to save us from sin, and to bring us everlasting life. Jesus taught, healed, forgave sins, and worked miracles to show us how much God loves us.

Jesus suffered and died to save all people from sin and death. Jesus is the **Savior** of the world, who saves us by his life, death, and **resurrection**.

Jesus rose to new life and invites us to share this new life with him. The resurrection fills us with hope. Jesus' resurrection teaches us that death is not an ending but rather a new beginning that leads us to new and everlasting life.

After the resurrection, Jesus shared his mission with the Apostles. He promised to send the Holy Spirit to be with them. Then Jesus returned in glory to his Father. Catholics call Jesus' return to God the **ascension.**

We Believe in the Holy Spirit

The **Holy Spirit** is the Third Person of the Blessed Trinity. The Holy Spirit is the love that is shared by the Father and the Son. The Spirit leads and guides us in living as followers of Jesus.

The Holy Spirit has been at work since Creation. With the help of the Spirit, the authors of the Bible wrote God's word. At **Pentecost**, the Holy Spirit gave the disciples the courage to share Jesus' good news. The Holy Spirit works in the Church today, helping us carry on Jesus' work. The Spirit works and lives in us. We are temples of the Holy Spirit.

About the Catholic Church

TEACHER REFLECTION

It is our belief as Catholic Christians that Jesus established the Church and set its course by forming the apostles and disciples as evangelizers and missionaries. We believe that at Pentecost the Holy Spirit revealed the Church to the world, and that the public mission of the Church began at that time. We profess in the creed that the Church is one, holy, catholic, and apostolic. These four marks describe essential features of the Church and its mission. We should be able to see and experience these characteristics of the Church in our parishes and in our nation, and in the work of the Church throughout the world.

You may want to review for yourself the teachings of the Church about the four marks of the Church in paragraphs 813–873 in the *Catechism of the Catholic Church.*

STUDENT REVIEW

Ask volunteers to read "About the Catholic Church" on page 332 in their books. Help the students learn the four marks of the Church—it is one, holy, catholic, and apostolic. Make sure that the class understands the meaning of each mark. Answer any questions the students may have.

About Mary and the Saints

TEACHER REFLECTION

Mary has always been a sign of God's special love for us. Mary's willingness to be God's servant, her saying yes to God, began our salvation in Jesus Christ. We believe that Mary, from the first instant of her conception, was totally preserved from the state of original sin. The Church calls this doctrine *the Immaculate Conception.* The Church also teaches that at her death Mary was assumed body and soul into heaven, where she shares in the glory of her son's resurrection. We honor Mary, the Mother of God, as Mother of the Church because she is the model of holiness for all of us.

You may want to review for yourself the teaching of the Church about Mary in paragraphs 963–972 in the *Catechism of the Catholic Church.*

ABOUT The Catholic Church

Catholics are followers of Jesus, and under the leadership of the pope and bishops, receive and share the Scriptures, worship God, celebrate the seven sacraments, and serve those in need.

The Church and her members are identified by four marks: one, holy, catholic, and apostolic.

The Church is **one**. We believe in one God—Father, Son, and Holy Spirit—one faith, and one Baptism. Our belief in Jesus unites us.

The Church is **holy**. God shares holiness with us. We are called to become holy and be filled with God's goodness.

The Church is **catholic**, or universal. The Catholic Church welcomes all people.

The Church is **apostolic**. The truths of our faith and our way of life come down to us from the Apostles.

The chief teacher of the Church is the pope. We believe that the pope represents Jesus on earth.

ABOUT Mary and the Saints

Catholics believe that Mary, the mother of Jesus, was born without original sin. This special gift from God is called the Immaculate Conception. From the first moment of life, Mary was filled with grace and lived a sinless life.

We honor Mary as mother of Jesus and mother of the Church. Mary is our mother, too. She loves and cares for us.

332

Catholics believe that Mary was taken up to heaven, body and soul, and shares in Jesus' resurrection. We call this belief Mary's assumption.

Mary is our greatest **saint**. Saints are special men and women who show us how to follow Jesus. We honor the saints and ask them to pray to God for us.

ABOUT Life Everlasting

We believe that one day Jesus will return in glory to announce that God's plan for the world is completed. We wait with hope for the time when God's perfect peace, love, and justice will be fulfilled when Christ comes again in glory. We work to bring God's kingdom to the world now.

Jesus teaches us that if we follow his example, we will be happy forever in heaven. Heaven is unending happiness with God and all who love God. If we have shown love for God, ourselves, and others, we will be together in heaven.

Those who have deliberately refused, in serious ways, to love God and their neighbor, and have not asked forgiveness, separate themselves forever from God and those who love God. We call this everlasting separation **hell**.

333

STUDENT REVIEW

Ask volunteers to read "About Mary and the Saints" on page 332 in their books. Clarify for the students the meaning of the Immaculate Conception—that Mary was born without original sin—and that she was filled with grace from the time she was born. This gift from God was given to her because she was to bear Jesus. She was to become the mother of God. Also explain the assumption (the action of Mary being taken up to heaven, body and soul, after her death). Ask: Why do we honor Mary? (*Because she is the mother of Jesus, mother of the Church, and loves and cares for us; she is our mother; she is our greatest saint.*)

About Life Everlasting

TEACHER REFLECTION

Our belief in new life forever, or life everlasting, has traditionally been described as the "last things"—the particular judgment; the realities of heaven, purgatory, and hell; and the final judgment. We believe that at the second coming of Christ all people will be gathered in Christ's presence, and that the truth of each one's relationship with God will be revealed. At the same time, the kingdom of God will come in its fullness, and humanity and the world will be transformed.

You may want to review for yourself the teaching of the Church about life everlasting in paragraphs 1020–1050 in the *Catechism of the Catholic Church.*

STUDENT REVIEW

Ask volunteers to read the section "About Life Everlasting" on page 333 in their books. Discuss any questions the students may have.

How Catholics Worship

The liturgical life of the Church is the Catholic community's way of celebrating what we believe. Through the signs of the sacraments and our participation in the liturgical celebrations, we renew our faith and gain an even greater share in the life of grace, God's life in us. Through the sacraments, we are challenged to follow ever more closely the way of Christ that leads to the realization of God's kingdom.

About the Sacraments

TEACHER REFLECTION

The whole life of the Church revolves around the Eucharist and the other sacraments. In the sacraments we encounter Christ and are enabled to live the life of faith more deeply. The sacraments of initiation—Baptism, Confirmation, and Eucharist—provide the building blocks for Christian life. Through them we are welcomed into the Church and are called to conversion and service.

The sacraments of healing—Reconciliation and Anointing of the Sick—recall the frailty of our human condition. The sacrament of Reconciliation provides us with an opportunity to acknowledge the reality of sin, to ask forgiveness, and to begin anew as disciples of Christ. Anointing of the Sick is a source of strength and consolation for those who are ill and those who are caring for them.

The sacraments of commitment—Matrimony and Holy Orders—celebrate publicly the calling to family life and to ordained ministry in the Church. These vocations are sanctified in the sacramental rites in which we are called to build the Body of Christ through example and service.

You may want to review for yourself the teaching of the Church about the sacraments in Part Two of the *Catechism of the Catholic Church*.

Catholics have a sacred history of **worship**. Worship is giving honor and praise to God. Through the sacraments and prayer, we praise, thank, adore, and ask God's help.

ABOUT The Sacraments

The **sacraments** are sacred signs that celebrate God's love for us and Jesus' presence in our lives and in the Church. There are seven sacraments. Through the sacraments, we are united with Jesus and share in God's life—grace.

The Sacraments of Initiation. We become full members of the Church through the three sacraments of initiation. The sacraments of initiation are Baptism, Confirmation, and Eucharist.

Baptism welcomes us into the Christian community, frees us from original sin and all sins, and unites us with Jesus.

During the celebration the priest or deacon pours water over the head of the person being baptized as he prays, "I baptize you in the name of the Father, and of the Son, and of the Holy Spirit (Rite of Baptism)."

We are born into a sinful condition that separates us from God. This condition is called **original sin**. Baptism frees us from original sin and all sins, and reunites us with God. We receive the Holy Spirit at Baptism.

Through the waters of Baptism, which represent life and death, we share in Jesus' death and resurrection. We are called away from sin to new life with Jesus.

Confirmation strengthens the new life we received at Baptism and makes us living witnesses of Jesus in the world.

During the celebration the bishop or priest lays his hand on the head of the one to be confirmed and anoints the forehead with chrism as he prays, "Be sealed with the Gift of the Holy Spirit (Rite of Confirmation)."

Confirmation is usually celebrated with a bishop. The Holy Spirit gives us special gifts to help us share Jesus' good news by our words and actions.

Eucharist celebrates the real presence of Jesus' Body and Blood under the appearances of bread and wine.

During the celebration the priest prays the words of consecration

over the bread and wine, which become the body and blood of Christ.

The Eucharist is our greatest act of worship. At the Last Supper, Jesus gave us his body and blood so that we could live forever.

The Eucharist makes Jesus' sacrifice on the cross and his resurrection from the dead present for us. The word *Eucharist* means "thanksgiving." During the Mass we praise and thank God for all our gifts, especially the gift of Jesus.

Jesus is truly present in the Eucharist. The bread and wine still have the appearance of ordinary bread and wine, but through the power of the Holy Spirit, they become Jesus' Body and Blood.

The Eucharist unites us with Jesus and the Church community. Jesus is also present in the people gathered to celebrate the Eucharist, in the word proclaimed, and in the priest who presides.

STUDENT REVIEW

Ask a volunteer to read "How Catholics Worship" on page 334 in his or her book. Then ask several volunteers to read aloud "About the Sacraments" on pages 334–335. Review with the students the definition of sacraments and original sin. Have the students list the sacraments of initiation on the chalkboard. Ask:

- Which sacrament frees us from original sin? (*Baptism*)

- Which sacrament makes us living witnesses of Jesus in the world? (*Confirmation*)

- Which sacrament celebrates the real presence of Jesus' Body and Blood under the appearance of bread and wine? (*Eucharist*)

- What is our greatest act of worship? (*The Eucharist*)

Then have volunteers define these three sacraments of initiation and describe how each one is celebrated.

Read aloud with the students the introductory paragraph "The Sacraments of Healing" on page 336 in their books. Have volunteers continue reading about Reconciliation and Anointing of the Sick. Ask a volunteer to name the two sacraments of healing (*Reconciliation and Anointing of the Sick*). Invite a student to write these two sacraments on the chalkboard. Ask:

■ What does the sacrament of Reconciliation celebrate? (*God's healing and forgiveness of our sins*)

■ What is the prayer of absolution? (*The prayer the priest prays during the celebration of Penance that takes away our sins.*)

■ What is sin? (*Our free choice to turn away from God and one another*)

■ What happens when we receive this sacrament? (*We are reunited with God and the Church community.*)

Discuss the sacrament of Anointing of the Sick. Ask:

■ What does the sacrament of Anointing of the Sick bring? (*Jesus' healing, comfort, and strength to the seriously ill, elderly, or those in danger of death*)

■ When the priest anoints the person with oil, what does he pray? (*That the Holy Spirit will help the person and that the Lord will save and raise the person up*)

■ How can we help people who are old or sick? (*By praying for them, visiting them, and giving them any help that we can*)

The Sacraments of Healing

The sacraments of healing—Reconciliation and Anointing of the Sick—we celebrate Jesus' forgiveness and healing.

Reconciliation celebrates God's healing and forgiveness of our sins. During the celebration the priest prays the prayer of absolution, ending with the words, "I absolve you from your sins in the name of the Father, and of the Son, and of the Holy Spirit (Rite of Penance).

When we sin, we freely choose to turn away from God and one another. Reconciliation reunites us with God and the Church community. In the sacrament of Reconciliation, the priest represents the loving forgiveness of God and the Church. We may celebrate the sacrament of Reconciliation whenever we need God's mercy and peace. We may celebrate the sacrament individually or communally.

Anointing of the Sick brings Jesus' healing, comfort, and strength to those who are seriously ill, elderly, or in danger of death.

During the celebration the priest anoints the person with the oil of the sick as he prays, "Through this holy anointing may the Lord in his love and mercy help you with the grace of the Holy Spirit. May the Lord who frees you from sin save you and raise you up" (Rite of Anointing).

Before the anointing, the sick may celebrate Reconciliation. The Eucharist may be received after the anointing.

We can help people who are old or sick by praying for them, visiting them, and helping them in any way we can.

336

The Sacraments of Commitment

In the sacraments of commitment, the Church celebrates two special ways through which people serve others by sharing their gifts. The sacraments of commitment are Matrimony and Holy Orders.

Matrimony celebrates the lifelong love of a man and a woman for each other. During the celebration, the bride and groom exchange marriage vows, promising always to be faithful to each other.

Through Matrimony the couple forms a partnership based on love. The man and woman promise to love each other in sickness and in health. They promise to be faithful to each other. Their love for each other is a sign of God's love for all people.

In **Holy Orders** bishops, priests, and deacons are ordained to serve the Church in a special way.

During the celebration, the bishop lays his hands on the head of the person to be ordained. Afterwards, he prays a prayer of consecration, or blessing.

Bishops, priests, and deacons are blessed to share in Jesus' ministry in a special way. Bishops carry on the work of the Apostles and lead dioceses. Bishops teach and serve the Catholic Church. Priests help the bishop in his ministry. Priests, like bishops, celebrate the sacraments, proclaim God's word, and help us become better signs of his kingdom. Deacons care for the poor and do other works of mercy. They may baptize, proclaim the gospel, witness marriages, and preside at funerals.

Read aloud with the students the introductory paragraph about the sacraments of commitment on page 337. Invite volunteers to continue reading aloud the paragraphs that follow about Matrimony and Holy Orders. Lead a discussion about the sacraments of commitment. Ask:

■ What is celebrated in the sacrament of Matrimony? (*The lifelong love of a man and a woman for each other*)

■ What happens during the celebration? (*The man and woman exchange vows, promising to love and be faithful to each other in marriage.*)

Discuss the sacrament of Holy Orders with the class. Ask:

■ Who receives the sacrament of Holy Orders? (*Bishops, priests, and deacons*)

■ What do bishops, priests, and deacons do? (*They share in Jesus' ministry. Bishops continue the work of the Apostles, teaching and serving the Catholic Church; priests celebrate the sacraments, as do bishops; and deacons care for the poor, baptize, proclaim the gospel, witness marriages, and preside at funerals.*)

About the Mass

TEACHER REFLECTION

Our celebration of the Mass is the primary source of renewal of our life in Christ. In the Mass we are once again welcomed into the community of the faithful, called to communion with others and service to others, and nourished by the Bread of Life. We are sent forth to exemplify the good news of the gospel in our everyday lives.

You may wish to extend the use of pages 338–341 by inviting a parish priest to demonstrate and explain the various vestments and sacramentals used at Mass.

You may want to review for yourself the teaching of the Church about the Mass in paragraphs 1322–1405 in the *Catechism of the Catholic Church.*

STUDENT REVIEW

Ask volunteers to read "About the Mass" on pages 338–341 in their books. Students can refer to this feature at appropriate times throughout the year to

- review the Mass and its major parts.
- learn some of the Mass responses and prayers.
- prepare for a class Mass.
- prepare for a First Eucharist if they have not received the sacrament at an earlier age.

Help the students learn the structure of the Mass. Write on the chalkboard the main parts of the Mass—Introductory Rites; Liturgy of the Word; Liturgy of the Eucharist; Communion Rite; and Concluding Rite. Have the students identify the elements of each section. Help the students understand how the Liturgy of the Word and the Liturgy of the Eucharist differ. Help them understand that in the Introductory Rites we prepare ourselves for the Liturgy of the Word and the Liturgy of the Eucharist. We pray for forgiveness and we praise God.

In the Liturgy of the Word we hear God's word in the readings from the Old and New Testaments and in the homily given by the priest or deacon. We profess our beliefs in the Catholic faith and pray for all God's people.

ABOUT The Mass

Introductory Rites

At Mass we come together to pray and worship as the family of Jesus.

Entrance Procession and Gathering Song

As the priest and other ministers enter in procession, we stand and sing a gathering song.

Greeting

We make the sign of the cross. The priest welcomes us by saying, "The Lord be with you." We answer, "And also with you."

Penitential Rite

As a community, we admit that we have sinned and we thank God for his gift of forgiveness. We pray the opening prayer.

Gloria

We sing or say this hymn of praise to God.

Liturgy of the Word

First Reading

The lector reads from the Old Testament or the Acts of the Apostles about God's love for us.

Responsorial Psalm

The song leader sings a psalm from the Bible. We join in singing a response.

Second Reading

The lector reads from the New Testament, usually from one of the letters.

Gospel Acclamation

Before the gospel is proclaimed by the priest or deacon, we sing, "Alleluia" or another acclamation.

Gospel

We stand in honor of Jesus as the gospel is proclaimed.

Homily

The priest or deacon explains the readings, especially the gospel, in a special talk called the homily.

Profession of Faith

We stand to declare our beliefs by reciting the Nicene Creed.

General Intercessions

We pray for the pope and the bishops, for our country, and for all God's people.

In the Liturgy of the Eucharist, we praise and thank God and ask that through the power of the Holy Spirit the bread and wine become the Body and Blood of Jesus. In the Communion Rite, the focus is on the special presence of Jesus in the Eucharist. After having offered ourselves and our gifts to God, we receive Jesus, God's greatest gift to us, in Communion. In the Concluding Rite, we are blessed and dismissed to continue serving God and others.

Liturgy of the Eucharist

Preparation of the Altar and the Gifts

We bring gifts of bread and wine to the altar as the table is prepared for the meal we are about to share.

Eucharistic Prayer

In this prayer of praise and thanksgiving, the priest addresses God our Father in our name. Together we sing a song of praise to God for his many blessings, especially for the gift of Jesus.

"Holy, holy, holy Lord, God of power and might. Heaven and earth are full of your glory. Hosanna in the highest. Blessed is he who comes in the name of the Lord. Hosanna in the highest."

Together with the priest, we call upon the Holy Spirit and ask that the bread and wine become Jesus' Body and Blood. The priest consecrates the bread and wine. We proclaim the mystery of faith. We sing or say these or other words of joy and praise, "Christ has died, Christ is risen, Christ will come again."

As the Eucharistic Prayer ends, we proclaim, "Amen."

Communion Rite

The Lord's Prayer

We pray together the prayer that Jesus taught us—The Lord's Prayer.

Sign of Peace

We offer each other a sign of peace to show that we are all brothers and sisters in Jesus.

Breaking of the Bread

While the priest breaks the host, we sing or say,

"Lamb of God, you take away the sins of the world, have mercy on us.

Lamb of God, you take away the sins of the world, have mercy on us.

Lamb of God, you take away the sins of the world, grant us peace."

Communion

Jesus invites us to receive the Eucharist.

Concluding Rite

Blessing

The priest blesses us in the name of God the Father, God the Son, and God the Holy Spirit. We answer, "Amen."

Dismissal

The priest tells us to go in peace to love and serve God and others. We sing a song of thanks and praise.

About Reconciliation

TEACHER REFLECTION

The grace of the sacrament of Reconciliation, or Penance, gives us the courage to admit our failures and wrongdoing, to ask forgiveness, and to renew our dedication to the Christian life. The experience of celebrating this sacrament in community can give us a better appreciation of the social consequences of sin and the need for reconciliation as a whole people. Reconciliation makes visible the mercy of our loving God.

You may want to review for yourself the teaching of the Church about Reconciliation in paragraphs 1422–1484 in the *Catechism of the Catholic Church.*

STUDENT REVIEW

Ask volunteers to read "About Reconciliation" on pages 342–343 in their books. Review with the students that Penance is another name for the sacrament of Reconciliation and that this sacrament may be celebrated individually or in community. Discuss with the class how the sacrament of Reconciliation of an individual is celebrated. Review a prayer of sorrow by asking the class to pray silently an act of contrition. (See page 5.) Point out that absolution is given by the priest, but forgiveness comes from God.

ABOUT Reconciliation

The sacrament of Reconciliation, or Penance, celebrates God's love and forgiveness through the Church.

Preparation I prepare myself for the sacrament of Reconciliation by thinking about my words and actions. This is called an examination of conscience. How do I fulfill God's commands to love him and to love my neighbor as myself? Am I sorry for having sinned?

Rite for Reconciliation of Individuals

Priest's Welcome The priest welcomes me in the name of Jesus and the Church.

Reading from Scripture The priest may share with me a reading from the Bible.

Confession I tell my sins to the priest. This is called my confession. He then suggests ways in which I might grow closer to God and asks me to say a prayer or do a kind act to help make up for my sins. This is called an act of penance.

Prayer of Sorrow The priest then asks me to tell God that I am sorry for my sins. I say an act of contrition.

Absolution Acting in the name of the Christian community, the priest extends his hands over me and asks God to forgive me. The priest forgives me in the name of the Father, the Son, and the Holy Spirit. This is called absolution.

Prayer of Praise and Dismissal After receiving absolution, I praise God with the priest. He says, "The Lord has freed you from your sins. Go in peace." I answer, "Amen."

Celebrating Reconciliation in Community

Sometimes we gather as a community to celebrate the sacrament of Reconciliation.

Introductory Rites   We sing an opening hymn. The priest greets us and invites us to pray for God's forgiveness.

Celebration of the Word of God   We listen to readings from the Bible. The priest reads the gospel and gives a homily.

Examination of Conscience   We examine our conscience and tell God we are sorry for our sins.

Rite of Reconciliation   Together we pray an act of contrition and sing or say The Lord's Prayer. Then, one by one, we tell our sins to a priest and receive absolution.

Proclamation of Praise for God's Mercy   When individual confessions are completed, the priest invites us to praise and thank God for his mercy.

Concluding Rites   The priest then blesses us. We sing a song of praise and thanksgiving.

Review with the students how reconciliation in community is celebrated. Point out that the entire community sings together and prays together, but that the examination of conscience and confession of sins to a priest is done individually. Absolution is given by the priest to each penitent, individually.

About the Liturgical Year

TEACHER REFLECTION

Just as we mark time by the yearly calendar and recognize the significance of certain days and seasons in our lives, so too the Church lives by the liturgical year. At the center of the liturgical year is the feast of Easter, which celebrates the mystery of the resurrection and our salvation in Christ. Throughout the year, we follow the journey of Jesus from his birth in Bethlehem to his death, resurrection, and ascension. On this journey we are reminded of the foundations of our faith and our call to live the gospel.

You may want to review for yourself the teaching of the Church about the liturgical year in paragraphs 1168–1173 in the *Catechism of the Catholic Church.*

STUDENT REVIEW

Ask volunteers to read the section "About the Liturgical Year" on page 344 in their books. Help the students review the feasts and seasons of the Church year. Use the visual of the liturgical year to help the students recognize the important events in Jesus' life and when these events fall in the Church calendar. Explain that the colors of the priest's vestments are associated with various seasons of the liturgical year: Green (Ordinary Time), Purple (Advent and Lent), Red (Passion Sunday, Good Friday, and Pentecost) and White (Christmas and Easter).

Lead a class discussion using the following questions.

- The Church year begins with what season? (*Advent*)

- What do we celebrate during the Christmas season? (*Jesus' birth; Epiphany, and Jesus' Baptism*)

- Describe the season of Lent. (*It is a time of prayer and sacrifice, a time of preparation for Easter.*)

- What are the holiest days of the year? (*The Easter Triduum—Holy Thursday, Good Friday, Holy Saturday, and Easter Sunday*)

Review with the students the dates of the six holy days of obligation. Explain that these days are called holy days of obligation because Catholics are required to attend Mass on these special days.

344

ABOUT The Liturgical Year

The **liturgical year** is the Church's official calendar of feasts and seasons. It celebrates all the important events of Jesus' life and Jesus' presence with us today.

The Church year begins with **Advent**. Advent is a season of joyful waiting. We prepare to celebrate the birth of Jesus at Christmas.

During the Christmas season, we celebrate Jesus' birth. We also celebrate the Epiphany and the Baptism of Jesus.

Another major season of the Church year is **Lent**. During the forty days of Lent we prepare to celebrate Easter. It is a time of prayer and sacrifice. The last week of Lent is called Holy Week. On the first day of Holy Week we celebrate Passion Sunday (Palm Sunday), when we recall Jesus' triumphant entry into Jerusalem.

The last three days of Holy Week are known as the **Easter Triduum** — the holiest days of the liturgical year. On Holy Thursday, we remember the Last Supper. On Good Friday, we remember Jesus' crucifixion. On Holy Saturday evening, at a special liturgy called the Easter Vigil, we celebrate Jesus' resurrection. We continue this celebration on the following day, Easter Sunday — the Church's greatest feast.

The Easter season lasts for fifty days. During this time we celebrate the ascension of Jesus and the coming of the Holy Spirit on **Pentecost**.

During the Church year we also have a season called Ordinary Time. During this season, we celebrate all that Jesus has taught us. We listen to the stories of his life proclaimed in the gospel readings at Mass.

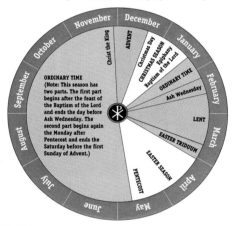

HOW CATHOLICS LIVE

The teachings of Jesus and the Church show us how Catholics live happy and loving lives.

 The Beatitudes

The Beatitudes are Jesus' teachings on how to find everlasting happiness. They teach us to love God and others, and promise us a place in the kingdom of heaven. Christians believe that they will be happy forever if they live the Beatitudes.

The Beatitudes	How We Live the Beatitudes
Happy are the poor in spirit. The reign of God is theirs.	We are poor in spirit when we know that we need God more than anything else in life.
Happy are the sorrowing. They will be comforted.	We obey God and trust in his goodness. We try to help those who are hurting. We know that God is with them.
Happy are the gentle. They will receive all that God has promised.	We are kind and loving. We use the gifts that God has given us to help others.
Happy are those who hunger and thirst for justice. They will be satisfied.	We work to help God's kingdom begin to take root in this world. We share the things we have with those in need.
Happy are those who show mercy to others. They will receive mercy.	We forgive anyone who has hurt us. We accept others and are patient with them.
Happy are the single-hearted. They will see God.	We show our love for God by loving our neighbor.
Happy are the peacemakers. They will be called children of God.	We try to bring God's peace to the world. We help people make up after a fight.
Happy are those who are treated unfairly for doing what is right. The reign of God is theirs.	We carry on Jesus' work in the world. We stand up for what is right, even though it is not always easy.

345

How Catholics Live

Morality is faith lived. To fully understand the demands of Christian morality, we need to recognize that it is based on the limitless love of God and the dignity of every human person as created by God. The focus of Christian morality is not rules, but relationships. The purpose of the Beatitudes and Commandments is to enable the relationship between God and ourselves to grow and to be expressed in our approach to our neighbor.

About the Beatitudes

TEACHER REFLECTION

The Beatitudes speak to the attitudes and actions that are to be characteristic of our lives as followers of Jesus Christ. They challenge us to live life fully; they speak to authentic happiness, and the happiness of the kingdom of God fully realized at the end of time. Happiness is not found in things, possessions, even in successes, but rather in developing right relationships with family, friends, and those with whom we work and associate.

You may want to review for yourself the teaching of the Church about the Beatitudes in paragraphs 1716–1724 in the *Catechism of the Catholic Church*.

STUDENT REVIEW

Ask a volunteer to read "How Catholics Live" and "About the Beatitudes" on page 345 in his or her book. This page can be used by the students as a reference feature throughout the year. Read aloud the Beatitudes with the students. Ask volunteers to explain in their own words what the Beatitudes mean. Then invite volunteers to read in the chart the explanation of how we live the Beatitudes.

About the Commandments

As the Commandments were first given to the Israelites, so they are proclaimed today to the new people of God and to all men and women of faith. The Commandments challenge us to deepen our relationship with God and to see the world around us from God's loving and caring viewpoint. Observing God's commandments is the first step to becoming followers of Christ and being called to greater holiness.

You may want to review for yourself the teaching of the Church about the Commandments in paragraphs 2052–2557 in the *Catechism of the Catholic Church.*

STUDENT REVIEW

Ask volunteers to read "About the Commandments" on page 346 in their books. This page can be used by the students as a reference feature throughout the year. Ask students to review the Ten Commandments. Invite volunteers to read in the chart how the commandments help us to live. Emphasize the importance of obeying the Ten Commandments. They are a guide for us to live as children of God.

ABOUT The Commandments

Jesus taught that it is important to obey the Ten Commandments. The Commandments guide us in living as children of God.

The Ten Commandments	The Commandments Help Us to Live
1. I, the Lord, am your God. You shall not have other gods besides me.	We believe in and love God more than anyone or anything else in life. We remember God's gifts to us. We talk to and listen to God in prayer.
2. You shall not take the name of the Lord, your God, in vain.	We use the names of God, Jesus, and all holy persons, places, and things with respect and love. We never say God's or Jesus' name in anger.
3. Remember to keep holy the Sabbath day.	We worship God by celebrating the Eucharist together on Sunday. We relax and do special things on Sunday in honor of God.
4. Honor your father and mother.	We love, respect, and obey our parents and all adults who care for us.
5. You shall not kill.	We show respect for human life by caring for all people. We never fight or hurt others.
6. You shall not commit adultery.	We respect our bodies and the bodies of others. We use our sexuality according to God's plan.
7. You shall not steal.	We never take things that belong to someone else. We are careful with other people's things. We do not cheat.
8. You shall not bear false witness against your neighbor.	We are truthful and honest. We never tell lies or hurt others by what we say.
9. You shall not covet your neighbor's wife.	We respect the promises that married people have made to each other.
10. You shall not covet anything that belongs to your neighbor.	We are satisfied with what we have. We are not jealous or greedy.

The Great Commandment

"You shall love the Lord, your God, with all your heart, with all your being, with all your strength, and with all your mind, and your neighbor as yourself" (Luke 10:27).

Jesus summed up the Ten Commandments in the **Great Commandment**, which teaches us that God's laws are based on love of God and love of neighbor.

The New Commandment

"This is my commandment: love one another as I love you" (John 15:12).

Jesus' love is the perfect example of how to live. Our love for each other is a sign of Jesus' love.

ABOUT The Works of Mercy

Jesus teaches that when we serve others, we serve him. The loving acts described in Matthew 25:31–46 are called the **corporal** and **spiritual works of mercy**. The Works of Mercy tell us how to respond to the basic needs of all people.

The Corporal Works of Mercy

1. Feed the hungry.
2. Give drink to the thirsty.
3. Clothe the naked.
4. Visit those in prison.
5. Shelter the homeless.
6. Visit the sick.
7. Bury the dead.

The Spiritual Works of Mercy

1. Help others make good choices.
2. Teach those who lack knowledge.
3. Give advice to those who are confused.
4. Comfort those who are hurting.
5. Be patient with others.
6. Forgive injuries.
7. Pray for the living and the dead.

STUDENT REVIEW

Ask a volunteer to read aloud "The Great Commandment" and "The New Commandment" on page 347. Invite the class to discuss how these two commandments sum up the Ten Commandments.

About the Works of Mercy

TEACHER REFLECTION

The lists of the Corporal and Spiritual Works of Mercy describe for us the concrete actions that are characteristic of those who are attentive to the presence of God in their lives. They direct us in our ministry to those around us, especially to the poor and less fortunate. Like the Precepts of the Church, the Works of Mercy are concerned with the welfare and growth of the community. Like the Works of Mercy, the Precepts call for our being attentive to our own needs and the needs of others, so that the Church can be marked by justice and holiness.

You may want to review for yourself the teaching of the Church about the Works of Mercy and the Precepts of the Church in paragraphs 2443–2449 and 2041–2046, respectively, in the *Catechism of the Catholic Church*.

STUDENT REVIEW

Ask volunteers to read the section "About the Works of Mercy" on page 347 in their books. Then have the class find the passage in Matthew that describes the Works of Mercy. Lead a class discussion on how the works of mercy outline ways for us to serve others with acts of loving kindness. Ask: When we serve others, whom also do we serve? (*Jesus*)

TEACHER REFLECTION

Sin is a conscious, deliberate choice not to do good; it is a rejection of a loving relationship with God and others. We are responsible for the consequences of our actions and our failure to act for the good. At the same time, we should remember the power of grace in our lives. Grace challenges us to live according to the dictates of conscience, which is informed by the word of God, the wisdom of the Church, and the advice of men and women of faith. With the help of the Holy Spirit, we are directed to live moral lives of holiness and generosity.

You may want to review for yourself the teaching of the Church about sin and grace, respectively, in paragraphs 1846–1876 and 1996–2005 in the *Catechism of the Catholic Church.*

STUDENT REVIEW

Ask volunteers to read the section "About Moral Living" on page 348 in their books. Discuss with the class how a person can tell if a sin is mortal. Have a volunteer explain the difference between mortal and venial sins. Ask volunteers to read "Helps in Living a Moral Life." Discuss how the Holy Spirit and God's grace help us live moral lives. (*The Holy Spirit helps us avoid sin, and guides our conscience; God's grace gives us the strength to choose what is good.*)

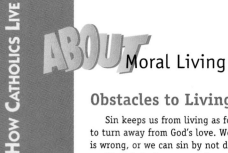

ABOUT Moral Living

Obstacles to Living a Moral Life

Sin keeps us from living as followers of Jesus. Sin is a free choice to turn away from God's love. We can sin by doing something we know is wrong, or we can sin by not doing what we know is right.

Mortal sin is a very serious refusal to live God's laws. Mortal sin turns us away from God and the Church community. However, even when we sin God's mercy and love never leave us.

There are three ways to tell if a sin is mortal.

- The action must be seriously wrong.
- We must know that the action is seriously wrong.
- We must make a free choice to commit the sin.

Mortal sins must be confessed in the sacrament of Reconciliation. Through Jesus, we receive God's mercy and forgiveness. We are reunited with God and the Church.

Less serious sins are called **venial sins**. Venial sins weaken but do not completely destroy our relationship with God and the Church community.

Helps in Living a Moral Life

Jesus calls us to live a **moral** life. We can live a moral life by following the teachings of Jesus and the Church. The Holy Spirit is always with us to help us make good moral decisions.

The Holy Spirit helps us turn away from sin and live as followers of Jesus. The Spirit guides our conscience—the ability to judge whether something is right or wrong. The Spirit helps us fight against temptation—a strong feeling that attracts us to do something wrong.

Catholics call God's loving presence in our lives *grace.* Grace gives us the strength to say no to selfishness and to act as the good people God created us to be. Grace helps us choose what is good.

ABOUT The Gifts of the Holy Spirit

The gifts of the Holy Spirit describe the ways the Spirit helps and guides us.

The Gifts of the Holy Spirit

1. **Wisdom** helps us know how God wants us to live.
2. **Understanding** helps us to be aware of all that God has taught us through Jesus, the Bible, and the Church.
3. **Knowledge** helps us to know that God is more important than anything else in life.
4. **Right Judgment** helps us make good decisions.
5. **Courage** helps us to be strong when faced with problems.
6. **Reverence** helps us to love God as our Father and to show our love in prayer.
7. **Wonder and Awe** help us to be filled with wonder and thanks for all that God creates.

About the Gifts of the Spirit

TEACHER REFLECTION

As Christians we have traditionally believed that the Holy Spirit is the source of those gifts that enable each of us to live the demanding life of a disciple of Jesus Christ. The Holy Spirit, the source of holiness, bestows these gifts when we are baptized, and they deepen in us as we become more open to growth in faith.

You may want to review for yourself the teaching of the Church about the gifts of the Holy Spirit in paragraphs 1830–1832 in the *Catechism of the Catholic Church*.

STUDENT REVIEW

Ask volunteers to read the section "About the Gifts of the Holy Spirit" on page 348 in their books. Invite the students to pray frequently to the Holy Spirit for help and guidance.

TEACHER REFLECTION

Every member of the Christian community is called by God to a particular role in the service of the Church. Although our vocation may be to serve as priest, religious or lay person; as teacher, missionary, or liturgical minister, we all derive our mission from our Baptism into the Church of Christ. Our vocation is strengthened by the Holy Spirit in Confirmation and encouraged by our participation in the Eucharist. Through prayer and our experience in the Christian community, we will be able to discern God's call to us and commit ourselves to our particular vocation in the Church.

You may want to review for yourself the teaching of the Church about vocations in paragraphs 871–945 in the *Catechism of the Catholic Church.*

STUDENT REVIEW

Ask volunteers to read the section "About Vocations" on page 350 in their books. Define *vocation* as a calling from God to live in a way that allows us to serve others. Ask:

- Is a vocation limited to certain individuals? (*No. Every Christian has a vocation.*)

- Who are some of the people who answer the call to devote all of their time to the ministry of the Catholic Christian community? (*Members, known as brothers or sisters, of religious communities; and ordained ministers—bishops, priests, and deacons*)

ABOUT Vocations

Many Ways of Serving

Lay Persons   Most Catholics live out their baptismal vocation as lay persons. Lay persons usually hold jobs in society and are either single or married. As part of their Christian vocation, lay persons often volunteer their time and skills in serving the local parish community, or even the local diocese. They may care for the poor, teach religious education classes, plan and lead the liturgy, help with parish organizations, or invite others to join the Church. In these and other ways, lay persons help the parish community fulfill its mission to reach out to all in the spirit of Jesus.

Vowed Religious   Some men and women choose to devote their entire lives to the ministry of the Catholic Church. These people join religious communities of sisters or brothers. Vows or promises of poverty, chastity, and obedience are taken so that the sisters or brothers can be completely devoted to their ministries and to becoming closer to God in community. Each religious community chooses particular ministries such as teaching, working with the poor, preaching, prayer and contemplation, nursing work, or parish work.

Ordained Ministers   In the Catholic Church, there are also ordained ministers — bishops, priests, and deacons. Baptized persons who are called to ordained ministry have the special vocation of leading the community in worship as well as serving in a wide variety of ministries within the Church.

Bishops are the chief teachers of the faith. They administer dioceses and celebrate the sacraments.

Diocesan priests serve in positions such as pastors of parishes, educators, and counselors. Priests who belong to religious communities may be assigned as pastors or teachers, or they may be assigned to the particular ministry of their communities.

Deacons   Most deacons are called permanent deacons. These men usually assist the pastor of a parish by leading the celebrations of Baptism and Marriage, preaching at Sunday Mass, and helping with parish management. Unlike priests, permanent deacons can be married and have families.

350

Glossary

absolution
the prayer of forgiveness prayed by the priest in the sacrament of Reconciliation *(page 217)*

abuse
violence toward someone or something *(page 139)*

adultery
being unfaithful to one's husband or wife by giving to someone else the special love promised in marriage *(page 145)*

Advent
four weeks of preparation before Christmas *(page 344)*

Anointing of the Sick
the sacrament of healing that brings Jesus' healing, comfort, and strength to those who are seriously ill, elderly, or in danger of death *(page 336)*

apostolic
one of the four marks, or qualities, of the Church that show its truth and its origin in God. The Church is apostolic, founded on and faithful to the Apostles' teachings *(page 332)*

ascension
the returning of Jesus in glory to his Father *(page 331)*

assumption
the taking up of Mary, body and soul, to heaven *(page 333)*

Baptism
the first sacrament of initiation, through which we are freed of original sin and welcomed into the Church *(page 334)*

bear false witness
to tell a lie *(page 175)*

Beatitudes
the teachings of Jesus on how to live happily; how Jesus lived *(page 75)*

Bible
the story of God and God's people; the written word of God *(page 328)*

Blessed Trinity
one God in three Persons *(page 330)*

catholic
one of the four marks, or qualities, of the Church that show its truth and its origin in God. The Church is catholic, or universal, open to all people *(page 332)*

Catholic Church
the Christian community which celebrates the seven sacraments and recognizes the pope and bishops as its leaders *(page 223)*

cheat
to get something from someone in a dishonest way *(page 165)*

commandment
a law given to us by God to help us live good lives by being loving people *(page 63)*

355

Using the Glossary

The glossary provides a reference for the vocabulary and terms of the Catholic religion that have been introduced in the chapter lessons of Units 1–5, in the Amen lessons, and in the *Our Catholic Heritage* section.

After you have presented the vocabulary in each chapter, you may wish to encourage the students to refer to the glossary to help them learn the definitions of the new vocabulary words and terms.

compassion
feeling another's pain and wanting to relieve it *(page 195)*

Confirmation
a sacrament of initiation in which we become fuller members of the Church and in which the Holy Spirit makes us stronger to live and share our faith in Jesus *(page 335)*

conscience
our power to judge whether something is good or bad *(page 43)*

consequences
the things that follow from a choice or an action *(page 25)*

Corinthians
the people who lived in Corinth, a city in Greece *(page 225)*

covet
to want something someone else has *(page 145)*

disciples
followers of Jesus *(page 83)*

Easter Triduum
the three holiest days of the year. On Holy Thursday, we remember the Last Supper; on Good Friday, we remember Jesus' crucifixion; on Holy Saturday, at the Easter Vigil, we celebrate Jesus' resurrection *(page 344)*

envy
wanting something that belongs to another *(page 163)*

Eucharist
a sacrament of initiation and of unity and love in which we receive the body and blood of Jesus *(page 335)*

examination of conscience
thinking about what we have said and done and how we may have sinned *(page 215)*

faithful
able to be trusted and depended upon *(page 143)*

Galilean
someone from Galilee, the land north of Samaria *(page 193)*

grace
God's loving presence in our lives *(page 17)*

Great Commandment, the
the commandment in which Jesus summed up the Ten Commandments by teaching us that God's laws are based on love of God and love of neighbor *(page 347)*

greed
wanting more and more things when they are not needed *(page 163)*

heaven
being with God forever *(page 95)*

hell
eternal separation from God and others *(page 333)*

high priest
a powerful leader of the Temple at the time of Jesus *(page 175)*

holy
one of the four marks, or qualities, of the Church that show its truth and its origin in God. The Church is holy because we draw our life from God and offer people the way to God *(page 332)*

holy days of obligation
the six special days celebrated by the Church in the United States *(page 344)*

Holy Orders
the sacrament of commitment in which bishops, priests, and deacons are ordained to serve the Church in a special way *(page 337)*

Holy Spirit
the Third Person of the Trinity who leads and guides us in living as followers of Jesus *(page 331)*

honor
to treat with respect *(page 123)*

Immaculate Conception
the belief that Mary, the mother of Jesus, was conceived without original sin *(page 332)*

in vain
in a disrespectful way*(page 115)*

Incarnation
our belief that God became man in Jesus *(page 330)*

inheritance
the money and property received by a relative usually from someone who has died *(page 185)*

justice
loving God and all people by treating everyone fairly *(page 73)*

lay professionals
nonordained persons who work full time in the Church community *(page 351)*

Lent
forty days of preparation before Easter *(page 344)*

light of the world
the lives of Jesus and his followers shining before others and lighting the way to God and happiness *(page 235)*

liturgical year
the Church's official calendar of feasts and seasons *(page 344)*

Matrimony
another name for the sacrament of Marriage, in which a man and a woman promise to love one another for the rest of their lives as husband and wife *(page 337)*

meditation
using our imaginations instead of words to listen to God speaking to us *(page 352)*

mercy
loving care, or compassion *(page 83)*

Messiah
the title for Jesus as God's chosen one who would bring peace *(page 330)*

moral
a choice between right and wrong *(page 345)*

mortal sin
a very serious refusal to follow the teachings of Jesus, one which turns us away from God *(page 348)*

neighbor
every man, woman, and child, especially someone who needs our love and care *(page 63)*

obey
to do what someone who is responsible for you tells you to do *(page 123)*

one
one of the four marks, or qualities, of the Church that show its truth and its origin in God. The Church is one in our faith, sacraments, and leadership *(page 332)*

original sin
the first selfish act of the first human beings, and the sinful condition into which we are born *(page 25)*

peacemakers
people who try to bring peace and friendship where these things are needed *(page 83)*

Pentecost
the day the Church began with the coming of the Holy Spirit upon the first disciples. *(page 344)*

prayer
talking and listening to God *(page 352)*

reconciliation
making up through sorrow and forgiveness *(page 183)*

reign of God
the time when God's peace, love, and justice will rule our lives and the world *(page 73)*

respect
to act with care toward someone or something *(page 123)*

resurrection
Jesus' rising from death to new life *(page 330)*

reverence
an attitude of respect and care *(page 117)*

Sabbath
the weekly day of prayer and rest: Sunday for Christians, Saturday for Jews, and Friday for Muslims *(page 115)*

sacrament
a sacred sign that celebrates God's love for us and Jesus' presence in our lives and in the Church *(page 334)*

sacraments of healing
Reconciliation and Anointing of the Sick—the Church's two sacraments of healing *(page 336)*

sacraments of initiation
Baptism, Confirmation, and Eucharist—the Church's three sacraments of welcome and belonging *(page 334)*

What is the relationship of fourth graders to their parents and other significant adults?

 Fourth graders need supportive reinforcement from parents and other adults. They need guidelines and rules to follow. They need to belong to a group, particularly a family group where there is love and approval. At the same time, the nine-year-old child acts more independently. This is sometimes expressed in talking back to adults and in outbursts of anger.

 What do the students need from me as a teacher to help them grow morally as the year goes by?

 Basically, they need to trust you as an adult who will accept them. They need to see you as someone who really cares for them. Here are a few specific ideas.

- Share in a positive way your thoughts and feelings about life and about God.
- Be patient, since children develop slowly.
- Allow for success, which enhances self-esteem, by assigning simple tasks that the children are able to accomplish.

- When correcting a child or the class as a whole, react in proportion to the behavior. Be as gentle and patient as possible. Try to remember that the children are only nine years old.
- Realize that the children need to belong to the group and to feel secure. They grow best through being loved by you as their teacher and by being socially accepted by other children. Help the children realize that God loves them and you love them despite their errors and wrongdoings. In discussing their actions, dwell on the children's good intentions, whenever this is possible.
- Discuss feelings of fear and anxiety, joy and happiness, sadness and anger as a part of the real experience of children's day-to-day life. Accept their feelings.
- Help the children realize that Christians are happy people. Make humor and laughter a part of each class.
- Realize that despite all the common characteristics of the nine-year-old children discussed in these pages, each child is a unique person. Teaching fourth graders can be a challenging and richly rewarding experience.

CLASSROOM ENVIRONMENT

Children learn best in an environment that is happy and secure. This environment should, of necessity, have the following characteristics.

First, there is reverence and respect for each individual in the class. The personal worth of each child is stressed when

- The teacher warmly welcomes each child to class, calling each one by name.
- The teacher treats everyone fairly, showing no favoritism to particular children.
- The teacher praises a child for what he or she may have accomplished.
- The teacher sends home special notes to children who may have missed a class because of sickness.
- The teacher enthusiastically responds to the children's ideas.

Second, a healthy environment is one in which there is a sense of caring among a cheerful community of people in the classroom. Such an environment is created when

- People share with each other.
- People cooperate as a group to get things done.
- People praise each other.
- Personal events such as birthdays and name days are remembered and celebrated.
- People are able to speak freely without fear of ridicule.
- People refrain from making judgments about each other.

Third, a healthy classroom environment is one in which there is a feeling that something of value is being accomplished. The children need to see that they have the opportunity to try new things and gain new skills as part of the experience of religious education. This happens in a practical way when

- Children take part in activities that allow each individual to be successful.
- Children enjoy working together.
- Children have a clear understanding of what is being taught.
- Children have their questions answered in a way that is meaningful.

- Children are presented with a variety of activities.
- A prayer life is cultivated and the children experience quiet time for reflection.
- Audiovisual material is a regular part of the class sessions.

Finally, a healthy classroom environment has a physical setting that is pleasant. Some factors that contribute to a setting conducive to learning are

- A room large enough to accommodate the members of the class comfortably, allowing plenty of roomfor activities.
- A room with windows.
- A room that is well lit and comfortably heated.
- A room that is made visually appealing through the use of pictures, posters, banners, flowers, and the children's art work.
- Chairs that are comfortable.
- Desks or tables that are roomy and the right height.
- Background music at appropriate times.

CLASSROOM MANAGEMENT

Teaching students self-discipline means equipping them with knowledge about socially acceptable customs in the world in which they live. It means, as well, helping them develop social skills such as making rules and cooperating in class. By the time the students have reached fourth grade, they have had the chance to learn and practice a number of self-discipline skills. These include listening, following directions, asking appropriate questions, and sharing classroom resources.

Fourth grade teachers should not automatically assume that the students have mastered these skills. Mastery means that the students are able to perform these skills without external prompting. Teachers should expect these skills to be used, but they should continue to teach the skills, reinforcing their mastery through encouragement.

By the time the students reach the fourth grade, their growth and development level are quite different from those of the very young child. They move away from thinking that rules made by adults are absolute. They know that rules change. They have friends whose parents run things differently from the way things are run in their own homes. The reasons that a teacher in grades 1, 2, or 3 might have given for following instructions no longer satisfy these students. They are moving toward a new level of maturity in which they act to accomplish goals.

Rule Making

Students in the fourth grade are very conscious of rules. They can comprehend the rules of getting along with each other in the classroom, as well as the consequences of breaking these rules. At this age the students are able to determine the rules of their classroom.

Classroom Rules   Fourth graders are able to help in determining the classroom rules. Brainstorm some rules that need to be set so that learning can take place. They should always be written out and posted in the classroom or in the hallway for everyone to see. The students should be reminded of the rules on a regular basis. Compliment your students for following these rules. Discuss with the students the following questions about each rule.

- What are some of the reasons for the rule?
- Who should follow it?
- What are the consequences of breaking the rule?

The members of the class should understand that this rule-making is always done within limits. You, as their teacher, reserve veto power. Explain to the students that an adult can often see the larger picture and may have to make a judgment call that the students will not understand. Assure the students that you will be as fair as possible in such situations. Let each student make a copy of the rules and bring them to the teacher to be signed. Allow the students to keep the list of rules.

Enforcement and Evaluation   Once rules are set, they should be viewed as a standard of operating procedure. Rules should provide ways of avoiding bad behavior and of introducing and reinforcing good behavior. Enforcement of rules should not be a form of punishment. Rules outline desirable behavior for students and provide a stable classroom environment in which to work and learn. Periodically, test the students on the class rules. Rules should be clear to both teacher and student. Ask:

- Is the rule clear to everyone?
- Do we, as a group, keep this rule?
- Is the rule really enforceable?
- Should the consequence of breaking the rule be changed or modifie

PLANNING

One of the keys to a successful religion class is good planning. This involves taking the time to look ahead. It means being willing to put in work time before class. Such planning is one of the marks of a dedicated and concerned teacher.

There are three special planning times: before the year begins, before each unit, and before actual class time.

Before the Year Begins

Planning starts as soon as you receive copies of THIS IS OUR FAITH. Here are some suggestions for getting started.

- Open to the Contents pages in the student text, noting the major areas of Catholic faith being covered.

- Familiarize yourself with the organization of the book.

- Study the Teacher Edition. The beginning pages of the Teacher Edition provide valuable information on the organization of the program as well as the features of the student text and the Teacher Edition. There you will find a description of the three steps used in every lesson plan. You should become familiar with the features of the student text and this three-step plan.

- Study the Scope and Sequence Chart that also appears in the beginning pages of the Teacher Edition. This will familiarize you with the overall theme of the year as well as with the developmental strands that run through the grade levels.

- Make a program calendar for the year by first determining the number of religion classes you will have. Other activities might include service projects, planning for liturgies, field trips, and so on. Isolate the days on which you will be able to conduct a class using one of the lessons in the student text.

Next, decide what lessons you will cover during the year and on what days these lessons will be taken. Examine the Contents page in the front of your Teacher Edition, noting that there are one introductory lesson, twenty core chapters, five unit review lessons, five Day to Day: Skills for Christian Living lessons, and thirty-one lessons in the Amen section, and Our Catholic Heritage, a reference section based on the *Catechism of the Catholic Church*. Each of the sessions is designed to provide you with at least a half-hour's worth of material to use with the students.

Before the Unit Begins

Each of the units of THIS IS OUR FAITH has four chapters that have been placed together because they cover related areas of Catholic faith. Become familiar with the overall development of each unit that you are about to begin teaching.

- Notice that in the Teacher Edition there is a page of information that begins each unit. This unit opener contains the unit aim, a doctrinal summary of each chapter, and the vocabulary. Reading these will give you a preview of the unit.

- For a more detailed overview of the unit, read through the chapters themselves, noting what they are seeking to achieve and the kinds of activities that are suggested.

Before the Class Begins

Experienced teachers have found it valuable to begin their preparation for next week's classes soon after the completion of this week's classes. Here are some steps they recommend.

- After your religion class is over and you have some time to sit and think, start asking yourself how the class went. What was successful? What did the students respond to most? What would you change if you could do the class over? Write down your observations on the pages of your Teacher Edition or in a separate notebook. You will also find this valuable when you teach the same lesson next year.

- Look ahead to the next lesson by turning to its Chapter Organizer in your Teacher Edition. Note the Objectives for the lesson.

- Review the Chapter Outline. This gives you an overview of the major activities that make up the lesson plan that appears in the book. Read through the lesson plan notes on the pages that follow. Make notes to yourself about what will work with your students and what will need to be altered or supplemented. Make any changes you feel necessary.

- Read the Background for the Teacher section of the Chapter Organizer. This will give you information about the theological content of the lesson as well as notes on the way the topic is approached in the lesson plan.

- Gather any supplies on the Materials Needed list that will not be readily available on the day of class. As you look through each lesson plan, you will find ideas for optional activities and additional information under Teaching Tips, Cultural Awareness, Curriculum Connection, Focus on, and Enriching the Lesson boxes that follow the basic lesson plan.

- During the days that follow this first preparation, review the lesson plan in your mind and in your heart. Ask yourself if you really understand what the lesson is trying to accomplish. Think about what you know about the topic and seek additional information if necessary. Pray to the Holy Spirit to guide you in your preparation.

- Finally, take time just before class (one-half day to a full day before) to review the lesson outline that you set down earlier in the week. Make any necessary changes. Make sure you have all the materials you will need for the class. Assign an approximate time that you will spend on each of the activities in the lesson plan. Mentally rehearse how you will conduct the class.

Try to make this procedure a part of your routine.

 What does it mean to adapt the lesson plan to your needs?

 Experienced teachers know that the lesson plans that appear in teacher manuals are only suggested ways to teach the chapters. They know their students and the kinds of activities they learn from best. They also know themselves and the kinds of things they do best in class. Experienced teachers take both of these into consideration when reviewing a lesson plan. They ask the following kinds of questions.

- What is really possible for me to accomplish in this lesson?
- What will the students be interested in?
- What is in this lesson that will work with my students?
- What do I have in my own experiences, interests, and talents that can complement or enrich this lesson plan?

Experienced teachers will make adjustments to the lesson plan that appears in the Teacher Edition, based on their answers to the above questions.

 Is there anything that I can read during the year that will help me be a better teacher?

 There are a variety of books and magazines available on becoming a better teacher. Two that should be read are *Sharing the Light of Faith: National Catechetical Directory for Catholics of the United States* and *The Creative Catechist* by Janaan Manternach and Carl J. Pfeifer, the authors of THIS IS OUR FAITH. Another helpful resource is the THIS IS OUR FAITH Program Director's Manual

LEARNING ACTIVITIES

Storytelling

Children love stories. The sessions of THIS IS OUR FAITH contain many stories from the Bible and from contemporary life.

Be totally familiar with the story. While telling the story, look directly at the students. It is always a good idea to have visuals on hand to illustrate main points, attitudes, or feelings reflected in the story. Keep the storytelling short and simple, interrupting occasionally to ask the students how they would react in similar circumstances. Make sure that you distinguish Bible stories from other kinds of stories.

Drawing

Children do not have the vocabulary or the experience to express themselves in words the way we do as adults. They are able, however, to express themselves through drawing.

In order to use drawing effectively, maintain an atmosphere of order in the classroom. An art activity is not a play period. It helps to play appropriate background music. Explain clearly what the students are to do and have all materials ready.

Be sure that you do not make judgments about the artistic value of the students' drawings. Praise their work, allow them to show their work to others, and ensure that specific insights they have expressed are respected. Above all, do not interpret meanings. Leave that to the individual.

Writing

Writing is a wonderful way for the students to gain insight into themselves and their faith. When we ask the students to write down their thoughts, they are forced to reflect on their ideas and feelings before putting their words on paper. Writing also brings up concerns and questions from the students' experiences that relate to your religion lesson.

In the THIS IS OUR FAITH program, such writing activity varies in the student text for each grade level. Generally, the activities include writing responses to questions, creating a story or poem, or writing personal prayers.

You should seek to create an atmosphere that encourages the students to write with openness and spontaneity. Don't indicate beforehand what you would write or what you expect them to say in their writing. Do not criticize their grammar and spelling, as you might in a language arts class.

Reading

In all the grade levels of THIS IS OUR FAITH, there are stories in the student text, both biblical and contemporary. There is also poetry to be read by the students. Each lesson contains some explanation of the teaching of Jesus or of various beliefs of the Catholic Church. All of these readings are set at the appropriate reading level for the students of that particular grade.

Reading is important because it is the primary way the students gain new information in their religious education class. Through the reading of the lesson, they are introduced to the vocabulary of the Catholic religion. They learn what the Church believes. They become familiar with the Scriptures through the reading of Bible stories and passages.

CHAPTER 1

How did I help my students see that the goodness of God is all around them?

CHAPTER 2

What did my students learn about the causes of evil and ways to fight against it?

CHAPTER 3

How did I help my students see the difference between temptation and sin?

CHAPTER 4

What new insights about the Holy Spirit did my students gain?

CHAPTER 5

How did my students learn to live the Great Commandment?

CHAPTER 6

How did I help my students to find the Beatitudes meaningful?

CHAPTER 7

How did I teach my students to practice the Beatitudes of peace?

CHAPTER 8

What were my students' impressions of the Ten Commandments as a code?

CHAPTER 9

How did I help my students see that God should be at the center of their lives?

CHAPTER 10

What did my students learn about honoring their parents and obeying all lawful authority?

CHAPTER 11

How did my students respond to the examples of radical nonviolence presented in this chapter?

CHAPTER 12

How did my students learn to be faithful to God?

CHAPTER 13

What were my students' attitudes toward greed and stealing?

CHAPTER 14

What points about honesty did my students have difficulty understanding?

CHAPTER 15

What were my students' reactions to Jesus' style of mercy and forgiveness?

CHAPTER 16

What did my students learn about bringing forgiveness to others?

CHAPTER 17

How did I help my students understand the need to express sorrow for sin?

CHAPTER 18

How did I help my students understand the Eucharist as a sign of unity?

CHAPTER 19

How did I teach my students to be lights to the world?

CHAPTER 20

How did my students see that they can make the world a better place in which to live?

ADVENT

How did my students learn to make a spiritual journey toward Jesus?

CHRISTMAS

How did I help my students see that they can bring the light of Jesus to others?

LENT

What did my students learn about the season of Lent?

EASTER

What were my students' reactions to the story of Thomas?

TEACHER'S
REFLECTIONS

END OF THE YEAR

How have I been changed by teaching the truths of our faith to others this year?

How did I improve my teaching skills this year?

What do I feel I have accomplished this year?

How did I help my students grow in faith?

What would I have done differently?

RESOURCE GUIDE

This Resource Guide provides a list of recommended books, videos, and music recordings for use with the lessons in the student text. The guide follows the organization of the text into five units and the Amen section. The following is an explanation of the formats used in listing the different categories of resource material.

Books Books are listed by title, author or editor, publisher, copyright date, and description. The chapter number or section title in parentheses refers to the place in the student text where the material is recommended for use. For example:

> *I Got Community.* Dale Gottlieb. Holt, 1995. A celebration of various individuals' contributions to the community in first person narration. (**1**)

Videos Videos are listed by video title, length, series title if applicable, company, copyright date, description, and student text reference in parentheses. For example:

> *Zip Your Lip to Gossip.* (25 min.) "Wooster Square" series. St. Anthony Messenger Press, 1990. Gossiping and telling things that are not true can hurt others and cause a lot of damage. (**14**)

Music Recordings Recordings are listed by title of the song or selection, title of the record album, company, copyright date, and student text reference in parentheses. For example:

> "Easter Rise Up." *Come Meet Jesus.* Pauline Books & Media, 1990. (**Easter**)

The Resourceful Teacher section ends with a list of frequently used publishers and media companies. An introductory note to this list, on page 392, offers advice about sources and scheduling.

Unit 1

Books

The Book of Creation. Pierre-Marie Beaude. Picture Book Studio, 1991. The Creation story as it might have been handed down through oral tradition. (**1**)

The Creation. Stephan Mitchell. Dial, 1990. Exploring the mystery of the Creation as explained in Genesis. (**1**)

The Story of Creation: Words from Genesis. Jane Ray. Dutton, 1993. The language of the first book in the Bible is used to tell the story of Creation. (**1**)

Adam and Eve. Warwick Hutton. Macmillan, 1987. Compelling watercolors highlight this interpretation of the mystery of Creation. (**2**)

And in the Beginning. Sheron Williams. Macmillan, 1993. Elements of Christianity and the original Creation story blend with the chosen people in an African setting. (**2**)

Down the Road. Alice Schertle. Browndeer Press, 1995. An illustrated story about independence, choices, the consequences of one's actions, and the love of one's family.(**2**)

The Woman Who Fell from the Sky: The Iroquois Story of Creation. John Bierhorst. Morrow, 1993. Sky Woman, with the help of her two sons, creates the earth. (**2**)

Fast Forward. Mary Jane Miller. Viking, 1993. A sixth-grade girl who cheated on a test wishes that she could fast-forward her life. (**3**)

Five-Finger Discount. Barthe DeClements. Delacorte Press, 1989. Jerry, whose father is in prison for robbery, also has a tendency to steal. (**3**)

The Robbers. Nina Bawden. Lothrop, 1989. Loneliness leads Philip into a friendship with a boy who steals. (**3**)

Fourth Grade Rats. Jerry Spinelli. Scholastic, 1993. Fourth-grader Suds has to decide between doing what is right and joining the Rats. (**4**)

Jerry on the Line. Brenda Seabrooke. Macmillan, 1990. A fourth grader talks to a lonely second grader each day on the phone, even though the conversations keep him from playing soccer. (**4**)

VIDEOS

Wild Irish Bloom. Mavis Jukes. Knopf, 1993. Twelve-year-old Iris encounters a number of problems (most of them caused by herself) that involve her family and friends. (4)

Videos

Countdown to Adventure. (30 min.) "Creation Celebration" series. Augsburg, 1990. Respect for creation in all its forms is the focus of this story about a zany scientist and his laboratory discoveries of the universe. (1)

A Long, Loving Look. (12 min.) Raven, 1982. A music video about the goodness of creation; it includes songs about raindrops, whispers, love, and gifts. (1)

St. Francis of Assisi. (18 min.) "Famous Men and Women of the Church" series. Don Bosco, 1988. Francis gave the Church a message of love and simplicity and a new religious order. (1)

Adam and Eve. (30 min.) "In the Beginning" series. CCC, 1994. Recounts the story of Creation, the mastery of God's handiwork, humankind's fall from grace through the first sin in the garden, the conflict between Cain and Abel, and Cain's betrayal. (2)

Adam & Eve. (20 min.) "Superbook" series. Crown, 1991. How it all began: the story of the earth's early days and its first man and woman, including the temptation of Adam and Eve and the consequences of their actions. (2)

Saints Gallery. (35 min.) Oblate Media, 1995. Program tells of the lives and deeds of persons who fought against evil and became saints because of their extraordinary lives. Martin de Porres is one of six saints featured in this review. (2)

Jesus, The Son of God. (30 min.) "Our Dwelling Place" series. Don Bosco, 1988. All people are children of God as shown through the events of Jesus' life, such as the boy Jesus in the Temple, Jesus' baptism, the temptation, and the healing of Jairus's daughter. (3)

One Good Turn. (14 min.) Brown-ROA, 1991. Story of two students and how they deal with cheating. Explores feelings of inferiority, rejection, acceptance, and being asked to "pay off" a friendship by cheating. (3)

The Temptation. (12 min.) "Lenten Gospels" series. Brown-ROA, 1991. Alone in the desert for forty days, Jesus is tempted by the devil. Viewers are challenged to reflect on the meaning of evil and the manner in which the devil appeared to Jesus. (3)

Jazz Band Blues. (10 min.) "Doing the Right Thing" series. Twenty-Third Publications, 1994. Bob wants Cindy to notice him, so during band class he plays a practical joke that backfires. Bob learns a hard lesson. (4)

Rock Ticket Trouble. (10 min.) "Doing the Right Thing" series. Twenty-Third Publications, 1994. Joey has been invited to a rock concert but can't go unless his science paper is done. He sees a paper that someone has left behind in the library and takes it to use as his own. Later, he pays a high price for going to the concert. (4)

Spin: Truth, Tubas and George Washington. (30 min.) "Secret Adventures" series. Oblate, 1994. After running against "Miss Popularity" for class president, Drea learns a hard lesson in truth and honesty. (4)

Music Recordings

"Canticle of the Sun." *Rise Up and Sing.* Oregon Catholic Press, 1984. (1)

"Song of Creation." *Celebrating Our Journey.* Resource Publications, 1996. (1)

"If Today You Hear God's Voice." *God Shines on You.* Oregon Catholic Press, 1995. (2)

"Let's Begin Again." *Our God Is Good.* Resource Publications, 1996. (2)

"Lead Me, Lord." *Rise Up and Sing.* Oregon Catholic Press, 1987. (3)

"O God, We Are Your Children." *God Shines on You.* Oregon Catholic Press, 1995. (**3**)

"Oh, How It's Good." *Our God Is Good.* Resource Publications, 1996. (**4**)

"Speak from Your Heart." *Rise Up and Sing.* Oregon Catholic Press, 1994. (**4**)

Unit 2

Books

Potato Kid. Barbara Corcoran. Macmillan, 1989. In spite of her protests, Ellis is chosen to take care of an underprivileged girl whom her mother takes in for the summer. (**5**)

Project Wheels. Jacqueline Banks. Houghton, 1993. In addition to all of Angela's problems with adolescence, she is also involved in a project to raise money for a wheelchair for a classmate. (**5**)

Stay Tuned. Barbarba Corcoran. Macmillan, 1991. Stevie befriends two homeless youngsters in New York City. (**5**)

Hannah on Her Way. Claudia Mills. Macmillan, 1991. Hannah is asked to repay Caitlin's kindness by letting Caitlin cheat on a test. (**6**)

Speak Up, Chelsea Martin! Becky T. Lindberg. C. Whitman, 1993. Third-grader Chelsea takes her mother's advice to stand up for herself and then has to face the consequences. (**6**)

Teammates. Peter Golenbock. Gulliver, 1990. Chronicles the life of Jackie Robinson, the first black baseball player to play on a major league team. Includes Robinson's search for justice and peace in tense situations. (**6**)

The Big Book of Peace. Ann Durnell and Marilyn Sachs. Dutton, 1990. Contributions from thirty-two writers and illustrations on the subject of peace. (**7**)

Peace Begins with You. Katherine Scholes. Little, 1990. Courage, strength, and responsibility are needed to achieve peace. (**7**)

Peace Tales: World Folktales to Talk About. Margaret Read MacDonald. Shoestring, 1992. Stories and proverbs directed toward achieving world peace. (**7**)

Monkey Island. Paula Fox. Watts, 1991. At age eleven, Clay finds himself homeless in New York City and struggles for the basic necessities of life. (**8**)

Teaching the Great Commandments. Anne DeGraaf. Standard, 1987. Excerpts from the Gospels of Matthew, Mark, Luke, and John, including parables, miracles, and other events from Jesus' life, are arbitrarily grouped as commandments. (**8**)

The Ups and Downs of Carl Davis III. Rosa Guy. Delacorte Press, 1989. A young black boy feels out of place in the South Carolina town where his parents have sent him so that he can "straighten himself out." (**8**)

Videos

Good Samaritan. (25 min.) "Animated Stories from the New Testament" series. Family Entertainment Video, 1989. "What is the greatest commandment?" asks the lawyer. Jesus answers with the story of the Good Samaritan, in this wonderfully animated video. (**5**)

Parables from Nature, Tape V. (15 min.) ECU, 1987. The second segment titled "Chuckie Chipmunk" deals with the parable of the Good Samaritan. (**5**)

Sammy: The Good Neighbor. (8 min.) "Parables for Children" series. Brown-ROA, 1993. A bluefish is traveling along when suddenly he meets a shark and is attacked. He lies wounded on the beach as other fish pass by. Finally, Sammy Squid stops to help. (**5**)

The Beatitudes. (10 min.) Paulist Press, 1993. Explores the meaning of the Beatitudes for fourth-grade children; focuses on the Beatitudes as a way to a happier life. (**6,7**)

God's Plan for Me. (10 min.) "New Creation" series. Brown-ROA, 1991. The first segment is a dramatization of "Blessed are the poor in spirit, the merciful, and the peacemakers." (**6, 7**)

The Hunger Next Door. (20 min.) ECU, 1987. Based on the true experience of one family, this drama explores the problem of hunger in America and what

proverbs directed toward achieving world peace. (**7**)

Monkey Island. Paula Fox. Watts, 1991. At age eleven, Clay finds himself homeless in New York City and struggles for the basic necessities of life. (**8**)

Teaching the Great Commandments. Anne DeGraaf. Standard, 1987. Excerpts from the Gospels of Matthew, Mark, Luke, and John, including parables, miracles, and other events from Jesus' life, are arbitrarily grouped as commandments. (**8**)

The Ups and Downs of Carl Davis III. Rosa Guy. Delacorte Press, 1989. A young black boy feels out of place in the South Carolina town where his parents have sent him so that he can "straighten himself out." (**8**)

Videos

Good Samaritan. (25 min.) "Animated Stories from the New Testament" series. Family Entertainment Video, 1989. "What is the greatest commandment?" asks the lawyer. Jesus answers with the story of the Good Samaritan, in this wonderfully animated video. (**5**)

Parables from Nature, Tape V. (15 min.) ECU, 1987. The second segment titled "Chuckie Chipmunk" deals with the parable of the Good Samaritan. (**5**)

Sammy: The Good Neighbor. (8 min.) "Parables for Children" series. Brown-ROA, 1993. A bluefish is traveling along when suddenly he meets a shark and is attacked. He lies wounded on the beach as other fish pass by. Finally, Sammy Squid stops to help. (**5**)

The Beatitudes. (10 min.) Paulist Press, 1993. Explores the meaning of the Beatitudes for fourth-grade children; focuses on the Beatitudes as a way to a happier life. (**6,7**)

God's Plan for Me. (10 min.) "New Creation" series. Brown-ROA, 1991. The first segment is a dramatization of "Blessed are the poor in spirit, the merciful, and the peacemakers." (**6, 7**)

The Hunger Next Door. (20 min.) ECU, 1987. Based on the true experience of one family, this drama explores the problem of hunger in America and what we can do to help. God's imperative to feed the hungry, house the homeless, clothe the naked, and visit the sick and imprisioned comes to life in this story. (**6, 7**)

Works of Mercy. (15 min.) Paulist Press, 1993. This video has powerful imagery that shows children what it means to reach out to others with the compassion of Christ. (**6, 7**)

The Commandments. (90 min.) Brown-ROA, 1995. This video details each of the Ten Commandments separately in ten segments. (**8**)

The Ten Commandments. (30 min.) CCC, 1995. Recounts Moses' journey to the top of Mount Sinai, where God makes a new covenant with Israel and reveals it in the form of laws carved in stone. (**8**)

Music Recordings

"Good Samaritan." ***Fingerprints.*** Pauline Books & Media, 1993. (**5**)

"Love Is the Greatest Gift." ***Celebrating Our Journey.*** Resource Publications, 1996. (**5**)

"God of the Hungry." ***Cup of Blessing.*** Oregon Catholic Press, 1989. (**6**)

"Jesus, You Love Us." ***Calling the Children.*** Oregon Catholic Press, 1988. (**6**)

"Blest Are They." ***Today's Missal.*** GIA, 1985. (**7**)

"Prayer of St. Francis." ***Glory & Praise.*** Oregon Catholic Press, 1987. (**7**)

"God Shines on You." ***God Shines on You.*** Oregon Catholic Press, 1995. (**8**)

"The Good News of God's Salvation." ***Calling the Children.*** Oregon Catholic Press, 1988. (**8**)

Unit 3

Books

The Believers. Rebecca C. Jones. Little, 1989. Nine-year-old Tibby gets involved in a fundamentalist cult. (**9**)

Our Church. Graham English. Liturgical Press, 1994. This book is about belonging to a church. It is about a

of the innkeeper. **(Christmas)**

Easter and Other Spring Holidays. Gilda Berger. Watts, 1983. The origins and ways of observing Easter and several Jewish holidays, including Passover, are explained. **(Easter)**

Elizabeth Bayley Seton: An American Saint. Elaine Murray Stone. Paulist Press, 1993. A middle-grade biography of Mother Seton, the first American-born saint and founder of the parochial school system. **(Saints)**

Walking with Jesus: Stories About Real People Who Return Good for Evil. Mary Clemens Meyer. Herald, 1992. Strong themes of peacemaking and Christian love permeate true life anecdotes that take place in the twentieth century. **(Holy Days)**

I Have a Dream. James Haskins. Millbrook, 1992. A well-researched biography, supported by excerpts from Dr. King's writings and speeches. **(In the Spirit of Jesus)**

Videos

Legend of the Christmas Flower. (40 min.) Oblate,

1995. Juanito and his grandfather encounter the true meaning of Christmas on a journey through the mountains. **(Advent)**

Martin the Cobbler. (27 min.) Billy Budd, 1980. Martin finds that when he meditates on the truth of Scripture, he opens his life once again to others and to God. **(Christmas)**

Mass of the Cross. (60 min.) Oblate, 1988. Florence Henderson sings accompaniment to a reenactment of the Stations of the Cross by youth. **(Lent)**

Last Supper. (33 min.) Brown-ROA, 1994. This video was filmed and dramatized in the Holy Land and Middle East. It depicts the Passover and the events of Passion (Palm) Sunday through Holy Thursday. **(Holy Week)**

The Mass for Children. (30 min.) Liguori, 1993. When some children are asked why they are unruly at Mass, it is discovered that they do not understand the Mass. A priest helps them by explaining the details of the Mass and answering their questions. Concentrates on real-life situations. **(Holy Week)**

Shrug: The Self-Doubting Thomas. (30 min.) "Secret

PUBLISHERS AND MEDIA COMPANIES

Many of the resources listed, beginning on page 383 are available from your school, parish, diocesan, regional, college, or university media center. Inquire there first. If you must seek further, the following partial list of publishers/distributors will be helpful. In all cases where you plan to use free or rental materials, confirm availability and make arrangements several weeks in advance of your scheduled use. Be sure to preview your selection before showing it to your class.

Bantam Doubleday Dell
Publishing Group, Inc.
1540 Broadway
New York, NY 10036
(800) 223-6834

Berkley Publishing Group
200 Madison Ave.
New York, NY 10016
(800) 631-8571

Billy Budd Films
235 E. 57th St.
New York, NY 10022
(800) 772-0380

Browndeer Press
See Harcourt Brace.
Brown-ROA
1665 Embassy West Dr.
Dubuque, IA 52002-2259
(800) 922-7696

Carousel Film & Video
260 Fifth Ave., Suite 405
New York, NY 10001
(800) 683-1660

CCC of America
6000 Campus Circle Dr.
Suite 110
Irving, TX 75063
(800) 935-2222

Crown Books for Young Readers
(Div. of Random House)
201 E. 50th St.
New York, NY 10022
(800) 733-3000

Crown Ministries Internat'l
9 Winstone Ln.
Bella Vista, AR 72714
(800) 433-4685

Dutton Children's Books
(Div. of Penguin USA)
375 Hudson St.
New York, NY 10014-3657
(212) 366-2000

EcuFilm
810 12th Ave., S
Nashville, TN 37203
(800) 251-4091

G.I.A. Publications, Inc.
7404 S. Mason Ave.
Chicago, IL 60638
(708) 496-3800
(800) 442-1358

Harcourt Brace & Co.
6277 Sea Harbor Dr.
Orlando, FL 32887
(800) 543-1918

Harper San Francisco
1160 Battery St., 3rd Floor
San Francisco, CA 94111
(415) 477-4444

HarperCollins Publishers
100 Keystone Industrial Park
Scranton, PA 18512
(800) 242-7737

Herald Press
(Div. of Mennonite Pub. House)
616 Walnut Ave.
Scottdale, PA 15683-1999
(800) 245-7894

Holiday House, Inc.
425 Madison Ave.
New York, NY 10017
(212) 688-0085

Henry Holt & Co., Inc.
115 W. 18th St.
New York, NY 10011
(800) 488-5233

Houghton Mifflin Co.
222 Berkeley St.
Boston, MA 02116
(800) 225-3362

The Lerner Group
241 First Ave., N
Minneapolis, MN 55401
(800) 328-4949

Liguori Publications
One Liguori Dr.
Liguori, MO 63057-9999
(800) 325-9521

Little, Brown & Co.
Time & Life Building
1271 Ave. of the Americas
New York, NY 10020
(800) 343-9204

The Liturgical Press
St. John's Abbey
Collegeville, MN 56321
(800) 858-5450

Macmillan Books for Young
Readers
See Simon & Schuster Children's.

Media Guild
11722 Sorrento Valley Rd.
Suite E
San Diego, CA 92121
(800) 886-9191

Millbrook Press, Inc.
2 Old New Milford Rd.
Brookfield, CT 06804
(800) 462-4703

William Morrow & Co., Inc.
1350 Ave. of the Americas
New York, NY 10019
(800) 843-9389

Nest Entertainment
(Family Entertainment Network)
6100 Colwell Blvd.
Irving, TX 75039-9833
(800) 452-4485

North-South Books
1123 Broadway, Suite 800
New York, NY 10010
(800) 282-8257

Oblate Media & Communications
7315 Manchester Rd.
Maplewood, MO 63143-9914
(800) 233-4629

Oliver-Nelson
(Div. of Thomas Nelson Pubs.)
Nelson Pl. at Elm Hill Pike
Nashville, TN 37214
(800) 251-4000

Oregon Catholic Press
5536 NE Hassalo
Portland, OR 97213
(800) 548-8739

Pauline Books & Media
50 St. Paul's Ave.
Boston, MA 02130
(800) 876-4463

Paulist Press
997 MacArthur Blvd.
Mahwah, NJ 07430
(201) 825-7300

Paulist Productions
17575 Pacific Coast Hwy.
Pacific Palisades, CA 90272
(800) 624-8613

Penguin USA
375 Hudson St.
New York, NY 10014
(800) 331-4624

G.P. Putnam & Sons
200 Madison Ave.
New York, NY 10016
(800) 631-8571

Pyramid Media
P.O. Box 1048
Santa Monica, CA 90406-1048
(800) 421-2304

Random House, Inc.
201 E. 50th St., 22nd Floor
New York, NY 10022
(800) 733-3000

Raven Press Ltd.
1185 Ave. of the Americas
New York, NY 10036
(800) 777-2836

Resource Publications
160 E. Virginia, Suite 290
San Jose, CA 95112-5848
(800) 736-7600

Scholastic, Inc.
555 Broadway
New York, NY 10012-3999
(800) 325-6149

Shoestring Publishers
P.O. Box 55552
Seattle, WA 98155
(206) 367-3174

Simon & Schuster Children's
200 Old Tappan Rd.
Old Tappan, NJ 07675
(800) 223-2336

Simon & Schuster School Group
P.O. Box 2649
Columbus, OH 43216
(800) 848-9500

Simon & Schuster Trade
1230 Ave. of the Americas
New York, NY 10020
(212) 698-7000

St. Anthony Messenger Press
(also Franciscan
Communications)
1615 Republic St.
Cincinnati, OH 45210
(800) 488-0488

Standard Publishing
8121 Hamilton Ave.
Cincinnati, OH 45231
(800) 543-1301

Stevens Publishing
3700IH35
Waco, TX 76706
(817) 776-9000

Gareth Stevens, Inc.
River Ctr. Bldg.
1555 N. River Center Dr.
Suite 201
Milwaukee, WI 53212
(800) 341-3569

Tabor Publishing
200 E. Bethany Dr.
Allen, TX 75002
(800) 822-6701

Twenty-Third Publications
P.O. Box 180
Mystic, CT 06355
(800) 321-0411

Vision Video
P.O. Box 2249
Livonia, MI 48151
(800) 588-8474)

Franklin Watts
(Div. of Grolier Publishing Co.)
Sherman Tpk.
Danbury, CT 06813
(800) 672-6672

Whitman Pub.
(Devin-Adair Pubs.)
6 N. Water St.
Greenwich, CT 06830
(203) 531-7755

For further information you may
wish to consult the following
publishers and/or distributors.

Alba House Communications
9531 Akron-Canfield Rd.
Box 595
Canfield, OH 44406-0595
(800) 533-2522

Ave Maria Press
Univ. of Notre Dame
Notre Dame, IN 46556-0428
(800) 282-1865

Candleflame Production
5536 N.E. Hassalo
Portland, OR 97213
(No Phone)

Cathedral Films
Religious Film Corporation
P.O. Box 4029
Westlake Village, CA 91359
(800) 338-3456

Child's World, Inc.
505 N. Highway 169
Suite 295
Plymouth, MN 55441
(612) 797-0155
(800) 599-7323

David C. Cook Pub. Co.
850 N. Grove Ave.
Elgin, IL 60120
(800) 3293-7543

Coronet/MTI Film & Video
4350 Equity Dr.
P.O. Box 2649
Columbus, OH 43216-2649
(800) 321-3106

Credence Cassettes (NCR)
115 E. Armour Blvd.
Kansas City, MO
(800) 444-8910

The Day Music
P.O. Box 14100
Nashville, TN 37214
(800) 251-4000

Gospel Films
Box 455
Muskegon, MI 49443-0455
(800) 253-0413

Landmark Media
3450 Slade Run Dr.
Falls Church, VA 22042
(800) 342-4336

Questar Video
P.O. Box 11345
Chicago, IL 60611-0345
(800) 544-8422

Star Song Publishing Group
P.O. Box 150009
Nashville, TN 37215
(800) 835-7664

Treehaus Communications, Inc.
P.O. Box 249
Loveland, OH 45140
(800) 638-4287

United States Catholic
Conference (USCC)
Publishing Services
3211 4th St., NE
Washington, DC 20017-1194
(800) 235-8722

Word Records & Music
3319 W. End Ave.
Nashville, TN 37203
(800) 876-9673

ACKNOWLEDGMENTS

Excerpts from the English translation of the *Catechism of the Catholic Church* for the United States of America Copyright © 1994, United States Catholic Conference, Inc.—Libreria Editrice Vaticana, are used with permission. All rights reserved.

The Church Is All of You, Thoughts of Archbishop Oscar Romero. Compiled and translated by James R. Brockman Copyright © 1984 by Chicago Province of the Society of Jesus. Published by Winston Press, Minneapolis, MN. All rights reserved. Used with permission.

Excerpts from the "Dogmatic Constitution on the Church (Lumen Gentium)" reprinted from *The Documents of Vatican II* by Walter M. Abbott, S.J. Copyright © 1966 by permission of New Century Publishers, Inc., Piscataway, New Jersey.

Scriptural texts used in this work are taken from the *New American Bible with Revised New Testament* Copyright © 1970, 1986 by the Confraternity of Christian Doctrine, Washington, D.C. and are used by permission of copyright owner. All rights reserved.

All adaptations of scripture are based on the *New American Bible with revised New Testament.*

Excerpt from *Pastoral Letters of the United States Catholic Bishops Volume IV, 1975-1983* Copyright © 1984 by the United States Catholic Conference, Washington, D.C. 20017. All rights reserved.

Excerpts from the English translation of *The Roman Missal* ©1973, International Committee on English in the Liturgy, Inc. All rights reserved.

Excerpts from *Sharing the Light of Faith: National Catechetical Directory for Catholics of the United States* Copyright © 1979 by the United States Catholic Conference, Washington, D.C. 20017. Used with permission. All rights reserved.

CREDITS

Cover art: Pamela Johnson
Marginalia art: Jill Wood
Helps for the Teacher art: Wendy Wassink Ackison
   and Robert Roper
Photo Credits: All photographs by Silver Burdett Ginn (SBG)
   unless otherwise noted. Page 368: The Stock Market.
   Page 369: Ronnie Kaufman/The Stock Market